THE BLOODY CRUCIBLE OF
COURAGE

Also by Brent Nosworthy

The Anatomy of Victory: Battle Tactics 1689–1763

With Musket, Sword and Cannon: Battle Tactics of Napoleon and His Enemies

THE BLOODY CRUCIBLE OF
COURAGE

*Fighting Methods and Combat
Experience of the Civil War*

BRENT NOSWORTHY

CARROLL & GRAF PUBLISHERS
NEW YORK

THE BLOODY CRUCIBLE OF COURAGE
Fighting Methods and Combat Experience of the Civil War

Carroll & Graf Publishers
An Imprint of Avalon Publishing Group Inc.
245 W. 17th St., 11th Floor
New York, NY 10011

First Carroll & Graf edition 2003
Second printing, December 2003

Library of Congress Cataloging-in-Publication Data is available.

ISBN: 0-7867-1147-7

Interior design Paul Paddock
Printed in the United States of America
Distributed by Publishers Group West

As always, I would like to first dedicate this book to my family—Mom, Alice, Enerria, Tristan, Xiomara and to all my friends, especially: Davie Sterling, Fred and Vickie Nagy, Roz Dotson, Hector Alemany, Angel Delgado, Debra Abrams-Wright, Gene Williams, "Jazz" Johnson, Connie Gray, and Dave Clarke. This work is also offered to the Black and "Spanish" communities in New York and Providence in return for such as warm and cordial acceptance of my family.

This work has spanned eleven years from start to completion and really is the culmination of twenty-six years of effort, a sizeable "slice" of anyone's life. I, therefore, ask indulgence to also dedicate this work to the memory of two men who have had a profound and indelible impact upon every aspect of my character: Harry M. Mendelson whose living example demonstrated the true meaning of the word *mensch*, and Alvin Robinson who by his vocal artistry has shown so compellingly that whatever is worth doing, must be done with the entire force of one's being.

CONTENTS

INTRODUCTION

A nyone even remotely familiar with the Civil War and its literature is aware of the tremendous number of works that have been written about this epic American struggle. Though probably an exaggeration, the claim that the number of books published on the Civil War equals the number of days elapsed since the close of the "Great Rebellion" is at least suggestive of the monumental amount of information available to anyone willing to frequent even a medium-sized library. Of course, a great many of these books are personal memoirs, regimental histories, and campaign studies written before the turn of this century. Printed in what today is considered to be limited quantities and often little more than pamphlets, relatively few of these are accessible to the majority of today's readers.

However, in recent years, a seeming cornucopia of significant works has been published and is widely available. It is not that uncommon for the "Civil War" section in a larger bookstore to monopolize three to five wall units, that is, fifteen to twenty shelves. Most of these books focus on particular aspects of the great American conflict, and works seemingly abound on each: the lives of most major commanders, the types of weapons used, major campaigns, as well as the tactics used by the combatant armies. William S. McFeely's *Grant: A Biography*, Robert G. Tanner's *Stonewall in the Valley*, Douglas S. Freeman's *Lee's Lieutenants*, John D. Billings's *Hard Tack and Coffee*, and Albert Castel's *Decision in the West: The Atlanta Campaign of 1864* are just a few of the great many that can be named.

Probably the most popular type of work, however, concentrates on an individual battle, and in-depth analyses exist for almost every major Civil War engagement. The Battle of Spotsylvania, for example, has been the subject of two recent weighty studies: *The Battles for*

Spotsylvania Court House and the Road to Yellow Tavern by Gordon C. Rhea and *If It Takes All Summer: The Battle of Spotsylvania* by William D. Matter. Gettysburg, of course, is a perennial favorite, and a plethora of works has been published about this gargantuan struggle. However, given the volume of existing information and material, authors are increasingly driven to limit their investigation to some particular aspect of this battle. The last several years alone has seen the publication of a number of these exhaustive treatments, such as David Martin's *Gettysburg July 1* and Harry W. Pfanz's *Gettysburg: The Second Day*, both of which focus on the action during a single day, while Thomas A. Desjardins has devoted an entire volume exclusively to the Twentieth Maine's action at Little Round Top, entitled *Stand Firm Ye Boys from Maine*!

This is indicative of a trend among Civil War historians. As the amount of information about each topic increases, subsequent works of similar ilk are often forced to turn up the degree of magnification, usually by concentrating on smaller and smaller subdivisions of the original topic, such as the examples cited on the Battle of Gettysburg. So the obvious question confronting any conscientious author considering a work on the Civil War is this: Is it really necessary for another work to be added to this literary mountain? One can hardly be blamed for concluding that the works defining the overall landscape have already been written, that there is little left to explore, and that all future work will be forever condemned to travel down well-known, well-charted informational highways.

A NEED

Despite this impression that "everything worth writing has already been written," one of the most basic informational needs for anyone interested in the Civil War has never been adequately filled: a single work devoted to the full spectrum of both the *fighting methods* and the *combat experience* during the entire Civil War. At first glance, this statement might raise the eyebrows of many knowledgeable Civil War buffs and researchers, who may feel that these two subjects have already received adequate treatment. After all, over the last 10 years, a number of works that touch upon some aspect of combat experience or fighting methods have been published and are widely available. Earl J. Hess's *The Union*

Soldier in Battle: Enduring the Ordeal of Combat, Reid Mitchell's *Civil War Soldiers: Their Expectations and Their Experiences,* and Gerald Linderman's *Embattled Courage: The Experience of Combat in the American Civil War* are all well-received books that explore what is was like to be a soldier during the great internecine struggle. On the more technical side, there are McWhiney and Jamieson's *Attack and Die: Civil War Military Tactics and the Southern Heritage* and Paddy Griffith's *Battle Tactics of the Civil War.*

All of these books, as well as many others—possibly hundreds—in some way touch upon either the nature of Civil War combat or the combatants' experiences or both. The very availability of existing literature, of course, forces one to ask if this area already has been adequately covered or is possibly even saturated with readily available information. One easy way of answering this question is to momentarily conjure up the ideal book about Civil War fighting methods and combat experience as well as the types of information that such a work would provide. A comparison of issues and information dealt with by this work and by those books mentioned would immediately tell us if there are indeed additional areas that remain to be explored and, hence, if there is still a legitimate need for additional publications.

Although the terms "how troops fought" and "combat experience" are readibly intelligible, and, in fact, seemingly self-explanatory, they nevertheless require some elaboration. Writers bent on taking the most simplistic approach would probably interpret combat experience as merely the way soldiers thought and felt on the battlefield. In the same vein, they might restrict the study of how troops fought to what is generally referred to as "tactics."

Unfortunately, reality always turns out to be a much more complicated affair, and even during the smallest engagements, there is invariably a complex interplay of physical and psychological forces at work. Although it is not the purpose of this work to delve too deeply into matters purely philosophical or psychological, a few words about the nature of combat experience and its relationship to fighting methods are necessary.

There is a tendency to interpret experience in an offhand way as purely the perceptual and cognitive appreciation of an ongoing stream of events, to look at experience only at the moments the causative events occur. The soldier's cumulative past and history, however, also play a vital role not only in shaping the nature of the combat experience but also on how the soldier interprets fast-breaking events on the battlefield and responds to them. What the soldier emotionally and psychologically brings to combat—his lifetime experience—obviously influences his feelings, attitudes, and potentially his behavior. In turn, behavior very definitely can influence and mold events. Deeply held, societally induced attitudes, such as political and religious beliefs, can greatly affect one's ability to engage in combat. Obviously, soldiers who possess an unquestioning belief in the "cause" for which they are fighting will fight with greater resolve and frequently continue to struggle, even knowingly lay down their lives, when less motivated troops would break and flee.

A soldier's competence is also largely a function of experience. Here we are not referring to idiosyncratic capabilities, such as personal strength, individual courage, and dexterity, which are particular ingrained qualities, but rather to the soldiers' collective ability to perform what is expected of them. The rank and file invariably entered the bloody arena with some sort of preparation, regardless of how brief or crude. Their officers, especially those at the higher command levels, meanwhile, brought a set of expectations and plans regarding what they would do and how they wanted their troops to operate. The soldiers' preparation took the form of "training," while the officers' expectations were molded by the body of military doctrine as it then existed, that is, the tactics, grand tactics, and even strategies at their disposal.

Training and military doctrine frequently affect both the combatants' expectations and capabilities and thus, to some extent, the course of events on the battlefield. Encountering defenders positioned behind a rail fence, an officer trained to esteem the virtues of cold steel was more likely to order a determined charge with lowered bayonets. Another officer who believed in the efficacy of firepower, especially that provided by the new rifle muskets and repeaters, would probably order his men to deliver a few volleys first. This is not to say that the outcome of even a portion of an engagement resulted simply from choice of tactics or methods to be used. A sizable gap has always existed between theory and what has proved practicable during the heat of battle.

Nevertheless, any work that aspires to be comprehensive has to address these issues. By necessity, not only must it examine how troops prepared and trained for combat, but it also has to take a detailed, structured look at the techniques, practices, and tactics that were actually used during the bloody crucible of battle. Completeness demands that it be very much a study of practice versus theory. On one hand, it is necessary to look at the art and science of war as adopted by the European intelligentsia. Then, we must look at how it was interpreted and understood in the American army during the period leading up to the commencement of hostilities in 1861. It is also necessary to describe the preparations that were taken—that is, the training methods and theoretical doctrine, such as tactical systems—and if and how these were actually used on the battlefield. Then all of these must be illustrated by real examples found on the Civil War battlefield.

Of course, variety was among the more noticeable characteristics of the American Civil War. Notable differences existed not only between North and South but also between East and West. This makes it important to investigate the similarities of and differences between methods used by the Union and the Confederacy, as well as those employed in the east versus those used in Missouri, Kentucky, and Tennessee. How did these vary according to terrain, such as river and coastal warfare, or fighting in and for forts and fortifications versus open-field engagements? What was it like to be in the infantry, artillery, or the cavalry? How did doctrine and the actual practices in the field evolve as the war progressed? A comprehensive work must tackle all of these issues. The same must be said of the available military technology. Not only is it necessary to look at the weapons that were available, but also it is necessary to examine how these were actually used or misused during battle.

Having established the foregoing model to evaluate the comprehensiveness of any work on Civil War fighting methods and combat experience, it becomes clear that the works published to date fail to provide all of the sought-after information. From this point of view, the material that does exist can only be characterized as providing "partial" answers. McWhiney and Jamieson's *Attack and Die* and Paddy Griffith's work on Civil War grand tactics offer largely contradictory explanations regarding the nature of civil war combat. In each, the choice of material and illustrations is subordinated to an overarching thesis. In *Attack and Die* this is that the bloodiness of the Civil War was the unavoidable result of a thoughtless proclivity towards the offensive, while Griffith argues that the Civil War was the last of the Napoleonic-style wars, albeit a poorly fought one at that. Neither work attempts to be encyclopedic, to cover the full range of tactical practices, such as the methods of the artillery, how the cavalry fought during the campaign, partisan warfare, and so on.

Probably Ian Drury and Tony Gibbons's *The Civil War Military Machine* is the single work that comes closest to comprehensiveness. Although this large-format book, with its copious illustrations, provides a full description of the available weaponry and in abstract terms of how the fighting varied from East to West, on land and on the river, and in and against fortifications and fortresses, its most conspicuous omission is the lack of anecdotal accounts. There are absolutely no examples of firsthand narratives of what happened on the battlefield.

Overall, the works that seek to describe the Civil War combat experience have managed to provide a more thorough treatment. Hess's *The Union Soldier in Battle*, Mitchell's *Civil War Soldiers*, and Linderman's *Embattled Courage* are all excellent, thoroughly researched works. None of these, however, attempts to link the experience of the engagement with the fighting methods at the soldiers' disposal.

The inescapable conclusion is that though there are works available that detail some aspect of combat experience and others that concentrate upon some aspect of tactics and weaponry, a comprehensive treatment of these combined areas together remains to be written. The goal of the present work, therefore, is to take the first steps on such a journey. *The Bloody Crucible of Courage*, however, has a second and equally important goal: to provide the context needed to understand the overall place of the Civil War in the evolution of military thought and practice. Since this can only be achieved by painting a detailed picture of the state of military science on the eve of the Civil War, Part One of this book first considers why it is important to examine fighting methods and the state of military art both in America and abroad in the decades leading up to the Great Rebellion.

PART I

PROLOGUE

PROLOGUE

Chapter 1

IS THE STUDY OF FIGHTING METHODS MEANINGFUL?

W hether because of the difficulty of the task or because most historians have traditionally been more interested in the chronological, political, or biographical dimensions of the Civil War, a comprehensive analysis of the fighting methods employed during this conflict has been largely overlooked. In most historical studies published before the 1980s, one finds detailed chronologies of troop movements, campaign analyses, and discussions of commanders' strategies. Relatively few of these works attempted to provide detailed descriptions of the actual fighting. They offered little more than a cursory comparative treatment of the tactics and fighting methods that were intended versus those that were used under fire.

A number of highly detailed battle studies have recently appeared. Although these works meticulously describe what transpired at each stage of the battle, even on a regiment-by-regiment level, the descriptions tend to be *neutral;* the events and actions are considered in and of themselves, rather than *comparatively* or *contextually.* We may learn, for example, that at a particular point during an engagement, such and such regiment resorted to "fire by files," but nowhere do we learn how and why this practice came about, its relative effectiveness, as well as its advantages and disadvantages. It is as though the weapons, fighting methods, and tactics somehow, as if almost by magic, arose after the fall of Fort Sumter. All too frequently, it appears those who study this great internecine conflict still believe that the formal, officially prescribed methods only possessed a theoretical existence and were not practiced on the field of battle, and even in those rare cases where they were applied in anger, they had no bearing on the outcome of the contest.

In fairness to Civil War historians, the information presented in the typical battle report that has come down to posterity appears to support this view. Most of the details that are provided are literally *incidental*. More often than not, a unit's actions appear to be a response to the circumstances in which the unit finds itself, rather than the progeny of predetermined doctrine. Suddenly the target of enemy artillery fire, an advancing infantry regiment opportunistically crouches behind a small undulation of the ground. A neighboring regiment finds itself suddenly outflanked and quickly wheels to meet the unexpected threat. The intent of the commander apparently plays but a subservient role, and in its stead there is powerful sense of spontaneity. The results of an action seem to be the unpredictable result of a complex interplay of random forces that lead to an unforeseen yet unavoidable conclusion. The idiosyncratic aspects of each engagement appear to greatly outweigh any discernible abstract qualities that lend themselves to categorization, and the historian can be forgiven for relinquishing the more challenging task of explaining the *why* and settling for the more prosaic task of delineating *what* has occurred and *when*.

This is not to say that these battle reports are completely devoid of tactical-level detail. Anyone willing to wade into the sea of primary sources can uncover seemingly innumerable examples of tactical practices found on the Civil War battlefield. However, most of these tactical specimens are highly fragmented descriptions, cursory mentions of only the most notable conduct during engagements. They rarely provide background explanations and almost never attempt to supply a broader context. This is neither unreasonable nor unexpected. The *Official Records* are by their very nature terse, pragmatically oriented records of individual engagements. Given the rigors of the campaign and the limited amount of time that could be devoted to administrative functions, these reports are sketchy, shorthand affairs that usually only recorded the most salient events of the engagement.

Fortunately, the Civil War historian has access to another type of primary source. In the decades after the "War Between the States," thousands of veterans decided to immortalize their experiences in the form of personal memoirs or by helping with their units' regimental histories. These works tend to have a different focus and treatment and often delve into what concerned the individual author and what he found interesting. It is from this corpus of material that one finds the most compelling evidence of tactical practices, how they were employed during battle, and sometimes even a commentary upon their effectiveness.

A Confederate Attack at Wilson's Creek

William Watson's account of the activity of the Third Louisiana Infantry during the Battle of Wilson's Creek (August 10, 1861, near Springfield, Missouri) illustrates the type of low-level information that can be gleaned through the judicious use of personal narratives. Although its officers penned four reports about the regiment's actions that day, little mention is made of a confrontation with Union regular infantry at the beginning of the battle. The regiment's colonel, Louis Hebert, says only that they encountered the enemy infantry at extremely close range (as near as 15 yards) as they deployed in a cornfield and implies that the enemy was quickly defeated:

> An advance was ordered, led gallantly and bravely by Captain Mcintosh. . . . The enemy was posted behind a fence and in the cornfield. The companies moved up bravely, broke the enemy, pursued them into the cornfield, and routed them completely.

In his memoir, Watson suggests the affair was much more hotly contested. Part of the skirmisher line in front of the regiment, Watson was in perfect position to see how the action began. As the two opposing sides neared one another, the skirmishers were forced to retire to within 15 yards of their respective lines. However, even this position could not be maintained for long. The men along the main line started to fire, and, intimidated by the bullets flying close over-head, the skirmishers on each side were quickly forced to rejoin their formations. The "featured event" had begun in earnest. Watson later recalled the mood at that point:

> Both sides were piqued and determined. It was a fair stand up fight, and the question was who would stand it the longest.

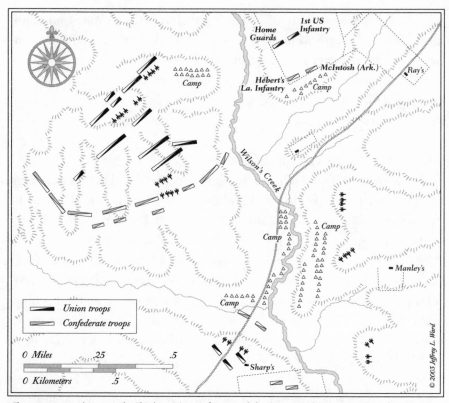

The engagement between the Third Louisiana Infantry and the First United States Regular Infantry took place in a field on the extreme right of the main Confederate line.

The fire was heavy on both sides, and bullets rattled like a hailstorm.

The Confederates were poorly armed, equipped with mostly smoothbores, while their opposition, part of the United States Regular Army, was armed with rifle muskets. As the rebels approached, the Union officers scornfully asked if they were "volunteers." When Watson's regiment answered in the affirmative, they were met with derision, and it was obvious that the Union officers expected to defeat their ragtag opponents easily.

Looking back, Watson felt that in spite the Union officer's invective and contempt, the Confederates actually possessed a slight advantage. Standing in brushwood up to their shoulders, the rebels were completely hidden whenever they stooped to prime and reload their muskets. In contrast, the Union soldiers were in open terrain and in full view. The Confederate advantage was only momentary, however; the smoke from the continuous musketry soon obscured both sides. Taking advantage of the limited visibility, the Union force attempted to work around the rebel flank, but the Confederates responded accordingly, and the effort proved futile.

The desultory fire continued for about half an hour, neither side able to administer a deciding blow. Then, as if by mutual consent, the fire slackened on both sides. The combatants had been firing and loading as feverishly as possible, and the much-needed lull allowed the infantrymen to regain their breath. As the smoke cleared, it was obvious that the Union soldiers had taken more than they had dished had out. The dead lay thick along their thinning line, and many of those still standing were visibly wounded, blood running down their faces from minor head wounds, suggesting, incidentally, that the rebel infantry were firing "buck and ball"—a musket ball and three buckshots. The Union officers who initially had been yelling commands and encouragement to their troops were now silent. Though the men were evidently angered at meeting with such stiff and unexpected resistance from rebel volunteers, their countenances still exuded a "fierce and determined look." Now it was the rebels' turn to mock their adversaries, and several yelled, "How about volunteers now!" The regulars' reply was unequivocal: A volley was immediately unleashed, and the contest was renewed with the same vigor as before.

Trading punch for counterpunch, the Confederates' advantage continued to grow. Thinking back at this engagement, Watson attributed the rebels' success to several causes, each small and difficult to notice at the time but which, when coupled together over time, rendered the final Confederate success inevitable:

It seemed to have become a test of rivalry between regulars and volunteers; both sides were thoroughly roused, and the combat was furious. They were of good metal and well disciplined, and maintained their phalanx by closing up to the center. They stood upright, and preserved their line well formed. This was fatal to them. Our line was not so well formed or the men so well disciplined, but they were as resolute and were better

marksmen, and the fighting being at close quarters the difference of arms was not much felt. We had the advantage of the
brushwood, but that was now getting too much trampled down
to afford much shelter.

Sensing they were gradually losing, the Union fire gradually slackened, and the men, now desperate, started to yell for the rebels to
come out in the open ground to fight at close quarters. This last
request was met with general approval by the rebels. Someone urged
his comrades to charge the Union line with bayonets, while someone
else cried, "Give them steel, boys." The challenge was immediately
accepted. A tremendous cheer went up, and the rebels rushed forward. The Union regulars broke, and most ran off toward the Union
center of the Union line of battle on Oak Hill.

A UNION ATTACK AT LABADIEVILLE

This part of the fight at Wilson's Creek had been a meeting engagement. The musketry had erupted almost immediately as the two sides
unexpectedly bumped into each other, and the officers had no time to
issue any instructions to their men. In an article that appeared in
Harper's Magazine during the war, Capt. John William De Forest of
the Twelfth Connecticut Infantry provided a compelling description
of a Union infantry attack that had occurred at Georgia Landing, near
Labadieville, Louisiana, on October 27, 1862. In this case, the Union
officers had the opportunity to prepare their infantry for the
upcoming assault, and one finds slightly different tactical dynamics.

Separated from the enemy by an uncultivated field and a strip of
woods, the Twelfth Connecticut began its advance unmolested by
enemy fire. Initially, the only challenge was posed by the intervening
terrain. First the regiment encountered a strong post-and-rail fence,
so common in Louisiana; then its men had to work their way around
thickets of thorny briars. Colonel Colburn and his officers energetically reorganized the line, directing the men to close up the gaps and
redress on the center of the regiment. These efforts preoccupied the
men and helped buoy their morale. Not only did it take their minds
off the horrors of imminent combat, but there was also a distinct
feeling of satisfaction in performing the series of drills.

Reaching the woods, Colburn and his officers learned from their skirmishers that the rebels were a quarter mile ahead, beyond some woods and a long, open field. Up to this point, the advance had been unopposed. However, when Union infantrymen finally set foot on the open field, the peaceful aspect of the operations immediately dissolved as the Confederate artillery opened fire. Branches and leaves above started to shake from the shells screaming overhead. Like those in every other relatively inexperienced regiment, the men instinctively ducked in unison, but without stopping or breaking. The Confederate gunners started to acquire the range, and the tempo of the firing increased. It was obvious that the artillery fire was directed at the regiment's colors. During the initial stages of the advance, Union artillery had been able to support the attack. Now, however, the advancing infantry had to advance through their own artillery's line of fire. It became necessary to halt the supporting artillery fire, and this noticeably lowered the men's morale.

Encountering another fence, Colburn emphatically ordered the regiment to push over the light obstacle. The companies on both flanks were temporarily stopped by dense patches of thorn bushes and bog and quickly had to file back into line as the remainder of the regiment continued forward. Approaching the regimental line at the run, the confusion seemed to spread throughout the formation. Once again, Colburn halted the regiment and redressed from the center. All the while, the Confederate artillery continued firing, and the shots could be heard coming in lower and lower.

The defending Confederate infantry finally unleashed its fire. The ragged file fire reminded De Forest of the rattle that could be heard as a boy ran a stick along a picket fence, only many times louder. Almost simultaneously, the "whit, whit" of the minié balls could be heard flying promiscuously around their ears. Puffs of dust in the field in front provided visual evidence of the enemy's hostile intent. Peering in the distance, one saw blue smoke, the unavoidable companion of musket fire in the days before smokeless powder, slowly spring up along the far edge of the field. To the right rose gray clouds of smoke, the telltale signs of artillery fire. Lying concealed behind a fence and in a ditch alongside a side road, the Confederate infantry was completely hidden from view.

The Twelfth Regiment continued to advance. The men's anxiety became more noticeable, and one of the color sergeants could be heard to wonder aloud, "Oh dear! When shall we fire?" After what must have seemed an eternity, the infantrymen were relieved to hear the lieutenant colonel order the regiment to halt and deliver a file fire, with the fire proceeding from right to left along the line in each company. The men in the regiment were too excited to wait their turns to fire, and one large battalion fire occurred as soon as the colonel's orders were uttered. Immediately, the attackers frantically began to reload, each "as if his life depended upon the speed of the operation." In the resulting pandemonium, the regiment's two center companies fell on the ground. The men had mistakenly responded to orders issued to the Thirteenth Regiment, which was slightly to their rear. The mistake, however, was soon corrected, and several officers quickly managed to get these men back on their feet.

Spontaneously, the entire regiment sprang forward. Colburn tried to stop the men in order to deliver a well-aimed volley, but it proved useless, and according to De Forest, the colonel "might as well have ordered a regiment of screeching devils to halt." Enemy canister and small arms fire colluded to seek the attackers' destruction. Yet, the Union infantry surged forward, loading and firing as fast as possible. Unconsciously, the men along the line pushed inwards toward the center. The formation was now three ranks deep, instead of the official two, and several of the lighter men were squeezed out of the line. As a captain, De Forest was supposed to position himself behind the rank and file, not only to reduce officer casualties but also to help prevent the more cowardly from slipping to the rear and escaping the crisis of the battle. To inspire his men and provide an example, though, De Forest ignored standing orders and kept slightly to the front of his company; he reasoned the company's two lieutenants were sufficient to prevent straggling. This was De Forest's first real action. Expecting a severe hand-to-hand contest at the end of the advance, he had drawn both his saber and revolver and was ready for any eventuality. The advance seemed interminable. De Forest recalled that in the frustration and nervousness of the moment, everyone appeared to be swearing.

So far, all of the firing had been directed towards the puffs of smoke produced by enemy small arms fire. No other signs of the enemy could be seen. About halfway across the field, at about the 250-yard mark, the advancing Union line finally saw the enemy. A body of Confederate infantrymen appeared to be running from the woods west towards their own front as though they had been hastily sent to reinforce the rebel line. However, the reinforcements got off only a single "sidelong" fire and then fled toward nearby bushes, "disappearing like partridges." The main rebel line continued to hold its position. It was not until the Union lines had advanced to within 100 yards that the defenders' resolve began to weaken. At that point, the Confederate artillery ceased firing, presumably to limber up and retire. A few seconds later, the men along the rebel line sprang out of the ditch and fled precipitously.

The sight of the enemy's backs proved too much of a temptation to the Thirteenth Connecticut Regiment. On their own, without receiving orders, its men unleashed a "stunning" volley. The two sister regiments, their men yelling and screaming, continued the advance, firing as fast as possible into the woods. The officers now redoubled their efforts to regain control, and after much effort, the Union line finally was halted. After a minute or two, the orders to cease firing were finally issued, and order was restored. The Union forces were victorious. A sense of shock settled on many of the participants. The defenders had failed to stand resolutely, and the battle was over before the true crisis had arrived.

After the battle, Confederate prisoners provided an insight into the relative effectiveness of the various offensive tactics that had been tried. The Confederate commander, Colonel McPheeters, felt he could easily hold off the Eighth New Hampshire, but as he watched the advance of the Twelfth and Thirteen Connecticut Regiments, he was heard to exclaim, "Those other fellows are coming sure!" Knowing that his command would be captured or annihilated if they broke after hotly contesting the position, he ordered his men to retreat immediately.

The prisoners also attested to the effectiveness of the fire-while-advancing style of attack. A captured Confederate captain explained how they were startled by this type of tactic. He and his men expected the Union infantrymen to utilize their usual mode of attack—to halt, fire, and then to proceed again—"not fire and come on all together," as he put it. Another captive soldier supported this view: "Your firing didn't hurt us, but your coming on yelling scared us." Apparently, the continuous firing of the attackers had suppressed the firing of the defenders. It was not that the Union small arms fire was necessarily accurate, directly hitting its intended targets. But the sound of all the bullets passing uncomfortably close by their heads and, even more annoying, the splinters hurled violently as the bullets glanced off the posts and rails, made the ditch in which they had been ensconced a "most disagreeable hole to be in." The effect was to spoil the defenders' aim and nullify the effectiveness of their own fire. Although the men in the Twelfth were roundly criticized for not following the colonel's orders to stop and deliver an orderly volley, De Forest felt the men had conducted themselves appropriately, under the circumstances:

> Notwithstanding our lieutenant colonel's criticism, I think we did wisely to blaze away while advancing, for, besides deranging the aim of the Southerners, it kept up the spirit of our own fellows, who thought they were doing as much harm as they received, and so felt they had a fair chance. Of course there was some danger to the front rank from the rifles of the rear rank; for instance, I had my neck slightly scorched by the fire of one of my own soldiers.

ALONG THE DEFENDING LINES AT CORINTH

Both of the preceding engagements have been examined largely from the attacker's perspective. However, what was it like to be the defender? How did those who awaited attack conduct themselves differently from those who advanced towards them? How were they influenced by the attackers' actions, and from their vantage point, were some of the attackers' tactics and methods more effective than others? In his published memoirs, *A Colonel's Diary*, Oscar Jackson provides a particularly informative description of the experience of the Sixty-third Ohio Volunteers during the Battle of Corinth (October 3–4, 1862), shedding some light on these questions.

On October 4, 1862, Confederate forces under Maj. Gen. Earl Van

Dorn decided to mount an aggressive assault against a series of Union batteries near the town of Corinth, Mississippi. In one part of the field, Phifer's brigade (Confederate) began to assemble for the attack against Col. John Fuller's First Brigade (Second Division) around 10 A.M. Streaming out of the woods, they started to form a series of large attack columns. In his after-battle report, Fuller indicated that his command had been attacked by four columns, each made of a regiment: the Sixth and Ninth Texas Cavalry Regiments, both serving as infantry, and two Arkansas regiments. Jackson claims these columns were holding as many as two thousand men apiece, much larger than a regiment, but this is extremely unlikely. Momentarily stunned by the size of the columns, the Union defenders stopped a desultory long-range fire that had already commenced. Taking advantage of the sudden calm, Colonel Fuller ordered his men not to resume firing until the enemy were about "to close upon them." The defenders did not have long to wait; as soon as the columns were formed, the Confederate assault began. On they came with a "firm, slow steady step." Their line of approach was somewhat oblique to the defending line; the attackers' right side started off slightly closer to the defenders' position than the left.

The strain on officer and men alike was almost unbearable as they awaited the apparently irresistible force slowly making its way toward them. Jackson, then in command of H Company, would long after remember his feelings of that moment:

> In my campaigning I had never seen anything so hard to stand as that slow, steady tramp. Not a sound was heard but they looked as if they intended to walk over us. I afterwards stood a bayonet charge with a yell and it was not so trying on the nerves as that steady, solemn advance.

Looking up and down the line, Jackson saw that the men in his company shared his sentiment. Each man along the defending line seemed to have his own way of dealing with the tremendous strain the soldier always feels before the start of battle. A few here and there could be seen nervously fidgeting, slowly bouncing from one foot to another. Others would nervously examine their weapons to see that everything was in working order: One man might be checking his primer, while the next was looking into his cartridge box. Another was adjusting his blouse or some other piece of clothing. But all were aware of the enemy's ineluctable progress across the field.

Realizing that his men probably expected a short pep talk, which in this situation was probably a good idea, Captain Jackson decided to say a few words to his company. In his memoirs, he remembered the substance of what he said:

> Boys, I guess we are going to have a fight. I have two things I want you to remember today. One is, we own all the ground behind us. The enemy may go over us but all the rebels yonder can't drive company H back. The other is, if the butternuts come close enough remember you have good bayonets on your rifles and use them.

When the enemy columns had advanced about a third of the way across the intervening field, Jackson's regiment was ordered to lie down on the ground. It was also instructed to fire by companies as soon as the enemy was sufficiently near. After the battle, Jackson would learn that the advancing rebels were actually unaware of their presence. The undulating ground in front of them effectively hid them from view. The attackers thought the men along the second Union line, who were clearly in view, were the only force they would have to fight.

Jackson appears to have been intent on fulfilling Fuller's plan for the defenders to withhold their fire until the right moment. As the front of the enemy's column approached the bank of a small stream 25 to 30 yards from the first Union line, Company H was ordered to stand up. Jumping in front of his men, Jackson pointed to a small bush, immediately in front of the company, that was 3 to 4 feet high. He ordered his men to aim at this level, and then issuing the orders to "Ready, aim," he nimbly jumped back behind the line before uttering the third and final directive, "fire!" This served as a signal to the entire regiment, and within a few seconds fire broke out along the rest of the line. Several companies of the Twenty-seventh Ohio were able to pour in an effective raking fire.

The sudden eruption of musketry from an unexpected location

came as a complete surprise to the advancing rebels. Before the battle, Jackson had been told by veterans that when a column was suddenly hit by extremely forceful fire, it would be stopped in its tracks, and the resulting jostling of men would make the sides of the column expand and retract, like a rope shaken from one end. This was exactly what happened. The smoke soon dissipated, and the fire had cut a swath into the closest column as deep as Company H was wide. All that was left was about 10 yards of soldiers on the ground, some motionless, others struggling in agony. Quickly the survivors deployed into line and delivered their own volley at extremely close range. However, the bullets struck the ground immediately in front of the defending line. Though showered with dirt and splinters, not a soldier in the company was injured.

Now the race was on to see which side would be able to deliver the next volley. The Union soldiers had the edge and managed to deliver their second volley before the attackers were able to reload. Not only had the defenders fired first and had a head start on reloading, but the attackers had lost valuable seconds while attempting to deploy after the first horrific volley. For five minutes, the desperate duel continued, but the advantage gradually accrued to the defenders, and the rebels finally were forced back in confusion. Recollecting the sight of the fleeing enemy, Jackson recalled:

> The enemy came to us in fine order, moving handsomely, but in retreating, every fellow went as suited him, and it appeared to suit all to go fast.

As the enemy quickly retreated, Jackson quipped to one of his men that they wouldn't have to fight this enemy again that day. He was quite surprised, therefore, when he saw the same enemy formations approach for a second time 40 minutes later. Although the Confederates began the advance with "slow, steady steps," they changed their tactics midstream and soon advanced at the double, the men yelling all the while. Again the Union defenders stood firm and unleashed a tremendous volley at very close range, and again the rebels went reeling back to their starting positions, not to return that day.

COMMONPLACENESS OF TACTICAL PRACTICES AND THEIR EFFECTIVENESS

Those studying tactical-level warfare generally employ two objectively identifiable criteria to gage the significance of various fighting methods during a conflict: *frequency of occurrence* of the methods and their *impact*. The tactical-level practices in the preceding engagements obviously meet the first criteria, *frequency of occurrence* being consciously or unconsciously employed in all three cases. Whether on the offensive or defensive, officers attempted to have their men employ an officially prescribed practice or something inspired by the individual situation. During the action at Labadieville, for example, the defenders attempted to thwart the attackers' plans with a medium-range fire that they hoped would stall the latter's advance. The Sixty-third Ohio Volunteers employed the converse defensive tactic at Corinth: The defending line patiently awaited the advancing enemy until the latter had approached to within very close range, and then the line emptied a withering fire into the noses of their foe.

The same can be said about offensive tactics. At Wilson's Creek, the Third Louisiana broke a stalemate with a bayonet charge, while the colonel of the Twelfth Connecticut Infantry at Labadieville ordered his men to periodically stop and fire before resuming the advance. The contest between Phifer's brigade and the Union Sixty-third Ohio Volunteers at Corinth is an even more convincing example, since the Texans consciously used two different methods of attack. Eschewing the use of their shoulder arms, the Texas infantry instead first relied on an uninterrupted advance directly towards the defenders. This first attempt unsuccessful, the commander and his officers decided to revise their methods. The second assault was conducted at a much quicker pace, which the Confederates hoped would frighten the defenders and destroy their will to resist.

This certainly is not to say that prescribed doctrine was always put into practice. The psychological stress of critical moments during battle created its own set of imperatives, and frequently there was a noticeable discrepancy between what the men were ordered to do and what they actually did under fire. At Labadieville, for example, the men of the Twelfth Connecticut Infantry—despite the orders to stop, fire, and reload—spontaneously continued to march on and, in effect, combined a determined advance with small arms fire to overpower their adversaries.

The second criterion used to judge the importance of tactics is whether the fighting methods had any effect on the other side or, even better, influenced the outcome of the engagement. In this regard, the preceding engagements are *suggestive* rather than *conclusive*. We learn from firsthand accounts of the defenders that in two of the examples discussed, the tactics employed by some of the attacking force intimidated the defenders more than those of others. During the affair at Labadieville, a captured Confederate infantryman claimed that the defenders had remained completely nonplussed by Union small arms fire but had been noticeably frightened by the determined advance. Oscar Jackson admits that at Corinth he and his men were much more intimidated by the slow, methodical advance employed during the first assault than the much quicker advance during the second.

The choice of tactics also occasionally influenced the result. At Wilson's Creek, the rebels' sudden determined charge broke a deadlock and handed the Third Louisiana Regiment a localized victory. A case also can be made that the firing-while-marching tactics of the Twelfth Connecticut Infantry substantially contributed to the victory at Labadieville. Clearly, these examples demonstrate that not all tactical practices were equal and some proved more effective, either because they caused the opponent to suffer a greater number of casualties or, more likely, had a much more devastating effect on the enemy's morale.

If, turning up the degree of magnification, one does find tactical practices frequently employed and also occasionally affecting the course of events, one must also conclude that the systematic study of contemporary fighting methods will meaningfully contribute to the overall understanding of the Civil War and its place in military history. The historian who pursues this type of research, however, must not be content with simply a descriptive and cataloguing role, but must simultaneously attempt to reconstruct a broader military scientific framework. For example, to what extent were the practices employed on the battlefield the result of officially accepted doctrine? What were the differences between practice and theory? Is it possible to identify regional variations or differences between individual commanders? Was there an evolution of practice throughout the war? How did the practices and methods employed on American soil fit in with the broader umbrella of military science of the time?

The problem, and this is why this approach has been conspicuously missing from the Civil War military historiography, is that such information is not easily obtained in large blocks. As seen, battle reports are fragmentary and provide the most skeletal of clues, when present at all. True, personal memoirs often provide more detailed explanations, but in this type of vehicle, the writer usually confines his observations to personal experiences or those of his unit. Rarely does the memoirist attempt to formulate broader, more general patterns. One can painstakingly go through a truly large number of battle reports and memoirs, extracting snippets that provide an insight to tactical-level practices, and like someone trying to assemble a giant jigsaw puzzle, meticulously reconstruct the "broader picture." However, not only would this require many lifetimes of Herculean effort, there is every indication that notable gaps in our knowledge and understanding would nevertheless remain.

Fortunately, another body of knowledge and intellectual tools exists, one that, if properly exploited, can not only facilitate and greatly expedite this task but also provide the needed insight into some areas that otherwise would forever be consigned to obscurity. Anyone sufficiently conversant with the nuances of mid-nineteenth century military science and its antecedents is able to look at a great many Civil War practices and recognize similarities to and differences from methods found elsewhere in military history.

While reading Watson's description of his regiment's behavior at Wilson Creek, for example, someone familiar with the Napoleonic Wars might be struck by the similarity between the procedural dynamics of this situation—a lengthy but ineffective firefight, followed by an immediately successful bayonet charge—and those encountered by General Duhèsme during the Battle of Caldiero. An account of this latter action is best left in Duhèsme's own words:

> I saw some battalions, which I had rallied, halted and using an individual fire which they could not keep up for long. I went there, I saw through the smoke cloud nothing but flashes, the

glint of bayonets and the tops of the grenadiers' caps. We were not far from the enemy however, perhaps sixty paces. A ravine separated us, but it could not be seen. I went into the ranks, which were neither closed nor aligned, throwing up with my hand the soldiers' muskets to get them to cease firing and to advance. I was mounted, followed by a dozen orderlies. None of us were wounded, nor did I see an infantryman fall. Well then! Hardly had our line started when the Austrians, heedless of the obstacle that separated us, retreated.

Similarly, while reading of the Twelfth Connecticut's attempt to fire while advancing at Labadieville, one is reminded of the "alternate firing" system described in Capt. Humphrey Bland's *A Treatise of Military Discipline* (1727.) This is the system, incidentally, that the Dutch infantry used successfully during the War of Spanish Succession (1701–14) and which served as the inspiration for a variant used by Prussian infantry early in Frederick the Great's reign (1740–86).

However, once again it is the engagement between the Sixty-third Ohio and Phifer's brigade at Corinth that provides the most intriguing example of obvious similarities of Civil War fighting methods and those found in other periods in military history. The experiences of Oscar Jackson and his men that day were similar to what they would have experienced had they (1) first been positioned along a defending French line assaulted by a British force during the Peninsular Wars (1808–14) which successfully repulsed the attackers; (2) a few moments later Jackson's force somehow magically found themselves along a British line that had to endure a vigorous French counterattack. The British method of attack at the time was to march in with a slow, deliberate step, the officers making every effort to slow down the advance and keep their men under control. The French infantrymen tended to rush in at the double, the men all the while shouting and hollering, the officers in front of the advancing line to serve as an example.

At first glance, even a cursory comparative analysis of previous European tactics and Civil War practices might appear to be a needless digression for a book that seeks to examine Civil War tactics and

combat experience. The subtle evolution of lower-level military practices during the seventeenth and eighteenth centuries seems to be far
removed from the methods used by Robert E. Lee's forces in northern
Virginia or Don Carlos Buell's in Tennessee. Nevertheless, there are
several compelling reasons why it is important to briefly look at military science as it existed just prior to the outbreak of the Civil War.
Later chapters will show that Northern and Southern armies did not
exclusively rely upon one or two officially endorsed tactical systems.
It is very easy to find examples of a wide assortment of tactical practices on the Civil War battlefield. Rarely, however, can one find
explanations of why these tactics were employed, what the officers
attempted to accomplish, or what, if anything, their sources of inspiration were.

In many respects, the situation of the tactically oriented Civil War
researcher is akin to that of the physical anthropologist studying the
evolution of humankind over the last two million years. Finding a
tiny, fragmented bone specimen, the knowledgeable anthropologist
draws upon a vast body of preexisting knowledge to identify the
species and the fragment's exact position within the animal's skeletal
structure. Rarely would someone find enough material to assemble
an accurate and complete picture without this background. This
informational framework is the result of the contributions of literally
thousands of anthropologists, formed after decades of analysis, spec-
ulation, and debate. This is remarkably similar to the situation confronting the military historian interested in Civil War tactics.

All of these considerations underscore the need for a quick preliminary look at the development of tactical doctrine throughout the
entire age of the musket (and this includes the rifle musket). This is
not to suggest that Civil War infantry tactics were simply a trans-
plantation of existing European tactics and that Union and Confederate officers were limited to tactical procedures handed down from
a European tradition. Though official doctrine prescribed by higher-
level military commanders, such as Beauregard, McClellan, and
Rosecrans, were indeed based on established European doctrine,
much of that devised by officers in the field was the result of their
own intellectual efforts and not earlier precedents. Thus, when,
during the Battle of Roanoke Island, Lieutenant-Colonel Maggi

ordered his men in the Twenty-first Massachusetts Infantry Regiment to fire while continuing to advance, it does not necessarily follow that this officer was aware of similar eighteenth century Dutch tactics. The value of a quick survey of European tactics is not that it necessarily points to the source of Civil War practices; rather, it shows the types of solutions that were devised by other tacticians, how these tactics fared in practice, as well as the strengths and weaknesses of each. This not only helps the Civil War historian to categorize practices described by otherwise fragmentary, top-level descriptions, but provides an informed basis from which he or she is able to more accurately determine why these tactics were employed and their probable utility or failure.

Chapter 2

ADVANCES IN SMALL ARMS, 1830–59

RENEWED FRENCH INTEREST IN RIFLES

Many readers probably take some intellectual enjoyment in the belief that the modern combat rifle owes its origin largely to events that took place on the American continent. According to this view, although the rifle had been known to Europeans as far back as the late sixteenth century, its first notable military use occurred during the American Revolution, when rifle-bearing colonists embarrassed the regular forces of his Britannic majesty George III. Albeit in a limited and tardy fashion, the British military eventually took note of these developments and the possibilities they offered. Their first response was the rather timid introduction of the Ferguson rifle and in slightly larger quantities the Grice, Willetts, Barker, and Galton muzzle-loading rifles among some of the British troops in 1776–77. Later, during the Napoleonic Wars, the 95th Rifle Regiment, armed with the Baker rifle, was generally successful against its French counterparts on the Spanish peninsula.

Learning from these events, the French military after Waterloo (1815) gradually took interest in rifled small arms. A series of developments culminated in the introduction of the Minié rifle, variants of which were so commonplace on the American Civil War battlefield.

When one takes a closer look at the history of the rifle musket, however, one is forced to conclude that the American Revolution's influence on the weapon's development was limited to the British army and in many respects represented an evolutionary cul-de-sac that abruptly ended with the close of the Napoleonic Wars.

The real impetus that stimulated the French to develop a more effective rifle came from North Africa. Although the story of the

Algerian Wars (1830–47) might appear to have little connection to the American Civil War, this conflict was actually one of the great military watersheds of the nineteenth century. There are several reasons why a study of the French military experience in Algeria in this present work is necessary. The entire doctrinal system contained within Casey's *Infantry Tactics* and Hardee's *Rifle and Light Infantry Tactics* originated with the French infantry's experiences in North Africa, and these were but translations of a work utilized by French chasseurs and Zouaves. When, during the first months of the Civil War, seemingly countless volunteer organizations donned exotic, loose-fitting garb with baggy red trousers, they were merely emulating the dress of the feared native soldiers in French service during the colonial wars. Today, when a U.S. Marine recruit at Parris Island is forced to climb rope walls and scamper over obstacles, he is following a training regimen first devised for the fierce Algerian fighters.

Probably the greatest impact of the Algerian Wars, however, was the effect it had on shoulder arms. The American Springfield rifle musket and its British cousin, the Enfield, were by far the most common small arms carried by the Civil War infantry. The development of the original version of these weapons in France between 1830 and 1846 is thus the story of not only the origin of both Enfield and Springfield rifles but also that of the military philosophy and doctrine that surrounded these weapons.

During the Napoleonic Wars the French did not follow British example but almost completely eschewed the rifle musket on the battlefield. Although they had periodically experimented with rifles during the ancient régime, they dismissed them because of the additional time required to load a rifle compared to a smoothbore. French riflemen during the Napoleonic Wars sometimes became so frustrated by the difficulty of loading and maintaining their weapons that they occasionally threw them away to pick up smoothbores. French authorities believed that the troops' ability to perform close-order drill and tactics was more important than a rifle's increased range and accuracy, also arguing it was essential that infantrymen be able to reload quickly to be ready to counter an enemy bayonet or cavalry charge.

With the return of peace in 1815, Western European powers

resumed their colonial expansion. Responding to repeated depredations by Algerian pirates, the French invaded Algeria in June 1830.
Thus began nearly two decades of desultory warfare in many ways
similar to that of the American Indian Wars in the 1870s and '80s.
The French soldiers were relentlessly pestered by irregular troops
that did not follow the "rules" of European warfare. These native
forces avoided set piece battles and relied upon a hit-and-run system
where every man took the advantage of shrubs, trees, and rocks.
Although dealing with a slightly later period, Lieutenant Colonel
Wilford's description of the British soldiers' experience against the
indigenous people of South Africa could have just as accurately portrayed the plight of the French in Algeria:

> What a melancholy object does a civilized soldier present, when
> loaded like a mule, and armed with a gun which will throw a ball
> with some certainty about the distance a man can throw a stone,
> pursuing an enemy who carries little more than the skin on his
> back, and at every rock and tree is a fortress.

The Arabs and Kabyles fought a hide-and-go-seek style of warfare
where the standard operating procedure was to spread out and hide
behind available cover and fire into the closely packed French
columns. Although notoriously bad marksmen, over time the Alge-
rians could still cause many more casualties than they in turn suffered. So, the French would throw out their skirmishers to try to
dislodge the natives from their protected positions. But not too far
away were Moorish horsemen, brandishing razor-sharp *yataghan*,
who would gallop forward and scatter the French skirmishers. The
French columns invariably rushed forward, but the enemy horsemen
immediately turned and fled to a safe position, only to attack again
as soon as the opportunity presented itself. Not content to simply play
hide-and-seek, the Arabs and Kabyles were able to strike back effectively. The French troops, encumbered with heavy equipment and
inappropriate clothing, were soon decimated without having struck a
proper blow in return.

Another problem arose from the difference in the effective range of
European smoothbores and the long matchlocks carried by their

Algerian opponents. Although seemingly equipped with primitive muskets, the Arabs and Kabyles had learned to deliver effective fire at relatively long ranges by elevating the gun barrels to a degree unknown to European soldiers. Confined to close-order formations, the French soldiers suffered more casualties than their irregular opponents. The French tried to bolster their infantry with horse artillery support. This failing, in desperation they even tried carrying around large-caliber wall guns, a long obsolete technology abandoned in Europe two hundred years previously.

AN IMPROVED RIFLE MUSKET

Realizing the ineffectiveness of the smoothbore musket against Algerian foes, Capt. Gustave Henri Delvigne, formerly of the Royal Guard infantry, tried to devise a muzzle-loading rifle musket that could be loaded as quickly as a smoothbore. For a rifled weapon to be accurate, there can be very little *windage,* the excess space between the projectile and the inside of the barrel. As the tight-fitting bullet is forced up the barrel, its sides enter the twisting rifled groove on the inside of the barrel, and the bullet spins. However, it is much more time consuming to ram a tight-fitting bullet down a narrow rifled barrel than to load a smoothbore, which tolerates considerably more windage. In trials conducted during the 1840s, for example, Prussian infantrymen armed with smoothbores were able to fire 10 volleys in 7 minutes, while those with jäger rifles only got off that number in 15 minutes.

Captain Delvigne devised an ingenious solution. His new musket was the same caliber as existing smoothbores, but a small "rebated" chamber (it had a smaller diameter) was added at the bottom of the barrel to hold the gunpowder. The musket ball dropped down easily and rested upon the shoulder of this chamber. The soldier then delivered several smart blows with a heavy ramrod, which flattened the ball slightly so that it expanded outwards, filling the rifled grooves and almost totally eliminating windage. While loading, there was enough windage so that this rifle could be loaded as quickly as a smoothbore, but once fired, it acquired all the advantages of the classic rifle.

Delvigne's new rifle was tested at Vincennes in 1834 with satisfactory

results. It possessed an effective range of 400 yards, more than double
that of the standard smoothbore. A less violent recoil and a more delicate
trigger facilitated better aim. Advocates claimed a soldier could fire as
easily lying down as standing. The new weapon was immediately
adopted by the *chasseurs à pied* sent to Algeria.

Unfortunately, the Delvigne rifle musket was unsuited to the trop-
ical clime. The inside of the barrel had to be well lubricated. The cartridges contained a wad of greased serge, which helped remove
powder residue and keep the barrel clean. In hot weather, however,
the grease would melt and drip into the charge, spoiling part of the
powder. The charge, now reduced well below the required sixty
grains, produced a weak and ineffective fire.

Another problem soon surfaced. The ball's trajectory depended
upon how the individual soldier rammed the ball and thus was unpredictable. If rammed too hard, the ball would be irregular in shape. If
not rammed hard enough, the ball failed to catch the grooves inside
the barrel and wouldn't spin. Both contingencies resulted in an
erratic trajectory. Once again, officers began to catch their men
throwing away the rifle muskets to pick up any of the more reliable
smoothbores they could find on the battlefield.

Although the Delvigne design was abandoned, it was the first in a
series of innovations that gradually transformed the rifle into the primary infantry weapon. However, it would require numerous other
inventors and experiments to find the optimal projectile, caliber, and
pitch and depth of grooves in the barrel, not to mention how much
powder should be used.

Delvigne's rifle musket had relied upon the traditional spherical
ball. However, Monsieur Caron, an artillery officer, followed by Captain Blais in 1833, experimented with elongated projectiles they
dubbed *cylindrical-conical bullets.* These slender projectiles were
subject to less wind resistance, yielding not only greater range and
accuracy but the same impact as larger calibers. In 1842 Captain
Thouvenin invented the *carabine à tige,* the "stem rifle." Thouvenin
got rid of the chamber in the Delvigne rifle and instead added a steel
pin, or stem, which projected 1½ inches from the bottom of the barrel.
Poured down the barrel, the powder settled around the stem. A wooden
sabot with a greased wad was attached to the cylindrical-conical

bullet, which slipped easily down the barrel and rested on the stem. The infantryman would strike the bullet three times with his ramrod, and the bullet expanded to fill the rifled grooves. Although the *carabine à tige* relied upon gentle rifling, its range was much greater than its predecessor. Its sight could be adjusted up to 1421 yards, and tests revealed that even at this range it could be deadly. Although its effective range was considered to be 600 yards, this was still three to four times the effective range of smoothbore muskets.

Captain Thouvenin's rifle saw a limited introduction in 1842, including a few units sent to Algeria. Its superiority firmly established, a number of French smoothbores were converted into rifle muskets by rifling the barrel and screwing in a stem at the bottom. This weapon saw service during the Crimean War over a decade later (1853–56), but by that time the new Minié rifle had seized the imagination of the pro-rifle school among the French military establishment.

Once again, a weapon that had shown so much promise during initial trials exhibited functional deficiencies during actual campaigning. Although the weapon could be successfully fired up to fifty times without interruption, a residue of burnt powder gradually built up. Since black powder is highly corrosive, the inside of the barrel had to be cleaned after each engagement. Unfortunately, to do this, a wash-screw had to be inserted down the barrel and positioned astride the pin, a procedure that obviously required dexterity, concentration, and patience, which were always in short supply during an action. It was also almost impossible to extract a bullet once it became stuck in the barrel. Considering the amount of ramrod pounding that was necessary, this problem was all too common. However, as with the Delvigne rifle, the greatest problem was that infantrymen were unable to ram the ball uniformly. Many rammed either too hard or too lightly, with the same undesirable results.

Both the Delvigne and Thouvenin rifles relied upon a human physical action to force the projectile into the rifled grooves. Capt. Claude Étienne Minié was intrigued with the problem and was determined to find a way to expand the base of the projectile mechanically to achieve a consistent and predictable trajectory. Returning to the old-style rifled barrel without a stem or a chamber, Minié instead altered the bullet to be fired. Hollowing out the base of the cylindrical-conical bullet, Minié inserted a thin iron cup. The bullet slid to its resting place on top of the powder with a gentle push of the ramrod, without the need to forcibly ram it down. When the charge exploded, gases filled the hollow cone and pushed the soft walls of the cup towards the walls of the barrel. Pressed against the barrel, the bullet filled the grooves, and there was no windage. This new form of musket was immediately recognized as a superior weapon and became known as the Minié rifle.

In 1846 all French chasseur and Zouave regiments in Africa received the new weapon. Its utility immediately demonstrated, a number of regular line regiments were also issued Minié rifles. Not only did the Minié rifle outperform its predecessors, it was also more reliable. Tests conducted at Vincennes in 1849 showed that at 15 yards the Minié bullet was able to punch its way through two boards of poplar wood, each ⅔ of an inch thick and separated by 20 inches. It was rumored that at 1200 yards the Minié bullet could penetrate a soldier and his knapsack and still kill anyone standing behind!

Despite some "teething" problems during the Crimean War, confidence in the new weapon remained high. The only obstacle to rearming the entire army lay in the expense that would be involved. There was a stockpile of more than 700,000 smoothbores, and it was difficult to justify the destruction of so many weapons that some argued were still serviceable. The solution was simply to convert these to rifle muskets. By 1857 the old muskets were being rebored with rifling grooves. The French Imperial Guard was the first to receive these converted rifles.

THE ORIGINS OF THE ENFIELD RIFLE MUSKET

The British army was not oblivious to the introduction of the new quick-loading rifle musket in France or to the breech-loading rifles adopted in limited numbers in Sweden, Belgium, and Prussia. Several new types of rifle muskets were examined. The Lancaster rifle, for example, was initially in contention but was set aside when its bullets were found to strip. The Duke of Wellington, still commander-in-chief of the British army, insisted that the ammunition for new rifle muskets have large enough caliber so that, in a pinch, it could be used in the traditional smoothbore.

In 1851 a British version of the Minié rifle, with a 0.702-inch caliber and weighing 10.5 pounds, was developed. Although it was officially accepted, trials soon revealed a problem. The weakness was not its range, accuracy, or ease of loading but the weight of the bullet. A conical bullet is considerably heavier than a spherical ball of the same caliber, and it was tiring to march with the regulation sixty rounds of the heavier bullets. The weight could be reduced by decreasing the number of bullets the soldier had to carry, but this was rejected outright.

A committee under the master general of ordnance, Viscount Lord Henry Hardinge, was convened in 1852 to study the problem. An acceptable rifled weapon had to be as easy to load as a smoothbore. It also had to possess as large a bore as possible to deliver a "crushing . . . close fire." The Hardinge Committee took a year to return with its recommendations. All infantrymen were to be armed with the three-groove 0.577-caliber Enfield rifle musket, which fired a cylindrical-conical bullet. This was the largest caliber for which the average infantryman could still carry both sixty rounds and a full knapsack during the rigors of a campaign. Barrels of smaller caliber and a larger number of grooves, although initially permitting more accurate fire, became fouled much more quickly. The Enfield charge was to be ignited by a percussion cap system, standard on all British shoulder arms from 1842 onward.

The Enfield weighed 2 pounds less than the old Brown Bess, and although the Enfield fired a heavier bullet, it produced much less recoil. It possessed greater accuracy at 300 yards and had a longer range, being effective up to 900 yards, the limit of its sights. Not only was the new weapon sturdier and simpler to manufacture, it also accommodated a wide range of projectiles, an extremely important consideration during this formative stage of the weapon's development.

Many other European armies soon followed the French and British and adopted some form of the rifle musket. In 1857 the Russians decided to arm 54 infantry regiments with a version of the Minié rifle. Portugal ordered 28,000 rifles from Belgium, while for general issue to their army, in 1854 the Austrians adopted the Lorenz rifle, which fired a conical bullet based on the Wilkinson-style bullet. The same year, both the Russian and the French governments adopted a plan to rifle all of their old smoothbore muskets. And of course, during Jefferson Davis's tenure as secretary of war (1853–57) the Americans produced what today might be termed an unauthorized knockoff in the form of the Springfield rifle.

EFFECTIVENESS OF THE NEW RIFLE MUSKETS

Soon after the Enfield's introduction, trials were performed to ascertain the new rifle's accuracy and range. It was also necessary to evaluate the performance of traditional smoothbore muskets, so that the two weapons could be meaningfully compared. During a speech in 1857 the chief instructor at the British School of Musketry, Lieutenant Colonel Wilford, sarcastically recalled the inaccuracy of the smoothbore musket in the hands of the typical soldier:

> Beyond 80 yards it lost all certainty of hitting a single man, at 200 yards it was uncertain even at larger bodies, and when screwed into a block or fired off at a rest, you might shoot all day at a target at 300 yards.

Although somewhat fanciful, Wilford's assessment of the "old service musket" was supported by some more pragmatically grounded trials. In 1841 the Royal Engineers concluded that the *maximum* range of the weapon varied between 100 and 700 yards, depending upon its elevation. Firing at a target twice as high and broad as a man at a 150-yards distance, it was able to hit the target three out of four times. Though doubled in height and width, when the target was moved to 250 yards, no hits were recorded and no balls ever retrieved. In another trial conducted during the early 1850s, a shooter with a Minié rifle hit a target at more than 1000 meters with 6 out of 100 shots, an accomplishment he was only able to achieve at 600 meters with a smoothbore. Incidentally, the new rifle musket possessed greater accuracy than a contemporary field artillery piece, which could only be expected to hit an 8-by-8-yard target at that range.

These experiments demonstrated that rifles using Captain Minié's "wedge projectiles" possessed both increased range and vastly greater accuracy. There was one characteristic of the weapons that caused some concern, however. Their projectiles possessed initial muzzle velocities well below those of older rifles and smoothbores. French tests revealed that a ball fired from a Thouvenin rifle musket possessed an initial velocity of 1408 feet per second, compared to 1023.6 for that fired from a Minié rifle, while Belgian trials found the British Enfield had an initial muzzle velocity of 1115 feet per second. In 1844 Major Mordecai of the United States Army had determined, using a musket ballistic pendulum, that the initial muzzle velocities of the U.S. model 1841 old-style rifle, the Brown Bess flintlock musket, and the pistol were 1750, 1500, and 947 feet per second, respectively. Thus, the velocity of the Minié rifle was only about 60% of those for traditional small arms. This had a profound impact on the weapons' performance. A faster bullet drops less *per distance covered*. Military men in the nineteenth century referred to the relatively straight line traveled by a fast projectile as a *flat trajectory* and the curved line of a slower projectile as a *rainbow trajectory.*

While evaluating the Minié and Enfield rifle muskets, the British also determined their trajectories. They found that for a bullet to hit a target 200 yards away, it would have to carry 21 inches above the line of sight at its highest point, compared to 42 inches for a bullet fired at a target 300 yards distant. In other words, if a new-style rifle musket was well aimed at an enemy 300 yards off, the bullet would pass over the heads of enemy soldiers between about 100 and 225 yards from the shooter.

The real problem was that when the rifleman sighted his rifle, the resulting arching trajectory meant he would strike the target only if the latter were within a narrow range of distances. If he sighted the rifle for a slightly shorter or longer range, he missed. When firing a weapon with a curved trajectory, the range of the target had to be accurately accounted for, so that the bullet was at an acceptable height when reaching the target. This narrow band was called the *dangerous space*. The depth of this dangerous space varied according to the speed of the bullet. The slower the bullet, the more curved the trajectory and, consequently, the narrower the dangerous space, which also depended upon the range of the target. The dangerous space for targets at extreme ranges could be as little as 10% of that for targets 100 yards away. French experiments to determine the dangerous

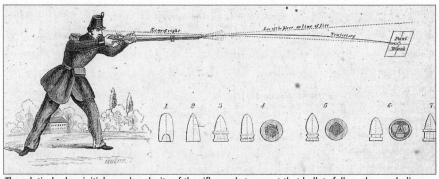

The relatively slow initial muzzle velocity of the rifle muskets meant that bullets followed a parabolic or "rainbow" trajectory. Accurate long-range fire required the shooter to accurately estimate ranges to within a few yards. *Scientific American,* May 11, 1861.

space for the Minié and the Thouvenin rifles showed that if the shooter adjusted his sights for 273 yards, the enemy had to be between 218.5 and 306 yards to be hit. However, at longer ranges the proper estimation of correct ranges became geometrically more important. If a shooter adjusted his backsight for 993 yards, the target was hit only if it was between 986.5 and 997.25 yards. The Enfield rifle was superior in this regard, with 60- and 40-yard dangerous spaces at 600 and 800 yards, respectively.

The infantryman armed with the new rifle musket had to elevate the barrel according to the range of the target, and this had to be done much more precisely when firing at distant targets. This, of course, had long been known to hunters and marksmen centuries before the Civil War. The problem was how to get ordinary soldiers to incline the rifle's barrel high enough to hit their opponents at long range. The solution was to add an adjustable *backsight* to the top rear part of the barrel, which the soldier raised or lowered according to the desired range. When the soldier looked through the back and front sights, he unconsciously elevated the barrel to produce the required trajectory. The backsight, by creating the impression that he was aiming "straight" at the target, duped the infantryman into raising his gun without triggering his fear that he was aiming too high.

However, even with a backsight, the soldier first had to accurately estimate the range of his target. If the weapon had an initial muzzle velocity of only 1000 feet per second, a relatively small error in the estimated range resulted in inaccurate fire. A soldier firing at a target

540 yards away who overjudged the distance by 33 yards would completely miss a 10-foot-high target. Even at shorter ranges, it was common to miscalculate ranges and fire so high as to miss even mounted officers.

This potential problem was even greater when charged by enemy cavalry. Repeated observations had demonstrated that cavalry could traverse the final thousand yards in approximately 4 minutes. They would cover the first 700 yards at a walk in about 3 minutes and the last 300 yards at a gallop in only 1 minute. Although a rifleman might be able to get off fairly accurate shots while the cavalry was still moving relatively slowly, it became increasingly difficult to assess the rapidly decreasing range once the charge began in earnest.

This was all no theoretical problem but a real battlefield challenge. At Antietam (September 17, 1862), for example, Confederate Maj. E. P. Alexander, an expert shot, decided to take a crack at the Pennsylvania Bucktails, who were running toward his position. Positioning eight men behind a rock to load for him, he started to unleash about eight shots a minute, starting when the Union infantry was still about 600 yards distant. Alexander would later recall: "I don't think I hit many, for distances varied rapidly, & all had to be guessed, but I did distinctly see one fellow drop at my shot."

These considerations may come as a surprise to modern readers. Rifles today have two if not three times the initial muzzle velocity of an Enfield or Minié rifle and consequently have much flatter trajectories. The trajectory of a bullet fired from an M16, for example, drops only 1 foot during the first 300 yards compared to 14 feet for that fired by a Springfield rifle.

Rifle Muzzle Velocity

Small Arms Type	Era of Use	Initial Muzzle Velocity (fps)
Brown Bess	c1689–1853	1500
Old style rifle	1778–1853	1750
Thouvenin (stem) rifle	1840s	1408
Flintlock pistol	1650–1850	947
Minié-type rifled musket	1850–56	1050
Enfield rifle	1858–65	1115

Krag-Jorgensen	Spanish-American War	2000
Springfield 1903	WW1	2800
M1 Garand	WWII	2800
M16	Modern	3250

Someone armed with a modern rifle does not have to make a range adjustment when firing first at a target at 300 yards and then at another at 200 yards. Using the same range setting will lead to some inaccuracy. However, a perfect shot would hit the enemy at 200 yards in the upper chest instead of the middle of the body at 300 yards, not an especially important difference in a combat situation.

SCHOOLS OF MUSKETRY

Soon after the adoption of the new rifle muskets, the French quickly devised a "scientific method" of range estimation, approved by the French minister of war in 1843 and codified in a manual entitled *Instruction sur le tir* (Instructions on Firing). Essentially the same system was adopted by the British School of Musketry at Hythe in 1853 and then by the Americans around 1858.

The French scientific method of rifle fire was predicated upon the assumption that soldiers armed with the new long-range rifle muskets were thoroughly trained in range estimation. For this to succeed, hundreds, possibly thousands, of rifle instructors would quickly have to be trained so that they in turn could return to their regiments and instruct the rank and file. To this end a musketry school was established at Vincennes. Each regiment sent a detachment that consisted of several officers, NCOs, and even one or two privates for a rigorous 4-month course. There was an encyclopedic approach by which participants were taught ballistic theory, how arms and munitions were manufactured, and the scientific method of range estimation.

As soon as the British adopted their version of a Minié rifle, the Enfield rifle, they encountered a similar need for a systematic approach to rifle training, and the School of Musketry was established in 1853 at Hythe. Attendees were given a 2½-month course of instruction similar to that at Vincennes, except that the British even more strongly emphasized practice of range estimation. Similar schools were established throughout Europe as other armies one by one adopted long-range small arms. Soon after the Springfield was adopted by the American army, a number of American officers pressed for the creation of a "school of musketry." There was some delay, however, and this did not occur prior to 1861, when the monumental events that erupted that year pushed these efforts into the background.

BREECHLOADERS

The idea of loading either a pistol or a shoulder arm at the breech end of the barrel was certainly not new. A number of arms utilized some sort of breech-loading mechanism, such as a number of pieces constructed by Marc Renede Montlaembert, Robert, and Casimir Lafaucheux in the eighteenth century. However, the first truly functional breech-loading small arm was unquestionably the Hall rifle, introduced as a trial in the U.S. army in 1823–24.

The first functional European counterpart was the Norwegian *chamber gun,* produced in limited quantities during the early 1830s. To load this latter weapon, the shooter placed a ball, a cone-shaped cartridge charge, and a cap into a cylindrical chamber. He then pulled the trigger, releasing a spring-loaded cock that hit the detonating cap. The mechanism proved to be relatively reliable, and in 1839 an official commission was set up to test the weapon. The resulting trials pitted the chamber gun against a Prussian jäger rifle. When firing at a target with a 2-foot radius, the Norwegian breech-loading rifle displayed greater accuracy when the range was within 205 yards. The jäger rifle musket was slightly more accurate at greater ranges. Impressed with these results, the Swedish government (Norway was then part of Sweden) purchased 400 breech-loading rifles and 50 pistols based on the same loading and firing mechanisms.

Similar experiments were repeated in 1845. This time competing against a standard smoothbore musket and the Prussian jäger rifle, the Norwegian breechloaders demonstrated notable superiority in both accuracy and rate of fire. Soldiers armed with the Norwegian rifle, the traditional musket, and the jäger rifle were able to unleash 10 volleys in 5, 7, and 15 minutes respectively. The breech-loading mechanism was still cumbersome, and the two rounds per minute was still far short of the seven to fifteen rounds allowed by later breechloaders, such as the Spencer and Henry rifles. Nevertheless, the Swedish king was still sufficiently impressed to order 500 of the new rifles.

Inspired by the new French approach to rifle muskets, in 1835 an arms manufacturer in Sömmerda, Germany, named Johann Nicholaus von Dreyse had begun to experiment with a muzzle-loading rifle with a new needle percussion system. Unfortunately, excessive ramming all too frequently led to premature explosions, and the inventor soon abandoned the muzzle-loading approach and concentrated loading at the breech instead. The rifle was quickly dubbed the *Zundnadelgewehr*, or "needle-igniting musket." Firing cylindrical-conical bullets, the weapon boasted a maximum range of 800 to 1200 yards, extremely impressive for the day. Unlike the percussion cap smoothbore, the detonating charge in the needle gun was ignited at its front and center, rather than at the rear. This, coupled with a more suitable center of gravity of the projectile, resulted in a greater force of propulsion.

Upon completion of a prototype in 1838, Dreyse began the arduous task of drumming up interest for the weapon among the Prussian military. Dreyse was more fortunate than most weapon inventors of the time, and his breech-loading needle gun was adopted by several regiments in the Prussian infantry in 1842. Its inventor claimed the rifle could be fired at six rounds per minute. Realizing the true potential of the new rapid-fire weapon, as most other Western countries cautiously experimented with some form of the Delvigne muzzle-loading rifle musket, Prussian authorities did everything in their power to keep their new acquisition a military secret. It would be another 15 years before other European powers cautiously began to experiment with breech-loading shoulder arms.

REVOLVERS (SIDE ARMS)

The idea of a pistol that could fire several shots in succession before its owner had to reload was certainly not new, and inventors had periodically essayed into this area from the early seventeenth century onward. Although Samuel Colt did not invent the "revolver," his ingenious side arm, where the chambers were rotated by cocking the trigger, was the first truly practical example of this genre. Unlike the breech-loading shoulder arms, which were met with nearly universal official skepticism in both Britain and the United States, the Colt revolver immediately was eagerly accepted by many mid-level officers in the British army. During the Eighth Kaffir War (1850–53), 500 Colt's revolving pistols were sold to British officers in the Cape Town colony. Reliable and highly accurate for a pistol, it met with general approval. In 1854 a report to Britain's Select Committee on Small Arms acknowledged the role played by the Colt revolvers during the African war and deemed it superior to any of its competitors. Not surprisingly, an increasing number of British officers carried some form of revolver during the Crimean War (1853–56).

The Great Indian Mutiny (1857–58), saw the first use of revolvers by mounted troops. On June 18, 1858, confronted with an overwhelming number of enemy cavalry led by the Rance of Jhansi, British Hussars pulled out their Colt revolvers and delivered a hitherto unknown volume of fire. Within moments the rebel cavalry was torn apart and completely repulsed, leaving 400 dead upon the battlefield.

RAPID-FIRE SMALL ARMS

The idea of using compressed air to hurl a projectile at an enemy dates back to the Napoleonic Wars, when the Austrian army introduced an experimental air gun. The weapon was never adopted by the Austrian infantry, and interest in other means to propel small arms projectiles lagged until sizable advances in metallurgy and engineering had accrued by the 1840s. At this time a few gun makers revisited the air gun, and several new prototypes appeared.

A few of the more creative inventors became fascinated with a new type of weapon that, at least theoretically, offered much greater potential, the rapid-firing small arm, in its modern form known as the *machine gun*. In 1846 a number of European newspapers enthusiastically touted the invention of an "electric gun" capable of firing 1000 projectiles per minute. The editors of *Scientific American* were critical, predicting that this would soon prove to be "humbug." The magazine's overtly acerbic tone is rather hard to understand since the same publication had proffered its own design for a rapid-firing device using compressed air pumps only several months earlier.

Both air gun and electric gun were only theoretical devices whose

This early design for a mechanical machine gun appears to have been nothing more than a concept at this stage. *Scientific American*, Aug. 27, 1846.

existence was strictly confined to the inventors' sketchpads and models. Jacob Perkins, an American expatriate living in London, had built a working model of a mechanical rapid-fire weapon in 1841, and its appearance probably precipitated the efforts toward the electric gun. Steam driven, Perkins's rapid-fire weapon was dubbed a "steam gun." Its inventor continued to refine the weapon, and in a later version on display at the Great Exhibition of 1851, it was able to fire 60 rounds a minute for up to 10 hours. These capabilities apparently impressed some British authorities, including no less than the British commander-in-chief, the Duke of Wellington. The duke was inclined to purchase some of Perkins's steam guns, but the entire venture evaporated with the appointment of Viscount Lord Hardinge after the death of the victor of Waterloo.

Perkins's invention was not the only mechanical rapid-firing gun to be exhibited at the Great Exhibition. We are told that a "war engine" designed by F. McGetteck was able to fire an astounding 10,900 charges in 10 minutes. Since this was never patented, it probably existed only as a nonfunctional model, and its rate of fire was only a theoretical capability calculated by its inventor. Another device patented in 1855 appears to have been developed to a more functional stage. W. Treeby built what he called a *chain gun*. In concept, it was remarkably close to the World War I machine gun. The charges, that is, the propellant powder, and the projectiles, were attached side by side to form a long chain. This was fed through the gun quickly, and each charge was fired rapidly in succession, about thirty-three times a minute. Although it received a favorable review from the *United Service Gazette,* which believed the weapon was ideal for defending a beach or an expansive open field, no interest was shown by British military authorities. Further development of these rapid-fire small arms languished until Messrs. Dickenson and Ross Winans, Confederate sympathizers in Baltimore, resurrected the idea of Perkins's steam gun in May 1861.

Chapter 3

DEVELOPMENTS IN
TACTICAL DOCTRINE, 1843–59

DOCTRINAL REACTION TO THE NEW WEAPONRY

I t did not take long for the more imaginative among Europe's military to think about the practical ramifications of the new rifled
small arms. Although there is little evidence that rifled artillery had any
impact on tactical theory before the 1860s, rifle muskets and
breechloaders immediately captured the imagination of some military
thinkers, who during the late 1840s began to propose new doctrine and
tactical systems.

Experimenting with the breech-loading needle gun, the Prussians
were not slow to appreciate the revolution in tactics that would
inevitably follow its adoption. Captain Wittich was one of the first to
write about its impact on existing fighting methods. In *Das Fahnlein
oder die Compagnie als die wahre tactische Einheit* (The Little Banner
or the Company as the True Tactical Unit), a pamphlet published in
1849, he predicted how the new rifles would affect combat and what
tactics had to be developed as a countermeasure. Wittich's analyses
were probably the single most thorough examination of the changes
that were likely to occur, and their impact was to extend beyond
Prussia. In 1852 Capt. Charles Chesney of the British army, in his
Observations on the Past and the Present State of Fire-arms, translated
a large portion of Wittich's tract, which now gained a European and
North American audience. Up to the Franco-Prussian War (1870–71)
most of the military theorists who sought to examine the impact of the
new weaponry touched upon issues first raised by Wittich.

Impressed with the needle gun, Wittich accepted the results of performance trials at face value. Wittich hypothesized that in the future,
firefights would take place at longer ranges. Infantry would be able to
unleash seven or eight rounds per minute and fire effectively at up to

600 to 800 paces. Possessing three to four times the range and six times the rate of fire of the smoothbore musket, the needle gun "must necessarily occasion a complete change in the whole tactics of war."

A defender who was able to inflict considerable casualties though his assailants were still at long range would have the advantage. It would be much more difficult for attackers simply to rush up and overwhelm an opponent. The attackers would be forced to deploy and first weaken the defenders with their own withering fire. It was also imperative to eschew the deep formations that had characterized the last half of the Napoleonic Wars. Even the battalion columns so commonly used by the French up to 1809 and later extolled by the internationally acclaimed military theorist Baron Antoine de Jomini now posed too much of a target. Instead, a much smaller column had to be employed. The 1843 Prussian infantry regulations, the inspiration for Wittich's writings, required the battalion to be divided into company columns, four ranks deep and separated from each other by the frontage they would occupy when deployed in line.

Of course, the rapid-fire capabilities of the new breechloaders posed new challenges, and even Swedish, Belgian, and Prussian tacticians doubted whether the breechloaders should be utilized up to their maximum rate of fire. Soldiers who fired five to eight shots per minute could consume the ammunition for an entire campaign during a single action. In many cases, especially when campaigning over mountainous countryside or in remote colonies, it would not be practical or even possible to increase ammunition supplies. Continued rapid fire could quickly exhaust an army's ammunition supply and seriously curtail its ability to continue active operations.

Captain Wittich therefore felt that long-range fire against enemy infantry should be restricted to the skirmishers. Men in formations should be allowed to fire only once the range was well within 600 paces. Of course, when threatened by either enemy artillery or cavalry, infantry would be allowed to fire at any practical range. Unlike the skirmishers of Napoleonic times, who could harass but not resist enemy formations, skirmishers now could be formed into small groups loosely equivalent to the traditional small squares. These skirmishers with their breechloaders could even keep cavalry at bay, especially when supported by friendly artillery.

Cavalry and artillery would be forced to adopt entirely new roles and tactics. Noting that the extreme range of the rifle musket now exceeded the range of heavy case shot, Wittich opined that the usefulness of light artillery would be tremendously reduced. Two platoons of proficient skirmishers, positioned 300 to 400 paces in front of the main force, would pick off artillerymen and silence the guns in minutes. Confidently, Wittich predicted that artillery, unless sheltered by protective cover, would be forced to operate at least a thousand paces from enemies armed with breechloading rifles. Horse artillery might prove the exception. No longer tied to following friendly cavalry, horse artillery would be kept in reserve until the right opportunity, then rush in, unlimber, and hold the important position until reinforced by friendly infantry. Nevertheless, the overall amount of field artillery available in the field would dramatically decrease. Military authorities would try to introduce heavier, longer-range artillery to replace the now inadequate field guns. These, however, could be drawn around the countryside only with great difficulty and would inevitably impair the movement of the other two arms.

The effectiveness of cavalry would also be severely curtailed. Skirmishers trained to rally in small, compact formations could hold off their equestrian enemies, even at long ranges. Cavalry would pose even less of a threat to regular formations. The only chance cavalry had of overturning formed infantry was if it somehow managed to catch the latter in flank by surprise. Henceforth, cavalry would rarely conduct headlong charges against enemy infantry. Deprived of its traditional role, Wittich felt that cavalry should be reduced to a small army reserve and a collection of divisional reserves. The Prussian officer argued that it would be advisable to equip all superfluous cavalry with a cavalry version of the breechloader so that they would be converted into "mounted infantry."

British "Battlefield Simulations"

Until 1850 most practical weapons trials were limited to simple, one-step operations, such as testing the weapon on a firing range. With the exception of William Duane, an American tactician writing in the early 1800s, virtually no effort was made to simulate how the new weaponry would perform under battlefield conditions. This was all about to change, however. Faced with the exceedingly optimistic French and Prussian appraisals of the new weapons and the tactical changes they would impose, the British military remained unconvinced and decided to conduct its own experiments to determine whether such optimism was warranted.

The new School of Musketry at Hythe provided the perfect setting. The first experiment, on Sept 17, 1853, evaluated the effectiveness of skirmishers with Enfields against an enemy line. Four skirmishers carrying "regulation Miniés" (the P51 Minié rifle) 200 yards in front of a 16-by-6-foot target fired 10 shots apiece at their own discretion. The target was hit 28 times out of a possible 40 shots, for a 70% hit rate.

In 1855 more elaborate trials were carried out to test the efficacy of these rifle muskets against infantry columns. Two targets were erected, each equivalent to the width occupied by thirty files and positioned to represent the first and last companies in a battalion in column at quarter distance (the distance between each tier of the column was equal to one-quarter of its frontage). The second target was placed 50 yards directly behind the first. The target in front, made of iron, prevented any bullets that hit it from striking the second target, too. Two groups of thirty-five skirmishers were provided thirty rounds per man. The first group fired as they advanced from 820 to 550 yards from the front target; the second group fired as they traversed the same space but retiring. The combined result was a 34% hit rate.

Of much more interest to the tactician was how these shots were distributed. Presumably, all the shots had been fired at the iron target in front, since the second target lay hidden behind this impenetrable obstruction. Of the 2100 shots, 379 had found their way to the first target. Throughout the experiment the distance of the target was unknown to the shooters, and they had to estimate the range, set their backsights accordingly, and then carefully aim and fire. At these ranges the dangerous space consisted of a relatively narrow band. Miscalculating the distance, the shooters frequently overshot their intended target. Fortunately, the second target was 50 yards farther, so 11% of the shots fired, 238 rounds, entered its dangerous space.

The practical significance of this was not lost on British military authorities. While the small dangerous space at longer ranges made it difficult to hit men along a line, deep columns were much more likely to be struck. At 450 yards the common soldier was twice as likely to hit a battalion in column compared to that in line; however, at extreme ranges he was six times as likely. Even if fire proved ineffective against linear formations at longer ranges, massed formations would still be a viable target. During the Napoleonic era, infantry and cavalry columns had been able to maneuver up to 300 to 350 yards from the enemy without loss from small arms fire. The 1855 experiment suggested that henceforth, these columns would find it much more difficult to conduct such preliminary maneuvers without suffering crippling losses.

Another experiment conducted at Hythe in May 1856 had equally important implications. This time the goal was to determine the effectiveness of the new rifles against field artillery at long range (610 yards, but the specific distance was unknown to the men). Sixty soldiers were placed in skirmish order, with an interval between each man. Of these, 23 had received extensive rifle training. They simulated firing against enemy artillerymen moving up into position. There were stuffed figures of eight artillerymen on foot, three drivers, a chief of ordnance, and a large, iron target 50 yards to the rear that represented six horses and a caisson. The skirmishers fired for 2 minutes. In that time each man fired about two rounds, and it was discovered that the six horse figures had been hit a total of twenty-two times, while the "men" had received seven hits. The experiment was repeated at 815 yards, where the men were allowed to fire for 3 minutes. The front row of skirmishers fired three times; the rear rank, twice. Now five out of the six horses were hit a total of sixteen times, while the eleven "human" targets were hit eight times. The experiment appeared to corroborate claims made by French and German tacticians that field artillery was now highly vulnerable to long-range rifle fire, to which it might not be able to adequately respond.

CAPTAIN GILLUIM: AN EXTREME ADVOCATE OF THE RIFLE MUSKET

Probably the most enthusiastic advocate of the new rifle muskets was Captain Gilluim of the Belgian Artillery. In 1856 Gilluim predicted that the new weaponry would change the very foundations of existing tactics. Wittich had felt the value of skirmishers would sharply increase but most infantry would continue to fight in traditional lines. In contrast, Gilluim felt that the greater range and much higher casualty levels would spell the end of close-order formations. More and more of the infantry would deploy as skirmishers, so that by the height of a battle, the entire army would consist of several lengthy lines in skirmish order. Gilluim also felt that the new infantry weapons would alter the way soldiers reacted under fire. Elevated from a mere cog in a mechanical formation and imbued with new-found confidence, the soldier would be transformed into a much more effective fighter:

> At great distances he will adjust his sights instead of firing at random: close to the enemy he will fire with more sangfroid than formerly, since he will feel confidence in his arm. It may be added the very occupation of thinking and adjusting the sights for different ranges will take from him all thought of danger, and he will find himself in as favorable a position as the artillerymen, whose coolness and sangfroid are proverbial.

BRITISH SKEPTICISM AND DEBATE

Despite the trials at Hythe, most of the British military did not share the unbridled enthusiasm of many Prussian, Belgian, and French theorists for the new rifles. Captain Chesney of the Royal Artillery was one of the first British officers to speculate about their probable impact. In his *Observations* (1852), Chesney described Wittich's views as overly optimistic. The changes imposed by the Minié rifle and the breechloader would be substantially more modest. He particularly rejected the idea that an engagement would devolve into a struggle between two lengthy lines of skirmishers, with the final result determined by "incessant fire"; skirmishers, even those armed with the new shoulder arms, would still be highly vulnerable to a sudden cavalry attack. Nor did Chesney think that the new riflemen could drive away field artillery as easily as many predicted. He argued that the extreme effective range of field artillery was still greater than that of the new rifles. A British 9-pounder firing heavy canister or solid shot in ricochet fire, for example, could annoy enemy riflemen operating 700 or 800 yards distant. Chesney concluded that with the exception of dense columns of troops—which, given their increased vulnerability to long-range fire, would no longer be feasible—the overall role and tactical methods of the three arms would remain largely unchanged.

Within 5 years of the publication of *Observations,* events would force the more progressive among the British military to take another look at the new weaponry and their probable effects. During the 1850s, a steady stream of inventions and improvements chipped away at the traditional conservatism: British infantry had adopted the Enfield, and experiments with rifled cannon were underway.

Since its establishment in the 1830s, the *United Service Magazine* had been one of the main forums for British military writing. The periodical, however, was a mirror of the conservatism then so prevalent among the British military. In its first fifty volumes, one finds little more than numerous rehashes of Napoleonic-style warfare punctuated with listings of recent promotions and news about the latest colonial expedition. By 1857 the need for an alternative vehicle of discussion and debate had become clearly obvious, and the Royal United Service Institute was established. Officers from all arms would air their views in its lecture halls and its journal.

In a lecture delivered on June 26, 1857, Lieutenant Colonel Dixon of the Royal Artillery was one of the first to talk about the implications of the new shoulder arms. Like Captain Chesney, Dixon felt that the new weapons would not alter the fundamentals of existing tactical practice and rejected the idea that close-order formations would be replaced by extensive clouds of skirmishers. Dixon argued:

> The impossibility of controlling or directing such irregulars would nullify all advantages likely to be obtained from each man being a good marksman. . . . A system would fall into pieces in the end from its inherent defects. An army would cease to act as a whole, and operations would be reduced to a multiplicity of small and insignificant attacks on isolated points.

This was the extent of agreement between the two writers, however.

Chesney had believed that the riflemen should be limited to a special rifle corps and should not be incorporated within the line regiments. Dixon argued that the best marksmen within each regiment should be trained with the new weapon and form its "flank company." This not only would provide a local tactical advantage but also bolster the ordinary soldiers' motivation by making possible "a proper spirit of emulation cultivated amongst the men [to] induce them to strive after such a distinction as promotion."

Like most other British officers of his day, Dixon believed that Prussian and French advocates of the new rifles had greatly overestimated their effective range. Officers would still have to coax and cajole their men to close within relatively short ranges, where the side whose men delivered their fire with the greatest "efficiency, coolness and determination" would be victorious. Infantry firefights would be conducted at "distances not materially varying from those at which they formerly attempted with inefficient means to do their duty." The maximum practical range during an engagement would probably be around 400 yards. Even at short range, line troops would still operate in close-order formations. Unlike a skirmisher carefully picking his targets at long ranges, the soldier in formation was to fire quickly to deliver the greatest possible weight of fire.

Despite his skepticism, Dixon had to admit that the greater range of the new rifles warranted a new maneuvering system. The old-time consuming maneuvers of the Prussian tactical school, the foundation of all Napoleonic maneuver systems, had to be abandoned. New maneuvering systems based on simplicity of execution and celerity of movement had to replace the standard evolutions, which were time consuming and risked higher casualties in the face of the longer-range rifle muskets.

Dixon also begrudgingly agreed with the Continental view that henceforth, the role of cavalry and artillery would be more restricted. No longer would it be feasible to commit cavalry at an early stage of battle, while the enemy infantry was still intact. Ponderous infantry squares would no longer be necessary. A two-rank line generally would be sufficient to repel a cavalry assault. Now cavalry should be kept as a reserve brought into play only after the enemy infantry was routed. The cavalry could still reap the fruits of the victory by pursuing the enemy fleeing the field.

Although Dixon felt that the artillery would be inconvenienced by the new infantry small arms, he believed that competent artillery officers could take effective countermeasures. Henceforth, artillery officers, even during the hottest engagement, must avoid posting their batteries in exposed positions. Dixon felt that despite the claims of the rifle's proponents, at longer ranges artillery would continue to enjoy an advantage. He pointed out that the ordinary rifleman with the unaided eye could not see, and therefore could not compensate for, inaccurate fire at long range. The artilleryman, however, could spot the location of shell bursts or see the earth spurting up several yards in front of or behind the intended victims and then adjust his range accordingly.

Given the range of the new rifles, Dixon correctly prophesized that fortifications would become even more important than ever before. Engineers would have to redesign these structures, however. The distance between key positions along a defensive work, always a function of the range of the defender's weapons, could now be increased. The main walls of the fortification positioned periodically in front of the main line would have to be moved farther to the front.

Both Chesney and Dixon served with the Royal Artillery, and perhaps their rejection of any doctrine which reduced the value of the artillery arm was colored by their membership in that branch of service. As others came forward at the institute to lecture on the need for new tactics, it became apparent that some British infantry officers were more optimistic about the importance of the new small arms on the future battlefield. On July 10, 1857, less than 2 weeks after Dixon's address, Lieutenant Colonel Wilford, the chief instructor at the School of Musketry, delivered another talk at the institution. Although Wilford's lecture largely focused on the various methods used to achieve accurate fire and how the weapon should be used during combat, the chief instructor also briefly speculated about its impact on combat methods more generally. Wilford was more optimistic about the rifle's practical performance than either Chesney or Dixon and believed that tactics had to be modified to accommodate the new weaponry. Battles would henceforth be fought at longer ranges. The traditional balance between the three arms—infantry, cavalry, and artillery—would also necessarily change. With their long-range weapons, infantry would not require the same amount of artillery support. Infantry would have the same effective range, in fact, as existing light field artillery, about 1000 yards. Like Dixon, Wilford emphasized that the design and use of outposts and field fortifications must also be modified to reflect the increased range of the defender's small arms.

Of course, all of this debate so far took place purely on a theoretical level. Events halfway around the world, however, soon afforded the British infantry an opportunity to test their new Enfield rifle muskets on the battlefield. When the Great Indian Mutiny erupted in May 1857, the new shoulder arms were just in the process of being distributed to a handful of British and native regiments. It did not take long for expert shots acting independently of the battalion to discover the greatly increased range and accuracy of the new weapon. Like the Algerian natives 10 years earlier, the Indian rebels at the start of hostilities were unaware of the new long-range threat. However, they soon learned they were in mortal danger as long as they were within 1000 yards of an expert shot. During the siege of Delhi, two enemy buglers perched atop an ancient archway were picked off simultaneously from far off by two sharpshooters. On another occasion an enemy leader in a crowd was picked off at 800 yards. (Some modern firearms experts feel these two incidents represent "lucky shots," since at this range individual soldiers were undistinguishable.)

Regardless of the exact range limit of the new rifle muskets, British sharpshooters soon learned that the Enfield could be used to destroy tactically more significant targets. During the relief of Lucknow (September 1857), two expert shots were able to crawl towards an enemy battery undetected and, handed a succession of loaded Enfields, quickly pick off all of the gunners and silence the battery. This accomplishment, once heard of in Britain, was sure to rekindle the debate regarding the effectiveness of artillery versus infantry. Cavalry was discovered to be equally vulnerable. A light company firing at enemy cavalry 700 yards distant was able to completely repel a charge after firing less than a minute.

Such news made its way back to Britain. Possibly inspired by these achievements, Captain Tyler expressed a very optimistic view of the impact of the new rifles on the battlefield when he delivered a lecture at the Royal United Service Institute entitled "The Rifle and the Spade, or the Future of Field Operations" on April 1, 1859. He agreed with others that field fortifications such as entrenchments, abatis, chevaux-de-frise, and so on would become more important. Greater efforts would now have to be taken to secure outposts. Ditches would have to be dug and other precautions taken to keep attackers at longer range. He adamantly disagreed with Dixon's opinion that the firefights conducted by ordinary infantry in formations would be limited to within a 400-yard range.

Though agreeing with the artillery officers that the smoke, uneven terrain, and confusion of the battlefield would probably preclude the effective use of the rifle to its full maximum range of 900 to 1000 yards, Tyler felt that it could still be used at long enough ranges to embarrass field artillery. He opined that firefights at the 600-yard range would be common and that cavalry and artillery, unable to stand before this new threat, would no longer play as important a role on the battlefield as formerly. True, artillery would attempt to counter the threat with long-range shrapnel, which in theory had a maximum range of 1050 yards. However, to be effective, shrapnel had to explode about 50 yards in front of the troops it intended to strike. The difficulty in getting a shell to explode at precisely the right place would limit its value in practice. Now highly vulnerable to this accurate small-arms fire, artillerymen, Tyler predicted, would have to find makeshift protection, such as heavy iron mantelets.

Tyler conjectured that henceforth, battles would be briefer. The rate of casualties would increase, and the troops would be unable to bear such withering destruction for long. The overall effect would be to produce decisive results more quickly. The most notable exception to this would be the struggle over key positions, such as houses and villages entrenchments that could be easily fortified and reinforced. Field fortifications would also become much more commonly employed than before. In such positions the defenders, armed with long-range small arms, would be more than capable of repulsing an infantry assault. To avoid needless casualties, the offensive commander would have to eschew daylight attacks and rely more heavily on shot and shell to destroy or neutralize such defenses. As to artillery, Tyler concluded that the:

duties of artillery will necessarily be modified, and as they will be called upon in the future, when employed to the best advantage, to act more against standing works, and less against moving masses of men at short ranges . . . they will be more stationary than heretofore, and will be better enabled to take advantage of a judicious combination of natural position and artificial protection, to secure them from the effects of their opponent's rifle fire. They will wisely avail themselves of the assistance of the spade . . .

This debate was not limited to the confines of the Royal United Service Institute. One can read how the same arguments began within months between artillerists and infantry officers on the other side of the Atlantic. The controversy can be found on the pages of works written by Lt. Cadmus Wilcox and Capt. John Gibbon. Both taught at the United States Military Academy at West Point, and one could reasonably assume both men passed their views to a number of cadets who would later serve as officers under these two arms during the American Civil War.

Theoretical Performance versus Psychological Reality

Although there was a debate about the details, in general British tacticians rejected the optimistic predictions the Prussians and Belgians made about the new guns. At the heart of this skepticism were psychological considerations. It was all very fine to establish extremely high hit rates on a target range, but this necessarily resulted in an overestimation of a weapon's true capabilities on the battlefield since it failed to account for how the soldier actually used it when under fire. During his lecture Tyler pointed out that regardless of the rifle's theoretical capabilities, "the dust, turmoil, smoke, and excitement of the battle-field will detract from the accurate aim of the men; and irregularities of the ground will much interfere with extreme ranges." The British tacticians were also concerned about the new rifle musket's relatively slow initial muzzle velocity. As already noted, this produced a more curved, parabolic trajectory than the old-style rifles, and this meant that at longer ranges the rifleman had to estimate the range of the target very accurately.

These concerns caused some British military experts to doubt whether the infantrymen could effectively fire at anything but relatively close range during combat. During his own lecture, Dixon of the Royal Artillery had pointed out that it is comparatively easy to train individuals to achieve very accurate fire on a firing range. The terrain is perfectly flat, and distractions, such as talking, laughing, or any unnecessary movements, are prohibited.

This, he observed, was an entirely different set of affairs from the extremely chaotic conditions invariably encountered during actual combat. All the training required to teach a soldier to judge distances accurately on perfectly flat target ranges would serve little practical purpose on the broken and undulating terrain on which battles were actually fought. A myriad of forces would distract the infantryman and destroy the presence of mind needed to judge distances and readjust the backsight. Not only was the soldier's line of sight frequently restricted by hills, hedges, and woods, but often his sight was obscured by the dust and smoke that invariably contributed to the pandemonium of battle. If this was not enough, whatever calmness and mental discipline he had was undermined by the confusion of battle. Hurrying from one position to another, he was as much the hunted as the hunter and invariably would be "excited by every circumstance which in battle may be considered to operate so powerfully to distort a man's judgement or his aim." Surrounded by smoke, most soldiers would be affected by the whistle of shells and bullets flying overhead, while shell, shot, and bullet decimated the ranks. Add to this the groans and shrieks of the dying and wounded. And, of course, the situation was even worse for infantrymen facing charging cavalry. The men's nerves would be tested to the extreme. The earth would literally shake for a hundred yards around and, gripped in paroxysms of fear, many of the men would lose control over their muscles and wobble from leg to leg.

This suggested to the more cynical among the British military that soldiers were simply unable to aim during the heat of battle. The best that could be reasonably expected was for the men to bring their rifles to the horizontal and try to "level" their weapons more or less according to the distance of their targets, much like their predecessors had sought to do during the eighteenth century and the Napoleonic Wars.

SMOOTHBORE VERSUS RIFLED MUSKETRY

Such observations led some, like British Captain Andrew Steinmetz in 1861, to argue that the smoothbore musket provided better performance at closer ranges, say within 200 paces:

> In fact, the trajectory of the smoothbore, at short distances was flat; the ball met a man who happened to be in the line of fire: the trajectory of the rifle, owing to the diminished velocity of the bullet by friction, can never be flat. If we could make the bullet spin without the loss of force by friction, of course the case would be altered; but that is impossible.

It was unanimously agreed that the new weapons not only could be fired effectively at much greater distances but possessed greater accuracy when firing beyond 100 or 150 yards or so. The concern arose from the rifle's performance within "point-blank" range. There were those who felt that under battlefield conditions a traditional smoothbore musket, such as the Brown Bess, was a more reliable weapon at these shorter distances. Those of this opinion argued that even at close range the projectile fired from a rifle musket displayed a much more curved trajectory than that of a smoothbore. At the very moment of a crisis, when an enemy infantry or cavalry charge reached the critical range, the infantrymen had to more carefully aim or level his new weapon in order not to fire either too high or too low. The discrepancy in performance between smoothbore and rifled weapons, as we have seen, stemmed from the difference in initial muzzle velocities.

CHASSEURS À PIED AND ZOUAVES

While the Prussians were beginning to revise tactical theory, the French introduced another tactical innovation, one which, though initially ignored by most other nations, ultimately would have a pronounced effect on the way European-style armies would conduct themselves on the battlefield. As the French minister of war, Marshal Soult had envisioned the creation of specially equipped infantry units and in 1833 was responsible for a royal ordinance calling for the formation of chasseur companies. These elite companies were to be armed with the Delvigne carbines and were to undergo special training different from the traditional Prussian system of maneuvers, which had been universally adopted throughout Western Europe since the mid-eighteenth century.

Although the proposed companies never came into existence, the concept of athletic-style training for soldiers as well as a new, faster maneuver system caught the imagination of a few farsighted military thinkers, in particular the Duc d'Orléans. Whether it did so because of the French troops' experience in northern Africa or some other considerations that have been lost to history is uncertain. What is indisputable, however, was the Duke's faith in the new fighting methods. A single company of chasseurs under the Duke's patronage was raised and stationed at Vincennes.

The duke was extremely impressed with the company's performance and soon wanted to expand the organization. On November 14, 1838, a royal decree authorized him to raise a full battalion of the new-style chasseurs on a provisional basis. Known as the Tirailleurs de Vincennes, this organization embodied a radically new approach to not only how the men would fight but how soldiers would be trained, as well. Emphasis was placed on what demonstrably worked, rather than on tradition. Not only were the chasseurs armed with new types of weapons; they were outfitted with a new style of uniform that completely broke with European military tradition. Setting aside the fancy but highly impractical habits (great coats) and breeches, long the hallmarks of the European soldier, they now wore wide, roomy pantaloons, a frock coat, and a light shako (a high, plumed hat). Unlike the rest of the infantry, whose training was generally limited to parade ground maneuvers and exercises, the Duke's chasseurs were allowed extensive practice with their weapons and had to complete a gymnastics course, which included leaping over obstacles and climbing. Like all other infantry regiments, they were also given fencing lessons.

Equipped with the Delvigne rifle musket, the chasseurs were taught the fundamentals of the "scientific" use of the rifle. At the heart of this complicated rifle drill was teaching the men to estimate ranges accurately, an essential precondition for effective long-range fire of any weapon with a significantly curved trajectory. In contrast to regular infantry, which always fired while standing or crouching in close-order formations, the chasseurs were taught to take advantage of all available cover and learned to fire while kneeling or even while lying on the ground.

The other half of the chasseur's armament consisted of the newly introduced "sword bayonet," which had a hilt and could be used by itself in hand-to-hand combat, as well as at the end of the rifle musket. The regular infantry was basically able to do little more than stand with their rifles and bayonets straight out before them. During their fencing lessons the chasseurs, however, were instructed on how to parry and thrust with the sword bayonet at the end of their rifles. They spent countless hours learning how to handle their weapons in combatlike situations, to guard themselves from charging horsemen, and to reply with a quick thrust at the rider or to hamstring his horse. These would prove to be invaluable preparations that would later allow the chasseurs to stand up to Arab cavalry, which had so easily ridden down other French skirmishers. The men responded well to the bayonet exercises, which noticeably increased their self-confidence.

Although expected to fight frequently in a regimental line like other infantry, the chasseurs were drawn up in two rather than the usual three ranks. It is tempting to assume that the Duc d'Orléans's interest in the two-rank line was the result of the repeated British successes with this formation during the Napoleonic Wars. Actually, the French chasseurs were forced to adopt the two-rank line for more practical reasons. The rifled carbine with which they were now armed was much shorter than the traditional smoothbores. If they had adopted a three-rank line, the carbines of the third rank would not have stuck out past the first rank, and inevitably, many of those in this front rank would have been scorched or even shot by those in the third.

However, probably the most significant innovation of the chasseurs was a new approach to maneuvering. Unlike other infantry, which performed most of their maneuvers at the ordinary step—90 paces per minute and only occasionally at the double quick—the Tirailleurs de Vincennes performed all maneuvers either at the double quick or the *gymnastic pace.* This latter step, already an extremely brisk 165 paces per minute (each 33.3 inches long), could be increased to a staggering 180 paces per minute.

The experiment was quickly dubbed a success by the French

military authorities, and Tirailleurs de Vincennes became a permanent organization on August 28, 1839, taking up residence at Fontainebleau. Although the unit impressed both the minister of war and King Louis Philippe, there were still sufficient skeptics to keep the Tirailleurs' true usefulness in doubt. To settle the controversy, it was decided to send the Tirailleurs to Africa to see how they would perform in actual combat. It became immediately obvious that the intensive gymnastic training had been a wise investment. In contrast to the other colonial troops, the Tirailleurs were in excellent physical condition and able to endure the rigors of an active campaign in the African clime.

The heavy version of the Delvigne carbine carried by the Tirailleurs also proved to be an instant success. The Arabs soon discovered that these new fighters bore little resemblance to the French infantrymen of previous campaigns. For the first time French marksmen were able to pick off the enemy systematically, even though the latter was scattered and trying to exploit whatever cover was available. The Tirailleurs were able to shoot down Arab sentinels at up to 400 to 500 yards, a hitherto unheard-of accomplishment.

Rather fortuitously, the Tirailleurs were brigaded with native soldiers known as Zouaves, who were themselves renowned for their bravery and rugged commando style of combat. The two organizations learned from each other, and the Zouaves soon adopted the new Tirailleurs maneuvers.

Stimulated by these successes in Africa and further motivated by political unrest in France, the Duc d'Orléans was authorized to raise nine additional battalions the next year, 1840. The duke felt, however, that the designation of Tirailleurs was too old-fashioned and not distinctive enough for such promising men. The ten battalions were now to be called *chasseurs à pied* instead. Even greater emphasis was placed on a scientific approach to sharpshooting, and a cadre of officers who were expert marksmen was sent back to Vincennes for further training. It was at this point that they adopted a formal method to teach the men how to estimate ranges accurately. Many other armies would later emulate these techniques, and it was in fact the same system that would be used by the First United States Sharpshooters during the American Civil War.

Five *chasseur à pied* battalions were sent to Africa, where they quickly distinguished themselves. As a result of the performance of the 6th Battalion at Oueh Foddah in 1842, the entire chasseur force, known after the Duke's death in 1850 as the Chasseurs d'Orléans, began to be ranked among the finest infantry in Africa. After hard-fought operations against the Flittas in 1845 and ensuing engagements at Zaatcha and Isly, among others, their reputation gradually spread among other military circles both in Europe and North America.

In 1845, under the guidance of Marshal Thomas Bugeaud, the various maneuvers employed by the chasseurs were codified into the officially sanctioned manual entitled the *Ordonnance du Roi sur l'exercise et les manoeuvres des bataillions de chasseurs à pied*, the "Instructions for the Evolutions and Maneuvers of the Foot Chasseurs." This required that all battalion maneuvers be performed at the gymnastic or triple pace. Moreover, unlike the traditional maneuvers, which required infantrymen to halt after completing each command, the chasseur maneuvers were performed in a continuous series of motions, without interruption after each stage. For example, the previous method of forming line from a closed column by companies required ten separate commands. In the chasseur version of this maneuver, all companies but the first would face left and then run into their final positions along the line to be formed. Once there they would face right and move into line. The entire operation was performed without even halting the first company.

The greatly increased emphasis on speed was not simply the result of the need to develop methods to counter the extremely quick, nimble, and ferocious Arab horsemen. French military authorities like Bugeaud recognized that in future wars in Europe, the chasseurs would be faced with enemy infantry also equipped with the new types of rifles. On the battlefield of the near future, speed could save lives. If infantry continued to rely upon the slow, processional methods of deployment, men would drop by the dozens before they could return fire or move forward to the attack.

The chasseur regulations of 1845 also prescribed a new system of skirmishing, which had been developed by the chasseurs and Zouaves during the Algerian campaign. Traditional skirmisher tactics called for the soldiers to move and fight along two extended lines. Although each was usually 4 to 8 feet from his neighbors, the men would occasionally crowd together when forced to move through constrictive terrain. Each man was assigned a fixed position along the lengthy skirmishing line and only occasionally deviated from the formation to take cover behind a bush or rock. The new system of skirmishers emphasized the role of small groups and localized initiative. Each skirmisher company was organized into tactical groups called *battle comrades.* These four-man *sections,* that is, two files, were to function as a single group and were never to lose sight of one another.

THE FRENCH BACKLASH AGAINST LONG-RANGE FIRING

Despite the string of experiments that seemed to prove the increased range and accuracy of the Minié-style rifle muskets, after the Crimean War, French military authorities began to doubt the practicality of long-range fire under battlefield conditions. The backsights on the Minié Pattern 1850, for example, had been sighted up to 900 yards, since infantry had been expected to use their weapon up to this range. However, as French military began to appreciate how the weapon would be used during battle—as the limitations of the high parabolic trajectory and the time and concentration needed to estimate the range accurately and set the sights accordingly became understood—the maximum range on the backsight was gradually reduced. Around 1858 the maximum range was reduced to 600 yards, and the following year down to 400 yards.

When the *chasseurs à pied* and Zouaves were given a new *carbine à tige* that same year, the weapon no longer even had an "elevating" backsight. The men were expected to use the simple flat backsight lying on the barrel when firing at targets up to 200 yards. When a firefight occurred at a longer range, the men were instructed to use their left thumbs instead. The light infantryman was to place his left hand across the lower band of the barrel, and the thumb would now become the "backsight." At ranges between 200 and 400 meters (about 432 yards), the soldier would keep the thumb pressed flush to the barrel and sight over his nail. Starting at 400 meters, he sighted on the "joint of the thumb" and aimed at the enemy's waist. When firing at ranges of about 600 meters (about 650 yards) the thumb would be erect.

Of course, this was easier said than done and required quite a bit of practice. This technique would be too complicated for any French cavalry armed with rifle muskets. French dragoons, for example, were ordered to use a much simpler method, one that had been employed by European infantry since about the 1780s. When firing at a target about 100 meters distant, they were instructed to aim at the enemy's feet. When the intended victim was about 200 meters away, they were to aim at the waist while they were to fire at the head when the range was 250 meters.

The French military's rationale for this backtracking from its earlier, more optimistic assessment of the maximum effective range of rifle muskets appears to have resulted from both economic and tactical concerns. Experience had demonstrated that in the excitement of battle, the infantrymen began to fire at too long a range and thus wasted a vast amount of ammunition. French writers around 1860 began to echo the cynicism expressed by some of the lecturers at the Royal United Service Institute several years previously. General Bonneau du Martray, for example, would conclude:

> As no one doubts that the rifle will play a much more important part in success of future battles than hitherto, it is the utmost importance to train good shots. We say, in the first place, that the use of the elevating sight is too slow and too difficult in battle; it will even cause the loss of some of the advantages of breech-loading. The determination of the distance, and, consequently, the adjustment of the sight, are liable to error, and the time required endangers the loss of the favorable moment for firing. . . . We think, therefore, that in the field we should abolish the use of the backsight. It is not absolutely necessary to hold the rifle at the shoulder to make good practice in firing.

These were the views that molded the French troops who in 1859 went to battle in Italy and who were seemingly totally vindicated by their performance. That conflict greatly influenced American thought just before the Civil War. Unfortunately, this last-minute change of French offensive doctrine has led to some confusion among future generations of military historians, arising from the use of the word *Napoleonic*, which has two different meanings, depending upon the time of use. Up to 1848 the term refers exclusively to Napoleon I. However, in military treatises and articles penned in the late 1850s, the meaning shifts and is used to characterize the new methods of Louis Bonaparte (Napoleon III), especially the turn away from long-range fire of the rifle musket and a renewed emphasis on the bayonet. This meaning of the term, when employed in the *Military Gazette*, for example, is also why the new *canon obusier* (gun howitzer) was known in the Americas as the "12-pounder Napoleon." A military analyst writing in the decade after the Civil War who lamented an unfortunate reliance upon "Napoleonic tactics" was more probably referring to the shift in French offensive infantry doctrine during the 1850s than he was to the conceptual armamentarium that underlay the true Napoleonic system used at the turn of the century. This is a subtle distinction that has unfortunately been lost to posterity.

Chapter 4

ARTILLERY PRIOR TO THE CIVIL WAR

O rdnance and artillery practices had undergone little change during the early 1800s, and had the Civil War erupted as a result of the Kansas Crisis in 1856, artillery on either side would have been very similar to that used during the War of 1812. Instruction manuals printed during the 1850s describe armament and procedures already in service for decades. The assortment of artillery pieces described in Gibbon's *The Artillerist's Manual*, which appeared in 1859, was virtually identical to those prescribed 8 years earlier by the official *Instructions for Heavy Artillery*.

American artillery was categorized into three classifications according to function. *Field artillery* was relatively light and mobile and accompanied the army in the field. *Seacoast* artillery obviously was intended for coast defense. Artillery for the defense of permanent garrisons and fortifications as well as those for destroying defensive positions were referred to as *garrison and siege* artillery.

Until 1860 the great preponderance of artillery pieces in American land service were smoothbore muzzleloaders. The basic design and functionality of artillery had been discovered early in its career. The two easiest ways of destroying an enemy target were either to shoot a solid mass directly towards it at high speed or, alternatively, to lob a heavy projectile on top of it. The first was by far the more popular approach, and most artillery was "guns" which shot a solid projectile at the target. These projectiles were effective against wagons, gun carriages, masonry, and, of course, humans. Since damage was caused by the weight and speed of the projectile upon impact, the greatest initial muzzle velocity was desirable. In order for the explosive gases to act as long as possible upon the projectile, the guns had to have long barrels. Projectile weight was also important; heavier shot not only carried farther but also permitted more accurate shooting. Guns were generally limited to a flat trajectory, usually not more than 4 degrees, since a curved trajectory caused the round shot to bury itself harmlessly in the ground.

In the early days the enemy frequently took shelter behind high, massive walls, such as a medieval castle or walled city, so it was often desirable to throw a large, heavy object onto the target. A massive projectile would be lobbed high up into the air, and the force of impact resulted from the velocity acquired as it descended back to the ground. This required a different type of artillery piece. To fire a heavy projectile, it had to have a large bore. However, since great velocity was not needed, it could have a short, stubby barrel. The resulting ordnance became known as a *mortar*. Usually, the barrel was elevated in a fixed position, at about 45 degrees to the vertical. The range was adjusted by changing the amount of charge that was used. Although mortars were not generally used on the battlefield, they were very useful during sieges. Parabolic trajectories meant projectiles could be fired over intervening obstacles to crush the roofs of buildings and subterranean vaults as well as troops on reverse slopes.

Centuries would elapse before the third major type of artillery was discovered. Eventually, advancements in metallurgy allowed the manufacture of the explosive shells. This looked like round shot, except it had a small hole on the surface for the fuse. The inside was hollow and stored the explosive charge of gunpowder. Obviously, an artillery piece that could hurl explosive projectiles could be highly useful during the day-to-day fighting of an extended campaign and on the battlefield. Unfortunately, until the 1830s and '40s, cast iron was not durable enough to withstand the enormous pressures experienced at high velocities, and shells were only effective when fired at less than 700 feet per second. Small charges had to be used, and the projectiles were thrown in a curved trajectory.

This created the need for a new artillery weapon, known as a *howitzer*, which made its first appearance during the Wars of Austrian Succession (1740–48). Although a howitzer looks similar to a gun, there are two noticeable differences. Since the projectile caused damage by explosion rather than the force of impact, projectiles with larger diameters and greater explosive payloads were preferable. And since range was achieved by a curved trajectory instead of greater muzzle velocity, gases in the barrel did not have to operate upon the projectile for quite as long. Thus, the resulting weapon had a larger bore caliber and a shorter barrel than a gun. The length of a howitzer's barrel was only four to six times its bore caliber, while guns typically had barrels that were twelve to twenty-four times the diameter of the bore. Unlike guns, in Britain both mortars and howitzers were referred to by the inside diameter of their barrel, such as a "10-inch howitzer."

Each of these weapons was capable of firing several different types of projectiles. Guns primarily fired solid shot. Howitzers generally fired explosive shells, but when forced by circumstance, howitzers could also fire shot. Generally called *round shot* in Britain and *solid shot* in the United States, these were simply spherical cast-iron balls. In the U.S. guns and howitzers were usually referred to by the weight of the solid shot they fired, so a "12-pounder" fired a 12-pound ball, while a "6-pounder" used a 6-pound ball.

Howitzers and mortars were designed to throw shells filled with explosives that would blow up when ignited by a fuse. The cast-iron shell was made thick enough to withstand the force of the explosion that propelled it. Also, to do maximum damage, it had to be able to penetrate wooden buildings and a few feet of earth.

The larger the interior space, the greater the explosive payload and the more damaging the explosion. In practice, instead of exploding into countless fragments, shells were scattered into a discrete number of larger sections. Shells fired by the 24- and 32-pounders broke into eighteen or nineteen pieces, thrown up to 600 yards, while 12-pound howitzer shells split up into twelve to fifteen pieces, scattered up to 300 yards. This explains their rather random effectiveness. People standing almost beside exploding shells were occasionally known to survive untouched, while more distant comrades might be killed. Nevertheless, shells were a highly useful tool, especially when firing against slowly moving cavalry. The noise and confusion of the exploding shells frightened the horses, making them unmanageable, which in turn forced the cavalry to regroup.

Shells had another useful purpose. Fired into wooden structures, the shells usually ignited the buildings when exploding, and this was an effective way of clearing a stubbornly defended town. Large shells could destroy earthen parapets. Burrowing into the earth before detonating, they acted like small mines. A 32-pounder howitzer could remove about 4 to 5 cubic feet of earth per shot.

A third type of projectile had long been used for short-range defense. Cast-iron balls were placed within a tin *canister* and packed in sawdust. As the canister was forced through the barrel, its thin metal skin was split apart, and the balls struck each other and were scattered. This increased the number of casualties that could be inflicted, while decreasing the need for accuracy. Canister could be fired from both guns and howitzers and was usually reserved for the last moments of an enemy assault.

Although *spherical case* had been invented by Henry Shrapnel in 1784, the first functional version was introduced in the British army only in 1804. It was recognized that the ability to fire multiple projectiles simultaneously was highly useful. However, because of range restrictions canister was generally limited to defensive operations. Shrapnel's projectile was in essence a type of shell. However, the internal space was filled with a number of musket or cast-iron balls, over which was poured molten sulfur to secure their position. In the center of these, a space was drilled out and an explosive charge inserted. Like an ordinary explosive shell, what was originally called a *common shell*, the internal charge was detonated by a lit fuse. However, spherical case, or *shrapnel,* as it was often called, was primarily an antipersonnel weapon. Casualties were caused by the numerous bullets and remnants of the shell rather than the actual force of the explosion. Since they were intended to be fired at people rather than buildings or earthen parapets, shrapnel shells had a thinner metal skin, which accounted for only about 50% of the total weight of the projectile.

Shrapnel was used with great success by the British army during the Napoleonic Wars. The artillerists determined the range at which it was to explode by inserting the fuse of the appropriate length. For maximum effect, fuses were timed to explode while the shrapnel shell was still in the air 50 to 75 yards in front of the targets. After the explosion, the iron balls and shell fragments, though dispersed, continued on, following the same general trajectory. Thus, unlike canister, its effectiveness continued undiminished for the entire effective range of the artillery piece. Canister was generally limited to targets within 350 yards, and the absolute range of the heaviest canister was less than 700 yards. Shrapnel had about the same range as solid shot and had been known to inflict casualties at 2000 yards. This had several practical ramifications. Not only could shrapnel be used offensively and not just as a response to enemy activity; it was no longer as necessary to thrust the artillery into the thick of the action, exposing it to musket fire and cavalry charges.

TRENDS IN AMERICAN ARTILLERY

Though the United States Ordnance Department had not been completely idle and some changes had been made to the artillery pieces over the years, one could characterize these changes as iterative in nature, not indicative of any fundamental modification in basic design or use. The only major developments for land artillery were the discontinuation of a 35-year experiment with cast iron and the return to bronze for field artillery, and the reduction of the number of different types of carriages and artillery pieces in the field.

The United States Artillery had almost exclusively relied on bronze in the construction of its field artillery from the Revolution up until the turn of the century. Bronze was favored because of its greater durability; it was less sensitive to the normal wear and tear, the inevitable result of firing. Unfortunately, bronze was also five times more expensive than cast iron, and the U.S. was dependent upon foreign sources for the necessary copper and tin. In 1801 Henry Dearborn, then secretary of war, motivated by a sense of economy, ordered the suspension of new bronze field pieces, pending the results of experiments that determined the effectiveness of iron versus bronze barrels. It was not until the early '30s that the required tests were conducted. In 1835 the Ordnance Board concluded that iron was generally unsuitable for field pieces, which henceforth must be of bronze, and the manufacture of bronze field pieces resumed the next year.

EUROPEAN ADVANCES IN ARTILLERY

During the seventeenth century there had been a seemingly endless variety of artillery, which of course created a logistical nightmare. The great French artillerist François de la Vallière was the first to attempt the systematic reduction in variety and an increase in mobility. Later in the century Jean-Baptiste de Gribeauval was to renew efforts in these areas, and he succeeded in reducing the number of artillery pieces to the 4-, 8-, and 12-pounders in the French army.

However the close of the Napoleonic Wars, the development of land-based artillery had reached a type of plateau and several decades would elapse before the next notable steps in its development would occur. No such stagnation characterized the development of naval artillery, though. By the early 1820s, a new artillery design appeared that solved a problem that had plagued artillerists for centuries. Although the idea of hurling large shells packed with a potent explosive payload had long captured artillerymen's imaginations, the strength of the available metals had continued to severely limit both the size of the shells and the velocity with which they could be fired. Larger shells required a much larger explosive force to propel them the required distance. However, if too great an explosive force was applied, the shell's payload itself would explode inside the howitzer and cause the destruction of the artillery piece and those around. Shells, as a result, had to be limited to smaller calibers.

In 1822 Lt. Col. H. J. Paixhans of the French artillery successfully constructed a long gun that had an especially designed chamber for the propelling explosive, so that the impact on the shell was reduced to within acceptable limits. Known as a *canon à bombes,* it was created for the French navy, which needed a weapon that could fire shells over the relatively long distances often encountered in coastal defense or ship-to-ship fighting. American journalists of the time refused to accredit this invention to Paixhans and argued that it was really the brainchild of Maj. George Bomford of the United States Army who used the new type of gun, a *Columbiad,* successfully during the War of 1812. According to this version, Bomford's plans soon fell into Paixhans's hands, and the latter, recognizing their value, worked to introduce this innovation into French service.

The British and American military were quick to recognize the importance of naval shell guns, and after a series of experiments, each developed its own variants of this new type of ordnance. Lt. J. A. Dahlgren quickly established himself as America's leading authority in this area. Under the auspices of the Navy, he went on to design extra-large coastal/siege artillery that would see significant usage during the Civil War. As far as who was responsible for the development of the shell gun, Dahlgren was firmly entrenched in the Paixhans camp. The American expert acknowledged that there were many who were responsible for the development of individual components within the new weapon, but it was the famous French artillerist who put it all together.

Although Bomford's, Paixhans's, and Dahlgren's combined contributions had solved the problems of firing large-caliber shells over long ranges in naval applications, they had done little to solve the problem for land-based artillery. In fact, by the late 1840s many among the more progressive military circles went so far as to prophesize that the introduction of the Minié and breech-loading rifles soon would spell doom for light field artillery. In his *Constitution militaire de la France*, published in 1849, Paixhans argued that a company of expert marksmen would quickly be able to pick off enemy artillerymen at 650 yards, where "almost every shot will take effect." At this distance the artillery's canister fire would be ineffective, and the artillery, deprived of an effective countermeasure, would soon be silenced. The British army, though, which could use shrapnel shells up to much longer distances, did possess such a countermeasure.

Not having yet adopted shrapnel, the French were more vulnerable to this threat, which they did not take lightly. In an introduction to *The Emperor's New System: Field Artillery*, penned in 1853, Captain Favé would write:

> Artillery should make an effort to increase their efficiency at long ranges; for, in proportion, as small arms reach perfection, the combatants will keep at greater distance from each other, and engagements will be decided at longer ranges. Since our last war [Napoleonic wars where firefights occurred within 120 paces], the percussion musket has replaced the flint, and rifles having a very long range, have been introduced into the

armament of the troops; the artillery, should therefore, seek to
increase their power at long range.

Unfortunately, solid shot did not work well at long range, where
most of the kinetic energy had been expended. Canister was of even
less use against the new, long-range shoulder arms, since the maximum range of heavy canister was 650 yards. At this distance British
skirmishers with the new rifle muskets in tests scored 27% hits in
only 2 minutes. Shrapnel and hollow explosive shells held much
more promise, since they were effective almost throughout their
entire maximum range. Ideally, artillery should be equipped with
ordnance that could fire shrapnel or explosive shells at long range
and then switch to round shot, before finally unleashing canister at
the close range.

The problem was that these projectiles required two different
types of ordnance: guns and howitzers. Unlike solid shot, which
had to be fired in a fairly flat trajectory, shrapnel had to be fired in
an arc. Up to this point, it wasn't possible to shoot hollow shells at a
high enough velocity so that they could be easily fired from a gun.
Given the existing state of metallurgy, the thin cast iron shell surrounding the explosives would break apart at higher velocities. Of
course, the shell's walls could be made sufficiently thick, but then
there was less room for an effective explosive charge. Rather than
increasing the thickness of the iron shell, artillerists chose to fire
hollow shells at a relatively low velocity instead, which could only
be performed effectively with a howitzer.

Despite Gribeauval's reforms, during the Napoleonic Wars each
army was still saddled with numerous types of artillery pieces, differentiated not only by type but also by the size of the projectile that
was fired. The first effort after the Napoleonic Wars to reduce the
mixed assortment of pieces and associated logistical complexities
was taken by the French military in 1828. The French army had lost
virtually all of its artillery during the closing stages of the Napoleonic
Wars and was now forced to completely rebuild its artillery arm. It
now had the opportunity to correct some of the deficiencies in its previous equipment. Impressed with British single-block trail carriages,
which had been noticeably more maneuverable than the French

counterpart, in 1827 French authorities adopted a simplified version of the British pattern. Field artillery was reduced to only four types: 8- and 12-pounder guns and 15- and 16-centimeter howitzers. However, to simplify logistics, only two types of carriages were to be employed. The 16-centimeter howitzer was mounted on a 12-pounder gun carriage, while the 15-centimeter howitzer sat atop that of the 8-pounder. This was a large step in the right direction, but it still did not solve the need for two different types of ordnance to fire shot and shell.

One of the first to work out the details of a completely practical solution was a young officer in the Swiss artillery, one Louis Napoleon Bonaparte. Prior to taking over the reins of French government after the 1848 revolution, the young Louis Napoleon submitted a proposal to create a single type of ordnance capable of effectively firing both shot and shell, functioning as both a gun *and* a howitzer. His basic idea was to exploit the new, stronger shells then becoming available so that they could be fired along relatively straight trajectories from a gun, rather than being limited to a howitzer. Until this point the heaviest propellant charge used in a howitzer was no more than about one-seventh of the weight of the shell and usually only about one-fourteenth. The low initial muzzle velocity meant that the shell followed a parabolic trajectory.

Charges equaling one third the weight of the projectile were used in guns. However, Bonaparte and other artillery engineers had studied the extensive experiments conducted by Captain Piobert at the Artillery Practice School between 1817 and 1825, as well as the results previously published by General Gassendi in his *Aide memoire*. The theoretical evidence suggested that a cannon, that is, a gun, using a charge of only one-fourth the weight of the projectile not only would possess all the propellant needed but also would cause less recoil and less damage to the gun. Advances in the way iron was cast eventually removed weight restrictions. Trials conducted with the new cast iron shells revealed that the weight of the firing charge to weight of projectile, and hence initial velocity, could be greatly increased. The French artillery engineers found that a charge equal to one-third of the weight of the shell was now feasible. These results had to be extremely exciting for French artillery engineers. For the first time it was possible to fire hollow shells at the same velocity as solid shot. It was now possible for a cannon to fire round shot and hollow shells, and the need for howitzers disappeared.

Existing doctrine had called for guns employing direct fire to use charges equivalent to one-third of the weight of the round shot being fired. Unfortunately, the one-third charge-to-projectile weight ratio was also the maximum ratio that the new cast iron shells could endure. Experienced artillerymen realized it was unwise to rely on a practice that pushed either the artillery piece or its ammunition to 100% of its capabilities, and they settled on a one-to-four ratio instead.

Since the propellant charge now was reduced from 2.0 kilograms (4.4 pounds) to 1.5 kilograms (3.3 pounds), the cannon barrel could be made of less metal, and the resulting artillery piece weighed only 75% that of its predecessor. By 1850 the new gun howitzer was ready to put through rigorous trials. The actual results were surprisingly close to those that had been suggested earlier by Piobert and Gassendi. The 15- and 16-centimeter howitzers demonstrated only a slight superiority to shells fired by the new 12-pounder gun howitzer, while round shot fired by the new piece was almost as effective as the older 12-pounder it would replace. Although all three of the existing artillery types each in its own way could slightly outperform the 12-pounder gun howitzer, these minor advantages in no way justified the logistical difficulties that arose from maintaining and supplying different types of ordnance.

The reduced weight of the new gun howitzer, coupled with significant engineering changes, produced a much more mobile and serviceable artillery weapon. The lighter barrel of the 12-pounder now could be mounted on a carriage closely resembling that employed by the older 8-pounder guns. The length of the first and second *reinforcements,* as well as the *chase,* was the same in both cases. Typically, howitzer carriages were subjected to greater wear and tear than guns. A howitzer was forced to fire at much higher elevations than that employed for direct fire, and much greater strain was placed on the carriage. To remedy this problem, the axis of the trunnions of the new 12-pounder was moved closer to the center of gravity of the entire piece. Although this modification slightly increased the amount of recoil, it also reduced the pressure upon the ground. It also more equally distributed the weight of the gun on the carriage. This meant that the piece was now much easier to handle. The limbering-up process became as easy as that used for an 8-pounder. Instead of four or five artillerymen painstakingly manhandling the piece, now two artillerymen could simply push down on the muzzle. The positioning of the trunnions also lessened the carriage vibration during quick movements that was so noticeably present on other types of ordnance.

Once he became emperor, Louis Bonaparte was ideally positioned to ensure that the new *canon obusier* received proper attention. Tests were duly conducted, and, pleased with the results, French artillery officially adopted the these gun howitzers. Mass production of the new artillery weapon began in earnest. By 1854 enough of the *canon obusiers* had been manufactured that French field batteries in front of Sevastopol, Crimea, were completely outfitted with the gun howitzer.

THE ADVENT OF RIFLED ARTILLERY

The French 12-pounder gun howitzer, or *12-pounder Napoleon* as it would soon become known in America, did much to temporarily restore French confidence in light artillery. Despite its apparent success, however, Louis Bonaparte continued to be troubled by the potential impact of the new long-range small arms on field artillery. By 1856 he began to believe that the gun howitzer was only a stopgap solution that would buy the old smoothbores at best a few more years of usefulness.

The permanent solution was to develop practical rifled artillery, whose effective range would be several times that of the new rifle muskets. The idea of rifling the interior of an artillery piece to increase its range and accuracy was by no means new; a number of military inventors had tinkered with the idea as far back as the early seventeenth century. One of the oldest known rifled artillery pieces was a breechloading device cast in 1615, which for many years was housed in a St. Petersburg arsenal. There is a chance that the Europeans were not the first to construct a breech-loading artillery piece. Volunteer officers walking along lower Manhatten during the Civil War were drawn to some ballast that had been removed from the *Flying Scud*, a clipper ship just returned from the Orient. Looking closely, they noticed this ballast consisted of old Chinese breechloaders, which they estimated to be at least a hundred years old.

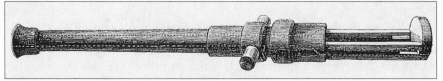

This eighteenth century Chinese breech-loading cannon was found by Union officers on Water Street in lower Manhattan. It had been used as ballast on a Yankee clipper ship returning from the Orient. *Scientific American,* Aug. 3, 1861.

By 1661 the Prussians were experimenting with shallow-grooved rifled artillery at Berlin, while a little more than 30 years later at Nuremberg (1694), some gunsmiths tried forging an artillery piece and then rifling the bore. By the mid-eighteenth century, the Swiss army possessed a few small rifled artillery pieces, while in England, Benjamin Robins worked on his own version, and a certain T. Senner constructed a breech-loading piece in Munich. Of course, all of these were experimental works, and it is improbable that any would have been serviceable in the field under battlefield conditions.

From the sketchy evidence left to us, it appears that the first truly battlefield-worthy rifled artillery was developed in 1816 by Capt. George Reichenbach, a distinguished mechanic who had served with the Bavarian army. A bronze piece with seven rifled groves, Reichenbach's rifled weapon fired pointed leaden projectiles. Reichenbach combined two rifling systems, each of which would later make a significant contribution to weapons technology: the use of an expanding projectile similar to that later employed by Minié, and the addition of metal buttons to the exterior of the projectile, similar to that later used by Colonel Beaulieu. Unfortunately, Reichenbach's invention was proffered to the Bavarian army at a most inopportune moment. The return to peace after years of warfare channeled the military leaders' focus to the demands of maintaining a peacetime army and only heightened the conservative establishment's suspicions of newfangled gadgetry. Although M. Ponchara, a French artillery officer, continued to experiment with rifled technology at about this time, it would be almost 20 years before any European military establishment would be willing to take a serious look at rifled artillery.

Next it was the turn of a Belgian artillery officer, Joseph Montigny, to take up the baton. A breech-loading rifled artillery piece, Montigny's invention was seriously considered by the Belgian military, at this time a highly progressive force in new weapon technology. Montigny's system was found to be too complex to be mass-produced, and it was simplified in 1835. Hearing glowing reports of the new invention, Tsar Nicholas invited Montigny to Russia and soon ordered 18- and 24-pounder prototypes. These were put through extensive tests, and the 18-pounder fired 1800 shots without mishap or jamming. Despite its impressive performance, Montigny's weapons fell victim to what plagued all previous efforts—deeply entrenched conservatism fatally mixed with insurmountable narrow-mindedness. A commission was set up to study the adoption of Montigny's rifled artillery system, but its president, General Samarrkoff, summarily rejected the plan.

Nevertheless, Montigny's efforts had succeeded where those of his predecessors had failed. Rifled artillery finally had caught the imagination of a wider circle of European inventors. In 1842 Col. Treuille de Beaulieu submitted a paper to the French Artillery Committee describing a new method of rifling guns. This was so far from their interest, they did not even bother to acknowledge its receipt. Elsewhere, though, the potential importance of rifled artillery gradually began to attract official attention, and the next 10 years witnessed intense competition between Maj. Giovanni Cavalli of the Sardinian artillery and the Baron Wahrendorf, the proprietor of the Aker Cannon Foundry in Sweden, to produce the first rifled artillery to be accepted by a European army. Both worked on breechloaders. The bore of Cavalli's gun (1845) had two rifled grooves, and its breech was protected first by copper wire, and then later by copper tubing, to prevent the gases from escaping. In addition to shallow, flat rifled grooves, the next year Wahrendorf coated the sides of the projectiles with soft lead so that they would more easily be pushed into the grooves and thus increase the spin. Incidentally, about this time (1850) Monsieur de Beaulieu, undeterred by the wall of silence with which his first submission had met, sent another proposal to the French authorities. This time at least they acknowledged receipt of the document.

In the early 1850s the Swedish military, deciding to take a closer look at rifled artillery, carefully considered both Cavalli's and Wahrendorf's systems of rifling. They had reservations about both,

and a Swedish officer named Engstroem decided to proffer yet
another system, this time by attaching hard wood bearings or buttons
to an iron projectile in lieu of a lead coating. General Timmerhaus of
the Belgian Artillery entered the arena in 1856. He invented a wad
that was attached to the projectile. Once the wad engaged the rifled
grooves, the elongated shot was rotated. As had happened with most
of his competitors, thorough trials revealed the inadequacies with
Timmerhaus's system.

The British developed their own homegrown variety of rifled
artillery during the early 1850s in the form of the Lancaster gun. This
piece did not employ a rifled groove. Instead, some type of twist was
imparted to the projectile by the shape of the bore. The bore was ellip-
tical and gradually twisted 90 degrees. This weapon, which appeared
so promising in the design stage, proved a failure during the Crimean
War. Rather than spinning, the projectiles tumbled, and all accuracy
was lost.

This was the state of affairs when Napoleon III asked his military
advisors what they thought about rifled artillery and whether there
were any rifling systems currently under consideration. The advisors
were vaguely aware of both Engstroem's and Wahrendorf's systems.
After some reflection they recalled also receiving a proposal from
Monsieur de Beaulieu, which, after being prodded by the emperor,
they finally decided to read. It was decided to test all three rifling
systems. The practical trials clearly demonstrated the superiority of
the Beaulieu's rifled artillery, a system that had sat on dusty shelves
for 14 years! Beaulieu's artillery was accepted officially, and a few
existing brass pieces were immediately rifled and sent to bolster the
troops embroiled in the ongoing Algerian conflict. These met with a
mixed reaction. The performance in action could not be criticized,
but they were very heavy and thus difficult to move over the rugged
Algerian terrain. The solution was simply to use lighter brass pieces!

Possibly awakened by the French experiments with rifled
artillery, other European armies seemed to renew their interest in
this type of ordnance. The focus appeared to split equally between
muzzle- and breechloaders. The British experimented with the
promising new Armstrong gun, while the Austrians and Prussians
continued to look at the Wahrendorf system. The Belgians, Dutch,

Russians, Sardinians, and Spanish continued to examine muzzle-loading rifled artillery. Though a number of countries had actively begun to experiment with rifled artillery, most remained unwilling to adopt the new weapon in any significant numbers. The Russians were the exception and quickly adopted the Beaulieu gun shortly after the French.

The general equivocation among other nations ended in 1859, when the Beaulieu gun demonstrated its value at Solferino during the short-lived Italian War. On two separate occasions during this battle, rifled artillery succeeded in disorganizing enemy cavalry at 2500 meters' distance and prevented them from charging. Though defeated, the Austrians managed to capture one of the new French rifled artillery pieces during this battle. They were sufficiently impressed with trials with the weapon after the war to order a 6-pounder version. Their stock of Wahrendorf guns were declassified as light field artillery and assigned to fortifications.

Ironically, the Belgians and Prussians at about the same time followed the reverse policy. Initially, authorities in the Prussian and Belgian armies became disillusioned with the Wahrendorf gun and adopted the Beaulieu system in 1859 and 1860, respectively. However, after rave reports about the Wahrendorf gun were published in the fall of 1860, both armies started to reorder 6-pounder Wahrendorf artillery.

Nevertheless, most other European armies still gravitated toward the French system. The Dutch army filled up the barrels of many old smoothbores with molten gun metal and then reamed and rifled the barrels, using a caliber similar to that of the Beaulieu gun. The Spanish army used the same process to produce 4-, 12-, and 24-pounder Beaulieu-style guns. These latter, incidentally, were used in anger during the Spanish-Moroccan War in 1860. The Italians were predisposed towards artillery designed by their native son Cavelli, but even they finally fell in with the French school of rifled artillery.

Clearly, by the opening shots of the Civil War, most of Europe's military had already begun the migration to rifled artillery, and by 1862 French writers claimed that smoothbores now had been completely supplanted by the new weapon. Not only that, but rifled artillery had also been christened in the crucible of battle. Though the early British efforts during the Crimean War and the Second Opium War were disappointing, French rifled artillery proved practical during the Italian War and while fighting alongside the British in China. Elsewhere, Spanish authorities were pleased with the performance of their rifled artillery during the Spanish-Moroccan War of 1860.

Chapter 5

THE REACTION OF THE AMERICAN MILITARY TO EUROPEAN DEVELOPMENTS

T he United States Army of the 1850s has occasionally been portrayed as a rather backward affair possessing a limited appreciation of contemporary military art, most of its resources spread out on the frontier and its attention held captive by Indian wars. There is some truth to this assessment. Asked to compare the American military with its European counterpart after his return from the Crimea, Maj. Richard Delafield concluded in his report to John B. Floyd, secretary of war under President James Buchanan:

> Our preparation in material, equipment, knowledge of the art of war, and other means of defense, is as limited and inefficient, as theirs is powerful and ready. . . . As a nation, other than in resources and general intelligence of our people, we are without the elements of military knowledge and efficiency of sudden emergency. . . . We possess a nucleus of military knowledge in the country barely sufficient for the wants of our army in time of peace.

On the surface Delafield's skepticism appears justified. Certainly, there were many officers who were unaware of the new weaponry and attendant tactical developments. Given existing military demands, much of the West Point curriculum was devoted to military engineering and fortifications, rather than European-style combat. Other than an ongoing, long-term trial of the Hall's carbine, there had been little official interest in the new experimental small arms. The official infantry maneuvers were based on the old post-Napoleonic French system, originally translated as *Infantry Tactics* by Winfield

Scott (later commanding general in the Mexican-American War, 1846–48).

However, as one takes a closer look, a more complex picture emerges. Much of the inherent conservatism had changed in 1853. With Jefferson Davis, the Secretary of War under Franklin Pierce, the War Department became noticeably more open-minded and progressive. This administration would issue the .58 Springfield rifle musket, experiment with breech-loading rifles, take the first tentative steps to test the rifled artillery just being accepted by a few European armies, and adopt a completely new light infantry tactical system. Capts. Alfred Mordecai and Delafield would recommend looking more closely at the reduction of the types of field artillery by adopting a single ordnance capable of firing both shot and shell.

Aware of the Hardinge Committee's recommendation in Britain to adopt the Enfield, the secretary of war was determined that the United States Army was not to be left behind. Col. Benjamin Huger was instructed to evaluate the British Enfield and Swiss rifle muskets along with a weapon manufactured by the Springfield (Massachusetts) Armory. These tests took place at Harpers Ferry, Virginia (now West Virginia) in 1853–54 and at Springfield in 1855.

If Davis had been influenced by the latest small arms developments in Britain, when it came to tactical theory, his attention shifted to France. This is hardly surprising, since the French military still enjoyed the highest reputation, based not only on the first Napoleon's great exploits but also on successful efforts in North Africa and the Crimea. Stimulated by the need to cope with the new military demands arising from colonial efforts in North Africa, French *chassuers d'Afrique* and Zouaves utilized a looser, more individualized tactical system that emphasized small-unit tactics and proscribed a rigid conformity to traditional close-order formations.

In a report to Congress in 1854, Jefferson Davis predicted that the adoption of a new rifled small arm would also necessitate corresponding changes in infantry tactics. The military had to be prepared to employ many more skirmishers, and Davis predicted that the traditional distinction between regular and light infantry would disappear and that the entire arm would be employed as "light troops."

These views merely echoed the sentiment of French tacticians, who had advanced the same argument since the introduction of the *à tige* rifle musket during the 1840s. It is hardly surprising that Davis and his staff, intimately aware of every technical aspect of the new small arms, were equally informed about corresponding tactical advancements. Any doubt about the source of Davis's inspiration should be put to rest by his decision on how to proceed.

In Davis's opinion a new infantry manual had to replace Scott's existing work. Col. William J. Hardee of the Second Dragoons was ordered to head a committee to write the new infantry manual. Although Hardee had served with distinction during the Mexican-American War, his main credentials for the present task, his fluency in the French language, stemmed from an episode much earlier in his career. In 1840 Hardee, along with two fellow officers, had been selected by Secretary of War Joel R. Poinsett to attend the Royal Cavalry School at Saumur, France. After a year they returned to teach the new cavalry methods to the Second Dragoon regiment.

In early 1854 Hardee and his staff began the translation of the *Ordonnance du Roi sur l'exercise et les manoeuvres des bataillons de chasseurs à pied*, the French manual for light troops. The work was completed on July 28 that year and met with eager approval from the secretary of war. That fall the new manual was tested at West Point using the Cadet Corps. The final version of the new manual was adopted on Jefferson Davis's order on March 29, 1855. Although it was originally published that year as *Rifle and Light Infantry Tactics*, Hardee followed Scott's example, and subsequent editions were entitled Hardee's *Tactics*, the title by which it is known today. Recruits who were forced into the seemingly endless practice needed to master the new light infantry tactics, however, often referred to the new system as the "Shanghai Drill."

The origin of the new manual was never a secret. A January 1858 article in the *Southern Literary Messenger* applauded Colonel Hardee's efforts, claiming that the fruit of his effort was an excellent translation of the original French document. Not all reviews were so flattering, and the New York *Courier and Enquirer* blasted Hardee's audacity for adding his name to the work. The article attributed the actual translation to a Lieutenant Bennet (actually 1st Lt. Stephan Vincent Benét, the grandfather of the well-known poet) and speculated that Hardee

Fire and Load Kneeling

Fire,
One time and one motion

Charge-Bayonet
One time in two motions

Shoulder Arms
One time and two motions

Illustrations in Hardee's *Rifle and Light Infantry Tactics.* One can detect the origin of Hardee's work by looking at the French uniform of the soldier in the illustrations.

probably had not even read the manual until the trials at West Point. Hardee did not escape such criticism even in his native South during the war. Benjamin F. Evans, a Charleston, South Carolina printer, painstakingly compared the two works and in a letter to William P. Miles (May 20, 1861) concluded that it was "word for word a translation and nothing but a translation." That Hardee had plagiarized a foreign regulation was common knowledge, and after the war Ulysses S. Grant, never known for his scholarship, would even note in his memoirs that Hardee's *Tactics* was "a mere translation from the French with Hardee's name attached."

Although this last initiative was rather theoretically oriented, French and British entrance into the Crimean War in 1854 afforded an opportunity to examine the latest developments in practice. Davis decided that a small military commission should travel to southern Crimea. The task was entrusted to a military engineer, an ordnance officer, and an engineer-cum-cavalry officer. On April 3, 1854, Maj. R. Delafield, Maj. A. Mordecai, and Capt. George B. McClellan received detailed telegraphic instructions for their impending assignment. Davis directed these commissioners to look at the new European small arms and recent innovations in French field artillery, in particular the gun howitzer, which eliminated the need for howitzers. The commission was also to observe what Delafield would later call the "auxiliary branches of the [military] profession," such as engineering, transport, and cartography, as well as veterinary and medical sciences.

Captain McClellan was the first to submit his findings to the new secretary of war. Although eventually published as *The Armies of Europe*, most of McClellan's attention focused upon the organization and methods of the Russian army, followed by a detailed discussion of European cavalry. Presumably, the title of the work was justified by a cursory sketch of the major European armies in the opening chapter. Regardless, McClellan's report was the first to be received, and this by itself guaranteed that it would receive the lion's share of attention.

The reports of the other two commissioners were much more technologically oriented. Both discussed the latest European developments in small arms and artillery, though Major Mordecai, the ordnance officer, provided greater thoroughness. His chapter on "rifled cannon" traced the most recent experiments with rifled artillery in Europe, starting with Wahrendorf's trials in Sweden in 1846, through Cavalli's efforts in Sardinia during 1854, to the Lancaster gun tested during the Crimean War, the display of the Krupp gun at the 1856 Paris Exhibition, and a vague mention of Joseph Whitworth's secret experiments in Manchester on April 12 of the same year. There was also mention of recent attempts to create extra-large mortars and guns, the most promising of which was a 13-inch gun manufactured by Horsfall & Co. at Woolwich (England) Arsenal in May 1856. In terms of hand grenades, Mordecai felt that the new French version held the most promise. A fuse was mechanically ignited by a small cord as the weapon left the infantryman's hand, and thus the grenade was remotely similar to that still used today. To describe the recent experimentation in small arms, Mordecai simply included a translation of Captain J. Schön's *Modern System of Small Arms* in his report. Reading through the Saxon officer's booklet, the War Department would learn of the step-by-step development of the self-expanding bullet and rifle musket and the various models that had been adopted by each European army.

Encyclopedic in scope, Major Delafield's observations ranged from the latest advancements in hospital wagons, stretchers, and amputation tables to such camp equipment as mess furniture, ovens, and tents. No innovation seemed too small or trivial. Delafield was also able to discern the significant, and his report noted the first use of telegraphic messages by the British to issue military orders, the Russian attempt to destroy enemy vessels with "torpedo mines," the electrical detonation of mines during siege operations, and the transport of troops from one theater of operations to another via steam-powered transport ships. Delafield was fascinated by two innovations that augured to transform naval operations: the first wartime use of what he called "iron-sheathed floating batteries" and iron mortar boats.

Because of McClellan's later notoriety, his report is still occasionally consulted by Civil War historians, a circumstance rarely shared by his two companions. Mordecai's and Delafield's reports, however, had a much greater practical impact at the time they were submitted. Their discussion of the widespread adoption of Minié-style rifle muskets lent credence to the decision of the American army to do the same. Both concluded that the artillery arm would have to pay close attention to two recent European trends, (1) the attempt to reduce the variety of field ordnance using a combination gun howitzer that fired both shot and shell and (2) ever-increasing experimentation with rifled cannon. Despite the change of administration by the time these reports were actually submitted, these conclusions were not completely lost on the American government. The ordnance department immediately began looking at the French gun howitzer, and in less than a year after Delafield turned in his report (May 7, 1858), a slightly altered version of this weapon was officially accepted by the United States Army.

As Delafield had pointed out, by the mid-1850s the American military found itself detached from the main current of military scientific thought. The commissioners' reports were the substantive first steps towards rectifying this deficiency. Taken together, the three reports served as a convenient first-stop reference that provided both their fellow officers and Congress a comprehensive introduction to contemporary military science.

However, the full impact of the Commission to Europe was not limited to the information provided by the reports. The three commissioners had returned to the United States with cartons filled with the latest military scientific writings. The commissioners had acquired no less than 317 separate military scientific works, plus hundreds of drawings, illustrations, and maps. These works encapsulated almost everything then known about European military science and dealt with every facet of military activity. Although artillery, infantry, cavalry, and engineering drill booklets comprised the largest single category, there were also many books on fortifications, mathematics, topography, surveying, and military justice. The latest technological developments were discussed in works such as *Manual d'Artillerie* (by Louis Napoleon), *Sur les shrapnels* (Charles G. Bormann), and *New Rifle Arms* (J. Schön), while the latest tactical theories were considered in Wittich's *Tactics of Light Percussion Arms*, Louis Napoleon's *Études sur l'artillerie*, and more. Unfortunately, it is not possible to determine who had access to these works and the extent to which they were actually read. In any case, within 2 or 3 years of their arrival, it is probably no coincidence that many of these works are cited in tactical and technical works authored by West Point instructors John Gibbon and Cadmus Wilcox.

It is clear that knowledgeable officers at West Point and the Virginia

Military Institute were intimately aware of the scientific principles associated with the new weaponry. They also understood the techniques necessary to achieve accurate long-range fire, the so-called scientific method of rifle fire first introduced by the French at Vincennes and adopted in a slightly modified form by the British School of Musketry in 1853. In 1858 Capt. Henry Heth of the United States Army wrote *A System of Target Practice*, which was chiefly a translation of the French *Instruction provisoire sur le tir*. A thorough treatment of how to fire the rifle musket "scientifically," the work remained in use for more than 5 years.

Breech-Loading Small Arms

Although the breechloader enjoyed some acceptance in German-speaking countries, this weapon was unable to make the same inroads in America as the French-inspired rifle musket. Once again reflecting Jefferson Davis's open-mindedness, Colonel Huger of the Ordnance Department tested the Sharps rifle during the winter of 1853–54. Patented by Christian Sharps in 1848, the early version exhibited a number of technical problems and was accordingly rejected. According to Huger's report not only did this shoulder arm lack the range of the Minié rifle musket, but

> after being fired four or five rounds, it was impossible to force the cartridge in, without bursting it. The firing was continued by separating the bullet from the cartridge, forcing it into the chamber with a stick, and afterwards pouring in the powder. The slide frequently becomes very difficult to move. When the arm was taken to the shop to be cleaned, after the firing was concluded, the slide could not be moved at all, until thoroughly soaked in oil, to soften the dirt around it. The paper of the cartridge is always left behind in the chamber after each shot, and is frequently on fire when the succeeding cartridge is inserted.

In August, Congress appropriated funds to purchase other breechloaders to be evaluated at West Point. Faced with what appeared to be insurmountable problems, further experiments were halted. Only in August 1857 would another board recommence the search for a suitable rapid-fire weapon. Although no one weapon was singled out for official approval, the Burnside rifle demonstrated the best overall rate of fire, accuracy, and reliability. However, for pure output of lead, the Sharps rifle, which could fire 18 times in only 50 seconds, placed first. When another board met the following year to consider the same issue, it similarly leaned towards the Burnside, but once again there was insufficient consensus to unequivocally recommend the weapon. Noting the great variety of breechloaders, the secretary of war's report to the 35th Congress in 1859 concluded that "some of these arms are best for one sort of service, whilst others answer best for another." The report did concede that great improvements had been made during the previous few years and was confident that "with some further encouragement, [additional] valuable results will no doubt be obtained. Some of these arms combine, in a very high degree, celerity, an accuracy of fire, with great force, at long range."

This view, however, was that of a small clique of progressively inclined professional military men. A majority of the American military and public did not hold so favorable an opinion of the breechloader. Skepticism arose from two entirely different considerations, the first technical, the other tactical and logistical. A military weapon must be much more reliable than a hunting or target rifle. As one writer so bluntly put it, to remain useful during a campaign, a shoulder arm had to be

> capable of being misunderstood, or misapplied, even by the most stupid. It must sustain unharmed the very hard usage of a class characteristically reckless and *mal adroit,* and it must equally resist exposure to weather and rough treatment during long campaigns. . . . The greatest difficulty is getting over the difference between a weapon that is unobjectionable as a gentleman's rifle or sporting gun, and one that will remain serviceable in the hands of common soldiers in the field—I might almost say, one that will not in his hands become wholly useless as a firearm in a few weeks.

The early American breechloaders were not durable enough to

withstand the rigors of military application. The single biggest problem was leakage of the explosive gases through the breech. The hot gases would eventually erode the metal in the area of the breech, thus allowing the gases to escape. This posed a hazard to its owner and greatly lessened the force of the projectile. Also, the breech mechanism consisted of moveable metal parts that were soon damaged or hopelessly fouled. In either case, the breechloader became completely ineffective, and the soldier might find himself without a functioning weapon at a critical stage of the battle. To some degree American cynicism regarding breechloaders was reinforced by some of the experiences with the Hall's carbine. Many troops issued this carbine encountered technical difficulties, and many had to be discarded.

Despite this rocky initial experience, the more far-thinking among the American military nevertheless believed that in the hands of specialized troops, reliable breechloaders could play a valuable role. Gibbon, for example, felt that these weapons were ideal for "superior marksmen" who as light infantry could exploit available terrain and terrorize the enemy with a rapid but accurate barrage of fire. Wilcox, who specialized in small arms and the new scientific method of aimed fire, felt the breechloader could be productively exploited in many other situations. Elite corps armed with breechloaders could be held in reserve until the climax of the battle, and then, when unleashed, their withering fire would decide the issue. So equipped, artillerymen could defend themselves more effectively when closely pressed. Troops in fieldworks would also benefit from breechloaders, as would escorts of supply trains and military engineers aiding the construction of trenches.

Common wisdom of the time strongly decried against arming the ordinary rank and file with rapid-firing weapons. It was feared that infantrymen would give in to the instinct for self-preservation and fire indiscriminately, without awaiting orders. Capable of expending all of their ammunition in a fraction of the time previously possible, troops might thus use up in a remarkably brief time the ammunition they were allotted for an entire campaign, and such fire, necessarily unaimed, would produce even fewer casualties than caused by troops armed with rifle muskets.

TACTICAL INFLUENCES

Although the protracted debate among Europe's military intelligentsia about the tactical implications of the new, longer-range small arms had not gone unnoticed in America, officers in frontier posts and volunteer state militia remained largely uninformed of these developments. To correct this problem, a number of American military scientific works appearing during the mid-1850s sought to describe both the new weaponry and associated practices. Some of these, however, were no more than mere catalogues of available equipment and techniques in the military armamentarium. In 1856, for example, the War Department published the *Report of Experiments with Small Arms for Military Service,* an in-depth discussion of recent experimental efforts. Although this work largely focused on the Harper's Ferry and Springfield experiments with the new stem and Minié rifles, its appendices provided lengthy excerpts from L. Panôt's discussion of the theory of motion of elongated projectiles, Lieut. Col. Charles Gordon's description of the British trials with the Enfield, and Gen. Howard Douglas's *Treatise on Naval Gunnery.*

In 1858 several American writers also began to proselytize tactical theories that sought to best exploit capabilities of the new weaponry. One of the first of these works was an article entitled "Modern Tactics," which appeared in the *Southern Literary Messenger* in January. The article provided a succinct but insightful look at the recent evolution of European tactical systems. Arguing that the entire American military should adopt the new French *chasseur à pied* and Zouave methods of fighting, it is hardly surprising that this semi-anonymous author, known only as "R. E. C.," agreed with the radical French and Prussian tacticians that there would be a total transformation of warfare. Henceforth, a much greater proportion of infantrymen would deploy as skirmishers. The heavy multibattalion columns used at Wagram and Waterloo were a thing of the past. To avoid senseless slaughter, a commander would have to use smaller columns, which would converge upon the intended point of attack, preceded by swarms of skirmishers. In most cases, especially when forced to assume the defensive, the troops, especially the artillery, would take cover behind temporary field fortifications.

Continued cavalry effectiveness could be achieved only through rapid charges delivered in much looser order than formerly. However, R. E. C. believed the most profound impact of the new small arms would be upon artillery. Accepting the view that the Minié rifle possessed a greater effective range than a 6-pounder and that appropriately armed skirmishers could soon pick off its crew, R. E. C concluded that the smaller calibers of light field artillery were obsolete. Unlike the more extreme advocates of the Minié rifle, however, he did not feel that all field artillery would be relegated to a secondary role. R. E. C. was one of the first American writers to speculate on the impact of the new French 12-pounder gun howitzer, capable of firing both shell and shot, which would play such an important role in the Civil War. This author placed a lot of confidence in this artillery piece, which would be able to respond to effectively accurate long-range rifle fire and would essentially neutralize the Minié's advantages.

The author of this article was almost certainly Raleigh Edward Colston, an instructor of French at the Virginia Military Institute who later commanded the Sixteenth Virginia Infantry Regiment. Colston was unabashedly influenced by French contemporary military thought, which he otherwise openly acknowledged as a guiding light to military theory and practice. One might argue that Colston's analyses were completely detached from mainstream military thought, the result of an unbridled francophilia that arose from his preoccupation with French language and culture. However, before dismissing Colston's views as an idiosyncratic aberration, his conclusions should be compared with those of two West Point instructors who soon would rise to moderate prominence.

Lt. Cadmus M. Wilcox (Seventh U.S. Infantry), who had taught at West Point from 1852 to 1860, authored the influential *Rifles and Rifle Practice as an Elementary Treatise upon the Theory of Rifle Firing* (1860). A thorough treatment of ballistics and the manufacturing and maintenance of arms and projectiles, this work also provided an exhaustive examination of the small arms currently used by the European armies, as well as a synopsis of the associated tactical doctrine. Although Wilcox did not cite his sources, his "Preface" explains that the work was a compilation of the "latest writings" and represented "what are regarded as the best French publications" used for instruction at Vincennes.

The same year Wilcox published his work, Capt. John Gibbon of the Fourth Artillery Regiment published *The Artillerist's Manual,* which gained an even wider readership. Although mostly dealing with ordnance and artillery practices, this work also tangentially discussed recent developments in small arms. Like Wilcox, Gibbon had been an instructor at West Point, and his writings were largely based on the notes he used to teach artillery tactics. *The Artillerist's Manual,* like *Rifles and Rifle Practice,* was an exhaustive treatment of its subject. Artillery students were walked through all of the recent ballistic experimentation and new theories. Once again, most of the content was extruded from foreign sources as Gibbon freely admitted in the subtitle of the work, *Compiled from Various Sources and Adapted to the Services of the United States.*

However, when it came to the effect of small arms on future warfare, the views of the two West Point instructors diverged. Wilcox's *Rifles and Rifle Practice* had largely been limited to an analysis of the new Minié-style rifle muskets, and given the author's preoccupation with this subject matter, it is hardly surprising that he shared the French and Prussian view that the new small arms would dramatically change how each of the three arms would operate on the battlefield. In many respects his views were a compromise between those of Prussian Captain Wittich and Capain Gilluim of the Belgian Artillery. Like Gilluim, Wilcox believed that the mere possession of a much more accurate weapon would transform the average soldier's performance under combat conditions:

> He will be inspired with more confidence, knowing the range and accuracy of his arm, at great distances he will no longer fire by hazard, but will use his elevation sights; at short distances, knowing the power of his rifle, he will fire with internal coolness, and with a certainty that the smooth-bore and round ball never could inspire.

Predicting that infantry fire henceforth would be twice as effective, it would no longer be necessary to fire a soldier's weight in lead to cause a casualty. The infantryman would now exhibit the same sangfroid under fire as artillerymen. Unlike the Belgian officer, however, he did not believe that the rifle musket's accuracy spelled the doom of close-order tactics. True, both sides would no longer be forced to deploy along lengthy lines and would tend to spread out over a much wider expanse, which would greatly complicate maneuvering onto the field. During the initial phases of an assault, furthermore, officers would struggle harder than ever to restrain their men from prematurely firing and wasting ammunition.

Like Prussian and French military authorities, Wilcox believed that opposing infantry could no longer march with impunity to within 300 yards of the enemy line. Rather, firefights would begin at about 1000 to 1200 yards and would continue until the attacker had approached to within 600 yards, where the fire would be "irresistible." It would become extremely important to shelter the men from enemy fire. Not only would it be critical to exploit all available terrain, but smaller, less dense formations had to be adopted. Infantry had to be deployed along only two ranks, and "small columns," similar to Prussian "company columns," should be used in lieu of battalion-sized columns.

Wilcox also believed that the infantry's increased capabilities would come at the expense of cavalry and field artillery. Cavalry would no longer be able to easily advance to within 1200 yards of an infantry firing line, and successful cavalry charges against infantry in position, though still theoretically possible, would occur more rarely than previously. Wilcox also agreed with the widely held view that the range of the rifle musket was now effectively greater than the field artillery it opposed and that field artillery no longer as a matter of course could be placed in front of friendly infantry. Field artillery would therefore necessarily play a less decisive role than formerly. Now considered to be highly vulnerable to well-directed small arms fire, artillery would have to be carefully ensconced behind protective terrain or withheld until a critical point in the battle. Field artillery would be largely deprived of any meaningful combined-arms role. Cavalry would now have to rely upon a preliminary infantry fire rather than artillery bombardment.

Predictably, Captain Gibbon took a markedly different view in his

Artillerist's Manual. He aligned himself much more with British lecturers at the Royal United Service Institute than contemporary French or Prussian military tacticians. Although conceding that the new rifle muskets would indeed augment the infantrymen's power, Gibbon rejected the notion that this necessarily led to the end of artillery's capability to play a vital role on the battlefield. Despite acknowledging that the effective range of the "oblong rifle-bullet" was at least 1000 yards, he felt that due to the ubiquitous confusion that characterized every battlefield, accurate fire at such extreme ranges would only be achieved by sharpshooters operating independently of close-order formations. For those constrained by rigid geometrical formations, Gibbon reiterated the argument, which was heard more and more frequently during the late 1850s, that the rifle musket would prove to be far less accurate and deadly than predicted by its proponents:

> In general, the infantry soldier, in the excitement of battle, does not make full use of the accuracy of the fire of his arm, which has led some to think that there is no great advantage in perfecting the accuracy of fire of arms intended for the use of the mass of troops.

Though Gibbon did not subscribe to this last view and felt the Ordnance Department was justified in adopting the more accurate rifle muskets, he nevertheless firmly believed that field artillery would more than hold its own against the new small arms. He pointed out that at 1000 yards it was extremely difficult for most infantrymen to adjust his aim according to the effect of each successful shot. To do this, it was essential for the soldier to know where the last shot hit and then to alter his aim accordingly. The trouble was that if the shot missed the intended target, all the soldier knew was that he had missed, so he could not determine whether the shot had been too high, too low, or had drifted too much to the right or left. In contrast, artillerymen almost always saw where their projectiles landed or exploded and were able to correct any error in aiming. Thus, during the first moments of a long-range exchange of fire, the rifleman's shots might be more accurate, but the situation would quickly reverse itself. Then the artillerymen would be able to:

let loose among his opponents a charge of from thirty to eighty musket bullets at a time, or send a solid shot through them with sufficient force to disable, perhaps kill, half a dozen, and disorganize as many more by its moral effect.

Captain Gibbon confidentially predicted that field artillery, far from becoming obsolete, would play an even more important role in the future and urged military authorities to invest in the effort needed to increase its efficacy rather than plot its demise.

New European Tactical Speculation

Colston's and Wilcox's tactical opinions echoed the same optimism that had characterized progressive Prussian and French thinking up to the mid-1850s. However, by this point, Napoleon III and his immediate coterie of advisors had gradually begun to retreat towards a more conservative point of view. Given how men tend to react under the pressures of battle, they thought the new weapons would never be used to their full potential, and the bayonet would continue to frequently decide the issue.

Both Wilcox and Gibbon were well aware of this recent change of opinion, which they each addressed in their writings. Believing that the frailties of human nature would always prevent the composure needed to handle the more complex weapons properly, Gibbon interpreted these developments as proof that field artillery would more than hold its own against infantry armed with the new weapons. In contrast, Wilcox, who had enthusiastically espoused the new infantry weapon, reacted with more reserve:

> It would seem difficult to justify this action of the French government; but as it knows well the advantages and defects of the elevating sight, and from practical knowledge in battle have had opportunities of judging of its usefulness, and whether or not the soldier, under the excitement of battle, avails himself of it or not, and it would be well to study the matter thoroughly before venturing to disapprove.

On their part the French military did not have long to wait to test this latest twist on infantry doctrine. Political events were to play a critical role in the surprisingly quick, and what would prove final, resolution of this debate, and Wilcox's admonition to "study the matter thoroughly," unfortunately, went unheeded in the excitement of the moment. In April 1859 the French found themselves allied with the Kingdom of Sardinia against the Austrians. This 3-month war, known at the time simply as the Italian War, ironically would have an intellectual impact in the United States far out of proportion to its military scope. The relatively sudden backtracking from the optimistic assessment of the long-range rifle muskets and how they would transform the ordinary infantrymen's role had initially been met with a certain amount of skepticism on the American side of the Atlantic. After all, a string of British, French and Belgian experiments all appeared to reaffirm the earlier optimism, and Wilcox's bewilderment about this sudden change of opinion seems to typify reaction among the American military, who were unsure of the reasons for this change.

A number of much-applauded events during the Italian War, however, changed all this and convinced most American military experts and the public that Napoleon III had been right once again! Prior to the commencement of hostilities, Napoleon III cautioned his men against an unthinking overreliance upon their rifle muskets. These weapons, warned Napoleon III, were "formidable only at a distance." It was essential that the men still unquestionably rely upon the skillful use of the bayonet, which he regarded as a peculiarly French arm. The French soldiers were again enjoined to advance quickly and with determination and decide the issue, as in their grandfathers' time, with the threat of cold steel, that is, by the "suddenness of the attack and the unabated vigor of practiced hands, lungs and legs."

Events on the battlefield appeared to demonstrate that the emperor's confidence had not been misplaced. Though a long-range exchange did occur between opposing riflemen at Montebello (May 20, 1859), the action was decided only when the French infantry rushed in and expelled the Austrian defenders from a churchyard at the point of the bayonet. Interviewed after the short war, a chasseur recounted how his regiment had similar success with the bayonet during the Battle of Magenta (June 4): "We don't care much about firing. . . . The bayonet . . . at Magenta the battalion didn't fire a shot; but we made lots of prisoners."

An American correspondent for the *Military Gazette* provided a more graphic description from Paris on June 28. Ordered to charge an Austrian eight-gun battery at Magenta, a task that the great Napoleon years before had adjudged impossible, the Zouaves ran forward in skirmisher order without firing a shot. As they ran, each Zouave kept a close eye on the enemy soldiers directly in front of him. Then, just when the latter were about to fire, the Zouaves threw themselves violently on the ground, and the otherwise murderous fire passed harmlessly over them. Quickly springing up, they set off again, until the enemy was about to fire again, whereupon they fell to the ground again. Thus, they quickly advanced to almost within bayonet range of the enemy line. There they hurled their rifles, bayonet first, into the enemy's bosoms. Lunging forward, each quickly withdrew his bloody weapon before the defenders had a chance to react and then impaled the victim's neighbor.

These accounts created a sensation among American readers. The correspondent for the *Military Gazette* praised Napoleon III for his fortitude in recognizing that the "Bayonet was still King of Arms." Writing a mere 4 days after the battle of Solferino, the American in Paris gloated:

> Many people supposed that the long range of muskets and rifles would do away with the bayonet charge, but what a mistake! Ah! This deadly, this devilish weapon, how it has become the king of the battles! . . . Gunpowder, crossbows, long bows, rifles, revolvers, and all the missiles they can send, are cast into the shade. Hurrah for the bayonet!

Contributors to the *Military Gazette*, which was the official organ of the New York State Militia, immediately took up this cry. In the next issue one writer offered the following panegyric:

> The Bayonet.—The public attention is constantly called to the fact that the bayonet is still a weapon of use, and must be relied on in all exigencies of war.
> It is always ready. No need of ammunition; no fear of failing

in its supply of food. It does its work ever so silently, surely and unfailingly.

Remarking that the only real question remaining was which bayonet to use, the traditional triangular version or the new sword bayonet, this writer pleaded with "our worthy friends at West Point" to render their verdict.

THE DEBATE REGARDING BREECHLOADERS CONTINUES

This was more or less the debate as it existed up to 1859. John B. Floyd had replaced Jefferson Davis as secretary of war in 1857, and indolence, myopia, and corruption replaced open-mindedness, pragmatism, and a sense of intellectual adventure as guiding traits at the highest level of the War Department. Formal testing of breechloaders, if not completely cast aside, was greatly reduced. The British government, which had been even slower to appreciate the potential of breechloading small arms than its American cousins, finally purchased a few Colt's revolving rifles for testing. On April 25, 1859, several marksmen fired the Colt weapons at a relatively small target 400 yards away. The results proved satisfactory, at least for military purposes. All 48 shots hit the mark, 17 were found to be within the 8-inch bull's-eye, while 24 others were clustered within a 2-foot square.

Here and there a few incidents showed that breechloaders could be useful in practice, and this momentarily placed these rapid-fire weapons back in the limelight. Sometime during 1858–59, while lending his support to make the Kansas Territory a free state, abolitionist John Brown used them to beat back a strong force of pro-slavery Missouri men. After his son was assassinated, Brown had purchased several Sharps rifles. This turned out to be a very wise investment. A few weeks later about a hundred Missourians raided the territory, looking for him. With a few men, Brown set an ambush. As the larger pro-slavery force approached to within 400 to 500 yards, Brown opened fire. His men handed him one Sharps rifle after another. His fire proved both rapid and accurate. Within minutes the raiders were beaten back, leaving behind about twenty dead, plus others wounded. An even more notable success for the breechloader was also soon reported from Italy, where Giuseppe Garibaldi's sharp-shooters, armed with the Colt's revolving rifle, enjoyed a series of victories over the Austrians.

The reputation of the breechloader did not gain appreciably despite these newsworthy achievements. In fact, the performance of the Colt's revolving rifle in Italy, if anything, amplified the debate. Reports filtered back that despite its rapidity of fire, it had proven unreliable in the field. The weapon had required constant care and would still frequently get clogged up. More pointedly, some of Garibaldi's officers complained about the tendency for some troops to fire too rapidly and waste precious ammunition. This latter criticism was sure to hit a bare nerve in the American War Department. As a result only a small number of Burnside, Merrill, Joslyn, and Maynard rifles were acquired by the United States Army for continued testing.

The success of the bayonet during the Crimean and Italian Wars and the seeming discredit of long-range fire tactics had another effect in America. The debate presented an opportunity to the more conservative to question the value of the new small arms in the first place. There were gunsmiths and officers who opposed the adoption of the Minié-style rifle muskets, arguing that they were not as useful as the long Kentucky rifles that had proved so effective during the War of 1812. The "Rifled Guns" article which appeared in the October 1859 edition of *The Atlantic Monthly* referred to the Minié, Lancaster, and Sharps rifles as nothing more than "bungling muskets," incapable of highly accurate fire and unable to withstand the rigors of a campaign. The author considered the Sharps rifle to be the most accurate and reliable of the breechloaders, but he had dug out too many of its bullets that had hit the target sideways to compare it favorably with the traditional American long rifle. Although the U. S. army had rejected breechloaders because preliminary tests had suggested a tendency to break and to jam, this writer had found both the Maynard and Sharps rifles to be sturdy and reliable.

The "Rifled Guns" writer felt that the real and insurmountable deficiency was accuracy. He compared the results of tests conducted by the Ordnance Department at Harpers Ferry with the findings published in 1848 by J. R. Chapman in *Instructions to Young Marksmen*. Chapman had reported that the Kentucky rifle exhibited an absolute deviation as low as 1.06 inch, and the "Rifled Guns" writer eagerly concluded that the Kentucky rifle was obviously more accurate than the Springfield and the Enfield and hence a more formidable weapon on the battlefield. Noting that the original optimism that accompanied the introduction of the self-expanding Minié bullets had largely dissipated as a result of the continued effectiveness of the bayonet during the just-concluded Italian War, he observed:

> No matter how perfect the gun, men in the heat and excitement of battle, will hardly be deliberate in aim, or effective enough in firing to stop a charge of determined men; the bayonet with most of mankind, will always be the queen of weapons in a pitched battle; only for skirmishing, for sharpshooting, and artillery, will the rifle equal theoretical expectations.

The article argued that only in America would a notable exception occur. Conceding that soldiers who did not grow up using firearms on a daily basis could never repel a determined bayonet charge simply by fire, he argued that for men trained to hunt since early youth and armed with highly accurate Kentucky long rifles, "firing is equivalent to hitting." The writer concluded that a defending line composed of such men would beat off even the most aggressive attacks, and even the "bravest of Wellington's army" would fail to penetrate a line of cotton entrenchments when faced with a "double line of Kentucky rifles."

As events would turn out, the opinions expressed in the "Rifled Guns" article were not some idiosyncratic, chimerical ranting of a lone military "iconodule." They reflected a type of technological right wing that would remain quite vocal in its opposition to the Minié version of the rifle musket until well into 1861. As will be seen in a later chapter, these arguments would be taken up again more than a year later after an article that appeared in the leading magazine for American inventors.

The Zouaves

Fighting alongside the *chasseurs d'Afrique* during the Algerian and Crimean Wars, the Zouaves had gained equal recognition and popularity.

Although the United States military never set about to study the fighting methods of the feared North African fighters as they did those of the *chasseurs à pied,* following the Crimean War the Zouaves captured the imagination of the American public. This popularity was not due solely to their reputation as ferocious and successful warriors, however. The new French light infantry tactics, with their increased emphasis on individual performance, appealed to American sensibilities. One of the first American essays to extol the virtues of these feared fighters appeared in the already cited "Modern Tactics" article in the *Southern Literary Messenger.* Colston's article argued that it was important for these innovative methods to be adopted in America. By this point (1858), one regular infantry regiment as well as the cadets at both West Point and VMI had officially adopted the new, French-inspired light infantry tactics. Colston went on to predict that in a few years the new light infantry tactics would completely supplant Scott's *Infantry Tactics,* an accurate prediction, as it turned out.

Zouave tactics would be a popular theme in American newspapers and magazines over the next few years. Attempting to explain their sudden popularity, a writer for *Frank Leslie's Illustrated Newspaper* reasoned: "Instinctively a military people, our young men were fascinated with the stories of the agile, impulsive, effective and somewhat dramatic movement of 'The Zouaves.'" A reporter for the *New York Times* would go one step further, arguing that traditional methods, by their excessive concentration on the "accuracy of lines and the precision of the marching," were not the most suitable for American troops. The "individuality, self-reliance, quickness and familiarity with the use of weapons" are all essential preconditions of the light infantryman, and therefore "to convert him into a machine soldier of Europe by drilling him exclusively in the old formations is a sheer waste of his most valuable qualities." This merely echoed Colston's original article, which had exclaimed:

> The new system is especially suited to the genius of the American people. It is in fact the bush-fighting of the American rifleman, rendered ten times more effective by the regularity of action which discipline produces, and by the improved weapon

[the Minié-style rifle musket] and the bayonet. . . . If the French have derived such advantages from the new system, what could not be expected from Americans trained in the same way?

Colston's plea did not go completely unheard, and several militia organizations patterned on the Zouave model soon sprang up around the country. The most famous of these was the United States Zouave Cadets of Chicago, established by Col. E. E. Ellsworth on April 20, 1859. Seeking to combine strict morality and clean living with rigorous exercise and drill, the troop practiced untiringly. Although the French Zouaves' exemplary conduct at Magenta only heightened the corps's reputation, it is improbable that the Zouaves would have had any meaningful impact on the American military were it not for the notoriety that the Chicago Zouaves gained in the summer of 1860. Those commanding the organization felt that their men had so completely mastered the Zouave drills that they could outperform any other military organization in North America. To prove the point, Colonel Ellsworth issued a challenge to all the militia and regular army organizations in the United States and the Canadas. Two reasons have been advanced to explain Ellsworth's sudden boastfulness, a quality that seemed out of place with his otherwise modest demeanor. One theory is that, awarded a flag by the National Agricultural Society without a contest, the Zouave Cadets wanted to demonstrate that they were indeed deserving of this prize. The second and more believable explanation is that Ellsworth was stung by the ridicule that was making the rounds among the Eastern militia and wanted to make these organizations eat their own deprecations.

In any event, a tour was planned that included most of the major cities in the Northeast and Midwest. On June 20 the Chicago Zouaves gave their first performance in Detroit, which was repeated over the next 2 months in Niagara, Buffalo, Rochester, Syracuse, Utica, Troy, Boston, Providence, New Haven, Hartford, Springfield, Philadelphia, Baltimore, Washington, Harrisburg, Cincinnati, and St. Louis. The most publicized demonstration, however, took place in New York City where a crowd of 10,000 spectators gathered around City Hall to witness the "practicable exhibition of athletic soldiership." The following

days the Chicago troop drilled in front of large crowds at Madison
Square Park and Fort Greene Hill in Brooklyn. The reaction of the
crowd was the same as it had been in every other city where the
Chicago Zouaves appeared.

Describing the precision and coordination throughout every
moment of the complex drills, a correspondent for *Scientific American*
likened the company's movement to that of a "collection of clocks."
This reporter was equally impressed with the effect upon the audience, noting that the overwhelming response of both casual spectator
and expert military observer had been one of "astonishment and
commendation."

But the audience was not simply impressed by precision. As Colston had mentioned, the new style of tactics was naturalistic and
meshed with the audience's sensibilities. Instead of standing upright
in formations like European troops, the Chicago Zouaves often lay on
the ground. Once they fired, they rolled over on their backs to reload,
before turning back onto their stomachs to fire again. Once the war
started, the Zouave methods of fighting weren't completely adopted,

The Zouves' exotic uniforms helped bolster the popularity of E. E. Ellsworth's United States Zouave
Cadets of Chicago. *Frank Leslie's Pictorial History of the War,* 1862.

but most Zouave units followed Hardee's or Casey's tactics; lying on the ground to reduce casualties and rolling over onto the back to reload were employed often enough. It was so natural, once it was adopted, few would remember how it had been first introduced among American soldiers.

ARTILLERY DEVELOPMENTS

Although relatively little progress had been made with rifled artillery in America before the Civil War, an officer in the Ordnance Department did effect another technological advance, one that would ultimately allow the production of much larger artillery calibers than hitherto possible. This, of course, was the discovery of a new "hollow" method of casting, which simultaneously reduced the possibilities of flaws in the cast-iron artillery piece while increasing its strength. This new casting method, which became known as the *Rodman principal*, would prove to be an important development with the advent of ironclads, when it became necessary to arm coastal defenses and fortifications with much larger and more powerful artillery.

Joining the army in July 1841, Lt. T. J. Rodman was immediately assigned to the Ordnance Department, where he remained for the next 25 years. Like a number of others, the young Rodman had been deeply affected by the explosion of the "Peace-maker" gun aboard the U.S.S. *Princeton* on February 29, 1844, which killed Secretary of the Navy Thomas Gilmer, among others. While attending West Point, Rodman had been taught that an artillery officer should expect a cast-iron piece to safely fire 2000 rounds. After the *Princeton* incident, which involved a wrought-iron 12-inch gun, Rodman realized that the "2000" figure was merely an estimate and no one had devised a method of scientifically determining the strength of each type of ordnance.

Paying closer attention to the casting process, Rodman soon observed that the system then in use created flaws in all cast-iron artillery pieces. At that time cast molten iron was simply left in the casting pit to cool gradually. Cooling from the outside, the metal shrunk inwards, which tended to separate the inner layer from the outer, thereby greatly reducing the strength of the metal and its ability to withstand explosive forces. Sometimes these weaknesses were invisible to the human eye, but Rodman reasoned they were there to some degree in all cast-iron pieces. Microscopic, they could not be detected until calamity struck. Late in 1844 the young lieutenant thought of a solution. With cold water piped in, the inside of the barrel would be cooled first, while the outside remained hot. Now, since the shrinkage started on the inside, as each successive layer cooled, it settled firmly on the one below it, thus obviating the stress that had tended to pull the layers apart.

Strictly speaking, Rodman's invention belonged to the United States government, and acting in good faith, the young Rodman made repeated efforts to convince those heading the Ordnance Department of its potential importance. Writing to Colonel Baker at the Watervliet (New York) Arsenal, Rodman sought the more experienced officer's advice. The latter curtly wrote back that any ordnance cast by Rodman's method would blow out at the breech. Rodman, not easily discouraged, remained convinced of the validity of his analysis and calculations. Rodman continued his efforts to secure official interest in his new system of casting. Ordered to Richmond to supervise the casting of some cannon using the traditional methods, Rodman stopped in at the Ordnance Office and explain his ideas to Colonel Bomford, who in General George Talcott's absence was acting chief of ordnance. Bomford was about to cast some of his own experimental ordnance. Though seeming to listen, Bomford ignored Rodman's advice and the next year, 1846, used the traditional methods when he cast his 12-inch gun. Still undiscouraged, Rodman made one final appeal in person to General Talcott, with the same result. This time, he asked whether there would be any impropriety if he cast his own pieces. Assured there was not, Rodman turned to the proprietors of the Fort Pitt Foundry (at Pittsburgh), Messrs. Charles Knap and Totten, who agreed to supply all the necessary resources in return for a 50% share.

In August 1847 a patent was taken out in Rodman's name, and the new partners soon manufactured a pair of 32-pounders using Rodman's principles of casting. The results were sufficiently promising that the Ordnance Department in 1848 agreed to sponsor its own trials with an 8-inch Columbiad, which it would cast. Though this weapon displayed greater strength and endurance than a standard 8-inch gun, the same experiment uncovered that the basic design of the gun was flawed. Although the project was delayed, the Ordnance Department never completely lost interest, and at least five other trials with 8-inch and 10-inch Columbiads were conducted over the next 9 years. In every case Rodman's "hollow cast" weapons proved to be much more durable than their traditional counterpart.

Unfortunately, a design problem that had first come to light in 1848 persisted throughout these tests: There was insufficient metal beneath the breech. The tests conclusively demonstrated the superiority of Rodman's hollow casting method. Although the Ordnance Department decided to alter the weapon's design in 1857, there were still 2 more years of delays. Finally, on November 16, 1859, the first official orders for Rodman artillery were placed, and 36 of the new 8-inch pieces were cast at Pitt Foundry.

Although these principles were originally unknown in Europe, the Rodman process did not long remain a secret. According to cannon developer R. P. Parrott, after delegates from the British Committee on Machinery visited the United States in 1854, the results of the recent Rodman tests soon spread among European military circles. During the Crimean War the British, though they never openly admitted it for fear of patent infringement, experimented with two 13-inch mortars cast using the Rodman system. During the siege of Sweiborg, the standard mortars had failed after 200 to 300 rounds. The Rodman mortars continued in service even after 2000 rounds had been fired. To allow extremely rapid fire, the Rodman mortar was suspended "like a pendulum." Capt. James Benton of the Ordnance Department remembers hearing that the resulting fire was so rapid that "they kept one and two balls in the air at a time."

Rifled Artillery in America
Interest in rifled artillery among European military establishments also did not go unnoticed in the United States. The first American tests of this new form of ordnance occurred around 1851. A standard 24-pounder was rifled out, and trials with the resulting rifled 32-pounder were conducted at Fort Monroe (at Hampton, Virginia). These first American attempts to produce rifled artillery were a disappointment,

and the matter was tabled until the middle of Jefferson Davis's tenure as secretary of war. Even before his departure for the Crimea, Maj. Alfred Mordecai had gained international recognition for the invention of a device to measure initial muzzle velocities of artillery and small arms projectiles. Returning to America in 1858, Mordecai threw his support behind the Beaulieu system, which had gained widespread acceptance in France, Austria, Russia, and Italy. Authorized to conduct his own trials at West Point, he was given a 42-pounder, not yet bored. Its 5.82-inch bore, that normally used for 24-pounders, was reamed out and rifled. Unfortunately, during the seventh round the projectile jammed and burst the experimental artillery piece. A similar fate befell a Sigourney gun being tested at West Point about the same time. This piece, which also used flanged projectiles, burst after only the fifth round! Although these failures permanently jaundiced the American military against both the Beaulieu and the Sigourney guns, they didn't completely undermine its faith in similar methods of rifling and projectile design.

Events afar, meanwhile, succeeded in redoubling interest in rifled artillery among the public and professional artillerists. French rifled artillery repulsed an Austrian cavalry charge with a few puffs at Solferino, while elsewhere France's allies the Sardinians used these weapons with equal effect. There were also vague rumors of the successful use of new breech-loading rifled artillery (the Armstrong gun) by the British during the Second Opium War, although these later reports would turn out to be specious. Excited by the possibilities offered by the new weapons, the *Military Gazette* reprinted lengthy sections of an article from the September 1859 issue of *Blackwood's Edinburgh Magazine* that represented the Armstrong gun as "no doubt, as yet, the most advanced stage of projectile development." Offering this statement for the delectation of their American military readers, the editors did not appear to expect any informed argument with this assessment.

Begrudgingly, the Ordnance Department inched along with its own evaluation of rifled artillery. Meeting in late 1859, the Board on Rifled Ordnance was charged with the systematic evaluation of two different types of rifled projectiles, those with flanges of cast iron that fit into the grooves of the gun and those with a cast-iron cup of softer metal that expanded from the force of the discharge. These projectiles had been submitted by a number of inventors, including Dr. Reed, Abbott, Gorgas, Rodman, and Sawyer. The ordnance used to fire them varied from a diminutive 3-pounder all the way to 32-pounders. The tests at Fort Monroe concluded, Brevet Colonel Hugur recommended the establishment of a permanent board to perform ongoing trials.

Spurred on by technological developments in Europe and growing war clouds at home, by the late 1850s an increasing number of American artillerists, inventors, and military engineers began to explore the possibilities offered by the new weapon. They would, however, receive little encouragement from American authorities. The Ordnance Department made it clear it was only interested in rifled artillery which utilized a system of flanged projectiles or better yet expanding projectiles, comparable to projectiles used by Springfield and Enfield rifle muskets.

Under Secretary of War Floyd's leadership, the Ordnance Department lost the progressive thrust that had characterized Jefferson Davis's tenure. Professor Daniel Treadwell, who during the 1840s had made substantial theoretical contributions to metallurgy and artillery design, encountered a decidedly unimaginative atmosphere when he visited Washington in February 1860. Believing that the combination of recent European innovations with his methods of strengthening artillery pieces would yield even more practical and powerful artillery, Treadwell requested an interview with Floyd. Treadwell would later recount that he found those he met within the Ordnance Department "as torpid as to any of the improvements of Europe, in rifled cannon, as they were to improvement in Naval matters in the Sandwich Islands." Floyd proved no different, and although treated with courtesy, Treadwell realized the secretary of war "knew nothing, cared nothing" about rifled artillery. Disappointed, Treadwell recognized the hopelessness of the situation and that all further efforts would be futile. Treadwell certainly was not alone in this sentiment, and it was no secret that the more progressive among the American military were offended by the myopic conservatism of the War Department under Floyd.

To compound the problem of lack of vision, evidence suggests

Floyd was also corrupt. Not only did Floyd quash the idea of a permanent Board on Rifled Ordnance, but, rejecting the cautions of the Ordnance Department, he forcefully worked for the adoption of the James system of rifled artillery. His motives appeared to have been politically or pecuniarily motivated. The James plan called for the rifling of existing smoothbore artillery pieces at a cost of $100 per weapon. Experience soon demonstrated this was an extraordinarily exorbitant price; the actual cost to the manufacturer was $10 apiece.

Born in West Greenwich, Rhode Island, about 1805, Charles Tillinghast James had risen to the rank of major general of the militia before his election to the Senate in 1852. After retiring from politics in 1857, James turned all of his attention to several military inventions and was soon credited with the creation of a new type of projectile for rifled ordnance. In 1860 Floyd appointed a board to consider James's new invention. Although the board did vote to recommend adopting the new James projectile and the artillery piece that had been designed to fire it, a controversy quickly flared up which prevented its official acceptance. Upon closer investigation, the minutes of the board's meeting revealed that some of the experts on the board had expressed a decidedly adverse opinion about the James projectile. Thus armed, some opponents to the James rifle were able to thwart its official adoption that year.

Robert Parker Parrott, the superintendent of the West Point Foundry, would also prove to be a key player in the development of American rifled artillery. Parrott began to experiment with his own rifled artillery sometime in 1857 or '58. He developed a cast-iron rifled cannon with a 2.9-inch bore, which became known as a "10-pounder." So that the piece could withstand the tremendous pressures that were associated with rifled artillery, the exterior of the tube was reinforced by a wrought-iron band near the breech.

Around the time Parrott was developing his rifled gun, another inventor was working on a projectile that, after a series of modifications, would become the mainstay of Parrott's new weapon. This of course was the Read projectile. Dr. Read had begun his work in 1856 and conducted a number of successful trials at West Point and Fort Monroe around the time of the Beaulieu and Sigourney fiascoes. Unlike his competitors, Read managed to fire over a thousand of his projectiles without mishap. Parrott first became aware of Read's invention in 1859 and was immediately impressed. So much confidence did he place in the Read projectile that he purchased a portion of Read's patent and became its exclusive American manufacturer. Throughout 1860 Parrott conducted his own experiments with the projectile, and he gradually proffered a series of modifications that led to a wrought-iron sabot that was pre-engraved so that it would fit into the rifled grooves. In 1861 he acquired his own patent for what was known as a "Parrott shell" during the war. This, however, was essentially a variant of the Read projectile.

Like Professor Treadwell, prior to the outbreak of the war, Parrott was unable to make any headway with the War Department, though not for any lack of desire or effort. Early in 1860 Parrott enjoyed a success in another quarter. In an attempt to secure the necessary armament for Virginia, a Commission for the Public Defense had been established. Col. Philip St. George Cooke, George Randolph, and Col. Francis H. Smith were sent to scout the Springfield, Harpers Ferry, and the West Point Foundries. They were especially impressed with Parrott's new invention, and Henry Wise, Virginia's governor, invited Parrott to send a prototype and 100 shells to the Virginia Military Institute for further trials. The necessary trials were quickly carried out in July by none other than Maj. Thomas J. Jackson and his pupils. Once again Parrott's invention passed all scrutiny, and Jackson passed on a very favorable report. During the Mexican-American War, Jackson had distinguished himself for a rare combination of talent and bravery, and his opinion was highly regarded. The Virginia authorities responded with an order for twelve Parrott rifles.

Back in the North almost a complete year had been lost to the indolence of Floyd's administration. True, the revised *Instructions for Field Artillery,* published that year, optimistically announced the trials of a 12-pounder gun howitzer that for the first time could fire shot and shell effectively. Though praising this effort, the New York editors of the *Military Gazette* pointed out this was but a first step, and they projected that when this new light 12-pounder was finally issued, "it will not only fire shot and shell with equal facility, but it will be rifled also." The only other tangible development occurred on

November 1, when the Ordnance Department recommended that about 50% of the guns guarding the forts and arsenals be converted to rifled artillery. This otherwise long delay caused inventors and the more knowledgeable among military circles to become infuriated as they saw war clouds gather on the horizon but still not a trace of preparedness at either the War or Ordnance Department. Frustrated, the editors of the *Military Gazette* lamented:

> Why is our Government so backward in the introduction of rifled cannon? France, Austria, Italy and England have their rifled cannon, and we are yet talking and experimenting. Recently, in China, the Armstrong guns have worked wonders— and in Italy the Sardinians have used rifled cannon with crushing effect, and Austria is arming her fortresses with them; and yet America, with all her inventive genius, cannot make a satisfactory rifled cannon. So it would appear! For why else is it that we have no rifled ordnance? We have the models of the Armstrong gun, the French Gun, and many others. These are all superior to the common smooth bore—why not take a better gun than the smooth bore, although not the best which can be? If we wait for any new and more perfect development of the rifled principle, we may find to our cost the truth of the saying, that "half a loaf is better than none."

Events were soon to demonstrate the wisdom of this sentiment!

Chapter 6

THE DEVELOPMENT
OF THE IRONCLAD, 1810–61

The idea of covering ships with iron plate is about as old as the idea of creating artillery capable of throwing explosive shells along a flat trajectory. In 1592, for example, the Korean admiral Yi Sung Sin had a "tortoise ship" constructed. The low-decked vessel was protected by iron plates studded with iron spikes to repel boarding parties. An oared vessel, it had a long ram to batter enemy ships. In 1613 the English traveler William Adam noticed a huge, Noah's ark–like monstrosity on his way to Osaka. The homely 800- to 1000-ton armored vessel was used to quash any would-be insurrections on the outlying Japanese islands.

This illustration originally appearing in *De Leone Belgico* (1588) shows the iron plated ship that the Dutch built to try to thwart the Duke of Parma's advance along the Scheldt River in 1585. *Scientific American,* April 28, 1894.

The Europeans were not behind in such efforts, and a vessel that might be construed as a proto-ironclad had already been constructed in the Scheldt River in 1585 to defend Antwerp against the Duke of Parma and his Spaniards. An unusually large, flat-bottomed ship, it had heavy iron plates attached to its wooden sides. If the illustration that appeared in the *De Leone Belgico* (1588) is accurate, the castle-like structure amidships had slightly slanted sides, each with four gun portals for on-board artillery.

These Korean, Japanese, and Dutch "ironclads," however, were anomalies, idiosyncratic affairs that were regarded as curiosities and failed to establish any intellectual precedent. French Col. Henri Paixhans and the Stevens family of Hoboken, New Jersey, were the first to systematically experiment with protecting wooden ships with iron plates in the 1810s. Shell guns could now inflict much greater damage upon enemy ships and at much longer ranges than hitherto possible, so to remain viable, men-of-war had to possess greatly strengthened defenses. Although John Ericsson would attribute the idea of attaching iron plates to a vessel to Robert Stevens, it was an officer in the French navy who merits this distinction. In 1810 Captain Jacques Phillip de Montgery proposed to cover French men-of-war with 4-inch-thick iron plates. Disillusioned with his navy after the defeats of the Nile and Trafalgar, however, Napoleon, vetoed the plan.

On this side of the Atlantic, it was Robert Stevens's father who put together the first tangible design for an iron-protected ship. Col. John Stevens, who in 1808 had built the *Phoenix*, the first oceangoing steamship, in 1812 proposed the construction of a saucer-shaped, propeller-driven "harbor-defense" vessel. Two features of Stevens's design proved to be prophetic. The propeller-driven method of propulsion allowed the ship to change direction quickly, so its guns could always be brought to bear against enemy targets. It was to have a relatively low profile, which Stevens likened to "a turtle, whose hard shell no enemy could crack." The Stevens family did not confine their efforts to design but conducted experiments with both armament and armor. In 1814 they developed an elongated shell that after extensive trials was rejected by both the army and the navy because it was prone to tumble.

The Stevenses were not alone in their interest in the use of iron to protect fighting ships. In the same year, Thomas Gregg proffered a design for his own iron-protected ship. On March 17 Gregg was issued a patent that *Scientific American* would later describe as an "almost exact model of the *Merrimac*." Its sides, angled at 18 degrees, were to be covered with iron plate. There was a sharp, iron prow, which was to serve as a ram.

A much more significant development occurred in 1820, when the Stevenses demonstrated that iron backed by thick planks of oak would reduce the damage of round shot. Unfortunately, this was several years before the first shell gun proved practicable. Seeing little need for such vessels, the United States government continued to reject John Stevens's proposals.

In France Colonel Paixhans's efforts met with greater success, and the French navy adopted his shell gun in the early 1820s. Certain that other powers would soon arm their own ships and coastal fortifications with the new weapon, Paixhans, in *Nouvelle Force Maritime* (1821), argued that France should develop ships that could withstand explosive shells. Like the Stevenses, he turned his attention to iron armor. Considering his proposal, the French *Comité Consultatif de la Marine* diligently analyzed all associated implications. It concluded that although it was possible to cover a large man-of-war with iron plate, not only would it be prohibitively expensive, but the number of guns had to be greatly reduced. Both conditions were unacceptable, and the proposal was promptly rejected.

Although interest in iron armor appears to have subsided for a few years, the proliferation of steam-powered vessels posed new opportunities and challenges. From the beginning some argued that it was imperative to protect the boiler room, since a direct hit would eliminate a vessel's motive power. On November 10, 1827, the British naval commander Charles Napier wrote to the Duke of Clarence to urge the use of iron plates to protect the boilers, engines, and paddle shafts of the steamship *Dee:*

> It has been proved, that a combination of oak timber, iron plates, bales of cotton, or reams of paper, four feet thick, will protect the boilers and engines against an eighteen pound shot, and without that protection, a steam boat is entirely useless in war.

A decade later in the United States, Capt. Matthew Perry made the same argument when advocating that iron bulwarks be added to the *Fulton II* in order "to cause all shot striking them from any direction to ricochet."

Growing likelihood of war between the United States and Great Britain in the late 1830s forced the Department of the Navy to revise its assessment of iron defenses for fighting ships. Despite their long series of rejections, the Stevens brothers continued their experiments and approached the government again in 1841. This time, however, they found a more attentive audience, and President Tyler appointed a board to evaluate their latest proposal. During their own trials conducted several years before, Robert and Edwin Stevens found that their 4-inch iron plate withstood shot fired by a 64-pounder, the heaviest then available. Repeating the same experiments at Sandy Hook, New Jersey, the official board confirmed these findings, and on January 13, 1842, it issued a favorable recommendation. The last hurdle was cleared on April 14, when Congress authorized a $600,000 contract to complete the project.

A Committee of Naval Affairs report to the House of Representatives on March 15, 1842, helps explain the government's apparent reversal of policy and why it had finally begun seriously to consider iron defenses on some vessels. The capture of San Juan d'Ulloa castle by the French fleet in 1838 had "struck too close to home." The threat of imminent war with Great Britain in 1841–42 conjured up specters of the British fleet's suddenly appearing in Chesapeake Bay, New York Harbor, or Boston Harbor. American military authorities realized that what had befallen San Juan d'Ulloa could also be the fate of American coastal cities. Many experts believed that no fixed-position coastal defense, regardless of its size or strength, could indefinitely resist a well-led enemy fleet. It would be necessary to bolster coastal defenses with movable batteries, especially in wide harbors, where enemy men-of-war could approach by a channel beyond the effective range of shore batteries.

There were two solutions. A fleet of small, mobile gunboats could be assembled, each armed with only one or two guns. Although unable to stand up to the large man-of-war, they could still preoccupy the enemy fleet, like fleas on a dog, while shore batteries inflicted more serious damage. However, this tactic was only feasible in calm waters. Not only did small vessels serve as rather poor gun platforms; they also were thrown about in stormy weather and easily scattered. Moreover, gunboats which relied on sail or "low" steam power would be easily outmaneuvered by new, more powerful "hi" steam vessels. An alternative approach was to deploy "floating batteries" at critical points in the harbor, which would be protected by massive wooden bulwarks similar to those used in shore batteries. There were two problems with this approach. Although floating batteries could be constructed to withstand even the heaviest shot, this made them extremely clumsy and easily outmaneuvered. Secondly, although thick wooden bulwarks could be made proof against even 64-pound solid shot, the explosive shells hurled by the new Paixhans shell guns would soon ignite the wood.

In Britain there was also a movement afoot to create iron-shielded floating batteries. As early as 1830 John Pode Drake proposed using 6-inch iron slabs to protect gun batteries. Five years later, he suggested a slightly less cumbrous version that relied upon 4- and 5-inch plates. Not discouraged, in official letters penned in 1841, Drake advocated the construction of "block ships" to be moored in harbors to obstruct enemy passage.

Back in the United States, by 1842 some on the Committee of Naval Affairs felt that a steam-powered, iron-protected floating battery was the best solution. Stevens was awarded the contract in February 1843. To meet its contractual obligations, the 250-foot long vessel was to be protected by 4.5-inch iron plates, covering all surfaces above the waterline that had to withstand both shot and shell delivered by 18- to 64-pounder ordnance. These plates were to be placed at a 45-degree angle to deflect as much shot as possible.

This floating battery was to have a 40-foot beam (the width at its widest point) and a 28-foot depth amidships. Its four boilers, placed below water level, would produce 900 horsepower, and the vessel was to be faster than any existing steam vessel. Fresh air would be pumped into compartments via a ventilation system. To reduce smoke, the boilers were to be powered with anthracite coal. The Stevenses intended to equip the floating battery with several guns "of the largest caliber (made of the same material as the one lately constructed by

Captain Stockton, viz. wrought-iron) . . . throwing shot to a greater distance than any now in use."

Because their plans were overly ambitious and beyond the technological capabilities of the time, the Stevenses quickly ran into difficulties and delays. They had to erect a huge, special dry dock at Hoboken, and each new component system had to be carefully developed and tested.

However, there were two developments that conspired to thwart the completion of the project. The first seemed harmless enough. Sometime in 1843–44, John Ericsson introduced a heavy, wrought-iron 12-inch gun. Up to this time the Stevens vessel's 4.5-inch plates were proof against all artillery that they were likely to face. The latest trials with Ericsson's artillery, though, demonstrated that it was able to pierce this armor. Feeling threatened, the Stevenses made a strategic error. Rather than completing the vessel, they redesigned the floating battery, in violation of all signed agreements, so that it could accommodate 6-inch armor, capable of withstanding the wrought-iron 12-inch guns. This seeming flagrant contempt for formal agreements, coupled with the prevalent skepticism about the newfangled iron vessels and repeated changes in the administration of naval matters—there were no fewer than seven different secretaries of the navy between 1841 and 1850—condemned the project to delays and finally to abandonment.

Robert Stevens's vessel was classified as a "floating battery." This was the same term used for large, moveable batteries which lacked propulsion and were towed, hardly surprising given their intended use. Ironically, this same term years later prevented the Stevens brothers from occupying their rightful place in history as among the first to advocate "ironclads" and incontestably the very first who attempted to build this type of vessel. Encountering some reference to the Stevens floating battery, historians usually conjure up an image of a ponderous vessel with extremely limited motive power and with little resemblance to Civil War ironclads. However, the Stevens floating battery was never intended for such a limited role. Fleeter than other ships afloat, it was well suited for ship-to-ship fighting. Unlike the later *Monitor*, for example, when not in combat the gun deck of the Stevens vessel was to be 7 feet above the waterline and hence seaworthy in rough weather. However, after decades of frustration, finally seeing a chance to sell their designs to the government in 1841–43, the Stevenses were astute enough not to quibble over terminology. If the government wanted to call their vessel a "floating battery," so be it, as long as they were awarded a contract.

By 1840, however, the Stevens brothers were not the only ones attempting to build "iron vessels of war." The previous year the British East India Company had acquired the *Nemesis,* a 700-ton iron-hulled ship with ⅜-inch iron plate. Coming under Chinese fire repeatedly during what would later become known as the First Opium War, the *Nemesis*'s armor was frequently breached; it was in fact struck no fewer than fourteen times during a single action. While testifying in front of the British Parliament in 1847, Captain Hall, the ship's master, recounted how one ball went "straight through the vessel, which made a hole as if you had put your finger through a piece of brown paper." At other times sharp rocks along the sea floor had gouged holes in her bottom. None of these holes proved dangerous, however, and they were easily repaired by driving in plugs of wood and oakum (tarred-fiber caulking) from the inside.

British shipbuilders began to construct several other iron "war vessels" over the next several years. In 1840 the British navy ordered its first iron ships, three small gunboats to serve as river craft in the Niger. John Laird, who had constructed both the *Nemesis* and the gunboats, then built some larger iron ships, hoping to convince the British Navy of their value. His optimism was misplaced, however, and one of the completed iron vessels was sold to the Mexican government and took part in the desultory fighting with the Texans in 1843. Although in Mexican service, it was still commanded by British officers, who later testified that, like the *Nemesis,* it had been frequently hit by 24- and 18-pounders, but all damage was easily repaired. Two other British iron vessels are worthy of mention. On April 6, 1846, the *Harpy,* slowly traveling up South America's Paraná River, came under heavy fire from permanent and field artillery on high cliffs at extremely close range, sometimes as close as 60 yards; 2 weeks later the *Lizard* had to run the same gauntlet. In both cases the ships, though hit, managed to pass and were easily repaired. Responding to the success of the *Nemesis,* in February and March 1845, the British government contracted for the construction of four iron ships to be built at Woolwich, outside London.

However, despite the performance of the *Harpy* and the *Lizard* under fire and the support of Sir George Cockburn, admiral of the fleet, new iron ships encountered insurmountable opposition over the next few years. The problem stemmed from a long series of trials in which iron plates were systematically subjected to solid shot at various ranges. French tests in 1834–35 indicated that the heavier naval ordnance could penetrate the iron plate then being considered to protect naval vessels. Those skeptical of iron ships or iron protection seized upon these results, arguing that they proved conclusively the impracticality of metal armor once and for all. The success of the Stevenses' experiments in 1841, however, seemed to reopen the matter. Learning of these latest developments, British naval authorities immediately performed their own trial in Portsmouth in 1842. Replicating the Americans' achievement proved elusive. Eight-inch and 32-pound shot were fired at fourteen iron plates that had been riveted together to form a shield 6 inches thick. Although none of the eight shots actually penetrated, both the iron and the timber behind it were greatly shattered. Although an assortment of metals was experimented with, none was found to be able to withstand close-range artillery fire. The difficulty stemmed from the methods to process iron then in use. In British tests, for example, laminated iron completely fragmented upon impact, thus affording little defense benefit. British cynicism only increased when in the United States, Ericsson's wrought-iron 12-inch gun finally punched its way through the Stevenses' plates. Though the Stevenses themselves believed they had found an acceptable defense in the 6-inch plates, there were those who remained convinced that both iron ships and iron-protected ships were inherently impracticable.

This was the state of affairs when the British Admiralty ordered its first iron ships in 1845. To silence critics, the next year Adm. George Cockburn ordered trials to be conducted near the Woolwich shipyards to test the effect of 32-pound shot against several ⅝-inch plates riveted together. Although Cockburn himself was pleased with the results, the sight of large holes in the plates seemed to bolster the arguments of the naysayers.

The argument that iron ships were unsound because at close

range a hole could be punched through the defensive armor probably strikes the modern reader as a rather specious argument, since
the recourse was to fall back upon wooden ships, which obviously
possessed even lesser defensive capabilities. However, although
solid shot from even medium-sized artillery could easily penetrate a
ship's wooden hull, such a vessel possessed much greater resiliency.
After solid shot punched a whole through a plank, invariably the
wood simply expanded to close up most of the hole. The writer of
"Iron-Clad Ships of War" (*Blackwood's Magazine*, November 1860)
assured his readers that he had frequently seen timbers, planking,
and spars struck by 3-inch projectiles, where, after a few hours, the
resulting perforations almost escaped detection upon even the
closest examination.

When a change occurred in the British naval administration later
in 1845, the new regime showed little interest either in the construction of iron vessels or in the screw propeller. Though it was too late
to stop the introduction of the latter, one of the new iron ships was
sold into civilian use; the remaining three were converted into troop
transport ships. This was the state of affairs for the next 9 years.
There was little official interest in either iron or iron-protected ships
in Great Britain or France.

An overthrow of the government in France and events during the
war between Russia and Turkey would soon force a complete reeval-
uation of this conservative position, however. Thus, by 1854 naval
authorities in Britain and France finally awoke to the vital importance of bolstering a ship's defense, especially when the ship was to
bombard coastal fortifications. In their own series of experiments, the
French finally obtained the first signs of encouragement in the early
1850s. Laminated iron 14.5 centimeters (5.7 inches) in thickness
was shown to stop all projectiles, though it was itself rendered useless thereafter. Encouraged by these results, a French naval designer
suggested the creation of a completely steam-powered vessel with
9-centimeter (~3.54-inch) iron plates riveted around the waterline
and amidships to protect the all-important, but especially vulnerable,
engine room.

Though the proposed vessel was never built, international events
would demonstrate the necessity of developing adequate defenses

against the Paixhans-type shell guns then being adopted by many European forces. The Turkish flotilla was completely destroyed by a Russian naval force under Adm. Pavil S. Nakhimov during the Battle of the Sinope on November 30, 1853. The engagement pointedly showed what henceforth would be the fate of wooden-clad warships unfortunate enough to encounter enemy vessels armed with shell guns. Napoleon III recognized the seriousness of the situation then unfolding. Faced with the specter of war with Russia, he realized that Russian fortresses and vessels equipped with shell guns could destroy French ships with little effective response from the French fleet.

Napoleon III had personally followed the various technological and engineering advancements with great interest and had already thrown his support behind continuing experimentation with new rifle muskets and a more general-purpose gun howitzer. During the Civil War, *Scientific American* speculated that Louis Bonaparte, who resided in New York early in his career, was influenced by the precocious Stevenses. Now as emperor he was reviving his interest in naval matters.

Renewed experiments in the feasibility of protective iron plates were hurriedly carried out in July 1854. The results demonstrated that the problem of iron fragmentation upon impact could be minimized, if not completely avoided, by backing the iron plates with very thick wooden walls. Such iron defenses, between 10 and 14 centimeters thick and supported by the wooden backing, were able to withstand both solid shot and explosive shell, even at close range. Encouraged by these results and goaded on by the emperor, the French minister of the marine finally decided in July 1854 to order ten shallow-draught, steam-driven, armored "floating batteries," armed with sixteen 60-pounders, whose upper decks were to be completely protected by 110-millimeter-thick iron plate. The specifications required these vessels to have a length of 174 feet, a beam of 13 meters, and a draft of 2.36 meters. The submerged screw drives were designed to propel these vessels about 6 miles per hour. Numerous difficulties were encountered during construction, so only five floating batteries were actually constructed: the *Congreve, Devastation, Foudroyante, Lave,* and *Tonnante.*

The concept of the construction of specially protected vessels to attack an apparently impregnable coastal fortification was certainly not new. Jean Claude D'Arcon's ill-fated assault on Gibraltar on September 13–14, 1782, the source of much ridicule, was still common knowledge among naval experts and military authorities. D'Arcon was a French naval engineer who suggested attacking the gargantuan rock with a host of rafts lined with sand, covered with cow- and oxhides, and reinforced with huge timbers. The topsides of a number of naval vessels were also cut down to near the waterline and similarly reinforced and protected. Sloped roofs were placed on them to deflect the sloping shot fired by the defenders. Despite all of these precautions, the result was a disaster. The first ship to catch fire, ironically, was the one carrying the Prince of Nassau and D'Arcon; the rest of the flotilla soon followed suit. Their masts cut down, both ships and rafts were unable to retire out of harm's way, and many of the crew went down with their vessels or were burned alive.

Despite this ignominious precedent seven decades earlier, French authorities decided to renew the experiment. Recognizing that a major war with Russia was inevitable, French authorities in August 1854 decided not only to pressure its ally Great Britain into building several of its own floating batteries but also to share all of its technological secrets. Upon reception of the French plans, Sir James Graham in September speedily conducted his own experiments. These proved successful, so the British agreed to build five floating batteries, which were slightly modified variants of the French pattern. In return, the British also agreed to build ten mortar vessels and twenty steam gunboats for the French navy, all based on existing British designs.

Originally, the French and British floating batteries were to be part of a combined naval and land force that would be charged with the capture of Kronstadt, on the Baltic Sea. However, the public outcry over events in the Crimea forced the abandonment of these plans, so the forces were rerouted to the Black Sea instead.

The new, ironclad floating batteries underwent their baptism of fire on October 17, 1855, when they, along with the rest of the Anglo-French fleet, were ordered to bombard Kinburn, where a Russian fort guarded the mouth of the Dnieper. Confident that their iron defenses would be proof against anything that the Russians could throw against them, the three French floating batteries—the *Devastation, Lave,* and *Tonnant*—slowly advanced in front of the conventional vessels to within 800 yards, where they opened fire. The Russian gunners meanwhile opened with everything they had. Fifteen minutes later the Allied mortar boats joined in, and for the next hour there was a tremendous exchange of shell and shot. Eventually, a fire broke out, compelling the Russians to abandon their guns. The Allies soon forced the defenders' surrender and took possession of the Kinburn fort.

The crew's confidence in their floating batteries turned out not to have been misplaced. One of these vessels had been struck by 63-pound solid shot, yet a flag captain wrote home that the Russian shells "broke against [the iron plates] like glass" and that the total damage was limited to the loosening of three rivets. Writing to the first sea lord in London after the clash, the commander-in-chief of the British Black Sea Fleet, Rear Admiral Lyons, would make a remarkably accurate prophecy when he advised his superior, "Still you may take it for granted that floating batteries have become elements in amphibious warfare, so the sooner you set about having as many good ones as the French, the better it will be for you." The admiralty took heed of Lyons's advice and immediately ordered the construction of four more floating batteries.

The French used floating batteries for several years; they nearly saw active duty again during the Italian War in 1859. Mobilized, they arrived in the upper Adriatic Sea before Venice the very same day the armistice that halted hostilities was signed. Had the dispute continued, they were meant to bombard Venice and Trieste. Not complacent with their initial success, the French decided to expand their program of ships with iron defenses, so in 1859 they authorized the construction of an "ironclad frigate." The completed vessel was christened *La Gloire.* At 250 feet long and with a 21-foot beam, the ship carried thirty-eight rifled 50-pounders and was protected by 4.3- to 4.7-inch iron plates. Her 900-horsepower engines allowed a maximum speed of 12 knots.

British reaction was immediate. Not only was there a sense that the French naval forces were gaining an edge over the heretofore seemingly insuperable British navy, but there was a fear in some quarters that Napoleon III, like his uncle, would embark on the stormy path of

French domination. The immediate response was to order the construction of Britain's own line of armored-plated ships. Thus, the *Warrior* and *Black Prince* were launched in short order to shore up the coastal defenses at critical coastal positions like Portsmouth, Woolwich Arsenal, and other major dockyards.

It was this last development that evoked passionate criticism from Capt. Cowper Phipps Coles, who during the Crimean War had achieved a certain level of fame with his "artillery rafts." Rather than relying upon coastal forts and fortresses, Coles had advocated the construction of a fleet of shallow-draft "iron-cased" vessels, which would a few years later become known in American parlance as *ironclads*. However, the vessels envisioned by Captain Coles were noticeably different from the iron-cased ships introduced by the French and represented an entirely different approach to naval tactics.

All of the British and French floating batteries built during the Crimean War, as well as the fighting ships built in 1859–60, like the *Warrior* and *La Gloire*, were designed to deliver broadsides with a relatively large number of artillery pieces directing their fire from either side of the ship at the same time. This was a system that had been employed since artillery had first been placed on ships during the

THE FRENCH IRON-PLATED FRIGATE "LA GLOIRE.

Encouraged by the success of primitive ironclads during the Crimean War, both the French and the British built iron-plated frigates at the close of the 1850s. The iron-plated *La Gloire,* from around 1860, is pictured here. *Scientific American,* February 16, 1861.

sixteenth century. During the mid-1850s a number of naval designers and tacticians began to propose a radically different approach to naval artillery and associated tactics. Instead of ships with a row of guns on either side, they argued that it was preferable to place one or two guns of larger caliber on a rotating platform, which allowed firing in any direction. Not only did this mean that larger ordnance could be utilized, but all of the preliminary maneuvering required to bring the guns to bear would be obviated.

It is still unsettled as to who first proposed this alternative to the traditional broadside arrangement. Captain Coles is certainly one of the candidates for this distinction. Like Napoleon III, Coles had been impressed with Russia's use of the Paixhans shell guns to destroy the Turkish fleet. Recognizing that the existing British men-of-war were likely to suffer a similar fate should they try to bombard Russian fortresses in the Sea of Azov, Captain Coles came up with a floating battery that was noticeably different from those based on the French model. Coles dubbed this raft-like affair armed with a 32-pounder the *Lady Nancy.*

His first attempt successful, Coles next proposed the construction of a number of rafts that from the outside appeared to be normal hulls but were constructed from empty mortar casks, which supported the gun platform on the deck and supplied the required buoyancy. The turret was protected by thick plates of iron sloped at 40 degrees. A single 62-pounder was housed in this iron cupola, which could be rotated 360 degrees.

The third of these rafts that were to be steam powered would tow the remainder. The plan was to proceed undetected under steam to the shallow waters near the shore, after having been supported by other ships in deeper water. The creation proved remarkably impervious to enemy fire. To offer a lower profile on the water during a fight, Coles had suggested that water could be pumped into some of the casks as desired. Projectiles, even 13-inch shells, which hit the hull between wind and water could destroy a cask or two, but their numerous brethren kept the raft afloat.

The Admiralty was so impressed that in November 1855 Coles was ordered back to Britain to explain his proposal to the lords commissioner in person. Unfortunately for Coles, Russia sued for peace, and his radical ideas were perfunctorily shelved. His interest nevertheless now highly stimulated, the imaginative naval designer continued his quest for a new type of armor-protected fighting ship. His next design was for a much larger vessel, one adorned with nine independent turrets, each housing two guns. Two turrets were staggered toward the bow, and two toward the stern, so that four guns at any given time could be fired, if need be, directly from the bow or stern of the ship. The remaining five turrets were placed directly in a single line so that they could deliver a ten-gun broadside in either direction.

Although many of Coles's ideas and designs must have struck most naval architects as highly original and unorthodox, if not downright bizarre, there were a number of similarities with the Stevenses' earlier designs. Both shared three fundamental principles: the use of water to protect most of the vessel, sloped armor, and the pumping of water into tanks to reduce a ship's profile on the water.

The similarity with the Stevenses' secret designs notwithstanding, Coles's were subjected to widespread censure in both the press and professional publications. Despite this rather public ridicule, there were those who felt that the captain's basic approach had merit. Delivering a talk at a British professional association in September 1861, a Doctor Eddy suggested the construction of a new type of gunboat, which even he, its inventor, acknowledged had been an outgrowth of Coles's ideas. As did the Stevenses and Coles before him, Eddy relied upon water to protect most of the gunboat's crew and innards. To achieve this, the ship had to have a very low profile, with most of the hull lying below the waterline. Enemy guns firing from a higher elevation thus had to be depressed. The gunboats were to have topsides sloped upwards to a central ridge to provide a nonperpendicular target, off which enemy shot would ricochet harmlessly. However, to achieve the maximum possible destructive effect, the guns themselves had to be eight feet above the water line. The two Armstrong guns were to be placed 4 feet apart atop a turntable that allowed full rotation. The armored sides of the "conical fort," which was described as an inverted "truncated cone," were sloped 45 degrees to deflect the incoming shots and minimize the amount of destruction.

Eddy envisioned that his agile gunboats would be easily able to outmaneuver their much larger and more cumbersome adversaries and thus more than neutralize the latter's otherwise overwhelming preponderance of armament. Though he used Coles's cupola, Eddy's design was different in one very significant detail. Unlike Coles's second design, with its fourteen guns in seven turrets, Eddy limited his gunboat's offensive punch to a single two-gun cupola to obtain the desired speed of about 16 knots. Was this an original idea, or had Eddy been influenced by Coles's original construction, which was actually used in the Crimea, or was it the result of a parallel series of developments that had been underway for several years in France? Unfortunately, not much more is known about Eddy's armored gunboat design, so it is impossible to answer this question with any certitude.

What is known is that French naval authorities began experimenting with rifled artillery on wooden ships in 1855–56. These tests demonstrated rather conclusively that the large, multigunned traditional fighting ships could be overpowered by much smaller vessels armed with rifled guns firing shells. Although the public's interest appears to have been fixated upon *La Gloire,* French authorities also became interested in smaller armored vessels that would carry far less, but heavier ordnance. According to the Paris correspondent for the *London Times,* Napoleon III ordered the construction of a number of tortoise-shaped armored gunboats in 1860, one of which was observed traveling from Bordeaux to Toulon in January of the next year. According to the correspondent, the vessel was

> composed of steel plates, and will be propelled by two screws and set in motion by a machine of 14-Horse Power engine. Carries but one cannon . . . . The mouth of the cannon will just pass over the back of the fish, which will present an inclined plane to the enemy, over which the balls will slide. The crew will be completely sheltered under this roof, of which the force of resistance is so well calculated that the heaviest shot or shell cannot ignore it.

Confidence in the new, smaller vessels was short-lived: The April

13 edition of *Scientific American* reported that the emperor had canceled further construction of this type of armored ship.

For many years it was widely believed that John Ericsson introduced the ironclad when he built the *Monitor*. In 1854 Ericsson had sent Napoleon III a proposal for the construction of an iron-protected ship with turreted guns and 6-inch iron sheets angled to deflect enemy shot easily. Since this description of a *New System of Naval Attack* was penned in 1854, it appears to predate Coles's efforts in the Crimea and suggests Ericsson could legitimately claim to have invented the progressive features of the *Monitor*. The problem, of course, is that most of these "innovative" features had already been embodied in the Stevens floating battery, which long predated either of Coles's or Ericsson's creations. So, other than in debating who was the first to propose gun turrets, Ericsson's proposal to French authorities is not relevant.

SUBMARINES AND MINES

Constructed during the American War of Independence, the diminutive *Turtle* was the world's first submarine. With the return of peace, the idea was not forgotten, and Robert Fulton continuously experimented with this type of vessel. Napoleon commissioned the famed American inventor to construct a submarine that could terrorize British shipping, but Fulton failed to complete the vessel successfully. Almost 20 years passed before a Russian engineer, Karl Andreevich Shil'der, resurrected interest in a submersible vessel. More successful than Fulton, Shil'der constructed a peculiar vessel. Two cylinders were attached to the top of the hull. These remained above the waterline and allowed the ship's captain and the pilot to navigate the small vessel, the main body of which was submerged. Projecting forward was a long spur. Attached to its end was a barrel with an explosive payload, which would be set off when ramming an enemy vessel. The most interesting feature was a separate floating dock that could be towed by a conventional vessel and housed three Congreve rockets.

Interest in the submarine waned for almost another 20 years, until in 1849 a noted Brooklyn inventor, Williard Day, inventor of a steam shovel, resurrected the idea. Day realized that there was a need for a submersible device that would allow workers to examine a ship's hull below the waterline without always going to the trouble and expense of placing the ship in a dry dock. He created what he called a "sub-marine telescopic examiner" for this purpose. The next several years witnessed a flurry of activity in this area, and several other patents were granted for submersible vessels and devices. In 1852 Day came out with an improved submarine explorer, while a few miles away in the Brooklyn Naval Yards, a French inventor successfully tested an underwater vessel for American naval authorities. On July 20, 1855, in France, Des Champ and Vilcocq were issued a patent for their "Deep Diving Boat."

Of course, the submersible vessel was not the only new naval technology being considered. Around the same time, inventors began tinkering with submersible and floating bombs. As early 1801 Robert Fulton, commissioned by Napoleon, attempted to construct a working "torpedo mine." The first experiments proved unsuccessful, and it was not until 1853 that the Russians introduced the first workable mines, which at the time were called *torpedoes*. The Russians experimented with chemically and electrically activated devices. Neither variant succeeded in doing much damage to British ships during the Crimean War. Meanwhile, in the United States, W. O. Stone, a mechanic in Charlestown, Massachusetts, invented a submarine rocket that purportedly was driven through the water like an ordinary rocket through the air.

The idea of using a submarine to sink enemy vessels was also considered, however. A British inventor, James Nysmyth, had drawn up plans for a "submerged propeller" that housed a large, underwater mortar, which projected out from its hull. The vessel, which was only partly submerged and in this respect resembled the Stevenses' creation, operated much like an ordinary ram. As soon as the vessel came up to the enemy ship, the mortar would fire, punching a large hole in the other vessel's hull below the waterline.

Other than the Russian mines, it is improbable that any of these inventions proved practical. Nevertheless, this litany of inventions shows that by the 1850s there was both widespread interest and knowledge about such creations and that the *H. L. Hunley* submarine, destined to gain fame as the first submarine to sink an enemy ship, did not arise in a vacuum.

PART II

THE BEGINNING OF THE WAR

T he ominous clouds of civil strife that had been gathering for decades periodically erupted into momentary flashpoints, such as the Kansas Crisis in 1856. However, after many years of grumbling and acrimonious debate, with the approach of the 1860 elections and the possibility that Lincoln would attain the presidency, the Southern secessionist movement was finally galvanized into action. Sensing the possibility of armed conflict in the not-so-distant future, on January 21, 1860, the Virginia State Legislature authorized $5 million to purchase arms and equipment, a truly vast increase from Virginia's 1859 military budget, a paltry $5,800. Later that year the Virginia Board for the Public Defense decided to send delegates to the leading American and European arms manufacturers. One far-reaching consequence was the arrangement for a Parrott rifled artillery piece to be sent to the Virginia Military Institute (VMI) for trials. Such preparations only intensified after Lincoln's election, and by December 15 Virginia's adjutant-general would report to the governor that besides the five divisional artillery regiments of the militia, 26 companies of volunteers had been raised, with 24 artillery pieces.

This activity did not go entirely unnoticed, and a number of Northern military men looked on with growing dismay. An article entitled "A Speck of War at Home" in the November 15, 1860, issue of the *Military Gazette* warned against the arming of the Southern militia, observing that such forces were intended against "their own brothers, and against no others." The article concluded with the hope that "prudent and wise counsels will prevail, that men will stop to count the cost and value of this Union." Unfortunately for the millions of Americans who would bear the full brunt of the impending storm, such optimism proved to be unfounded. There were some in the North, however, who were unwilling to leave the fate of the Union to either chance or calm heads. In the December 10 edition of the *New York Herald*, James C. Kerrigan recommended that New York City's militia establish a military organization to "protect the municipal rights of the city and the constitutional rights of the citizens of the country, in the event of a revolution in the country."

This appeal certainly was no cry in the dark, and during the following weeks similar sentiments were heard elsewhere in the North, especially after the seizure of Fort Marion in the harbor of St. Augustine, Florida (January 7, 1861) and the *Star of the West* incident (January 9). The following dispatch from Boston appeared in New York papers around New Year's Day:

> There is no disguising the fact that Massachusetts is ready to respond promptly to any demand made upon her for troops to sustain the Union and the laws. I learn to-day, from the highest authority, that seven thousand troops can be put into marching orders on twenty-four hours' notice, and that one hundred and forty-five thousand men are enrolled in the militia of this State. Of this number twenty thousand could easily be mustered.

The day this warning appeared, General Abbot returned from Washington and recommended that New Hampshire be placed on a "war footing." Less than 2 weeks later, Buffalo newspapers reported that a local armory was to strengthen its two militia regiments by recruiting 2000 men. By January 21 similar movements were reported underway in Troy, New York, Philadelphia, and Worcester, Massachusetts.

Nevertheless, this was a minority reaction, and most Northerners still believed that Southern saber rattling was mere braggadocio and all would be smoothed over by compromise. When the storm finally broke, the Federal government was caught largely unprepared. Shipments of small arms to the south were halted. However, it was widely believed that Buchanan's secretary of war, John B. Floyd, had sabotaged Union efforts to prepare for a rebellion by ordering arms to be relocated from arsenals in the North to their counterparts in Southern states and ensuring that the regular army was scattered among small, ineffective garrisons.

Whether because of incompetence, injudicious optimism, or the surreptitious actions of secessionists within the War Department, the army had remained essentially the same the decade leading up to early 1861, with many of its 15,500 effectives distributed along the western frontier. The navy also had meager resorces. Its 9000 men and officers worked six screw frigates, five steam sloops, twenty sailing ships, and several gunboats, for a total of 1200 guns. These figures suggest a slightly inflated picture of the American navy's actual strength. Of the five screw frigates, only one was actually in commission. In April 1861 several other craft were laid up out of service in the dockyard in Norfolk, Virginia, only a hundred miles from Richmond. In sum, there were no reserves, no transport—in fact, little or no organization for war.

Worse yet, the Federal government couldn't even guarantee that it could maintain the relatively small human resources that had been at its disposal. Among the officer class, there was an obvious division of loyalty, and a great number of officers elected to resign in order to serve their "country," which in these cases meant their individual states. The same applied to future officers learning their trade at the United States Military Academy at West Point. Interestingly enough, the same trend was not found among the common enlisted men, the great majority of whom remained in the service of the Union. A substantial portion of the regular forces had to be left along the frontier, since their removal would leave the western territories open to depredations of hostile Indians. Even if the entire regular army became available for operations against the rebellious states, however, it still was grossly inadequate to deal with the crisis at hand.

To rectify these deficiencies, Lincoln immediately responded to the fall of Fort Sumter on April 13, 1861, with a call for 75,000 militiamen. This force was to consist of 94 regiments, each of 780 men, to be raised by the loyal states. The number of regiments to be supplied by each state was more or less proportionate to its population. The District of Columbia, for example, was to contribute 1680 men. Although the men were originally to be supplied by state militias, this immediately proved inadequate, impractical, and in some cases illegal. State authorities in Connecticut, for example, found state laws did not allow for the commander of its militia to respond to the president's requisition. The state's governor met his quota with a call for volunteers, instead. In most cases, the existing militia organizations lacked the required number of men and had to accept volunteers to make up the balance.

When Lincoln issued his April 15 proclamation, in effect a declaration of war against the seceding states, the Northern capital was virtually defenseless. If the capital was to be saved, militia and even some volunteer organizations had to be mobilized immediately. There were several tense days as Lincoln and the pro-Federalists within the city awaited their arrival. In desperation, Senator Lane of Kansas raised a company of seventy-five men to protect the president. Stationed at the East Room of the White House, one half slept while the remainder stood guard. The first outside troops, a modest five companies of 500 Pennsylvanians, arrived on April 18, followed the next day by the Sixth Massachusetts Infantry. Lacking barracks and facilities, it became necessary to quarter the men temporarily in the House of Representatives and the Senate Chambers, then not in session. Throughout the capital, the first incipient measures were taken to erect defensive works. Key public buildings were protected by sandbags and barrels of flour, while whatever ordnance that could be found was placed to command the approaches to important buildings.

To get to Washington City the two regiments had to march through Baltimore, then predominantly secessionist in sentiment. (Although the District of Columbia was established in 1790, most Americans used the map-maker's fiction and referred to the city as "Washington City." The even shorter term "Washington" appears to have increased in popularity after the Civil War.) The Pennsylvanians managed to make their way through, meeting only cold, hostile stares. The next day the citizens in the streets were both more firmly resolved and better prepared to oppose the movement of Union troops through their city. First bricks and stones flew, and then shots were fired at the Massachusetts men. The latter immediately returned the fire, and twelve citizens were killed, and dozens wounded. A delegation from the city approached Lincoln to protest what they considered the "pollution" of their soil by Northern troops. Remaining adamant, Lincoln announced his intention to continue with troop movements through the city. Learning of this, malcontents immediately set about cutting the telegraph wires through Maryland, tearing up stretches of railroad tracks, and wrecking a number of bridges. Washington was now an island surrounded by hostile rebels and their sympathizers.

Several days passed, and fewer than 1500 militiamen had arrived to garrison Washington. The situation dramatically improved on April 24–25, when almost 3000 militiamen and volunteers from New York, Rhode Island, and Massachusetts made their way into the capital. It was obvious, however, that even if the mandated 75,000 militiamen were raised, not only would a much greater force be required, but the men would be forced to stay with the colors for a much greater time than was initially anticipated. On May 3, therefore, a call went out for 300,000 volunteers, who were to remain in service for 3 years.

Following Lincoln's proclamation, there was a flurry of activity in almost every Northern state to raise the required quota of men so desperately needed to defend the nation's capital. The First Regiment Rhode Island Detached Militia was among the first of these regiments to arrive, and its history during this period is representative. On April 16 Governor Sprague instructed the state militia commanders to gather their men immediately. At 8 A.M. the next morning in Providence, cannon's signaled militiamen to assemble at prearranged meeting places. Most responded without hesitation. The Newport Artillery, for example, was on the wharf at Newport by 11:30 A.M. Boarding a steamer at 1 P.M., the company set off for Providence. Later that day it marched to the Railroad Hall on Exchange Place, where it settled in for the night. Here the various militia units were clothed, equipped, and gathered together to form the First Rhode Island. On Saturday, April 19, the regiment boarded the steamer *Empire State*. Arriving at New York the next day, it was transferred to the *Coatzacolcos*, a military transport, which proceeded to Chesapeake Bay on the 21st. (By tearing up large sections of railroad track, Southern sympathizers from Maryland had made it more difficult for the troops to reach the capital, so, unlike the regiments that would follow in the months to come, these first regiments had to be shipped to a port on the Chesapeake Bay.) From Annapolis, the regiment would have to march the last leg of its journey. The regiment began its march to Annapolis Junction on April 25 and soon after reached its destination, the capital.

Fortunately for the North, the interruption of rail activity between Baltimore and Washington proved short-lived. Mechanics in a Massachusetts regiment not only managed to re-lay the torn-up track but also repaired a damaged engine. The rail line reopened, and troops and supplies once again could be sent expeditiously to Washington. The flow of volunteer troops into the city increased, and by the end of the month the capital was defended by 10,000 volunteers. The moment of immediate crisis had passed!

The regiments coming from the northeast continued to follow this travel itinerary. Within a few weeks transports no longer had to travel all the way into Annapolis but disembarked their soldierly cargo at Elizabeth Port, New Jersey, where the troops were loaded onto trains. The railroad network was much less extensive than it would become by the early twentieth century, and some regiments were forced to take a rather circuitous journey. The experience of the Second Rhode Island is illustrative. During the 2-day ride, the train slowly worked its way westward through New Brunswick and Trenton, New Jersey; Easton and Harrisburg, Pennsylvania; before heading back to the southeast through York and on to Baltimore. These were the days before rival railroad lines had learned to share depots and train stations, so upon arriving at Baltimore, the men had to detrain and march through the city to the Washington Station. Once there, they boarded a second train and traveled the last leg of the journey to Washington City. Although today a modern train is able to traverse the distance separating the two cities in about 40 minutes, the lack of signaling equipment meant a train frequently had to be shunted on sidings to let another train with the right of way pass. As a result, it often took up to 5 hours to cover these last 40 miles.

Judging from period memoirs, the 2- to 3-day train ride could be characterized at the very minimum as a "memorable experience." Not only did the troops endure several sleepless nights, but as the summer wore on, the close press of humanity packed into the boxcars made it even more difficult to bear the stifling heat and humidity. When compiling his regiment's history years after the war, Edwin Marvin of the Fifth Connecticut Volunteers remembered the night journey to Harrisburg as the "the most disagreeable night of the service." The novice soldiers had managed to catch only a few moments of sleep on the steamer. Once on the trains the best that could be managed was only a few seconds of slumber at a time. The train made frequent stops, and the men were allowed to get off at Harrisburg, York, and Baltimore to procure meals and refreshments at local restaurants. All too often refreshments meant filling up oneself and one's canteen with whiskey or beer. When the train finally pulled out, many of the men were "pretty well soaked and sodden." Intoxication manifested itself in all the usual forms. Some were irritable and garrulous, while others sat stunned in an alcoholic haze. All were exhausted. Yet, there was not enough room to stretch out and fade away into slumber. As soon as anyone started to doze off, he invariably bumped into his neighbors. Startled, they awoke, and the affair as frequently as not was closed by a short but cogent exchange of expletives. All this transpired in a ubiquitous pall of stifling tobacco smoke.

> We were dead played out, and we could no longer entertain each other with thrice told yarns; indeed, we were cross and irascible; we wanted to sleep, but we could not even do that. We did catch cat-naps sitting, standing, lopping and leaning, but these were entirely unsatisfactory, as the minute we let go of ourselves to sleep we lurched heavily upon someone else, and so gave occasion for a rude awakening and lots of talk. We wished for morning, but it would not come; we wished for the end of our journey, but no one knew when and where that was to be, and so we wore away one of the most wretched nights of our service, till, the daylight was beginning to give us glimpses of a wooded, mountainous country about us, we came to the long looked for halt.

The trip from the northeast to Washington City via Harrisburg was probably the exception, however. By the summer most regiments from New York and New England took the train to Camden, New Jersey, detrained, and embarked upon steamboats, which in turn conveyed them to the foot of Washington Avenue, Philadelphia. They then boarded a second train to Baltimore.

HOW RECRUITS WERE RAISED

The different types of "calls," such as militia versus volunteer, and varying local circumstances meant that in practice there was no single method by which the required regiments were raised in each state. Obviously, after the first call for 75,000 militiamen in April, existing militia units served as cadres around which complete regiments would be formed. The Tenth Massachusetts Infantry Volunteers were thus formed from the old prewar Tenth Massachusetts Volunteer Militia, while the Thirteenth Massachusetts Infantry was based upon the Fourth Battalion of Rifles. In Pennsylvania the Duquesne Grays, a unit that had served with distinction during the Mexican-American War, became Company B of the Twelfth Pennsylvania.

Such militia units were no longer available when it became necessary to respond to the May 3 call for volunteers, so other means of organizing regiments had to be found. Probably the most prevalent method was to raise individual companies in nearby towns and counties and then organize these into regiments at a common point of rendezvous, as was the case with the Fourteenth Massachusetts Infantry. Other times a prominent personage was appointed colonel and allowed to raise the requisite number of men almost any way he saw fit. Such was the case with the Fletcher Webster Regiment in Massachusetts. No source of potential manpower was overlooked, and colleges and universities provided their share of recruits. There were cases where almost an entire class of undergraduates enlisted together to form their own regiments, and the tutors and professors served as officers.

In May the War Department also issued an organization standard for the volunteer infantry regiments. Infantry regiments had to have between 844 and 1024 men and officers. Originally, a regiment was to be organized into a ten-company unit, made up of one grenadier company, a light company, eight standard companies, plus a fourteen-man regimental staff. In practice, however, the regiment consisted of ten regular companies. Each company at maximum strength had 101 men and officers. The establishment authorized by the New York State adjutant general on July 2, 1862, approximates that utilized by the early 3-month volunteer regiments:

Regimental Staff

1	Colonel
1	Lieutenant-Colonel
1	Major
1	Adjutant
1	Regimental Quartermaster
1	Surgeon
1	Assistant-Surgeon
1	Chaplain
1	Sergeant-Major
1	Regimental Quartermaster-Sergeant
1	Regimental Quartermaster
1	Regimental Commissary-Sergeant
1	Hospital Steward
1	Principal Musician
14	Total

Company of Union Infantry

1	Captain
1	First Lieutenant
1	Second Lieutenant
1	First Sergeant
4	Sergeants
8	Corporals
2	Musicians
1	Wagoneer
64 to 82	Privates
83 to 101	Total

Although this organizational structure appears to have been almost universally followed, there were at least a few examples of more idiosyncratic regimental structures. The Thirty-sixth Illinois started the war boasting both infantry and cavalry elements. Its ten infantry companies were supplemented with two cavalry companies with ninety-one and ninety-five men and officers, respectively. This arrangement appears to have been quite useful for its reconnaissance and picket duties in southwestern Missouri on the way to Pea Ridge (March 6–8, 1862). A few of the early regiments, such as the First Rhode Island came equipped with a light artillery company. The Second New Hampshire had a Dahlgren gun for its own use in late July.

When formed in *order of battle,* that is, in line, the companies had to place themselves in strict, officially prescribed order according to the seniority of company captains. The following sequence had to be maintained from right to left: the 1st, 6th, 4th, 9th, 3rd, 8th, 5th, 7th, and 2nd companies. This practice can be traced back to seventeenth-century European military procedure. It had been designed to ensure that the company led by the most veteran captain was positioned on the right flank, the company commanded by the next most experienced captain was posted on the left, while that of the third captain was in the middle of the regiment.

As the months passed the War Department continued to fine-tune the organizational structure of the expanding military machine. In June it was announced that nurses would not be allowed to attach themselves to individual regiments. Instead, nurses whose credentials were acceptable to the War Department would be allowed to serve at government military hospitals.

Faced with an influx of immigrants into the service, the next month the War Department decided that henceforth a functional command of English was an essential precondition for anyone seeking service in the Union army. This resolve proved short-lived, however, the temptation to accept large bodies of eager, able-bodied men proving too much to resist. In August it was decided to accept foreign-speaking individuals as long as they entered regiments whose men spoke the same tongue. This itself proved to be a short-lived compromise, and 5 days later the entire set of restrictions were revoked.

Height restrictions were also lessened at the same time. The existing height requirement was reduced from 5'4" to 5'3". Union military authorities also tried to eliminate an abuse that soon made an appearance. States such as New York, Illinois, and Massachusetts eventually each raised dozens of volunteer regiments. In an effort to gather the requisite number of officers, each succeeding wave of regiments naturally would try to induce volunteer officers with existing regiments to resign from service there and sign up in their service. Needless to say, this was highly disruptive. To curtail this problem, the War Department during the late summer declared that any officers who resigned from a volunteer regiment would be ineligible to serve with any other.

ACTIVITY IN CAMPS

66 "Informed" opinion on both sides optimistically prophesized that the conflict would be quickly resolved. "It will be all over in 90 days" was the most common prediction. Those on the Northern side were convinced that they would quickly defeat the rebels and force the contumacious states back into the Union. With equal conviction Southerners believed that all they had to do was stand up for their rights and present a strong countenance, and they were certain to repel the first Federal army foolish enough to set foot on their soil. In these first few months, the ever-present patriotic fever seemed to smite civilian, military, and ecclesiastic alike. In towns and cities from the coastal areas of New England all the way to the northern Midwest, demonstrations of patriotic enthusiasm were the order of the day. Fervent speeches decrying Southern treason—or, conversely, Northern oppression—and military bands and militia practicing in the town squares punctuated the otherwise predictable evening routine.

To accommodate the thousands now flocking to their country's colors, scores of camps were established throughout the countryside. Unlike later in the war, when a self-conscious effort was made to sequester new recruits in order to distance them from their former civilian past, at this early stage instruction camps were frequently set up adjoining or even inside large cities or towns.

Although some of the men streaming to the colors had previous military experience, possibly as volunteers during the Mexican-American War or, if immigrants, in some European army, a great majority of the men were complete novices to the rigors of military life. Regardless of how transient the upcoming struggle was likely to be, the troops still had to be trained in the basic drill. Generally, each regiment was treated as a separate camp and surrounded by its own chain of sentinels. Instruction covered basic parade ground maneuvers, such as how to march and form the basic formations and, of course, how to perform the manual of arms. The men were also shown the rudiments of sentry duty and were constantly inspected by their officers. The first few days and weeks were spent learning the "school of the soldier," which included basic military functions, such as how to deport oneself as a soldier, march in step, handle one's shoulder arm, and so on. These mastered, the military novices moved on to drilling in companies and then in battalions.

Officers, meanwhile, were taught the sword exercise and practiced with their pistols. More theoretical subjects, such as outpost duty, were left to the evening. In the smaller camps, the number of men available limited the scope of drilling, so exercises were conducted on a small-unit level. However, in camps where several regiments had been brought together, a few brave officers attempted regimental and even brigade-sized maneuvers. Maj. Gen. Jacob Cox would recount that when he arrived at Fort Dennison on April 29, the as-yet unarmed men were kept busy marching in single line, by file, in changing direction, and in forming column of fours from double ranks.

Many veterans would remember these early camps for the long days, the hard work, the discipline that was quickly instilled into the troops, and the ardor with which both men and officers pursued their new profession. Col. Benjamin F. Scribner, who commanded the Thirty-eighth Indiana Infantry, recollected how in his first camp it seemed that everyone, officers and rank and file alike, vied with one another to master the soldier's duties. In some cases the regimen was so demanding, the discipline so strict, that resentment arose among the men. Dexter Butterfield, a sergeant with the "Abbott Grays," that is, the Second Massachusetts, would recall that while stationed at Camp Andrew, the men thought that the drilling was needlessly severe and the officers were being unduly harsh. With the advantage of hindsight, he had to concede that the entire regiment would later come to appreciate this thoroughness. In Butterfield's opinion, as a result of these efforts, "the officers made out of the raw material one of the best, if not the best, regiment that ever left the state, and we were acknowledged to be the best company in the regiment."

Not all veterans shared this rather rosy picture of these early training camps and were more cynical about such first efforts to convert raw recruits into a semblance of a military machine. Remembering back to this early stage of the war, General Sherman would concede, "We had good organization, good men, but no cohesion, no real discipline, no respect for authority, no real knowledge of war." Many of the early volunteer regiments were made up almost entirely of inexperienced civilians, all the way from buck privates up to the colonel. Not surprisingly, such organizations initially experienced the greatest difficulty performing the most rudimentary drills. Officers of the Sixteenth New York, for example, during the first week found it difficult to get their men to keep step or to march out exactly when ordered. Military protocol required that the men advance after the order "FOR-WARD! . . . March!" The men in this regiment tended to jump the gun and start off after the word "FOR-WARD!" The correct method of stacking arms at the end of the drill in many cases proved to be a more persistent problem. Many regiments had to wait weeks if not months for their shoulder arms and naturally remained uninstructed in their use. Usually, the officers in these regiments suddenly found themselves stymied as they ordered their men to stack their arms after the first drill with actual weapons. John Donaghy, who served with the 103rd Pennsylvania for most of the war, informs us that his company was able to stack arms only "after much experimental bungling." Colonel Scribner records a similarly embarrassing experience while his men trained at Muldrough's Hill.

The situation was not appreciably better among the companies formed from prestigious militia units, even those who had served in the Mexican War. Before the war, the "Duquesne Grays" had been considered the crack volunteer unit in Pittsburgh. Of course, its ranks were greatly expanded after Lincoln's call to arms. The result was that new recruits had to learn everything from scratch, while experienced volunteers had to unlearn everything previously taught. Donaghy was forced to concede that the result was that the company "drilled [no better] than those around us, in fact not so well as some of them."

There was much less standardization than during later campaigns. Many of the newly formed regiments were first taught the discarded Scott's *Tactics*, only to start over again with Hardee's *Tactics*. However, Hardee's *Tactics*, so closely associated with a high-ranking officer now in Confederate ranks, was soon officially discarded, and a new translation of the same source was adopted, the so-called Casey's *Tactics*. Once again, whatever was learned had to be set aside, and the study of tactics started all over again. It was not unheard of for officers in various companies to utilize different approaches to maneuvers in the same brigade or even the same regiment. Though the Ninth Ohio and the Second Minnesota Volunteers were brigaded together with the Eighteenth U.S. Infantry Regiment, the two regiments employed entirely different sets of "tactics." The former was composed entirely of German immigrants. Despite all official regulations to the contrary, the regiment followed a tactical system used by the Prussian army, with which many had previously served.

In some regiments nearly every company commander had his own pet drill. Even when a common system was enforced, lacking the presence of an expert tutor, officers were left to make their own interpretations. This type of problem plagued the 103rd Pennsylvania for quite some time. The adjutant, necessarily a spectator to all the regiment's exercises, noticed that Donaghy's methods did not correspond with the colonel's. Hoping to standardize the regiment's maneuvers, he asked the colonel whether all drills should be conducted

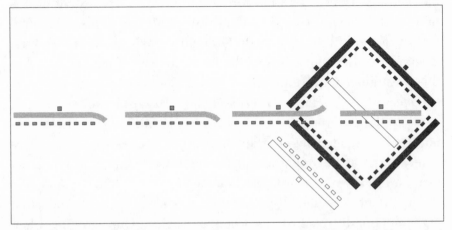

A maneuver from *Hardee's Rifle and Light Infantry Tactics.* Not only was this method of forming a square faster than its Napoleonic equivalent, but the oblique fire from its front face produced an effective raking fire.

"according to the book." The colonel of course responded in the affirmative. Nevertheless, in subsequent exercise the colonel, who couldn't seem to wean himself from officially discarded tactics, continued with his own unique systems of movements. The problem came to a head when the brigade was ordered to perform the regulation movements under the knowledgeable eye of General Silas Casey. Needless to say, there were many blunders and embarrassing moments, and several days later the colonel received a communiqué scolding him for his negligence. The more conscientious officers of course made every effort to rectify their lack of knowledge and experience. Someone walking around a camp in the evening would often see a newly appointed officer with a copy of the drill manual or some other work on basic tactics, struggling to acquire the rudiments of his new profession.

Although lack of uniformity of drills could be an embarrassment during a review and an inconvenience on the battlefield, the first Northern volunteer regiments were saddled with a much more important deficiency in combat preparedness. And unlike the inadequacies in drill and maneuvers, which were apparent to officer and spectator alike, this deficiency remained largely unnoticed. All too frequently, the men entered their first campaign without having had any training or practice on how to use their weapons. This was especially true among northeastern regiments, where most men had never handled a musket before mustering into service. The extent of this problem has been revealed by Capt. Edwin Marvin in his regimental history of the Fifth Connecticut. Originally raised as the Colt's First Regiment of Revolving Rifles, the large number of men attracted to this prestigious unit waited more than 2 months to be mustered into service. Col. A. G. Hazard, president of the Hazard Powder Company, wrote to the governor and offered to supply 50,000 pounds of gunpowder for target practice. Captain Marvin assures us that unfortunately, this was the only time any mention was made of teaching the men how to use a rifle or target practice.

The effects of such ill-preparedness became evident when that regiment finally reached the front in August. One morning when about forty men came off of picket duty, it was decided to have a little fun while firing off the round that had been loaded the evening before, a task that was required of all pickets before they returned to camp. About a hundred yards away, the broad side of a barn proved to be too much of a temptation. The men fired a volley at the harmless foe. The men were sadly disappointed when they checked the results of their seemingly fearsome fire. Only four bullets had found their way to the building, though it was 20 feet long and 15 high. Of these, only a single bullet hole was within the height of a line of infantrymen. Had these shots been fired in anger, the volley that seemed so impressive would at best have inflicted a single casualty at the enemy line only 100 yards away.

Convinced that this incident evinced the shooting capabilities of the average New England troops in the summer of 1861, Captain Marvin felt that most Union infantrymen from the East knew as much about how to fire and operate their weapons as they did a camera "if they had been then and there called upon to photograph the enemy's line of battle or any particular man in it." In the years following the Civil War, Captain Marvin was deeply chagrined that so many hapless youths had been allowed to go into their first battle without adequate training:

It was a cruel mistake and caused a great waste of life, and to a large extent was chargeable with the impression which widely prevailed, at first, that the rebels were the better soldiers simply from the fact that some of the first engagements proved them better shooters than the Union troops from the east.

The Confederate Camps
Stationed in California before the war erupted, E. P. Alexander had to work his way by rail through Cleveland and Cincinnati before proceeding to Chattanooga, Atlanta, and finally Richmond. As he wended his way through Ohio and Tennessee and the states farther south, he was able to visit a number of military camps on both sides. Ever the keen observer, he mentally noted the differences between the Northern and Southern camps of instruction. Not only were the Northern camps larger, generally housing a regimental-sized organization, but they were better organized. The men were neatly attired in blue uniforms, and on more than one

occasion, Alexander noticed that the Union volunteers had been issued rifle muskets. This was in stark contrast to camps then being set up in the rebellious states, which were much smaller, usually having a company or so of men, noticeably more disorganized, and not as well equipped. The men rushing to serve the Southern cause were handed a motley assortment of uniforms, brown, gray, and even blue, and the vast majority had to settle for old-fashioned smoothbore muskets.

On a more basic level, however, Southern officers faced the same challenges as in Federal camps. Lacking a consistent course of instruction, drills and tactics varied from camp to camp and even from officer to officer. George Eggleson, who initially served with the First Virginia Cavalry, found the results at the camp he first attended to be "signally funny." The most impractical maneuvers of every sort were most scrupulously inculcated into the martial novitiates, and predictably, the result of these incongruous teachings during battalion drill "closely resembled that of the music where each sang the chorus to the tune he knew the best."

Looking back, veterans would have mixed opinions about the effectiveness of this early training. Recollecting his experiences at Camp Curtain, Joseph R. Orweig, another veteran of the Confederate cause, wondered at how quickly the raw recruits had been molded into effective martial material. As a result of the "long and severe training," several companies, even an entire regiment, could be maneuvered adroitly even on the battlefield.

Eggleson proffered a much more cynical assessment. In his view the men were "simply a mob of rather ill-armed young gentlemen from the country." Despite the conscientious efforts of a handful of West Pointers and cadets from the Virginia Military Institute, these eager youths only received basic military discipline before being rushed half-prepared into the field, and an entire year of hard-fought campaigning would elapse before they fully appreciated what it was to be a "modern soldier." In retrospect Eggleson wondered how these men had been able to fight so successfully:

> They were as ignorant of the alphabet of obedience as their officers were of the art of commanding. And yet they acquitted themselves reasonably well, a fact which can be explained only by references to the causes of the insubordination in camp.

This passage hits upon some of the fundamental qualities of the Confederate soldier that would initially lead to victory, as well as the limitations of his character that would ultimately contribute to his defeat. The sense of independence, freedom, and the inalienable right of democracy was much stronger among the men filling the Confederate army than their Northern cousins, who fought for the preservation of the Union. Accustomed to a freer, out-of-doors life, with its rigorous regimen of hunting, field sports, and other sylvan activities, they had little experience with any type of subservience. They were used to obeying only when forced by special circumstances, and then only when there was an immediate and compelling reason.

These attitudes had been inculcated into the Southern worker and gentleman alike and were not easily set aside even after they entered military service. True, on the exercise field they obeyed their officers, partly because they realized it was an unavoidable necessity and partly because they succumbed to a sense of novelty; they were curious about the drills under study. According to W. H. Morgan, who served with a company that was originally part of the Twenty-eighth Virginia Infantry, as the Confederate forces began to concentrate around Manassas, General P. G. T. Beauregard issued a general order that admitted that strict military discipline would not be enforced. To ensure proper order and operational efficiency, commanders would instead rely upon the "good breeding" of the men. After the war George Eggleson would claim that he was unable to recall a single situation in which a captain dared to offend his men by either appointing or demoting a noncommissioned officer without first submitting the matter to his men for a vote.

There was a pervasive democratic feeling that the men were as good as the officers. Frequently, this appeared to be borne out by practice and habit. Unlike today, when it is an infraction of military discipline for an officer to fraternize with the men, it was not that uncommon during this early period for Confederate company officers to mess and sleep among their men. Officers and men quarreled, even fought, without consideration of rank. After all, officers within the regiment for the most part had arisen from the men, chosen by democratic election rather than through gradual incubation within a strict, formal militaristic system. Up until December 1861 even many of the corporals were elected.

Social standing was a more lasting distinction. Eggleson provided an apt description of the ever-pervasive, rigid class stratification of Southern society: "The line of demarcation between gentry and common people is not more sharply drawn than in Virginia. It rests then upon an indeterminate something or other, known as family." Of course, colonels and general officers were not quite so slavishly sensitive to their men's feelings, and many an order or directive was issued that, if it did not lead to an open protest, caused the men to harbor silent resentment, especially during the summer months of '61.

While the Second Virginia Infantry camped at Camp Lee in June, for example, a soldier was arrested for shooting at a squirrel within the camp. To the Virginian soldiers this appeared to be an "outrage on the rights and liberties of a freeman and an insult to the honor and dignity" and for a time dampened the ardor and enthusiasm of the men's patriotism. Another example of how the rank and file could be offended by what they considered to be an infringement of their rights, regardless of the rank of the officer responsible for the orders, occurred a month later. Marching to Piedmont to entrain, a company known as the Botts Grays espied a coach that was a little more comfortable than the others. A few minutes after they entered the car and made themselves comfortable, Lt. A. S. "Sandy" Pendleton, a staff officer for Col. Thomas Jackson, entered, explained that this was an officer's coach, and ordered everyone to vacate the car immediately. Indignant, the infantrymen retorted they were every bit as good as the officers and remained where they were. Pendleton eventually left, and the Botts Grays retained the coach for the rest of the journey.

So strongly entrenched was this democratic sentiment that during the first 6 to 9 months of the war, some of the more popular men refused to stand for elections and even rejected promotions when these were proffered. The higher the social standing or the greater the wealth, the more patriotic it was to serve in a humble capacity. It was inevitable that such laudable sentiment eventually would succumb to reality, and before the first year was over, those that had previously eschewed prominence were now seen vying for commissions during elections.

Despite their disciplinary peccadilloes, once on the battlefield the

Southern men under the leadership of Beauregard, Joseph E. Johnston, and Lee possessed sufficient discipline and military acumen to repeatedly best their Northern cousins. The very men who the day before in the safety of camp had been so fractious and who did everything to avoid discomfort and distasteful duties, instantly endured unimaginable hardships and privation once on the march.

If their general demeanor belied their resolution and capacity to fight, so then did their appearance. Heros von Borcke, a Prussian officer who served on J. E. B. Stuart's staff, remembered his first impression of a Confederate camp, which he characterized as "a novelty tome in the art of castramentation [the systematic method of laying out a military camp]." Unlike European camps, where tents and even horses were arranged with geometrical precision, the Confederate camp had a definite haphazard appearance, with the horses scattered about, some tied to bushes, some to trees, and others still left to graze as they chose. Von Borcke had to admit, however, that it was amazing to see the instant transformation as soon as the men received orders to break camp, as well as the rapidity and discipline with which this was accomplished. Others noted this deceptive appearance. E. P. Alexander, noted Confederate artillery commander, had noticed that the Northern soldiers in general had "more flesh and better color" and speculated that a neutral observer at first glance would probably have thought them to be better fighting material than their Southern counterparts. Throughout the war Alexander would find it paradoxical that his comrades would seemingly fight all the harder as they grew "thinner and more ragged and hungry looking." Once again, Eggleson's memoir seems to supply the answer:

> These men were the people of the South, and the war was their own; whereas they fought it of their own accord, and not because their officers commanded them to do so. Their personal spirit and their intelligence were the sole elements of strength. Death has few terrors for such men, as compared with dishonor, and so they needed no officers at all, and no discipline, to insure their personal good conduct on the field of battle.

Lt. Col. William Ripley of the First United States Sharp Shooters attributed another reason for the early Confederate successes: "Man for man they were the superiors of their northern antagonist in the use of firearms." According to Ripley, the majority of the Southern men had been inured to the use of firearms since childhood, having been taught to hunt either to supplement the family's dietary intake or, if of a higher social status, purely as sport. Their Northern foe, in contrast, had for the most part come from the farm, the office, or the local store.

THE PRESS AS ADVISORS

Many officers received assistance from what today would probably be regarded as an unexpected resource. Recognizing that large numbers of their readers were flocking to the colors and many would serve as volunteer officers, many newspapers, magazines, and journals printed articles to advise those who now found themselves in a military profession. On April 24, a week after Lincoln's appeal for 75,000 militiamen, the *New York Times,* for example, carried a short article entitled "Suggestions from an Old Soldier," which offered the most rudimentary advice to the soon-to-be soldiers. Novices were admonished not to drink too much water on a march. If possible, they should carry water mixed with a little vinegar in the canteens—even better still, cold coffee—and if forced by thirst to drink while on the move, they were best advised to swish one or two gulps around the mouth and throat before spitting it out. Readers were especially warned against sitting down while on sentry duty, regardless of how tired they became. If they succumbed to this temptation, fatigue would set in all the more rapidly. The article urged the new soldiers to rub down their guns with sweet oil. They should take care of their comrades during forced marches, helping carry the weapons and load of those who were about to fall behind. But most of all, the *Times* article strongly advised soldiers to "avoid spirituous liquors as you would poison."

During the next few weeks, practical advice in some form or other would be proffered in almost every newspaper in the country. Seemingly elaborating upon the above dietary advice, another "old soldier," this time in the columns of the *New York Post,* cautioned that volunteers should also studiously avoid "strong coffee and oily meat," citing General Scott's belief that this indulgence had cost the life of many a recruit during the Mexican War. Noting that during a campaign a greater number of soldiers die from sickness than "by the bullet," the veteran campaigner suggested that the recruit should let his beard grow to protect the throat and lungs from a sudden chill; he was also urged to wash daily in warmer weather to prevent "fevers and bowel complains."

Most of the *Post*'s article, however, dealt with the necessary accoutrements that the martial novitiate should purchase before setting off to war. The new recruit had to remember that "a sudden check of perspiration by chilly or night air" could lead to illness and death and therefore was cautioned never to abandon his blanket. For extra warmth the soldier was advised to line his blanket with brown drilling (a twilled cotton fabric). Though this added 4 ounces to the soldier's burden, it was well worth the extra effort and ensured the needed warmth on a cold night. The soldier in the Western theater was also advised to spend $1.50 and purchase a small India rubber blanket (standard issue for most Eastern troops), which he could spread on the ground before going to sleep or over his shoulders while on guard duty during a rainstorm. The best "military hat" was that made of light-colored, soft felt with a high crown for ventilation space immediately above the head. This could be tied up in a "continental" style in fair weather or turned down during rainy weather or when the sun was too strong.

However, of all the magazines, journals, and newspapers, the *Scientific American* appears to have most consistently served as a means of popular military instruction during the first months of the conflict. Unlike its modern counterpart, the *Scientific American* of the day was primarily targeted toward inventors, manufacturers, and progressively minded machinists. Its pages provided a litany of mechanical inventions as they were introduced.

However, with the eruption of the Civil War, attention quickly turned to matters military, and soon the magazine was filled with articles such as "Learning to Shoot—Careful Loading of Rifles," "Disabling Canon," and "Practical Warfare." The magazine usually either explored innovations in military technology or focused on specific procedures, but occasionally, it also provided more general background information about newly emerging military scientific theories or about the state of military science in general. In early 1861 *Scientific American* unabashedly declared that the French military intelligentsia was the center of the martial world and the most worthy of emulation. The January 19, 1861, edition of *Scientific American*, for example, touted Napoleon III as no less than the "most shrewd and far-sighted ruler of men now living." Two weeks later the magazine explained why Napoleon III was so frequently mentioned on its pages:

> Napoleon III, is the ruling spirit who has effected the entire revolution that has recently taken place in the equipment of soldiers, in all armies, with the rifle instead of the musket; and he has given more attention to this subject, perhaps, than any other person living.

Some of this praise was unwarranted. Though Napoleon III did play a role in the adoption of Beaulieu's rifled artillery, the development of the Minié rifle musket had begun long before his rise to power. That said, it certainly was true enough that a "revolution" in the art of war had been underway since the late 1840s, and the French military was at the heart of this change. During the 1850s there was at least a cadre in every western European army that felt the new long-range small arms would substantially alter the conduct of war. As seen in earlier chapters, many prophesied that engagements would take place at longer ranges, and some even questioned whether field artillery would continue to play an important role, since it was believed that it would now inevitably be suppressed by highly accurate fire from distant marksmen.

Traces of these views appear in the American press early in the war. Less than a month after the fall of Fort Sumter, *Scientific American* published an article that summarized some of the more progressive European tactical theories. Entitled simply "Practical Warfare," the article warned its readers that "a complete revolution has been effected in the army exercises in Europe within ten years, and a few of our citizen soldiery seem to be aware of the fact." Observing that the new weaponry made the old-style Napoleonic column obsolete, it explained that

> in the olden times, the solid columns and the desperate charge

generally won the battle; but light, active troops, spread over an extended field with good rifles, would soon slaughter the best drilled columns in the world, armed with smooth-bores muskets and handled in the old-fashioned pasteboard style. Modern tactics require a more extended field with room for maneuvering, hence greater care is necessary in handling the soldiers, and more intelligence on the part of the soldiers is necessary for taking up proper positions, to save themselves and harass the enemy to the greatest advantage. Formerly the position of an army could be approached within 300 yards without experiencing injury from enemy fire. With the modern rifles, they could not approach men nearer than 1000 yards. Cavalry must now keep at a respectable distance until they can dash in under the cover of smoke, or be preceded with riflemen and artillery.

The article undoubtedly referred to the experiments conducted during the mid-1850s at Hythe and Vincennes. The sentiment expressed in this article was congruous with that of an article that had appeared 10 days before (May 1) in the *New York Times*, which argued that it was imperative that the volunteers be taught how to fire their weapons and afforded sufficient practice:

Especially should attention be paid to sharp-shooting. By target-firing, men should be brought to such perfection in the use of the musket, and of that infinitely more useful weapon, the rifle, as should ensure every bullet discharged in battle its victim. The musket is principally valuable as the handle of the bayonet, the rifle in the hands of the marks man is a bayonet that stabs at a long range; and cannot be grasped by the adversary. At the South, skill in sharp-shooting is almost universal. At the North it is extremely uncommon. If our raw recruits, instead of wasting time in clamoring after equipment and learning needless evolutions, will consume every hour in target practice, they will be able to give a better account of themselves.

Incidentally, the *Times* reporter had diagnosed the trap into which most of the new recruits and their inexperienced volunteer officers had already fallen. Most volunteers regardless of rank displayed servile and punctilious preoccupation with parade ground maneuvers and officious uniforms. *Appearance was confused with capability and performance.* The May 1 *Times* article ended with the warning that the volunteers were best advised to redirect their attention to substance, which in this case, was concentrating upon their ability to use their weapons effectively:

> The soldiers of GARIBALDI, they will remember, wore red shirts and slouched hats, and were as incapable of the evolutions which distinguish our crack regiments, as of the feats of BLONDIN; and yet they never suffered defeat. Their success lay in courage and the mastery of the rifle. The campaigns in Sicily has, in fact, many lessons for our soldiers in this crisis.

However, the belief that long-range firefights would be settled by accuracy of fire was no longer cutting edge doctrine. During the late 1850s Napoleon III resurrected the doctrine of advancing to within close range and deciding the issue by a bayonet charge. And once again, we find some familiarity with these latest military theories among American journalists. By the summer of 1861, the editor of *Wilkes' (N.Y.) Spirit of the Times,* a sporting magazine, found himself in Washington as a volunteer soldier. In a letter to his paper, he theorized about which weapons would prove to be most effective during the actual crucible of battle:

> Some importance has been attributed to the fact that the Southern men, as a general thing are better marksmen than the soldiers of the North, and that they will consequently possess a great advantage, through such superiority, in the hour of battle. But while I do not believe this is the case to any great extent, I would not, even if I were to give much consideration to this fact; for in battle but few special shots are made, and the coming struggle is not designed to be a contest of mere marksmen or evolution. War began with the spear for its weapon: after a variety of changes, through several centuries, it

yielded its refinements, and under Napoleon III on the fields of Magenta and Solferino, comes back to the spear again.

This is nothing more than a rather poetical reiteration of Napoleon III's approach to infantry tactics, and to prove his point, the author of the letter cited the recent accomplishments of the Zouaves and the *chasseurs d'Afrique* during the Italian War, when they overthrew their enemies by rushing into the Austrian ranks:

> On this plan the coming war between the North and South will surely be contested; . . . and may Heaven help those under the edge of whose bayonets these "pet lambs" shall succeed in getting. . . . The saber bayonet is also to be distributed throughout the entire army, and I feel certain, from what I have gathered through military men, the actual embrace of battle, man to man, is what the Northern captains of this war intend to rely upon.

As far as the tactical doctrine mandated by official orders and instructions that would be issued is concerned, this prediction proved entirely correct. As will be seen in a later chapter, commanders on both sides, such as McClellan, Beauregard, and Rosecrans, would indeed instruct their men to withhold their fire until they were sure of hitting their intended victims, aim low, and then charge in with lowered bayonets.

There is some evidence that Southern papers occasionally echoed the same debate. On May 20 1861, the Pawtucket, Rhode Island, *Manufacturer and Farmer's Journal* told its readers of a dispute about tactics then taking placing among some prominent rebel officers. General Robert E. Lee believed that the impending war would largely be determined by the efforts of the artillery arm. Most of his brother officers, on the other hand, felt that "in every battle the southern volunteers will, at any sacrifice, seek the closest quarters possible, and decide the fate of the hour with bowie knife and bayonet." Apparently, at this early stage of the war, not everyone was impressed with General Lee's potential to command. Writing about the relative merits of each side, the author of the Pawtucket article opined:

The difference in these two opinions is accountable to the fact
that the first comes from purely a theoretical old soldier, who
has to do with "man machines" all his life, while the other
emanates from those who understand the calibre and spirit of
the volunteers.

Though appearing in a New England newspaper, this article was
most likely excerpted entirely or in slightly modified form from a
Southern newspaper. At least half of the articles that appeared in
small-town newspapers were actually taken from the counterparts in
large cities. Undoubtedly, the Pawtucket *Manufacturer and Farmer's
Journal* would have cited the source if it had been from a Boston or
New York newspaper. However, culling information from a rebel
newspaper, the editors apparently did not feel themselves bound by
the niceties of journalistic protocol or copyright legalities.

FREEDOM AT WASHINGTON

The opportunity to thoroughly train the torrents of troops then
rushing to the colors proved to be of short duration. In the West most
of the newly formed regiments were assigned to a number of regional
armies and immediately began to take part in active military operations. Meanwhile, in the East a great part of Union forces were
quickly rushed to Washington City. Once there the training in many
regiments lost its rigorousness. Almost everyone believed the rebels
would be dissipated with a show of force and a few shots of cannon,
and there was generally an air of gaiety, similar to that often found in
a summer militia encampment. Soldiers strolled through camp and
city in a wide variety of military raiment, the abundance of long dress
coats with numerous buttons an indicator that such uniforms had
been designed for appearance rather than functionality. In the volunteer regiments there was an unmilitary promiscuity between the men
and their officers, and the latter frequently ate and slept with the
rank and file.

Among the numerous volunteer regiments, there was little of the
rigorous discipline usually associated with a professional army.
Passes from camp were easy to come by, and the streets of Washington were filled with bands of men and officers determined to have

a good time. In a speech delivered at the twenty-fifth anniversary of the First Battle of Bull Run, Edwin Barrett, a 3-month volunteer and an assistant surgeon with the Fifth Massachusetts Infantry, recounted his usual daily itinerary up to McDowell's advance towards Manassas. His time was about equally divided between chores and training at the regimental camp and various so-called errands into the capital. Most of these were official work in name only. He was rarely supervised, and while on duty in the city was able to make a number of visits to Congress, where Barrett admits being engrossed by the debates. On other occasions he would meander up to the Union outposts to look at the rebel pickets a short distance away. This was apparently a popular sport at this period, and while so engaged, he bumped into Hannibal Hamlin, the vice-president, who was doing the same.

THE LACK OF CADRES

Union volunteer regiments were saddled with an even greater limitation than the lack of experience and training among the men. The majority of officers in these regiments were initially as ignorant of military art and practices as the recruits they led. Though some volunteer officers had served in militia units or in the Mexican-American War, most came from completely civilian backgrounds. When it came to the campaign and battlefield, inexperience at the command level was a more serious problem than a comparable problem among the men and would take much longer to rectify. After all, raw troops led by veteran officers could continue to be trained even after the start of active operations. Moreover, experienced officers take every precaution to protect their men from needless danger during combat and the campaign.

One solution would have been to form cadres of experienced military professionals by distributing officers from the regular army among the volunteer units. Gen. Winfield Scott, firmly convinced that the regular forces, despite their small numbers, would be responsible for most of the fighting, emphatically rejected this option. The volunteers would be relegated to secondary functions, such as guarding supplies and garrisons behind the lines.

Many young officers in the regular army wanted to accept commissions in the volunteer organizations, but their resignations were refused, and they were forced to continue within the regular army. Experienced officers in volunteer regiments were generally limited to West Point graduates who had not entered the army after graduation, officers who had retired or for some other reason had left the regular army, or those who had served in foreign service. The Mexican War of 1846–48 had been the last war that utilized traditional methods of warfare, so veterans of this conflict were eagerly sought after. It wasn't uncommon for those who had served as enlisted men now to be offered commissions in the volunteer regiments, and those who had been subaltern officers might find themselves being made lieutenant colonels or even colonels. The experience of B. F. Scribner is illustrative in this regard. Scribner had served with the Second Indiana Volunteers at Buena Vista. Faced with the necessity of raising two thousand men for the Indiana Legion in 1861, Governor Morton turned to Scribner to organize the Seventh Indiana.

There were not enough experienced officers, and a majority of the new officers in the volunteer regiments came from civilian life: lawyers, mechanics, businessmen, and of course politicians. Many of course had served before the war with state militias or some form of home guards. Unfortunately, in practice this provided a less useful experience than one might expect. All too often these organizations were but infrequently mustered, and even when activated, they practiced small-unit drills and learned "no more instruction or discipline than was required to quell a riot or take part in a procession."

The Confederate army was better off. Not only did it have more than its share of officers and West Point graduates, but many of the officers drawn from civilian ranks had gained a modicum of experience while attending the military academies sprinkled around the Southern states. Unlike the North, the breakaway states had no preexisting standing army. As they enlisted, these officers (Grant estimated Southern officers had made up 30 to 40% of the original officer class of the U.S. Army) were given commissions in the "provisional army," but Southern military authorities were free to assign them as they saw fit. In practice the officers tended to serve with the volunteer organizations raised in their native states, and in this way the experienced officers were much more evenly distributed among the new regiments being formed than in the North, where almost all active officers were ordered to remain in the regular army.

Chapter 9

ARTILLERY AND IRONCLADS
AT THE BEGINNING OF THE WAR

I n addition to providing practical advice on the do's and don'ts of
military life, the newspapers and popular magazines played
another important role. Not only did they attempt to present a broader
picture about newly emerging military scientific theories than that
offered by any drill book, they sought to make the American public
aware of recent military technological developments, which were more
seriously considered abroad.

This provided much-needed emotional support for American military inventors, who had received little more than rebuffs and rejection from the War and Navy Departments. It also applied pressure on
public officials to assume a more progressive stance. This would
prove to help sway official policy during the summer of 1861, when
the Navy Department was vacillating on whether or not to experiment
with the new "iron plated ships" that had been the cause of so much
controversy in France and Great Britain for several years. Later in
the war it would also give legitimacy to the gun manufacturers who
had advocated breechloaders and eventually helped thaw the government's icy view of these weapons.

Prior to the Civil War, the American army was not only small;
much of its attention was focused on the Western frontier. Although
importance was paid to coastal fortifications, less attention had been
placed on European-style close-order tactics. When it came to experimentation with new weaponry and fighting methods, the American
military establishment had been a follower rather than a leader.
During the 1840s and '50s, the industrial age had continued to take
hold on both sides of the Atlantic, and technological innovation
slowly but ineluctably crept into many aspects of everyday life.

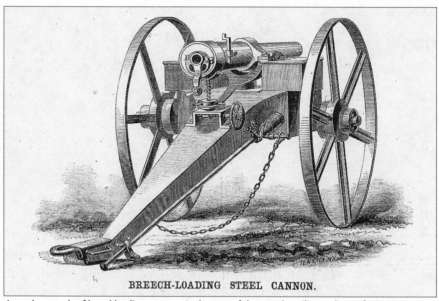

BREECH-LOADING STEEL CANNON.

An early example of breechloading cannon. At the start of the war, the military editors of *Scientific American* were wary of breech-loading rifled artillery, such as the one pictured here, and instead endorsed muzzleloaders like the Beaulieu cannon. *Scientific American,* Vol. IV, no. 3, January 19, 1861.

Though the United States could boast more than its share of inventors and engineers, very little effort was directed toward the military arena. Patents for new varieties of ice skates, fire escapes (at this point a device that firemen brought to tall burning buildings), farm threshers, and the like greatly outnumbered those for new weapons or assorted military paraphernalia.

Americans interested in military innovation looked toward Europe. Affluent families often subscribed to several prestigious British magazines. The wife might curiously leaf through the pages of the *London Illustrated Times* for the latest fashions. More than a few American inventors and scientists subscribed to the (London) *Engineer.* A sharp-eyed person interested in recent military developments would read of a new mechanically activated hand grenade, which had been used to try to assassinate Napoleon III in 1858. The reader would also learn of French experiments and resulting successes with "deep diving devices" (submarines) during the same period. Even the most casual reader would notice the fanfare accompanying two other new weapons whose advocates claimed they would profoundly transform the very foundations of war. These were the new breech-loading Armstrong rifled artillery piece, introduced with the accolade of the British press, and the large, iron-plated frigates then being built in France and the United Kingdom.

As the threat of war loomed ever larger, mention of matters purely military became much more frequent in American magazines and newspapers. In January and February 1861, *Scientific American* provided several articles about the new European rifled artillery. Its readers learned that opinion in Europe had been split along two lines. The British military had invested in costly experiments with the Armstrong breechloaders, while Napoleon III and the rest of Europe were content with muzzle-loading rifled artillery.

Although the American press enthusiastically endorsed the new British breech-loading rifled artillery pieces introduced in 1858–59, the United States government had serious reservations. The Armstrong gun had been introduced during the Second Opium War (1856–1860), but its performance failed to meet expectations. The lead band around the projectiles was usually forced off as it left the barrel, frequently maiming, even killing, hapless British skirmishers in front of the battery. If this was not bad enough, the vent on the gun was frequently defective, which soon rendered the piece inoperable. Citing the Armstrong's disappointing performance, *Scientific American* declared itself a staunch supporter of the French stance for muzzle-loading rifled artillery. In contrast, writers for the *New York Times* continued to recommend the Armstrong gun until May 1861, mentioning this weapon several times in association with iron-plated vessels of war, the other new military innovation which had captured the American public's imagination, just as it had the Europeans' the previous year.

As reports trickled back from Europe, the pendulum of popularity started to swing in the opposite direction, and the American press turned its back on breech-loading technology and focused instead on muzzle-loading rifled artillery. The February 2, 1861, edition of *Scientific American* explained the almost universally accepted objections. Given the existing state of metallurgy, the breech-loading mechanism was heavy. Contrary to our expectations, artillerymen found muzzle-loading field pieces both more convenient and quicker to reload. The ramrod and projectile together were considerably lighter than the ponderous breech mechanism. Moreover, the extreme heat in the breech area caused the metal to expand suddenly and then retract gradually as it cooled, eventually causing the parts to buckle or strip.

This remained the majority opinion among American artillery experts throughout the Civil War. Testifying before the Joint Committee on the Conduct of the War in January 1864, Gen. William F. Barry reiterated these objections almost verbatim. His wartime experience had shown that muzzle-loading rifled field artillery had indeed proven to be more practical and convenient in the field. This was all the more regrettable because since the advent of the ironclads, the caliber of fortress and coastal artillery had been greatly increased and it was difficult to load a 200- or 300-pound projectile at the muzzle. A breechloader that could ameliorate these problems would make it much easier to load the ultralarge caliber pieces and would be ideal in fortifications and on ships.

Despite these limitations a few breech-loading artillery pieces were used by both sides during the war. Shortly after the fall of Fort Sumter, a group of Northerners living in Britain purchased six wrought-iron Whitworth breechloaders, which they donated to the Union forces. Falling into an administrative abyss, these were discovered 6 months later lying abandoned on Staten Island. General Barry, then McClellan's chief of artillery, had the pieces brought to Washington City. Examining the Whitworths, Barry concluded that they were too delicate for campaign duty. The manufacturer's instructions advised keeping the moving parts in the breech mechanism constantly lubricated with the finest-quality machinery oil. The dusty and muddy roads in northern Virginia would have wrought havoc on such intricate mechanisms and have soon rendered them useless.

These problems were compounded by the design of the Whitworth bore. Unlike with other artillery pieces, its bore was a hexagon with a turn to produce the necessary rotation. This meant that the projectiles had to have a hexagonal-shaped cross section, something that was much more difficult to manufacture than cylindrical shells. Not only did each projectile have to be carefully lathed by hand, but the unusual cross section also yielded a much smaller internal volume.

Thus, the shell carried less explosive powder and was less effective than those fired by other artillery pieces of the same caliber.

The accuracy and range of the Whitworth, however, compared favorably with other weapons. So, when Union outposts across the Potomac complained of incursions by Confederate reconnoitering parties, Barry sent across two Whitworth artillery pieces, which proved very useful. On another occasion, when Hooker and his army were stationed below Budd's Ferry, he received two Whitworths on loan, once again compliments of General Barry. Since the Whitworths were capable of very accurate fire at extremely long rages, Union artillerymen using them were consistently able to hit individual farmhouses 3 miles distant. In Virginia the Confederates also obtained a few Whitworths, and a few of these were employed at Antietam. Although designed as breechloaders, when presenting mechanical problems, Whitworth artillery could be used as ordinary muzzleloaders.

THE JAMES GUN

Until the cannon shots that disturbed the serenity of Charleston Harbor, people harboring "treasonous intentions" had shown greater interest in rifled artillery than had their Northern counterparts. Northern newspapers repeatedly reported that Southern states were stockpiling considerable quantities of this new ordnance. Although these fears were not completely unfounded—Alabama, for example, had ordered rifled artillery from Northern manufacturers—the quantity was greatly exaggerated. Despite the overall optimism that war would be avoided, Northern authorities began to interdict the southward flow of ammunition and arms. Artillery destined for Alabama was confiscated by Rhode Island officials and handed over to its Providence Corps of Artillery.

At the outbreak of hostilities, the Ames Company of Chicopee, Massachusetts, was manufacturing 20 pieces of smoothbore artillery for the Federal government. Shocked out of their complacency, the local citizenry looked around to see how they would arm the numerous volunteer corps then being raised. A number of prominent New England patriots agreed to pay for rifled artillery from Ames for local volunteer artillery companies. The manufacturer wired the government to ask permission to fill the order and eventually was allowed to do so. Looking for an acceptable design, the company settled on the 14-pounder rifled bronze gun designed to fire the James projectile. This projectile, incidentally, appears to be nothing more that the Belgian Charrin Projectile, for which Charles Tillinghast James seems to have been able to secure a patent in the United States. It is not known whether James, previously a major general in the militia and then a U.S. senator, contributed to its design or whether the gun was so designated simply because it fired the new James ammunition.

Lincoln's initial call to arms led to the creation of numerous volunteer artillery batteries, and as in Chicopee, there was a scramble to acquire the required materiel. Many Northern volunteer artillery batteries were only able to obtain outdated small-caliber smoothbores. An 1861 work by John P. Curry, *Volunteer's Camp and Field Book,* described how these ineffective guns could be converted into rifled cannon. The volunteer artillerymen were to bore the 6-pounder barrels and then snugly insert an iron or brass liner with a gently spiraling rifled groove. This conveniently converted the old 3.67 caliber guns into the 3.80 caliber utilized by the James projectile, and these hybrid pieces also became known as *James guns* or *James rifles.*

Thus, there were two different types of ordnance with exactly the same name used even in high official circles. Warren Ripley in his *Artillery and Ammunition in the Civil War* provides an interesting example of just how far up in the Union military organization this confusion permeated. The search for reliable and effective ordnance during the first 2 years of the war involved the highest-ranking officers. Maj. Gen. George McClellan was no exception; consulting with artillery experts, he decided to inquire about the 3.80-caliber James gun. In June 1862 he wired Secretary of War Edwin Stanton to order James "steel rifled guns" since "these guns have been tried by others in whom I have confidence." Stanton's reply sent back in the late afternoon verged on open sarcasm: "James is not known as a manufacturer of guns and it is not known that he makes any pretension of having invented one." Stanton then reminded McClellan that this was the same type of gun that McClellan refused to recommend several months previously. Undaunted, McClellan persisted and sent another missive that evening. He explained that one of his most reliable artillery officers had experimented with the James gun and had pronounced it to be the "best he had seen."

During the first year of the war, the James gun, even the makeshift variety, enjoyed a good reputation among artillery officers. When Union Gen. Irvin McDowell's army advanced to Bull Run in June 1861, it possessed a number of James rifles. After the battle Confederate E. P. Alexander would report the capture of nine such weapons. During the bombardment of Fort Pulaski, the Union attackers had converted a number of smoothbore calibers to rifled guns using the James method. After capturing the fort, Brig. Gen. Quincy A. Gillmore compared "James guns" to Parrott rifles, claiming that for the purposes of effecting breaches in fortification walls, both the James and Parrott projectiles "seem to be all that can be desired."

Despite such endorsements, the popularity of the James gun or rifle soon waned. The James projectile quickly developed an evil reputation as unreliable and even dangerous. The problem appears to have two origins, one that applied to the so-called James gun conversions, and the other intrinsic to the James projectile itself.

Prophetically, John Curry had cautioned that the process of carving out the groove had to be left to expert hands, since if the rifled spiral was "turned too much," the piece could explode when fired. Not only did excessive rifling fail to increase accuracy and range, but it also interfered with the projectile's natural course. The trick was to impart only enough rifling to negate the windage. Curry's fears soon proved real. Being a new weapon with an entirely new bore caliber, extensive practice was required to establish the relationships between amount of charge, angle of elevation, and range. The new rifled weapon was supported by about the same barrel thickness as the 6-pounder from which it had been converted and could only accept the same charge. Unfortunately, the conical shell was necessarily heavier.

It became immediately apparent that the James gun exhibited several fatal flaws. Whether because the craftsmen who rifled the barrel imparted too tight a spiral, the artillerymen succumbed to temptation and increased the propellant charge, or there was some intrinsic flaw that escaped detection, all too often the tremendous pressure that built up within the barrel caused either the breech or the shell to burst. Neither was a particularly pleasant experience. To the gunners it seemed that half the time the gutta-percha that had been wrapped around the shell to ensure that it "took to the rifling" was stripped off before exiting the mouth of the barrel. The projectile, instead of following the rifling, then was forced across the grooves, very quickly wearing down the brass or iron liner which had been inserted into the tube.

Regardless, the fate of the weapon was effectively cast in October 1862 when General James was himself killed when a shell exploded prematurely while he was presumably trying to solve these deficiencies. Having fallen into disfavor, there is no evidence that any James rifles were manufactured after this date, though in the West a number of James guns appear to have remained in service until the last year of the war.

PARROTT ARTILLERY

Although Parrott had been experimenting with rifled artillery for several years and successfully produced several prototypes, his efforts remained unknown to even knowledgeable artillery officers until April 1861, when the shock waves from recent events shook even the conservative Ordnance Department. Colonel Craig, then chief of ordnance, ordered Capt. James Benton at West Point to test the Parrott rifled artillery. Gen. William F. Barry would recollect that he saw his first Parrott, a 30-pounder, while stationed at Fort Pickens about this time. Fortunately, the replacement of Craig by Col. James W. Ripley as chief of ordnance did not derail the growing support for Parrott's artillery. Ripley immediately overturned the government contract with James to convert smoothbores into rifled pieces and ordered ten 10-pounder Parrotts on May 23. When Barry returned to the field a few weeks later, he stumbled across several batteries armed with several Parrott artillery pieces. Pleased at this success, Parrott now turned his attention to the development of a rifled weapon for seacoast batteries and in the fall of that year, introduced a 100-pounder piece. Encouraged even more, Parrott designed ever larger ordnance and before long began manufacturing 200-pounder, 8-inch, 10-inch, and 300-pounder weapons.

PICTORIAL HISTORY OF THE WAR OF 1861.

A side and rear view of a 30-pound Parrott rifled artillery piece with projectile. *Frank Leslie's Illustrated Weekly,* May 10, 1862.

BIG BETHEL

When it came to rifled artillery, Confederate authorities did not lag behind their Union counterparts. A Parrott rifled artillery piece had been sent to VMI for trials, and, impressed with the results, Virginia authorities ordered twelve pieces. Unlike so many other efforts to secure rifled artillery, this Virginia initiative proved successful, and the guns and requisite ammunition managed to reach Virginia before the fighting had started in earnest.

One of the Parrotts found its way into the command of Maj. George W. Randolph, who commanded the Howitzer Battalion. Randolph's five artillery pieces took part in the engagement at Big Bethel, Virginia, on June 10, 1861. Though a small force with only three Navy howitzers, a rifled howitzer, and a Parrott rifled gun, Randolph's motley command occupied central stage during the events that unfolded. Posted on either side of the road leading to Hampton Roads, the Howitzer Battalion lay right in the path of the advancing Union infantry columns. One of the rifled howitzers was accidentally "spiked" when the priming wire broke inside the vent while the howitzer was withdrawn to protect the rear against encirclement.

Of the remaining artillery pieces, the Parrott was the most actively employed. At the start of the action, its crew had directed solid shot immediately in front of an advancing enemy column about 600 yards away. The shot ricocheted into the dense formation, whose men immediately scattered to either side of the road. Some hours later a second Union column attempted to advance upon the Confederate artillery. Though Randolph ordered the rifled howitzer forward, this proved unnecessary, as once more Union efforts were stymied by the fire of the Parrott. Though his entire command had fired only eighteen solid shot and eighty shells, spherical case, and canister over 4½ hours, the results had been decisive.

Major Randolph was as perspicacious as articulate, and his report is a highly informative account of the desultory engagements that characterized the opening weeks of the war. There were a number of defects in Confederate artillery and equipage that became manifest during the stress of combat. The Borman fuses used by Confederate navy howitzers were defective. The 5-second fuses would explode after only 2 seconds, in front of the intended target. The wire primers used to ignite the charge broke so easily that they had to be discarded. The limbers for the howitzers also proved incommodious. Since the advent of horse artillery in the 1750s, many artillerymen sat astride the limbers and were able to advance at the horse's gait, greatly increasing a battery's mobility. Unfortunately, the small size of the limbers for the navy howitzers prevented this practice. These howitzers were drawn by only two horses, and the extra weight of a man on the limber proved hazardous. To rectify this problem, Randolph recommended that in the future these pieces should be drawn by four horses.

Randolph was very impressed with the performance of his Parrott gun, however. True, as with the howitzers, there had been problems with the fuses used in the shells. These fuses could not be cut down to less than 4 seconds, so they could not be employed when the enemy had closed to within 500 to 600 yards. Standard practice required artillerymen to substitute their own shorter fuses; however, they found that they could not extract the original fuse from the shell. Other than this, Randolph adjudged that the "power and precision" of the Parrott made it a "very desirable" weapon.

The affair at Big Bethel was a tiny action compared to the large, set-piece engagements that would punctuate the next 4 years. At the time, however, it gained attention out of all proportion to its strategic significance. Not only did it presage a series of embarrassing Union defeats, but it marked the first use of rifled artillery in anger on American soil. Word about the effectiveness of the new weaponry spread rapidly on both sides. Possibly to ease the stinging embarrassment of defeat, Union officers reported that they had faced an estimated twenty rebel artillery pieces, many of which were rifled. This implied that the new Parrotts were more effective than the smoothbores. The reputation of rifled artillery spread even more rapidly on the Confederate side. After all, the Confederates knew that the cause of the Union discomfiture had largely been due to a single Parrott. Moreover, Maj. Thomas Jackson's praise of the weapons after the earlier trials at the Virginia Military Institute had had its own effect. Hundreds of Jackson's pupils were now Confederate officers, and the views of the distinguished veteran of the Mexican War carried much weight.

AMBIVALENCE ABOUT IRONCLADS

Before the rigors of the Bull Run campaign showed the frailties of an aged Winfield Scott, the veteran commander-in-chief devised a strategy that would be pursued throughout the war. Known as the Anaconda Plan, like its namesake that wrapped itself around its victims and crushed out all life, the strategy called for the systematic economic strangulation of the rebel states. This was to be achieved by a two-pronged strategy: to separate the populated eastern states of the South from western food-growing states and to interdict supplies from abroad. The United States Navy would enforce a massive blockade of the southern Atlantic coast and the Gulf of Mexico. Meanwhile, another force would construct a series of fortified positions along the Ohio and the Mississippi Rivers from Louisville past Memphis, Vicksburg, and New Orleans. This plan, incidentally, was developed before the formal commencement of hostilities. In a memorandum to Secretary of State William Seward dated March 3, 1861, Scott warned against an invasion of the Southern states, arguing that such an effort would incur an immense national debt, take years of fighting, and require an army of 300,000 men. He countered with the Anaconda Plan.

Scott quickly convinced Lincoln to endorse the plan. When later that month Gideon Welles was appointed secretary of the navy, he was directed to implement the first phase of the operation, the blockade of the southern Atlantic coast. With ninety ships, 1200 officers, and 6400 seamen, on paper the U.S. Navy appeared to have sufficient resources for the task. Much of this strength was illusory, however. Almost fifty of the ships were sailing vessels, which would quickly prove to be completely outmoded. Out of the forty steam-powered ships, five were considered to be completely "unserviceable," nine were laid up in the "ordinary," and seventeen were on foreign service off Africa, South America, and in the Pacific, leaving only seven in the Home Service, available for action.

The problem was compounded by the conservatism of those leading the Department of the Navy. It appears that Welles and his immediate subordinates underestimated the magnitude of the struggle now facing them. Like most of those in the North, at this early stage they probably thought, at least unconsciously, that the rebellion would collapse with the first defeat the Union forces would assuredly inflict upon them. As a result for months the navy failed to take even the most basic step of ordering the return of the widely dispersed ships in the Foreign Fleet.

The *New York Times* continued to recommend the Armstrong gun until May 1861, mentioning this weapon several times in association with the iron-plated vessels of war then capturing the American public's imagination. Although these more robust fighting ships had been discussed for several years in technical and scientific journals, such as the *Journal for the Franklin Institute* and the *Military Gazette,* the American public at large became aware of these new fighting ships only with the publication of a series of articles in *Blackburne's Edinburgh Magazine* that started in November 1860. The American edition, published in New York City, was to have an impact not only on public opinion but also on how the armored ships would be viewed by posterity. Up until this time armored vessels, such as *La Gloire* and the *Warrior,* were known to British naval architects as "iron-cased ships" and were referred to variously in the American press as "mailed ships," "iron plate ships," "armored ships," and sometimes just as "floating batteries." The *Blackburne* articles, authored by a Briton, used the term "iron-clad vessel," and it was by this term that the new iron-protected ships would become known in history.

Scientific American meanwhile published numerous articles on the new iron-cased ships, on how they were to be constructed, their effectiveness, and so on. The January 1861 edition of *Scientific American* reported a British Parliamentarian's assessment of the new "iron frigates." Writing to the *London Times,* Mr. Vivian boasted that "the best wooden war ships are useless in her presence [the *Warrior's*] as the old musket is before the Minié rifle." The editors of *Scientific American* agreed completely and concluded, "It appears to us that such a frigate could walk through a entire fleet of wooden ships as easily as a life guardsman could cut his way through a regiment of pasteboard soldiers." However, the *New York Times* (May 8, 1861) did not possess the same unqualified confidence in the new iron-protected ships. In May it cautioned the American government to avoid the costly British and French experiments and instead to send two competent naval experts to Europe to investigate the latest developments for themselves. The *New York Times* did nevertheless applaud the efforts of Captain Coles, R.N., who had vociferously agitated for the adoption of the revolving turret, which, protected by extra-thick iron, would be able to rain terror with one or two heavy breech-loading rifles, such as the Armstrong rifled cannon.

With the prospect of a lengthy war, one would expect the Department of the Navy not only to have made every effort to increase the number of available ships but to quickly and energetically utilize the most modern and effective technology, as well. Rather curiously, the U.S. Navy appeared slow to respond to the recent developments abroad. It certainly was not from a lack of awareness or information. Welles and his associates, by their own admission, were very well aware of the latest developments in the use of iron plating on ships. In his July 4, 1861, report to a special session of Congress, Welles acknowledged that

> much attention has been given within the last few years to the subject of floating batteries or iron-clad steamers. Other governments, and particularly France and England, have made it a special object in connection with naval improvements; and the ingenuity and inventive faculties of our own countrymen have also been stimulated by the recent occurrences toward the construction of this class of vessel.

Welles's major concern was expense. He thought that workable ironclads could be produced only after significant expenditure of money and lengthy trials. By early July Welles decided to lay the issue before Congress. He recommended that Congress authorize the establishment of a board of competent officers to assess the usefulness and feasibility of the new ironclads and recommend whether or not several should be constructed. The bill to appropriate funds to construct one or more "iron-clad steamers or floating batteries" appears to have met little resistance in the Senate, and by July 16 the bill had entered the House of Representatives. Unfortunately, when some representatives attempted to resurrect a much older government project, the bill became mired in debate.

The *Warrior* and *La Gloire* were not the only iron-protected vessels that had gained notoriety. A vessel mothballed for years on a Hoboken dry dock and periodically the butt of public ridicule quickly came back into public attention. In February 1861 the *New York Mirror* started to agitate for additional funding to complete the Stevens floating battery. Only 2 years before, the *Military Gazette* had declared this experimental vessel suitable only for "exhibition to visitors, at three cents a head, as a monument to folly."

By July this was no longer the view of much of the press and the public. On July 16 the *New York Enquirer* argued that had the Stevens floating battery been available, the fall of Sumter might well have been averted, and it asked its readers to urge Congress to take action. This sentiment was echoed in *Scientific American,* which had long supported experimentation with new iron-protected ships. However, probably the most complimentary view of the Stevens floating battery took the form of a full feature article in the August edition of the magazine, which was accompanied by a large lithographic illustration, which, with the advantage of hindsight, shows the battery looking remarkably similar to Ericsson's ironclad, which would later gain such renown. The author of this article concluded that

> most of the best features of modern marine practice and naval
> defense were 20 years ago embodied in the designs of this
> vessel, viz., high steam, the screw propeller, hollow and fire
> water-lines fore and aft, the iron hull, the box or tubular-bridge

framing, the link-motion and steam reverse gear and inclined armor. The improvements designed at that early day, and not yet adopted in the best practice—still ahead of the times—are the two screws for rapid turning, the water-armor during action, and the ability to rise rapidly to the surface; the use of guns heavy enough to protect themselves, instead of loading the ship with armor to cover them, the ability to fire, so to speak, a *broadside* in every direction, and the system of ventilation described. And yet the government is advised to throw away this work, and to build mailed ships on modern principles! We would urge the public, for their own sake, to instruct themselves and their representatives in this matter before it is too late.

There were those among the House of Representatives who were influenced by this increasing chorus, and immediately there was an effort to amend the bill as formulated by the Senate. The suggested changes were the seemingly insignificant alteration of a few words. "Construct," for example, was changed to "complete," and "iron" became "iron or steel." Nevertheless, this was a thinly disguised effort to secure funds to complete the Stevens floating battery. If the bill had called for the completion of an ironclad steamer, the funds could be awarded to anyone who had a partially built ironclad, and, of course, there was only one candidate, the one in dry dock in Hoboken.

The argument in favor of resurrecting the Stevens floating battery arose as much from political concerns as it did from technological considerations or possible cost savings. The original incentive to fund the development of the Stevenses' battery had arisen from the fear that the British would use Bermuda to springboard into coastal American cities. A similar specter arose among knowledgeable shipbuilders and military men in 1861, the result of the seemingly sudden surge in European naval technology. A report submitted to the British House of Lords on June 11 provided the results of recent trials of artillery against iron-cased vessels. These latter had proven completely proof against shot and shell fired by traditional cannon at all ranges and even against heavy rifled artillery fired at ranges greater than about 450 yards.

The fact that by 1861 neither Britain nor France had commissioned any new large wooden men-of-war for several years was not lost on the more perceptive American shipbuilders, such as Donald Mackay, who had traveled to Britain and France to examine the iron-cased vessels for himself. Mackay returned to the United States and claimed that these two foreign powers would soon have up to twenty large iron-cased naval vessels, and the fear immediately arose that they could interrupt the intended naval blockade of the Southern coast or even attack Northern cities at will. E. H. Derby, a friend of Mackay's and apparently an expert in naval matters, soon began to implore Federal authorities such as his friend former secretary of the navy, James K. Paulding, and many representatives to Congress to allocate funds without delay to build American iron-cased ships.

These efforts proved effective, and not only did some members of the House attempt to modify the Senate's bill to appropriate funds for the construction of iron-clad steamers, but they also proposed a separate bill that would grant $812,000 to complete the Stevens floating battery. There were those who vehemently opposed any effort to reconsider the battery, though. Representative Owen Grimes was foremost among those in opposition, on the floor arguing that any new moneys spent to revitalize the Stevens project would produce the same results as the original funding. Also intended as a ram, the Stevenses' vessel had been equipped with an expensive 8000-horsepower engine. Citing articles recently published in the British *United Service Journal*, Grimes pointed out that the British Navy rejected rams after their own trials with this type of vessel had proven to be an abysmal failure.

Hampered by the limited resources that were available and forced to extemporize, the Confederate authorities had exhibited no such conservatism, at least as far as the new type of iron-protected vessels was concerned. An iron-protected floating battery, known as the Charleston Raft, was constructed in Charleston Harbor a few weeks before the attack on Sumter. Its two 32-pounder and two 42-pounder artillery pieces were placed behind sandbags, while all vertical sides were faced with iron plates. Steamboats were to push the raft forward until it reached the Sumter, where a scaling party would use ladders to scale the walls of the fort. It appears the project produced trepidation on both sides, in the fort's defenders because of what its guns could do and in the attackers because they feared it would capsize and sink.

In the months that followed, a few Southerners attempted even more ambitious projects. On May 28 the *Mobile Tribune* reported that Colonels Bonner and Flemming, with Colonel Hardee's permission, began the construction of a "steam floating battery," which obviously was to possess its own motive force. Although it is not clear whether this vessel was ever completed, 6 weeks later the *Boston Journal* claimed that the rebels had covered a large tugboat with railroad iron and built another vessel from heavy timber covered completely by iron. Known as the New Orleans Battery Ram, this vessel was the size of a normal steamboat; however, its cabin had slanted sides covered with railroad iron so that any round shot that struck would be deflected. It also had a very sharp iron prow to ram enemy shipping. However, probably the most innovative of its features was its offensive armament. Hoses attached to its boilers could spray boiling hot water onto the crews of opposing vessels. Both the converted tug and the ram were to hunt Federal ships then blockading New Orleans.

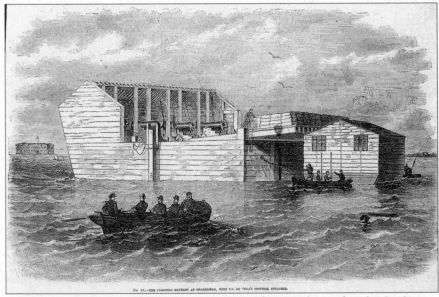

Confederates constructed the Charleston Floating Battery to take part in the assault against Fort Sumter in April 1861. The barge-like vessel hooked to its stern was Doctor Vegas' floating hospital. *Frank Leslie's Illustrated Weekly,* March 30, 1861.

OTHER INNOVATIONS

Two other new types of weapons were introduced during this early stage of the war. In both cases the Confederates, probably more strongly driven by a sense of urgency, again took the lead. During the second week of May, many newspapers in the North announced that Confederate sympathizer Ross Winans, who had become a millionaire by operating a line of cigar steamers (a type of ship), had commissioned a Mr. Dickenson, a Baltimore inventor, to build a rapid-fire mechanical gun pattern on the Perkins steam gun design. The bullets were poured into a hopper that fed into the rear end of the barrel. Like the Gatling gun that would come after it, it had a number of barrels that quickly rotated. However, the rotation was driven by a steam engine, and hence the weapon was dubbed the Baltimore Steam Gun. It purportedly could fire three hundred 2-ounce balls a minute to an effective range of 100 yards, and the gunners were protected by a thick iron shield that resembled a railroad cow-catcher. The gun weighed 6700 pounds, so it probably could only have been used for static defensive situations.

Since Winans was a known Southern sympathizer, the publicity stirred Union authorities into action. Two infantry companies and two artillery pieces from Mortimer's "Flying Artillery," commanded by Maj. A. M. Cook, were ordered to seize the invention and apprehend its inventors, which they did without incident. Dickenson and the gun were brought to Annapolis under guard. This ended the short and somewhat inglorious career of the Civil War's first "machine gun."

Coincidentally, that same week Union authorities seized another newfangled machine of war that Confederate sympathizers tried to sneak out of the North. On May 18 the *New York Times* would report tremendous excitement in Philadelphia when a "submarine boat" was discovered aground an island in the Delaware River. The craft was the invention of Brutus de Villeroi, a French citizen who was probably trying to take the submersible vessel clandestinely to his customers, probably a group of Confederate businessmen in the South. Apprehended, de Villeroi and three others protested that they were testing the invention for the Union Navy, but when the story was found to be untrue, the submarine and its crew were confiscated.

Chapter 10

ARMING THE INFANTRY

THE CHOICE OF SMALL ARMS

W ith all the hoopla about recent innovations in weaponry, one would have expected some official interest in breech-loading shoulder arms, which had already been partially adopted by several European armies and enthusiastically supported by a growing number of British and American inventors. Although the first efforts to devise an effective breechloader place took place in the Germanic regions of Europe during the 1830s and '40s, interest in the new type of small arms quickly spread to Great Britain and then to the United States.

When the war started, there were those among the American public who felt that the breech-loading rifle, with its potential for extremely rapid fire, would prove to be more valuable than either the rifle musket or the Kentucky long rifle. Several official governmental reports had briefly endorsed the continued testing and even the tentative adoption of breechloaders. A report submitted to John Floyd as secretary of war had concluded that "the highest efficiency of a body of men with firearms can only be secured by putting into their hands the best breech-loading firearms." Moreover, as the first militia and volunteer units were organized in response to Lincoln's call for 75,000 troops, there were a number of efforts to arm a few local volunteer corps with breechloaders.

Interest in the new weapon ranged all the way from the very highest of authorities down to those responsible for individual units. Two weeks before the First Battle of Bull Run, the president of the new Confederacy personally requested that J. E. Brown, Georgia's governor, furnish a ten-company volunteer regiment. Jefferson Davis specifically asked that the five mounted companies be equipped with "breech-loading carbines." John J. Pettus, governor of Mississippi, also took steps before the eruption of hostilities to secure breechloaders for his state's militia. Writing to Floyd on the last day of 1860, he requested that the Federal arsenals advance Mississippi its 1862 quota of firearms and if possible to send "Map [sic] patent breech-loading rifles." Most probably, Pettus was referring to the Maynard rifle. Though it is highly unlikely that Union authorities gave any credence to such a request at this stage of the crisis, Mississippi officials somehow did manage to procure a supply of Maynard rifles, and the First Mississippi Infantry (Provisional) in early 1861 was in part equipped with this weapon.

There was a corresponding interest in repeaters and breechloaders on the Northern side. In the weeks following the surrender of Fort Sumter, generous donations from New York City and its residents attempted to arm at least a portion of Colonel Ellsworth's Zouaves with breechloaders. Federal authorities quickly intervened, however, and the Zouaves were equipped with more standard fare. After the humiliating events at Bull Run, Rhode Island Governor Sprague requested and received permission from the secretary of war to augment his state's contribution to the Unionist effort with the formation of the Burnside Rifle Company, which presumably would be armed with the weapon patented by their namesake. Several weeks earlier Governor Andrews of Massachusetts had asked to be allowed to arm an entire regiment with the same weapon. Even the Union army's aging commander-in-chief, Winfield Scott, displayed some interest in breechloaders. Corresponding with Scott (June 6, 1861), Maj. Gen. Benjamin Butler thanked his superior for his suggestion to arm some flank companies with the new weapon. He went on to explain that he had appropriated 200 Sharps rifles that were originally intended for the "Naval Brigade" and had given them to several companies in Colonel Duryea's command.

However, one of the most serious efforts to arm a Northern regiment with breechloaders was undertaken by Samuel Colt, who, as the inventor of the Colt revolver, was already wealthy and influential. Upon Lincoln's call for volunteers, Colt immediately began to negotiate with Connecticut and Federal authorities to gain permission to raise a regiment of men armed with his revolving rifle. Hundreds of men were actually raised as the Colt First Regiment of Revolving Rifles and were temporarily stationed at Colt's Meadows. Although a Federal agent had verbally accepted Colt's offer, negotiations broke down when the men in his regiment refused to enlist for the 3 to 5 years that were the terms of regular service. They wanted to commit to the ordinary 90-day enlistment offered to all the other volunteers. Connecticut offered to accept the regiment into its quota of state volunteer regiments.

However, feeling slighted by his regiment's refusal to enter Federal service, Colt in turn rejected this alternative and withdrew his offer to arm the regiment with Colt's revolving rifles. The Colt First Regiment of Revolving Rifles was formally disbanded on June 20, its men transformed into the Fifth Connecticut Volunteer Regiment and armed with rifle muskets instead. Blinded by his own arrogance and inflated sense of self-importance, the famous inventor lost sight of the true goal of the moment, the creation of an effective fighting force to preserve the Union. In retrospect, we can say he also lost a golden opportunity to demonstrate the value of the rapid-fire breechloaders on the battlefield.

Despite these pockets of support for the experimental breechloaders, the overwhelming majority of officers, gunsmiths, and the general public looked upon the new weapon with suspicion. The men in the First Regiment of the Mississippi Army, though armed with rifles purportedly capable of firing "twelve times a minute" and at ranges up to 1600 yards, quickly became the butt of sarcasm. Mississippi veterans of the Mexican-American War derisively referred to the Maynard rifles as "pop-guns," and a local newspaper, the *Intelligencer* of Oxford, Mississippi, after painting a satirical picture of the regiment at a fancifully effective rifle practice, sarcastically concluded that there was "nothing to do with a Maynard rifle but load her up, turn her North, and pull trigger. If twenty of them don't clean out Yankeedom, then I'm a liar, that's all." The point being made was that since the story told was a bold-faced lie, then the conclusion was obviously bogus, as well.

Despite John Brown's feat with a Sharps rifle in Kansas and the successes of Garibaldi's troops armed with Colt's revolving rifles in Italy, general skepticism about breechloaders continued unabated. It will be recollected that there were three general criticisms of these weapons: mechanical unreliability during the rigors of a campaign, inaccuracy, and the excitable soldiers' potential to spend vast amounts of ammunition without inflicting commensurate injury on the opponent. Up until the outbreak of the war, the debate among the American military had largely been carried out on the pages of the *Military Gazette*, the official organ of the New York State Militia. This intellectual contest could be characterized as a split decision. No clear consensus about the practicality of the breechloader emerged. Some writers felt that it was the way of the future; others that it was forever doomed to the realm of impracticality.

Upon the fall of Fort Sumter, the great majority of the *Military Gazette*'s staff and contributors, however, were called into active service, and the journal ceased publication at the end of April. As a result there was no official or even semiofficial forum for debate about the military arts and sciences until the appearance of the first issue of the *Army and Navy Journal* in August 1863. The resulting vacuum was filled in part by *Scientific American*, on whose pages informed opinion was supplied by the likes of Oliver Winchester, James Eads, and a number of others connected in some way with the North's military efforts.

Vociferous in their support of "mail-clad" fighting ships and rifled artillery, the editors of *Scientific American*, perhaps unexpectedly, were not strong supporters of the breechloaders, either for small arms or for artillery. During the months leading up to the fall of Fort Sumter, the magazine published several short articles and letters which espoused a position even more conservative than that of Col. James W. Ripley, then the head of the Ordnance Department. Not only did the military editors reject breechloaders; they did not even have a favorable opinion of the new self-expanding Minié bullets. They recommended the retention of the old-style rifle muskets, which had been used by their fathers and grandfathers. Though acknowledging that both the Minié rifle musket and breechloaders allowed more rapid fire, they argued that neither of these types of small arms were reliable or extremely accurate. Those opposing breechloaders also arugued that the repetitive opening and closing of the breech mechanism led to the leakage of explosive gases, and this distracted the soldier, if not causing outright injury. These opinions, mostly specious and hardly new, echoed the rather conservative views that had already appeared in the *Atlantic Monthly* and the *Military Gazette*.

However, unlike the extreme technological conservatives—who believed that the breechloader and even the rifle musket, which suffered from intrinsic flaws, would never fire accurately enough to be useful on the battlefield—the military editors of *Scientific American,* even at this early stage of the war, believed that the limitations of breechloaders stemmed from the individual designs and existing technology. They reasoned that in theory there was nothing "to prevent a breech-loading rifle from being made to carry as accurately as any other." The February 2, 1861, editorial immediately drew criticism from some of the magazine's readers, who argued that even rifle muskets using self-expanding bullets could never be as accurate as those forcefully rammed home with a patch. A New England gunsmith reasoned that the basis of accuracy in any rifle was uniform force applied to the projectile as it sped through the barrel. He argued that the very process of ramming down the ball made it adapt to the irregularities of the barrel, so on its return journey back up the barrel, it would conform perfectly to the inside surface of the barrel.

Although these latter sentiments represented a minority point of view, most informed opinion favored the introduction of the rifle musket that fired self-expanding bullets, and the growing consensus had turned decidedly against the use of breechloaders. Thus, Floyd's endorsement of breech-loading rifles proved to be but a fleeting aberration in the government's overall stance toward these highly controversial new weapons. Unfortunately for many rifle manufacturers and the advocates of the new magazine guns, Col. Ripley, a career officer in the Ordinance Department, was appointed the chief of the Army Ordnance Department in May 1861. Events would quickly show that Ripley was anything but progressive. He appears to have frequently subordinated both common sense and his country's best interests to the vagaries of his own personality and ego. This was amply demonstrated during Oliver Winchester's first visit to the Ordnance Department soon after the outbreak of the war. Winchester's presentation of the new Henry rifle completed, Ripley superciliously retorted that he believed that "nine-tenths" of officers would prefer to be armed with a flintlock musket than any breechloader or "magazine" repeater.

Winchester would later remember encountering only one coherent objection to breechloaders within the Ordnance Department. It was feared that men armed with the rapid-fire small arms would quickly and indiscriminately expend all of their ammunition. This certainly was not a new argument, and the profound waste of ammunition on the battlefield had been a major concern to tacticians, military analysts, and government authorities since the mid-eighteenth century. French Marshal Maurice de Saxe's observation that to kill a man in battle, the man's weight in lead must be expended was frequently quoted, and several published works provided statistical analysis of the effectiveness of small arms fire based on actual battlefield results. It was reported, for example, that the Duke of Wellington's infantry inflicted one casualty for every 800 shots during the 1813 Battle of Vittoria on the Iberian Peninsula.

The proliferation of the new rifle muskets during the Italian War in 1859 in fact resurrected this concern. Rifle muskets using self-expanding bullets had originally been hailed as highly accurate weapons, and there was an expectation that on the whole, fewer rounds would be wasted. Rather disappointingly, despite the increased range and accuracy of the new rifle muskets firing self-expanding bullets, the same low ratio of casualties versus shots fired was observed during the Italian War. A medical and surgical gazette published at Lyon and cited in the American press at the time noted that during the Battle of Solferino (June 24, 1859) the Austrians fired no fewer than 8,400,000 rounds, which resulted in 2000 men killed and 10,000 wounded. In other words, it required 700 rounds to hit an enemy target and 4200 rounds for a kill.

This prompted one wag writing for *the New York Commercial* to suggest that the great French marshal's estimates had proven to be an understatement, observing that these statistics showed it required on average 272 pounds of lead to cause a single death. The low rate of hits was ascribed to the overwhelming tendency of combatants to fire without aiming or even adequately leveling their weapons to obtain the proper range. The general consensus among American military professionals was that these tendencies would only increase if infantrymen were equipped with rapid-fire weapons. A weapon capable of firing ten to fifteen rounds per minute could soon fire off the equivalent of the amount assigned to a soldier for an entire campaign.

Faced with all of these opinions, the Ordnance Department decided upon what had emerged as a centrist policy. Not only would breechloaders not be adopted, but those volunteer organizations, such as Ellsworth's Zouaves, which had been partially equipped with these weapons would be stripped of these "costly breech-loading toys."

INFANTRY ARMAMENT
Union Small Arms

If asked what type of firearms were carried by the Civil War infantrymen, probably there would be a temptation to say that Union infantrymen were equipped with rifle muskets, usually of the American Springfield or the British Enfield patterns, while initially, the Confederates were mostly armed with percussion cap smoothbores. Although this is true enough as a one-sentence generalization, the reality was not so straightforward. Lt. Col. Ferdinand Lecomte, an observer sent to America by the Swiss army, noticed "all methods" of rifle muskets among Union infantry. Some regiments indeed were lucky and received modern Springfields. During the first 2 years, however, many Northern regiments, especially those from Western states, such as Minnesota, Illinois, Kentucky, and Missouri, were armed either with several rifle types or even with obsolescent smoothbore weapons. The men in the Second Minnesota Volunteers when they were mustered into service, for example, carried a diverse range of both of rifled and smoothbore weapons. There was no standardization even of caliber size. Originally, the Eighth Kentucky Volunteers were able to arm themselves only by disarming local rebel sympathizers and confiscating "borrowed" weapons, mostly small-bore hunting rifles and shotguns.

Even regiments raised in more populated areas encountered difficulties. When the Thirty-sixth Illinois showed up at the U.S. arsenal at St. Louis, for example, only A and B companies were fortunate enough to receive Enfields. The remainder of the regiment was handed remodeled old-pattern Springfield muskets. One of its companies, known as the Waynes Rifles, made up of local marksmen, was so disgusted that the men refused to take any weapons. Both the Kentucky and Illinois regiments had to put up with these weapons for almost 2 years. The Second Minnesota regiment didn't receive Enfield rifles until March 29, 1863.

Although there was a greater availability of modern weapons in the East during the first months of the war, some Eastern regiments found themselves in a situation similar to that of their counterparts in the West. The First Rhode Island Infantry, for example, was sent to the front in the weeks preceding Bull Run equipped with old flintlock smoothbores that had been remodeled for percussion caps. The Second Pennsylvania Heavy Artillery Regiment (originally the 112th Pennsylvania Volunteers) was initially even worse off, armed only with clubs and a few old muskets. These were put aside for Austrian rifle muskets on March 15, 1862, which proved to be only a stopgap measure, and these were traded in for Springfield rifle muskets shortly thereafter.

Aware that some other regiments received new Springfield or Enfield rifle muskets, many men grumbled to the folks back home about the weapons they received and grumbled about supposed "deficiencies." Lt. William Clark, Thirty-sixth Company E, Illinois, speculated, "We shall be equally in danger from the muzzle of squirrel rifles and the breeches of our own muskets, and caught there like a rat between a trap between muzzle and breech . . ." It wasn't uncommon for men also to berate lesser known European weapons, such as the Austrian Lorenz .54 rifle musket. Although some Union troops in the West were issued some inferior, near-defective specimens, overall this proved a more than adequate weapon, and the men in the 104th Pennsylvania Infantry, and the Sixty-first and the Fifth New Jersey Infantry Regiments, for example, were vocal in their appreciation of the Austrian weapon.

This lack of standardization continued well into the second year of fighting, even among Union troops in the East. However, of the five New Jersey volunteer regiments mustered into service in the summer of 1862, for example, one regiment received Springfields, two were armed with Enfields, and two others received the Austrian Lorenz rifle musket.

CONFEDERATE SMALL ARMS

Edward Porter Alexander, chief of ordnance for Beauregard's army after Bull Run, estimated that originally only about 10% of the infantrymen in the Confederate army in Virginia were armed with rifle muskets. At this early stage a great majority of the men carried percussion cap smoothbore weapons, and a few possessed only antiquated flintlock muskets, though here and there one encountered clusters of Mississippi and Austrian rifles. These latter, however, soon gained an evil reputation for clogging after only about 20 rounds. The problem appears to have been more the result of a slight discrepancy with the caliber of the ammunition used than from any intrinsic problem with the weapon itself. Ammunition for the .54-caliber Mississippi rifle varied from .520 to .538, while bullets for the Austrian Lorenz were between .537 and .54.

Fortunately for the Confederates, however, the overall situation was improved by their initial victories, when, for example, hundreds of rifle muskets were captured after the Battle of the First Bull Run. Nevertheless, this was but a partial solution, and by the early spring of 1862, the Confederate capability to supply newly raised units with adequate weaponry reached a crisis. Rifle muskets, pistols, even sabers were all in extremely short supply, and the desire to arm most of the infantry quickly with rifle muskets was scuttled.

From an exchange of letters from officers in the field and central authorities, we learn of the makeshift arrangements that had to be made to compensate for the shortages. Unlike the Union authorities, who, to simplify logistics, tried to impose a homogenous armament within each regiment—if need be, by taking away the better weapons—the Southern leaders purposely chose to arm the flank companies with the best arms and directed the remaining, "center" companies to arm themselves with whatever shoulder arms could be had. On April 21 Maj. Gen. J. C. Pemberton instructed Brig. Gen. Maxcy Gregg to take any rifle muskets possessed by the two center companies of Colonels Colquitt and Gibson and distribute these among the flank companies of the Twelfth and Thirteenth South Carolina Volunteers respectively. This policy was reiterated in orders sent to Maj. Gen. T. H. Holmes and Brig. Gen. J. R. Anderson by General R. E. Lee over the next 2 weeks, and again in instructions issued by Asst. Adj. Gen. W. H. Taylor at roughly the same time to Gen. D. Leadbetter in Chattanooga. Once again both commanders were ordered to strip all rifle muskets from the center companies and distribute these among the flank companies. The center companies were to be armed with "state" weapons, that is, whatever could be supplied locally.

This idea was also not completely unknown in the North, and a few Union regiments employed the same practice. It is unclear whether the idea of providing the flank companies with superior weapons was based upon the advocacy of the reformist European theoreticians before 1856, or whether it was simply the result of trying to stretch the few available rifle muskets systematically across the regiment.

The string of Confederate victories that summer during the Seven Days' Battles and the Second Bull Run campaign, coupled with increased production capabilities on home soil, greatly alleviated the South's small arms shortage, at least in the East. Captain Fitzgerald Ross, an observer sent over by the British army to monitor the Confederate army, estimated that by the time of Lee's Pennsylvania Campaign in June–July 1863, all but Hood's division had finally been supplied with Enfield and Springfield rifles. In his personal memoirs General E. P. Alexander confirms this observation, claiming that Gettysburg was the first battle in which the Confederate infantry was "entirely rid" of smoothbore muskets. Modern small arms experts, such as Joseph Bilby, feel that the smoothbores were slower to disappear, though.

Small Arms in the West

If the Union infantry regiments in the West found it difficult to obtain modern small arms, their Confederate counterparts faced an almost impossible situation. Here a regiment that found itself uniformly armed with a recent model of a smoothbore percussion cap musket could count itself lucky. Many regiments in the Deep South and the West continued to carry obsolescent arms well beyond Gettysburg and Vicksburg. Operating in the trans-Mississippi states, Gen. W. L. Cabell would report on Feb. 27, 1864, that the majority of some of his regiments continued to carry smoothbores. In his report Cabell explains why he simply did not consolidate all his rifle muskets into a single regiment. Invariably, the various regiments were required to throw out a small body of skirmishers, and this task was most effectively performed by those with long-range weapons, i.e. rifle muskets. Arming the flank companies with these weapons ensured that these skirmishers could be taken from the regiment in hand, without picking and choosing men from a number of different organizations, which would have been a time-consuming, disruptive task.

The backwoodsmen of Tennessee, Kentucky, Arkansas, and adjoining Western states and territories were certainly no strangers to small arms and marksmanship. Hunting was often relied upon for a substantial portion of their families' subsistence. When the call to arms came in spring 1861, fervent patriots of these states showed up carrying their squirrel rifles, shotguns, or whatever else they used or could get their hands on. In many cases these would be the only weapons available to the newly formed regiments, especially those from the more rural regions. Of General Price's six to seven thousand Missourians, several thousand initially had no weapons whatsoever. The men in Brig. Gen. James H. McBride's command, coming from hill country in the southwest corner of the state, had very primitive arms.

When General Bragg ordered Nathan Bedford Forrest on a raid into Tennessee, the latter remonstrated that his men were inadequately armed for the task. In addition to the shotgun and squirrel guns that were so common, some of his men were only armed with flintlock muskets from their grandfathers' time! Forrest of course was never at a loss as how to overcome whatever challenges came his way, and he was able to equip many of his men with Sharps rifles captured after the successful engagement at Lexington on December 17, 1862. This problem would long plague Southern commanders.

It is only fair to point out, however, that not all regiments in the Western theater were forced to such a primitive assortment of weapons. The Third Louisiana Infantry Regiment, for example, right from the beginning was slightly better off. Its light company carried Springfield rifles and saber bayonets and therefore was referred to as the "rifle company." The other companies appear to have been uniformly armed with late-model smoothbore percussion cap muskets. Capt. Fitzgerald Ross estimated that during the first 2 years, three quarters of the weapons carried by both sides in the Western theater of operations were either smoothbore muskets or Austrian rifles. Although this is a considerable overstatement, there were some who didn't feel this was a particular disadvantage and who enthusiastically subscribed to the already-discussed theory that a regiment that had two companies equipped with longer-range rifles, which would serve as "rifle" or "flanking" companies, was sufficiently armed.

ARTILLERYMEN'S SMALL ARMS

Although the artillery's main armament was the ordnance its men had to transport, load, aim, and fire, the exigencies of the battlefield meant that the artillerymen occasionally had to personally defend themselves against charging enemy cavalry or infantry that managed to reach the guns and engage them in hand-to-hand combat. Prior to the war the official stance was that whatever protection was needed in such cases was to be provided by either local infantry or cavalry support. Although a few artillery officers had lobbied to arm artillerymen with the new repeating side arms, this had been soundly rejected. Authorities declared that the artillerymen had to be made to continue to fire, whatever the threat, until ordered to retire. A succinct description of this rationale is preserved in Gibbon's seminal work on American artillery:

> The proposition made to arm cannoneers with small-arms, such as revolvers, short rifles, etc., is calculated to do more harm than good. They should be taught to look upon the pieces as their proper arm of defense, to be abandoned only at the very last moment. The fate of many a battle has turned upon the delivery of a few rounds of grape or canister at short range upon an advancing column.

Artillery officers and sergeants were more fortunate, being allowed to carry revolvers from the start of the war.

These were the official regulations; in practice many men and even entire batteries took it upon themselves to acquire more effective side arms and discard those they felt were useless. Most artillery officers, for example, didn't have much confidence in the saber. Although some officers required their men to maintain their sabers and their scabbards in spotless condition in order to appease superior officers during monthly inspections, they then ordered these weapons to be kept in the regimental wagon during both drills and actual engagements with the enemy.

Although the official regulations prohibited the ordinary gunners from carrying revolvers, it wasn't unheard of for artillerymen to arm themselves with these new inventions. When the men in the company that would in a few weeks become Battery A of the First Rhode Island Light Artillery learned they were to embark on a train for Baltimore, the scene of civil unrest and attacks by the local population on arriving Union troops during the first weeks of the war, most of the men in the company took the precaution of arming themselves with revolvers.

There was little standardization, however, as the men in each regiment chose small arms they preferred or which were most readily available. In her history of the Nims' Battery, the Second Massachusetts Battery of Light Artillery, Caroline Whitcomb claimed that its men armed themselves with "sevenshooters," that is, Smith and Wesson revolvers—not to be confused with Spencer rifles which were also known as "sevenshooters"—although some modern weapons experts feel this is probably an exaggeration. Early in the war, NCOs in the First Wisconsin Battery were unofficially issued .44 Colts, although the men and drivers were expected to rely upon the regulation saber. Not trusting this weapon, the men resorted to dornicks (rocks) and clubs, which proved highly effective in close-in fighting. Feeling the need to take similar precautions, the teamsters equipped themselves with French revolvers, although if we believe some of the memoirists, these proved to be of extremely dubious value. Rather sarcastically, Daniel Webster claimed that these could

> send a ball through a tent—if you stood close enough for the powder to burn a way through it. For the purpose of offense, defense or suicide they were nowhere as compared to the "unloaded gun."

Again, some modern experts believe that such out-of-hand dismissals of exotic European small arms is apocryphal, the result of more pervasive cultural trends that influenced those writing their memoirs, long after the conclusion of the Civil War.

As the war progressed, however, an increasing number of batteries were overrun and captured, and it became obvious that neither a rifle musket nor the saber was the most effective of the weapons then available for personal defense. In 1863 the Ordnance Department finally sanctioned the distribution of revolvers to ordinary artillerymen, and many, but not all, batteries ended up with this superior means of self-defense at close range.

SHARPSHOOTERS

The use of expert marksmen during campaign operations and on the battlefield dates as far back as the late 1700s, and many examples can be found during the American Revolution and the Napoleonic Wars. Not surprisingly, one encounters officers discussing how and where to employ these specialized troops during the preparations for war from November 1860 onward. Almost every major combat throughout the 4-year struggle saw at least some men detached from the main forces to ply their deadly trade against selected targets. In most cases these sharpshooters were selected from crack companies or occasionally from among the best shots in a regiment. From the point of view of their function, they were an *ad hoc* unit employed to meet the particular circumstances of the individual situation.

Before long a number of units, companies, and regiments were raised especially for this role. In August 1861 Maj. Gen. John C. Frémont (the 1856 Republican presidential candidate) called for the creation of one company of sharpshooters and one of "pioneers" in each regiment in his command. Few details are provided other than that the sharpshooter company was to contain all the best marksmen in the regiment. The pioneers were charged with cleaning the roads, removing obstacles, and so on. Although it is unclear the extent to which these orders were carried out, we do know that another specialized unit raised under Frémont's authority, the Frémont Body Guard, participated in a successful charge at Springfield, Missouri (Oct. 25, 1861). Although this elite group was armed with Colt revolving rifles, considered a very desirable shoulder arm during this early period, it appears to have relied upon tactics that demand a *high rate* of fire rather than *accuracy* of fire. During the charge each man in the bodyguard purportedly emptied two Colts revolvers and his rifle without stopping to reload, for a total of eighteen shots delivered in rapid succession.

Larger units would be raised that would be devoted to an expert skirmishing and a sharpshooting role, such as Birge's Sharpshooters (Fourteenth Missouri, which became the Sixty-sixth Illinois on November 20, 1862) and the Yates Sharpshooters (Sixty-fourth Illinois). The most famous of all sharpshooting regiments, however, were the two associated with Col. Hiram Berdan. From the moment the first salvos against Fort Sumter heralded the start of the Civil War, Colonel Berdan realized there was a need for a select corps of highly skilled sharpshooters for special duty during which highly accurate small fire was required. Placing ads for expert marksmen in various Northeastern newspapers, Berdan was overwhelmed with volunteers and by the first week in May was already prepared to send twenty-six five-man detachments to Washington City.

Berdan's appeal was so successful that it was soon decided to organize an entire regiment of sharpshooters. The First United States Sharpshooter Regiment was formed during the early summer of 1861 in order to concentrate several hundred of the best marksmen in the Union into a single organization. To join the regiment, however, the prospective recruit first had to publicly demonstrate proficiency as a sharpshooter. The qualifying trials consisted of ten shots at a target 200 yards distant. The shooter was allowed to use any type of rifle without a telescopic lens and could fire from any position as long as the weapon's butt rested upon his shoulder. When all his shots were examined, the total distance from the center of the target could not be greater than 50 inches. There was no lack of applicants and good shots, and the regiment quickly filled its quota.

Originally, the marksmen admitted into the regiment were allowed to bring their own target rifles for campaign use. After all, equipped with telescopic lenses, these were the most accurate long-range rifles money could buy. Unfortunately, the realities of campaigning immediately showed the impracticality of this plan. Most target rifles were considerably heavier than their military counterparts. Most were at least 15 pounds, while some were as much as 30, whereas the Enfield and Springfield rifles each weighed only about 9 pounds. Although a 15-pound rifle didn't appear to weigh much on a target range, it would certainly prove to be a heavy burden on an extended march to an infantrymen burdened with knapsack, haversack, blanket, canteen, and overcoat. Not only were many of these fancy weapons too bulky, but none had been designed to withstand the rigors of an active campaign. The sophisticated sights and the sensitive hair triggers constantly failed, and unlike on the range, in a critical combat situation, this could result in something more serious than a momentary inconvenience or poor score. The assortment of target rifles also quickly imposed logistical problems: It was simply impossible to supply ammunition systematically for all of the numerous rifle types brought in by the marksmen.

It became obvious that privately owned weapons would have to be replaced by a single type of small arm. However, Gen. James W. Ripley, chief of the Ordnance Department, took a very conservative approach to infantry armament and lobbied to arm the sharpshooters with the standard Springfield rifles. This of course was an extremely shortsighted policy, one that would have lessened much of the sharpshooter regiments' usefulness, especially when accurate long-range fire proved necessary. After some discussion among themselves, the sharpshooters requested that they be armed with a modified military version of the weapon then being produced by the Sharps Manufacturing Company.

After a considerable amount of argument, lobbying, and correspondence back and forth, Ordnance backed down from its original position and in March 1862 ordered that one of the regiments temporarily be equipped with Colt revolving rifles. The plan was to replace these later with the Sharps rifles that the men wanted. Most of the two sharpshooter regiments were quickly armed with the Colts, but the Michigan and New Hampshire companies held onto their nonmilitary target rifles for a while longer. As it turned out, some of the marksmen were not satisfied with the new weapon. Many complained that although the Colt revolver was a pretty rifle to look at, unfortunately, it was inaccurate and unreliable—occasionally even dangerous to its owner. However, the Colt was later used very successfully by Rosecrans's men in the

West, and the sharpshooters' complaints were probably theatrics designed to cajole authorities into giving them the weapon they wanted most, the Sharps rifle.

In practice the type of weapon Berdan's sharpshooters were given does not appear to have greatly affected their performance in the field. Starting from the siege of Yorktown, they enjoyed a long string of successes, including notable accomplishments during the Seven Days' battles, Chancellorsville, and Gettysburg. Union veterans would long remember how the Andrews Sharpshooters coolly picked off Confederate officers at long range during this last battle.

BREECHLOADERS IN THE CAVALRY

During the late 1850s breechloaders started to be issued in the British cavalry in limited numbers, and some Sharps carbines were used in anger during the closing stages of the Indian Mutiny. British opinion about this weapon and its capabilities appears nearly identical to that held by Garibaldi's troops who were equipped with the infantry version. The tape primer was not always reliable. It tended to become brittle in very hot conditions and soggy in extreme humidity. The carbine would also become progressively fouled and more and more difficult to load. However, the manufacturer of the weapon had foreseen this problem, and early models came equipped with ramrods to load the weapon from the muzzle in a crisis.

Unlike its pedestrian counterpart, the United States cavalry was not slow to realize the potentialities offered by the new breechloaders and repeaters that were becoming available with increasing frequency during the late 1850s. The use of firearms by mounted troopers had been a problem as long as the cavalrymen had been armed with muzzleloaders. Inserting the ball and charge down the barrel and then ramming it home was of course more difficult atop a moving horse. True, the advent of the percussion cap to some extent had simplified the loading process. However, it still required great dexterity and concentration to load the weapon and insert the cap while mounted and in motion. Forced to fumble around, the cavalryman would often drop the cap. And once in proximity to the enemy, reloading became impossible.

In *Volunteer's Camp and Field Book*, one of numerous works on military art and science hurriedly published during the first months of the war, John P. Curry extolled the virtues of the new breechloaders and repeaters and explained their advantages for cavalry operations. Two new inventions had eliminated the need to insert a percussion cap manually each time the trooper loaded. The new breechloaders utilized bullets in which the projectile, the propellant charge, and the detonating charge were all housed inside a single cartridge. Not only did this simplify and speed up the loading process, but it also meant that the new rifles, especially those that utilized metal cartridges, could be fired in all weather, even the most violent rainstorm. A few of the new rifles utilized the Maynard primer or tape cap. This consisted of a roll of detonating charges which automatically advanced each time the hammer was cocked, much like a child's cap gun. Both inventions seemed to solve problems still posed by the percussion cap. Even the single-shot breechloaders, such as the Sharps rifle, could be fired four or five times faster than the muzzleloaders they were to replace. The Maynard system, however, proved impractical and was abandoned about 1860.

Chapter 11

UNPREPAREDNESS:
BULL RUN AND ITS AFTERMATH

T he period separating the fall of Fort Sumter, April 14, 1861, and the Battle of Bull Run, July 21, might be characterized as the Civil War's halcyon days. Stirred on by the vigor of patriotism not yet tempered by the horrible carnage of the battlefield, and further stimulated by the promise of glory and a quick return to home and hearth, day after day the men toiled to master their new martial profession in an environment that, if Spartan, was nonetheless imbued with camaraderie and common conviction. True, the period was not completely devoid of fighting, but what did occur was limited to the contests of pickets and the occasional small-scale action, such as the fight at Big Bethel on June 10.

All this would quickly change on July 16, when Maj. Gen. Irvin McDowell initiated the first full-scale operation by pushing his forces forward to directly confront Gen. Pierre G. T. Beauregard's forces, by now firmly ensconced behind Bull Run Creek, between Manassas Junction and Centreville, Virginia, and only 25 miles southwest of Washington. The prevalent belief among the Union populace was that the mere appearance of a bold advance was all that was required to scatter the rebel forces. There were some among the more experienced of the regular Union officers, however, who had their reservations about this optimistic assessment. Looking upon the sea of recently raised volunteers, the martial limitations of this human materiel were noticeable to the discerning eye. A few days before the Battle of Bull Run, a regular officer cautioned a volunteer officer with the Second Rhode Island Regiment that under pressure of actual combat, these novices would not meet expectations: "Your men will make splendid soldiers to advance, but they will not know how to retreat."

This proved to be an all too accurate prediction. The first telltale signs of these shortcomings began to appear during McDowell's advance towards Centreville. Capt. William H. P. Steere, who served with a Rhode Island volunteer regiment, remembered that the advance had more the feeling of a "pleasant ramble" than a serious military offensive in search of the enemy. The volunteers' discipline frequently faltered, and even when they remained in their ranks, the men amused themselves with conversation, laughter, and jokes. In his memoirs Gen. William Tecumseh Sherman admitted he and his officers exerted little control over their men. Every time the column passed a stream or a spring, the volunteers broke ranks and filled their canteens. Strawberry and blackberry patches were also an irresistible temptation. All of these factors conspired to slow down the march, and the result was that on July 17 the Union force, instead of reaching Centreville, only advanced seven miles. The continuous dawdling exhausted both officers and men, and the former lacked the experience to recognize the problem and its consequences. In a rare moment of criticism, Col. G. F. R. Henderson, one of Stonewall Jackson's early biographers, attributed part of the delays to the lack of "good marching qualities" and the inability to carry the prescribed weight of even light marching order for any great distance.

Even when the commander ordered a halt, the few precious moments of rest were generally mismanaged. Veteran regular troops used to the rigors of campaigning against Indians in the West quickly ate their next meal, realizing that the next opportunity to do so might not occur again for hours. The volunteers usually just lay down and, if possible, took a short nap. Though more refreshing in the short run, it proved to be a pernicious habit that robbed the men of their energy as the hours passed. Also, not yet having acquired the basics of military economy, when they did eat, the raw troops also consumed more than the regular troops did. On July 20 General McDowell would report that he was "somewhat embarrassed by the inability of the troops to take care enough of their rations to make them last the time they should."

AT BULL RUN

If these shortcomings were an annoyance to officers during the march, they would prove nearly fatal to the Union cause during the First Battle of Bull Run. The heat experienced that day, combined with the intense physical activity that is part of any battle, produced extreme thirst. Despite the urgency of the situation and the importance of maintaining a cohesive fighting formation, Sherman remembers that at the height of the battle, many of the men along the firing lines left the ranks and went to Sudley Springs to refill their canteens, just as they had while on the march during the preceding days.

Despite such breaches of discipline, the men on both sides stood and fought bravely for most of the day, though other telltale signs of the men's inexperience soon became evident. As Burnside's brigade began to attack the Confederate left flank, Union artillery was quickly brought into action—first the pieces that followed the Second Rhode Island Volunteer Infantry, then Griffin's and Ricketts's batteries. Lt. Albert J. Monroe remembered that the sensation of coming under small arms fire for the first time reminded them of the explosions of "bunches of crackers." Looking back at this first action with the experience of 4 years of hard fighting, Monroe realized that the Union artillery committed two very basic errors. The Union batteries had been unlimbered much too close to the enemy lines, sometimes as close as half pistol range (about 20 yards), and had they faced a more experienced Confederate force, they would have been completely overrun and the guns captured after a single desperate charge. The inexperienced gunners also fired too quickly and made little effort to select their targets carefully and make every shot count. According to Monroe the artillery fire was directed merely at the smoke surrounding a rebel battery and was "exceedingly rapid, everyone appearing to feel that the great object was to make as much noise as possible, and get an immense quantity of iron into the enemy's line in the shortest possible space of time, without regard to whether it hit anything or not." Fortunately for the Union artillery, however, at this early date neither side understood the "rudiments of the art of war," so for at least a brief period, the artillery was left free to ply its attempts at destruction.

Just as artillerymen had to learn to cope with hostile musket fire, so did the infantry vis-à-vis artillery fire. In fact, one of the most unsettling experiences for novice troops was the sound of an

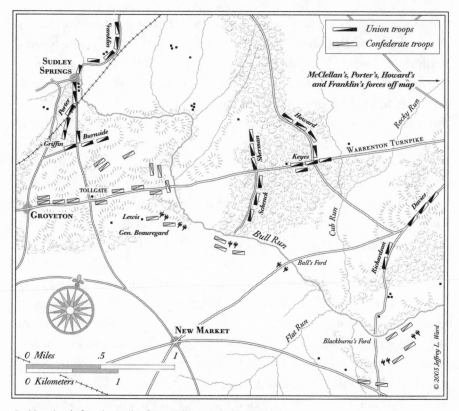

Positions just before the Battle of First Bull Run (July 21, 1861).
This is based on a map prepared by Captain A. W. Whipple that accompanied Irvin McDowell's after-battle report.

incoming artillery shell. Lt. Joseph Favill, who had enlisted with the Seventy-first New York State Militia Infantry in April, described the reaction of the regiment when fired upon by artillery for the first time at Bull Run:

> Suddenly a loud screeching noise overhead sent more than half of the regiment pell mell to the other side of a fence that ran along the road side. Here we crouched down flat on our bellies, just as a shell exploded a little beyond us. It was from the rebel batteries in front, and the first any of us had ever heard, and it certainly did seem a terrible thing, rushing through the air like an immense sky rocket, then bursting into a thousand pieces, carrying death and destruction to everything in its course. The stampede was only momentary, but very funny; the boys

jumped back again; in fact, almost as quickly as they had dispersed, and then stood steady in the ranks, watching the advance of the Rhode Islanders.

Also like the artillerymen, the infantrymen tended to give in to their impulses and fire too quickly during their baptism of fire. Once again we are indebted to Lieutenant Favill for a vivid description of how the men in the Seventy-first New York conducted themselves during their first firefight:

We marched immediately, reached the crest of the hill, and amid the rattle of musketry, the booming of the guns, and the screeching of the shells, lay down and commenced firing. Before we had time to get well at work, along came Griffith's light battery at full gallop scattering the right of our regiment badly; we got together again as quickly as possible, but were five or six files deep, narrowing the front of our regiment, and rendering about half of us useless. I was in this struggling crowd, and with many others, tried hard to get the line straightened out, but the objection many of the fellows had to take the front rank prevented our doing much of anything.

These types of problems certainly weren't limited to the Union side, and here and there in the memoirs of Confederate veterans, similar observations are occasionally found. Bela Estvan, a Hungarian originally in Austrian service, and who served as a Confederate cavalry colonel, would recall the hesitancy and confusion of Confederate sharpshooters during the final days leading up to the collision at Bull Run. Ordered to select available Union targets, they would actually ask permission to fire before each shot: "May I fire? I think I can hit him." George Baylor, at this point serving with the Second Virginia Infantry, would never forget observing the first volley delivered by the Thirty-third Virginia in anger and his disgust as the latter raised their muskets at a 45-degree angle and he realized that none of the bullets would hit their mark "unless [the Yankees] were nearer heaven than they were generally located by our people."

All these deficiencies were little more than inconveniences, however.

The great majority of troops on both sides passed the most basic test of the battlefield. Regardless of their inexperience, clumsiness, and lack of finesse, they held their ground and continued the fight throughout the morning and early afternoon.

The most profound implications of the troops' inexperience, especially those on the Union side, would only manifest itself late in the afternoon, between 4 and 4:30, when the infantrymen along the Union right suddenly and seemingly without explanation gave up the fight and collectively started to walk off the battlefield. One of those present at this strange event was William Russell, the noted journalist for the *London Times*. He would later confide that though he had seen every sort of raucous event, "from Irish wakes to pitched battles," he had witnessed nothing more strange than that Union flight, the soldiers quickly retiring "when there was nothing to run from." All cohesion, all order, seemed lost in but a matter of moments.

Many others, however, despite the "indescribable confusion," were struck by the calmness of the men's demeanor. There was no terror or panic, just a collective resignation that the day's fighting was over, and there was nothing more to do than to get back to camp. Serving with the artillery attached to the First Rhode Island Regiment, Lieutenant Monroe was in a position to observe the men closely at the start of the flight. What he saw reminded him of workers getting off of work at the end of a hard day's labor:

> The scene was such as to remind one of that which can be seen daily in any large manufacturing town or village, when the operatives, let loose by the expiration of their hours of labor, all set out for their respective homes. During working hours the system of work is maintained, but upon the ringing of the bell, all depart according to their respective bents and wills. So upon this field the general impression seemed to be that of the day's work was done and that the next thing in order was repose.

Capt. James R. Fry, at the time assistant adjutant general on McDowell's staff, would note that there was "no special excitement, except that arising from the frantic efforts to stop men." Monroe noticed a very large and powerful man, who served as a field officer with what he thought was a Maine regiment, coaxing, threatening, and even physically manhandling whomever he could get his hands on in an attempt to stop the rout and restore order. His exertions were of no avail, and the human torrent continued unabated. Such heroics were a minority reaction even among officers; most had succumbed to insouciance and walked away among the men.

What was the cause of so strange a transformation? Why did troops who had so stubbornly contested the issue all day give up within moments and walk away en masse? In an early history of the great conflict, John G. Nicolay attributed the breakdown to the loss of regimental organization. Men and officers became mixed, the parent units now undecipherable. According to this author by 4 o'clock the 12,000 Union volunteers on this side of the field had completely lost any semblance of cohesion and could no longer be handled as a military organization.

This is not to suggest that the Union discomfiture happened simply because the Union troops somehow became physically displaced, the formations disrupted, and the spatial relations between men and their officers irreparably muddled. The real cause of the breakdown lay in the psychological realm and was attributable to the limitations of troops not yet inured to the vicissitudes, the stress, the extreme demands of battle. Inexperienced troops lack a certain flexibility, and although they can initially fight as hard as, possibly even harder than, veterans, once pushed past a certain threshold, they completely crumble, and no effort can restore them for the remainder of the day. Probably better than any other American writer, Col. B. F. Scribner of the Thirty-eighth Indiana Infantry Regiment described the difference between raw and experienced troops:

> Old soldiers when overpowered or taken at a disadvantage may yield ground; but they will keep together as if attracted to each other by a sort of moral gravitation, and will halt when threatened by missiles of the enemy. On the contrary, when raw troops become panic-stricken they cannot be rallied within the noise of battle. Not having acquired the cohesion which long association and discipline give, they will so disperse that much time and effort must be employed to collect them for further

duty. But old soldiers will unconsciously reform their ranks, even as cavalry horses are said to have done when abandoned by their riders, who embarked on ships.

Earlier in the day the Confederates had been affected by the same phenomenon and only because of fortunate circumstances were able to avoid disaster. Beauregard, in his own account of Bull Run, written for the seminal *Battles and Leaders of the Civil War,* admitted that a panic engulfed the Confederate line when Bee's troops were pushed back when the Union line was extended by the arrival of Heintzelman's division on the Union right and Sherman's and Keyes's brigades out toward the left. Fortunately, what saved the Confederates at this point was the presence of a strong, extremely well-led force, Thomas Jackson's brigade, whose example helped calm the panicked soldiers and around which they were able to re-form.

INEXPERIENCE OF VOLUNTEER OFFICERS

The need to raise a volunteer army five times the size of the standing army, coupled with Scott's refusal to allow regular officers to transfer to the newly formed regiments, meant that most states recruited new volunteer officers from almost every conceivable background. Reflecting an underestimation of the severity of the upcoming conflict, many of those selected to fill even the highest officer ranks were political appointments. During the first months it was common to encounter volunteer captains, colonels, even generals who were completely ignorant of the military art. The resulting variety in experience and skills created a pernicious problem that would plague the Union forces for much of the war. In his history of the Sixteenth New York Infantry, Newton Curtis, who served with the regiment, speculated that "in no battle of modern times, in which thirty-five thousand men were engaged, was there so small a number of officers educated in the science and the art of war" as at Bull Run. According to Curtis at this stage of the war, there were only two officers with formal training in military art in Slocum's brigade and only five or six in the twelve regiments that made up Franklin's division. This situation wasn't confined to McDowell's army: Many brigades in the West had an equally small percentage of experienced officers.

The lack of adequate officer training affected every aspect of military operations, from the type of tactics and grand tactics that could be employed on the battlefield to how the human resources were managed during arduous forced marches. Many officers failed to understand such a basic concept as the long-term importance of protecting their men's health. They didn't appreciate the combined weight of the knapsack, haversack, canteen, gun, and 40 rounds, physically demanding more from their men than could have been reasonably expected. Little attention was placed upon the proper selection of camps and the necessary sanitary conditions. The result was a significant amount of unnecessary losses due to disease and illness. In his memoirs Judson Bishop, colonel of the Second Minnesota Regiment, estimated that during the first year his regiment suffered about 20% casualties from this source. Three years later, after marching 480 miles during midwinter, the same regiment lost only 3% to illness, despite the facts that tents were no longer available and half of the men were new recruits with only a few months of active service.

Raw recruits could learn the manual of arms in several days and after several weeks could maneuver in a passable fashion. A few months of hard campaigning usually were sufficient to mold the martial novice into an experienced soldier. NCOs and officers have always had a much longer learning curve and require much greater time to season. Of course, officers, like the men they commanded, learned more quickly when they were placed within an experienced cadre, where they would benefit from the advice and example of the experienced officers. Unfortunately, Scott's adamant insistence that all regular U. S. Army officers remain with their original units precluded this possibility. Though the policy was reversed in 1862, so regular officers could now transfer to volunteer organizations, the damage was done. The lure of leadership positions in the new regiments had worn thin, and most officers elected to stay with the regular forces.

Of course, valuable experience was gained as a regiment saw more and more active service. Unfortunately, a number of Union volunteer regiments were soon affected by a related development. A regiment in the field could try to maintain regulation strength by a stream of new recruits, which could be injected into the regiment as it sustained losses from the crucible of battle or the rigors of campaign. In practice there were two problems with this. The recruiting effort necessarily meant the detachment of a few officers to supervise this replacement effort. After the effusive rush to enlist subsided after the first few months of war, as the grim realities of military life became common knowledge in even the most out-of-the-way village or farm, many regiments found it difficult to entice and train the needed amount of men.

Partly to put a stop to this drain of resources and partly because Union military leadership thought the rebellion would be crushed with the upcoming summer campaign, on April 3, 1862, the War Department ordered the disbandment of all recruiting operations of existing regiments. This turned out to have been only a temporary measure, for recruitment by the existing regiments resumed later that year.

From this point on many of the new recruits were funneled into new regiments rather than used to bolster understrength regiments in the field. There were two reasons. Many of those who came to the colors preferred the new regiments since there was a training period before they were sent into battle, and there was always the possibility that peace would come first. Also, throughout the war much of the recruiting was actually performed by individuals who sought a commissioned rank in the regiment about to be formed. No such incentive existed in established regiments, whose officer rolls were already filled. The solution that most states adopted, therefore, was simply to raise new regiments rather than actively nourish those already in the field.

Although this was the most expeditious way of collecting warm bodies, it certainly was far from the best manner of maintaining effective fighting organizations in the field. Several thousand years of martial experience had repeatedly demonstrated that a fighting organization reaches its optimal performance only after acquiring sufficient practical campaign and battlefield experience. A veteran regiment learns to fight more effectively, to become better at surviving, than one composed exclusively of recruits. Unfortunately, eliminating a regiment's ability to replenish its strength with recruits meant that it could never obtain its full potential, regardless of any increase in the abilities of its soldiers. The regiments would diminish in size and hence effective strength with each successive engagement. The other side of the coin was that the newly raised regiments required the same learning curve that the veterans had already gone through and were condemned to commit the same errors. These problems persisted as long as completely new regiments entered the field.

Although by the start of the 1862 campaign, the general level of officer competence had substantially improved over that of the previous year, many egregious examples of officer incompetence were still encountered. The problem was felt to be common enough to warrant state military authorities in Pennsylvania, for example, to convene an Enquiry Board at Harrisburg to test the competence of volunteer field officers from that state. Those failing these tests were expeditiously removed from active service.

In his memoirs Capt. John Donaghy provided a detailed example of how officers' inexperience could severely affect the men's combat performance and limit their ability to cope with crises of battle. During the Battle of Fair Oaks (May 31, 1862), the 103rd Pennsylvania Infantry Regiment, severely attacked and greatly outnumbered, was rapidly pushed back and largely dispersed. Donaghy and a portion of his company ran into the flank of the Ninety-sixth New York, then marching forward in a column of fours. The enemy appeared, and the Union regiment's colonel decided to send out skirmishers to meet the approaching threat. However, this officer only issued the cautionary warning "Deploy as skirmishers" and failed to follow with the actual command. Confused, his men stood motionless, despite an irritated repetition of the cautionary statement.

Donaghy, partial to skirmishing tactics, ordered his comrades to break out into skirmish order, which they did with noticeable legerity. The Ninety-sixth Regiment, however, remained unresponsive. Its men, completely unprepared for a stand-up confrontation, panicked and fled, forcing Donaghy and his skirmishers to retire again. As they neared the rifle pits in the rear, they joined a mass of men from Wessells's brigade. Now flooded with a torrent of stragglers, the rifle pits proved to be indefensible, and the milling crowd continued its confused retreat backward. It was only when the fleeing mass reached the rear of their camp that officers systematically attempted to rally the men. Unfortunately, in the excitement of the moment, these officers disregarded the proper procedure required by the official tactics.

Some shouted, "Form here!" while others directed the men to some other spot along the line. Though willing to stand and fight, the men were bewildered.

Donaghy saw the problem and knew the solution. Approaching the senior officer present, Col. Joshua Howell of the Eighty-fifth Pennsylvania, Donaghy asked if he could act as the colonel's adjutant and form the line. Howell consented. With two sergeants from his company as guides, he gave the order "Right dress!" The men immediately obeyed, and there were soon about 300 men in line, an accomplishment that would not have occurred had the more senior officers been left to themselves. The rallied force now advanced to its camp and was able to delay the enemy until instructed to fall back.

UNION REACTION TO DEFEAT AT BULL RUN

The immediate result of the unexpected Union defeat at Bull Run was surprise and consternation. As with all deep humiliation, there was a certain amount of denial among the soldiers who had participated in the affair. Approaching artillerymen attached to a Rhode Island regiment a few days later, Lieutenant Monroe attributed the defeat to lack of discipline and opined that the Union soldiers not only needed a much more rigorous training regimen but had to completely change their mind set. To underscore the urgency of these changes, Monroe advised his men, "We had to come down to regulations, the same as in the regular army, and should consider ourselves almost as state convicts." Not surprisingly, his men were initially indignant.

Meanwhile, the Confederates made their way closer to Washington City, and rebel flags flying from advanced outposts could be seen from the dome of the Capitol. Panic set in among the city's populace, just as it had in mid-April. A stream of fresh regiments continued to arrive, and the lines defending the city were reinforced. A cordon of defensive works was hastily thrown up. The capital once again secure from enemy attack, calm was gradually restored throughout the North.

Although the enthusiasm of the early months was gone, never to return, a less ostentatious but more determined resolution set in. The men now recruited had to enlist for 9 months, rather than the hopelessly optimistic 3-month term required after the fall of Fort Sumter. Since it was realized that it would not be enough for them simply to show up for battle, the troops arriving in Washington were immediately subjected to much stricter discipline and intensive training. Officers would share a similar fate. Most officers stationed in the capital had up to this point enjoyed considerable freedom; passes into the city had been easily obtained and how they passed the evenings was usually left to their discretion.

All this changed overnight. Col. William Franklin was appointed commander of Fort Ellsworth, one of the works protecting Washington. His policies typified the new tone of the military administration. The movement of both men and officers was now restricted. Colonels were now instructed never to issue passes to more than two officers and two men at one time. All passes now automatically expired at 5 P.M. the day they were issued, thus drastically reducing the time men and officers could be separated from their regiments. To set an example, officers who came to his office to plead for extended passes were placed under arrest, though no charges were actually preferred. The motley array of differing uniforms also disappeared. The general air on the streets of Washington changed profoundly. The near-carnival atmosphere evaporated overnight, and a new sense of sobriety prevailed.

McClellan soon replaced McDowell as Union commander, and a concerted effort was made to reorganize the army into a more effective military machine. Regiments were brigaded together and assigned to divisions. The nearly continual training and drill assumed a new sense of urgency. Before Bull Run most regiments trained in isolation; now brigade-size exercise became more common. Fraternization between officers and their men was now strictly forbidden. Recruits with previous military experience were more fully appreciated than they had been in April and May, and their comrades in arms paid more attention to their advice.

A soldier could master formal procedures, such as the manual of arms and the maneuvers on the parade ground, but other important competency could only be acquired through actual experience. Though often softer, or less defined, than officially prescribed drills, such knowledge and abilities could be vital to staying alive under fire or avoiding disease during the campaign. Gradually, experience taught that the infantryman was best advised to take off his socks before wading into a ford, a precaution that greatly reduced the blistering of feet, and to make an extra effort in the evening to gather hemlock boughs for a comfortable bed. As they gained experience, soldiers learned to distinguish between the reports of musketry aimed in their direction and those pointed away. Pragmatism was of the essence. The 90-day recruits had placed much attention on fancy, gaudy clothing. They had carried around heavy knapsacks stuffed with personal effects, which proved terrible encumbrances during a march. Such frills, considered so important early on, were now discarded as unimportant.

The Southern soldier in particular proved a quick learner and such burdens were soon set aside. By his second campaign the rebel soldier typically had only the clothing he wore plus a few essentials. At the beginning of the war, many Union volunteers were also heavily encumbered with unessential material, and like their Southern foes, they quickly pared down what they carried on the campaign.

This was as true on a company and battalion level as it was for the individual soldier. At the beginning of the war, each Union regiment was equipped with six mule wagons for the headquarters and company tents, quartermaster stores, the hospital outfit, and officers' baggage. Taking up as much space on the road as the regiments themselves, such wagon trains greatly slowed down the army's rate of advance. As the war progressed, the number of wagons per regiment was greatly reduced. Instead of keeping shovels and axes on a company wagon, for example, soldiers, especially those among Western regiments, learned to appoint two or three men as "pioneers." Charged with clearing the way of obstacles, they marched with the necessary implements at the front of the regiment. The unit became increasingly self-sufficient, and the regimental wagon train was correspondingly reduced in size.

PART III

INFANTRY
AND CAVALRY

Chapter 12

THE REALITY OF THE BATTLEFIELD

W hen one considers the large number of engagements that occurred during the Civil War and the great number of individuals who participated in these actions, the variety and types of experiences encountered during the heat of combat appears to be endlessly varied. If this were true, the task of categorizing and understanding the soldiers' experiences would be extremely difficult, if not impossible. Of course, many of the Civil War soldiers' experiences were indeed idiosyncratic, their nature inextricably tied to unique situations, representing one-of-a-kind events that bore little resemblance to those experienced elsewhere on the same battlefield or during other engagements. Flipping through memoirs and biographies, a great many examples of these unique combat experiences are found. Conversations between soldiers and the extraordinary and strange actions of individuals fall within this category.

One of the most strikingly unusual occurrences was witnessed by Carl Cameron, who served with the First Wisconsin Battery of Light Artillery during fighting near Tazewell, Tennessee on Aug 3, 1862. The enemy having finally been repulsed, Cameron's attention was drawn to the dead body of a rebel infantryman, over which stood a tall, lanky Union infantryman. Noticing abdominal fat protruding from the large, bloody hole in the Confederate's lower stomach, the infantryman quickly cut off a piece with his bayonet. Bending over, he then proceeded to calmly and methodically grease his shoes with human fat.

Anyone willing to read enough firsthand accounts will eventually find many other examples of the curious, and the bizarre. Fortunately, most wartime experiences were much less individualized and more inextricably tied to the events from which they originated. Rather than being caused by a unique set of events, they were the result of commonly occurring situations. During the 4 years of internecine strife, innumerable times a defending line stood anxiously awaiting the oncoming storm, as waves of attackers surged forward amid the hail of shot, shell, and Minié bullet. On countless occasions artillerymen feverishly plied their trade and did their best to wreak death and havoc upon the enemy, despite the rain of enemy small arms and artillery fire.

Before dissecting the various doctrines and practices that were used during the Civil War, it might be useful first to create a generalized sketch of what it was like to fight in a large-scale action during this era. What follows therefore is a collage of experiences taken from the memoirs of many veterans and others, assembled to form a typical picture of the Civil War battlefield experience.

Before the Battle

Standing upon an elevated position to the rear of the Confederate's lines at the First Bull Run (July 21, 1861), a European observer would later compare gazing down upon the impending battle to looking at a large panoramic painting which hung in a much more peaceful setting. Reduced by the distance to mere dots, the troops, horses, and wagons could be seen crisscrossing the field "like swarms of bees." Long columns of infantry would be moving toward the intended battle line, while the artillery worked its way to the flanks and other advantageous positions. With bayonets glittering in the bright sun, from a distance the approaching enemy would appear to march in perfect order. Between the lines field officers could be seen riding back and forth, urging their men on and providing last-minute orders and directions. Even when the desired lines of battle were quickly formed, to a combatant ruminating upon the possibility of imminent death, the interval felt like an eternity.

Dust meanwhile would rise up to form long, sinewy, and dark, cottony chains of clouds as the artillery, ammunition wagons, and ambulances flew toward their destinations. If the advance posts had failed to detect the enemy's movements, such clouds of dust beginning to peep over the distant horizon would provide the first telltale signs of the enemy's approach. Experienced officers could usually not only discern the enemy's direction of march but also whether the moving force was infantry or cavalry; dust clouds thrown up by cavalry rose higher and were thicker than those generated by infantry. On a sunny day the type of gleam from the enemy's muskets and bayonets in the distance also revealed the direction they were heading; the glitter seemed brightest whenever the enemy was approaching the observer.

As the enemy closed to about 2000 yards, groups of men and formations began to be discerned, and cavalry could be distinguished from infantry at about 1200 yards. It was only at about 600 yards that the unaided eye could start to see the blurry forms of individual soldiers. During the 1850s a group of French officers set out to methodically determine what a soldier with average eyesight could discern at various ranges. Although a European study carried out under peacetime conditions, its findings nevertheless are germane to those interested in the American Civil War. After all, the average optical capabilities of the American soldier were probably the same as that of his French counterpart. Although most field and staff officers by Civil War times were equipped with field glasses and were no longer as bound to the limitations of the naked eye as their grandfathers had been during the War of 1812, the following chart, which summarizes the study's observations, describes what the typical soldier would have observed as enemy forces approached over relatively flat, open terrain.

Approaching Cavalry

Approximate distance	What is distinguishable
650 yards	The rate of motion—walking, trotting, galloping; the direction of the movement—advancing or retiring; the brilliant part of the accoutrements—helmet and cuirass; the color of the uniform—red, white; the breastplate, the plume, the blade of the lances.
430 yards	The saddlecloth; the rates of motion and its direction; the helmet and the cuirass; the bright colors of the uniform; the shoulder belts of the horsemen in front.
325 yards	The colors of the saddlecloth; the reins of the bridles on horses with light saddlecloths, seen sideways; the scabbard of the horseman's sword, seen on his left; the shaft of the lances; the epaulettes, the hair of the head.

215 yards	The saddlecloth; the reins of the bridle on horses with dark saddle cloths; the blade and scabbard of the sword; the shaft of the lance; the carbines slung; the principal parts of the uniform and equipment.
110 yards	The soldier's body; his shape and arms; his weapons and equipment; the details of his uniform; harness; the line of buttons on his jacket, holster, and cloak.

Approaching Infantry

Approximate distance	What is distinguishable
650 yards	The movement of companies marching, advancing, or retiring, the red color of infantry.
430 yards	The direction of their march and the movement of their muskets.
325 yards	The barrels of the rifles or carbines; the rifle at the shoulder, the different parts of the uniform.
215 yards	The color of the uniform; the badges of the belts or shakos; the hilts of the swords, the cartridge box.
110 yards	The different parts of the body; the movements of the men individually; the form and color of the uniform.

Source: Adapted from Steinmetz.

If they were still far enough away from the enemy, nearby friendly troops in front might be seen carrying their knapsacks, or "bureaus," as they were sometimes called. These of course would be unslung and heaped into company piles as soon as an action was imminent. Here and there along the line, regimental flags flapped in the breeze. Someone gazing upon a Confederate force during the early days of the war would have noticed five to ten times as many flags as during later campaigns. At first each company carried its own flag, but this caused so much confusion that only a single flag per regiment was retained. The company officers positioned themselves behind their men along the line to ensure that there were no shirkers and everyone performed his duty. If the observer were close enough, the field officers could be heard yelling out orders encouraging or cautioning their men. The adjutants then repeated these orders along the line.

With the first roar of the artillery, the poetical appearance of the battlefield instantly vanished as the deadly struggle began in earnest. The attacking side began its advance seemingly in perfect order. Clouds of smoke leapt up furiously here and there in the distance as the enemy's artillery began its defensive fire. The enemy's batteries frequently remained unobserved, and smoke rising from the tops of ridges, behind clumps of trees, or within hidden hollows or valleys was proof that the defenders had carefully placed their pieces to take advantage of available terrain.

The projectiles speeding on their way towards the intended targets, it took only a few seconds for little, white puffs of smoke from the exploding shells to rapidly dot the field, many exploding over the attackers' heads. A survivor of the carnage at Antietam (Sept. 17, 1862) would recall that long after the actual event, these would appear peaceful in the mind's eye:

> Every one of them exploded just as nicely as they could wish, squarely over our heads, shaking its fragments among us, leaving only a harmless cloud of smoke to roll peacefully away, as if satisfied with its work and glad to return to its proper home in the atmosphere.

The men's actual reaction during a battle was rarely so serene, however. Hundreds were killed or severely wounded by such shell bursts. Bodies would lie scattered below each puff, and small groups of wounded men could be seen slowly limping back to the rear, many forced to use their muskets as crutches. Nevertheless, as the lines of attacking infantry continued their seemingly inexorable motion forward, gaps would appear, and the lines became increasingly more ragged. As the attacking formation continued forward, it left in its wake a trail of the dead and dying.

How far the attacking lines were able to advance and, in fact, their ultimate success or failure depended upon a myriad of factors. Foremost among these were the determination and commitment of the troops on both sides, leadership, the amount of defending artillery, and, of course, many unforeseen circumstances. The majority of attacks were able to advance to within 100 to 150 yards of the enemy, and many were able to close to within "pistol range," that is, within about 20 paces or so. The defenders might open fire at long range, trying to stymie the assault at an early stage, but if experienced and well led, they would withhold their fire. If the defenders did hold their ground, the barrels gleaming in the sun would inevitably be leveled. Then followed a short pause that seemed an eternity both to the intended victims in front and those along the line anxiously awaiting the orders to fire. Suddenly, there was a tremendous burst of fire, a tremendous, withering volley, and a light bluish smoke rose up along the length of the defending line. Unlike the smoke from artillery, which leapt higher into the air, that from musketry rose more lazily, even hanging over the ground on a breezeless day or clinging to the foliage, if any was present.

The effect of the volley, delivered at such close range, was frequently devastating. Someone glancing at the attacking line a moment after the defender's volley might be reminded of a gale. The line of men appeared as if blown down by a "blast from a tempest." Dismayed by the sudden horror, in most cases the leading elements would run back in complete disorder. The panic contagious, the second line, if close enough behind, and sometimes even the third line would be carried along by the routed tide. Most often the rout would continue back for 150 to 200 yards, until the panicked men found refuge in a hollow or behind undulating ground. The enemy artillery would relentlessly continue to ply the ranks with metal and cause more casualties than ever. Riding among the disorganized masses of men, officers would grab the regimental colors and scream at the men to rally and reform. Eventually, the officers' efforts would have an effect, and here and there among the milling crowd, small portions of a line would start to form, much like crystalline structures coagulating around isolated precipitants in a chemical solution. As the process continued, these isolated sections of line gradually stretched out until the whole mass was once more re-formed.

But other points along the attacking line might have more success. The attackers sometimes succeeded in advancing to close range, and then it would be the defenders' turn to panic and flee. At other times the attacking line would be neither routed nor immediately

victorious but would stall, and its men, despite the officers' exhortations, began to fire individually, and the battle quickly became general. The individual shots merged into one continuous sound,
producing a thundering roll or crackle of musketry, punctuated periodically by booming of the artillery. Almost deafening in volume, the
deadly cacophony drowned out the officers' commands, as well as the
men's screams and groans. Thomas L. Livermore, a Union sergeant
during the Seven Days' battles (June 25–July 1, 1862), likened the
"piping tones" of the minié balls as they whizzed above to "a very
small circular saw cutting through thin strips of wood." Coming all
too close to the men's heads, the bullets reminded him of large blue
flies that sometimes flew high and at other times seemed to pass close
to one's ears. One Northern newspaper correspondent would describe
his impressions of being fired at: "You hear a drop, drop, drop, as a
few of the skirmishers fire, followed by a rattle and roll, which sounds
like a falling of a building, just as you heard the bricks tumble at a
great fire."

Most often the sharp, noisy rattling of the musketry would soon be
swallowed by the booming of the artillery. To John Robson, who
fought on the Confederate side, this thunderous sound reminded him
of "a mighty, rushing wind, [which] rises, swells, lulls, and roars
again along the line." In a moment much of the soldiers' surroundings were wrapped in smoke, and on a windless day it was possible
for the entire battlefield to be enveloped. At Antietam a group of
newspaper correspondents, civilians, and even a few officers scampered up an incline hoping to gain a panoramic view of the murderous contest. George Noyes later recalled that they saw only the
"usual battle panorama"; the smoke prevented them from distin-
guishing a single battery or brigade. A. F. Hill of the Eighth Pennsylvania Reserves recalled that during the Second Battle of Bull Run
(August 29–30, 1862), the smoke was so dense that he could not see
the enemy in front lying in wait. He never forgot the sound of the
Minié bullets striking and crushing the bones of those around him.

The battle, or "the ball," as it was often referred to, was now in full
swing. The artillerymen would hear a "wack, wack" as Minié bullets
struck the wheels and the guns. Very occasionally, a caisson loaded
with artillery ammunition would explode, and for a few seconds parts

of the charred wagon and mangled bodies of men would rain down throughout the immediate area. Sergeant Foster's description of his regiment's experience during the First Battle of Fredericksburg (December 13, 1862) provides a universal description of the sheer horror of any hard-fought contest during the Civil War:

> No one who has not witnessed such a scene can form any idea of the awfulness of that hour, the fearful screeching of the shells, the ominous buzzing and the vicious whistling of canister and the endless, "ping ping" of the minie balls, while the reports of the musketry was one continual crash and, far and above all, the thunderous tones of hundreds of cannon, completely drowned the encouraging shouts of the officers. The whole line was enveloped in a cloud of sulphurous smoke, almost hiding the regiments from each other and through which crimson flares of the muskets and cannon darted fiery tongues. What carnage! Comrades fell all around you, mangled and bleeding, the colors go down, but are raised to fall again and again, the line moves forward with decreasing speed until when past the center of the plain it finally stops, fires a few spasmodic volleys, wavers, breaks and flees to the protection of the bank from whence it had started. Then, without delay, it reforms, moves up the bank and the tragedy is re-enacted.

A momentary breeze would occasionally push aside the low-lying smoke clouds, and if the infantryman could detach himself from loading and firing his weapon, he might see "thousands of busy reapers in the harvest of death" and the effects of the carnage. Occasionally, shot (solid cannonballs) would be seen skipping along through the enemy's formations. When this happened, the gap produced in the enemy's ranks was "for an appreciable instant like the splash produced by striking the surface of water with a stick." This gap was produced as much by men quickly dodging out of the path of the incoming projectile as it was by the physical destruction of those not fortunate enough to see the deadly missile or be able to get out its way. This dodging or ducking motion was an involuntary reaction based on the strongest instinct for survival. It also occurred whenever

the troops heard a shell passing overhead. As one veteran would
recount in his regimental history:

> It was always interesting to notice the men of the army when-
> ever a rebel shell came their way. It was impossible to resist
> the temptation to 'dodge' it, and the men could do this with
> better precision than drill—all dodging together.

During the War of Independence, the motion of men's heads in
unison had reminded an observer of ducks. Everyone agreed, and
the term *duck* stuck. This reaction was so predictable that someone
standing at a distance could trace the path of an invisible projectile
crossing the battlefield by the successive ducking of heads, reminiscent of the "waving of grain in the wind." This tendency was
greatest, of course, among newly raised regiments as they experienced their baptism of fire. Officers would do their best to curtail
this reaction, explaining that the projectiles traveled more quickly
than the sound they made passing through the air. Once they heard
any projectile, it had already safely passed by, and conversely, the
shell that would hit them could not be heard. No matter how much
the officers cajoled their men about ducking, however, the tendency
continued under fire nearly unabated.

About 25 to 35% of Civil War artillery was still smoothbore. When
these pieces fired solid round shot, the opposite situation was occasionally encountered. It was not uncommon for round shot ricocheting at extreme ranges to travel at comparatively slow speeds, as
little as 4 or 5 feet per second. Sometimes a soldier was foolish
enough to try and stop a slow-moving cannonball with an arm or leg.
Unbeknownst to the hapless soldier, the round shot was spinning at
very high speeds and possessed enormous centrifugal energy. It
wasn't unheard of for such a seemingly harmless cannonball to tear
off an arm or a leg. Other times the soldier was lucky enough just to
be thrown backwards head over heels, and for a moment it would
appear to his comrades that he was following the cannonball that he
had just tried to stop.

The battle meanwhile raged on in all its fury. Even after many of
the frontline formations had long been committed, the generals and

their staffs could still be seen in frenzied activity. Their horses now foaming with sweat, couriers and staff officers furiously galloped from one command to another, handing out written instructions or verbally passing on important orders. Here and there brigades, even divisions, wheeled and then set off to occupy some vulnerable position or, conversely, to exploit some newly discovered enemy flank.

Despite standing orders to the contrary and all the efforts of the officers to effect compliance, all too often the artillery and infantry on both sides would fire continuously. Sorely pressed and forced to beat off successive infantry assaults, some batteries started to deplete their ammunition. If they were lucky, ammunition wagons soon would be ordered forward to restock their ammunition.

Artillerymen were rarely limited to a single type of projectile. If the range was great, they probably would start by firing shell, then switch over to solid shot, and then finally to canister. Veteran soldiers could even differentiate between enemy shells fired from smoothbores and those coming from the new rifled ordnance. Fired upon by Union artillery, George Neese, who served with Chew's Battery, attached to "Stonewall" Jackson's forces in the Shenandoah Valley, immediately noted that "from the clear whiz of the shell" all eight enemy pieces were rifled.

At the Battle of Slaughter's Mountain, Virginia (August 9, 1862), or Cedar Run, as it became known in the North, the gunners in Rockbridge Battery were mystified when they heard Union shells reminiscent of "the shrill note of a tree-frog [but] on a big scale." In the weeks following the battle, some of the men speculated about what "new engine of war" they were facing. Their curiosity was finally answered when they captured the Union stores at Manassas Junction, where two guns different from anything seen before were found atop a railroad flatcar. The cannon turned out to be the 3-inch Ordnance rifles soon to become quite popular among both Union and Confederate artillerymen.

The farmers and shopkeepers who filled the volunteer armies were initially surprised that they occasionally could actually see the shot and shells that were sent over to put an end to their existence. This was possible when they were standing directly along the path of fire and, of course, if they happened to be looking straight ahead that moment. Neese remembered his first experience of being fired at by a Federal battery:

> March 23 '63—the first shell they fired at us from a battery on our right was a twelve-pounder, and I saw it flying in its graceful curve through the air, coming directly towards the spot where I was standing. I watched it until it struck the ground fifteen yards in front of me. . . . I was . . . surprised shell could be so plainly seen during its flight. . . . I for a moment forgot danger linked in the black speck that was descending to earth.

The percussion shell exploded upon impact, covered Neese with dirt and debris, and brought his attention back to the realities of the battlefield.

This experience taught Neese not to look at these incoming shells so dispassionately. During a later engagement, once again Neese noticed a projectile hurling directly toward him. This time he quickly moved 8 feet to the side, and lucky thing for him he did so, as the shell landed exactly where he had been standing!

Not surprisingly, as with Neese, the fact that artillery shells could frequently be seen by the intended victims sometimes proved to the reason for their survival. Trooper Harris with the Fifth Michigan Volunteer Cavalry was talking to a friend named Pennington at Gettysburg, when the latter yelled, "Jump!" Both troopers instantly rolled out of their saddles and onto the ground. A second or so later a shell buried itself harmlessly in the ground 30 feet to their rear. Frederick Phisterer, who fought with the Regular Brigade of the XIV Army Corps, would recollect another notable example at Murfreesboro, Tennessee (noon, December 31, 1862). His line had ample opportunity to observe the rebel shells on their inbound flight. One man returning from the rear was working his way back to his position in the very front line of infantry. The men in the rear ranks suddenly noticed a ball fast closing in upon the very spot where the man was walking. Fortunately, the soldier also noticed the danger and quickly made a "profound obeisance." The ball hit a few feet in front of the man and then ricocheted up. It certainly would have decapitated him had he not taken the evasive action. His comrades in the rear, relieved of the nervous suspense and reacting to the ludicrousness of the situation, broke out in laughter.

Of course, after dark it was no longer possible to see ordinary shot and percussion shells. However, it was still possible to detect fused shells, though it took an experienced eye to recognize a potentially lethal threat. Edward Moore in the Confederate Rockbridge Battery explains that he and his companions were fooled at Antietam:

> It was now dark, and our range had been accurately gathered. After each discharge of our opponent's guns, what appeared to be a harmless spark of fire, immovable as a star, repeatedly deceived us. It was the burning fuse in the head of the shell which, coming straight toward us, seemed stationary until the shell shot by or burst.

BEING HIT

As the battle intensified, the zip, zip, zip of small arms fire could be heard along the lines. If both sides were still several hundred yards apart, both bullet and shell seemed to fly about in an "indiscriminate, aimless sort of way," and anyone could be hit randomly. Inevitably, casualties would start to mount. It might begin with a single man fortunate enough to receive only a slight wound. Occasionally, some such struck by bullets escaped serious injury. If this casualty possessed enough strength and stamina, he might be able to work his way back to the rear.

After the Battle of Labadieville, Louisiana (October 27, 1862), the first lieutenant of Company D of the Twelfth Connecticut would tell Captain De Forest that during the regiment's advance, he saw two of his men fall and roll over. At first he thought they were shirkers trying to escape. It appeared that as they rolled over and over, each man was "struggling to squirm undermost in order to escape the bullets." The lieutenant hit the top man with the flat of his saber and yelled for them to get back into their ranks. One was able to get up immediately and, grabbing his rifle, ran to rejoin his company. The second, however, simply pointed to a bloody hole in his trousers and remained on the ground. The incoming bullet had hit the first man's rifle with such a force as to knock him down.

Glancing off the rifle, the bullet entered the second man's thigh, felling him with the other.

As the two sides closed, the trickle of casualties was sure to soon become a torrent. A.F. Hill served with the eighth Pennsylvania Volunteer Reserves at Gaines's Mill (east of Richmond, June 27, 1862). Despite having to load and fire as fast as possible, Hill couldn't help noticing his comrades' reaction when hit by small arms fire:

> Here a man would suddenly start, drop his gun, and limp away—the blood flowing from a wound in his leg; another would suddenly spring in the air, uttering a piercing shriek, then fall back, quivering—lifeless—his eyes staring vacantly—his teeth set—his hands clenched till the fingernails cut into the palms. Another would sink to the ground without a groan—without a grasp for the suddenly departing breath. Another would convulsively clasp his hand to his breast—perhaps brow—a moment stand, then stagger, reel, and fall to the earth gasping for breath—the hot blood gushing from his wound.

At Labadieville, De Forest witnessed just such a reaction. Immediately after the defending rebels delivered their second volley, he heard a "sharp crash" of broken bones to his right, followed by someone yelling "Oh!" in pain and horror. Forest turned to his right just in time to see the color sergeant fall slowly backward, with a stare of "woeful amazement" as the blood literally gushed from his mouth. Though the bullet had hit Sergeant Edward squarely in his front teeth and exited behind the left jaw, the sergeant determinedly clung to the colors as he fell.

In his own memoirs Samuel Wing, a private in the Third Maine Infantry, would claim that many popular accounts of the battlefield created a mistaken conception of combat experience. Many writers, especially newspaper correspondents and popular writers, frequently talked about a "river of blood" in their accounts. This seemed especially the case among those after the war who would attempt to describe the truly hellacious conditions and events where the action had been intensely contested, such as at Bloody Angle, the Hornet's

Nest, and Bloody Lane. In reality, such were figures of speech, rather than actual fact. Wing pointed out that unless one was talking about a small stream in which there accumulated numbers of dead and dying, there was no such thing as a river of blood! Ordinarily, the ground and grass roots absorbed any blood flowing from an unfortunate victim almost as fast as it left the body. Wing also noted that in the first years after the war, many writers claimed that fife and drum were used to drown out the shrieks and screams of those dying or severely wounded. He maintained that during his whole battlefield experience, he never even heard a shriek. Firstly, given the "roar of the cannon and whistle of bullets," which far surpassed anything civilians would ever hear at a Fourth of July celebration, no musical accompaniment was necessary. But more to the point, Wing noticed that "the first effect of a [grave] wound is numbness, and the wounded seldom speak above a whisper, which is hard to hear in time of battle."

THE WOUNDED

Of course, not everyone was engaged in the death struggle along the front lines. Many had to wait nervously in some reserve formation in the rear. Others had to stand guard over a wagon train or command post in some safer place. These fortunates would anxiously follow the course of the battle by listening to the decreasing or increasing rattle of musketry and booming of artillery, or by tracing the progress of the dense clouds of smoke that rose over every battlefield.

Though for the moment spared the risk of bodily harm, they would be subjected to another form of horror, which was the inevitable result of any hotly contested engagement. The empty ambulances would gallop off to pick up the passengers that were sure to be awaiting them. Then, not too many minutes later, there would emerge the procession of stragglers, followed by the wounded. The first, scared and embarrassed, tried to remain as inconspicuous as possible; the latter totally focused on a single overriding objective: to reach the rear and much-needed medical attention. Some would come along limping quickly, still carrying shoulder arms; others more severely wounded were only able to drag themselves slowly and painfully. Occasionally, one might see an officer helped off the field by several of his men, possibly a general in a blanket with a soldier holding each corner. In many regiments musicians were frequently employed as a type of primitive medics, whose duty was to act as stretcher-bearers and carry the wounded back to the surgeons' area. The ambulances, which had set off so quickly, now could be seen slowly making their way back fully laden with their ghastly cargo.

In large-scale actions where the eventuality of combat was known several hours in advance, hospitals were established in the rear. Many of the more grievously wounded would be unable to survive the journey unless they first received lifesaving medical attention on or near the battlefield. Surgeons on both sides therefore set up, usually in relatively sheltered areas near the front lines, what euphemistically could be called first aid stations to perform their craft.

In reality these had more in common with the bespattered slaughterhouses that reeked of blood and whose floors were covered with chopped-off animal parts. William Blackford, who at this point was a cavalry lieutenant in J. E. B. Stuart's command, would never forget encountering the surgeons' tables during the First Battle of Bull Run. Trotting in a column of fours toward the sounds of battle, the regiment entered a "shady little valley," whose contours and flora sheltered the unfortunates from both the sun and enemy projectiles. But the sights, sounds, and smells of that place were unforgettable and would be forever etched on the mind of anyone who chanced upon the scene. By the time Blackford's regiment rode by, the surgeons had been practicing their trade all morning. Blackford's own words probably best describe what the cavalrymen saw:

> Tables about breast high had been erected upon which screaming victims were having legs and arms cut off. The surgeons and their assistants, stripped to the waist and all bespattered with blood, stood around, some holding knifes and saws, cut and sawed away with frightful rapidity, throwing the mangled limbs on a pile near by as soon as removed. Many were stretched on the ground awaiting their turn, many more were arriving continually, either limping along or borne on stretchers, while those upon whom operations had already been performed calmly fanned the flies from their wounds. But among these last, alas! some moved not— for them the surgeon's skill had not availed.

The "prayers, the curses, the screams, the blood, the flies, the sickening stench of the horrible little valley" proved too much for many of Stuart's troopers, and Blackford remembers seeing more than one trooper leaning sideways over the saddles and violently vomiting as the column continued its trot toward the sound of the roaring battle.

Though such scenes would become commonplace as the war dragged on and the number of large-scale actions multiplied, they never seemed to lose their effect on the observer. Forced to walk through just such a field hospital, Abner, a Union veteran, saw his own share of horrors. Here he noticed an "endless procession of agony from the ambulances to the hospital, an endless procession of death from the hospital to the burial ditch." His most vivid recollections were of four men walking past him, each holding a corner of an army blanket. When he looked closer, to his dismay Abner noticed a trickle of blood dripping from the folds and inside a pile of arms and legs! The surgeons and their assistants here had certainly been busy trying to save the lives of their charges the only way they knew how—amputation. A few moments later another ghastly sight presented itself. A soldier was slumped against the corner of a wall, his blood still pulsing though the top of his head had been shot away. The sufferer was vainly grasping for life, if only for a moment or two more.

E. R. Hutchins, who served as an assistant surgeon with the Union's Army of the Potomac, remembers that the situation after the first Battle of Fredericksburg was particularly trying:

> On the closing night in this battle I took a train of ambulances filled with wounded across the river on our retreat. There was no shelter, and there was a cold drizzling rain. We laid the poor sufferers on the ground, and at daylight the sight was pitiable. During the evening, before the retreat was ordered, I was stationed in a large church, doing my duty as assistant surgeon. Occasionally, a shot or piece of shell would land in the church, wounding or killing some one or more who had already suffered. The lights were finally ordered put out and each surgeon was compelled to stand just as he was when darkness came upon us. A step or two taken was liable to end on some poor

sufferer. The groans and moans, the pleading for water, and even begging to be killed were entering every heart, and made the stoutest quail.

THE AFTERMATH

No matter how many men had been brought to bear, how important the position, how desperate the fight, the engagement would sooner or later come to an end, usually later that same day before nightfall. Even those fortunate enough to escape without injury did not really escape unscathed. They would be completely exhausted, some even psychologically devastated. Provided by a veteran of the Mexican-American War, this account of a soldier's state at the end of a hard-fought engagement describes the universal experience of battle:

> Fighting is very hard work, the man who has passed through two hours' fight has lived through a great amount of mental labor. At the end of a battle, I always found that I had perspired so profusely as to wet all my clothes. I was as sore as if I had been beaten all over with a club.

In most cases one side or the other, if not clearly victors, could at least boast command of the battlefield. Parties of infantry then would be detailed to scour the ground and bring in the wounded. Discarded arms from friend and foe alike would be piled in stands and later systematically retrieved. Others not officially directed, if they were not injured nor just totally worn out—physically and emotionally—might walk the field, just for curiosity's sake.

A roving band of curiosity seekers might come up to an embankment, ditch, or thicket of bushes and trees where the action had been particularly hard fought. Here bodies would be found in numbers, in many positions, as death often caught its victims unaware. Henry Davidson, who fought as a Union artilleryman on the left of McCook's division at Corinth (May 27, 1862), describes just such a situation. The rebels had stubbornly held onto a thicket 200 yards in front of a Union battery. Determined to crush the enemy in front, his battery fired 279 rounds of shell and canister. After the battle Davidson found the ground around thickly populated with the enemy dead.

Almost all the branches were sheared off as if a "tornado of hail" had swept through. Many men were struck down just as they were reloading their weapons; others seemed to be peacefully reclining back against a log, tree, or pile of dirt. What struck Davidson was that the "fatal messenger reached its victim, leaving them almost as natural as life."

If the weather was either warm or damp, the "sightseers" would notice a nauseating moldy odor. Sgt. Thomas L. Livermore would always remember this smell. He always attributed it to the pervasive presence of fresh blood, though he reasoned it could have also been simply the smell of the torn soil.

One of the most vivid descriptions of the aftermath of a Civil War battle has been left by E. R. Hutchins, who recorded his observations after the first Battle of Fredericksburg. That night, cautiously walking around the Union perimeter of the battlefield, our observer noticed

> mangled forms, rent and tossed, as if maddened beasts of the arena had run riot among them. Limbs flung from their bodies, and half trampled in the mire. Grave faces, stark and stiff and deadly pale, looking like phantom lights. They looked like something neither dead nor living, with a fixedness that was more than stillness. There were open eyes that saw not, and hands still grasping muskets with a clutch that no living strength could loose. Horses, cannoneers, dismounted guns, crashed wheels, overturned gun carriages, the tongues upright in the air, and the yokes swinging like gibbets on high.

Depending upon the temperature, the surrounding area soon began literally to take on the most unpleasant atmosphere as the corpses started to rot. During the war there was actually some debate as to who would decay more quickly, a Confederate or a Federal soldier! The fighting at Antietam was so desperate that Union forces were unable to bury all the dead. Three days after the fighting, many of the corpses started to bloat and discolor. Jacob Roemer, who walked over the field, claimed he could distinguish a rebel from a Union soldier by the color of the skin. The Confederate dead by this point were all swollen and black, while the skin of those on the Union side remained white. Roemer attributed this to the lack of salt in the Confederates' diet. Edward Moore, who fought under Stonewall Jackson, remembers seeing exactly the opposite after the First Bull Run, however. Here Moore claims it was the Union soldiers who were swollen and blacked, while the rebels remained white! Once again, he reasoned that the difference lay in the diet of those in the opposing armies.

Usually, after the wounded were cleared, the burial parties made their way onto the field to perform their grim task. If permitted by the overall strategic situation and with sufficient human resources, the bodies would be removed, and a crude but organized graveyard hastily created. If the exigencies of the campaign demanded prompt movement or there were not enough laborers, the dead were buried where they fell. This was particularly the case after especially heavy fighting, where the ground sometimes was covered with corpses. When this happened, the fallen often were interred in the most makeshift of graves. Sometimes it seemed that only a few shovels of dirt were hastily thrown over the bodies.

It was not uncommon for soldiers a few days later to walk over the same ground and see here and there an arm or a leg projecting up through the ground. This seems to have been a common occurrence during the Peninsular Campaign in '62, where the watery ground prevented more elaborate ceremony. Lt. Josiah Favill recounts how after Fair Oaks all that could be done was to dig a little ditch around each of the fallen and then throw the dirt thus loosened over the body. The heavy rains soon rendered these efforts futile, and entire heads would soon appear above the ground, creating the most gruesome of scenes. As the months passed, the situation would only worsen.

R. H. Peck, who served with the rebel Army of Northern Virginia, had an experience similar to Favill's as he traveled over the many battlefields around Richmond. There was one spot in particular that was etched on his memory. Early in the spring of 1863, he chanced to pass over the site of an engagement that had taken place the previous July. He would always remember crossing a field where the Yankees had delivered a determined charge. It was only with difficulty that he could keep from stepping on bones still wrapped in torn bits of blue uniform. There had been so many corpses that the rebels simply threw the dead Union soldiers in gullies, which they covered as best they could with earth. When the spring rains came, the shallow covering was completely washed away, and the ground was strewn with skulls for half a mile along the streamlets. Some soldiers had little respect for the deceased and sought to take advantage of this carnage. While crossing the ghastly little field, Peck noticed a man from his regiment who had been a dentist before the war. Busy examining the skulls to see if they contained any gold fillings, he had already extracted quite a number and had his haversack completely full of teeth.

Writing many years after the cessation of hostilities, W. W. Blackford would recall that he had found it not only interesting but extremely instructive to ride over the battlefield after a hard-fought contest—provided that the dead and wounded were as of yet unmoved. Not only could a dedicated soldier heighten his understanding of the relationship between strategy and the topography of the contested real estate, but he could also gain a sense of the tactics used in each part of the battlefield and its effectiveness. The density of casualties simultaneously indicated both offensive and defensive positions, their relative strengths, and sometimes even the result of each action in the drama. Walking over the Second Bull Run battlefield at the end of the first day of action, Blackford noted how each "front" was sharply defined, the rows of the dead in nearly perfect straight lines, as though the troops were "lying down to rest." This was the telltale sign that these men had been mowed down by a withering volley or the onset of a quickly executed file fire. Individual fire would produce a more ragged line of bodies. The bodies were then more randomly scattered behind the lines, telling the melancholy tale of those who struggled to reach the rear during their last moments after receiving a mortal wound.

Of course, where there had been repeated charges over the same stretch of ground, such distinct lines of casualties gradually became blurred, as each attacking impulse left its dead at a slightly different point along the advance. By the end of the second day of the Second Bull Run, Blackford would observe that the ground in front of the Confederates was:

so thickly covered with the fallen that it looked like one vast blue carpet. I do not mean that the ground was really entirely covered, but at a distance, one body obstructing the vision of several yards beyond, the effect was that described.

This phenomenon, although statistically rare when considering all 7000 or so Civil War actions, engagements, and battles, certainly was found at most of the hardest-fought battles, such as Bloody Lane at Antietam, the defense along the railroad cuts at Second Bull Run, the Hornet's Nest at Shiloh, Spottsylvania, and Cold Harbor. When it did occur, the very concentration of casualties posed a challenge to any ordered formation that attempted to cross over previously contested ground. John McLaughlin, who fought with Union forces at Antietam, recounts how only with difficulty was his regiment able to traverse Sharpsburg Road, the ground by this point littered with rebel dead and wounded. In one particular case the rebel casualties lay "in long lines or ranks in ghastly mechanical regularity," and the greatest exertion was required to step over the dead and dying.

A glance at the dead could also tell a keen observer about the effectiveness of the weapons that had been directed against each area:

For there lies the harvest they have reaped, each sheaf distinctly labeled with the name of the reaper in the wound received. Artillery tears its sheaves out by the roots and scatters the fragments, while infantry mows them down in well heaped windrows.

An experienced observer could also tell whether the casualties had been caused by bayonet, small arms fire, or artillery. Obviously, an explosive shell often mangled its victims, and it was not uncommon for body parts to be thrown outward in concentric circles from the center of the explosion. Solid shot, on the other hand, would decapitate, tear off a limb, or possibly punch a large hole through an otherwise undisturbed body. Although to an untrained eye the difference between a bayonet wound and that caused by small arms could only be ascertained by close scrutiny of the victim, living or otherwise, the battlefield habitué quickly learned to differentiate between the two wounds at a glance, even from afar. Capt. Oscar Jackson, who served in the Western theater remembers how an old veteran pulled him aside and claimed he could tell who was shot and who had been bayoneted to death at a single glance. One simply had to look at the faces. Those who had been killed by bayonet wounds "have a contorted appearance, as if cramped, that enables them to be selected from a pile of dead from those who were otherwise slain." These of course were extremely rare cases, only one or two instances likely to be found on a major battlefield.

Regardless of the lessons of war that could be gleaned, most soldiers were unable to remain dispassionate, remembering that the dead laying about them had been breathing, walking souls just a few short hours before. Somewhere a mother would never see her darling son again, a wife would be forever separated from her husband, a son his father. Years later while writing his memoirs, Colonel Bishop of the Second Minnesota couldn't help but contrast the difference in feelings during and immediately after the battle:

> Men can, in the enthusiasm and excitement of battle, see and take part in the murderous work without realizing how horrible it is, but to go over the field the day afterwards, and in cool blood to gather up the mangled and suffering victims, gives a life-long impression of the cruelty of war and of its pitiful waste of human life.

Despite the saddening, melancholic feelings that were inevitably engendered, many, if not most, men succumbed to an unfathomable fascination bordering on morbid voyeurism. Walking over the ground after the Battle of Iuka, Mississippi (September 19, 1862), Capt. Oscar Jackson remembers being impelled by a strange curiosity to look at the dead men's faces and their wounds. Paradoxically, almost perversely, there was something about the exercise that reminded him of a picnic during more peaceful times, one seemed to hunt for the dead bodies "as for strawberries in a meadow."

Chapter 13

LIFE DURING THE CAMPAIGN

THE CONFEDERATE EXPERIENCE

During the first rush to the colors, Confederate recruits placed a premium on high boots, long gloves, fancy caps, and heavily padded coats with long tails and numerous buttons. Their knapsacks were crammed with everything potentially useful: extra underwear, towels, combs, brushes, blocking, looking glasses, needles, thread, buttons, and even bandages. Often weighing up to 50 pounds, all this made marching a torturous experience.

Always a stern taskmaster, experience soon demonstrated that fancy apparel and a motley collection of accoutrements not only were unnecessary, but they were also harmful encumbrances that sapped men's energy and slowed down the march. For the infantryman, at least, the sturdy, functional appearance of large boots was illusory. The narrow heels quickly wore out more on one side, and very soon the foot soldier had to constantly worry about twisting an ankle as he stepped on the countless rocks, and other minor obstacles encountered during the day's march. Once wet, high boots were always a challenge to put on quickly when answering roll call and very difficult to take off at the end of the day. Long gloves proved worse than useless; so encumbered, the infantrymen could not handle an axe, load his musket, or even buckle a harness.

Events soon forced the Civil War soldier to brave the harshest elements: torrential rainstorms, windy days, and in the winter even blizzards and sleet storms. It is natural to think that a large, seemingly warm overcoat would be highly valued and only discarded in extreme circumstances. The long overcoat, however, soon met the same fate as boots and gloves. It was not worth the inconvenience of carrying around a bulky coat throughout the summer and other warm weather, simply for a small benefit when it finally turned cold. Most of the men threw them away, confident that they could either serendipitously find a replacement when needed or just do without. A few determined souls continued to carry their overcoats all year round. The short jackets and double-knit wool breeches were much warmer than the modern would suspect, however, and by this point, out in the field day after day for months, the men's bodies had become so acclimatized to weather extremes that they were able to endure changes in the climate with remarkable indifference.

As a result, short, single-breasted jackets almost ubiquitously were substituted for the long, tailed overcoats. The Southern version quickly was dubbed a "gray jacket." The legions of parasitical arthropods that invariably infested the garment, incidentally, were known as "graybacks." Cotton garments were considered more desirable than flannel and "merino," not only because they were easier to wash, but, more importantly, because they were much less attractive to insects. Wide brogans now replaced the useless boots for infantry, while gloves were discarded. The regulation French-inspired kepis eventually fell victim to the same trend. Gradually, most men chose to substitute the soft felt slouch hat, which not only was much more comfortable but afforded greater protection from the elements.

At the beginning of the war, almost everyone attempted to carry one or two changes of clothes. The men expected to be able to wash their soiled clothes in cauldrons of hot water and then store the clean clothes in the knapsack until needed. Unfortunately, during active campaigning hot water was rarely available. The alternative, a cold-water wash, neither cleaned the clothes nor got rid of the fleas and lice and was a waste of time and effort. The most common solution was simply not to wash one's clothes. Most men possessed only the clothes on their back, which they wore until frayed and torn, at which point they would scrounge around for timely replacements. The real advantage was not so much that there was one less housekeeping task to perform but that the heavy knapsack could now be cast aside. Not only did this cumbersome appendage chafe the neck and shoulders; it was heavy to carry and more than anything else wore the soldier out during a long march.

By his second campaign the rebel soldier typically only had what he wore, plus a blanket, gum-cloth, haversack, and a canteen slung over this shoulder. On the belt hung the heavy cap box and cartridge box. Some soldiers were even known to throw away these boxes and place their contents in their pockets. Some even cast aside their haversacks, squeezing smoking tobacco, pipe, and a small bar of soap into their pockets, along with the powder and bullets. Contrary to the new recruit's expectations, the revolver was found to be as useless as "heavy lumber" and was quickly sent back home.

In his *Detailed Minutiae of Soldier Life*, describing what it was like to campaign with the Army of Northern Virginia, Carlton McCarthy claimed that the canteen was not used as much to store water as it was to convey buttermilk, cider, or sorghum back to camp after foraging expeditions. Many even dispensed with the canteen and relied upon the tin cup they carried in their haversack to meet all of their liquid vessel needs. McCarthy tells of one very ingenious Confederate infantryman who devised a way of dispensing with the canteen. After each victorious engagement, this soldier would walk the battlefield and pick up whatever canteens he could find. Then he would give these to those in his regiment who needed a canteen, with the proviso that they allow him to take a swig whenever he wanted. McCarthy estimated that at any one time this soldier had made this same arrangement with about forty of his comrades.

The company equipment underwent similar reduction and now was limited to a skillet and a couple of frying pans.

THE MARCH

Other than a small percentage of troops on permanent garrison duty, during the campaign season most soldiers on either side were rarely stationed in one place for lengthy periods. There were a few notable exceptions, such as when the Army of the Potomac was assembled across from Fredericksburg in preparation for an assault against this key Confederate position, but these were exceptions caused by strategic considerations. One finds innumerable instances of a regiment, division, even an entire army rushing off at the last moment to seize some objective or to counter the enemy's plans.

The march became a part of daily routine, and frequently, the men found themselves on a long advance during extreme heat, severe rainstorms, or winter blizzards. A description from the Nineteenth Massachusetts marching through Virginia during the summer months is probably typical of the summer experience:

> The sun was now well up and the air intensely hot, causing the perspiration to run out and, running down the face, drip from the nose and chin. The salty liquid got into the eyes, causing them to burn and smart and it ran from under the cap, through the dust and down the sides of the face which was soon covered with muddy streaks, the result of repeat wiping upon the sleeves of the blouse.

Marching along roads on a clay bed proved particularly problematic. On a hot, dry summer day, the thousands of stomping feet and horses' hooves would quickly pulverize the clay into a fine, flourlike dust, which frequently lay on the ground several inches deep. Riding along these roads, cavalrymen often found they couldn't see their comrades riding just a few paces to the side or front. Infantrymen were especially affected whenever they had the misfortune to be passed by either artillery or mounted troops. Men in the 102nd Illinois would remember one particularly memorable occasion when while marching toward Frankfort, Kentucky on October 8, 1862 they were pulled off the road in a narrow place to let a cavalry force pass. They were soon enveloped by a large cloud of dust. Later that evening they experienced an even greater dust bowl when once again they were forced off the road to give an artillery train the right of way. This time the dust "filled the atmosphere from hill-top to hill-top and veiled the face of the rising moon."

Marching along limestone beds often produced a like effect. During Buell's great 300-mile race to Louisville at the end of September 1862, Colonel B. F. Scribner of the Thirty-eighth Indiana Volunteers would forever remember his emotions as he gazed upon his men during this memorable forced march:

> It was a rare and touching sight to see these poor fellows so covered with limestone dust that their garments, beards, hair and visages were all of the same color, all seeming old and gray

with the dust and bending under the burden of their guns and knapsacks, limping along with blistered feet. They appeared more like grim spectres than young and sturdy men.

Marching conditions only got worse as the weather changed. If it was miserable to march along clay or limestone roads in sunny, dry weather, it quickly became a nightmare when it rained. A rebel soldier who served in the command of Gen. John Breckenridge (vice-president under Buchanan and Southern Democrat presidential candidate in 1860) during 1861–62, recalled that this army, sometimes 55,000 strong, was often accompanied by a thousand wagons. In the fall and spring, the rain, which often turned to sleet, seemed to fall "four days out of seven," and the men were forced to camp without tents in a dripping forest or in wet fields, thoroughly chilled, lying all the while in wet clothing, often without even the benefit of a fire.

Not surprisingly, the Confederate army suffered great losses from desertion and sickness. The towns along the route were left full of the sick. During one particularly grueling 30-mile march, one quarter of the division fell by the wayside and had to be collected by the rear guard, and soon every available wagon and ambulance was filled up with exhausted stragglers.

The back roads that now bore the burden of hundreds of wagons and artillery pieces, not to mention the tramping of thousands of feet, quickly became a quagmire. As this happened, the roads became a little lower than the ground on either side, so that even an hour's rain would turn the sooty dust into "liquid mud, and so change a man's personal appearance that his own mother could not have recognized him." The roadway thus transformed, soldiers would find it extremely difficult to make headway. The inches of dust was now a murky guck that sometimes enveloped a leg up to the shins and was so sticky that it was difficult to draw out the foot in order to take the next step. This extra effort added greatly to an already exhausting effort and accelerated the rate at which men fell by the wayside. Cavalrymen would encounter similar difficulties, and the horses' hoofs would sink so deeply into the mud that the riders would have to dismount and struggle ahead one pace at a time like the infantry.

Wagons and artillery experienced even greater difficulty. Becoming hopelessly stuck, wagons would be abandoned, and their mules were doubled up, even tripled up, with other teams in an effort to continue the advance. The artillery couldn't be abandoned at any cost, and it was not unheard of to attach 24 mules or horses to a single piece. Sometimes even such massive motive power proved insuffi- cient, so 20-foot prolongs were attached to the piece, and branches and wood rails were slid under the wheels. Then the gunners, assisted by whatever infantry was at hand, would take a running start and try to yank the artillery piece out of the quagmire and onto drier ground, should any exist. During this Herculean effort, it was common for horses and mules to break their legs, and the wayside would eventually be littered with dead and dying animals and exhausted men lying prostate on the water-soaked ground.

As the rain continued to fall, the brooks and streams would swell and flood. What had been an easy ford but a few days earlier now was transformed into a dangerous, raging current. Col. Judson Bishop, who commanded the Second Minnesota Regiment, remembers how difficult it was to cross the Elk River at Tullahoma, Tennessee, after a severe rainstorm had flooded the river the previous day and knocked out the bridge. A rope was strung across the river to prevent the men from being carried away by the current. The men took off their clothes, cartridge boxes, and knapsacks, tied them all together in a bundle, and hung them from their bayonets. With one hand on the rope and the other raising their muskets in the air, the men waded through the stream in single file. At some points the water reached up to their necks, and although no one in Bishop's regiment was drowned, many lost their bundles and were forced to remain naked until some other clothing was found.

As bad as this was, conditions worsened during the winter. Made to continue forward during a forced march during a blizzard, the men's clothing would eventually become soaked. As the snow piled up, the baggage and artillery trains would lag behind, and so disap- peared the men's hopes for tents, blankets, a quick change of clothing, or other amenities that might have made conditions a little more tolerable when the order finally came to halt that evening. Then, after scavenging the surrounding forest for firewood, log fires would be kindled, and the men would try to thaw out their clothing, now frozen solid with sleet and caked mud. Unfortunately, as soon as one side warmed up and a man turned around, the other side would freeze again. Despite the cold, the men gradually succumbed to fatigue and, lying together in groups for warmth, drifted off into a cold, miserable sleep.

IN CAMP

As troops flocked to the colors on both sides, those responsible for planning an upcoming campaign probably intended the troops to be fed by company messes, and initially, each company was equipped with a few frying pans and skillets. Events would soon prove that the "best laid plans of mice and men aft gang aglee," and the men would frequently be left to cook for themselves. Those fighting for the Confederacy all too often even had to procure their own food. This was partly due to logistical entropy. The same considerations that prompted the individual soldier to lighten his load applied equally to company and even regimental equipment. Many units soon dispensed with company wagons, and the few remaining frying pans and skillets were carried by the soldiers.

The availability of food became an issue as soon as the first Confederate army began assembling in the Manassas area. Writing to his family in the weeks before the First Battle of Bull Run, William Montgomery of the Palmetto Guards (Second South Carolina Volunteers) constantly complained of the shortage of food and the lengths he and his comrades had to go just to find something to eat. On one occasion he and a friend walked 3 miles to beg an old woman to sell them some food. Their pleas were answered, and they were given some bacon, cornbread, butter, and coffee. Whatever rations they did receive consisted of sea biscuits and coffee without sugar. A few weeks later Montgomery reported in a second letter that the situation had worsened and their extemporaneous food-gathering expeditions now ranged up to 5 miles from camp. The situation did not improve, and Montgomery began to try to get his brother to visit him and bring something "nice" to eat.

The experiences of the Confederates during that first summer, however, were but a mild precursor to the extreme privations both

Cooking in a temporary camp. Men from the Nineteenth New York Volunteers are seen baking bread in a temporary camp. *Frank Leslie's Illustrated Weekly,* September 14, 1861.

sides, especially those fighting in the Western theater, were to frequently experience during active campaigning. Even under the best of circumstances, the rations were meager—once again, especially on the Southern side. Two or three days' worth of rations were often distributed at a time, and many of the men would cook and eat the entire lot at one or two sittings. An army on the offensive could outpace its supplies, and Southern armies found themselves in this situation more frequently than armies fighting for the Union. Approaching a house along the road, some men would break ranks and attempt to purchase or, if the population was sympathetic to their cause, entreat for food. George Montgomery would never forget the delicious raspberry jam or the beautiful visages of the young women who supplied such much-appreciated snacks during the long march of the Maryland campaign.

Supply problems more commonly arose out of a sudden reverse or the need to strategically maneuver quickly to counter an unexpected threat. Rudely pushed back in an undesirable direction, the men in the defeated army often had to trudge days through uninhabited land. A company with a crack shot, if they were lucky, might enjoy roasted squirrel or fowl. But most would have to settle for an ear of corn or some unidentifiable flora that would serve as an ersatz vegetable. The rebels in General Zollicoffer's command found themselves in such a situation after a repulse at Mill Springs, Kentucky, on January 19, 1862. Soaking wet from continuous rain, the men in the Nineteenth Tennessee were forced to go to sleep that night in the open and on empty stomachs. The next evening, after a full-day trek, each man received but a small piece of beef, apparently appropriated from some farm since it was "warm from the slaughter." Most of this was immediately roasted on a campfire and consumed, but some men conscientiously saved a few remnants, which they ate before setting off the next morning.

The third evening after the engagement, each man received a hatful of meal, without lard or salt. This posed something of a challenge to cook. After mixing and rolling it up, some men baked it on flat rocks in the fire; others rolled it into strings, which were then wound around their ramrods and held over the fire until cooked.

This austere regimen continued until the Confederate force reached Gainesboro on January 27, where, meeting up with the steamer *Nashville*, the men finally received tents, clothing, and best of all, adequate provisions. Incidentally, this was not the last time the men in this regiment had to endure extreme privation. Later that year they had to subsist several days on "sick flour," so named for the most likely result. Lacking lard or grease, the men used salt and water to work this into biscuits. Unfortunately, the result was so hard that in order to eat them, some men first had to carve holes in their centers, fill them with black powder, and blow them apart!

The tendency to simplify what was carried also affected the prevailing art of castrametation (designing a camp). The tents that had dotted the early Confederate camps of instruction completely disappeared as soon as the fighting began in earnest. Most men carried a gum-cloth and a wool blanket that together were rolled up lengthwise, the gum-cloth on the outside, looped up over the left shoulder, and tied under the right arm. At night the men would pair up and place one of the gum-cloths on the ground. Lying down, they would cover themselves with the two blankets, followed by the other gum-cloth, which protected them from any form of precipitation, whether rain, snow, or sleet.

The exigencies of the campaign, however, often denied the men even these primitive comforts! A sudden enemy attack on an unsuspecting encampment forced a precipitous retreat and the loss of one's belongings. A decisive reverse on the battlefield had the same effect. It was not that rare that the men had to sleep without blanket or oilcloth. William Worsham of the Nineteenth Tennessee recalls one such night after their retreat from Mill Springs in January 1862, when the men were forced to recline on the wet ground.

Taken off guard after a sudden winter storm, the men sometimes found themselves without blankets. In desperation, a dozen soldiers were known to sleep in layers, just the way someone might arrange logs. Four men slept on the ground. Another four slept on top of them but perpendicular to those below them. Those on the third layer lay along the same axis as those on the ground. After 1 or 2 hours, everyone would get up, and each layer would rotate, so that everyone spent the same amount of time in the second layer, which was the warmest. Spooning was a more prevalent sleeping pattern. Each man would lie on his side, with his knees tucked into the back of the knee joints of the man in front of him. The pattern thus formed by several men reminded them of spoons placed in a dining set, hence the name!

Daylight, when it finally came, did not end the men's hardships, as they would awake to new problems. The teams' harnesses would be completely frozen, and the wheels of the carriages immobilized. Valuable time had to be spent chopping and digging away the frozen earth from the spokes and felloes (rims).

The harshness of such conditions and their effects upon man and animal explain why campaigning was kept to a minimum during the deep winter months.

THE MARCH TO THE SEA

The Civil War soldier generally had to endure a tough, Spartan-like existence bereft of amenities, where even the necessities of life were frequently in short supply. There was one notable episode that stood in marked contrast. This of course was Sherman's famous March to the Sea. For the first time the Union troops enjoyed an abundance of food, a moderate amount of comfort,

Plate 1. The Baltimore steam gun, a dubious weapon constructed by Southern sympathizers, was loosely modeled on the Perkins steam gun of the 1840s. It was quickly captured by Union cavalry and never saw action. *Frank Leslie's Illustrated Weekly, May 18, 1861*

Plate 2. De Villeroi's "submarine boat" was seized by Union authorities on May 16, 1861 in the Delaware River near Philadelphia. As with the Baltimore steam gun, its operators were trying to reach Confederate forces when captured. *Frank Leslie's Pictorial History of the War, 1862*

Source of lithographic engravings: Providence Public Library
Photography: William Keyser
Original illustrations: Stewart Gibson

Plate 3. In this depiction of the Battle of Big Bethel (June 10, 1861) between General Piece's and Colonel Magruder's troops, Zouave skirmishers are seen in the left center and Bendix's assault column on the right. Colonel Townsend on horseback can also be seen sending out two companies of skirmishers. *Frank Leslie's Pictorial History of the War, 1862*

Plate 4. Much of the little spare time in camp was spent performing necessary tasks, such as washing clothes and cleaning weapons. These experienced soldiers had learned to hang from a branch the weapons they cleaned. *Frank Leslie's Pictorial History of the War, 1862*

Plate 5. In the months following Fort Sumter, the northern public was haunted by the specter of rebel masked batteries lying in wait to ambush unsuspecting Union forces. The June 17, 1861 attack on a train carrying some of General Schenck's troops by a masked battery greatly heightened these fears. *Frank Leslie's Pictorial History of the War, 1862*

Plate 6. As this illustration of Union forces taking advantage of a rail fence at Laurel Hill shows, men and officers were quick to exploit whatever cover was available (Battle of Bealington July 8, 1862 at 5 P.M.). *Frank Leslie's Pictorial History of the War*

Plate 7. Soldiers had to fight in all weather, inclement or fair. Here, a portion of McClellan's forces led by General Morris had to fight their way across Corrick's Ford during a rainstorm (July 13, 1861). *Frank Leslie's Illustrated Weekly, Aug. 3, 1861*

Plate 8. An "infernal machine" (submerged mines) discovered by the steamer *U.S.S. Resolute.* These submerged explosives had been set afloat by the Confederates on the Potomac River to destroy a Federal flotilla. *Frank Leslie's Pictorial History of the War, 1862*

Plate 9. Nowhere were the "horrors of war" more noticeable than at the rear of the lines as shown in this artist's depiction of the First Battle of Bull Run. *Frank Leslie's Pictorial History of the War, 1862*

Plate 10. Infantry repulsing a cavalry attack seems to validate the old adage "If Foot could be brought to know their own Strength, the Danger from which they apprehend from Horse, would soon vanish." This is especially true, as in this case, when they were supported by artillery on one flank and friendly cavalry on the other. *Frank Leslie's Pictorial History of the War, 1862*

Plate 11. Cavalry, especially partisans and guerrillas, often had to work
their way through difficult terrain. Here, men from General Rosecran's
division working their way through a forest near Laurel Hill, Virginia on
their way to attack Rebel entrenchments at Rich's Mountain. *Frank Leslie's
Illustrated Weekly, Aug. 31, 1861*

Plate 12. The scene of infantrymen pushing a wagon out of a rain-soaked mud-hole was repeated innumerable times on the Virginia Peninsula during the summer of 1862. *Frank Leslie's Illustrated Weekly, Aug. 31, 1861*

Plate 13. Union infantrymen "foraging" in a local farmer's yard. Food supplies were not always available when needed, and soldiers on both sides were often forced to take matters into their own hands. *Frank Leslie's Illustrated Weekly, Sept. 28, 1861*

Plate 14. Cooking facilities and the food tended to improve once the army was settled into a semi-permanent position. *Frank Leslie's Illustrated Weekly, Nov. 2, 1861*

Plate 15. Artillery supports an attacking column, while the low lying smoke along the defending line shows that the latter has opened long range small arms fire, which would probably have been ineffective. Note the closed column of attack on the right. *Frank Leslie's Pictorial History of the War, 1862*

Infantrymen building a road. The Independent Regiment of Cincinnati builds a road across islands in the Ohio River. These were connected to either shore by a "bridge of boats." *Frank Leslie's Pictorial History of the War,* 1862.

and, compared to the ordeals of the previous months, a relative lack of fighting.

The first part of Sherman's 1864 campaign had taken place in very rough, often mountainous countryside of northwestern Georgia, where Joseph E. Johnston's forces had contested the Union advance every step of the way. The nearly continuous fighting took place over a relatively uninhabited region where the solder had neither opportunity nor time for even modest amenities.

All this dramatically changed after mid-November when Sherman's forces advanced out of Atlanta on their march toward Savannah, Georgia. Most of the Confederate forces in the area had been sent to join Hood's reckless bid to recapture Nashville, so Sherman's advance met with little organized opposition. Daily campaigning was certainly not completely devoid of danger, however. Now operating in small groups, the Confederate opposition periodically mounted surprise attacks, and there was a real danger of being taken prisoner if the proper precautions were not taken while foraging for supplies. The changing landscape also made a difference. In contrast to the rugged, thickly timbered mountain ranges earlier on, the countryside to the southeast of Atlanta was much more hospitable. The relatively level land, punctuated with an occasional minor elevation, was both populated and richly cultivated. Earlier,

during the hotly contested portion of the campaign, at night the soldiers had been forced to sleep on the barren earth, which was both
uncomfortable and damp. The countryside now was covered with a
tough, wiry grass much like those in the bottomlands of Illinois, and
the soldiers benefited from a much more relaxing sleep.

However, it was the abundance of food that posed the most dramatic difference, although no thanks to the quartermasters. The lines
of communications having purposely been severed by the destruction
of rail lines back to Chattanooga, all subsistence now came from
daily foraging. The dietary cornucopia offered by the rich Georgia
countryside at harvest time, however, more than made up for what
had been abandoned in Atlanta. The crops bountiful, there appeared
to be an unlimited supply of corn, sweet potatoes, and other crops at
hand. Every plantation was well stocked with cattle, pigs, and
poultry. Its smokehouses were filled with hams and cured bacon,
while the pantries were replete with butter, honey, molasses,
sorghum, syrup, apples, home-style jelly and preserves, and pickles.

Every morning, details were sent off to forage for food and other
provisions. Initially called foragers, these groups soon became known
as "bummers." The exact procedure seems to have varied widely. In
the Second Minnesota Infantry, for example, this detail consisted of an
officer and ten men. In the better-led regiments, such men were armed
and acted as a group so as to be able to withstand a sudden ambush.
Breaking ranks, the foragers would set off and get as far in front of the
main column as they could. After an hour or 2, they would leave the
road and head to the closest plantation. There, seizing a cart or carriage and the requisite beasts of burden, they would start to gather all
the goods they could find. Many, not content to limit their efforts to
husbanding foodstuffs, would seize whatever else they could find, the
silverware, chandeliers, even women's clothing.

The task soon accomplished, the foragers returned to the road to
wait for their company to come along. Standing alongside the road,
their appearance often ranged from the ludicrous to the grotesque.
Some would be waiting in a rickety old cart, some in a fancy coupé
carriage, while others stood holding onto a steer or two. As soon as
the company came up, the booty would be distributed to carry on
the march, and here and there men could be seen marching along

with pieces of pork or other varieties of meat stuck onto their bayonets.

Despite the abundance of food, the campaign was hardly play. Occasionally, small groups of rebels were encountered who did their best to annoy Sherman's army and obstruct its advance. Fallen trees blocking the roads had to be removed. Such obstacles were sometimes so extensive that the columns were forced off the main road and had to find an alternate path forward. This in turn usually meant the construction of *corduroy roads,* where a solid road base was formed by placing longs side by side.

Railroads had to be destroyed, and the men soon learned ingenious ways of bending the iron rails into unrecognizable masses, through the judicious admixture of hot fire and elbow grease. And, of course, there were occasionally the ever-unpopular night marches.

Even when the Union troops had a clear march forward, there were telltale signs that there was a war being fought. Plumes of smoke frequently dotted the horizon, a sign that a commercial establishment or the home of a prominent rebel had been set ablaze. Cotton fields, acknowledged to be the "currency" of the South, generally met the same fate.

Yet, despite the seeming unending effort, solace could be taken. The war was nearing an end, not tomorrow, not next week, but sometime in the foreseeable future.

Chapter 14

THE PSYCHOLOGICAL BASIS OF TACTICS

I t is impossible to formulate hard and fast rules about how soldiers perform under various combat conditions, and unfortunately, there are no genuine universals which predict unerringly how everyone will react to a particular situation. Nevertheless, one can still identify general trends. Just as one can catalogue the sights and sounds encountered during a battle—the screaming, oft erratic sounds of shot and shell whizzing by, the sight of an unfortunate comrade momentarily staggering back before falling prostrate on the ground—it is possible to piece together the *sensations and emotions that arose from these perceptions*. The historian not only is able to recreate what was seen and heard but can reconstruct the buildup of anxieties, from the first fleeting doubts as the enemy appeared, followed by an unendurable tension before the action became general, through to the dissipation of fear as the combatants became completely engrossed in the frenzied physical exertions that accompanied the moment of crisis.

Thus, it is possible to assemble an "emotional landscape." No longer preoccupied with the purely *perceptual*, an attempt is made to paint with broad strokes a picture of the *psychological* forces encountered at different stages of the battle, such as how combatants felt when they unexpectedly faced a cavalry charge or when they assaulted a prepared artillery position. This is potentially useful since the resulting lexicon not only describes the diverse emotions encountered on the battlefield but also links these with the type of event that evoked each emotion.

This is not to suggest an overly mechanistic model of human behavior on the Civil War battlefield. Faced with a rapid fluctuating series of life-and-death situations, the soldier did not always act predictably. After all, regardless of his personal inclinations, a soldier's behavior has always been tempered by a sense of patriotism, camaraderie, political and religious conviction, and most importantly, the desire to avoid the shame of dishonor.

The comprehensive cataloguing of emotions and causative events must appear to be an impossible task, subject to endless variation. Fortunately for the historian, most combatants fought in a limited number of close-order formations. Their every movement was theoretically prescribed by official procedure and under close scrutiny of their officers. In the overwhelming majority of cases, the ways in which men were able to vent their emotions were equally restricted. Not free to leave their positions in line or column, their physical means of coping with the kaleidoscope of emotions were usually limited to small, barely observable motions.

As the soldiers entered the battlefield, there was usually a short period of introspection, as participants nervously pondered their likely fate. Capt. G. B Adams of the hard-fighting Nineteenth Massachusetts, for example, never forgot the tenseness of the men as they waited to advance into battle. Faces turned pale as the men anxiously clutched their {rifle} "muskets." This was not an idiosyncratic reaction peculiar to a regiment or even this arm of service; infantry and cavalry alike displayed the same nervousness and introspective tendencies before an action.

In his memoirs Lewis Stimson proffered similar observations. Stimson's unit was frequently called upon to push in Confederate skirmishers. Although these were mostly "demonstrations," in which the simple act of threatening the enemy skirmishers usually had the desired effect, there was enough "firing, shot, shell, and bullets" for the riders not to take their well-being for granted. Not used to battle, Stimson initially was embarrassed by his own taciturnity, but looking around, he was quickly relieved to see that even the most experienced officers were similarly affected:

> It was quite noticeable, the hush would come as we rode into the zone of firing. I don't mean that anyone flinched, but they all grew quiet. And they had all been at it for three years, and many had been wounded.

This quiet self-absorption was momentary, and as the two sides neared, heightened anxiety became evident, especially for the defenders, who, confined to a more passive role, had to endure the nerve-racking ordeal of awaiting their opponent's approach. A careful observer with the presence of mind to dispassionately look around would see even the bravest struggling to control themselves. Many took solace in seemingly trivial actions. One might check if his rifle was in working order or if he had enough rounds in his cartridge box; another might fidget with his clothing. A third would count the buttons on another's coat or whisper a commentary about the shot and shell that rained around them. For some the physical tension would be so great that the equilibrium of the body was temporarily disturbed, and they would involuntarily shift their weight from one foot to another or twitch their fingers.

As the two sides neared one another, the tension continued to mount, and many consciously struggled to maintain self-control. Trying to cope with their own nervousness, officers frequently broke out into an unholy stream of invectives as they screamed the orders in an attempt to be heard over the whistle of bullets and growing din of the battle.

Inevitably, the terror would subside as the action engulfed the soldiers and physical exertion replaced anticipation. Capt. John De Forest of the Twelfth Connecticut likened the uneasiness to intermittent "throbs of pain." Once the paroxysm of anxiety dissipated and the fear of personal safety passed and the soldiers were fully engaged, they often became as "tranquil as if [the fear] have never came near." Though not exempt from these feelings, veterans who had learned to identify truly dangerous situations were quicker to recover and immerse themselves into the task at hand, whether to join the charge or withstand an assault. Less-experienced troops, however, were not always slower to break. Sometimes their very naiveté proved an asset. Buoyed by a simple physical activity, such as a rapid advance, they could sometimes be made to charge unhesitatingly when more experienced troops equivocated, even refused. De Forest observed that "a regiment of well-drilled greenhorns, if neatly brought into action, can charge as brilliantly as veterans."

Operating in relatively small groups, sharpshooters, skirmishers, and aides-de-camp possessed much greater flexibility than those in formation. They were also freer to follow their instincts of self-preservation. Suddenly fired at, a skirmisher did not have to remain in the open but could hide behind a tree or take whatever evasive steps were expedient. However, even men within large formations were occasionally forced to seek nearby cover, such as when fighting in a dense wood or attacking enemy field fortifications. The enemy fire having become much too hot during the assault on Confederate Fort Gilmer (outside Richmond, September 29, 1864), S. M. Coursey of the Second Pennsylvania Heavy Artillery reflexively sought cover behind a stump no taller than 6 or 7 inches off the ground. Diving down, the Union soldier lay as flat as he could, hoping to be screened by this minimal protection. Unfortunately, a rather overweight comrade decided to seek shelter behind the same scanty protection, and completely out of his mind with fear, he was unaware of Coursey's presence even while lying on top of him. Only with difficulty was Coursey finally able to wiggle out from under the other soldier and find another stump behind which to hide.

However, even when able to act alone, the soldier was rarely free to ignominiously minimize the risk of injury or death. The dictates of duty or the need to display a courageous countenance tempered one's instincts. Once again Stimson's memoirs provide an illuminating example. During one of his first engagements as part of General Birney's staff, Stimson rode in a queue of officers three or four abreast. Following the general as he meandered from position to position on the battlefield, Stimson began to notice that regardless of which way the informal column twisted and turned, he was always on the "windward side," that is, the side closer to the enemy and more exposed to bullets. Alerted, Stimson looked for the reason. The next time the column turned, he noticed that his fellow officers, all more battle-seasoned than himself, subtly checked their horses for a moment, then regained their position in column, only now on the side closer to friendly troops.

Even after the battle became general, it was inevitable that for some the strain would become unbearable and they would seek a means of escape. Here and there, a trickle of stragglers fell out of line and searched for a safer place. Many congregated among the wagon trains in the rear. However, this was "jumping from the frying pan into the fire." According to Col. Benjamin Scribner, who led the Thirty-eighth Indiana Volunteers, this was among the most "miserable and unhappy places" to be while the battle raged:

> Here the stragglers collect to palliate their cowardice, and, to mitigate the contempt they are conscious of deserving, they proceed to magnify the dangers and destruction at the front, and to invent disasters that have overtaken the army. Thus the shirks are kept in a continuous turmoil of fear and anxiety.

Of course, most soldiers managed to control their fears and remain in line. Who stayed and performed his duty, and who broke, was not always predictable. Appearances could be extremely deceptive. All too often, the so-called manly soldier, who exuded strength, braggadocio, and all the trappings of courage on the drill ground and during the march, crumbled when he found himself within the bloody crucible of courage. After several campaigns Stimson, whose memoirs display considerable psychological savviness, totally lost confidence in what he termed the "constitutionally brave man, the man who was thought not to even think of danger." Stimson concluded:

> Let him once get scared and the chances are he will be scared through and through and without control of himself. . . . The man who appreciates danger and faces it is the one who can be trusted to keep going.

Abner, a Union private, agreed with this assessment and concluded that during combat "the word 'bravery' has no significance to the combatant; men are heroes or cowards in spite of themselves." In his own memoirs Samuel Wing of the Third Maine evinced even greater cynicism. Coupling his experience of how others conducted themselves under fire with his own feelings and struggles, Wing opined that if left to their own inclinations, all soldiers would run away if not for the inescapable ignominy that would follow. The advice offered by his sergeant before one battle seemed to aptly sum up the real situation:

Talk about courage; there are none here but would do the same thing [run away], if it was not for the shame and disgrace attached to it; I judge all by myself. I do not go into a fight because I like it, and would not go in, if I was not ashamed to run.

The greatest test did not occur during the heat of the action but when the men were left to their own thoughts and anxieties, such as when they waited idly for their part in the action to begin when positioned on at the periphery of the engagement or in the rear as the part of the reserves. According to Abner:

The true perspective of danger is observed and comprehended by the man attached to the edge of a battle—not in it, but near enough to feel its pulsation and get an occasional shock of its power. . . . The bravest front, bolstered by pride and heroic resolution, will crumble in the presence of the agony of wounds. Wading through bloody fields and among the distorted dead bodies of comrades, dodging shells, and posing as a target to hissing bullets that whisper of eternity, is not conducive of action, much less thought. The shock from a bursting shell will scatter a man's thought as the iron fragments will scatter the leaves overhead.

RECOGNITION OF THE PSYCHOLOGICAL DIMENSION

That combatants became preoccupied with physical activity after the initial bout of fear subsided was not lost upon some of the more thoughtful. After the war the extremely perspicacious Colonel Scribner would publish one of the rebellion's most insightful memoirs, chronicling not only the actions, trials, and tribulations of the Thirty-eighth Indiana but also how the novice volunteer officers slowly acquired the art of war. Lt. Col. Judson W. Bishop, who commanded the Second Minnesota Infantry, in his own memoirs observed that it was rare that opposing lines "face each other with equal nerve and determination." In his experience, if one side was determined to stay and fight, the other invariably would change its mind and retire.

Scribner had also noticed this tendency and concluded that success often went to the side that somehow managed to hold out even an instant after both groups of combatants had become "impressed with the idea that they will all be killed" and begun to consider flying for safety. A profound realization, one that had been understood by only a select few in eighteenth- and nineteenth-century Europe, Scribner's observation is worthy of elaboration. During a hotly contested engagement, there eventually will come a moment where one side or the other breaks. This is the *ultimate* moment of the crisis. Just before this moment, maybe a few seconds but as short as a heartbeat, there occurs the point where the men on that side start to equivocate, where they have "second thoughts" about continuing the action and think about retiring. This could be called the *penultimate* moment of the crisis. The penultimate moment is marked by the beginning of *a thought or emotional process,* such as panic or even more reasoned thoughts, such as the need to retire. The ultimate moment is indicated by a physical activity, such as turning one's back, stopping, or running away.

In many engagements one side quickly gained a moral and possibly physical advantage over the other, such as when attackers prematurely assaulted an entrenched position reinforced with artillery. In this case, at the penultimate moment one side thinks about retreating, while the other does not. In our example, the defenders, aided by stout works and friendly artillery, remain determined to hold their position, as the attackers start to equivocate. In other engagements both sides might be equally effected and equivocate at roughly the same time. As improbable as this sounds, it was much more common than might be expected. This frequently occurred when two bodies of cavalry charged one another or when a determined infantry assault appeared to the defenders to have a chance of success.

Some officers realized that when both sides underwent this emotional crisis simultaneously, anything that could prolong the friendly troops' morale even for a few moments longer could win the day. In Scribner's words, it was necessary to employ

> every incentive that can influence the actions of man . . . required to make him overcome that instinct of nature which prompts him to avoid danger, and to incite and fortify him for the performance of duty.

This had been understood by some European military authorities from the end of the seventeenth century onward. A love of one's country, a sense of honor, ambition, or the fear of disgrace long had been regarded as powerful motivations which could prod soldiers to endure conditions from which they would otherwise try to avoid or escape. It was this desire to evoke esprit de corps, patriotism, a feeling for a cause, and the desire to avoid disgrace that prompted officers to appeal to their men in impromptu speeches during the moments that immediately preceded some critical action. Often these addresses were single-sentence admonitions, such as "Fire low," "Stick to your company," or "Don't let your regiment down."

Apart from these short appeals, officers and drill sergeants could only attempt to cultivate psychological motivators between engagements. Here and there, however, some officers realized that in a critical moment the men's morale, if for at least a few brief moments, could be positively affected by the activity of the officers themselves and NCOs or by some action the men were ordered to perform. A few of the more observant eventually realized that once their men became preoccupied with some engaging activity, such as loading and firing, the initial bout of fear subsided, and the men's performance returned to manageable levels.

However, the activity that would momentarily serve to divert the combatant's attention from the face of death did not have to come from the official tactical armamentarium. It could be some sort of *incidental,* or even *accidental,* action. What De Forest in his memoirs characterized as an irrepressible "swearing mania" is probably the simplest example of the latter. Officers and NCOs sometimes broke out into the most effusive litany of curses, swearing, and blasphemy. Ironically, the very butts of such verbal abuse, the men being pushed and ordered forward, seemed to benefit from these insults. Not only did it help take their mind off the carnage that surrounded them, but the very emotion inspired them.

Lt. Col. Benjamin F. Winger would write about just such a reaction among his men during the hellacious fighting in front of Petersburg on June 16, 1864. The Second Regiment of Pennsylvania Heavy Artillery, standing in a clump of woods, was subjected to a deadly cross fire from Confederate artillery in Petersburg to their front and Fort Clinton on their right:

As the shells burst and solid shot and shells of the enemy
began knocking and tearing the trees to splinters, our boys
began to twist and wobble. The officers said they must stand
straight in line and take what comes till we made the charge. .
. . Whilst I do not think it proper to do violence to the third
commandment, it did seem that the only thing to be done was
to do a lot of good, hard swearing, and, with a corporal behind
them, to prevent shirking, I gave orders to fix bayonets, and
every fellow went into the charge with alacrity. They thought
if the officers could swear till a blue streak went up, they
could afford to be brave.

On their part officers frequently were not only tolerant of such lewd-
ness, a flagrant violation of the declared values of the age, but cog-
nizant of its value: "In the excitement of the charge it seemed as if
every extremity of language was excusable, providing it would help
towards victory."

It had long been understood that the moment when an officer
ordered a charge was a critical moment, and various methods had
been devised to stir the men into action. An officer drawing his sword
and pointing towards the enemy or, in the case of cavalry, sounding
the charge are examples of minor motivators that helped stir up the
required emotion.

A few American officers resorted to a time-honored technique.
Tradition tells us that during the Crusades, just before Douglas and
his Scots encountered a host of Saracens, the bold Scottish leader
drew a golden ball hanging from his waist. Throwing it among the
enemy horsemen, he cried, "There goes the heart of Bruce!" Wildly
stirred up, the Scots rushed in and defeated the Saracens. Similarily,
as the Thirty-eighth Indiana Infantry, outside Atlanta (August 1864),
attacked through a rebel abatis during the Battle of Jonesboro, the
color-bearer was killed, and his body fell upon the regiment's standard. The men, hesitating in the face of this inauspicious omen,
started to take shelter from the deadly fire, but there was no time to
lose. The rebels, who had wavered as the Union line approached the
earthworks, now started to rally. Sensing the urgency of the moment,
Lt. Joe Redding rolled the dead body off and lifted the bloodstained

flag back into the air. Mounting the earthworks, he flung the flag towards the enemy, yelling, "Boys, there it goes!" Then, without looking back, he leaped into the enemy's ranks. Instantly innervated, the Thirty-eighth rushed after him. The flag was recaptured, and the rebels were pushed out of the position.

This tactic of an officer single-handedly rushing in and stirring up the troops behind was also used on at least one occasion by Union cavalry. Col. Charles Russell Lowell used similar theatrics at Waynesborough, Virginia, September 28, 1864. Forced to quickly counter an unexpected assault by Confederate cavalry who were trying to stop the destruction of a railway bridge, Lowell rode up and ordered the Third New Jersey cavalry to countercharge their rebel counterparts. The men in this regiment, drawn up in columns of squadrons, had witnessed a series of reverses, so not surprisingly, the men had lost their nerve and remained motionless even after Lowell had ordered the front squadron to sling their carbines, draw their sabers, and advance to the charge. Captain Bliss, who had just led several unsuccessful attempts to stop the rebels and who was forced to retire back to the Third New Jersey's position, describes what happened next:

> The captain in command of the squadron said, 'Corporal Jones, are you afraid?' and the corporal made no reply. The men wavered and Colonel Lowell said, 'Give a cheer boys, and go at them,' and at once, putting action to words, spurred his horse at a gallop towards the enemy, followed by myself, both waving our sabres. The squadron at once cheered and followed. After going a short distance, Colonel Lowell drew out to one side to be ready to send the other troops to the support of the squadron, and I was left to lead the charge.

Whether the men surged into the fight from a sense of shame or an instinctive reflex to follow someone displaying obvious bravery, this motivation by example had succeeded where direct orders had failed. It is impossible to determine whether Lieutenant Redding's and Captain Bliss's actions were completely spur-of-the-moment decisions, or whether they arose from the pragmatic stratagems, ruses, and ploys subtly imbricated into the officers' collective unconscious through daily discussions during the march and in the tent.

There is no such uncertainty associated with the next example of how some Civil War officers had their men perform certain actions, raising morale or stabilizing emotions so that they could perform their duty more effectively even under the most trying of conditions on the battlefield. Noticing that his men were becoming uncontrollably wild during the Battle of Shiloh (April 6–7, 1862) Col. August Willick ordered his Indiana men to cease firing. While still directly in front of the enemy, who continued to fire, he drilled his regiment in the regulation manual of arms. Surprisingly, his men performed this task as though on parade. Once they regained their composure, Willick ordered his men to fire. Now their shots were observed to be "deliberate, steady, and effective." The colonel had realized that one of the surest ways of restoring the troops' presence of mind was to have the troops perform actions that had become second nature by constant practice.

Willick wasn't the only Union colonel to use this artifice. During the Battle of Antietam (September 17, 1862) Col. Edward Hincks ordered the Nineteenth Massachusetts to halt and then ordered them to perform the manual of arms. The next year Colonel John DeCourcy did the same with the 22nd Kentucky Regiment, and Joseph Hayes had some of the men in the Eighteenth Massachusetts perform the manual of arms while awaiting Pickett's Charge at Gettysburg.

THE REBEL YELL

Almost certainly the most frequent and tactically significant of these psychological ploys, however, was the rebel yell, used by the Confederates in the great majority of engagements to bolster the men's courage and determination as much as to scare the enemy. Rather than some pre-agreed-on technique, this battle cry almost certainly arose spontaneously during the early days of the war. Kirby Smith's troops are known to have used this yell when they took some Union infantry in flank during the late stages of the fighting at the First Bull Run. According to a Confederate veteran, the men opened their mouths as wide as they could and yelled their loudest over and over again as long as their breath lasted. The result was "one continuous shout of mingled voices, without any intermission, unison or time . . . a commingling of shrill, loud sounds, that rent the air and could be heard for a distance of two miles or more." Observers estimated that this cacophony could be heard 1, possibly 2 miles away.

Union infantry invariably used a very different type of cheer. His duties as a sergeant often brought W. H. Morgan uncomfortably close to Union infantry formations and he had ample opportunity to observe his opponents at the crisis of battle. The Union men cheered, "Hip, hip, huzza, huzza, huzza!" in unison and in time, unlike the rebel infantrymen; it struck Morgan as "coarse and harsh." This cheer was very similar to British practice, from which it probably originated. While fighting against the French army in Spain, the British tended to use a very controlled approach where the officers did everything to keep the men's emotion in check until the final moment before a charge. Then at close range the British infantry would deliver a well-leveled volley, shout their two or three cheers, and rush in with lowered bayonet, almost always with the same result: the complete discomfiture of those who opposed them.

In adopting the boisterous and continuous rebel yell, the Southern infantry had espoused a very different martial tradition. Soldiers in many parts of the world favored much more aggressive offensive tactics than the British; instead, every effort was made to secure victory with the first assault. The attackers were worked up to an emotional frenzy and rushed in with as noisy and bellicose a manner as possible to intimidate their enemy into submission. During the Napoleonic Wars, French officers, for example, usually ran in front of the advancing lines with upraised swords to encourage their men by example. In the Near East attacking Turkish and Mameluke horsemen would rush in as fast as their horses could carry them, all the while yelling, screaming, and using every other trapping of ferocity imaginable. The Scottish warriors, to whom many of the Southern insurgents traced their ancestry, had always employed similar practices, while fighting their hated British foe and there was nothing the British infantryman found more threatening than a screaming Scotsman with claymore and target coming at him. Typically, the style employed by the Confederate infantry fell much more in this school of attack than the highly disciplined, calculated approach used by both the British or German-speaking armies.

Chapter 15

INFANTRY DOCTRINE

CHANGING CONCEPTION OF TACTICS

T oday the term *tactics* generally refers to the movement and use of troops to secure a localized advantage over the enemy. It is no longer simply seen as the application of force at the right time and place to achieve the maximum impact on the enemy; modern military professionals associate a large number of issues with this term. Someone talking about air force tactics, for example, might include the need for rigorous pilot training, repeated realistic simulations, the characteristics of weapon systems, as well as physical limitations of human responses in high-G environments and how pilots tend to react in real combat situations. It has long been recognized that for a tactic to be effective, it must be *situational,* that is, it must be appropriate for the situation in which it is applied. It is no longer thought of as merely the unthinking application of a simple pre-formulated drill or procedure.

Tactics originally possessed a much more limited meaning and has evolved slowly over time. Unfortunately, there is an all-too-common tendency for Civil War historians to limit what legitimately falls into this area of military science simply to the routines described in period drill manuals. This has largely occurred because the most widely used American drill manuals of the period all included the term *tactics* in the titles—Scott's *Infantry Tactics*, Hardee's *Rifle and High Infantry Tactics*, and Casey's *Infantry Tactics*—thus suggesting that the tactical domain was limited to the contents of these volumes.

This, however, is a rather simplistic view of tactics, even in the context of mid-nineteenth-century military science. During the early 1700s the term had generally referred to the methods of deploying an army on the battlefield and the subsequent maneuvering around unfavorable terrain once the battle began in earnest. Tactics was approached from a purely mechanistic perspective and was viewed as a series of routine steps or procedures, such as the methods used to form line and the method of fire to be delivered when charged by enemy cavalry. Forces that affected performance, such as those that added to or detracted from the soldiers' will to fight, were not consciously considered.

The vast watershed of experiences afforded by the Seven Years' War and the Napoleonic Wars allowed the more reflective among European tacticians to more thoroughly appreciate the full range of forces and dynamics at play on the battlefield. Although offering a fairly standard definition of tactics in *The Spirit of Military Institutions, or Essential Principles of War,* General Auguste Marmont, who had served with the French army during the Napoleonic Wars, expanded the tactical domain when he sought to explain the types of competency required to implement any tactical initiative effectively:

> Tactical talent consists in causing the unexpected arrival, upon the most accessible and the most important positions, of means which destroy the equilibrium, and give victory; to execute, in a word, with promptness, movements which disconcert the enemy, and for which he is entirely unprepared.

The marshal was merely echoing more radical thinkers of the time, such as A. H. Bülow, who saw tactics as a type of mental "fencing" wherein the two antagonists, using a series of thrusts and counterstrokes, struggle to deliver the final and crushing blow. A number of years before, the Prussians started to move beyond a purely mechanical interpretation of tactics. Frederick the Great realized that to be effective, tactics had to account for the situations in which they were applied. A technique that was effective in one situation might be totally inappropriate in another. Frederick recommended, for example, that inexperienced troops sometimes deliver a volley or two while still out of range to become familiar with the sights and sounds of battle, a practice strictly prohibited for veterans.

This illustrates the other tactical layer that began to be self-consciously addressed. The soldier's physical actions could affect how he felt, so appropriate tactics in a situation could positively affect the troops' morale. The walk, trot, charge doctrine and the cavalry column of attack were both designed by the Prussians to bolster their troops' morale at the critical moment, while simultaneously demoralizing the enemy cavalry they faced.

Although the psychological dimension of tactics was temporarily lost with the death of Frederick the Great, it gradually was rediscovered during the decades following the Napoleonic Wars, as reflected in the writings of such luminaries as Bugeaud de la Piconnèrie, Captain Lewis Nolan, and Fortuné de Brack. Unlike most other military thinkers, who limited the discussion to principles and common routines that could arise on almost any battlefield, these authors were willing to deal with highly specific situations that might affect even small groups of soldiers. Like Frederick, they sought to provide rationales for their recommendations. To inflict the most deadly results, for example, de Brack explained that the cavalryman must learn to thrust with the sword turned sideways so that it would enter between the ribs. Cautioning against thrusting with too much force, he went on to observe that many a trooper was sidelined for the remainder of a campaign with a strained elbow or shoulder after successfully impaling an enemy.

The significance of such observations is probably greater than meets the eye. Although Nolan and de Brack wrote decades before Freud would popularize the formal study of the human mind, their writings nevertheless displayed psychological awareness. While discussing tactical solutions, both always considered how troops tended to perform during actual conditions. de Brack, for example, explained that cavalrymen could use their pragmatic understanding of how the adversary tended to react during a life-and-death struggle at close range. When slashing at an enemy horseman, De Brack suggested always to aim at the neck, since when threatened, an opponent reflexively crouched, and so by aiming low the saber would still at least strike the victim's forehead.

Bugeaud was probably the most aware of the psychological dimension. Noting that combat always consisted of "a moral part and a physical part," he concluded that the *moral*, what today would be called the psychological, was the more important of the two and that successful tactics imparted a positive psychological effect to those employing them and had a negative impact on the enemy. Physical activity on the battlefield was never psychologically neutral but had a psychotropic effect, either positively or negatively affecting troops' morale, depending upon how appropriate the action is to human nature and the circumstances in which it is employed.

Although traces of this more noticeably psychological approach to tactics can be found as far back as the early eighteenth century, these views were almost always presented only as fragmentary asides. Official regulations and formal treatises had a much more narrow scope and a distinctly procedural focus. The more pragmatic nuances were mostly passed on during discussions on the parade ground or in the barracks and thus would appear to have been permanently lost to posterity.

Fortunately, it is possible to recreate a very detailed picture of the evolution of tactics throughout the musket era by expanding the primary source material to include period memoirs and the full range of military treatises. One can then identify the subtle regional differences, such the Dutch and later Prussian tendency to rely on firepower, versus the French resolution to settle the affair with lowered bayonet. It is also possible to see how these doctrines evolved over time. Again, it must be emphasized that the fighting methods employed during the Civil War were not limited to existing European tactics. A preliminary survey of European tactics, however, does allow for a more thorough, accurate, and meaningful comparative analysis. It also is another source of information and clues about many Civil War practices that, unexplained in Civil War literature, would otherwise remain forever enigmatic or misunderstood.

Throughout the flintlock era there had been two main schools of thought regarding how infantry should attack. Each advanced opposing views about the role of firepower during the assault. One side argued that the quick assault performed without stopping to deliver fire was the most effective. The other view held that any advance without periodically stopping to fire was doomed to failure because the casualties inflicted by the defenders would never be returned. All offensive tactics were ultimately based on one of these two fundamental approaches, or the attempt to combine these opposite tactical philosophies, such as the original Dutch tactical school or the later Prussian attempt, during Frederick Wilhelm I's reign, to fire while advancing.

According to the *à prest* doctrine employed by many French commanders after 1690, the infantry was to advance in an orderly fashion and with a deliberate gait until 50 to 70 paces from the enemy. Prior to the 1750s, French infantry did not employ cadenced marching, and initially, the ranks were often left about 13 feet apart. This meant that when the advancing line was about 50 paces from the enemy, the advance temporarily stopped and the ranks quickly closed to 1 or 2 feet apart. As soon as all was ready, the march resumed. However, the pace was speeded up, and the men advanced *à prest*, that is, with a quickened step. Following the established doctrine, French officers would prohibit their men from beginning to fire until they ordered them to do so during the final moments of the assault.

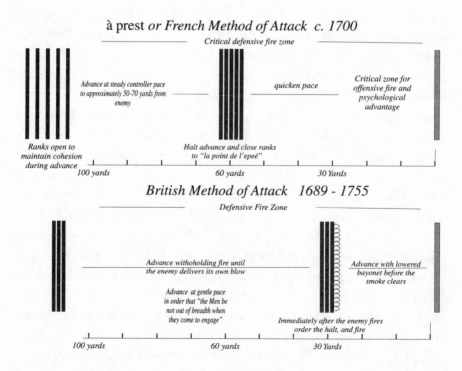

The French *à prest* attack was emotionally volatile and relied upon the troops' élan. In the early 1700s, the British usually placed more importance on a controlled approach before the bayonet charge.

Dutch Method of Attack 1690-1713

Defensive Fire Zone

Advancing as 'slow as the foot can fall'

Advance at steady controlled pace to approximately 60 yards from enemy

From the right, platoons advance in succession halt, kneel, lock, present and fire

Halt and deliver battalion fire

| 100 yards | 60 yards | 30 yards |

Wolfe's Method of Attack   1756

Defensive Fire Zone

Advance at steady pace until fired upon

Advance in silence

When ordered to charge, give a 'war like shout' and advance with lowered bayonet

Halt and deliver a cool and well levelled fire with pieces carefully loaded

| 100 yards | 60 yards | 30 Yards |

Wolfe's genius was to combine Prussian reliance on firepower with a bayonet charge at the critical moment. The officers were enjoined to control their men's emotions.

Prussian Method of Attack 1748-1763

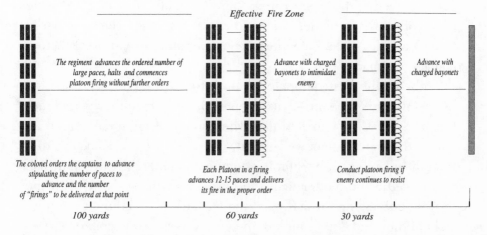

Effective Fire Zone

The regiment advances the ordered number of large paces, halts and commences platoon firing without further orders

Advance with charged bayonets to intimidate enemy

Advance with charged bayonets

The colonel orders the captains to advance stipulating the number of paces to advance and the number of "firings" to be delivered at that point

Each Platoon in a firing advances 12-15 paces and delivers its fire in the proper order

Conduct platoon firing if enemy continues to resist

| 100 yards | 60 yards | 30 yards |

The Prussians were inspired by the Dutch school of offensive tactics. They employed a slightly different, simplified form of platoon fire, however.

According to Marshal Nicolas de Catinat, who commanded the French Army of Italy during the 1690s, this tactic provided the attacker with a psychological advantage during the final moments of the attack. If the defenders fired at the attacker at any time during the last 100 paces of the approach, they were incapable of fire during the final seconds, precisely the time when a psychological edge was extremely critical. Realizing that they could no longer fire and that the approaching enemy still could, the defenders would be demoralized as they fought their fears and did their best to stand their ground. The attackers, on the other hand, having not yet delivered their fire, became all the more confident, realizing they had the ability to fire on a now-defenseless enemy.

The response to this tactic was for the defender to withhold his fire until the very last second. The defender not denuded of his fire would never become as demoralized as the attacker hoped. The threat of this countermeasure led most officers favoring the *à prest* assault to believe that the attacking force should withhold its fire until about 20 to 30 paces from the enemy, stop and deliver fire, and then run into the enemy before the latter could recover from the blow and return the fire. If this was executed properly, the defenders would be incapacitated and thrown into temporary confusion by this murderous volley fired at extremely close range. They most likely would be unable to fire in the few seconds the attackers needed to cross the last 20 to 30 paces. Faced with an onrushing foe, the clouds of smoke from the whole offensive formation, having fired at once, and the necessarily heavy casualties, the defenders almost certainly would break before contact was made.

Probably the best rationale for this offensive tactic was provided by the Marquis de Santa-Cruz, a Spanish military authority and tactician. Santa-Cruz believed that when an attacking force neared an enemy that made use of well-timed volleys, the attacker was at a distinct disadvantage if he simply attempted to ignore the fire and rush in and settle the matter with the lowered bayonet. Faced with the terrible buzzing and whistling of the musket balls and the unsettling sight of the dead and wounded, the attackers would become increasingly consternated. Less-experienced men were particularly affected by the ordeal. Many, now extremely agitated, would begin to fire despite their officers' wishes. Trembling and exhibiting much-diminished muscular control, these shots, totally unaimed, ended up being directed "as much at the sky as the earth." The result was that when and if the attackers made it to 20 or 30 paces from the defenders, their numbers were diminished through casualties and desertion, and whatever forces did remain were no longer in order. The defenders, who remained relatively composed, could easily send the attackers reeling back if at the right moment they counter-attacked with lowered bayonets.

To counteract this possibility, sometime in the late 1600s, the Dutch devised a method of assault in which the attacking force periodically stopped and a portion of the formation delivered a volley, before stepping off with their comrades once again. The attacking formation would march with shouldered arms until it had approached close enough to inflict meaningful casualties upon the defenders. Capt. Humphrey Bland estimated this distance to be around 60 paces. While continuing to march, the men in the battalion now advanced with "recovered arms," which in this case meant the musket was held pointing straight up a few inches in front of the soldier. A few moments later the rightmost platoon in the battalion would quickly advance until its rear rank was even with the front rank elsewhere along the front. At this point its men would halt, kneel, lock, present, and fire. The other platoons meanwhile continued to advance "as slow as the foot can fall" so the battalion's cohesion was not lost. This slow, deliberate gait also allowed the men who fired to reload while they continued to advance.

After the rightmost platoon fired, the one on the left flank would spring forward and fire. Then it became the turn of the second platoon from the right, followed by the second platoon on the left. This process of alternating fire between platoons on the right and left of the battalion continued until all platoons had fired. As soon as all the platoons had reloaded, the battalion would switch from the slow, deliberate method of marching to a more normal pace. At some point the platoons in the battalion would recommence the *alternate fire* just described, so it was expected that the defenders would be subjected to two or three complete fires by the time the attackers were 20 paces or so distant. At this point the entire battalion would fire before rushing in with lowered bayonets. Bland informs us that this method often caused the defenders to break after a single round of firing, and even when the attackers had to advance to close range, there were usually few casualties inflicted on the advancing forces.

Despite its virtues, this Dutch method of firing while advancing was difficult to perform and demanded the highest level of discipline. A Prussian variant evolved during the mid-1700s. Frederick the Great's father, Frederick William I, held these Dutch methods in great esteem, and the epitome of the martinet, he compelled his infantry to spend countless hours unerringly repeating the newly introduced cadenced manual of arms. In this cadenced version, every man along the firing line performed the same step at the same instant. The expectation was that the men, now firing much more quickly, would crush the opposition by sheer weight of fire. Although there is little evidence that this tactic ever caused the expected casualties, its psychological impact became apparent during Mollwitz (1741), the Prussian infantry's first battle under the young Frederick the Great. The cadenced manual of arms and this quick-fire system quickly became *de rigeur* throughout most of Europe, and Allied tactics could be found advocating this method of attack as late as 1811.

Ironically, just as the Prussian cadenced manual of arms and quick-fire system were gaining in popularity, there was a British officer who was honing his own tactical system. Though only adopted on a widespread basis more than 50 years after his death, this new tactical doctrine nevertheless had a monumental impact upon how the British infantryman would conduct himself against the French on the Iberian Peninsula and at Waterloo. In 1755 Lt. Col. James Wolfe wrote a set of instructions for his Twentieth Regiment of Foot. Unlike many of his peers, who had a decided preference for either the exclusive reliance upon the bayonet or the musket during an attack, Wolfe advocated a compromise in which the two weapons worked synergistically to produce a total impact greater than the sum of the components.

Wolfe recognized that as much as the officers urged their men to fire repeatedly, once the two sides had advanced sufficiently close, one side or the other would quickly break into a bayonet charge. Specifically rejecting the Prussian quick-fire system then coming

into vogue, Wolfe enjoined his men to deliver "a cool and well leveled fire, with the pieces carefully loaded," arguing that this was
"much more destructive and formidable than the quickest fire in confusion." The manner in which his regiment was to conduct the bayonet charge was consciously different from how it was normally
conducted by other British regiments in those days. Instead of yelling
or crying out, they were to remain completely silent, even if every
other regiment along the line was yelling at the top of their lungs.
Only when ordered to charge were they to give a "war-like shout" and
then immediately rush in with lowered bayonet.

Later generations would attribute the continuous string of British
victories over the French between 1808 and 1815 to the greater firepower capabilities of the British line and the more accurate fire of the
British infantrymen making up this formation. This largely ignores
the sea of available memoirs and official reports and appears to be a
rather self-serving effort to reinterpret historical events in terms of
newly acquired sensibilities among late-nineteenth-century historians that arose from rapid-firing weapons and such new quantitative
conceptions as rate of fire and firepower. More recent studies suggest
that a quick but deadly close-range fire followed by a determined
bayonet charge, wherein the soldier's emotions where effectively held
in check to the final moment, was the real reason for British victory.

INJUNCTIONS TO FIRE LOW

By the mid-nineteenth century, most of the more mechanical tactical
approaches to infantry attack and defense had long been obsolete.
The Dutch method of periodically firing during the forward movement
had been abandoned by the Seven Years' War (1756–63), while the
Prussian system of robotically attempting to fire three rounds per
minute finally had been cast aside by the end of the Napoleonic Wars.
It was recognized that both systems required tremendous sangfroid
(coolness under fire), something that exceeded the capabilities of all
but a few crack corps.

To be effective, tactics had to accommodate how infantrymen actually acted during the heat of battle. The consensus was that the most
that could be demanded of the men was to advance until within
medium range, deliver one, possibly two well-directed volleys and

then rush in with the bayonet. Of course, there were subtle regional differences. The French, for example, favored a very aggressive assault, in which every effort was to work the men up into a frenzy early in the charge, while the British emphasized the need for men and officers to maintain complete control and reserve until the final moment, when all hell's fury was unleashed.

The advent of the longer-range small arms during the 1840s forced some military scientists to reevaluate these tactics. Some argued that the introduction of the new weapons meant that traditional tactics that relied on dense formations advancing to extremely close ranges had to be discarded and that henceforth, firefights would be conducted at much longer ranges. However, the spirited quick attack with lowered bayonets nevertheless survived this new ideological threat. From about 1853 onward Napoleon III and his advisors began to have second thoughts about revisionist tactics that emphasized long-range firefights. The success of the French Zouaves and chasseurs during the Crimean War and their even more brilliant exploits during the Italian War appeared to justify the French leader's return to traditional form of aggressive attack, whereby the issue would be settled with the threat of cold steel.

These trends were well known to the more knowledgeable among the American military prior to the Civil War. The American military had long self-consciously emulated French practices, and all American tactical systems from Scott to Casey were no more then word-for-word translations of French drill booklets. The rival tactical doctrine, advocating long-range firefights and use of the "scientific method" of aiming rifle muskets, was also no stranger to the American military and public, having its share of proponents at West Point and in the popular press. Given the long-term role of the French military as a source of inspiration and guidance, on the one hand, and the conviction of those who advocated new tactics for the new weapons, on the other, one would expect that both of these tactical motifs would have manifested themselves once the Civil War had started in earnest and would influence the doctrine prescribed by commanders and high-ranking officers on both sides.

Of these two opposing systems, the scientific method, requiring systematic aim, was the more conspicuously absent from the Civil

War battlefield. Several books were printed or reprinted which described how to obtain accurate long-range fire with the rifle musket. Captain Henry Heth's *A System of Target Practice*, for example, was reprinted in 1862, although in this second printing the captain's name had been removed, since the author of the first edition was now fighting for the Confederate cause. Relatively few organized attempts, however, were made to systematically employ this method of aimed fire on the Civil War battlefield.

The first and most notable of these attempts is provided by the First and Second Regiments of Sharpshooters. The soldiers accepted into these regiments spent months laboriously mastering the same system that had been taught at Hythe and Vincennes, learning to estimate the range in order to properly sight their weapons, an essential precondition for accurate fire. The accomplishments of this corps the next year in front of Yorktown are some of the most impressive instances of highly accurate long-range fire and provide incontrovertible evidence of the utility of the scientific method of aiming when conducted by expert marksmen acting as individual sharpshooters. On the Southern side Patrick R. Cleburne seems to have most appreciated the potential benefits of a systematic, practiced approach to aiming, insisting upon its adoption.

The noisy, aggressive, French-style attack seems to have fared better on American soil. Civil War literature provides countless examples in which infantry conducted an aggressive attack that culminated in a quick charge with outstretched bayonets. How many times does one run across a Union veteran who recounts in his memoirs the extreme difficulty with which the defending line endured the notorious rebel yell and the whirlwind rush that always followed? This precipitous charge, in both the uncontrolled emotion that was vented and the sheer speed, bears many resemblances to the French version of the infantry bayonet charge. In both, men and officers from the start threw away all reserve and caution, and total emphasis was placed on the success or failure of the first attempt.

THE AMERICAN DOCTRINE OF ATTACK

This was the situation often found on the field. However, what about the theory?! A thorough search of the *Official Records* yields a number of tactical instructions issued before the start of a campaign or engagement. Significantly, these formal instructions called for a much more controlled approach than the wild, frantic efforts that have become so closely associated with the Civil War battlefield.

Before the start of hostilities, on the Southern side only Lee felt that the upcoming fight would be dominated by technological advances, particularly among the artillery arm. The overwhelming consensus was that, following the French example in the late war in Italy, the bayonet would once again prove to be the "queen of the battlefield." The doctrine implicit in tactical circulars and orders issued on both sides reflected this sentiment. Both Beauregard and McClellan issued orders that described how their infantrymen were to conduct themselves under fire during an upcoming campaign. The tactical doctrine in both cases is virtually identical. Sensing the impending Union drive into Virginia, Beauregard, who then commanded the (Confederate) Army of the Potomac, issued General Orders No. 41 on July 17, 1861. In addition to evoking a sense of patriotism of a "free people" against "an odious government" Beauregard emphasized that

> great reliance will be placed on the bayonet at the proper juncture, but above all it is enjoined upon officers and men to withhold their fire until directed. . . . In firing, each man should take aim, and never discharge his piece without a distinct object in full view.

Beauregard believed this tactic, coupled with the "superior intelligence" of his soldiers, would make up for the training and experience of the regular army they expected to face.

Almost a year later, with his army poised ready to advance up the peninsula towards Richmond, Major General McClellan issued corresponding instructions to his Union troops. After reminding the men that they were to leave their knapsacks with the regimental wagons, he implored them to make absolutely certain that their arms were in perfect order and that they had at least forty rounds in their cartridge boxes and twenty in their haversacks and pockets. McClellan enjoined his troops to "preserve discipline" and "to obey promptly and intelligently all orders they may receive." As they neared the enemy, McClellan, echoing an admonition taught to West Pointers in Dennis Mahan's *Elementary Treatise*, felt it was imperative that the men

> preserve in battle perfect coolness and confidence, the sure forerunners of success. They must keep well together; throw away no shots, but aim carefully and low, and above all things rely upon the bayonet.

In a series of circulars and general orders, commanders on both sides repeated similar injunctions throughout the war. Rather than the work of inexperienced dilettantes who had gained their positions through influence and politics, these were penned by such respected military leaders as Sherman, Burnside, and Rosecrans (who before Chickamauga enjoyed a reputation as a competent commander) on the Northern side and Longstreet, Magruder, and Hardee on the Confederate. When these doctrinal instructions are considered collectively, the prescribed infantry tactics could be reduced to several key elements: Withhold fire until presented with a good target, aim low with deliberation, and when circumstances were favorable for aggressive action, charge in with lowered bayonet.

However, it was generally agreed that these tactics only could be carried out if the infantrymen obeyed the officers' orders. In instructions issued to his troops in front of Richmond prior to the Confederate counterattack that precipitated the Seven Days' Battles, Gen. James Longstreet emphasized the importance of self-control under fire. It was imperative that the men along the line "preserve a quiet demeanor and self-possessed temper." This was especially critical for raw, inexperienced troops entering battle for the first time. According to Longstreet, although the "fiery noise of battle [would appear] indeed most terrifying," the recruits could maintain the required equanimity if they remembered that they could rely on their fellow soldiers as long as they never lost sight of them; their comrades in turn were relying upon them. Then all would be well, provided that they also remembered to "aim low."

Brig. Gen. James G. Blunt, commander of the First Corps of the

Union Trans-Mississippi Army of the Frontier, offered similar words of advice to his troops a few days before the battle of Prairie Grove, Arkansas (December 7, 1862.) He enjoined his men not to shout but to keep quiet so as to hear their officers' orders. Above all, he cautioned them to ignore "idle rumors or the words of unauthorized persons." This was indeed useful advice. So many times an otherwise determined line of men would waver and break because of some false rumor about being outflanked or isolated.

All of these tactical instructions emphasized the importance of a controlled, deliberate fire. Men were never to start firing for the sake of producing a rapid fire, simply because others around them started to do so, or just because they happened to see the enemy. Officers on both sides continued to advocate this approach throughout the war. Despite the enormous amount of fighting experience accumulated by May 1864, Maj. Gen. James. B. McPherson still found it necessary to explain to his men that

> it is not the rapid, continuous roll of musketry, delivered in a hasty manner, which shakes an enemy, checks his advance, and drives him from the field, but the accuracy with which it is given.

Maj. Gen. Gouverneur Kemble Warren entertained a similar opinion. In Circular No. 109, distributed on August 1 that year, Warren emphasized that the officers had to do everything to control their men and ensure that they saved their fire, since "one good volley well put in will render the enemy's line powerless."

Such various letters and orders demonstrate that officers almost universally extolled their men to "aim low." This was equally the case among the Confederates as among the Union military, and this instruction was repeatedly issued up until the closing stages of the war. In a letter to Gen. John McNeil, Rosecrans recommended that troops aim at the enemy's shins when firing, while Maj. Gen. T. C. Hindman's instructions ordered the men to fire at their knees.

Col. William Phillips, in a circular issued to the Army of the Frontier in January 1864, offered similar instructions. He urged his men to fire at the knees of the enemy infantry. However, if the enemy was on horseback, the men to fire at the rider's lower body. Incidentally, the circular ended with this rather ambiguous set of instructions:

> Those who are still in arms are rebels, who ought to die. Do not kill a prisoner after he has surrendered. But I do not ask you to take prisoners.

If there was almost universal agreement that the men should withhold fire until "short range," there seems to be no clear consensus as to what was meant by this term. In a letter to Brig. Gen. E. B. Brown dated October 6, 1864, Rosecrans prescribed that men withhold their fire until the distance between adversaries had been reduced to a "deadly range." Three weeks before, in a September 27 letter to General McNeil at Rolla, Missouri, General Rosecrans appears to have provided an empirical definition of what he considered to be a "deadly range" when calling for his men to reserve their fire: "till they can see the whites of the enemy's eyes." Major General Hindman, in his instructions to the First Corps of the Trans-Mississippi Army, seems to place a maximum limit at which a soldier who was carefully aiming should direct fire at an individual enemy soldier. Hindman's orders give essentially the same instructions as did Rosecransz: "Wait till you are certainly within the range of your gun, then single out your man, take deliberate aim."

When it came to prescribing the type of fire system to be used, there was a greater disparity of opinion. In an 1864 letter to Gen. McNeil, Rosecrans felt that generally, the infantry should deliver a volley by one half of the line. Here he was presumably referring to what was frequently called *fire by wing* or what in Britain was sometimes known as *fire by half-battalions*. As to its effectiveness, Rosecrans maintained, "No troops west of the Mississippi will stand such a fire." General Warren of the Army of the Potomac ordered his officers to do the same to allow only 50% of the men to fire at one time, but in a slightly different manner. His August 20, 1864, instructions required that the fire alternate between the first and rear ranks.

Earlier in the war (September 22, 1863), while commander of the Army of the Cumberland at Chickamauga, Rosecrans had advised Maj. Gen. George Bibb Crittenden, who commanded the Twenty-first

Army Corps, that the men manning rifle pits were to "fire by volley and by ranks." The various general orders and circulars on either side do not appear to have elaborated much further. General Beauregard, however, in his series of circulars issued to the soldiers of the Army of the Mississippi during 1862 and 1863, advised against the use of *file fire* except for skirmishers firing as individuals. He argued that file fire "excited the troops and renders their subsequent control difficult." Instead, he recommended the use of fire by wing or *fire by company*. This view would be echoed by Gen. William B. Bate 2 years later during the Atlanta campaign. He instructed his officers to avoid file fire at the beginning of the battle, except for skirmishers, who, if they wished, could use this type of fire. Instead, the officers were to utilize the same type fire systems prescribed earlier by Beauregard, fire by wing or company. In either case the fire was to be delivered alternatively by front and rear ranks.

Incidentally, Beauregard's and Bate's views about file fire represented a departure from the majority opinion in the French army during the Napoleonic Wars. Writing a detailed set of tactical instructions for his corps while at the Camp de Montreuil-sur-Mer in 1804,

Scouts from the Ninth Indiana Volunteers encounter their Confederate foe during a skirmish. *Frank Leslie's Pictorial History of the War,* 1862.

Marshal Michel Ney spoke highly of the then relatively new type of fire system, arguing that "a soldier . . . can aim much better than he is able to do when firing at the word of command given by the officer." He concluded that "fire by files which besides is very brisk, does more real execution than a regular fire." The marshal did concede, however, that once file fire began, all semblance of order was quickly lost, and it was next to impossible for the officers to put an end to the firing should the need arise. Apparently, this latter consideration forced American officers to reassess the value of fire by files.

File fire was frequently used in practice, however. Not only did many attempts to use more controlled fire quickly devolve into file fire, but there is also at least one case on record of an army commander specifically ordering its use. On August 19 1864, Maj. Gen. Oliver O. Howard, who then commanded the Army of the Tennessee, ordered that Gen. William B. Hazen ensconce two regiments in a "secure place near the skirmish line." These were ordered to fire by files for half an hour. The seeming fury and confusion that would necessarily result was intended to give the impression of a general assault. Howard of course intended the real blow to fall elsewhere. File firing, though not encouraged by tacticians, tended to be commonplace on the field of battle. Testifying before the military commission set up to investigate the evacuation of Maryland Heights and subsequent surrender of Harpers Ferry during Lee's Maryland Campaign, Maj. William H. Baird explained that it was "almost impossible" to get inexperienced troops to fire by volleys when under fire. Regardless of the officers' efforts, they almost always fire by file instead.

THE EFFECTIVENESS OF FORMAL METHODS OF ATTACK

Tactical doctrine that called for troops to advance within close range and conduct a bayonet charge probably strikes many modern readers as hopelessly obsolete after the adoption of the new rifle muskets. During recent decades a number of historians, reflecting this view, have argued that the bloodiness of the Civil War, the great preponderance of failed attacks, and even the overall Confederate defeat was in fact attributable to a tactical system that should have been discarded along with the smoothbore muskets. In the preface of *Attack and Die*, for example, McWhiney and Jamieson opined:

Offensive tactics, which had been so successfully used by
Americans in the Mexican War, were much less effective in the
1860s because an improved weapon—the rifle—had vastly
increased the strength of the defenders.

The most commonly evoked images of the Civil War appear to support this view, foremost among these the sanguinary attacks of
Hooker's infantry through the cornfield at Antietam, Pickett's Charge
at Gettysburg, and the repeated but fruitless Union attempts to
advance against Longstreet's corps at Fredericksburg. The very massiveness of Pickett's Charge at Gettysburg, and the regularity with
which successive waves of Union troops were dashed apart before the
sunken Telegraph Road on Marye's Heights, suggest that regardless
of the attackers' resolve and exertions, regardless of the weight of the
attack or the tactics used, all attempts to discomfit ready and well-
placed defenders necessarily were doomed to failure. A statistical
study of the overall success rate of the attacking army versus its
defending counterpart during major Civil War battles also seems to
force similar conclusions. In a great majority of major Civil War battles, the army on the overall offensive was unequivocally defeated.
First and Second Bull Run, Cross Keys and Port Republic, Kernstown, Malvern Hill, Murfreesboro, Fredericksburg, Chancellorsville, and Gettysburg are obvious examples. During the first three
campaigns, only a handful of instances of the attacker emerging victorious from a large set piece battle can be cited: the Confederate
assault on Lexington, the First Battle of Winchester, Gaines's Mills,
Chickamauga, Lookout Mountain, and Missionary Ridge. All of this
suggests that by 1861 traditional methods of attack had indeed been
rendered ineffective by advances in weaponry.

Intuitively, a won-lost evaluation of the effectiveness of tactics
appears compelling and not easily challenged. However, as common-
sensical as this analysis appears, it not only violates an understanding
of some of the most basic and pervasive principles of military science:
It systematically pushes aside a great body of evidence that must also
be considered. Military science has long differentiated between the
tactical, grand tactical, operational, and *strategic* levels of military
activity. During an engagement or battle, a commander and his officers

necessarily use elements from all levels. So, a commander might pursue a clever strategy to place his foe at a disadvantage before the onset of the fighting, and his infantry might employ effective tactics, but his subordinate officers fail to properly implement his plans, and because of this, the overall attack fails, and the battle is lost. The elements on each level never operate in a vacuum but are influenced, sometimes greatly so, by other levels of activity.

Long recognizing this complex interplay of tactical, grand tactical, and strategic elements during a battle, military scientists have always attempted to evaluate the procedures and concepts on each level by the degree to which they achieve their immediate objectives. One evaluates the effectiveness of file fire, for example, by its ease of implementation and the number of casualties it inflicts. Similarly, an assault is successful if the attackers take its localized objective. Now, obviously, battles and large engagements consist of numerous tactical operations, so a particular assault can succeed, but the battle still be lost.

As one applies this more detailed type of analysis to Civil War battles, it becomes apparent that many more assaults are successful on a purely tactical level than is commonly recognized, and in many battles the attacking side loses not because of a failure of tactics but because of errors made on a grand tactical or even strategic level. The Confederate assault during the first day of Shiloh, albeit a surprise attack, managed to gradually push Grant's army out of its camps and back towards Pittsburg Landing. One encounters a similar dynamic during the first day of the Battle of Murfreesboro. That summer at Gaines's Mills John B. Hood's Texas Brigade plus a force under D. H. Hill pushed back Morel's division. There were numerous successful Confederate offensive actions on the localized level at Chickamauga. Near end of the battle of Antietam, A. P. Hill's Division successfully attacked Issac P. Rodman's Third Division (IX Corps) on Union left flank. During the first day of Gettysburg, Early's Division swept away Howard's XI Corps from north of the city. When the full spectrum of engagements is considered, one is able to identify dozens of cases in which an attack succeeds in taking its tactical objective.

Nevertheless, despite localized successes, it is clear that the rifle musket and rifled artillery were at least slightly more effective than the weapons they replaced, and during the Civil War, the defender could repel an attack more readily than formerly. Certainly, the battlefield was not transformed to the extent originally predicted by Captains Wittich and Gilluim. Rarely, if ever, did opposing formations of infantry face off at the 600- or even 400-yard range that Captain Tyler and Lieutenant Colonel Dixon had anticipated before the war. Paddy Griffith's assertion that in 1864 the average firefight between opposing infantry in formations was 141 yards is probably closest to the mark. Though this appears to be a very modest estimate of the average range, when compared to the 90-yard or so average during the Napoleonic era, it nevertheless represents more than a 50% improvement.

However, the dynamics of attack and defense were probably even more affected by the proliferation of rifled artillery and increasingly effective concussion and percussion shells. The ability to fire explosive shells accurately beyond 1000 yards deprived the attacker of two very potent tools. To charge effectively, cavalry usually required time to form for the charge and then had to set off slowly to maintain order and not blow the horses prematurely. Now cavalry that remained stationary in the 500- to 1000-yard range would be immediately scattered with a few artillery shells. Battalion columns held in waiting within this same range would suffer the same fate. Not only were they vulnerable to rifled artillery and the new shells, but they could also suffer casualties from even relatively inaccurate small arms fire.

However, these heightened capabilities were a matter of degree, rather than an obviously profound transformation. It would take several seasons for even the more perspicacious of officers to really appreciate the new weaponry and the changes in tactics that were demanded. Until then reliance upon the older methods seemed to remain the most reasonable choice.

Line

Column of Companies at half intervals

Intervals equal to one half company frontage

Column of divisions at quarter interval

Column of Companies at full intervals

Intervals equal to company frontage

Column of divisions at half interval

Columns were differentiated by function, width and density. Columns of companies and columns of divisions were the most common. These could be either *open* (at full distance) or *closed*, depending upon the distances between the tiers in the formation.

Chapter 16

CAVALRY—THE BEGINNING

THE BEGINNING

T he Civil War erupted at a point when the role of cavalry on the battlefield was debated by both the European and American military. By the late 1840s, Captain Wittich had theorized that with the introduction of the Prussian needle gun, cavalry would no longer be able to make headlong dashes into infantry formations and would cease to pose a major threat during battle. The only way cavalry could continue to play any role at all was to be armed with the new breechloaders and function as a type of "mounted infantry."

Though more conservative in their estimates of the practical effectiveness of the Enfield rifle musket, as we have already seen, some prominent British officers speaking at the Royal United Service Institute also felt the glory days of the mounted arm were a thing of the past. Like Wittich, Captain Tyler, who lectured on the impact of the rifle musket upon field operations, felt that the new small arms henceforth would greatly restrict the role of cavalry and artillery and that neither would play as prominent a role during combat as formerly. This was in line with the views of Lieutenant Colonel Dixon, who two years earlier (1857) had prophesized that from then on, cavalry would be limited to a "special reserve for determining the rout of infantry when in disorder from the action of artillery or other causes, and for reaping all the fruits of a victory by pursuing a broken army."

Although French-speaking military authorities also initially believed that the new Delvigne rifle would definitely affect how cavalry was to conduct itself during battle, they were generally more optimistic about this arm's continued importance. Gen. Jean Baptiste Renard of the Belgian Army argued that the weapon's impact on cavalry methods would be quite minimal and pointed out that recent practical trials had demonstrated that the traditional smoothbore muskets pierced the cuirass when the cuirassier had approached to within 38 yards, while at the same distance the rifle muskets only indented this protective gear. He also argued that the exaggerated curvature of the rifle musket's trajectory would reduce its accuracy at long range.

Seemingly influenced by such arguments, Gen. Louis-Jules Trochu, regarded as one of the most competent officers in the French service during the Italian War of 1859, instructed infantry officers to withhold their men's fire until the enemy cavalry had approached to within 40 paces, fire, and then countercharge with lowered bayonet. The French general felt that accurate fire could be achieved only when the enemy horsemen began their charge at a walk, at about 700 meters. Unfortunately, at this lengthy range the "dangerous space" (where a bullet following a highly curved trajectory might strike the enemy) was too shallow, and misjudgment of distance by the men would lead to an ineffective volley. This would waste the crucial first fire and thereby cripple the defensive capabilities of the infantry line.

Some other French cavalry experts held a slightly different view of the matter. General Bonneau du Martray, for example, believed that the introduction of rifled small arms and rifled artillery would force a more profound change of cavalry tactics. However, just like the knights of old, who had to completely change their habits and practices with the introduction of small arms long ago, cavalry in the 1850s should "rejoice and take pride in this prospect, which will furnish them with numerous opportunities of being useful, with an increase in the sphere of their activity." Here Du Martray was alluding to the experience of French cavalrymen who had been armed with new rifled carbines during the Algerian Wars. Although he felt that mounted skirmishers could not match their infantry counterparts, they could still render extremely important service against equestrian foes.

After the disappointing performance of the French cavalry during the hostilities of 1859, the Randon Commission was set up to study the need for French cavalry reform. This commission concluded that as an interim solution cavalry should be given rifled carbines, and

Napoleon III intended that the cavalry ultimately be armed with breechloaders. All cavalry had to be trained to fight as skirmishers when needed. However, probably the most drastic recommendation was the way cavalry was henceforth to charge infantry in line. Rather than the direct, head-on charge, which in its existing form had been authored by Frederick the Great, French cavalry were now to employ a *raking charge,* during which they approached the enemy infantry from the right, in order to avoid the new, more powerful small arms fire. Once near, they were to ride along the front of the opposing infantry position. This technique certainly was anything but new: Illuminaries such as Frederick the Great and General Auguste Marmont had both championed this technique. However, rather than some secondary method used in specialized situations, this technique was to become the primary method of attack.

The French assessment of cavalry's future role appears to have had little impact on American military thinking, and the more pessimistic Prussian and British views on the matter seem to have gained the upper hand in America. In 1859 Capt. Cadmus Wilcox declared that cavalry in the future would no longer approach with impunity to within 400 yards but under ordinary circumstances would instead start to suffer crippling small arms casualties at about 1200 yards. Examples of this position can be found in the American press as early as May 1861, when an article entitled "Practical Warfare" appeared in *Scientific American.* Its author predicted that henceforth, long-range fire would settle most engagements and that attack by close-order columns was no longer feasible. The same article opined that cavalry's role would also be greatly restricted and that for the most part cavalry would have to keep a "respectable distance" until an opportunity presented itself, when the mounted force would "dash in under the cover of smoke, or be preceded with riflemen and artillery."

During the opening months of hostilities, such a pessimistic assessment of cavalry capabilities was largely confined to professional circles, and the prevalent view among the public and the press was that mounted forces would play a role in the resolution of the upcoming conflict. The riotous attack of Baltimoreans upon the Sixth Massachusetts Militia, for example, prompted many to think about effective countermeasures. The Northern press was foremost in this effort, and an April 23 item in the *New York Times* urged the Federal government to send the 450 "well mounted" cavalrymen then stationed at Carlisle, Pennsylvania, to be armed with lances and rushed to Maryland to quell these disturbances. The journalist's argument was that this mounted force would be more effective than 1500 infantrymen. This argument was picked up by other Northern newspapers, and over the next few days, articles appeared that recommended sending 400 mounted troops then stationed in Washington and other experienced regular cavalry that had returned to the East from the Indian territories.

The military administration under Gen. Winfield Scott did not share the public's optimistic assessment of the usefulness of cavalry on American soil. During the initial rush to arms, the governors of New York, Indiana, Minnesota, Iowa, and Pennsylvania made offers to raise cavalry regiments, which were peremptorily declined by the secretary of war. The federal government in fact refused to accept volunteer cavalry until after the ignominious defeat at Bull Run, when it became clear that the conflict would take longer to resolve than first thought. Planning to fight in the rough, densely forested, mountainous terrain of what was then western Virginia, McClellan repeatedly asked for mounted troops to act as scouts, but his requests consistently fell on deaf ears. Only in July was he authorized to raise a single company of volunteer cavalry for 3-year service. Displaying initiative, McClellan was able to procure a few extra mounted companies by appealing directly to the states in his military department.

Scott's attitudes undoubtedly were the result of his experience during the Mexican War and intermittent outbreaks of violence on the frontier. The campaign in Mexico had not been conducive to large-scale cavalry actions, and much of the fighting had devolved into the siege and assault of walled cities and fortresses. Though cavalry played a more important part on the frontier, small contingents were distributed among a series of outposts and were relegated to patrol, escort, and mail delivery roles.

A Change of Attitude
The attitudes of the high-level Union military would begin to change

with the stunning and humiliating Union defeat at Bull Run. During the battle the First Virginia Cavalry, led by the flamboyant and inimitable J. E. B. Stuart, rather fortuitously stumbled upon an opportunity to trounce a Union infantry regiment and gain undying glory for the Southern cavalry arm. Beauregard had ordered Stuart to charge the left flank of the Union attack on his own left flank, but the independent-minded colonel decided it was easier to attack the right flank of this force and thus divided his regiment to go around either side of Thomas "Stonewall" Jackson's line. As Stuart and about 150 of his men moved to the right of Jackson in a column of fours, they entered the outskirts of a woods and soon saw troops garbed in red running towards the Confederate rear, away from sounds of a heated firefight. Given the direction and their frenzy, Stuart at first thought they were Confederate infantry ignobly running away, and he admonished them to stand and fight. However, spotting the Stars and Stripes carried by one of the men, he realized these were enemy troops and immediately ordered his men to form line on the right (the rear of the column obliqued left) and charge.

In his poignantly penned memoirs, Lt. William W. Blackford provides a somewhat heroic picture of the action. The red-clad Zouaves, though caught off guard, were able to "front face" and get off a volley, which, though at point-blank range, inflicted hardly any casualties. The enemy line was momentarily enshrouded in smoke, and neither side could see the other. Blackford's horse, Comet, rushing forward and unable to change its course or pull up, bowled over two Zouaves, who were thrown through the air like rag dolls. With no time to even reach for his revolver or saber, the lieutenant could only grab his carbine, which had been slung over his shoulder. Stuart's account in his official report, as brief as it is, is probably more accurate. It is unclear whether any of the defenders actually awaited the charge, and the affair was over in a matter of moments. The New York Fire Zouaves almost instantly scattered.

From that moment onward the Southern Black Horse cavalry became a force that struck fear into its Northern adversaries. Talking to Union soldiers upon his arrival in Washington City the day after the battle, Capt. James H. Stevenson heard the most incredible stories about the exploits of the now-feared Virginia Black Horse cavalry and would write: "These men astonished the crowd of eager listeners with some of the most marvelous stories of the prowess of the 'rebels' . . . The Black Horse Cavalry were like demons mounted upon fiery dragons, and their swords fearful to think of." In his own memoirs Willard Glasier, a Union cavalryman, recalled the public's reaction during the weeks following the debacle and how almost everyone now sought an antidote in kind: "A peculiar enthusiasm in this direction was perceptible everywhere. It was as though the spirit of the old knight-errantry had suddenly fallen upon us." Incidentally, this dread of the Black Horse cavalry did not soon dissipate. After the battle of Williamsburg the next year, J. E. B. Stuart would boast that the Union infantry faced with the specter of the Black Horse was transfixed with fear and "ventured not to the open ground, so essential to [the Union's] own development and artillery maneuver."

It was in this atmosphere that the cry to raise cavalry regiments became both more frequent and more assertive. Senator Ira Harris of New York called for the formation of a cavalry unit, which, when finally formed, became known as the Harris Light Cavalry Regiment. Despite the enthusiasm the initial Union efforts to organize cavalry regiments in the East met with lugubrious results. Most of the new troopers had never touched a saddle, let alone ridden a horse. The horses, most of which were used to the common bridle, rebelled when curbed bits were inserted into their mouths. The rebellious mounts struck Glasier as "monstrous kangaroos" whose awkward riders had "taken lessons in somersaults," and he had to admit the Southern cavalry's contempt for these "mudsills and greasy mechanics" might not have been totally misplaced.

The newly raised cavalry regiments in the South did not experience the same degree of teething problems. Their recruits had grown up riding horses. Though certainly not lacking in horsemanship and natural talent, Confederate cavalry regiments possessed a tendency that would make itself felt several years later. A captain of hussars in the Imperial Austrian Service, Fitzgerald Ross had been sent to closely examine every aspect of the Southern troops. He characterized the Confederate cavalry as really a type of mounted infantry; though there was no standardization of weapons. Some showed up with sabers, others with pistols; almost all the recruits brought muskets, in the use of which they had been trained from earliest youth. There was little or no time for regular cavalry drill and the saber, which Ross believed was the "true arm of real cavalry." Ross's remarks appear to be neutral observations, more a type of taxonomical reflection than an attempt to malign Confederate cavalrymen.

In fact, Ross concluded that the Confederate authorities "act judiciously in taking their men as they found them, and not trying to establish the European system." The broken and wooded nature of most of the terrain, as well as the frequent fences, was not conducive to classical cavalry doctrine and precluded large-scale charges. Ross did feel, however, that the practice of cavalrymen's supplying their own horses did affect the way in which the Southern cavalry tended to fight. According to Ross, a cavalryman who had his horse killed or permanently disabled would be transferred to the infantry, unless he was able to replace his mount. Ross theorized that the troopers, fearing this, dismounted, placed their valuable mounts to the rear, and then fought on foot. Modern research, however, suggests that many Southern cavalrymen were given opportunities to replace lost mounts, and this protectiveness might have been less of a consideration than suggested by Ross.

ARMING THE CAVALRY

Cavalry traditionally had been armed in one of two different sets of weapons, depending upon the function it was to serve. Heavy cavalry, responsible for the main brunt of fighting on the battlefield, usually carried a side arm and a straight sword. Dragoons and light cavalry generally were armed with a slightly curved sword and a carbine and/or pistol. The principal purpose of the American cavalry had been to patrol the vast Western frontiers, and the functional specificity so characteristic of European cavalry had been set aside. As a result, by the mid-1850s the U.S. military only distinguished between "cavalry," dragoons," and "mounted rifles." These distinctions only further blurred with the need to raise a large number of cavalry units as it became clear the internecine conflict wouldn't be resolved within 90 days.

By 1854 the Colt revolver had replaced the single-shot model 1842 pistol, but both dragoons and cavalry regiments continued to be armed with some sort of sword. This long continued to be the official policy of Union military, and during the reorganization of the Union army after First Bull Run, Gen. George Stoneman still elected to arm all but two squadrons in each regiment with revolver and saber; the two "flank companies" received carbines. This practice might have had more to do with the limited number of carbines available than a reflection of pure doctrine. As greater numbers of carbines became available, they were gradually distributed among entire regiments.

For the Confederate authorities the choice of weapons was also governed more by availability than the theoretical capabilities of each. At the start of the war, those who could, armed themselves with revolvers and sabers, as was the case reported by the inspector general of the Confederate Army for Stuart's cavalry on May 23, 1861. However, 6 weeks later Maj. Gen. Irvin McDowell would report that much of the Virginia cavalry his reconnaissance parties had faced were irregularly armed with whatever they could get their hands on— double-barreled shotguns, pistols, fowling pieces, and a few carbines and sabers.

The situation was even less promising in the west, where in Missouri, Kentucky, Tennessee, and Mississippi, an even greater preponderance of the cavalry initially was armed with weapons supplied by local civilians. In Missouri most of General Thompson's cavalrymen (Pillow's Army of Occupation) carried shotguns and old-fashioned squirrel rifles. This problem certainly wasn't confined to the Southern side, and in his memoirs Sgt. E. Tarrant of the First Kentucky Cavalry (Union) remembered how even after A, B, and C Companies were armed with Sharps rifles and saber bayonets, the remainder had to be content with muskets, probably percussion cap smoothbores, for what seemed an interminably long time.

CHARGE DOCTRINE

The method of attacking an enemy cavalry or infantry prescribed by various period American drill manuals was essentially the same as that which had been introduced by Frederick the Great more than a century before. Although there were many regional variations, the majority of cavalry charge doctrines adhered to the same basic precepts. To maintain order as long as was possible, the cavalry began the advance at the walk and then, after 50 to 150 paces, broke out in a trot. When sufficiently close to the enemy, the troops began to gallop. The exact distance when this last transition occurred depended upon the cavalrymen's training and varied from army to army.

There were some American officers, however, who recommended a much shorter charge than that demanded by the traditional European system. In *Volunteer's Camp and Field Book,* a book written specifically for volunteer officers rushing to serve their country in early 1861, John Curry recommended a different tactic, especially when faced with superior numbers. Threatened with an enemy charge, the cavalry was to begin its movement as though it was beginning a countercharge. However, as soon as it reached 20 to 30 yards of the enemy, while at an "easy gallop," it was to unleash a volley with its carbines or pistols toward the center of the opposing formation. The troopers were to quickly replace their revolvers in the holsters or throw the carbines around their necks, then immediately seize their swords, which all the while had been dangling from their right wrists. Dividing up into three or four small columns, the friendly cavalry was to immediately work their away around the enemy's flank. Curry felt that this charge at a controlled gait was preferable to the hell-for-leather charge of the opponent. Traveling much faster, the enemy not only would take longer to turn to either side but would be unable to pull up suddenly for fear of being ridden down by the rear ranks, throwing the formation into hopeless confusion.

If not in the exact wording, then in the details Curry's method of attack was nothing more than the tactics that had been employed by the British Light Dragoons since first introduced at the start of the Seven Years' War. That these light cavalry tactics had remained current up to the start of the American Civil War is not surprising since they had been utilized in a slightly altered form throughout the Napoleonic Wars. Col. Fortuné "Mademoiselle" de Brack recommended similar tactics when light cavalry was attacked by heavy cavalry, such as cuirassiers. De Brack had served with distinction as commander of a guard lancer regiment under Napoleon and was well known throughout the nineteenth century for his courage and thoughtful approach to the art of war.

Regardless of possible influences on Curry's tactical thinking, one occasionally finds American officers in the field advocating similar tactics. Intending to cross Roger's Gap, Tennessee, Gen. George W. Morgan, who commanded the Seventh Division of the Army of the Ohio, instructed his cavalrymen always to "boldly and fiercely" countercharge when attacked by enemy cavalry. Like Curry, he specifically ordered them to a make a short charge. In order to guarantee that the horses were not blown, the countercharge was to commence only when the enemy had approached to within 50 yards. Coincidentally, this was exactly the same charge doctrine employed by the British and the Dutch during the War of Spanish Succession, 150 years earlier.

There were certainly enough neophyte officers who eagerly embraced this aggressive charge doctrine with its reliance upon a gallop and an outstretched sword. During an action that took place near Henrytown, Missouri, in late 1861, finding two of his companies attacked by a rebel force, Maj. Clark Wright commanded them to stand, return the enemy's fire steadily, and then instead of trying to reload, charge in with their outstretched sabers. The result was total success. Panicked, the Confederates broke, fled, and were chased for over 1½ miles during a running fight. There were some on the Confederate side who also espoused the traditional cavalry charge. Col. Angus W. McDonald, for example, lamented that none of his companies possessed either sabers or pistols. McDonald complained this deficiency deprived his men "of the weapons adapted to a cavalry charge" when faced with a well-equipped enemy, and should they meet in hand-to-hand combat, his men would be forced to resort to "clubbed rifles and shot-guns against revolvers and sabers," a situation he characterized as most unequal.

ALTERNATIVE TACTICS IN BROKEN TERRAIN

As much as some officers wanted to employ these shock tactics, the nature of much of the ground frequently conspired against their use and was one reason for the paucity of true cavalry-style tactics at this stage of the war. The *Official Records* is filled with reports of officers who explained that though they initially wanted to order a charge, they had to change their plans and come up with a tactical substitute.

Col. John D. Stevenson of the Seventh Missouri (Union) Infantry complained that his regiment, lacking in rifles or carbines, had to engage in costly hand-to-hand fighting. Apparently, rebel "bush-whackers" took refuge in places unapproachable by an equestrian force. His cavalry had to dismount and rush in to where they could use their revolvers and sabers.

A few months later Maj. Charles H. Town of First Michigan Cav-alry, in a report of his regiment's conduct during a skirmish at Mil-ford, Virginia (June 24, 1862), complained that his men were unable to best their rebel opponents since the rough, broken terrain where they invariably encountered their foe precluded the effective use of either the saber or the revolver. The rebels had positioned themselves on the fringe of dense woods that could not be charged directly by the cavalry. Forced to dismount, the Union men started to advance upon the rebel line, when Major Town noticed that he was outflanked on either side by forces armed with muskets and rifles. Only twenty or so of his men had carbines, and realizing the revolver was no match against longer-range weapons, he ordered his men to retire.

This oft-repeated criticism of the saber couldn't be ignored: The weapon was effective only in open terrain and was practicably use-less in a thick forest. Here troops armed with long-range shoulder arms had a distinct advantage. The troopers armed with sabers or revolvers either had to rush in to neutralize the enemy's advantage or give up the fight. Rushing in wasn't always feasible, especially when the defenders dismounted and ensconced themselves upon steep, broken hillsides. Unable to even approach the defenders, the cavalry had to keep outside of range and were reduced to "little more than spectators."

The same Clark Wright whose men successfully had charged home at Henrytown was frustrated when he attempted to use the same tac-tics during an action near Sugar Creek, Arkansas, on February 16, 1862. After his men unloaded their pistols and carbines, Wright once again ordered a charge. This time the brush proved too dense, and the horsemen were unable to advance quickly enough. He aborted the charge, and the men relied upon firepower to fight their way through the enemy position. This proved to be a very common problem, especially in the West. During the Battle of Shiloh, for example, at least one entire

Union cavalry regiment was on the field ready for action throughout the second day of the engagement, but the broken nature of the battlefield prevented its participation. The Fourth Illinois Cavalry Regiment several times was ordered to advance and charge the enemy's lines, each time it was ordered back before the charge could commence.

This all-too-common experience induced many officers to think about alternative tactics and weaponry. In theory, one could arm troopers with carbines in addition to revolvers and sabers, so that they had a suitable weapon for every occasion. When transferred to the Military Department of North Carolina, Gen. Ambrose Burnside found that cavalry regiments armed with sabers and revolvers were frequently at a disadvantage for lack of longer-range small arms. Writing to the secretary of war on June 24, 1862, he observed that though "sabers and pistols . . . is a most excellent general rule to adopt, in any cavalry, . . . in this thickly-wooded country a great portion of the skirmishing has to be done on foot, which renders carbines very necessary" and requested that General Ripley send, naturally enough, 1000 Burnside carbines.

However, carrying all three weapons wasn't that practical. It was cumbersome, especially during a fast-paced engagement. A more practical way to achieve tactical flexibility was to arm one or two companies in a cavalry regiment with sabers and the remainder with carbines. Then the regiment could employ either saber or long-range fire, depending upon the circumstances. The Second Iowa chose this solution. Its men were divided into several "saber companies," while the remainder fought dismounted as a "battalion of riflemen." If the situation called for an even greater force to hurl at the enemy, the saber companies from several regiments could be momentarily grouped together into an ad hoc formation, such as that used by Philip H. Sheridan, then colonel of the Second Michigan Cavalry, during an action near Booneville (July 1, 1862). Two saber companies from the Second Michigan and two from the Second Iowa worked their way around the enemy's left flank by a circuitous route and fell on its rear, while those with carbines and rifle muskets engaged the enemy from the front.

Of course, an even simpler solution to the inadequacies of saber tactics in rough terrain was simply to discard edged weapons and substitute fire tactics instead. To many, especially those from the South and Southwest, the saber charge—which required much practice and complete conformity of action of everyone along the charging line—probably seemed to be both contrived and unnecessary. After all, it appeared both more natural and more effective in open terrain simply to ride quickly up to the enemy and empty one's revolver or carbine in their faces. Texan cavalry in particular relished these tactics. An engagement at Rowlett's Station (Woodsonville, Kentucky) on December 17, 1861, provides an excellent example. During a chance encounter between a 1400-man Confederate force under Gen. T. C. Hindman and the Thirty-second Indiana, which was guarding a railroad bridge over the Green River, a small but determined body of Texas Rangers charged the Union advance guard then strung out along a skirmish line. Caught off guard, the Union infantry was almost overthrown as the Texans advanced to within 15 to 20 yards and emptied their revolvers. Forming small rally squares, the Union skirmishers replied with an even more deadly fire and drove off the rebel cavalry. The act was twice more repeated, but each time with the same result.

Those who favored reliance upon firepower simply had their cavalry dismount and fight on foot as mobile, light infantry when the engagement took place upon more difficult terrain. This practice certainly wasn't new. It is believed that dragoons, a type of cavalry that originally had been designed to move on horseback but then fight on foot, was introduced by Charles de Cossé, Marshal de Brisac, who commanded a French army in Piedmont (northwest Italian region) about the year 1600. The extent to which dismounted cavalry was employed during the Civil War was without precedent, however.

Although in most cases dismounted fighting started as an impromptu reaction to fast-unfolding events, it quickly became systematized. As soon as the commander gave the order to fight on foot, all of the troopers immediately dismounted. Three quarters of the men would run forward, either into line or in skirmish order, depending upon the circumstances. The remainder took the horses to the rear, where they would remain throughout the engagement. The number of men guarding the horses was not set in stone, and should the front line be hard pressed, the horses would be tied together in groups of fifteen to twenty so that many of the men in the rear could join the fight. Frederick Whittaker, a Union cavalryman, estimated the entire process took less than 2 minutes. Whittaker claimed that cavalrymen on foot tended to fight more effectively than infantry in the same situation. Not only were they usually fresher, having ridden to where the fighting was to take place, but they were generally more enthusiastic, often regarding a momentary fight merely as a break from routine.

HAND-TO-HAND FIGHTING

Examining cavalry charges in greater detail, one notices that a much higher percentage of these actions resulted in melees than their counterparts during the Napoleonic Wars. During earlier wars the result of most charges was one side or the other breaking and precipitously flying from the field, the victorious side in pursuit. Glancing through Civil War literary references, examples of close-in, hand-to-hand fighting are not uncommon. The Seventh Missouri Infantry (mounted), armed with only revolvers and sabers, for example, had to approach to extremely close range in order to grapple with its Confederate adversaries, armed with longer-ranged weapons, during a skirmish in Lafayette County, Missouri (March 10, 1862). Charged by enemy cavalry with drawn sabers at Cane Hill (Boston Mountains, Arkansas, November 1862), Col. Emmett Mac-Donald reported that his Missouri Cavalry (Confederate) fought hand to hand with those brave enough to approach to contact, but these were so few that the Union cavalry was quickly forced to retire.

This type of fighting quickly broke down into individual fights, in which one might assume that experienced regular cavalrymen and their officers would enjoy an advantage. These free-for-alls possessed all the characteristics of a modern street fight, however, and a ferocious disposition and a willingness to kill or be killed were as important as formal training with the available weaponry. The *Official Records* and veterans' memoirs are filled with examples of men observed to perform prodigious feats. During the already cited action at Henrytown, Missouri, after empting his revolver, Lieutenant Montgomery of the Frémont Battalion of Cavalry (Union) flailed with his sword until it was "doubled up." Still not satiated, he then attacked his seventh victim, whom he knocked unconscious with a single punch.

The previous year a skirmish at Frankfort, in western Virginia (June 26, 1861), had witnessed an even bloodier melee between Confederate cavalry and a small mounted patrol that had been detached from the Eleventh Indiana Infantry. Col. Lew Wallace would write of the affair:

> I would simply say of this skirmish, that it was one of the boldest, most desperate, and fortunate on record, abounding with instances on the part of my scouts of rarest coolness, skill, and courage. What makes it most singular is that, for a considerable portion of the time, it was a hand-to-hand fight, carried on with pistol, saber, bayonet, and fist. One man, Louis Farley, killed six rebels; another (Grover) killed three; David Hayes, the wounded corporal, killed two, and received all his wounds while in hot pursuit at the very tails of the rebels' horses.

At least one observer noted that occasionally formal training could even be a disadvantage during these free-for-alls. In his memoirs Captain George Baylor of the Twelfth Virginia Cavalry recounted witnessing a situation in which the rigid approach of formal training actually worked against a West Point officer. During a cavalry brush in front of Madison Court House, Virginia on June 21, 1863, a Confederate trooper named B. C. Washington engaged in hand-to-hand combat with Maj. Samuel McIrwin of the Second New York Cavalry. McIrwin, like all formally trained cavalrymen, was under strict orders to hold and use his saber with his right hand. Common practice was predicated on the assumption that the adversary was equally well trained and all held their weapons in their right hands. In this case his opponent, trooper Washington, was left-handed and—like most Confederate troopers, not overly bound by the niceties of the theory of saber fencing—had grasped his saber in the way he felt most comfortable, with his left hand. The contest was over almost as fast as it started. Washington struck first, but, well trained, the Major easily parried the blow. Unfortunately for the Union officer, the saber's design was to guard against a blow from a right-handed antagonist.

Checked, Washington's saber slid very quickly down the blade. Since McIrwin's saber's guard was on the other side of his hand, Washington's blade wounded his hand, forcing him to drop his weapon, and he was forced to surrender. The major later conceded he had never been instructed in the use of the saber against a left-handed man.

The fatalities inflicted during the fighting at Henrytown and Frankfort notwithstanding, a great majority of wounds caused by the saber did not prove lethal, as in the foregoing example. Most military authorities had long agreed that a *thrust* wound was many times more likely to maim or kill than a *slashing* blow. Writing at the end of the Seven Years' War, the French general François de Grandmaison had observed that while a single stab wound frequently proved fatal, cavalrymen who suffered in excess of twenty cutting wounds often survived! In his instructions to his French lancer regiment, de Brack entertained a similar view when he pontificated:

It is the points alone that kill; the others serve only to wound. Thrust! Thrust! as often as you can: you will overthrow all whom you touch, and demoralize those who escape your attack, and you will add to those advantages that of always being able to parry and never uncovered.

The most deadly situation actually occurred when one side considered itself vanquished and tried to flee beyond the reaches of their now-victorious foe. Inevitably, a hot pursuit followed, and the defeated cavalry could suffer tremendous casualties. Although one might expect the fleeing forces, motivated by sheer terror, to quickly outdistance the pursuers seeking their destruction, the all-too-common reality was that the victorious pursuers, worked up into a blood lust would gallop along with the same reckless abandon. The difference, of course, was that the defeated cavalry, with their backs to their pursuers, were unable to fend off any blows that might come their way.

An example of just how much damage even a single pursuer could inflict upon fleeing cavalrymen is provided by George Bliss's actions at Waynesborough, Virginia, September 28, 1864. A captain in the First Rhode Island Regiment, during the late afternoon engagement, Bliss had actually commanded several small detachments from various other corps during an impromptu attempt to repel a sudden attack on Union cavalrymen who had been in the process of destroying a railway bridge. All of his defensive attempts were at first unsuccessful.

Bliss had been forced back with a few stalwarts to the Third New Jersey Cavalry, which was made to countercharge the advancing Confederate cavalry only through the personal bravery of its colonel and Captain Bliss. Bliss, trying to set an example for his initially reluctant troopers, precipitously advanced about a hundred yards in front of the first squadron, which finally started to advance to meet the rebels. While Bliss was looking back to see that his men were following him, his horse jumped over a barricade that Bliss himself had earlier ordered constructed across Waynesborough's main street.

Unfortunately for Bliss, seeing a small enemy force approaching the flank, the captain of the regiment's frontmost squadron stopped the regiment's advance and wheeled the men to meet this latest treat. Unaware of these developments and believing he was closely followed by his men, Bliss plunged into the Confederate force in front, who just a moment before had stopped its own advance, turned, and fled in the greatest of haste, also unaware of the last-second threat to the Union flank. This situation of a single Union rider chasing a large body of veteran Confederate horsemen would be laughable in the extreme if not for the potentially fatal implications. What happened next is best left in Bliss's own words:

> ... jumping my horse over the low barricade, dashed in among the rebels, only to find myself making the attack single-handed. I had ridden past a dozen of the enemy before I discovered my desperate situation. They were retreating in a loose column of fours, and so I rode in among them there were three files on my left and one on my right. ... There was but one chance; fifty men behind me were shouting "Kill that d—— Yankee." To turn among them and retrace my steps was impossible; my horse was swift and I thought if I could keep on until I came to a side street, I might dash onto that, and, by making a circle, reach our lines.

Captured near the end of this affair and held prisoner by those whom he attacked, Bliss, after a series of amiable discussions, was able to reconstruct exactly what happened in what must have been only a few moments. Bliss had determinedly ridden into the fleeing Confederate column and frantically started to rain blows to the right and left with the cutting edge of his saber. Noting the wounds inflicted and the personal experiences, Bliss and his captors determined that he had delivered six blows. Although Capt. Morgan Strotten and W. T. Hanes escaped by dodging their heads, four others were not so fortunate and received nonfatal slashing wounds. Breaking through the three files of Confederate riders on his left, Bliss attempted to escape through the first side street, but the enemy horsemen, now free to fire at their prey, quickly brought down his horse, and Bliss was soon captured.

Incidentally, the actual process of capturing the Union captain revealed another potential problem that could occur during a cavalry melee. Although Captain Bliss had signaled that he wished to surrender, one of the Confederate horsemen churlishly attempted to stab him in the back with an outstretched saber. Fortunately for Bliss, the rebel cavalryman didn't realize that to kill one had to turn the blade sideways so that it could pass through the rib cage. Bliss was nearly knocked out of the saddle by the unexpected blow but survived with several extremely painfully bruised ribs!

MOVEMENT AWAY FROM SABER CHARGES

Almost from the very beginning of the conflict, there were those that felt that Southern cavalry needed more than the revolver-saber combination. When on April 11, 1862, Ambrosio José Gonzales, the chief of artillery for South Carolina and Georgia, proposed an elaborate system of coastal defense for the Southern coastline, he felt that cavalry called upon to defend coastal batteries was much more suitably armed with double-barreled shotguns. Not only was this weapon readily available, but it was also a particularly vicious weapon when aimed at close quarters at small boats packed full of Northern invaders. Given the wide dispersion of the pellets, the mounted trooper had a much greater chance of hitting his intended target than when armed with conventional carbines or rifles. This was especially true when firing while in motion.

This opinion was to be echoed by other cavalry officers, especially among those in the West. Unable to purchase an adequate supply of revolvers, William R. Hunt, an ordnance officer in Memphis, implored the Confederate secretary of war to order that these weapons be stripped from infantry officers and private soldiers and distributed among the cavalry, who were much more in need of them. In the same letter Hunt also hinted that arming the cavalry with shotguns might be a reasonable alternative and alluded to Col. Nathan Bedford Forrest's opinion that the shotgun was the "best gun" for cavalry service.

As it turned out, Confederate authorities in Richmond had been leaning in a similar direction, if only for logistical reasons. By late 1861 revolvers had become scarce in the West, and by early 1862 this deficiency had become general throughout the Confederacy. It became extremely difficult to arm new cavalry organizations with this weapon. Responding to the governor of Georgia's offer to raise new cavalry regiments, on February 24 J. P. Benjamin, the Confederate secretary of war, stipulated that two cavalry regiments would be accepted provided that they were armed with sabers and carbines or double-barreled shotguns. Benjamin added that lancers would be accepted and that Richmond would even provide the lances. However, less than a month later, Benjamin reversed his views regarding the acceptability of sabers. Writing to the governor of Alabama on March 17, he explained that double-barreled shotguns were the most suitable weapons for cavalry and that "after a month or two sabers are universally discarded as useless, *men not being thoroughly trained to the use of that arm*" [italics mine].

There were those on the Confederate side who if they did not necessarily support the use of sabers, nevertheless continued to advocate the use of edged weapons. While writing to Robert E. Lee on March 21, John B. Magruder, charged with the defense of the Virginia peninsula, agitated for the adoption of lances and shotguns, arguing that not only were lances easier to come by than sabers, but they could be fashioned by any carpenter and much more effective in battle. Angus W. McDonald held the opposite view. Instead of a long lance or even a saber, he wanted his men armed with a short, half-pound hatchet, which presumably he felt would be much more wieldy in close-in fighting.

Although these early efforts to consider alternative armament for cavalry were driven either by logistical considerations or highly individuated circumstances, such as the need to defend the coasts, there are signs by the beginning of the second year of the war that there were many cavalry officers who believed that sabers, and hence charge tactics, were either impractical because of the rough terrain or obsolete because of the advent of long-range and relatively quick-fire small arms. An article that appeared in the January 25, 1862, edition of *Scientific American* was indicative of this trend and probably best presented the underlying rationale. Arguing that the government was wasting millions to maintain this now useless arm, the writer recommended authorities immediately get "rid of this arm of service." To support his argument, the writer excerpted a passage from an unidentified European military writer:

Let the horse be ever so swift, the sabre ever so sharp, or the rider ever so bold, the conical ball is too much for him. A charge of cavalry upon a body of properly armed infantry bids fair to be henceforth impossible. Two hundred yards has been fixed by the best authority as the proper charging distance, and in bygone days it was only at two hundred yards that the fire of a squadron began to tell, and saddles to be emptied. But now-a-days the iron rain patters on the horsemen before they get within half a mile of the foe. If they quicken their pace to close, the maddest charge will not bring a dragoon horse on the bayonet in less than three minutes, and when he arrives he is blown and disabled. "When he arrives"—if he arrives, we should say; for even in traversing eight hundred yards at the top of his speed he receives half a dozen volleys from practiced sharpshooters. To send cavalry in such service has a swifter messenger in his cartouch box than the fleetest hussar.

Once more the influence of Captains Gilluim and Wittich and their followers is seen surfacing among American opinion! The *Scientific American* article also appears to reflect a growing opinion among those serving in the field. On April 7, 1862, Brig. Gen. J. M. Schofield would write to Gen. James Totten that despite their clamor to be armed with edged weapons, his men had "no more use for a saber than for a columbiad."

This antisaber sentiment could be found among some cavalrymen throughout the war. The October 17, 1863, edition of the *Army and Navy Journal* published a letter similar to the tirade against cavalry published in the *Scientific American* 18 months earlier. Convinced that sabers had proven not to be useful weapons and were merely encumbrances dangling from the troopers' waists, this officer could not decide whether this uselessness was the result of inadequate training in proper weapon use or of obsolescence caused by the recent advances in small arms. As evidence the anonymous writer cited the action at Jonesville, Virginia, that had taken place that January, where the Ninth Pennsylvania Cavalry, fighting dismounted, presented an almost laughable appearance:

> Each with a muzzle-loading rifle and long sabre at his side, was ludicrous in the extreme. The sabres prevented the use of their rifles effectively as light troops when dismounted, and, conversely their rifles would have greatly interfered with the use of their sabres, on horseback. . . . These weapons do not belong together. They should have hung their sabres to their saddles on dismounting.

He concluded that 80% of cavalrymen should be, in effect, mounted infantrymen, who, armed with repeating or breach-loading rifles, were to fight dismounted in skirmish order. The remaining fifth should be properly schooled in the use of the saber and charge tactics.

MOUNTED INFANTRY

Although the first reference to "mounted infantry" in the *Official Records* was penned on November 27, 1861, at Camp Marion (Virginia) by C. J. Colcock, lieutenant colonel of the Confederate Lower Squadron Mounted Infantry, *Dyer's Compendium* mentions that a twenty-seventh Regiment Mounted Infantry (Union) had been organized in Missouri in May that year. There were probably a number of such small, ad hoc organizations that were brought together without the federal government's, possibly even their states', authorization. After a skirmish near Paris, Tennessee (March 10, 1862), for example, an officer of the Fifth Iowa Cavalry would report that he had captured Captain Couts, of "Stock's mounted infantry."

Strictly speaking, the concept of mounted infantry was anything but new, and its use predated the musket by more than 50 years. With their introduction in the early seventeenth century, dragoons were originally intended to be a type of mobile infantry that would quickly ride to where they were needed in the countryside or on the battlefield and then dismount and fight as infantry. As time passed, dragoons increasingly became just one more type of cavalry, which, like the others, would fight almost entirely as an equestrian force. The original purpose of dragoons was never totally forgotten, though, and as part of their formal training, they continued to learn how to fight on foot. Interest in "fast infantry" was rekindled with the introduction of the needle gun and the *carbine à tige* during the 1840s, when, as we have seen, tactical theoreticians such as Wittich expected regular cavalry to give up its traditional methods and become a form of "mounted infantry."

The experimentation with mounted infantry during the Civil war does not appear to be related to these relatively obscure developments among the radical western European military intelligentsia, but appears to have arisen from indigenous factors. During the first year of war, experiments with mounted infantry were sporadic and appear to have been the result of individual efforts rather than the result of official policy. This would begin to change on Aug 23, 1862. When faced with a growing Indian war on his frontier, Alexander Ramsey, governor of Minnesota, urgently requested to be allowed to raise a battalion of this arm, and Halleck gave permission 2 days later. There is evidence that Ramsey was not the only one interested in mounting infantry during that summer. It was just about this time that Col. Mortimer D. Leggett of the Seventy-eighth Ohio Infantry jubilantly reported the success of his "mule infantry" during a skirmish at Bolivar, Tennessee (August 30). Proclaiming that this force moved "with the celerity of cavalry, yet fight as infantry," he recounted how twice during the engagement this infantry atop their horses quickly changed positions and thwarted the enemy's attempt to outflank the Union position.

Portions of the Minnesota battalion were mustered into service by mid-October. History does not record the service provided by this force. However, records show that whether influenced by this development or the product of completely independent forces, a number of high-ranking officials would press authorities in Washington for permission to raise similar battalions. On October 15, 1862, James F. Robinson, governor of Kentucky, telegraphed Secretary of War Stanton to allow the Fourteenth Kentucky to form two battalions of mounted infantry, one at Maysville and the other at Paducah. State authorities were not the only ones thinking about providing some of the Union infantry with a more expeditious means of locomotion. As a countermeasure to incursions of rebel partisans then laying havoc to Union communications and its supply effort, Brig. Gen. Thomas Davies suggested to Grant that the entire Second Division, Army of the Tennessee, be given mounts, a request that he would repeat directly to Halleck near year's end.

When ordered to increase the strength of his cavalry arm, Maj. Gen. John A. McClernand would reply that although his assigned territory did not have the resources to supply any more men, he could compensate for this deficiency by collecting the required number of mules and pack horses and thus mount about one-fifth of the existing infantry force. In order not to demoralize his men, the ersatz cavalrymen would not be required to tend to the horses after each journey. McClernand provided a rationale for his stratagem:

> Thus mounted, the infantry would be prepared to perform the double duty of men on foot and on horseback. By rapid movements they could retard the advance of the foe, cut his communications, destroy his trains, and harass him at every step. In like manner they could rapidly pursue a retreating foe and continually annoy and distress him. To add to their efficiency I would also provide them with a suitable number of mountain howitzers to meet any demand for artillery service; and for the same purpose I would supply each battalion of cavalry with two pieces of the same character.

CAVALRY VERSUS INFANTRY

During the Napoleonic Wars the cavalry arm had played a crucial role on the battlefield. Although it had long been recognized that "if Foot could be brought to know their own Strength, the Danger from which they apprehended from Horse, would soon vanish," the mounted trooper remained a threat that could best the footman should the latter ever expose a weakness. Probably Marshal Joachim Murat provided the most spectacular example of what could be achieved when his Reserve Cavalry destroyed or disrupted the center of the Russian army at Eylau (February 8, 1807).

Naturally, many of those who joined the cavalry at the start of the Civil War hoped that the arm would relive the glory of bygone days, and J. E. B. Stuart's seemingly effortless success against the Fire Zouaves during First Bull Run only heightened these expectations. However, as the struggle began in earnest, repeated efforts to reproduce these results proved frustratingly elusive. At Shiloh the Fourth Illinois Cavalry Regiment several times attempted to charge, but each time the charge was aborted. Meanwhile, on the Confederate side two of Nathan Bedford Forrest's biographers credit the great Confederate leader with a daring charge against the Union defense that up to this point had frustrated General Cheatham's Second Division. Despite heavy defensive fire Forrest's horsemen were able to approach to within 40 yards, when they were bemired in a morass.

During most Civil War battles, a preponderance of the struggle rested upon the efforts of the infantry and artillery. This is not to suggest that the mounted arm was totally excluded. However, when it did play a part, cavalry generally was introduced during the later stages of the contest and then almost always was directed against its enemy counterpart, such as during Second Bull Run or the third day of Gettysburg. One finds relatively few instances in which cavalry purposely charged enemy infantry deployed in line and ready for the assault. The terrain over which many of the battles were fought of course was a contributing factor. Many battles, such as Chancellorsville, the Wilderness, Lookout Mountain, and Missionary Ridge, were contested on extremely rough terrain that precluded the use of cavalry. In other cases the opposing forces lacked sufficient cavalry for it to be meaningfully employed.

A few cases can be found in which cavalry did charge the pedestrian arm during a set piece battle, but these charges were launched only after the opposing infantry had been thoroughly shaken by friendly infantry or demoralized by a sudden turn of events. One such example occurred during the autumn of 1863 near the Culpepper Court House. Stuart and his command had been ordered on October 9 to cross the Rapidan to capture a Union signal station on Stonehouse Mountain. Stuart's force set out the next day, and once across the Rapidan headed toward Culpepper Court House, catching up with some retreating enemy troops near Griffinsberg. At this point, Company B, the Jefferson Company, of Twelfth Virginia Cavalry, the Baylor Light Horse, commanded by then-Lieutenant Baylor, was acting as General Stuart's bodyguard.

Nearing Culpepper, Stuart and his men noticed a regiment of Union infantry on their right, seemingly in an isolated position and quickly marching parallel to the Confederate column in a desperate attempt to regain its own support near the town. In his memoirs John Esten Cooke, who at the time was an aide to Stuart, recollected that he had never seen Stuart more excited:

> He was plainly on fire with the idea of capturing the whole party. The staff scattered to summon the cavalry, and soon a company came up at a full gallop.

As Stuart's column hastened its own pace to cut off the enemy infantry, the column began to be thrown into some confusion, and it was clear that unless charged, the enemy would effect its escape. Looking around and sending off his aides in all directions, Stuart quickly realized that the only available cavalry was Baylor's small detachment. Baylor recollects feeling that the proposed undertaking was a "rash and dangerous" one, but the orders were both unambiguous and emphatic, so there was nothing he could do but comply. Baylor's company began its charge just as the Union infantry debouched into open ground. Noticing the Confederate charge, the Union infantry faced to their rear and double-quicked a few steps up a slope. Once in position atop the small rise, the Union infantry once again quickly faced about, the long line of gun barrels fell, and a single volley was hurled against the small band of Confederate horsemen. Both Cooke and Stuart reported that this volley was delivered when the Confederates had closed to 30 yards. Baylor, who actually led the charge, conceded that it was delivered when his horsemen were still 100 yards distant. In any case the volley was too high, going over the cavalrymen's heads, and little loss was inflicted.

The Confederate cavalrymen, however, were unable to make good their initial success. An impassible ditch lay between the would-be victors and the panicked Union infantry. The latter unceremoniously threw off their knapsacks, and most were able to escape unscathed, the ground littered with discarded guns, knapsacks, and blankets.

LACK OF CAVALRY CHARGES

It is natural to attribute this lack of formal cavalry charges against infantry to the increased range and accuracy of the new small arms. According to this explanation, now the infantryman could fire effectively while the mounted threat was still at long range, and the cavalry would be decimated before it was able to close. There is some evidence that the cavalry's performance was much less restricted by these new weapons than moderns believe. Received wisdom assumes that, threatened with enemy cavalry, the infantryman would continue to fire throughout the latter's charge, except for the final few seconds when it would "guard against cavalry."

Period tacticians, however, generally believed that once a cavalry charge began, the defending infantry would be able to fire only once, possibly twice. Several trials conducted to determine the length of time required to conduct a charge found that a cavalry regiment required about 7 minutes to attack an enemy 1000 yards distant. The first 400 yards were covered at a trot in about 4 minutes, the next 400 yards at a "round trot" in 2 minutes, while the last 200 yards at gallop in 30 seconds.

There was less agreement about the best method that the defending infantry could employ to defend itself, however. In the late 1700s many military thinkers accepted the adage that Frederick the Great's Prussian infantry had been able to fire three rounds per minute in volleys and five rounds per minute when they fired individually. By the end of the Napoleonic Wars, experienced officers realized that this rapid rate of fire was impossible to maintain under battlefield conditions. Two schools of thought emerged. Some believed it was best for the infantry to fire about three volleys into a fast-approaching cavalry. Others, however, believed this was unobtainable and the infantry should withhold its fire until close range, then unleash one deadly volley.

Now, there is some indirect evidence that as long as the infantryman was armed with a muzzle-loading weapon, the last tactic was generally both the most effective and practical. Thomas Bugeaud, although he had risen to marshal by the later stages of the Algerian War, had started off during the Napoleonic Wars in a much more humble capacity. Extremely observant, Bugeaud's memoirs are chock-full of deeply insightful anecdotes and analyses. However, one of his most intriguing and seemingly counterintuitive observations was about the distribution of casualties during an infantry-versus-infantry engagement. The amount of casualties absorbed by the attacker would gradually increase as he neared and tended to be the greatest when he had closed to within 150 to 100 paces. According to Bugeaud, however, if the attacker remained resolute and continued to approach, the rate of casualties then actually declined during the last stages of the assault. This anomaly clashes with our expectations, since one would assume that as the attacker approached, he offered a better target, and there was an increased likelihood of hits.

A passage in a mid-eighteenth-century military scientific treatise, *Essai sur la tactique de l'infanterie* (Geneva, 1761), not only corroborates Bugeaud's observation but provides a compelling explanation. Its author maintained that once the enemy infantry had advanced to within 120 paces, a regimental commander was best advised have his men withhold their fire until the last moments. In theory, there was enough time to fire again and reload; it would take the enemy about 40 to 50 seconds to advance the remaining distance and only about 20 seconds to reload a flintlock musket. The problem stemmed from how the men reacted to the sight of the approaching enemy during the last moments. Regardless of what they were ordered to do, as soon as their enemy advanced to within about 80 paces, the men stopped whatever they were doing and prepared themselves to face the enemy with their bayonets. The instinct for survival overpowered training and doctrine.

These observations about infantry-versus-infantry engagements might appear to have little to do with the feasibility of *cavalry charges against infantry* during the Civil War. However, anyone who has studied the experience of battle during the eighteenth century and the Napoleonic period knows that the sight of a fast-approaching enemy cavalry formation was many times more intimidating than the sight of oncoming enemy infantry. One of the most vivid descriptions of just how psychologically trying it was to brave a cavalry charge was provided by a British cavalryman, William Thomkinson, who survived the Peninsular Wars (1808–1814):

It is an awful thing for infantry to see a body of cavalry riding at them at full gallop. The men in the square frequently begin to shuffle, and so create some unsteadiness. *This causes them to neglect their fire* [italics mine]. The cavalry seeing them waver, have an inducement for riding close up, and in all probability succeed in getting into the square, when it is all over.

Thomkinson was quick to point out that the men, fixated with the approaching threat, neglected their fire. This reaction certainly was not limited to European soldiers. In his remembrances of the battle of Corinth, Oscar Jackson recalled that many in the Union infantry had a similar reaction as they awaited a Confederate infantry assault. Many of the men along the line seemed to bounce, standing a while on one foot and then on the other.

The rifle musket involved the same general method of loading and possessed a potential rate of fire roughly comparable to the older smoothbore muskets. This meant that as long as the great majority of Civil War infantry was armed with Enfields and Springfields during the final stages of a charge, when the cavalry was at full trot or even gallop, the defending infantry would experience the same psychological dynamics as just described.

This did not mean that charging cavalry would break through the defending line with impunity. During the Napoleonic wars, though cavalry often was able to approach defending infantry, the latter, with their serried ranks of outstretched bayonets, was still usually able to hold the horsemen at bay. When this happened, the cavalry usually

had to circle around the defending formation, as Ney's cavalry did at
Waterloo, or they were soon forced back by well-controlled fire by
ranks. In this regard many Civil War cavalry regiments enjoyed a distinct advantage. Their European predecessors had been armed with
single-shot flintlock pistols. Those Union or Confederate troopers
armed with Colt revolvers in a similar position, instead of retiring,
could unleash a sufficient volume of fire to cause numerous casualties. As soon as sufficiently large gaps appeared, the defending line
was doomed.

An example of just how deadly this tactic could be is provided by the
massacre of a detachment of Thirty-ninth Missouri Infantry by a large
group of rebel guerrillas led by Bill Anderson and George Todd. Spotting a small band of bushwhackers, the soldiers chased their prey but,
as it turned out, were led into a trap. Anderson and Todd's men were
alerted by the initial chase and advanced toward the Union infantry.
When they were half a mile from the latter, they split into three groups.
Todd and about sixty-five men were to work their way around the left,
while another group went to the right. Anderson and the remainder were
to attack frontally. As soon as he spotted the rebels advancing, the
Union commander, Maj. A. V. E. Johnston, ordered about ninety of his
men to dismount and form line with fixed bayonets along the crest of a
hill, while thirty-five Union troopers, the "fourth men," held the horses
in the rear. Anderson and his men charged as soon as they cleared the
forest. The defenders fired a volley, but only three attackers were hit;
most of the shots were high. Frank James, many years after the incident,
would vividly recall the final moments of the fight:

Up the hill we went yelling like wild Indians. Almost in a twin-
kling of an eye we were on the Yankees' line. They seemed terrorized. Hypnotized might be a better word . . . Some of the
Yankees were at "fix bayonets," some were biting off their cartridges, preparing to reload. Yelling, shooting our pistols upon
them we went. Not a single man of the line escaped. Every one
was shot through the head . . . My brother, Jesse James . . .
killed the commander of the Federal troops. Only several men
holding the horses were able to escape.

The popularization of six-shooters did not mean that cavalry could automatically defeat infantry. There were also a number of developments that worked against the effectiveness of the traditional cavalry charge against infantry. Although infantry with rifle muskets rarely fired at enemy lines at more than 400 paces, a deep formation might prove to be too much a temptation and entice the defender into a long-range but still effective fire. The longer range of the rifle musket, therefore, made it difficult to set up carefully prepared attacks. It became increasingly impractical to use true columnar formations. Moreover, by 1864 soldiers on both sides and in most theaters of operations routinely erected "hasty entrenchments" whenever they had an opportunity. The appearance of these ad hoc defensive works would afford greater protection to the defending infantry and made cavalry charges less likely to succeed. Finally, there was the appearance of breechloaders and repeaters. Infantry armed with these more rapid-firing shoulder arms obviously could have beaten back any cavalry charge with ease.

It is ironic that before the advent of hasty entrenchments and repeaters, the cavalry and its officers were insufficiently trained to conduct true cavalry charges, and by the time they acquired the experience to conduct these potentially devastating tactics, the infantry had acquired new tactical assets to render the traditional cavalry charge ineffective.

PART IV

THE WEST AND SPECIALIZED FORMS OF WARFARE

Chapter 17
FIGHTING IN THE WEST

Although portions of Virginia so hotly contested by rebel and Union armies were difficult and broken, most of the Western theater proved to be more inhospitable and disruptive to both day-to-day campaigning and battlefield activities. This was as true during Zollicoffer's 1861 campaign, as he led his rebel army through Kentucky, as it would be for Sherman's forces 4 years later, as they pushed their way through the north Georgia mountains towards Atlanta.

The roughness of the terrain, coupled with its sheer expansiveness, complicated every aspect of military operations. Frequently, an army would advance hundreds of miles, stretching its communications and supply lines to the limit. A difficult situation even when traversing populated areas with cultivated farmlands, such advances verged on the impossible when moving through unending forests and hills with a few widely dispersed roads. This dramatically affected every aspect of logistical planning, such as transmitting orders and keeping the armies fully supplied in food, arms, and ammunition. True, the extensive river systems that wend their way through the Western states frequently provided an alternative system of travel and supply. However, the exigencies of campaigning all too often sent combatant armies into areas not easily reached by rail or even river transports. Then Confederate and Union armies were forced to rely on whatever roads were available, and this meant trudging along backwoods lanes or even cow paths toward some unnamed locale destined for immortality but which hitherto had never graced any map.

Quickly thrown on the defensive, the Confederates were the first to learn how to interdict these routes. Unlike the European countryside, where a blocked road usually had little military impact, since the troops usually could take to the open fields and circumvent any obstruction, in the Western theater a small force defending a critical juncture along a road could effectively thwart even a large-scale offensive operation for days by closing down the only avenue of advance. On both sides of the road often lay expansive forests with dense underbrush. Frequently, the road meandered through lowlands surrounded by high, impassible hills and mountains. The simplest defensive expedient was to cut down some timber, which, when thrown across the road, served as an instant strongpoint.

Ordered to Bowling Green, Kentucky, to join the rest of Ormsby Mitchell's Third Division of the Army of the Ohio in February 1862, the progress of the Fourth Ohio Cavalry was temporarily interrupted by just such an effort. At first the rebels failed to appreciate that the woods on either side of the road were passable; quickly outflanked, they were forced to fall back. Such delaying tactics proved much more effective as the division neared Nashville, however. The Confederate rear guard soon learned to choose points that were not as easily outflanked. Fighting their way slowly forward, the Ohioan cavalrymen had to dismount and climb over a seemingly endless succession of obstacles. Armed with axes, spades, picks, jackscrews, and long ropes and hooks, the Michigan Engineer Corps following the Ohio cavalry chopped up the impedimenta and dragged it aside. Before long the road was reopened to the artillery and wagons following in the rear. However, no sooner had they cleared one set of felled trees than they had to start over again with the next. Dead animals placed in ponds were a greater nuisance, making it difficult to find suitable drinking water.

Even when the advancing Union forces were lucky enough to find themselves unopposed, the elements seemed to conspire against them. Insufferable heat in the summer, deadly cold in the winter, and periods of seemingly endless rain in between added to the already onerous rigors of the long march. This was particularly a problem early in the conflict, when the green troops failed to take the necessary precautions for a long trek in the heat.

A veteran commissioned to write the regimental history of the

102nd Illinois Volunteers would recall how his regiment fared during its first real "forced march," as it advanced out of Louisville on October 3, 1862. The men were still naïve enough to fill up their knapsacks, while the commander was sufficiently inexperienced to push his men far beyond what could have been reasonably expected. Though advanced in season, it was unseasonably hot, and water was not to be had. Though the march started off well, men soon started to fall by the wayside, at first singly, then in twos and threes and finally by entire squads. Still, the march continued well into the night. By midnight three-quarters of the regiment had been left behind along the roadside. It was only by 10 o'clock the next morning that most of the stragglers had come up to rejoin the regiment, and the march resumed.

MOUNTAINS AND MOVEMENT

Although it was always difficult to move a large army successfully through a large forest, it was probably the mountainous regions, such as in parts of Georgia, Kentucky, and Tennessee, that posed the greatest challenge to operations. Artillery was particularly affected. The steep grades made it extremely difficult to drag artillery pieces that could weigh as much as 4000 pounds up an ascent. Coming down the other side was frequently as dangerous as the ascent had been arduous.

Just how difficult it could be to transport artillery over this type of difficult terrain is poignantly illustrated by the trials and travails of the artillery that accompanied Gen. George W. Morgan's Seventh Division of Army of the Ohio during the summer of 1862. Intending to surprise the rebel force that guarded Rodger's Pass in eastern Tennessee, on June 7 Morgan's force was directed to leave the Big Creek Gap road and follow a goat's path so narrow and steep that it was generally thought impassible to cavalry and artillery. Undaunted, General Morgan ordered the two 20-pounders and two 30-pounder Parrott rifles in the siege battery to proceed across the mountain first. The 30-pounders, weighing 3500 pounds, were each pulled by twelve horses, while eight horses were attached to each 20-pounder (1750 pounds apiece) and caisson. Each wagon was hauled by the regulation six mules.

Feeling that it was unlikely that anyone was foolish enough to cross at this point, the Confederates left the pass unguarded, and at first the progress of the expeditionary force went unopposed. The road up the mountainside followed a tortuous path sometimes so steep that the horses were unable to get a firm footing. Artillerymen, with the aid of ropes and tackles, would hoist the horses, wagons, and artillery up these inclines. With the loads too heavy for the small number of artillerymen assigned to each piece, many infantrymen had to hand their muskets to their comrades and pitch in. Other times, when the outside edge of the road was bordered by a sheer drop of hundreds of feet, a shallow trench was dug near the inside edge of the road. The inside set of wheels of the limbers, caissons, and wagons were placed into this track so that the vehicles could not veer toward the other side of the road and inadvertently fall over the precipice.

Then, suddenly, the road would plunge precipitously downward, and although it had been with the greatest backbreaking effort that men and officers had managed to haul the siege battery up the mountain, they quickly learned that the descent was even more difficult and perilous. It was critical that the wagons and artillery proceed down the road at a controlled pace. If a weighty load picked up speed, it would become unmanageable and careen down the road, killing the horses and men it ran over and destroying any wagons and other pieces that were still methodically working their way down the mountain.

To prevent this, a handspike was thrust through the rear wheels to prevent them from turning. A dozen men held these wheels and thus served as an additional brake. The wagons were allowed to slide slowly down the fast-falling road. In more difficult spots a cable attached to an axle was wrapped around a tree, and the men then patiently lowered the artillery inches at a time. Of course, sometimes there were no trees to which to attach a cable. Then some of the artillerymen in front of the artillery had to hold the pieces back with a dozen or so prolongs. This was a dangerous and backbreaking affair, the men carefully walking backward, all the while struggling to hold back the heavy artillery piece and keep it from careening out of control.

A BATTLE IN THE WEST

The vast regions of continuous forests and mountain ranges also influenced the face of battle. Unlike a battle fought over relatively open ground, where a general could observe disposition of opposing forces from nearby high ground and presumably formulate a reasonable battle plan, engagements fought over extremely rough terrain meant that the commander's view was restricted to the immediately adjoining area. At best, officers could only guess what was transpiring by carefully listening to the crackle of musketry and the booming of artillery fire and by watching the smoke rising above the trees, in order to determine the location from which they originated and any changes in their intensity. As the commander and field officers became less able to issue meaningful orders, subordinate officers were required to seize the initiative, and the bravery and ability of smaller groups of men became a more determinative factor. The battlefield fractionalized into numerous small piece actions; chance assumed a much greater role.

Novice troops, inexperienced and confined to a particular spot or formation, would have even less idea of what was going. To these men the distant popping of skirmishers' muskets were the first signs of the impending action, followed a few minutes later by first the report of a few ordered volleys, then the inevitable roar of continuous firing. This was the signal that the fighting had begun in earnest.

Seasoned veterans, however, would seize upon other precursor signals that would warn them that a general engagement was imminent. The columns that had been advancing at a steady gait would begin to hesitate perceptibly, somewhat reminiscent of a swarm of bees hovering over a spot, seemingly undecided whether to alight, continue on, or return from where they came. The next sure telltale sign was a heightened level of activity among the officers and couriers, who would soon be seen galloping to and fro, while the colonels would gather around the divisional generals seeking further instructions. The general officers would peer ahead with their field glasses. After brief conferences, the colonels would return to their regiments and, with the help of the company captains, concentrate on steadying their men. A series of sharp orders would be issued to the men, and the sound of clashing accoutrements and arms announced that action was imminent.

Next followed a brief flurry of activity, as formations jockeyed during the last moments to occupy some important position or redress some just-noticed fault in the general deployment. The infantry columns would open up, as the cavalry, with "jingling spurs and clanking sabers," trotted forward to some advanced position, and the ammunition wagons and ambulances struggled to catch up to the main body of the infantry.

The regiment would remain stationary for a while, sometimes a long while, but eventually a courier rode up to its colonel. After a short conversation the colonel would order the regiment forward. John Robson, who fought with the Fifty-second Virginia Infantry, describes what would frequently happen next:

> 'Attention 21st,' or whatever the number may be—'forward!' and away goes the whole regiment to the front. You can see them marching quick and strong in columns, for a bit, and then you hear the Colonel say 'front in line, march!' then on they go, up the hill to the fence, which the men jump over, and you hear the guns—pop! pop! bang! bang! The familiar "Rebel yell" breaks fourth, and the firing grows in volume—quick, spiteful, rattling, you, perhaps, think this is a battle, and I imagine it would pass for one in Revolutionary times, but it is only skirmishers advancing now, and they trot along cheerfully, about ten or fifteen feet apart, firing and loading rapidly, calling funny remarks to each other, laughing, shouting and cheering—but advancing.

The inexperienced observer could hardly be faulted for concluding that the battle now had begun in earnest. Incredibly, such sights and sounds of activity and confusion, however, merely indicated that the enemy's skirmishers had been driven in and his position "developed." The skirmishers would be ordered to cease firing, and here and there artillery battery could be seen galloping into position and unlimbering. The artillerymen ran up to their pieces and started to load as fast as possible, then stepped aside an instant before they were fired. Some pieces managed to fire at a brisk three rounds per minute. One after another a sheet of fire flew from the muzzle, the shells screaming over the lines and a second or two later exploding among the enemy's ranks.

Meanwhile, the skirmish line to the left and right of the artillery continued to pop away, as the brigades behind formed in line preparatory to the attack. The skirmishers on both sides were now pinned, unable to advance or retreat without risking nearly certain death, and forced to lie flat on the ground, hiding their heads behind trees or whatever else was available for partial protection. The brigade finally began its advance. The sound of a thousand ramrods rattling down the barrels was immediately followed by the long, drawn-out, "Forward," and the brigade started its determined advance. In a few moments the advanced skirmishers were reached. Succored, these men jumped up and, encouraged by their comrades, ran to the flank of the formation or simply joined in the charge.

The battle had begun in earnest.

TERRAIN AND THE DAY-TO-DAY FIGHTING

As much as the rough terrain in the West influenced how troops were able to move around and act upon the battlefield, it probably had an even greater effect on the minor operations during the day-to-day campaigning. Small-scale, independent operations abounded, either in the form of partisan warfare carried out by irregular forces led by the likes of William C. Quantrill and John H. Morgan, light troops under Nathan Bedford Forest, or even regular volunteer regiments, such as the First Kentucky (Union) Cavalry. Much of this kind of fighting took on a catch-as-catch-can aspect, as opposing forces, each pursuing its own set of loosely formulated objectives, unexpectedly stumbled into one another.

The chaotic nature of this type of fighting is admirably demonstrated by an engagement that took place on May 5, 1862, when Union forces under Gen. Ebenezer Dumont attempted to surprise Morgan at Lebanon, Tennessee. After capturing one of Gen. Robert B. Mitchell's wagon trains at Pulaski on May 3, Morgan and his partisans holed up in Lebanon the next night. After a number of false starts, the Union pursuers finally caught up about 1 A.M.; halting 4 miles from the town, they remained completely undetected. In their saddles all day, the Union troopers were exhausted but, despite a torrential rainfall, gathered some fence rails before lying down to rest.

Dumont and Colonel William W. Duffield, who commanded the Twenty-third Brigade, were determined to seize the opportunity and attack Morgan's men before they awoke. The plan was for the First Kentucky Cavalry to rush down the main road into the center of the town. To cut off the rebels' avenues of retreat, Major George Wynkoop's Seventh Pennsylvania would enter the right side of the town, while the Fourth Kentucky Battalion, under Col. Green Clay Smith, approached from the left.

After a short prayer the signal was sounded to begin the attack. The First Kentucky Cavalry charged, first at a trot and then hell-for-leather down the road. The Confederate pickets a mile outside of town only noticed their attackers just before being ridden down. A few were able to discharge their weapons, thus sounding the alarm. Morgan's men had quartered themselves in various college buildings around the town's outskirts, but as soon as the pickets fired, the men attempted to get to their horses in the livery stable. However, the precipitous arrival of the Union cavalry forced most to seek shelter in several buildings adjoining the public square: the courthouse, a hotel, and a large college building.

Surging ahead unopposed, the leading elements of the Union cavalry column entered the town about the same time as Morgan's pickets and were unopposed until they reached the far side of the public square. Here they encountered a hastily organized line formed from those who had not been able to gain the relative safety of the surrounding buildings. As a forlorn hope, cavalry Company C had advanced a slight distance in front of the main column and was the first to engage. A lieutenant and several men burst through the opposing line, while the rest of the company passed around either side of the enemy formation. However, the remainder of the regiment bore the brunt of Confederate fury. Enveloped by the enemy line in front and numerous other Confederates ensconced in several buildings on their flanks, they were subjected to a lively cross fire. That morning there was little breeze, and a pall of smoke quickly enveloped the street level.

Recognizing that the severest threat came from those inside the college building, Col. "Frank" Wolford, who commanded the First

Kentucky (a.k.a. the Wilder Riders), ordered about a hundred men to attack the building. Outnumbered, the occupants tried to flee, but many were killed or captured. The engagement now seemed to divide into a number of different focal points, as the attackers closed in on several strongly defended positions in a bid to drive them out of the town. Rounding up as many of his men as he could, Wolford now turned his attention to the hotel, which so far had resisted capture. Firing out of the windows on the upper floors, its defenders had the advantage of elevation and posed a deadly threat to the Union cavalrymen on the street. The Union troopers, still mounted, returned fire, though with little effect.

The situation quickly became even more confused, and no one at this point appears to have had any strategic sense of what was happening or what to do next. With little regard for his personal safety, Wolford did everything he could to direct and inspire his men. He soon became the focal point of the Confederate fire, and within moments several shots tore through his clothing. Finally, one struck the brave officer in the hip. The heavy fire started to unsettle the horses and make them unmanageable. It became impossible to reload, and most of the Union troopers were momentarily forced to pull back. The line of dismounted Confederates that had met the Union charge at the start of the engagement reappeared in front of one of the buildings around this point. Half of these men were garbed in blue overcoats taken from the wagon train captured 2 days earlier. Although they had gray uniforms on underneath, in the confusion of battle, it was easy to mistake this body for Union troops. A number of the attackers were captured after walking up to the blue-clad Confederates. Most conspicuous among these were Honnell, the regiment's chaplain, and Col. Frank Wolford himself.

Despite these setbacks the Union cavalry gradually gained the upper hand, pushing the Confederate partisans back building by building. After an hour and a half, Morgan's forces had nowhere to go in town and finally made a break for it in a northeasterly direction. Not all of his forces were able to escape, however. About fifty men and fifteen officers had barricaded themselves in the upper stories of the Odd Fellows' Hall, a large brick building, and had apparently remained completely undetected by the Union forces as they began to secure the town after the defenders had fled. The now-victorious Union cavalry only became aware of their presence after a deadly volley from the building severely wounded two careless troopers who had been casually walking down the street. The Union forces soon surrounded the building, which they threatened to set on fire unless the occupants surrendered within 10 minutes. Not surprisingly, the defenders complied precipitously. The main body of Morgan's men, then in full retreat, was also threatened by Union forces who dogged their heels. The chaplain of the First Kentucky was able to escape by guile, while those guarding Wolford were slowed down by the colonel's injuries; overtaken, they soon had to relinquish their prized captive.

This affair certainly was of little strategic importance, and Confederate partisans, including those led by Morgan, would continue to pester Union forces for most of the war. Its interest to those studying the Civil War is that it is representative in its ad hoc aspects of a myriad of engagements in this theater during the 4 years of desperate fighting.

Chapter 18

IRREGULAR TROOPS AND GUERRILLA WARFARE

THE ADVENT OF GUERRILLA WARFARE

T he practice of sending out small bodies of troops to harass the enemy and interfere with the latter's logistical operations had long been an accepted part of European warfare. Two types of troops had been generally assigned to this type task. Light cavalry, such as hussars and *chasseurs à cheval,* were frequently sent out to scour the countryside and attack enemy convoys and scatter their reconnaissance parties. Smaller organizations called *partisans* were also raised specifically for the independent operations demanded by the *petite guerre,* as the day-to-day campaigning was called. Unlike the light cavalry, which was organized into regiments, in the early 1700s partisans were generally company-sized units that often contained both cavalry and infantry elements. In western Europe all of these troops were uniformed and theoretically followed the accepted conventions of war.

During the eighteenth century most of the conflicts between western European countries were motivated by hereditary disputes, balance of power issues, or simply the avarice of monarchs. The civilian population, especially those in large town and cities, remained relatively unaffected and were not emotionally involved to any great degree. This certainly was not the case with the Spanish citizenry, though, after Napoleon's armies invaded the Iberian Peninsula. Large numbers of peasants banded together and did everything they could to discomfit the invaders, such as to attack and kill the procession of stragglers and the wounded that fled the battlefield, especially after a defeat. The flow of ammunition, food, and other supplies also came under attack anytime the French military was so foolish as to try to send forward insufficiently protected small detachments.

In the English-speaking world, the term *guerrilla* has become inextricably associated with those that carried out such acts. This term is derivative of *guerra,* the Spanish word for war, and originally referred to the petty war conducted by detached parties, generally in the mountains. This function traditionally had been performed by partisans, and those who engaged in this sort of fighting were known as *guerrilleros* or *partidas.*

As the term *guerrilla* spread to other linguistic communities after the Napoleonic Wars, it took on a new, powerful connotation. Guerrilla warfare began to refer to an irregular band of men who renounced the accepted rules of warfare. The men joined together because of conviction or a sense of patriotic duty rather than because of law or levy. Receiving neither pay nor provisions, they furnished themselves with whatever they were able to seize or steal. Lacking the formal structure and training to utilize the formal tactics and strategy of regular military units, they could only rob, kill, or destroy. It was impossible to take prisoners. Operating generally within enemy-controlled territory, this new brand of warriors usually had to pass themselves off as peaceful citizens until it was time to come together once again and undertake their clandestine activities.

Although many military authorities continued to regard independently operating troops as partisans, increasingly in the English-speaking world, they were referred to as guerrillas. In *International Law, or Rules Regulating the Intercourse of States in Peace and War,* for example, U.S. Gen. Henry W. Halleck treated the terms *partisans* and *guerrillas* as synonymous. This subtle change in terminology was neither a fad nor a cosmetic issue but reflected an important change in the European, and hence the American, cultural and political landscape. Military authorities now had to acknowledge the advent of a new factor that now could highly motivate a large sector of a country's citizenry: nationalism!

PARTISAN AND GUERRILLA WARFARE IN AMERICA

If the Civil War had been fought over prairies in the northwestern part of the continent or the highly cultivated, relatively flat land found over much of western Europe, guerrillas and partisans could have played but a minor role. As it was, America in general, and the

South and West in particular, were ideally suited, both in geography and culture, to support guerrilla warfare. The land occupied by Union troops in northern Virginia, for example, was dotted with forests and intersected by hills, gullies, and other types of difficult terrain. True, there were many farms, houses, hamlets, and villages throughout the countryside, but within a short horse ride, there was almost always sanctuary in the form of some sort of rough terrain where a small group of men could hide and elude pursuit. And of course, the countryside of Missouri, Tennessee, western Virginia, Kentucky, Mississippi, and Arkansas was even more favorable for irregular warfare.

Two other factors which contributed to the popularity and success of this new style of warfare lay in the character of the people fighting the war, especially among those on the contumacious side. Regular warfare, in which the individual fought as part of an organized unit, though requiring bouts of bravery and a certain amount of stamina, on the whole was much less demanding, both physically and psychologically, than guerrilla warfare. Fighting a conventional-style war, the soldier followed the officers' orders, and his motions generally conformed to the formation. The guerrilla usually operated in very small, informal groups, upon occasion even individually. There was a much greater need for initiative, decision, and intelligence. This type of warfare also involved much greater risks: the destruction of one's property, even death. Unlike the regular soldier, who, when caught, could expect to be taken prisoner, the guerrilla faced summary punishment. Those supporting the South's Second War of Independence were generally driven by strong conviction and the willingness to endure privation and hardships so long as they obtained their freedom.

Regardless of its potential suitability, irregular warfare was slow to appear during the Civil War. With the exception of some irregular actions in Missouri, almost all of the fighting during the first 15 months of hostilities followed a conventional format. Opposing forces faced off against each other in a series of chance skirmishes and engagements or the occasional set piece battle. Once or twice, such as at Fort Donelson (Tennessee, February 1862), there was even a fleeting effort at a formal siege. During the first few months, both sides believed that the war would be over after one or two major battles, and everyone intent on fighting rushed to join a local regiment. Even the lack of any sort of strategic success during the first campaign failed to completely quell the initial optimism, and in early 1862 probably most combatants still hoped for a relatively speedy resolution to the conflict.

Not surprisingly, it was the Southern side that first deviated from traditional warfare and started to adopt more unconventional methods of fighting. One finds evidence that some Confederate officers wanted to organize partisan units from the beginning of hostilities. Henry A. Wise, who served as a brigadier general, originally applied to raise an "independent partisan command," which, "subject only to the general laws and orders of the service," would presumably be free to confuse and harass Union forces by constant motion and quick raids. Maj. Gen. M. Lowell made a similar request to Beauregard on May 12, 1862. A large number of those seeking to serve their cause joined "partisan companies" which were raised specifically for independent and detached service. The formation of such companies had been sanctioned by the Confederate Congress with the passage of the Partisan Ranger Act in 1862. Some Confederate state and military district authorities even resorted to such troops for defense. Gen. Earl Van Dorn, for example, requested that Gen. J. S. Roane use every means in his power to defend Arkansas, including the appointment of "partisan officers."

True guerrilla activity appears to have erupted in both Missouri and Tennessee in mid-July 1862, however. Col. J. D. Bingham, quartermaster of the Seventeenth Army Corps, testified before a board of inquiry that this problem appeared around Nashville after the Union capture of Murfreesboro, while Brig. Gen. John M. Schofield felt it originated in Missouri with the creation of a number of bands under Porter, Poindexter, and Cobb. In Tennessee the guerrillas immediately set about threatening the Union supply lines and foraging efforts. Trains and wagon convoys were attacked, as were small, unguarded groups of foragers. Towns and occasionally even fortified positions were attacked and momentarily captured. The intent was to force Union commanders to retain large numbers of valuable troops in the rear, who otherwise would have been more productive employed. It was also a convenient way of securing much-needed supplies, small arms, horses, and even the occasional artillery piece.

In Missouri many partisan and guerrilla leaders spent much of their time and effort devoted to clandestinely raising troops in Union-held territory. They would sneak into an area and organize, arm, and provision squads and companies, who were then spirited away to the south, taking great care to avoid Federal soldiers and Union state militia. The effort paid off, and secessionists from Missouri formed 12 Confederate regiments and three artillery batteries in the Trans-Mississippi Department.

Not limited to Missouri and Tennessee, the horrors of irregular war quickly sprang up in Louisiana, northern Mississippi, and Arkansas—anywhere in the Southern states where there was a Union army of occupation. Not content simply to disrupt the enemy's activity, guerrillas soon moved against segments of the civilian population. The property of anyone supporting the Union cause, even by

A Confederate party from Colonel Magruder's command setting torch to a village. This type of guerrilla warfare would become almost commonplace in the Western theater and then in the deep South during Sherman's March to the Sea in late 1864. *Frank Leslie's Illustrated Weekly,* Aug. 7, 1861.

only verbal support, became fair game. Under the cover of darkness, the farmer's crops were stolen, the horses taken from his barn. Stage-coaches and mail carriers were robbed of valuable Federal currency. Telegraph lines were cut, rail lines were torn up, bridges and trestles set ablaze, tunnels blown up.

METHODS OF GUERRILLA AND PARTISAN WARFARE

The most important tactical element in irregular warfare has always been the element of surprise. This was as true for N. B. Forrest, who often wielded brigade-sized forces, and fought regular Union troops in what amounted to pitched battles, as it was small, independently operating groups of bushwhackers, who might pick off a small squad or the lone sentry. Exploiting the advantage of a sympathetic popula-tion and the cover of darkness or foreboding terrain, the partisan band would fall upon the unsuspecting victim, quickly seize or destroy what it came for, and then withdraw as quickly as it came to avoid the retribution of the large Union counterforce that was sure to follow.

Knowledge of the land was a key ingredient in this method of war, and many of the most successful of these fighters had learned the required stealth from constant hunting or experience during the Indian wars. Sent to track down various bands of partisans that were causing mischief in Texas in early 1864, Capt. Richard Murphy was impressed with just how much these groups were able to avoid detection. It was difficult to pick up their tracks. When partisans came to a road, they would cross it at a rocky place, where little trace was left, or they would spread blankets over the road to achieve the same results.

Bushwhackers employed numerous other means of deception. Union uniforms were occasionally among the captured supplies. It wasn't uncommon for the Southern men to don these uniforms to con-found their enemy by their false appearance. Early in his career Morgan, during a raid on the Union railroad lines, successfully passed his men off for those of the Eighth Pennsylvania Infantry. Bushwhackers employed another form of deception. They would either steal or forge paroles (written passes) that authorized their presence in certain areas of the countryside. Stopped by patrols, they

Skirmishers taking advantage of cover. A group of skirmishers, possibly sharpshooters, take advantage of the cover provided by a rail fence. The action illustrated here took place near Munson's Hill, Virginia, on August 31, 1861. *Frank Leslie's Illustrated Weekly,* Sept. 21, 1861.

would simply show these passes and then, once the threat had passed, would resume their way to a rendezvous with their comrades.

Though lacking the organization, strength of numbers, and strategic vision of the likes of Forrest or Morgan, many ad hoc bands nevertheless devised countless ways of disrupting Union operations. Probably the simplest yet most effective tactic was simply to attack and harass small parties of Union soldiers, such as isolated pickets and vedettes or those foolish enough to leave the marching columns or camp.

The potential dangers facing small parties of Union soldiers traveling beyond the picket lines are illustrated by an experience that befell two members of the First Kentucky Cavalry. Captain Wilson and surgeon Stanway on November 10, 1862, rashly visited Company D, which was on detached duty 10 miles from the regiment's camp. Returning at dusk, the two leisurely rode through a cedar forest under a clear, moonlit sky, totally engrossed in an animated conversation. Before long four riders surreptitiously coming out of the forest got the drop on them and demanded their surrender. Though staring at a pistol aimed at his eyebrows, the doctor drew his own revolver with great legerity and felled one of his assailants with his first shot. The bushwhackers returned fire immediately, and their shots grazed Captain Wilson's skull and clipped his mustache as he feverishly attempted to draw his own revolver, which had been buckled into his holster.

To make a serious situation even more desperate, more than a dozen additional guerrillas rode out of the forest to help their colleagues subdue the pair, who now blazed away at their attackers. One bushwhacker advanced to within an arm's length of the doctor, who for the second time in the space of a minute or two found himself staring down the barrel of a pistol. Before the rebel could fire, Stanway nimbly knocked the enemy's pistol down with his own revolver. The gun still discharged, however, and the doctor's leg was shattered. Sensing he was about to loose consciousness, the doctor let himself off his horse and collapsed on the ground.

Prolongation of the fight was senseless, and Captain Wilson bolted into the forest to make his escape on his horse, known in the First Kentucky for its speed. Before he could get completely away, however, his horse received a severe flesh wound in the breast. Jumping off, Wilson managed to dive into the forest and evade his pursuers. Now thoroughly disoriented, Wilson couldn't find his way back to camp and had to spend the night in the woods before eventually making his way back to the regiment the next morning. Stanway, meanwhile, lying helplessly on the ground, was robbed of his clothing and valuables.

Outnumbered by as much as ten to one, Captain Wilson and the surgeon were lucky to have survived this fracas with only a grazed temple, clipped whiskers, and in the case of the doctor, a shattered leg that would take months to mend. A great many stragglers and other Union soldiers who ventured outside of the protective pale were not so fortunate, and their involvement in the great internecine saga and life itself came to an abrupt and permanent end.

Sgt. E. Tarrant, who rode with the First Kentucky Cavalry (Union), remembers that the introduction of guerrilla warfare was a two-stage process. First there was the appearance of partisan organizations led by Morgan, Forrest, and others. This was quickly followed by guerilla bands that were aided and abetted by local citizens. The fighting soon became especially bitter and quickly took on the form of a vendetta, as the prewar bloodletting between the abolitionists and slave owners was rekindled. Not content to raise troops and gather provisions, the guerrillas immediately began to rob and murder any "Union men" they stumbled upon. Houses were occasionally set ablaze to chase Union families out of the area. One guerrilla leader went to the unheard-of extreme of shooting the wives of two local men who brashly decided to take arms for the Union cause.

Revolvers and shotguns were the favorite weapons of partisan troops and bushwhackers. Frequently, these fighters carried several revolvers. After a raid upon Lindley, Grundy County, Missouri, in July 1864, Maj. Rezin A. De Bolt reported that the local citizens had been robbed by men each carrying a shotgun and two to four revolvers apiece. Each fighter was thus able to generate a tremendous amount of firepower up close and in a short span of time. Usually armed with only a rifle musket or carbine, and possibly a saber and a revolver, the Union forces opposed to these partisans and guerrillas felt themselves outgunned and relatively powerless.

Some partisans and bushwhackers purposely chose to carry only a revolver. At the beginning of his career as a partisan, John Mosby was issued a rifle and a saber, which he dragged around for the first year despite never using them. Later on Mosby had the opportunity to seize many a Spencer, a weapon he found invaluable, but in his memoirs the famous partisan colonel could only deprecate the sword, claiming,

> The only real use I ever heard of their being put to was to hold to a piece of meat over a fire for frying. . . . The sabre and lance may have been very good weapons in the days of chivalry. . . . But certainly the sabre is of no use against gunpowder.

In his own memoirs James Williamson, one of Mosby's followers, provided a more reasoned explanation of Mosby's opinion of the saber. It must be remembered that all of Mosby's actions and fighting were by necessity clandestine affairs, in which the advantage of surprise was everything. As guerrillas crept up upon their intended targets, it was critical to be absolutely silent. Anything that generated noise had to be either discarded or left behind. Sabers tended to clank, and carbines tended to rattle, in the saddles as they approached; so most men just carried revolvers, as deadly a weapon as one needed in a close-in fight.

UNION RESPONSE TO PARTISANS, GUERRILLAS, AND RAIDERS

Faced with the specter of omnipresent bands of guerrillas operating with impunity behind the front lines and astraddle lines of supply and communications, high-ranking Union officers came up with a number of ways to counter the threat. One of the most obvious was to send in more troops, and this is what the beleaguered state of Missouri did in the summer of 1862. On July 22 all able-bodied men in the state were to repair to the closest military post to join the state militia. It was hoped that this new force would be sufficient to exterminate the guerrillas that posed such a problem.

The War Department, on its part, demanded that Union forces take increased precautions against ambuscade. P. H. Watson, the assistant secretary of war, wrote to the military authorities in Alabama and Missouri explaining that Gen. Horatio Wright in Florida stopped sentries from being assassinated at night by ordering the pickets and guards to automatically fire at anyone approaching them, without even first giving the normal challenge, "Who goes there?!" Watson advised those in the West to do the same. Some officers went further and took measures to reduce the enemy's opportunity to hide in rough terrain while they snuck up on their prey. As soon as irregular warfare broke out in May 1862, Brigadier Gen. J. D. Cox, for example, ordered his men to burn the underbrush around their encampments and sentry posts.

Other officers chose a more defensive response. In August 1862 Gen. N. P. Banks, Second Corps, Army of Virginia (Union), advised William O. Redden, who commanded a force at Front Royal (in the Shenandoah Valley), to fortify his position, reasoning that few defenders were required in such a strong point since Confederate irregular forces would never be audacious enough to attack. This would free most of Redden's force to seek out and destroy the rebel guerrillas. Operating in the West, Gen. J. M. Schofield ordered his subordinates to employ a parallel strategy, as far as the cavalry was concerned. All small posts were to be abandoned, and the cavalry concentrated into larger bodies to "strike the guerrillas quickly and with vigor." About the same time General Buell similarly pooled his cavalry together into larger bodies.

Overall, the assumption of more defensive postures merely played into the Confederates' hands. There were fewer patrols and consequentially less reconnaissance. Roving bands of Confederate guerrillas had an even easier time moving through Union-held territory and attacking vulnerable targets. Even when they concentrated their forces into larger, stronger forces, the Union military still found it extremely difficult to counterattack and pursue a suddenly appearing group of irregulars. Benjamin Loan, a brigadier general of the Missouri State Militia, which had been called largely to deal with the incursions of marauders infesting the state since the summer of 1862, complained to Gen. Samuel Curtis in St. Louis that it was almost impossible to eliminate the threat:

It is much easier to catch a rat with your hands in a warehouse filled with a thousand flour barrels than it is to catch a band of guerrillas where every, or almost every, man, woman, and child are their spies, pickets, or couriers.

Much of the problem stemmed from the rough terrain. Following the trail of retreating Confederate irregulars near Tchefuncta, Louisiana, men in the Twelfth Connecticut Infantry, though often able to hear their wily adversaries, were only able to snatch "dissolving views" of them. After a skirmish at Sibley, Missouri (October 6, 1862), Capt. D. H. David led a small expedition to track down Quantrill and his men. The hot pursuit led through the worst thickets David had ever encountered. To make matters worse, the band of marauders would split up every so often, only to reunite at some agreed-upon spot a little later. When the Confederates suddenly changed direction and headed into new and equally perilous woods 3 days later, Captain David was forced to call off the pursuit. His men had only eaten three times during the entire episode, and their horses were played out. In his report David concluded that guerrillas could never be taken by pursuit; rather, they could only be beaten "by strategy." Col. William R. Penick, who had led the Fifth Missouri

Militia Cavalry on a similar wild goose chase, had come to the same conclusion and argued that the only effective way of dealing with Confederate guerrillas was to "make it unhealthy for the neighborhoods where they harbor to allow them to remain among them without giving information to us," that is, to exert pressure on the civilian population that supported the secessionist cause.

This was the exact approach that would be settled upon by higher Union authorities and which proved much more successful than any tactical measures. Union authorities did not consider most involved in "petty war" to be legitimate soldiers but as "band of robbers" who engaged in "systematic plunder and murder." As such they were not entitled to the conventions of war, and some Union commanders issued instructions for these "bandits" and "murderers" to be summarily executed as soon as they were captured. Such extreme measures were not commonly employed, however. The Confederate commanders in the West simply threatened to reciprocate the gesture with captured Union troops.

A much more promising tactic was to hold local citizens accountable for guerrilla activity in their areas, and from May to July 1862, a spate of official proclamations proclaimed the consequences for anyone caught providing aid to the Southern cause. In Missouri, Brig. E. B. Brown promised that anyone caught harboring guerrillas would suffer the harshest punishment that could be imposed by a military commission. Even suspects against whom there existed insufficient evidence would be incarcerated and freed only after a heavy bond was posted. Around the same time, the Union Army of Virginia took even more comprehensive measures. Whenever a railroad, road, or telegraph was damaged, all citizens within 5 miles had to report to military authorities and then repair the damage. If guerrillas fired upon soldiers from a dwelling, that house was to be burned down immediately. On June 23 that summer, the Military District of Missouri implemented a similar plan. Sympathizers were to be charged $5,000 for every Union soldier killed by guerrillas and $1,000 for each soldier wounded. They were also responsible for the full monetary value of all property destroyed.

Never known as a pushover, Gen. W. T. Sherman immediately took draconian steps to discourage rebel artillery from firing upon passenger steamboats. Henceforth, each steamer carried a number of Southern sympathizers. Sherman wrote to Confederate Maj. Gen. T. C. Hindman informing him that any Confederate artillery attack on these vessels was thus an attack on its own people.

These measures taken as a whole seem to have had an effect. Sherman believed that the depredations of the guerrillas were finally working against the local citizenry, even among those who espoused the Confederate cause. Noting a lull in such activity around mid-September 1862, Sherman speculated in his reports that the Tennessee farmers had tired of their patriots, who apparently were unable or unwilling to differentiate between Union families and secessionists as they helped themselves to horses and provisions. A few months later in a letter to the Union general-in-chief, Grant himself predicted that guerrilla activity would soon slacken off. Faced with guerrilla attacks along the line of supply, the men in his army had to live off the land, and within a few weeks there would be little left in north Mississippi to support the guerrillas.

TACTICS OF NATHAN BEDFORD FORREST

No discussion of partisan warfare during the Civil War is complete without some analysis of the tactics and methods used by Nathan Bedford Forrest. Forrest's exploits span the full gamut of military operations. Most of his earliest essays in the military art fell within traditional venues. By 1862 a colonel of a cavalry regiment, he led his troopers against enemy infantry at Shiloh as well as both infantry and artillery during the attempt to break out of Fort Donelson.

Only later that year did he seriously focus on the type of operations for which he will be forever remembered, as a successful raider and partisan leader. The raid on Murfreesboro in July 1862, his expedition into west Tennessee in December that year, his pursuit and capture of General Streight and his cavalry as the latter attempted to lead his own partisan attack against Confederate resources in north-western Georgia in May 1863—these are but a few of the daring and successful-against-great-odds exploits that deservedly have become part of Civil War folklore.

Neither Forrest nor his men were bushwhackers, only capable of attacking an unsuspecting adversary while made invisible by the cover of terrain or darkness. During the war, however, there was never any shortage of naysayers, and Gen. Braxton Bragg remained an implacable critic even after the sterling performance of Forrest and his command during the Battle of Chickamauga. Indulging in a tirade against his cavalry officers in general and Forrest in particular, Bragg was heard to remark, "The man is ignorant, and does not know anything of cooperation. He is nothing more than a good raider." The general's eye was probably jaundiced by envy. Not only was Forrest the partisan leader par excellence; when necessary he could very competently employ conventional methods of war. He led his command as regular (dismounted) cavalry during the bloody fighting the first day of Chickamauga and again during the storming of Fort Pillow (April 15) during the 1864 west Tennessee expedition. It is this dual capacity—one day his men fighting as an irregular band of partisans, and the next fighting as desperately and effectively as any regular regiment—that makes this Confederate commander so exceptional in the annals of war.

Of course, part of these abilities stemmed from Forrest's character and general military acumen. Called upon to characterize Forrest's military qualities, his official biographer, Gen. Thomas Jordan (C.S.A.) concluded that Forrest was

> Cool in the presence of confusion, clear in his comprehension of the possible, untiring in his activity and personal energy, ready and affluent in resources to remove or surmount obstacles that would paralyze most men.

Forrest was a rare combination of calculating tactician and ferocious warrior. Almost from the beginning he displayed remarkable *coup d'oeil*. Literally meaning a "stroke of the eye," this referred to an officer's ability to quickly survey the landscape and appraise every feature for its potential military significance. Attempting to escape detection after his successful raid on Murfreesboro, Forrest showed remarkable presence of mind and the ability to exploit available terrain. Finding himself nearly boxed in by hostile forces, he quickly formed his men into a column of fours and calmly led them to a dry creek bottom, where they remained unobserved to a large

Union force that soon passed nearby. His actions at Parker's Cross-roads are an even better example of self-possession under the most unexpected and trying circumstances. Whether surprised by the unexpected appearance of enemy troops in his front or a sudden attack in the rear, he consistently was able to adjust his plans rapidly to meet the ever-changing exigencies of the battlefield

Part of the secret of Forrest's frequent successes went beyond his force of personality, daringness, or general military competency. The great partisan leader also developed several tactical methods that would repeatedly stand him in good stead. The most prominent of these techniques, what today would be called a *pincer movement*, was developed early in his career. Suddenly approaching a Union rear guard during the affair at Sacramento (December 28, 1861), Forrest garnered about 150 of his men and then quickly advanced toward the enemy. His men only began firing when about 120 to 75 yards from the enemy. Intimidated by the aggressiveness of the Con-federate partisans, the Union cavalry appeared about to retire. Not wanting the prey to escape, Forrest ordered his own men to with-draw. This had the desired effect. Seeing the rebel cavalry inexpli-cably flee, the Union cavalrymen regained their composure, took the bait and followed Forrest's men. However, Forrest was now rein-forced by the remainder of his command, which had come up. In a position to renew the offensive, Forrest ordered Major Kelly to work around the Union right, as Lieutenant Colonel Starnes went around their left. Soon thereafter, Forrest and his mounted men charged the center with a fiendish yell. Attacked on both flanks and intimidated by the onrush of seeming berserkers in front, the Union cavalry broke in complete disorder.

Forrest would use this technique of using frontal forces to pin an enemy in position with while threatening its flanks and rear time and time again, usually with minor variations to suit the circumstances of each situation. At Brice's Crossroads (June 10, 1864), for example, Captain Morton's artillery galloped to within 60 yards of the Union line, unlimbered, and delivered a withering fire, while the remainder of Forrest's forces simultaneously attacked the enemy's flanks.

Eighteen months earlier at Parker's Crossroads (December 31, 1862), Forrest had used an interesting defensive-offensive variation.

His command had bumped into a comparably sized Union force moving along the Huntingdon road. As usual Forrest went on the attack, but several hours of hard fighting failed to break the enemy's resolve. He ordered Col. A. A. Russell's Fourth Alabama Cavalry to work its way around the rear, while the Confederate artillery was repositioned on the flanks to produce a more effective cross fire. Until this time the Union force had become increasingly demoralized, but, misinterpreting the Confederate movement to their front, they thought that a portion of the rebels had retired. Reinvigorated, they immediately charged into what amounted to a trap. They were quickly and decisively repulsed by Forrest's artillery, which belched deadly canister fire. Russell's forces, now in position, attacked from the flank and the rear, while the remainder of Confederates advanced frontally. The Union discomfiture was immediate and complete.

There is one other ingredient of Forrest's success that must be mentioned: an almost maniacal ferocity. Many times the general and his men found themselves in situations in which ordinary troops would have failed. Victory then stemmed from a "success at any cost" attitude. During the final stages of Forrest's relentless pursuit of General Streight and his raiders, the desperate Union commander attempted to set a trap for the Confederate force. The road ran through a thick forest with dense underbrush. Streight's men erected a barricade at a sudden turn in the road. This would force Forrest and his men to cross a field and over a small crest, behind which waited 500 Union soldiers. The road and field were lined with Union marksmen who intended to pick off the Confederates as soon as they fell into the trap. On came Forrest's men in a column of fours. As soon as the enemy skirmishers started to fire, Forrest ordered a charge, rather than attempt to back out of the position. The Confederate cavalry advanced so quickly that the sharpshooters had little time to set up their shots, and few casualties were taken. Now it was Streight's turn to be surprised, and his men were soon scattered by the charging cavalry.

Chapter 19

RIVER AND COASTAL WARFARE

Despite all the public discussion about the potential of the Stevenses floating battery and European iron-mailed ships, the federal government was remarkably slow to take action in the months after the fall of Fort Sumter. Seemingly impervious to the pressures of war and the need for celerity, a board charged by Congress during midsummer 1861 to investigate the feasibility of iron-protected ships took 6 weeks to return with markedly ambivalent findings. Admitting that its members had little practical experience with "naval architecture" and that there was no consensus among experts, the report equivocated on the central issue. Though it conceded that these heavily protected vessels could be very useful for coastal and harbor defense, the board concluded that they could not possibly be used to attack fortifications. Apparently preoccupied with their use vis-à-vis coastal fortifications, the board failed to consider ship-to-ship encounters seriously. Nevertheless, the board ultimately approved three proposals to build what later would be known as *ironclads.* Bushnell & Company of New Haven, Connecticut, was authorized to construct a vessel that when completed would be christened the *Galena;* Merrick & Sons were to build the *New Ironsides;* while John Ericsson received approval to begin constructing a floating battery that he would call the *Monitor.* Of the three, Ericsson's creation would gain the lion's share of acclaim after its success against the C.S.S. *Virginia* (a.k.a. the *Merrimac*) at Hampton Roads (March 9, 1862).

Before the war Ericsson had a rocky career marred by disappointment and several embarrassing scandals, including the infamous *Princeton* disaster. The onset of the war seemed to reinvigorate

Ericsson's hopes, and he immediately resurrected his plans to construct an iron-protected fighting vessel. Signing a contract with the government on October 5, 1861, Ericsson and his associates immediately began construction and would complete the project in hitherto unheard-of time. In his article "The Union and Confederate Navies" in *Battles and Leaders of the Civil War,* Prof. James Soley told his readers that the Swedish-American inventor had had a relatively easy time securing the contract. His interview with the board lasted a mere 2 hours, and it in turn came to a favorable decision after only 2 hours of closed-door deliberation. Of course, Soley admits that he relied on Ericsson's version of these events.

During the decades that followed the war, a number of pamphlets appeared that attempted to provide the story behind the ironclads and the famous engagement at Hampton Roads. *The First Monitor and its Builders,* a short pamphlet that appeared during the 1880s, provides a less flattering account than Soley's. Francis Wheeler, its author, claims that Ericsson initially was unable to interest the board in his plans. Whether the authorities' reluctance was based on lingering resentment because of the *Princeton* tragedy or because of a series of scandals involving Ericsson in the 1850s is impossible to determine. John A. Griswold and John F. Winslow at the time were in Washington to adjust some claims in connection with iron plating for Bushnell's *Galena.* Learning of Ericsson's predicament, the two decided to use their influence to help the inventor. After an unsuccessful conference with Commodore Smith, a member of the board, Griswold and Winslow decided to try to circumnavigate the board and see President Lincoln. Meeting with the two businessmen, the president was impressed with their sincerity and conviction and decided to prevail upon Commodore Smith. Another meeting was set up between Griswold, Winslow, Smith, the secretary of the navy, and others, including the president. Though Griswold and Winslow made an impressive presentation, Commodore Smith remained resistant. However, the matter seems to have been settled when, in his closing remarks, Lincoln declared that the project had merit. A few days later Ericsson received the contract.

Regardless of how Ericsson obtained the contract, the result was the same. The inventor exerted every bit of his physical and psychological being to bring the project to fruition. The vessel was to be assembled at the Continental Iron Works in the Greenpoint section of Brooklyn, and on October 25 a contract was signed by Thomas F. Rowland, its owner, and Ericsson, Winslow, Griswold, and C. S. Bushnell. Work began immediately. The hull, side armor, and decks were constructed at the Greenpoint firm. The turret was fabricated by the Novelty Iron Works. The "port-stoppers," the heavy metal guard that protected the two turret guns (11-inch Dahlgren smoothbores), were forged at the Steam Forge in Buffalo, while the turret mechanism was assembled by the Delamater Iron Works. The various components were shipped to Greenpoint, where they were assembled into place on the vessel. The turret, however, was so large that it had to be transported in sections and, once in Greenpoint, riveted in place by Rowland's men.

Largely due to Ericsson's indefatigable efforts to oversee and expedite the project, his armored vessel was completed in "record time" and launched at Greenpoint, Brooklyn, on January 30, 1862, 101 days after the contract was signed. Lt. John L. Worden assumed command 2 weeks later, and two trials runs occurred, the first to Wall Street in lower Manhattan and the other to Sandy Hook, New Jersey. One problem immediately surfaced: The vessel was difficult to steer and could not be brought to full speed when moving forward. The remainder of February was spent making the myriad of adjustments to solve such shortcomings.

By March 6, however, the problems had been corrected, and the *Monitor* and the tug *Seth Low* set out for Hampton Roads, where the ironclad was desperately needed to counter the *Virginia*, whose appearance in those waters was expected at any day—a very accurate foreboding, as the morrow would show. Although the *Monitor* left New York Harbor with the prospect of fair weather, she soon encountered rough seas, which for a few worrisome moments threatened to delay the journey. The inclement weather abated just at the critical moment and Lt. John L. Worden and his charge arrived near Fort Monroe at 4 P.M. on March 8, in time to hear the last booming choruses in the altercation between the *Virginia* and the Union ships of war.

IRONCLAD VERSUS IRONCLAD

The Confederate Navy showed none of the reluctance to experiment with iron-protected vessels that had raised such controversy in the North, and very early in the war, the decision was made to build what ultimately would become the C.S.S. *Virginia*. Summoned to Richmond on June 1, 1861, to help Chief Engineer W. P. Williamson and Lt. J. M. Brooke draw up the necessary plans, John L. Porter, a navy "constructor," brought a model of an iron-protected vessel that he had built in 1846, a time when, it will be recalled, the Stevens floating battery had captured the public's imagination. It is possible, however, that the vessel the South ultimately created was influenced by other developments. In addition to the model patented by Thomas Gregg in 1814, which *Scientific American* described as an "almost exact model of the *Merrimac*," there was an Austrian gunboat that had recently been publicized in some Northern newspapers. The vessel had taken belated part in the Italian War of 1859, and a detailed description and illustration appeared in *Frank Leslie's Illustrated Magazine* on February 9, 1860. Though lacking any motive power, this vessel had a similar appearance to the *Merrimac*.

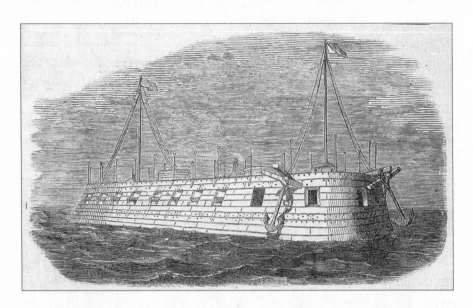

An Austrian ironclad, circa 1859. The Austrian floating battery named the *Spitfire* was constructed to defend the Porto di Malenocco at Venice around 1859. Its appearance is similar to the *Virginia* and embodied the theory of "angulated" defensive armor discussed in the press. *Frank Leslie's Illustrated Weekly,* Feb 9, 1862.

Lieutenant Brooke, who drew up the final designs, initially envisioned that the iron-protected, angled walls above the hull would stretch from bow to stern. The extreme weight of this protection, however, would severely limit the vessel's length and beam. He soon realized that the hull would be below the waterline and much less vulnerable to artillery. It thus became feasible for the hull to extend beyond the iron-cased covering above the surface.

The lack of one vital necessity almost scuttled the project at its inception. There were no new engines available for the proposed vessel in the entire Confederacy. Although Brooke and Porter were able to meet this challenge, the solution they chose had unforeseen consequences that later would greatly limit the vessel's performance at the moment of greatest consequence, when it unexpectedly found itself confronted with its nemesis, the U.S.S. *Monitor*. Discovering the half-burned remnants of the U.S.S. *Merrimac*, which had been set afire by Union forces evacuating the Norfolk naval yards, Porter suggested that its hull and engine be used instead of those specified by the original design. There was one problem, however. The *Merrimac* had been an oceangoing vessel and had a 22-foot draw, almost double that specified by the ironclad design. Under the circumstances, however, there was no choice but to utilize what was available.

The designs were quickly revised, and the new vessel was now to weigh 3200 tons, to be 263 feet long, and accommodate a 320-man crew. The protective 4-inch iron-plate armor sloped 35 degrees and was backed by 24-inch pitch pine. Despite the importance of the project, progress was slow. The required iron sheathing, provided by Tredegar Ironworks, in Richmond, Virginia, the only source of rolled iron plates in the South, was delivered at an excruciatingly slow pace. The ship's armament consisted of two 7-inch rifled artillery pieces, two 6-inch rifles, and six 9-inch smoothbore cannon.

A 4-foot cast-iron prow that was to serve as a ram was secured to the bow. One writer suggests that Southern spies in Brooklyn provided information that led the vessel's designers to conclude that this prow initially was not long enough to penetrate the *Monitor*'s overhanging armor, so it was lengthened without regard to the concomitant reduction in strength. Regardless of whether this actually occurred or the prow's weakness was simply the result of faulty workmanship or design, the weakness not only influenced the tactics that the *Virginia* could employ but possibly predetermined the very result of the Herculean struggle with the *Monitor* on March 9.

Unlike the *Monitor*, whose builders labored to complete it in the shortest time possible, the launching of the *Virginia* appears to have been forestalled by strategic considerations. Apparently, the original plan was to wait until the *Monitor* appeared near Hampton Roads, Virginia, come out and sink her, and then destroy all of the other vessels in the area at will. In early March an outcry among the Southern public and its press forced the authorities' hand, and the *Virginia* was ordered to undertake its trial run on March 8, well before the appearance of its long-expected adversary. Accompanied by the gunboats *Raleigh* and *Beaufort*, the *Virginia* got underway and steamed down the Elizabeth River around noon. There was no lack of potential targets. The frigates *Minnesota, Roanoke,* and *St. Lawrence* were anchored off of Fort Monroe, along with several gunboats. Several miles to its left, near Newport News, were the frigate *Congress* and the sloop *Cumberland,* both sailing ships, with 50 and 30 guns, respectively.

The *Virginia* chose to go after the *Cumberland* first, the better armed and more distant of the two enemy vessels near Newport News. The *Roanoke, St. Lawrence,* and *Minnesota* meanwhile got "under weigh" in an effort to join the Union vessels then under attack. Under fire from Confederate batteries at Sewell's Point, they kept close to the opposite side of the navigable channel, but the *Minnesota* and the *Roanoke* were soon aground and out of action. The *Congress* and the *Cumberland* soon found themselves in a similar predicament. Espying the Confederate ironclad in the distance, both vessels attempted to get underway. There was little time and even less breeze, however.

The gunboat *Zouave* was the first vessel to open fire, followed by the pivot guns on the *Cumberland*. The *Virginia* ignored the six shots from the *Zouave*'s 30-pounder Parrott, which bounced harmlessly off of its iron shell, and continued to close toward its intended victims. As the ironclad passed the *Congress,* she unleashed a broadside, which was defiantly returned by the Union frigate. Turning its attention to *Cumberland*, the *Virginia* fired at its pivot gun. Delivered at close range, the salvo proved devastating and instantly killed nine or ten of the pivot gun's crew. The next round demolished the *Cumberland*'s after pivot gun. The *Virginia* continued to close on the *Cumberland*, oblivious to shot and shell fired by the Union frigate and sloop, as well as the shore battery at Newport News, which had just begun to fire.

Moments later the ironclad rammed into the *Cumberland* just under the forerigging on the starboard side. The iron prow forced in the ship's planks and timbers below the waterline, creating a hole that one witness claimed was large enough to "drive through a horse and cart." The *Virginia* quickly attempted to back out of the *Cumberland*'s side, but the tides caught the ironclad, turning it to the side and snapping the iron ram. The damage to the enemy vessel was all that could be desired, though. Shuddering once or twice, the *Cumberland* quickly listed over to port and then sank.

The *Virginia*, supported by wooden ships armed with shell guns and reinforced by the *Patrick Henry* (formerly the *Yorktown*), *Jamestown*, and *Teaser* of the James River gunboat flotilla, now turned her attention toward the *Congress*. The latter had slipped her anchor, loosened her foretopsail, and, with the aid of the *Zouave*, attempted to escape. These efforts proved futile, and the *Congress* also was soon aground. As she approached from the stern, the *Virginia* renewed its fire with devastating effect. Both vessels exchanged fire for about an hour. However, it was a most unequal affair. Realizing that all effort to extricate the frigate and even resistance was futile, the officer in charge (Lieutenant. Pendergrast, after Lieutenant. Smith was killed) signaled the surrender. As the *Zouave*, on the far side of the *Congress*, pulled away, it began to fire at its adversary again, and many on the *Virginia* as well as those on shore thought that the surrendered vessel had reneged on its white flag. The gunboat *Beaufort* sent a boarding party to claim the Union vessel as a prize, but the shore batteries prevented this Confederate force from remaining on the *Congress* beyond capturing twenty Union sailors. Unable to seize the captured Union frigate, the *Virginia* fired hot shot into the helpless vessel, which soon was ablaze. Many of the sailors not completely debilitated escaped by swimming to shore or to small boats that came to pick them up.

Hours before, when the *Minnesota* had attempted to come to the rescue of the *Cumberland*, it had run aground on a rise that separated the north and south channels, about halfway between Old Point Comfort and its destination. Though still in a position to fight, she could not escape and ultimately was at the ironclad's mercy. However, after all the misadventures that had befallen the Union squadron that day, fate finally smiled on the up-to-now losing side. It was now 5 o'clock, and the tide was falling. Both of the *Virginia*'s pilots refused to lead the iron monster towards the hapless *Minnesota*. Reluctantly, the *Virginia*'s commander, Commodore Franklin Buchanan, who had himself been injured, reluctantly ordered the ironclad back to the Elizabeth River. The destruction of the *Minnesota* would have to wait till the morrow.

Fortunately for the Union cause, just as the engagement was winding down, the U.S.S. *Monitor* reached Fort Monroe after its 2-day journey from New York. By 9 P.M. that night, she reached the *Roanoke*. After the pilot, Samuel Howard, came on board, she then proceeded to the *Minnesota,* where she quietly stood guard. Its crew finally was at liberty to rest for the few hours that remained until daybreak.

When morning came, it was quite foggy. Despite this, around 7:30 A.M. first a column of black smoke and then the *Virginia*'s smokestack were espied off Sewell's Point. Before the Confederate vessel managed to approach, the fog dissipated. The completely windless day greatly assisted observation, and it was a perfect day for the 40,000 spectators who lined the shores to watch the historic contest about to begin. Steaming beside the ironclad could be seen two side-wheel steamers and two screw-driven gunboats, all wooden vessels. Approaching to within a half mile of what it thought was just the defenseless *Minnesota,* the *Virginia* fired its first salvo. A small tug near the former's side was blown up, killing and wounding 17 men. Although a fire broke out on the frigate, it immediately returned fire.

It was at this point that the *Monitor* made its appearance. She had steamed in so quietly during the night that neither the soldiers on the shore nor on the enemy vessels were aware of her arrival. Even when morning dawned, the *Monitor* was initially invisible to those on shore and aboard the *Virginia*. Most of its hull was beneath the waterline, and its turret was within the shadow of the large warship she was to protect. Few on shore had any idea about the true nature of the "tin can on the shingle" that was now trying to work its way around the *Minnesota* and interpose itself between the Confederate ironclad and the frigate. To those favoring the Union cause, the situation seemed desperate, and they must have had the same expectations as those who witnessed David standing up to Goliath. One Union observer thought the diminutive Union vessel had about the same likelihood of success as "a rat attacking an alligator."

The Confederate ironclad managed to unleash a second salvo into the *Minnesota*. Before she was able to get off a third, the *Monitor* finally managed to interdict any further action against the disabled Union frigate. Realizing that this was no place for wooden ships and that the outcome of the engagement would be determined solely by the ironclads, the small steamers and gunboats fell behind. The *Monitor* meanwhile headed directly for the *Virginia*. For a moment the *Virginia* stopped its engines to allow its officers to get a better look at their adversary. This pause lasted but for a moment, however. Those on board the *Virginia* knew this was the *Monitor*, which had been expected in the area for the last several weeks. Getting underway once again, the larger ironclad fired a tremendous salvo at the *Monitor*. Those on the shore gasped and expected the Union vessel to be completely destroyed. Much was their surprise after the smoke cleared to see the Union ironclad not only still afloat, but completely undamaged. The *Monitor* fired back as she headed directly toward the *Virginia*'s starboard.

As the two ironclads passed one another heading in opposite directions, they each unleashed a salvo while only a few feet apart. Both vessels remained undamaged and circled around to get at the adversary once again. With its rotating turret, the *Monitor* was able to continue firing. From his position aboard the *Virginia*, Lt. John Wood estimated that the *Monitor* was able to fire once about every 7 or 8 minutes and that almost every shot struck, quite an accomplishment when the difficulties of controlling the turret's motion are considered.

This pattern of circling around and crossing paths appears to have repeated. Unfortunately, existing accounts are so conflicting that it is impossible to create a detailed chronology of all the actions that occurred, except to say that both vessels kept up a lively fire and sharpshooters attempted to pick off Union sailors by firing through the gun ports. Eventually, the gunners in the turret ran out of ammunition and the *Monitor* had to withdraw temporarily in order to transfer additional ammunition from the hull. This done, she once more entered the fray. Of course, the *Virginia* had originally wanted to finish off the *Minnesota* and at one point attempted to slip by the Union ironclad and approach the disabled frigate. The *Monitor* reacted quickly, and Commodore Worden attempted to ram the *Virginia*'s screw propellers, which would have proved fatal had he succeeded.

During the struggle both ironclads encountered a number of mechanical and operational problems. Some of the difficulties experienced by the *Monitor* were design issues; others were teething problems inevitably experienced by all new technologies. The problems of the *Virginia* stemmed from its size and basic design and the relatively minor but cumulatively significant damage gradually sustained during the day's fighting. It will be recalled that it had been decided to substitute the already constructed hull of the U.S.S. *Merrimac*, an ocean-going vessel, for that called for by Lieutenant Brooke's original plans. The extra 10 feet of draft greatly influenced the Confederate ironclad's movements. The ironclad had to greatly restrict its movements to a few narrow channels for fear of running aground, a fatal occurrence during a hard-fought struggle between two equally balanced contestants. Even with these precautions the *Virginia* went aground once or twice during the fighting, but it was able to work itself free before its adversary was able to exploit its momentary vulnerability. With its 12-foot draft, the *Monitor*, in contrast, was able to go almost anywhere she wished and several times during the engagement was able to retire to relative safety while its men either tended to the wounded in the pilothouse or restocked the ammunition in the turret.

The *Virginia*'s navigational problems were exacerbated during the fighting. Early in the fray the smokestack was shot away. It became increasingly difficult to obtain a sufficient draft of air into the boilers for the engine to operate at peak efficiency. The result was that the vessel's effective speed gradually decreased as the contest wore on.

In his chapter on the first fight between ironclads in *Battles and Leaders*, John Taylor Wood, who served aboard this rebel vessel, claimed that they had been at a disadvantage since the *Monitor's* rotating turrets allowed its gunners to constantly fire at the *Virginia*, regardless of the relative positions of the two combatants. This advantage, however, was largely illusory. Unbeknownst to the crew of the *Virginia*, the gunners in the turret found it extremely difficult to accurately aim their pair of guns. There were two problems. The apparatus used to rotate the turret proved faulty. Given the tremendous inertia of the turret, it was difficult to turn the turret and to get it to stop in the required position. This was an even more serious problem than it sounds, since the artillerymen could not see anything out the gun port but a very narrow band in the direction the gun was pointing. They saw their target for only a moment or two as the turret rotated, but it would continue to turn after they tried to stop it. The only solution was to fire the gun on the fly, for the brief moment the guns pointed at the target while the turret was rotating.

The position of the pilothouse near the bow of the long, slender hull only compounded the problem. The two occupants, the pilot and the commander, were the only individuals on board with a clear, panoramic view of their surroundings. Unfortunately, they were physically separated from the gunners to whom they issued orders and directions. There was a speaking tube between the pilothouse and the turret, but this, unfortunately, was destroyed early in the action. Two men, both landsmen unfamiliar with the technical maritime jargon of the gunners, the commander, and the pilot, had to run between the two centers and sometimes misreported the instructions. It was difficult to implement even the simplest of instructions, such as the "target is to the starboard." The various directions had been painted on the floor in the turret, but these were soon hopelessly erased by the constant scuffling of feet as the men moved around the turret. The pilothouse posed another problem. It was impossible to fire directly over the bow, which made it impossible to solve the inertia problems simply by pointing the *Monitor* at the *Virginia*.

After the *Virginia's* first salvos, all directed at the *Monitor's* turret, the vulnerability of the pilothouse was noted, and Commodore Franklin Buchanan, the *Virginia's* commander, directed that the artillerymen now aim at this part of the *Monitor*. Eventually, after about 2 hours into the fighting, this tactic paid off. A shell exploded right over the peek hole out of which Worden was looking. Blinded by burnt powder and iron fragments, the *Monitor*'s commander was knocked unconscious, and the ironclad was forced to return to shallower water and stop for about 30 minutes in order for some of the crew to make their way along the top of the hull and pull their commander to safety. On her part the *Virginia* started to run out of ammunition, and the rate of firing slackened. Her commander decided to try to ram her foe with her damaged prow. Patiently, Thomas Catesbyap Jones, filling in for the injured Buchanan, maneuvered his vessel into position before finally striking. The ship "was unwieldy as Noah's ark," and the *Monitor* was able to turn enough at the last moment that the *Virginia* only delivered a glancing blow and no damage was inflicted. The *Monitor*, with its rotating turret, was able to capitalize on the proximity of the enemy vessel and fired two rounds while only a few feet away. Both struck the *Virginia* near the after pivot gun halfway up the iron shield. This shield was pushed in 3 inches and the men behind were knocked over by the force of the concussion.

The two vessels, now moving in opposite directions, did not choose to reengage. The *Monitor*, maneuvered by the pilot and Lt. Green, retired to Old Point. Later that afternoon, however, she returned and placed herself near the *Minnesota*, which was finally gotten afloat once again. The *Virginia*, visibly listing, headed toward Sewell's Point.

Despite the appearance that the 4-hour, hard-fought engagement was a draw, it proved to be a strategic victory for the North. The possibility of wholesale destruction of Union fleets, shipping, and coastal cities—which loomed as a very real threat the previous evening—had now dissipated. Though quickly repaired, the *Virginia* would never pose the same threat. Twice more she would sally out into Hampton Roads and try to goad the *Monitor* into another action. However, there were no longer vulnerable wooden ships anchored between Fort Monroe and Newport News, so there was no pressing need to comply. The *Virginia*, thought to be unable to pass the forts blocking passage out into Chesapeake Bay, was forced to retire back to the Norfolk navy yards. With the Confederate withdrawal 2 months later, she was scuttled on May 11.

IRONCLADS VERSUS FORTIFICATIONS

The Union government's initial aversion to armored gunboats does not appear to have extended to its policy on how the war in the West was to be waged. On April 29 engineer James B. Eads wrote the secretary of the navy to propose shore and floating batteries that could control traffic along the Mississippi and Ohio Rivers in order to blockade the rebellious states. If Eads's overall plan was bold, the means he proffered was rather conventional. His idea of a floating battery was merely a steamboat, reinforced with thick cotton bales for added protection, with a "a complement of 32-pounders." He recommended that the government convert the *Benton*, a particularly strong, twin-hulled snag boat, used to raise sunken steamboats. Although this vessel had only a 5-foot draught and could be navigated through most rivers, Eads felt it advisable for the vessel to be accompanied by two lighter vessels that could negotiate even shallower waters.

Records show that the federal government began to seriously consider the use of self-propelled floating batteries to secure the Western rivers, and the chief engineer of the U.S. Army was brought in to analyze the necessary characteristics of such vessels. In a June 1 memorandum, Gen. Joseph Totten concluded it was not feasible to construct a propeller-driven "armed steam vessel." Instead, these river gunboats should be shaped like a bateau (with flat bottom and curved up at both ends) and powered by two side-wheels. No more than 170 feet long, 28 feet wide, and a draft of 5 feet, their total weight should not exceed 395 tons. The chief engineer was willing to defer to the opinion of Samuel Pook, who he conceded was an experienced shipbuilder officially connected to the U.S. Navy. Judging from the contract that was entered with James Eads on August 7, Pook appears to have favored a slightly larger type of gunboat. Eads was to build seven gunboats, each of which was to be 175 feet long, 50 feet wide, with a 6-foot hold. These were to be completed by October 10, 1861. The agreed-upon specifications only required that the boiler and engines be protected by iron plates.

Unlike in the East, where there was a definite lull in open hostilities following the fall of Fort Sumter, both sides immediately jockeyed for strategic locations along the upper Mississippi in Kentucky and Missouri during the summer of 1861. Unwilling to wait for the completion of Eads's gunboats, Commander John Rodgers of the U.S. Navy purchased three steamboats with conventional side paddle wheels that were immediately modified for their new martial roles. These gunboats, the *Lexington, Tyler,* and *Conestoga,* were about 180 feet long, with a 42-foot beam and a 6-foot draft, and could achieve 7- to 10-knot speed. Protected by additional 5-inch oak bulwarks, these quickly became known as *timberclads.* Offensive armament appears to have varied, from the *Tyler,* which had a pair of 32-pounders, to the most heavily armed, the *Conestoga* which had four 32-pounders and four 8-inch Dahlgrens.

Eads and his crews, meanwhile, continued to construct the seven specially built gunboats. Although the government initially had envisioned only limited iron protection, those lobbying for iron protection of fighting vessels gained the upper hand by mid-September, and it was decided to extend iron protection to all of the above-water portions of the vessels.

Eads did not have to wait long to see the value of his efforts. In early February Gen. Ulysses S. Grant and Flag Officer A. H. Foote received permission from Halleck to use a combined armored gunboat and conventional infantry force to attack Fort Henry on the eastern side of the Tennessee River. Conventional wisdom taught that a naval force that attacked a coastal or river fortification required a three-to-one superiority in artillery power. Whether because he did not have a high regard for Fort Henry or because he thought that the armored protection of the gunboats and the infantry accompaniment substantially altered the equation in his favor, Foote believed that the fort could be overpowered with mere parity of artillery.

Foote's force consisted of four armored gunboats, the *Essex, Carondelet, Cincinnati,* and *St. Louis,* augmented by the three timberclads. On his part Grant commanded 23 infantry regiments. These embarked on a motley collection of steamers, which set off from Paducah, Kentucky, on February 2. While retiring after a reconnaissance of the area around the fort on February 5, the *Essex* came under fire while 2½ miles from the enemy position, considered to be a remarkable distance at this point during the war. Although a round went through the officers' quarters, there were no casualties. In light of the

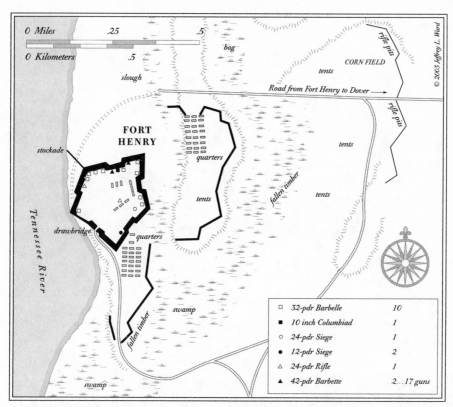

Fort Henry and its outworks. As can be seen by the surrounding swamp, the fort was unhappily situated on low ground, making it a vulnerable target to naval artillery fire.

unexpected long-range capabilities of the fort's artillery, Grant and Foote modified their plan of attack. Instead of coursing up the main channel and being exposed to all of the fort's artillery at long range, it was decided to cautiously wend their way up the "island chute," the channel, between Panther Island and the eastern bank. This was much narrower than the main channel, so the flotilla had to be organized into two divisions. The first consisted of the four armored gunboats steaming abreast, followed by the three timberclads. There was so little room in the chute that the *Carondelet* and the *St. Louis* had to be lashed side by side, and they remained in this state throughout the day's operations. Unfortunately, this meant that only the guns in the bow could be brought into action. Thus, eleven Union artillery pieces were pitted against eleven in the fort.

Apparently the old adage that inaccurate fire only emboldened the

The upper portion of the Union ironclad *New Era* was protected with boiler iron. The hull below the waterline was made out of well-seasoned timber. Plying the Missouri River, it was armed with 10 Dahlgren guns and carried 100 men. *Frank Leslie's Illustrated Weekly,* Oct 26, 1861.

enemy applied also to naval gunnery, so Foote cautioned the gun crews against injudicious long-range fire. The orders to get under way were issued at 10:50 the next morning, and by 11:35 the flotilla had passed Panther Island. The gun crews had taken Foote's orders to heart, and there was no firing until the first division was past the tip of the island and about 1700 yards from the fort, when the *Cincinnati* unleashed one of its guns, the signal to begin the bombardment. At this early phase of the action, the artillerists on the armored gunboats elected to fire shell, which initially were thrown along a rainbow trajectory. However, as the vessels continued to approach their target, the muzzles of the guns were gradually lowered. On the *Essex,* for example, the first shots were fired at a 7-degree elevation, which was lowered to 6 degrees, 5 degrees, 4 degrees, and finally to 3 degrees inclination. The fuses were correspondingly shortened from 15 to 10 and then 5 seconds.

As they reentered the main channel, the gunboats closed towards one another and seemed to offer the defenders a single face that periodically erupted into flame and smoke. The fort's battery was commanded to temporarily abjure from returning fire. The defenders only had two long-range guns, a 128-pounder Columbiad and a 6-inch rifled cannon. Their eight 32-pounders, two 42-pounders, and five 18-pounder siege guns possessed modest ranges, and it would be a waste of ammunition to fire prematurely. The gunboats meanwhile began firing more rapidly as they advanced. The men manning the bow guns worked furiously, and it was exhausting labor. Frequently, an officer would order the men working the guns to change places with those assigned to guns that could not be brought into action. There would be a temptation for the relieved men to stand around and encourage those who had just taken their places, but to remove them from danger, an experienced officer would forcibly order them to their new positions.

So far all the projectiles had headed from the gunboats to the fort. About 20 minutes after the *Cincinnati* had begun firing, the defenders finally began to reciprocate. For a few minutes the Union officers stationed on the spar decks remained nonplussed, eagerly watching the action. Quickly, the shot and shell became too hot, and they scurried below. Events soon demonstrated that even those behind thick iron plates were still at risk. The gunboats had now neared to about 600 yards from the fort. For 20 minutes both sides hurled as much shot and shell at one another as humanly possible.

The Confederate battery was the first to draw blood. Piercing the *Essex*'s casemate just above a porthole, a shot penetrated its middle boiler. What followed was an interplay of pandemonium and carnage. One man was decapitated by the round; several others were instantly scalded to death by the jet of steam and boiling water that spewed out of the ruptured boiler. In a desperate bid to escape an excruciating death, others jumped through the ports. The pilots dead or dying, the guns and boilers unattended, the *Essex* lost all motive power and, breaking formation, started to drift.

The rest of the Union flotilla relentlessly continued towards the fort and soon dealt out retribution that more than compensated for the damaged *Essex*. To compound their problem, the defenders had more than their share of bad luck. First, the 6-inch rifled cannon burst, placing not only its crew hors de combat but many of those working adjacent guns, as well. A few minutes later a priming wire became jammed in the Columbiad's touchhole, and the Confederates lost their only other effective gun. If that was not bad enough, soon after, the gunboats succeeded in striking two of the 32-pounders, which again caused numerous casualties. The defensive fire now ineffectual, the gunboats were free to select their targets with impunity. Survivors in the fort would later recount how the gunboat shells burst through the fort like a minié ball through a board. Now, the Confederate defenders essentially defenseless, the fort surrendered. In his report Grant asserted that the entire action, from the first shot to the surrender, lasted only 1 hour, though the declaration of Gen. Lloyd Tilghman, the fort's commander, that the decision to surrender occurred at 1:55 suggests that the engagement lasted more than 2 hours.

Of course, the capture of Fort Henry was only half of Grant's strategic objective; there remained Fort Donelson about 12 miles away on the Cumberland River. This second objective would prove to be a much more formidable challenge. Not only did Fort Donelson contain a vastly larger garrison, it was also much more favorably situated. Unlike Fort Henry, whose earthen walls and batteries were myopically placed almost at river level, Fort Donelson was positioned atop 120-foot bluffs that dominated the river below. The fifteen guns on the river side of the fort were divided into three batteries: The first was about 20 feet above water level, the second at the 50-foot level, while the third straddled the top of the bluffs.

A few days after the capitulation of Fort Henry, towed by a tugboat, the *Carondelet* anchored about a mile downriver from Fort Donelson. Grant had ordered its captain, Henry Walke, to demonstrate in front of the fort to prevent the arrival of enemy reinforcements. The captain carried out his instructions at 12:50 P.M. on February 12, when, within 3 miles of the fort, he dropped anchor and fired about a dozen rounds at the fort. The defending gunners, most of whom were novices, were literally practicing artillery drill when attacked and declined to return fire. The gunboats did inspire Union infantry on the other side of the fort to initiate a few skirmishes. It was important to unmask the enemy's batteries in order to determine their position and size.

Grant ordered the *Carondelet* to return the next day and bombard the fort more vigorously with its bow guns, partly to unmask the batteries and partly to cover his own investment of the fort on the landward sides. This time Captain Walke's gunboat approached a heavily wooded point on the shore about a mile from the enemy's position and proceeded to fire. Emboldened by the defenders' continued stoicism, the *Carondelet* continued to approach. The defenders, once again caught in the middle of their artillery drills, at first abstained from firing, just as they had the day before. The gunboat's fire was deadly accurate and soon became too destructive to ignore. Lieutenant Dixon ordered the fort's rifled artillery piece and the Columbiad to begin firing. The first few shots overshot their mark, but the third from the Columbiad struck home. Seemingly unfazed, the *Carondelet* continued to fire. First Lieutenant Dixon was decapitated, and then the Columbiad was rendered temporarily unserviceable.

The 128-pound round shot from the Columbiad had caused much more damage than was apparent. Striking the corner of the broadside casemate on the port side, it deflected off the barricade surrounding a boiler, hit the beams of the upper deck, and destroyed a steam heater. The wounded were transferred to the *Alps*, and the damages repaired. The *Carondelet* then recommenced its firing, which continued to dusk, when the gunboat finally retired. That day the gunboat fired a total of 139 70-pound and 64-pound projectiles.

The bombardments on February 12 and 13 proved to be only preliminary exercises; the real combined naval and ground assault was reserved for February 14. Late on the 13th, the three armored gunboats, the *St. Louis, Louisville,* and *Pittsburgh,* and two timberclads, the *Tyler* and *Conestoga,* joined the *Carondelet.* This force set off at 3 P.M. the next day. Once again the armored gunboats were in the first line, with the timberclads following a thousand yards to the rear, the whole moving at a "moderate speed." The attack was no surprise to those in Fort Donelson; they could see the large, dark brown billows of smoke slowly approaching from miles away. After some hesitation and debate, the defenders started to shell the still-invisible Union naval transports with the Columbiad. However, before a second shot could be fired, the armored gunboats appeared from around a bend. The shelling continued until the attackers had approached to within 1½ miles, and then the Columbiad and the rifled gun began to fire solid shot, ricocheting it off of the water to improve the chances of hitting the target and causing damage near the waterline. Unfortunately for the fort's defenders, the rifled gun quickly jammed, demoralizing the men and placing the entire burden on the Columbiad until the gunboats would enter the range of the Confederate 32-pounders.

The *St. Louis*, the flagship, now about a mile from the fort, was the first gunboat to return fire, but it was soon joined by the three other gunboats, and then the timberclads behind, which lobbed conical shells. The battle now became general, with each side gradually picking up the pace of the fire as the gunboats continued to near. The firing soon reached a crescendo. As at Fort Henry, the gunboats were only able to use their bow guns, so this portion of the day's events devolved into a duel between the twelve guns on the gunboats versus the ten in Fort Donelson. The Union vessels could only approach to within 300 to 400 yards. Any closer, and the bow guns could not be sufficiently elevated to reach the top batteries on the bluffs.

The Confederate batteries quickly gained the upper hand, however. The two top-level batteries, enjoying the advantage of height, were able to fire at the thin, vulnerable top armor of the Union gunboats. By the end of the engagement, the *St. Louis* was struck by fifty-nine rounds, four of which hit "between wind and water." One round that hit its Texas deck killed the helmsman and wounded Flag Officer Foote. Another went through its wheelhouse and carried away the wheel. The *Pittsburgh* took two shots in the bow, one of which damaged a bulkhead, broke pipes, and wounded some of the crew. Other rounds destroyed her steering capabilities, and the vessel dropped out of the fight, drifting downriver at the mercy of the strong current. The *Louisville* suffered similar damage with the same result. To make matters worse, some of the shells fired from the timberclads fell short and exploded on or very near the gunboats in front of them.

However, much of the Confederate gunners' fury was directed towards the *Carondelet,* whose incursions had so annoyed the Confederate batteries during the previous 2 days. One shot from the Columbiad severed the gunboat's anchor and, careening over the vessel, took with it part of the smokestack. Several rounds tore into the armor, weakening the boat's defensive capabilities. The pilothouse was struck, and a pilot was mortally wounded. The boat davits securing a lifeboat were destroyed, and the lifeboat dropped into the water. To add to the confusion, a rifled gun on the port side exploded, wounding many.

The bow guns on the *Carondelet* continued to fire, but with the other gunboats having dropped out of the fight, she was completely overpowered by the concentrated might of all three Confederate batteries. Increasingly, her side armor was damaged by solid shot fired at short range and ricocheting along the water. Two 32-pound shots hit between wind and water, and the vessel started to leak. The *Carondelet's* gun crews continued to fire unceasingly, no longer to inflict damage on the enemy but simply to sustain the large pall of smoke that obscured the vessel's exact position. The Union attempt to destroy the Confederate river batteries and demoralize the defenders had failed. Now only a land-based escalade or a long, drawn-out formal siege held any prospect of success.

THE RAM VERSUS IRONCLAD

After studying mathematics at the École Polytechnique in Paris as a young man, Charles Ellet, Jr., returned to America to apply his knowledge to the construction of the large, highly engineered iron bridges then proliferating throughout the country. He soon became the chief engineer of the James River and Kanawa Canal. Before long he submitted to the city of St. Louis a design for a suspension bridge over the Mississippi. He soon after designed and constructed a suspension Fairmount bridge over the Schuylkill River, the first major bridge of this type in the United States.

In 1854, on behalf of the Virginia Central Railroad, Ellet traveled to England as a consulting engineer. While waiting to make the transatlantic journey, the highly talented engineer learned of the *Collins* disaster, in which the large liner was sunk by the much smaller *Artic*, which had struck the former amidships. Ellet was fascinated by the incident and immediately saw the military application of a fast vessel with a sharp, reinforced prow that would intentionally ram a larger but slower and less maneuverable warship. This was the very time that the Russian navy was trapped in Sebastopol's harbor, and the Russian Admiralty was seriously considering scuttling its ships to deprive the Allies of this prize. The American engineer offered to command a few small, fast vessels that would ram and sink the enemy men-of-war. His proposal was positively received, but before he was able to go to St. Petersburg, the tsar died, and the project was dropped.

Returning to America, Ellet concretized his ideas in a pamphlet he personally published in December 1855. Although a popular work, it was coldly ignored by Naval authorities, who were loath to accept a suggestion from someone with no formal naval experience. Snubbed, Charles Jr. returned to his long-term professional concerns and for the time set aside his interest in the notion of rams.

Like Ericsson, however, Ellet resurrected these plans with the eruption of hostilities between the two American moieties. A pamphlet in which Ellet described the ram and its advantages was well received. *Scientific American* on February 22, 1861, endorsed Ellet's views and argued that all "iron war steamers" should have strong iron prows which could be used offensively. After a meeting with Secretary of War Stanton on March 14, Ellet was dispatched to Fort Monroe, were he was to convert several small steamers into rams. However, receiving little or no cooperation from General John Ellis Wool, to whom he was assigned, he was unable to make any progress and quickly resigned. Ellet returned to his civilian activities, and little more happened that is germane to this story until February 1862.

The ram certainly was not new to American naval authorities. The British Navy had recently constructed and tested ram steamers. Representative Grimes reported to Congress that during the 1850s the British had briefly experimented with the ram but soon became disillusioned with this type of craft. This did not deter a few in the South to undertake a similar venture. James Edward Montgomery, a former riverboat captain, tried to interest the Confederate government in this new naval tactic but initially met with the same frustration and rejection as his Northern counterpart. Though spurned by the navy, Montgomery received approval from the Confederacy War Department to convert some steamboats into rams to help defend Memphis from Union armored gunboats (ironclads). Crewed by local landsmen familiar with the local waters, these vessels were protected by cotton bales and armed with one or two guns.

The new ironclads had dominated the public's attention in February and March 1862. In May and June attention temporarily shifted to the fast-moving and relatively agile ram steamer. Grant's Army of the Tennessee, now commanded by Gen. Henry W. Halleck, lay siege to Fort Pillow, the last remaining strong point that stood between the Union army and Memphis. On April 12 these ground forces were reinforced by Foote's armored gunboats and a number of mortar boats. From that point onward, these large mortars hurled mammoth shells into Fort Pillow approximately once every 30 minutes. The mortar boats were necessarily clumsy, ponderous affairs, totally incapable of defending themselves if attacked by water. For added protection every night an ironclad slipped down the Mississippi to the more exposed mortar boats to protect them from a surprise attack.

On May 10 it was the *Cincinnati*'s turn to stand guard over mortar boat No. 16. Convinced that their guns were sufficient to repel any assault that the Confederates could launch at them, the Union armored gunboat commanders failed to take the precaution of remaining at "steam's up." The possibility of being attacked appears to have been inconceivable, and that morning the crew was busy "holy-stoning" (scrubbing the deck), and the steam "was down."

Mortar boats first introduced during the Crimean war were used with good effect during the siege of Island No. 10 and Fort Pillow in Tennessee. *Frank Leslie's Pictorial History of the War,* 1862.

Suddenly, large, puffing columns of deep, black smoke appeared on the horizon downriver, the harbinger of most unpleasant tidings. The size, number, and direction of the plumes told the Union crewmen that a number of enemy steamers, in all probability the Confederate River Defense Fleet, were making their way upriver and that attack was imminent. Montgomery's fleet consisted of eight rams: the *Little Rebel, General Bragg, General Sterling Price, General Earl Van Dorn, General Sumter, General M. Jeff. Thompson, General Beauregard,* and *General Lovell.* From the distance of the rising smoke, the surprised crewmen and their officers realized that they had about 8 minutes to try and get up steam, much too little time to do so using standard procedure. In desperation the engineers threw oil and other inflammable matter into the fire, and the *Cincinnati* slowly swang out into the Mississippi. Soon the individual enemy steamers became recognizable. In the forefront was the *General Bragg,* which was traveling sufficiently fast that the billow in front of the bow was 10 feet high.

The *Cincinnati* withheld its fire until the approaching Confederate ram was at extremely close range, then unleashed its starboard battery of four 42-pounders. Though obviously absorbing frightful punishment, the *General Bragg* continued to close. At the last minute the Union gunboat desperately tried to swerve to minimize the impact. The attempt was partially successful, and the ram was only able to gouge a 6- by 12-foot section out of the gunboat's amidships. The *Bragg*'s bow became momentarily stuck in the *Cincinnati,* and before she was able to work its way loose, the latter was able to empty another deadly broadside into the Confederate vessel.

Though the *Bragg* was severely damaged and now floating out of action down the river, the *Cincinnati*'s troubles were far from over. A second Confederate ram, the *General Sumter,* now could be seen approaching her stern. Two 6-inch guns aboard the gunboat managed to get off two rounds each, but this failed to thwart the enemy's intentions. The *Sumter* managed to strike the *Cincinnati*s fantail at full speed, destroying the rudders and a portion of the hull in the stern. If that was not bad enough, a third Confederate ram, the *General Lovell,* struck the gunboat on her port side, while sharpshooters picked off any Union crew member who was exposed. Water pouring in on three sides of its hull, the *Cincinnati* soon went down, bow first.

Its crew scrambled first to the hurricane deck and then to wheel-house, which, given the shallowness of the water at that place remained above water.

Fortunately, it was just at this point that the remaining Union armored gunboats arrived. The *Benton,* the Union flagship, steamed into the fray and delivered a salvo from its 9-inch Dahlgren guns on the bow, then continued to maneuver and delivered in succession broadsides from its starboard, stern, and port sides. Several of the Confederate vessels attempted to ram her, but, maneuvering out of the way or repelling the attempt with the pure brunt of artillery, the *Benton* managed to reload and deliver several shots. The Union mortar boat did not remain idle during the attack and it fired shells over the Confederate rams. This boat, however, was soon silenced by the *General Earl Van Dorn,* which bypassed the Union ironclads and fired two rounds from its 32-pounder through the mortar boat's blinds. The *Mound City,* another Union gunboat, meanwhile was rammed by first the *General Sumter* and then by the *General Earl Van Dorn,* which managed to circle back. Severely damaged, the Union ironclad headed for the shore, where she sank in 12 feet of water.

The *Sumter* itself could not escape unscathed, however. A few moments later a 50-pound shot fired by the *Carondelet* penetrated her boilers, and there was a tremendous explosion. The *Sumter,* now dead in the water, floated slowly downstream. Overpowered and suffering from the Union gunboat artillery, the Confederate River Defense Fleet was finally beaten back.

History would record the action, which would become known to posterity as the Battle at Plum Point, a Confederate victory. After all, the Confederate River Defense Fleet had sunk two "ironclads," the *Cincinnati* and the *Mound City.* The success was largely illusory, however. Only a few Union crewmen and officers had been wounded, and both vessels were soon raised and returned to active duty. Although the Confederates seemed to fare better in terms of the damage to their vessels, one lost and two damaged, they had suffered extensive casualties. Moreover, the Union sailors also developed a sense of confidence that would stand them in good stead a month later in the naval battle for the true prize of that campaign, Memphis.

The siege of Fort Pillow continued until May 29, when the occupants blew up as much of the fortifications as they could and then hastily beat a retreat. General Beauregard's strategic withdrawal from Corinth, Mississippi, in the face of Halleck's massively superior numbers on May 30 now made the Confederate occupation of the fort unfeasible. The Confederate River Defense Fleet retired downriver and anchored at Memphis.

RAM VERSUS RAM

During the night of June 5–6 an enemy tug had steamed near the Union river fleet, now near Memphis. It ran aground, and, having to abandon the vessel, its crew then set it ablaze so that it would not fall into Union hands. A wise precaution during normal combat conditions, this was a foolish action during a clandestine nocturnal probe. Aware of this reconnaissance effort, Flag Officer C. H. Davis suspected that an attack was imminent. Determined not to be taken off guard as his forces had been at Plum Point, Davis ordered his gunboats to be ready for action, and each gunboat built up enough steam to get underway quickly, should it receive orders to do so. Davis apparently expected Ellet's rams to join them shortly, and if the Confederate River Defense Fleet attacked, he intended to counter with a combination of his own armored gunboats and Ellet's rams.

No effort had been made to contact Ellet, however, and when his rams approached Davis's gunboats, he was completely unaware of the night's events or Davis's plans. His first inkling that anything was amiss was when an enemy shot whizzed over the bow of his flagship, the *Queen of the West*. Davis's and Ellet's combined command suddenly found itself attacked by the Confederate River Defense Fleet.

Two of Davis's armored gunboats had dropped their stern anchors prior to the action, and they now began to fire upon the advancing Confederate rams with their bow guns. Ellet had long awaited the eventuality of battle, and he quickly ordered his own rams forward into the fray. Up until this point Ellet's vessels had been advancing at "half speed" effectively in two divisions: four of his most powerful rams in front—the *Monarch*, the *Lancaster*, the *Switzerland*, and his own *Queen of the West*—followed by the remainder towing a large barge or simply tagging along behind. Ellet's intention was to attack with the front four rams, but the plan quickly unraveled.

On the *Lancaster* confusion among the officers, combined with pilot error, caused the gunboat to be backed onto the riverbank. Its rudders were damaged, and the vessel was out of the action before it really began. The captain of the *Switzerland* misunderstood Ellet's hand signals and thought his gunboat was to remain a half mile behind as a reserve.

Davis's gunboats had spread out as soon as they spotted the advancing enemy and began to fire quickly. A low-lying wall of smoke soon stretched across the Mississippi. The *Queen* and the *Monarch* sprang forward at full speed into these clouds. Once through, the *Queen* headed directly for the *General Lovell,* near the middle of the line of advancing Confederate rams, while the *Monarch* went after the *General Price,* on the right. At first the *Queen* and the *Lovell* continued to make straight for each other, and it appeared that a colossal collision would destroy both vessels. At the last minute, the captain of the *Lovell* changed his mind and ordered his ram to turn away. This equivocation settled the *Lovell's* fate, however. Struck cleanly in her vulnerable amidships, she was cut almost in two and sank in a matter of moments, and those unable to jump clear of the wreck were drowned. With Ellet and his crew's attention focused on the *Lovell,* the *Beauregard* delivered a glancing blow that sheared off the *Queen's* starboard wheel. Crippled, the *Queen of the West* headed slowly for the Arkansas bank and was now out of the fight.

The *Monarch* and the *General Price* meanwhile continued to close, but once again, at the very last moment, both vessels turned just enough to substitute a glancing blow for a head-on collision that would necessarily have been fatal to both. Although the *Monarch* escaped undamaged, the *General Price* suffered a caved-in bow and the loss of a side wheel. She also began to take on water.

The other Confederate rams had not remained idle, and as the *General Bragg* caught up to the leaders, she focused on the *Monarch.* The 32-pounder on its bow began to fire; however, its gunners were quickly chased off the deck by sharpshooters on the Union ram. The *Beauregard* also turned its attention to the *Monarch,* which was still attempting to disengage itself from the *Price,* and for a few moments the Union ram was threatened on both its port and its starboard. Breaking free of its victim, the *Monarch* proved quicker and more agile than either of its foes and nimbly slipped between them. Unable to change its course in time, the *Beauregard* inadvertently slammed into the *General Price*.

Turning around, the *Monarch* rammed the *Price*, delivering what proved to be a coup de grâce. Once again circling around to gain headway, the *Monarch* next charged the *Beauregard*, already slightly disabled by the unfortunate collision with the *Price*. Davis's armored gunboats had been firing all the while, and one of their shots struck the *Beauregard* about the same time that she was rammed by the *Monarch*. Penetrated by an artillery shot, her boiler exploded, causing devastating casualties. The *Monarch* attempted to tow the sinking *Beauregard* to shore, but its prize sank in shallow shoal water. The *Price*, crippled by three collisions, also attempted to make its way to shore but met with the same fate as the *Beauregard*.

The Union gunboats had kept up a lively fire all the while and scored a number of hits on the Confederate rams that had not been engaged by either the *Queen* or the *Monarch*. The *Little Rebel*, for example, endured a heavy battering, and its boiler exploded before its captain decided to disengage. Beaching on the Arkansas bank, its crew fled into the woods and escaped. She was soon followed by the *General Bragg*. The *Jeff Thompson* went aground further downriver, where she was blown up by her crew. Artillery fire from the Union gunboats appears to have been particularly effective that day, and the *General Sumter* became another casualty and soon was run aground on the shore. Only the *General Van Dorn* managed to flee back down the river and escape. The Battle of Memphis was a decisive Union victory. Compared to seven ships completely lost to the Confederate side, only two Union rams were damaged.

ERICSSON AND THE ORIGIN OF THE IRONCLAD

The Herculean contest between the *Monitor* and the *Virginia* and the ease with which the latter sunk or destroyed several wooden men-of-war convincingly demonstrated that the days of the wooden fighting ship had ended. Journalists on both sides of the Atlantic decided to investigate the history of this innovation. It is natural to assume that the Swedish-born inventor John Ericsson would assume a preeminent role in these accounts. The debate between those who had urged the adoption of iron-protected ships and those who had stubbornly stood in their way, however, had long been on public record. Thus, it was impossible to completely overlook the role played by those others who had for so many years vociferously but fruitlessly argued for their adoption. In 1863 *Scientific American* explained that although European naval engineers and architects were proud of Cowper Coles's role in the development of the rotating turret, they nevertheless concluded that Robert and E. A. Stevens were the true inventors of the ironclad. As if to dispel any doubt about this assertion, a few weeks later an article in the *Cornhill Magazine* about the recent "naval revolution" avowed to its British readers that the Stevens floating battery was indeed the "first iron-cased ship ever commenced."

A few tried to establish an even longer lineage, however. In the weeks following the *Monitor-Virginia (Merrimac)* duel, Senator Cowan of Pennsylvania petitioned for a pension for the widow of Thomas Gregg, arguing that her husband's patent of an iron-protected ship in 1814 represented the first tangible step in the development of what had become known as the ironclad. Acknowledging the role played by Captain Montgery's advocacy of iron ships during the 1820s, the *Army and Navy Journal* in September concluded rather sarcastically that the lengthy delay between his pioneering efforts and the engagement at Hampton Roads "represented the necessary time between the conception and the execution of an idea."

Unfortunately, within a decade of Appomattox, the role played by the Stevens family had been completely forgotten, and only Cowper Coles remained to challenge Ericsson's claim as the true inventor of the ironclad. In the public's mind, the role played by Ericsson in the development of the ironclad gradually expanded. In a pamphlet entitled *The First Monitor and Its Builders* (1884), Francis B. Wheeler credited Ericsson as the inventor of the vessel that had been so successful at Hampton Roads. Of course, Wheeler was literally referring to the invention of a *Monitor*-class ironclad, rather than necessarily the entire genus, but this was a subtle and implicit distinction that was probably lost on most of his readers.

The next step was taken during the publication of the highly influential *Battles and Leaders* in the late 1880s. In his introduction to the "First Fight of Iron-clads" chapter, John Taylor Woods claimed that

this single fight "revolutionized the navies of the world," who, immediately abandoning wooden ships, hurriedly started to construct ironclads. When one recalls that the American legislature was aware of
the British and French moratorium on wooden fighting vessels by
1861 and the threat of the proliferation of the new iron-protected vessels, Woods's claim is clearly inaccurate. In his own chapter,
"Building the Monitor," Ericsson provided a more accurate account
of its origin, noting that the construction of the British *Warrior* and
the French *La Gloire* had actually influenced decisions in Washington and Richmond.

There were several attempts during the early 1890s to trace the
origins of the ironclad prior to the Civil War. In an 1893 article in the
Graphic, Comdr. C. N. Robinson of the Royal Navy pointed out that
the first European "iron clad" had actually been constructed in
Antwerp in 1585, and the story was picked up on the American side
of the Atlantic by *Scientific American.* Such efforts to more accurately
trace the early story of the ironclad proved futile, and it is clear that
by the mid-1890s the myth of the *Monitor* as the first ironclad had
firmly taken hold.

One of the problems was purely terminological. Seeking to
unravel the story of the new type of fighting vessel, later generations
unconsciously chose the obvious approach and limited their
research to vessels already consciously categorized as "ironclad."
Of course, pre–Civil War vessels of this type had not been known by
this term but had been referred to by a motley collection of labels,
such as "mailed ship," "armored protected ship," "iron-protected
ship," "iron-cast ship," and "floating battery." The use of this latter
term to refer exclusively to a nonpropelled floating gun platform only
occurred after the popularization of the term *ironclad* during
1861–62, but originally, *floating battery* referred to even self-propelled floating gun platforms.

Chapter 20

DEVELOPMENTS DURING THE WAR

A s the War Between the States dragged on, there was a gradual accumulation of collective martial experience. Volunteers who had joined the service with no experience and little military skill not only mastered formal procedure but learned how to proficiently perform the innumerable tasks demanded by the exigencies of day-to-day campaigning. It is not unnatural, therefore, that there would be an evolution of practice, and new tactics and methods were occasionally introduced. These ranged from organizational changes, such as the introduction of the corps system, to how the types of small arms ammunition that was distributed were used.

SHARPSHOOTERS

The operations in front of Yorktown would witness the advent of another tactical phenomenon, the widespread use of expert marksmen or sharpshooters, whose task was to pick off important targets, such as the enemy skirmishers, officers, and artillery crews. The use of sharpshooters was by no means new to warfare. The British and German Allies, for example, had frequently resorted to expert shots to bring down French officers during the second half of the Napoleonic wars. Charged with the evaluation of the feasibility of defending Fort Moultrie (Charleston, South Carolina), Maj. Robert Anderson cautioned in November 1860 that several nearby "sand hillocks" afforded perfect cover for enemy sharpshooters while they easily picked off defenders along the parapets of the fort, their greatly increased lethality made possible by their longer-range, more accurate weapons. And once hostilities commenced, it didn't take long for sharpshooters to ply their deadly trade in earnest, especially in the

West. Reports about the engagement at Belmont, Missouri, the siege of Fort Donelson, and the Battle of Shiloh, to name but a few, all pay tribute to the prowess of sharpshooters.

Despite these precedents the exploits of Berdan's specialists in front of Yorktown, Virginia, in April 1862 mark a new chapter in the use of sharpshooters on the battlefield and during the daily campaign. Henceforth, not only were they employed more frequently and in greater numbers, but they became part of the normal fabric of daily warfare. Prior to this, no matter how successful, they had remained some sort of special operation, an unpredictable military aberration which, encountered only sporadically, did not have to be constantly feared or taken into consideration.

There had been earlier sieges before Yorktown, such as at Fort Donelson, but these were fleeting affairs in which the opposing forces never really settled down to the more prosaic tasks required by formal siegecraft. The lengthy Confederate lines of prepared defensive positions posed quite a different situation at Yorktown. Most of the Union infantry turned to strengthening existing fortifications, erecting fieldworks, and building approach roads, while the responsibility for more active operations shifted to the artillery, skirmishers, and other forms of specialized troops. During the first few days, well-served Confederate artillery, ensconced behind earthworks, walls, and other defensive protection, pestered those who attempted to approach and threatened to impede Union operations significantly.

Berdan's sharpshooters took up the challenge. Taking advantage of whatever flimsy cover was available, small groups of the First United States Sharpshooters cautiously advanced closer to the enemy entrenchments and started to harass enemy skirmishers and artillerymen, who had been operating unmolested. Lieutenant Colonel Ripley in his memoirs remembered one of these exchanges. The men in Company F had advanced to within about 500 yards of the powerful line of breastworks that extended from the main rebel fort at Yorktown to the low ground at the head of Warwick Creek. Hiding behind a large farmhouse and adjoining outbuildings, a few picked men were ordered to take a few shots in order to determine the exact range to their intended victims. Thinking themselves safe behind their seemingly strong fortifications, the Confederate artillerymen continued to fire upon Union positions. The first few shots of the Union sharpshooters were but a momentary prelude to the main event, though. The range now ascertained and communicated to the rest of the sharpshooters, Ripley ordered his command to fire. Their effectiveness soon became apparent to observers on both sides, for within an hour all of the Confederate guns within a thousand yards had been silenced, their crews killed, wounded, or driven off.

On their side the Confederate marksmen were quick to reciprocate. Hiding in a series of rifle pits and behind clusters of bushes in front of the main line of works, they in turn wreaked their vengeance on Union artillerymen, who also began to suffer heavy losses. Although Berdan's sharpshooters quickly turned their attention to their enemy counterparts, the effort initially proved fruitless. The rebel sharpshooter would take a well-aimed shot, and although the resulting puff of smoke disclosed his position, he simply hid within his hole until the inevitable return fire completely subsided. Then he would unleash another deadly shot, and the whole process would be repeated.

Ripley remembered one Confederate sharpshooter whose audacity and marksmanship raised his opponent's ire. Pvt. John Ide, a native of New Hampshire in Company E, stepped up to the challenge. One of the few men in his company who still carried his own target rifle with a telescopic sight, his shots struck uncomfortably close to their intended victim. Quickly, the affair devolved into a personal feud between the two expert marksmen; most of the other sharpshooters momentarily stopped firing to watch this long-range duel. The rebel marksman soon proved himself the master, and Ide fell dead, shot in the forehead while standing up to aim. The Confederate triumph was short-lived, however. Confident that the threat was over, and made cocky by success, he became even more daring and exposed himself to view. The rebel marksmen turned his attention back to Union artillerymen who all the while had been firing at the Confederate lines. Once again focused on his original targets, he failed to notice that a Union officer had recovered Ide's target rifle and was waiting for his next appearance. The shot fired, its projectile struck its mark, and both antagonists in the original duel now lay dead.

PICKING OFF OFFICERS

The Peninsular Campaign was to evince another tactical practice that was very much akin to sharpshooting. In an effort to demoralize surrounding troops, there began a deliberate attempt to single out officers as targets in preference to the enemy rank and file. In his memoirs, when recollecting that his colonel advised his men to fire at mounted men whenever they appeared, James M. Dinkins, then a private in the Eighteenth Mississippi, rationalized that even at this early stage (April–June 1862), they were aware that Union commanders had already issued similar instructions. Richard Wheeler in his memoirs offers corroborating evidence that supports this assertion. After the battle of Fair Oaks, Col. John B. Gordon's men claimed that they had heard a Union officer order his troops to "shoot that man on horseback" as Gordon rode along his lines.

This practice would prove as popular and as efficacious as sharpshooting in general and would be prevalent throughout the war in every theater of operations. Before the Battle of Prairie Grove (Fayetteville, Arkansas, December 7, 1862) Brig. Gen. James G. Blunt, who commanded the Union Army of the Frontier, set similar instructions down on paper. He urged his shooters to direct especial attention to Confederate officers, and failing this, they were to pick off the enemy artillery horses. So common did such practice become that Union soldiers unfortunate enough to have darker than normal uniforms were sometimes mistaken for officers. The regimental history of the Nineteenth Massachusetts Infantry would claim, for example, that many a private at Fredericksburg was singled out because he had recently received a new uniform, one that was a darker blue than that specified by the regulations.

Once again, these tactical developments, strictly speaking, were not true innovations but owed their origins to previous foreign wars. As we have seen, near the close of the Napoleonic Wars, the Allies increasingly attempted to target French officers. Regardless of intent, this remained a limited practical threat as long as almost all of the combatants were armed with the relatively inaccurate smoothbore muskets. All this changed, however, with the introduction of the *carabin à tige* and the Minié rifle muskets. The *Military Gazette,* the official publication of the New York State Militia, reported that during the Battle of

Montebello, Italy, May 20, 1859, 50% of all French brigadier generals had been killed, and 75% of all colonels killed or wounded. The resulting post-bellum analysis concluded that this unprecedented casualty rate among high-ranking officers was due to their ostentatious dress in the presence of an enemy now armed with weapons that in competent hands could be accurately fired beyond 600 yards. The Austrians, having taken some precautions, had suffered less in this regard. Rank was no longer distinguished by epaulettes, *croix d'honneur*, and so on but by the presence of stars and unique facing colors. The French quickly followed suit, and Napoleon III soon prohibited the use of epaulettes in French service.

Faced with an identical situation and the same unfortunate results, a number of Union officers adopted the same obvious solution. When required to supervise hazardous picket duty, officers increasingly began to shed all signs of senior rank and make themselves indistinguishable from the rank and file. In fact, so great was the danger to officers in exposed positions that during the Peninsula Campaign of 1862, standing orders required Union officers to take these precautions. Called to take his turn as general officer of the day in charge of the picket lines, Col. Samuel K. Zook of the Fifty-seventh New York Infantry took off his shoulder straps and donned enlisted men's clothing.

Both problem and solution would continue for the duration of the war. Desiring to see how events were unfolding during the Battle of the Crater (Petersburg, July 30, 1864), General Grant, accompanied by an aide and an orderly, rode up to where a regiment stood in reserve. Grant dismounted and unceremoniously took off his coat, turned it inside out, and then put it back on. Next he traded his officer's hat for a private's cap. Thus looking like a common private, he unobtrusively walked up near the crater to perform his own personal reconnaissance. Of course, this type of precaution was only possible when an officer was detailed for some expected or scheduled event and had time. It was rarely possible during an engagement, when officers, totally preoccupied with the events around them, would not have time to change clothing.

BUCK AND BALL

In an effort to prepare for operations in the Pensacola, Florida, area, on March 17, 1861, George Deas, acting adjutant general, instructed the Baton Rouge Arsenal to send Brig. Gen. Braxton Bragg ammunition for artillery and small arms. This included a request for 50,000 "buck and ball" cartridges. The ammunition referred to consisted of a single ball and several small (.30-calaber) buckshot pellets, so called because they were traditionally used to hunt large game, such as buck deer. This certainly was no lone request, and one can find other requests for this type of ammunition even prior to the outbreak of hostilities. In January that year the governor of Louisiana had asked the state legislature for authorization to purchase 200,000 buck and ball cartridges, along with 5000 flintlocks and 3000 percussion cap smoothbore muskets. Interest in this type of ammunition certainly was not limited to the states then contemplating secession. Finding that his troops were short of ammunition during an expedition to Newport News in May, Gen. Benjamin Butler wrote to the Virginia Military District (Union) and requested that buck and ball be immediately sent. Gen. George H. Thomas appealed for these cartridges in September 1861.

Buck and ball was used only in smoothbore muskets, and one would expect the demand for this ammunition to have dried up as troops switched over to rifle muskets as the war progressed. Not only does a careful examination of the *Official Records* reveal that this trend this did not occur, but the requests for buck and ball actually continued throughout the entire war. Furthermore, a number of Union infantrymen who by 1863 had ample opportunity to be armed with Springfield or Enfield rifle muskets, purposely chose to stick with their old smoothbores. Among these were the Sixty-third, Sixty-ninth, and Eighty-eight New York regiments and 116th Pennsylvania of the Irish Brigade, as well as the Twelfth New Jersey Regiment. The chief ordnance officer of the Army of Virginia (Union) requisitioned 800,000 cartridges in August 1862; the governor of Pennsylvania requested 2,000,000 buck and ball and 1,000,000 .58-caliber cartridges on September 17, the first day of fighting at Antietam. On the Confederate side Lt. Gen. John C. Pemberton, during the siege of Vicksburg, enjoined Col. Josiah Gorgas, chief of ordnance, to maintain a "constant supply of field and small-arm ammunition (especially buck and ball)."

Officers attested to the effectiveness of buck and ball in their after-action reports. During the operations at New Madrid, Missouri, around mid-March 1862, Maj. Gen. John P. McCown became apprehensive that the Federals would land troops from their gunboats, so he ordered regiments to be placed *à cremaillere,* in a series of squares placed en echelon. Col. A. J. Brown's Fifty-fifth Tennessee, equipped with 60 buck and ball cartridges per soldier, was positioned on the vulnerable flank of this formation. Of course, this is only indirect evidence of the ammunition's destructiveness, an inference drawn from the position of the various regiments along the defensive formation.

More direct testimony of the buck and ball's capabilities were provided by officers during the fighting in the Virginia peninsula that summer. Reflecting upon events that had just occurred during the Seven Days' battles, Confederate Gen. Paul J. Semmes attributed his troops' ability to inflict significantly more casualties than they suffered to their use of buck and ball, their steadiness, and the accuracy of their fire. No idle boast, this explanation was shared by least one Union general, Innis N. Palmer, who proffered the same explanation in his own battle report after the Battle of Malvern Hill.

It is tempting to regard this advocacy of buck and ball and hence the retention of smoothbore muskets as a type of grassroots movement by a few reactionaries who, in spite of overwhelming evidence and logic, wanted to hold onto their beloved but now obsolete weapons. There were those with a formal appreciation of the current weaponry and tactics who also endorsed this sentiment. Probably the most articulate among this group was G. L. Willard, a major in the regular U.S. Army and colonel of the 125th New York Infantry. Willard made his case in a pamphlet entitled *Comparative Value of Rifled & Smooth-Bored Arms*, published privately in February 1863. Once again, like Gibbon and Wilcox before him, Willard drew heavily on foreign sources that provided detailed data on the trials associated with the new rifle muskets. Basing his conclusions upon the experiences of the first two years of fighting, the colonel contended that only a fraction of infantry should be armed with the rifle musket, one regiment per brigade of volunteers, as well as one battalion in each regular U.S. Army regiment. Those armed with rifle muskets should be as thoroughly instructed as light troops tended to be. The back elevating sight should be removed from all small arms, other than those intended for skirmishers or sharpshooters. Willard admitted that the new rifle musket was indeed more effective than its predecessor when handled by an expert who acted independently of a formation, and he acknowledged that skirmishers had assumed a more important role as a result. He argued that "under certain circumstances, the arms formerly employed [smoothbores] were more effective than the new ones, particularly when at close quarters."

The problem stemmed from the need to readjust the backsight accurately as the distance to the target was reduced every 100 yards or so. Willard argued that experience during the first two Civil War campaigns showed that the average soldier, once under fire, never readjusted the backsight. Should he use the two sights to aim when the enemy had approached to within close range, the shot would fly over the assailants' heads. Willard preferred the smoothbore musket. Although it had a much shorter range, it had considerably higher initial muzzle velocity, and Willard argued this meant that up to 200 yards it had a "flat trajectory." There was no need to calculate ranges, so at this critical juncture the infantryman just had to level his weapon, which was all he could manage to do anyway as the enemy neared.

Willard's pamphlet has recently been republished with an excellent new introduction by William C. Goble. Unfortunately, there has been a tendency for many readers to regard Willard and his arguments as a curiosity and the data he cited as chimerical. Neither Willard's arguments nor the data used to substantiate his claims were new, though. Even the new rifle musket's most ardent supporters, such as Cadmus Wilcox in America and Lieutenant Colonel Wilford in Britain, had openly acknowledged the weapon's characteristics, and this is the reason why the "scientific means of firing" had been developed. However, the appearance of the *Comparative Value* pamphlet showed that there were those fighting in the Civil War who believed that the way soldiers tended to act under fire precluded any weapon with such a slow initial muzzle velocity from being used effectively by the average soldier constrained to operate within a close-order formation. This is a view, incidentally, that conformed closely to the predictions made by Captain Tyler and Lieutenant Colonel Dixon at the Royal United Service Institute in Britain several years previously.

HEAVY ARTILLERY

In order to secure the capital, a substantial force had been permanently stationed in Washington and the surrounding fortifications. However, by the third year of the war, many of the regiments on the Union front lines had participated in a number of engagements, and casualties and disease had thinned the ranks to only a fraction of their official strength. Given his determination to break through the Confederate armies and attack Richmond, Grant recognized that a number of the full-strength garrison units would have to be reallocated among the various corps within the Army of the Potomac.

During late 1863 and the spring of '64, a number of existing infantry regiments in Washington, as well as some newly raised units, were converted to "heavy artillery" regiments. For example, during winter 1863 the Eighteenth Maine officially became the First Maine Heavy Artillery. Ostensibly, they were to operate the heavy artillery that garnished Washington's fortifications. However, when it came to their training and their ultimate use, one could say that these regiments had a split personality, also being well drilled in close-order infantry tactics. The Second Pennsylvania Heavy Artillery regiment won drill tournaments, for example.

Each of the heavy artillery regiments was organized into three battalions. Instead of the ten companies in a standard infantry regiment, these regiments now were to have twelve "batteries" (which, when they functioned as infantry, were essentially companies), each of 150 men. The regiment's staff consisted of a colonel, a lieutenant colonel, and three majors (each commanding a battalion.) Each company was led by a captain, two first lieutenants, and two second lieutenants. Unlike with regular infantry regiments, there was neither a regimental quartermaster nor an adjutant, these functions being fulfilled by senior lieutenants.

During the 2 or so years these regiments served in a garrison capacity, the daily regimen consisted of drilling and manning the fortifications. Sometimes they would be ordered to help erect new fortifications, while an occasional scare of a threatened Confederate surprise attack seasoned their otherwise uneventful routine. The constant, repetitive drilling and practice during their 2 years of garrison duty resulted in the creation of highly disciplined units. They were thoroughly disciplined and were superb troops, as their subsequent records show.

The switch to a heavy artillery organization demanded that an additional 800 men be added to a 1000-man infantry regiment. Although this meant that 44.4% of the newly formed heavy artillery regiments were raw recruits, events during May and June 1864 were to demonstrate that the esprit de corps and iron discipline were not significantly affected by the expansion. Veterans would explain after the war that the 50 new recruits learned quickly from the cadre of 100 experienced soldiers in each of existing companies. Even the men added to the L and M Companies, which had to be totally created from scratch, appeared to follow the same accelerated learning curve. This was a far cry from the situation in 1862, when most of the regiments' officers knew little more than the rank and file they were charged to train.

The men in these heavy artillery regiments would show their mettle as soon as they were given the opportunity. General Grant observed in his memoirs: "These artillery troops fought with the steadiness of veterans. . . . The reputation of all these new arrivals [was] as well-disciplined veterans worthy to be classed with an equal number of regulars."

Despite such accolades, after the war some of the veterans admitted that at the onset of their first real campaign, in the late spring of 1864, these heavy regiments had a lot to learn about the realities of the American battlefield. Ensconced in the fortifications surrounding the national capital, the garrison regiments had been sequestered from the experienced fighting troops and unfortunately were unable to benefit from the latter's experience. They were as yet unfamiliar with the benefits of the "scattering, covering, and crawling up" methods, which by this stage in the war had been universally adopted by the veteran troops in the Army of the Potomac. They therefore started the campaign determined to conscientiously employ the formal closed-order drill prescribed by the drill manuals.

The horrors of the battlefield and the instinct for survival quickly forced attitudinal changes, however. Within several days the former garrison troops, who were already extremely experienced with pick and shovel, albeit in a different context (building fortifications), "could out dig the diggers."

THE ADVENT OF "COLORED TROOPS"

Men of African descent were given an opportunity to prove their martial qualities early in the country's history, standing side by side with their white compatriots at Bunker Hill (June 17, 1775) and again at the Battle of Rhode Island (August 29, 1778.) In fact, by the height of the American Revolution, as much as 8% of Washington's army might have been "men of color," and there were at least some black men in almost every major engagement. In 1812 Andrew Jackson called upon the patriotism of black men to come to his aid.

Despite these precedents, during the Great Rebellion authorities on both sides were reluctant to call upon this potential wealth of fighting material. Far from exploiting this source of manpower, instead bowing to political considerations, authorities initially ordered Union troops initially ordered to return any fugitive slaves—generally depersonalized by the term contraband—to their Southern owners. Many soldiers gradually found methods of noncompliance, however, and increasing numbers of slaves found their way to freedom.

The Confederates were actually the first to renew the experiment. The New Orleans *True Delta* reported in late April 1861 that a regiment of 1400 free "colored men" was to be raised to repulse any attempt by the "mean, false, and dastardly Black republicans" to seize that city. Though this regiment appears to have participated in a grand review later that year, the sentiment against arming black men was so strong that the unit was disbanded and the experiment abandoned.

The attitude of most of the public was hardly different in the North. Probably a majority of the Northern populace regarded the sons of Ethiop with aversion, harboring the most uncomplimentary views of their capabilities. The prevalent view at the start of the war was that slaves, beaten into total submission for so long, had long lost any claim to manhood and at best were only capable of passively enduring pain and indignation. Those of a less charitable bent circulated more vicious opinions. So intense was this sentiment in parts of the Northern states that in 1861 the New York chief of police felt justified in closing down a group that attempted to recruit freedmen, without the niceties of consulting existing laws or ordinances. Even most ardent abolitionists, who for so long had worked passionately for their freedom, doubted whether black soldiers could have any meaningful use.

As it became apparent the war would not be over quickly, a few Union officers began to revisit the issue. Congress itself set up the situation. The Union Articles of War were altered in March 1862, and Union soldiers were now forbidden to return fugitive slaves. On his own initiative Maj. Gen. David Hunter set free the slaves in Fort Pulaski (Savannah) and on Cockspur Island, Georgia, on April 12, 1862. Three weeks later he expanded this policy to all slaves in Georgia, Florida, and South Carolina. Given the enormity of the potential political repercussions, however, Lincoln quickly annulled these acts.

Though most senior Union officers opposed admitting black men into armed service, the desperateness of the situation gradually forced a more pragmatic policy. In June slaves of Southerners actively involved in the rebellion were considered to be free, and in July Lincoln authorized Gen. Rufus Saxton to arm 5000 volunteers of African descent. This led to the formation of the First South Carolina Volunteers, which afterward became the Thirty-third United States Colored Troops.

The real impetus for raising black troops, however, came as a result of the Battle of Antietam. Emboldened by the first major Union success in the East, Lincoln penned the preliminary draft of what would become the Emancipation Proclamation, which went into effect on January 1, 1863. Three weeks later the governor of Massachusetts was authorized to set up separate units for black troops. On May 22 a Bureau of Colored Troops was set up in the War Department, and the organization of black regiments, which were designated as "colored troops," began in earnest. Black men were officially proscribed from the officer class, and the highest position to which they could aspire was that of non-commissioned officer, such as sergeant or corporal.

The gradual proliferation of black infantry organizations did not mean that there was total confidence in the plan. Even Union authorities at the highest levels initially envisioned that these black troops would serve primarily in a logistical capacity to help free up white troops who could be shoved into the forefront of the fighting. Writing to Grant on July 11 and 2 weeks later to General Banks, Henry Halleck advised using these controversial troops to garrison important positions. Even Lincoln at first appears to have held the same view. Although confiding to Grant that the black troops were a "resource which, if vigorously applied now, will soon close this contest," he envisioned that they would be used solely in a support role along the banks of the Mississippi River.

Many Union officers were far more skeptical and in fact resentful about these developments. Some white troops, feeling insulted that former slaves would be wearing the same uniform, threatened to desert should colored troops actually be raised, and the white officers who applied for service with blacks were frequently referred to as "nigger officers" by their peers. The black rank and file was occasionally exposed to more physical forms of insults. In his report Col. James S. Brisbin recounted the indignities that the troopers in the Fifth U.S. Colored Cavalry were forced to bear:

> On the march the colored soldiers, as well as their white officers, were made the subject of much ridicule and many insulting remarks by the white troops, and in some instances petty outrages, such as the pulling off the caps of colored soldiers, stealing their horses, &c., were practiced by the white soldiers.

Of course, there was an even more caustic reaction among their Southern enemies. At first the Confederate government refused to exchange captured black soldiers, and on May 1 it even promulgated legislation that called for the execution of these unfortunates and their officers. The threat of like measures being handed out to captured Southern officers forced Confederate authorities to follow a more reasoned course, and this legislation, with the exception of several grisly atrocities, was generally not carried out.

Gaining firsthand experience with the new source of recruits, a few Union officers began to gain confidence in black soldiers and wanted the experiment to be conducted on fair terms. General Butler, who had earlier insulted Brig. Gen. J. W. Phelps when he ordered that the latter's "contrabands" work on fortifications, by late 1863 had his stance on the use of blacks for servile labor. Finding that some of his subordinates harbored considerable prejudice against black soldiers, he issued unequivocal orders that they were to be treated fairly and that any violations would be stringently punished. Writing to Secretary of War Stanton, he insisted that it was important that "Negro troops" had "first-class officers" so that their true fighting abilities could be accurately assayed. Other commanders, such as in Brig. Gens. George L. Andrews in Louisiana and Q. A. Gillmore in South Carolina encountered the same obstacles and took similar steps to resolve these problems.

About 50,000 freedmen and recently freed slaves rushed to the Union colors during 1863. Realizing that the future of the entire experiment with black soldiers rested upon the success of their first experiences in combat, those commanding these controversial troops were did not want to hurry the newly raised black units prematurely into battle. At this point a single well-publicized rout during battle, a mutiny, or even a spate of desertions would have completely undermined the credibility of all the black regiments then being organized, and the entire essay would have ground permanently to a halt. In general, commanders took every precaution to ensure their men were more than adequately trained and prepared for the ultimate test that surely was to come.

One of the first indications of these black soldiers' true mettle was their unexpected rapid progress on the drill ground. Almost every officer who served with these regiments and who later penned his memoirs would comment upon the black troops' proficiency during parade and on the march. Thousands of spectators flocked to Camp Whipple (Arlington Heights, Virginia) during early 1864 to watch the Fourteenth U.S. Colored Infantry as it trained. One spectator emphatically predicted to its colonel, Thomas J. Morgan, that "men who handle their arms as these do, will fight." Even such a seasoned disciplinarian as Gen. George Thomas was forced to concede that he "never saw a regiment go through the manual of arms as well as this one."

These troops' desire for perfection seemed to reflect a different set of values towards drill and officers than that usually encountered among white troops. Henry S. Clapp, an officer with the Twenty-third Colored Infantry, found these men to be generally more obedient and deferential to their officers than the soldiers in the more democratically oriented white volunteer regiments. Although one might naturally attribute this mind-set to a docility born of congenital slavery, officers in these regiments were forced to conclude it owed its origins to an entirely different set of psychological factors. According to Capt. George Sherman of the Seventh Colored, these soldiers consistently displayed

> great eagerness to learn their duties, and an interest in them that could not be excelled. They gave themselves up to the work before them, wholly and without reserve, while the officers of the regiment seemed imbued with an earnest determination and a common ambition to make the regiment second to none.

Elaborating upon this observation, Thomas W. Higginson, colonel of the First South Carolina Volunteers (Colored), felt that these troops routinely exhibited a greater range of emotion, from heartfelt jocularity to deep and grave pensiveness, and they seemed to be able to more easily make the transition from one type of emotion or mind-set to another, according to circumstance. As a result Higginson was surprised to discover that he was able to maintain discipline and control with a "looser rein" than with the white volunteer company he previously commanded. Being more attentive, these men made fewer mistakes, they "rarely mistake their left for their right," for example, and learned more quickly.

The joviality and kindness of these troops was deceiving, however. Underneath they were tough, extremely tough. In an article for the Rhode Island Soldiers and Sailors Society, Capt. James H. Rickard of the Nineteenth Colored Troops provided a telling example. Sent out as a skirmish line one day, the newly formed unit found itself attacked by what it thought were rebels. In reality the attackers were a group of white Union soldiers dressed in gray who had been sent out to test the Nineteenth's resolve. Unfortunately, one of the black soldiers was struck in the forehead by a minié ball, which took out a piece of bone the "size of a half dollar." The man was removed to a nearby hospital, where he convalesced for a few days before he returned to the unit in full fighting condition—minus a portion of the bone in his forehead, of course.

Although black troops would be involved in several desperately fought engagements in 1863, such as at Fort Wagner (Charleston, July 18), most of these men had to wait patiently until 1864 before they would finally be thrown wholesale and as a matter of course into the forefront of a major battle. In almost every case the black troops conducted themselves with great valor. The courage of the Fifty-fourth Massachusetts at Fort Wagner is now so well known as not to require elaboration. So too was the conduct of black regiments in

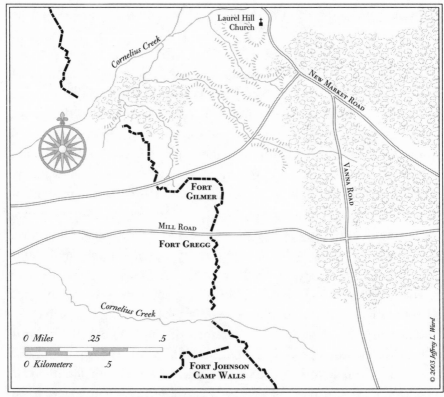

Fort Gilmer and environments. This would be the site of the heroic attack of the Seventh Colored Infantry against heavily defended Confederate defenses.

Gen. Edward Ferrero's division during the Battle of the Crater at Petersburg (July 30, 1864). In both cases the black troops fought bravely, and although defeated gained great respect among the rest of the Union army.

One very much lesser known incident does deserve mention, since at the time it as much as any other influenced informed opinion on both sides. This was the Seventh Colored Infantry's assault on Fort Gilmer (outside Richmond) on September 29 that year. The Ninth Maine had just failed in its attack against the Confederate position. The target had been a defensive "curtain" consisting of rifle pits 500 to 700 yards distant. Four black companies under Capt. Julius A. Weiss's command were ordered to form line in a slight declivity that afforded some protection. As they assembled in the formation, enemy artillery opened fire. The advance was sounded, and the tiny attacking force advanced forward at the ordinary quick step, seemingly nonplussed by the shell and shrapnel fire (spherical case) that now swept the advancing line from the front and right flank. The colored troops continued to advance, forcing the Confederate gunners to switch to canister. Yet, on the brave lot came, hopelessly outnumbered. Remember, it has long been held a rule that to achieve success, the attacker should have a three-to-one numerical advantage. But here it was the defenders who enjoyed such numerical superiority.

When about three-quarters of the way across the field and now exposed to enemy musketry, the men were finally ordered to charge, which they did with great alacrity. The defenders appeared momentarily stunned by the audacity of the small band of attackers, and for a few seconds all defensive fire ceased, before resuming with even greater determination. The attackers reached and jumped into a 7-foot ditch at the foot of the Confederate entrenchments. Unfortunately, many were killed just as they reached the lip of the ditch. After resting a few moments, the men attempted to escalade the rebel position. Unable to reach the top easily, the men paired up, and one climbed upon the other's shoulders, all the while showered with hand grenades.

Of course, thus encumbered, they became "sitting ducks," and they were easily picked off as soon as their heads appeared over the earthworks. Despite their heroic efforts, it was hopeless, and the attackers eventually were forced to surrender. The casualties had been staggering. More than a third of the force's 150 men lay dead or dying; numerous others were grievously wounded. This action is cited not because of what it accomplished in terms of the physical objective—the assault was hopelessly doomed from the onset—but rather because of the gallantry with which this impossible task was conducted.

One can only appreciate the dimension of these men's valor, their determination to struggle on at any cost, when one compares their efforts to another charge, which, though equally ill fated, has gained its participants immortal fame. Faced with similarly insurmountable defenses at Colquitt's Salient on the eastern portion of the Petersburg defenses a few months before, the First Maine Heavy Artillery, though mounting five or six assaults, only managed to close to within 60 to 80 yards of the defender. Not only did the tiny band of the Seventh Colored Infantry then brave the storm of shell, shrapnel, canister, and small arms to reach the very foot of the defensive works, but once there they then struggled to storm the works despite the rain of hand grenades and deadly point-blank small arms fire. To the defenders, it must have appeared that they faced a new breed, one not subject to the ordinary laws of physical destruction and daunted morale.

In orders issued 2 weeks later, General Butler proffered what was probably the general reaction to this bold attempt to take Fort Gilmer:

> The colored soldiers, by coolness, steadiness and dash, have silenced every cavil of the doubters of their soldiery capacity, and drawn tokens of admiration from their enemies—have brought their late masters, even, to the consideration of the question whether they will not employ as soldiers the hitherto despised race.

That even many Confederates had been impressed with the Seventh Regiment's effort was no idle boast! On October 6 the *Richmond Whig* provided a firsthand account of the affair, told from the vantage point of one of the defenders. The later freely admitted, "Those fellows [the black troops] fought well." After the war another defender, in a piece written for the *Southern Historical Society*, opined that this was the nearest that Richmond came to falling during this period. No less a personage than Robert E. Lee was so impressed that when a bill authorizing the use of black troops for the Confederate cause was being debated in December that year, the great Southern general argued that the recent attack on Fort Gilmer proved beyond any doubt that black men would fight.

By the war's end no fewer than 178,975 black troops had fought under the Union colors. Out of this, 36,847 would never return home. Truly, these slaves and sons of slaves had pulled their own weight in this great American drama. Never again would Americans of African descent be completely relegated to the sidelines during times of national crisis. In recent years the "buffalo soldiers," as native Indians called the wooly-haired riders of the Ninth and Tenth United States Cavalry regiments, have finally been assigned to their rightful place in American history both for helping to "pacify" the West and for their contribution to the victory at San Juan Hill, Cuba (July 1, 1898). The tradition firmly established, black troops would fight with the same conspicuous bravery and determination during the First and Second World Wars. No longer segregated into separate units, black men and other minorities fought bravely alongside white compatriots during the Korean and Vietnamese conflicts, and a "person of color," Gen. Colin Powell, finally reached the zenith of American military authority as the chairman of the Joint Chiefs of Staff during the Gulf War (January–March 1991). He has obtained even more responsibility as the Secretary of State during the Second Gulf War.

PART V

ARTILLERY

Chapter 21

GRAND TACTICS
DURING THE CIVIL WAR

N o matter how thoroughly researched, how detailed the analysis, any work seeking to be a comprehensive study of Civil War military practices cannot limit itself to tactics. It must also investigate what transpired on the grand tactical level. Lower-level minutiae, such as how individual battalions changed formations, maneuvered around the battlefield, and conducted themselves during attack and defense, all fall within the domain of *tactics*. If tactics can be defined as the use of weaponry and formal systems of troop movement to derive a localized advantage over the enemy during combat, then *grand tactics* can be thought of as the methods used to manipulate larger bodies of troops to win an engagement. The focus thus shifts from individual battalions and regiments to brigades, divisions, and corps-level organizations and is the purview of commanders and field officers.

Grand tactics is never a completely separate system but is always inextricably connected to available tactics and weaponry. Linear warfare, the predominant grand tactical system throughout the eighteenth century, is an excellent example. The advent of the flintlock and socket bayonet in the late seventeenth century completely transformed the art of warfare on every level. The socket bayonet greatly increased the musketeer's ability to defend himself from enemy cavalry. Not only could the flintlock be fired more quickly than its predecessor the matchlock, but the disappearance of the lit match meant that the ranks and files in a formation could be brought much more closely together. The result was that pikemen were soon considered completely superfluous, and the deep 6- or 8-rank battalion formations (incidentally, a French battalion was roughly comparable in size to an American regiment) were reduced to five, four, and even three ranks.

These thin formations, though capable of delivering more firepower frontally, had highly vulnerable flanks. The solution was to abandon the old checkerboard pattern of formations and place infantry battalions side by side. Infantry battalions now sometimes formed two lengthy, continuous lines that stretched across most of the battlefield, hence the term *linear warfare*. On relatively flat, open terrain, cavalry was placed on either flank of the infantry, again along two lines. When on ground unfavorable to the effective use of cavalry, the equestrian arm was kept as a reserve in a distant third line.

Linear warfare, however, was not without its own distinctive set of limitations. Through the process of stringing battalions along a line increased the infantry's defensive capabilities, especially against cavalry, it also created a relatively inflexible system. The multibattalion line became a single grand tactical entity, in effect a type of "quantum unit" that under ordinary circumstances was difficult to subdivide into smaller grand tactical elements. The first reason for this lay with the intrinsic nature of the line, while the other stemmed from the command structure then in use. An offensive force, by definition, had to be distributed equally along the entire front. The success of the movement fell almost entirely upon the troops in the first line. If these were thwarted or pushed back, those along the second line invariably gave way. Once any portion of the line was ordered forward, in most cases the remainder had to follow. Not to do so would have meant that the portion of the line that advanced would have highly exposed flanks and there would have been a gaping hole in the part of the line that was left behind.

Up to the French Revolutionary Wars (1792–1800), officers, even those at the higher levels, were neither trained for, nor expected to display, independence or initiative on the battlefield. Brigade, major, and even lieutenant generals spent most their efforts making sure that their commands conformed to the army's overall actions and movements. The deployment of the cavalry and infantry in two separate large blocks had a similar effect and usually guaranteed that the two arms operated independently of one another. There was little of what now would be called "combined arms operations." All of these factors conspired together to ensure that the main force of an army functioned as a single entity, one that necessarily attacked frontally and acted along a *single axis of operations.*

Gifted commanders understood these limitations and devised ways of working around the potential problems. Probably the notably effective examples were invented by the Duke of Marlborough and Frederick the Great. Marlborough, for example, frequently anchored portions of the line on whatever broken terrain was available, such as villages and woods. Each portion thus *appuyed* (anchored) could act more independently than its counterpart along a single expansive line. When faced with the necessity of overthrowing some strong point, such as a village or troops posted along a hollow way or behind hedges, Marlborough formed what during the Civil War would be called "columns of attack" by placing a series of lines, one behind the other.

Frederick the Great resorted to a different set of grand tactical tools to defeat his foes. Linear warfare tended to be particularly bloody. When opposing commanders and their officers decided to have their infantry fire, the law of averages meant that the amount of casualties was about the same on both sides. When two hostile lines confronted one another frontally, it was difficult for one side or the other to gain a significant advantage. Frederick solved this problem through the creation of an effective means of suddenly attacking one of the enemy's flanks. After the War of Austrian Succession, he devised the *march by lines* as a means to work around the enemy's front quickly. During the Seven Years' War, he occasionally positioned battalions *en echelon,* from which position they were then used to perform an *oblique attack.*

A number of unrelated tactical developments meanwhile were introduced, each of which was relatively inconsequential but when taken together ultimately revolutionized how warfare would be fought on the European battlefield. This new system has become indelibly associated with the young military genius who attempted to subjugate Europe and thus is usually referred to as Napoleonic warfare. Although popular opinion generally reduces Napoleonic grand tactics to large skirmisher screens followed by myriads of battalion columns, an accurate enough top-level description for the first several campaigns during the

French Revolutionary War, it fails to deal adequately with the diverse range of grand tactical methods encountered when one looks at all the French campaigns during this period. Recent research suggests that the French frequently employed much greater grand tactical flexibility, often fighting in regiment- and brigade-size lines even during the early 1790s.

There was also a transformation of these methods over time. Up to the zenith of French capabilities around 1805–1806, the French infantry gradually evolved slightly different tactical slants, depending upon the specific foe they expected to fight during an upcoming campaign. The French employed large defensive squares to ward off vicious, highly skilled Mameluke horses during the Egyptian campaign. Just before the Austerlitz campaign (1805), Napoleon advocated large, multibattalion, mixed-order formations (generally, a battalion in line, with a battalion column behind each flank), while the *carré oblique* (oblique square) was both advocated and actually used in the 1806 struggle against the Prussians. French grand tactics from 1809 became increasingly heavy handed, as the pool of competent NCOs and officers became ever more diluted due to casualties and their enemies' increasing adoption of French practices. In desperation French commanders occasionally resorted to large, multibattalion columns, seemingly to punch their way through the defender's position.

One would have to wait until the 1830s and '40s for the next major grand tactical system to evolve, as the gradual digestion of experience gained from the Napoleonic Wars was permitted by a lengthy peace. Although most contemporaries regarded the grand tactics described in Baron Antoine de Jomini's works as simply a distillation of the most important principles of Napoleonic warfare, this separate system deviated from Napoleonic grand tactics in several extremely important ways. Unlike Frederick the Great and Napoleon, whose innovations were forged during the crucible of battle, Jomini made his contribution to the evolution of the art of war during peacetime conditions. Although the baron had seen active service during the Napoleonic Wars, his real interest was military history and theory, rather than active campaigning. With the return of peace after Napoleon's final defeat at Waterloo, Jomini was finally able to devote all of his efforts

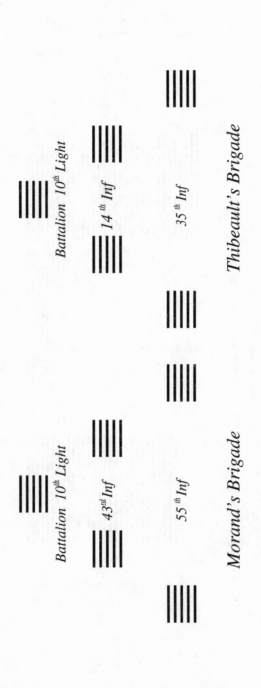

St. Hilaire's Division at Austerlitz

Battalion 10ᵗʰ Light

Battalion 10ᵗʰ Light

43ʳᵈ Inf

14ᵗʰ Inf

55ᵗʰ Inf

35ᵗʰ Inf

Morand's Brigade

Thibeault's Brigade

The formations employed by French Napoleonic armies gradually became more sophisticated as commanders gained experience. To cope with Russian uhlans and Cossacks, Napoleon and his commanders ordered the adoption of these heavy mixed order formations during the 1805 campaign.

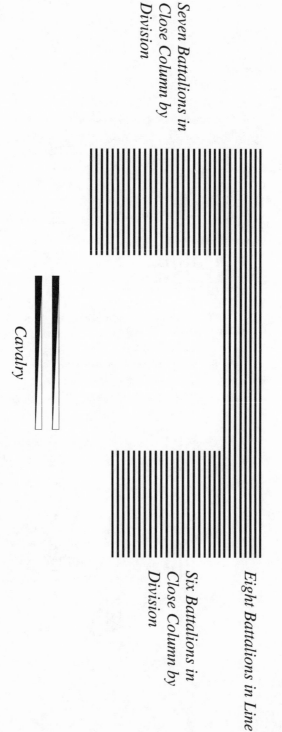

MacDonald's Column at Wagram

Seven Battalions in Close Column by Division

Eight Battalions in Line

Six Battalions in Close Column by Division

Cavalry

Losses in the officer class eventually forced French commanders to simplify their tactics and grand tactics. According to Bugeaud, this resulted in monstrous columns, like Mac-Donald's massive column at Wagram, that characterized a French "tactical bankruptcy" during the later Napoleonic period.

to his writings. During the next 25 years, he published a number of works that, providing a comprehensive treatment of the strategic and grand tactical dimensions of modern warfare, would have a tremendous impact on military thought. In this regard *Precis de l'art de la guerre,* originally published in 1838 and introduced to the English-speaking world in 1854 as *Summary of the Art of War,* was his most important work. Although this tome deals mostly with the strategic and operational dimensions, two entire chapters were devoted to tactical and grand tactical issues.

Of the five building blocks that formed the tactical foundation of his system, four had been popularized during the Napoleonic period. In addition to the traditional line, Jomini acknowledged the utility of skirmishers, rows of battalions in column, massive columns, and small squares. Despite the veneer of progressiveness, Jomini's grand tactical system was remarkably conservative—one could even say reactionary. According to the practice of the day, the overall manner in which an army was deployed was referred to as its *order of battle.* Jomini categorized the recommended grand tactical formations into twelve possible archetypes known as *orders of battle.* The simple parallel order, used by European commanders since Louis of Baden and the Turkish wars, Jomini deemed the least useful. Affording little opportunity for tactical skill, this formation handed both opponents an equal chance of success. Parallel lines with one flank *en crochet,* that is, with one side thrown back or refused, sometimes could be useful in defense.

However, a commander-in-chief who found himself on the offensive was better advised to select one of several different orders of battles, depending upon circumstances. A leader wishing to concentrate forces to attack a particularly important position along the enemy line of battle could advance with a deployed line reinforced either on a flank or in the center. The reinforced part of the line consisted of several narrower lines one behind the other, or it could consist of a series of battalion-sized columns of attack. Someone wishing to attack an enemy flank could resort to an oblique attack, instead. Here the attacking force primarily advanced in deployed line but approached the intended part of the enemy line at an angle, typically between 10 and 45 degrees. The outside part of the attacking line was to be reinforced by a narrower line directly behind where the deployed line

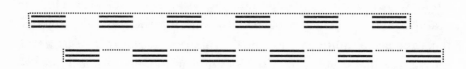

Although French Napoleonic armies also employed "lines" of battalion columns, to ensure tactical flexibility, they had fewer battalions along the line. Jomini's more extensive "lines" are indicative of the intention to form a line before engaging the enemy.

would contact the enemy. Finally, Jomini also felt that the commander could choose to attack *en echelon,* which could be a series of battalions placed in either a V or an "inverted V" formation.

Jomini's influence quickly spread beyond France and into other military establishments, including that in America. In 1844 Henry Halleck was sent to France to inspect that country's latest developments in permanent fortifications. Whether Halleck had been familiar with Jomini's writings prior to this trip is unclear. However, during a series of lectures at the Lowell Institute in Boston the next year, in his treatment of tactics and army organization, Halleck essentially regurgitated Jomini's opinions in their entirety. His lectures a resounding success, Halleck published an enhanced version of the lecture notes as the *Elements of Military Art and Science* in 1846. In his preface Halleck candidly acknowledged that the ideas expressed in his book were a synthesis of the latest European thought and admitted that "no pretension is made to originality in any part of the work."

CIVIL WAR GRAND TACTICAL SYSTEMS

Looking at the full panorama of battles that punctuated the 4 years of incessant fighting in the Civil War, one finds a tremendous amount of variation on a grand tactical level. One in fact encounters most of the grand tactical systems in use since the adoption of the flintlock musket and socket bayonet.

Linear Grand Tactics

The traditional linear system, with its emphasis of fighting in line, was by far the most common grand tactical system employed on the Civil War battlefield. One finds instances of multibattalion linear formations from Bull Run all the way to the final stages of hostilities in the spring of 1865. This is not to say that these linear grand tactics always employed the same geometrical structure or were guided by the same principles. Civil War linear formations took many forms. One occasionally finds the series of lengthy lines similar to those employed by Marshal Daun or Prince Henry during the Seven Years' War. Grand tactical formations modeled on Jomini's linear order of battle also can be found, as well as the brigade- and division-sized lines popularized by the French during the Napoleonic Wars. The

Jomini's division and corps formations addressed command and control concerns. Divisions from the same corps often were placed behind one another to minimize the organization's frontage.

confusion that inevitably arose from fighting in rough, forested terrain also meant that an army, corps, or division was forced to rely on a more ad hoc linear approach whereby individual regiments, even brigades, though in line, might not have the same direction as their neighbors.

The initial deployment of Gen. Albert Sydney Johnston's Confederate forces at Shiloh is an excellent example of a classical linear grand tactical formation. Hardee's corps of two divisions plus Gladden's brigade formed the first line, with its cavalry on either flank, while Bragg's corps was deployed in line 800 yards to the rear. Also in line, Polk's corps formed the reserve. This specific grand tactical structure is much closer to that used in the mid-eighteenth century than it is to, let's say, Jomini's linear order of battle.

Not only did the placement of Hardee's cavalry mimic a system that started to fall into disuse during the Seven Years' War, but the manner in which the three lines were formed utilized an archaic relationship between command structure and grand tactical formation. In Jomini's system the troops in each division were deployed equally along the first and second lines, the first directly in front of the second. This minimized the frontage of each division and made it easier for the divisional commander to control his troops. The system employed by the Confederate army at Shiloh meant that each corps was stretched out several miles, making it virtually impossible for the corps commanders to maintain command control once the battle started. During the battle this problem became so great that it was agreed that Bragg would command all Confederate forces in the middle, Polk those in the center, while Hardee took charge of the left, regardless of their original corps assignments.

Of course, most of the linear formations found on the Civil War battlefield were not as extreme. Hundreds of cases can be found of Union and Confederate forces fighting in regiment-, brigade- and division-size lines. To some extent this was due to a precedent set at the turn of the nineteenth century. Popular accounts have often portrayed French Napoleonic armies always fighting in column when on the offense. Recent studies have shown consistently that Napoleon's armies used a much more diverse array of tactical formations, utilizing regiment- and brigade-sized lines much more commonly than had been thought. Among French officers line and column were probably equally regarded as fighting formations. Most French officers would have felt equally comfortable attacking an enemy in a brigade-size line or a column of attack. The choice depended upon the circumstances and what the remainder of the brigade or division was doing. American practice during the war varied from that used by French Napoleonic armies in one significant way. Civil War commanders tended to place much more emphasize on the need to fight in line.

Napoleonic Grand Tactics

Although the great majority of Civil War formations and grand tactical techniques were directly derived from or inspired by the traditional linear system, one can also find grand tactical elements more closely associated with the Napoleonic era. This includes the occasional use of not only the large multibattalion columns of attack that signaled the degeneracy of the French military art during the final phases of the Wars of the Empire, but the more articulated and sophisticated battalion columns that were an officially sanctioned part of the French grand tactical armamentarium, as well. The *Official Records* and literally thousands of personal memoirs that have been passed down to us provide numerous references to "deep formations," "dense columns," and so on. Union reports contain references to Confederate attacks by deep formations at the Battles of Gaines's Mill, Corinth, Chickamauga, and Franklin, as well as during the Atlanta Campaign. Such tactics were not limited to the Confederate side, and Union commanders utilized deep columns during the Knoxville Campaign in late 1863 and at the engagement at Cloyd's Mountain (southwest Virginia, May 9, 1864).

One must be careful about these accounts, however, and not uncritically assume that there was actually a multibattalion attack column in every case. Since most reports are devoid of detail, one is rarely able to identify the type of formations that were actually used. One of the more credible accounts of a deep Confederate column has been provided by Capt. Oscar Jackson in his published memoirs. During the Battle of Corinth, the Confederates formed a series of large columns as they poured out of the woods opposite his regiment's position. Jackson estimated these columns to be formed from several different regiments. Although Jackson unfortunately did not go into additional detail about the width, depth, and density of men, his account suggests there were at least four regiments placed one after another, and the frontage of the formation was larger than a double company, being either a half or an entire battalion wide. A little later, when describing how his regiment stopped the first of these columns with a deadly fire delivered at 30 yards, Jackson mentioned that the enemy column appeared to be as deep "as his company was long [that is, wide]." If true, the Confederate regiments had to have been placed one behind the other, with little or no spacing between them. In this respect they were at least vaguely similar to the gargantuan monstrosities that the French employed at Wagram and Waterloo.

Probably the largest "column of attack" during the Civil War, however, occurred during the Overland Campaign in 1864. During the repeated attempts to storm the Bloody Angle at Spotsylvania, on May 12 Hancock's corps formed a massive column 20,000 men strong! Barlow's and Birney's divisions were positioned in the first tier of the attack. Mott's division was held a little behind in a second tier, while Gibbon's division was placed still farther back in reserve.

To accommodate the different type of terrain they had to traverse, the two frontmost divisions adopted a formation different from the others. Barlow's division was assembled in two lines of masses: Brooke's and Miles's brigades were along the first "line," while Brown's and Smyth's were positioned along the second. Each regiment along these lines was in a "double column on the center," or two companies wide. There was a 5-pace space between each regimental column and 10 paces between brigades. Because a part of the division would have to pass through woods, Birney's and Mott's commands were deployed along four lines, thus yielding a depth of eight men. The distance between lines was close but apparently somewhat varied. In his originally unpublished memoirs, General E. P. Alexander estimated that that Birney's formation had a total depth of 50 yards. Barlow's division, which only had to march across an open field, was organized in a much denser formation. Brooke's and Miles's brigades were in column of attack along the first line, while Smyth's and Brown's brigades were identically deployed along the second.

The four brigades all consisted of two regimental masses apiece. Each ten-company regiment was formed in a close column two companies wide and five deep. The resulting column was twenty men deep and probably less than 100 yards from front to back. The brigade's pioneers were distributed along the front of the column to clear away the logs and trees in enemy abatis.

The use of large multibattalion columns during the Napoleonic era, however, had been a statistical aberration, just as it would be during the Civil War. The real hallmark of officially accepted French practice had been a reliance upon much smaller, battalion-size columns. During this period tacticians relied upon several different methods of categorizing columns, depending upon whether they wished to describe its frontage, density, or function. The most common descriptor referred to the width of the column. Hence, a *column of companies* was one company wide; the width of a *column of divisions* was equivalent to a division of a battalion, which in the American service was two companies wide. The most common type of column during the Napoleonic era had been columns of companies and columns of divisions. Either type could be open or closed. In an *open column* each tier was spaced so that the distance between each successive tier was equivalent to the width of the column. In a *closed column* each tier was densely packed, 2 or 3 paces from the one in front.

Regardless of their width and density, after maneuvering onto their assigned positions on the battlefield, these French battalion columns usually functioned as *columns of waiting* until the division commander decided to commit them to the contest. Meanwhile, these columns were positioned at "full interval" relative to their neighbors on the left and the right; that is, the space between battalion columns was equal to the width of the battalion when in line. This allowed greater flexibility and made it possible to deploy quickly into line should the commander deem it necessary. Alternatively, they could simply advance and assault the enemy as a *column of attack*.

In fact, Civil War records yield examples of battalion columns deployed in exactly this Napoleonic-style arrangement at the start of an engagement. Just before the start of the Battle of Shiloh, all of the elements in Gen. Daniel Ruggles's rebel division were positioned along a 2-mile stretch between Bark Road and Owl Creek on the left in "line of battle." Each of Ruggles's battalions was in double column at half distance, a two-company-wide formation in which each tier in the column was separated from those to its front and its rear by a distance that equaled the frontage of a company. The orders to employ this type of formation were issued the previous day, and there is some evidence that the idea came from Gen. Braxton Bragg himself. These battalion columns were placed along two "lines," and it appears that following a common practice of the day, the second row of columns was placed so that it rested directly behind the spaces between the columns along the first line. We know from Union reports filed after the battle that at least a part of the actual Confederate attack was conducted in these columns. The Seventeenth Kentucky Infantry, for example, found itself attacked by two small Confederate regiments advancing at double-quick time in close columns doubled on the center, columns that were two companies wide.

Union commanders used a similar grand tactical formation on at least two occasions. During the second day of fighting at the Second Battle of Bull Run, Maj. Gen. John Pope ordered Brig. Gen. John F. Reynolds with his Third Division to attack in a row of open column by companies. The First Pennsylvania Rifles (the Bucktails) advanced in front as skirmishers, with Cooper's battery following behind in the center of the "line." The five regimental columns were placed in line with the artillery. When ordered by Major General Thomas to form his division into a column of attack on June 15, 1864, during the Atlanta Campaign, Gen. John Newton placed five regiments "column doubled on the center," that is, by column of divisions, in each tier of the column.

A New Type of Column of Attack

If multibattalion columns of attack and "lines" of battalion-size columns could be traced back to well-known European antecedents, there were two Civil War grand tactical formations whose intellectual ancestry cannot so easily be identified. The first of these was a formation often adopted by Union divisions at the start of a battle; the other was a method often used to conduct a large-scale assault of an important part of the enemy line of battle. Frequently, a division-size force deployed along one or two battle lines, followed by a "line of columns" in reserve. This formation differed from the Napoleonic equivalent in one very important way. Although frequently employing a multitiered grand tactical formation, French divisional commanders had tended to leave all the battalions in column until it had become necessary to establish a firing line. The emphasis was flexibility until the very last moment. In contrast, by ordering that first one or two lines were to be deployed at the start of the engagement, the Union field officer from the outset had committed to a more linear style of fight.

Certainly, the most detailed set of tactical instructions that prescribed this sort of formation was issued by Maj. Gen. Don Carlos Buell during the weeks following the Battle of Shiloh. Issued during the relatively calm period that followed this important Union victory, it is the product of deliberate thought rather than a hurried, ad hoc reaction to the exigencies of day-to-day campaigning. The three brigades in the division were to form battle lines from right to left according to their number. Two regiments from each brigade were to deploy along the first line. The second line was to consist of only three regiments, one from each brigade, to be positioned directly behind the middle of the two regiments from the same brigade in column along the first line. The distance between the first and second lines was to be 370 paces on open ground and only 200 paces when it was necessary to fight on broken terrain. The third "line," 200 paces in the rear of the second, was to consist of three regiments in double column directly behind the regiment from its brigade along the second line. If the division was on either flank of the battle line, one of the regiments in the second line was placed *en echelon* so that it extended beyond the flank of the first line, in order to support these troops should their flank be suddenly threatened. This practice, incidentally, was modeled on the formations employed by the Prussians during the Seven Years' War.

A flank company from each regiment along the first line was thrown out to provide a skirmisher screen for the whole formation. After feeling out the enemy's position and beginning the attack in earnest, officers were to reinforce this screen with a second flank

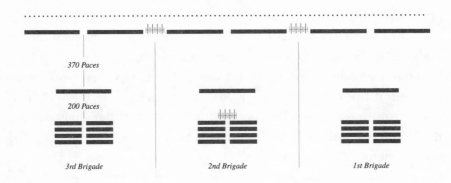

Buell's Proposed Formation for a
Division April 1862

370 Paces

200 Paces

3rd Brigade   2nd Brigade   1st Brigade

After the battle of Shiloh, General Buell ordered his senior officers to employ this grand tactical formation, very similar to Baron de Jomini's recommended division and corps disposition.

company from each regiment. Two of the artillery batteries in the division were to be placed along the first line on either side of the central brigade, while the third battery was placed near the center of the third line. If there was any cavalry attached to the division, it was to await orders sheltered from enemy fire behind the line of columns that formed the third line. The divisional commanders were to remain in the third line, where they could observe the events as they unfolded and oversee all grand tactical activity. Brigade commanders, on the other hand, were to be in harm's way along the first line.

Rather than Major General Buell's own idea, this grand tactical system appears to have been an integral part of the Union army's grand tactical tool chest. When preparing for the intended Mine Run campaign in late November 1863, Maj. Gen. William French, for example, ordered the divisions in the III Corps to adopt a similar formation. The regiments in the first two lines were to be deployed, while those in the last "line" were to remain in "column of attack," which in this case almost certainly referred to a column of companies or divisions. The Union armies in the West were usually smaller than those in the Eastern theater, and it was less practical to maintain a third "line." During the Battle of Murfreesboro, for example, Gen.

William Rosecrans ordered that all the divisions in the Army of the Cumberland deploy along two "lines": The regiments along the first line literally deployed, while those along the second were to remain 200 yards back in "close column, half distance on center." Rosecrans's rather clumsy and contradictory terminology was referring to a column in which each tier was separated from the one in front by half the width of the company or division.

There are numerous examples of similar grand tactical formations applied on a smaller scale. It was common for a Union brigade to have one, sometimes two, deployed lines supported by one or more regiments in column. During the Union advance toward Corinth in June 1862, for example, the Twenty-second Brigade was formed along two deployed lines 70 yards apart, while a third regiment was formed in double column at half distance 100 yards farther back. During an action at Bull Run Bridge on August 27 the same year, the Third New Jersey Infantry was positioned in double column at half distance 200 to 300 yards to the rear of the interval between the First and Second Regiments, which were deployed in line. Similar brigade-level line and column formations were used during the fighting at Murfreesboro and during the Chickamauga Campaign.

The second truly distinctive American grand tactical formation is illustrated by the tendency for Union commanders to resort to a series of lines to attack an important position. Although this type of formation was often referred to as a "column of attack," it really was a series of linear formations that were to reach the enemy's position in succession. Lacking the massiveness of the huge columns of attack occasionally encountered at the end of the Napoleonic period, it served as a means of feeding additional forces against the enemy infantry rather than a means of simply overawing the defenders and crushing their will to stand and fight. The Second Battle of Bull Run affords one of the earliest examples of this new American-style type of column of attack. Ordered to support Gen. Fitz-John Porter's attack against Jackson's position on the second day of the battle, Brig. Gen. John P. Hatch drew up his command in seven lines, each succeeding line 50 yards behind the one in front. The first six lines consisted of half of a brigade each, while Gen. Abner Doubleday's brigade formed the seventh. It is not clear how long the rear lines remained in this

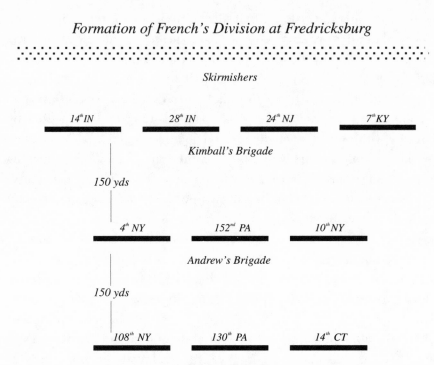

Formation of French's Division at Fredricksburg

Skirmishers

14thIN   28th IN   24th NJ   7thKY

Kimball's Brigade

150 yds

4th NY   152nd PA   10thNY

Andrew's Brigade

150 yds

108th NY   130th PA   14th CT

Palmer's Brigade

Union commanders seemed to take a page from the Duke of Marlborough and frequently formed attack columns from a series of battalions in line, one behind the other. This avoided the denser Napoleonic battalion columns that were now vulnerable to long-range small arms.

column of attack, and Hatch, who commanded this division, insinuates that during the ensuing assault some of the brigades in the rear obliqued slightly to the right in order to able to fire at the defending troops.

This rather deep succession of lines appears to have been an accepted part of Union doctrine, and a similar formation is encountered a month later during the engagement at Crampton's Gap (September 14, three days before Antietam). In this case, however, lines in the column of attack were kept much farther apart. Maj. Gen. Henry W. Slocum ordered his First Division to form a six-line column of attack 200 yards behind an extensive line of skirmishers. The Fifth Maine and Sixteenth New York Volunteers formed the first line of the column, while Newton's and Torbert's brigades followed, each deployed along two lines. The sixth and last line consisted of the Ninety-sixth Pennsylvania Volunteers. Each brigade was 200 yards behind the one in front.

So far this rather linear column of attack had been used as a divisional formation whose frontage was necessarily less than two regiments wide. However, a few months later during the Battle of Fredericksburg, when Maj. Gen. Darius N. Couch's II Corps was ordered to attack Marye's Heights, the same type of principles were applied to several divisions, and the columns of attack were expanded to brigade frontages. The main assault against Marye's Heights was delivered in succession by divisions commanded by French and Winfield S. Hancock, both deployed in nearly identical attack formations. Each division advanced in three successive brigades in line, 200 paces apart, so the Confederate defenders along this part of the field had to face no fewer than six successive attacking waves. More accurately, since the survivors of the front lines in each of these lines often continued to advance informally in a deep, amorphous mass, the rather ineffective attacking force was reinforced at least five times. Although Major General Couch had been ordered to employ this multibrigade formation the day before the battle, he and his divisional officers had been given the latitude to decide upon the most appropriate distance between the brigades in line.

The wide columns of attack found at Fredericksburg present an anomaly. True, division-size columns of attack were resorted to during the final days of the war, when on April 2, 1865, the Second Divisions of both the Union VI and IX Corps were ordered to attack a fortified part of the Confederate line in front of Petersburg. However, after that, Fredericksburg linear columns of attack generally were smaller. Examples of brigade-size columns of attack are found during the Chattanooga-Ringgold and Atlanta Campaigns, the fighting before Port Hudson, Louisiana, in June 1863, and then again at Spotsylvania on May 6 and Cold Harbor on June 3, 1864.

Given the American military's predilection for French military drill and tactical practice, this linear quality of both the Union multitiered, division-level formations and columns of attack appears to be a deviation from the principles that had characterized American military thought since the turn of the century. A study of European and American warfare in practice yields no obvious precedent, nor can one find a prescription of these types of formations in any drill booklet, regulations, or monograph devoted to contemporary tactics. The closest to a model which may have influenced the American military is found in Jomini's *Summary of the Art of War*. However, rather than being a model applied in an unaltered form on the Civil War battlefield, Jomini's work provided inspiration that was both conceptual and fragmentary. It was more a case of taking certain elements of Jomini's grand tactical formations, such as the orders of battle he recommended, and transforming them into other formations, which, though new, retained some important characteristics of Jomini's original model.

Jomini had recommended the use of the "parallel order" reinforced either on a flank or in the center when attacking an important portion of the enemy line. A hybrid formation, Jomini's concoction was a synthesis of (1) the traditional two-line army formation used throughout the eighteenth century with a (2) rather deft version of the Napoleonic concentration of force. The main battle line was reinforced by a series of narrower lines at the point of attack. Now, if one ignores the traditional line dimension of Jomini's grand tactical formation and focuses on the series of narrow lines in front of the area to be attacked, each 70 to 200 yards behind the previous, one is left with a formation virtually identical to the Civil War linear column of attack. It is possible that Union military authorities, realizing the impracticality of army-size battle lines, discarded this element but retained Jomini's method of throwing a succession of narrow waves against the fortified part of the line.

This may also explain the origins of the divisional formation prescribed by Buell after Shiloh. Although Jomini did refer in *The Art of War* to a deployed line supported by a second "line" of battalion columns, he recommended this formation only when on the defensive. When on the offense, Jomini recommended that the attack force be arranged in two lines of "thin columns." During his discussion of how troops should be arranged for battle, Jomini provided several pages of charts that show how corps and the divisions within each could be arranged on the field. His suggestion for how two corps, each containing three divisions, could be deployed in a "thin formation" is interesting in this regard. The first corps was placed alongside the second corps. Jomini recommended that the first and second divisions in each corps be deployed along a line. The three brigades in the third division of each corps were to be positioned along a second line. However, since there were six brigades along the first line, a full interval had to be maintained between brigades along the second line. In a note that accompanied the chart showing this arrangement, Jomini added that although each brigade in this army-level organization was usually deployed in line, the commander, should he choose, could maintain the troops along any of these lines in a double column deployed on the center.

ASSESSMENT OF JOMINI'S GRAND TACTICS

Although Jomini's writings had been largely ignored by American military authorities during the 1840s and most of the 1850s, his *Summary of the Art of War* was finally adopted as a textbook by West Point in 1859, thus guaranteeing that his writings would have at least some impact on the American army that entered the Civil War. Interest in Halleck's *Elements of Military Art and Science* intensified roughly around the same time, and starting in 1859 this work was reprinted in each of 5 consecutive years. Given the similarity of doctrine and its treatment, it is not surprising that the popularity of these two authors rose in tandem. After McClellan's removal in late 1862, Halleck became general-in-chief of the Union armies, and as such, one of his many responsibilities was to advise which types of grand tactical systems were to be used. It is only natural, therefore, that the general would exert pressure upon his subordinate generals to utilize what he had already expatiated upon in his published works. Presumably, he would have encouraged his fellow officers also to study those writings that served as his own source of inspiration, in particular Jomini's *Art of War*. This would explain the popularity of Jomini's works in the Union army and the reason for the publications of three editions of this work during the war.

Despite the critical acclaim showered upon both authors and the popularity of Jomini's grand tactical system, and hence Halleck's, it would eventually prove to be an unfortunate development, one that would not only substantially contribute to the bloodiness of the Civil War but a few years later similarly fetter the French army when it moved against the Prussian army in 1870–71. Regardless of his intention to produce a practical system for contemporary European armies, as far as his methodology and source of inspiration, Jomini remained firmly entrenched in the past, the distant past. The result was a hybrid grand tactical system, a type of a collage formed by the admixture of practices taken from several earlier periods.

On a purely grand tactical level, Jomini's *Art of War* represented a synthesis of several elements of the Napoleonic system with a number of static elements associated with linear warfare. As one examines Jomini's and Halleck's twelve "orders of battle," for example, one cannot help but notice the linear qualities of virtually all of these grand tactical formations. Seven of these formations required the army to deploy into line, in one form or another. An eighth recommenced the deployment in echelon introduced during Frederick the Great's time, while three others recommended the use of a series of narrow lines to concentrate against the actual point of attack. Only one of the twelve orders of battle allowed the use of massed columns, and even in this case, the columns were to be connected together in a "line" that stretched across the entire front.

The noticeably static quality of Jomini's system contrasts starkly with the pure Napoleonic system, which had placed much greater emphasis on several versatile but very powerful *concepts* rather than upon the strict adherence to officially prescribed *formations*. Designed to facilitate the greatest concentration of force at a critical time, Napoleonic grand tactics possessed important dynamic qualities unavailable to a commander who limited himself to the older linear system. French Napoleonic armies were able to operate along *multiple axes of operations*. Rather than being forced to commit all of his troops to a single large-scale offense, the commander could orchestrate the attack into a series of *phased assaults*. Able to rapidly go in and out of line and columnar formations, it was no longer necessary to protect the flanks of individual infantry battalions by deploying battalions along long lines. It became feasible to intermix cavalry and infantry brigade- and division-size formations, which in turn permitted a new level of *combined arms support* than was hitherto possible. Not only was there was no need, but it was actually undesirable, to maintain large corps or army-level formations, and

Suchet's Division at Jena

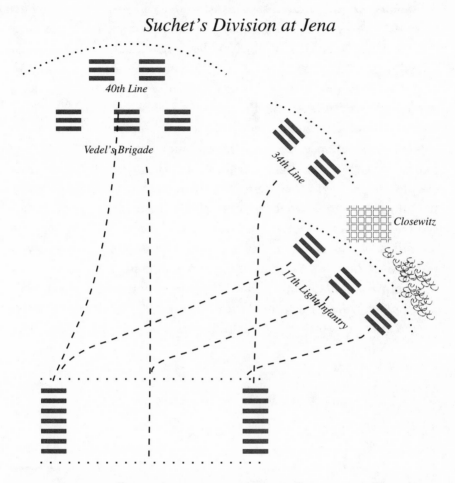

Suchet's attack during the battle of Jena on October 14, 1806, demonstrates both the articulation and flexibility of the Napoleonic Grand Tactics. Components of the French division were able to act semi-independently and along *multiple axes of operations*.

during battle responsibility for tactical-level decisions were completely relegated to division commanders.

The adoption of Jomini's grand tactical system meant the discard of a conceptually oriented calculus for a lexicon-based system. In modern terminology one can say the Napoleonic system was *concept-driven*, while linear warfare and Jomini's system was *rule based*. Generals were now encouraged before a battle to select a large grand tactical formation from the small set of approved orders of battle. Their selection determined how the troops would fight throughout the contest.

Napoleonic grand tactics were markedly different in this regard. With the exception of a few occasions, such as immediately prior to the Battle of Austerlitz, when Napoleon specifically ordered large, mixed-order formations to be used, French generals were generally free to maintain their divisions in one of a large number of possible configurations. In a typical French division, some of the battalions could be deployed in line, while others remained in column. There was no expectation to position the battalions into their "final" configuration before the fight began. Quite the opposite: The whole system encouraged maintaining the division in a waiting configuration until a favorable opportunity to attack the opponent arose. Often the battalions in the division would maneuver into a series of different formations before finally approaching the enemy and resolving the affair either with firearms or the threat of cold steel. Not only did this help camouflage the commander's intentions and help deceive his opponent, but it also made it easier to take advantage of unexpected situations that arose. There were also seemingly endless possible variations.

Jomini's Twelve Orders of Battle

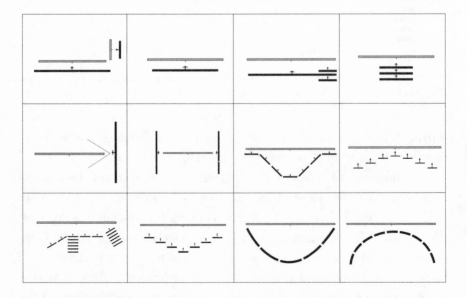

Jomini's grand system is noticeably more linear than the Napoleonic grand system it replaced.

Jomini's orders of battle offered few of these capabilities. Jomini offered only a dozen or so orders of battle, and all of these had to be formed before the start of the engagement. There was little room for maneuvering once the order of battle was formed. The individual battalions generally remained in the same position relative to the others until they were to engage the enemy. The linearity of these orders of battle helped to restrict the commander's operations to a single axis of operations. It also worked against interspersing cavalry with the infantry and minimized combined arms support. Since individual divisions, like their eighteenth-century counterparts, were forced to become a part of a larger whole, their positions and movements had to conform to that of the corps- or army-size structure, which in turn discouraged or made impossible any initiative on the part of individual division commanders.

With Jomini's system's renewed emphasis on linearity, the attempt to employ this system led to higher casualties during the Civil War. Napoleonic grand tactics sought to destroy an enemy by bringing an overwhelming force to bear against a vulnerable portion of its position, for example by assaulting the enemy's flank unexpectedly. Suddenly faced with overwhelming odds, the opponent's will to fight collapsed, and there would be a wholesale rout. Though relatively few casualties would be inflicted during the actual crisis, the enemy would be defeated, and many would be captured or become *hors de combat* during the relentless pursuit that followed.

Linear warfare, on the other hand, maximized the amount of casualties required to create a breakthrough. Sometimes when two lines confronted each other, one side would break as its men lost their nerve. More often, however, both sides initially braved it out, and a horrific and lengthy firefight ensued. When large numbers of similarly armed infantrymen fired at each other at medium range, both sides tended suffer the same magnitude of casualties. During lengthy firefights the rate of fire quickly decreased. Less aware of the mounting casualties than they would be if they were subjected to one or two devastating volleys, the participants continued in their deadly task. The casualties continued to slowly accrue, and if the firefight went on long enough, the casualty rates would climb to higher levels than if both sides had simply exchanged well-ordered volleys and one side or the other quickly fled.

That Jomini should prove to be such a conservative, retrogressive intellectual force should hardly be surprising to anyone even remotely familiar with his life. After serving briefly with the French army as a volunteer staff member from 1798 to 1800, Jomini shifted his attention to more scholarly efforts and wrote the *Traité de grande tactique*, a five-volume analysis of the Seven Years' War, which was published in 1805. Napoleon was sufficiently impressed with Jomini's efforts that he promoted the young officer to staff colonel, and it was in this capacity that Jomini served in Ney's corps during the 1805 Ulm Campaign and the 1806 Prussian Campaign. This was a rather serendipitous appointment, for Marshal Ney had emulated a series of Frederician maneuvers during the camp de Montreuil-sur-Mer in 1804, and the young Jomini and the great marshal presumably had occasional opportunities to exchange views on the Prussian monarch's art of war.

Although Jomini by 1813 had become Ney's chief of staff, he defected to Russian service after Ney's recommendation that Jomini be appointed a general of division was rejected. Jomini stayed in Russia for the remainder of his military career, and it was within this notoriously conservative military, political, and social environment that Jomini wrote the works that were to have such widespread influence on mid-nineteenth-century military thought.

Jomini's works were published variously in Paris and Brussels, and the bulk of his readership was officers involuntarily enmeshed in the aesthetics and mores of the French Restoration, which permeated all aspects of daily life. The return of the traditional monarchy brought with it a renewed emphasis on the legitimacy of the traditional power structure. If not rejected outright, elements of the radicalism that characterized the previous 25 years were minimized and woven into a broader traditional framework. These social dictates applied as much to military doctrine and practice as they did political ideology and neoclassicism in art. The practice of delegating tactical authority to division commanders at the expense of the commander in chief's ability to maintain total control now struck a discord, and any system that led a return to army-size structures, and hence the reestablishment of the commander in chief's control, could be expected to be looked upon favorably by military authorities.

Chapter 22

AMERICAN ARTILLERY DOCTRINE

B y the end of 1862, it had become clear that the war was going to be a hard-fought, prolonged affair and a number of long-term efforts would have to be undertaken if full military potential was to be achieved. The publication of several treatises on artillery was one such area of effort. A number works on various aspects of artillery already existed, such as Gassendi's *Aide-mémoire a l'usage des officers d'artillerie* (1844) and Piobert's *Traité d'artillerie theorique et pratique*. Both were highly regarded, and Gassendi's work had continued to be considered the standard reference on artillery until the advent of rifled artillery in the late 1850s. However, apart from being written in a foreign language and thus inaccessible to most American artillery officers, both treatises limited themselves exclusively to technical issues and lacked the tactical and grand tactical relevancy so desperately sought after by the American belligerents.

Eighteen sixty-three would prove to be a bumper year for American treatises on artillery. In the North a second, expanded version of John Gibbon's *The Artillerist's Manual. Instruction for Field Artillery* was purportedly translated from the French by Gen. R. Anderson, but the actual effort was carried out by Capts. William H. French and William F. Barry, both of whom would be promoted to general rank early in the war. Both works, though published in 1863, had been started before the war. The Confederate authorities were no less ambitious, and two similar works appeared during the same year in the South: *Andrews' Mounted Artillery Drill,* compiled by Lt. Col. R. Snowdon Andrews and published in Charleston, and the *Ordnance Manual for the Use of the Officers of the Confederate States Army,* by Col. Josiahs Gorgas, chief of ordnance.

All of these were highly technical works intended to provide all the detail artillery officers needed to properly maintain and use ordnance. Lengthy sections were devoted to how to prepare gunpowder and how to manufacture the projectiles and fuses. Usually, these rather dry descriptions were accompanied by exhaustive mathematical treatments about how to calculate the ideal trajectory and the corresponding charge to be used, the optimum rifle twist for a given type of ordnance, and so on. There was little discussion about how artillery should be employed on the battlefield.

Anyone interested in piecing together Civil War artillery doctrine must manipulate the bits and pieces of information provided by an assortment of such works contemporary to the war. However, two sources are particularly useful in this task: Maj. Joseph Roberts's *The Handbook of Artillery* and Gibbon's *Artillerist's Manual*. Though Gibbon and Roberts both had served in the Fourth U.S. Artillery Regiment before the war, when it came to assembling their respective works on artillery, there was little commonality in treatment. Roberts devoted the better part of a chapter to contemporary artillery doctrine. As commandant of Fort Monroe (Hampton, Virginia) for most of the war, Roberts obviously possessed a more than adequate understanding of military engineering, fortifications, and siegecraft. Hardly original, Roberts provided what might be considered a consensus among Europe's more conservative military thinkers on how artillery should be used. Rigorously schooled in the military science of the time, Roberts took an approach to artillery usage that reflected a distinctly "theoretical" orientation. As one wades through his artillery tactics, it is easy to conjure up images of a West Point instructor sketching vector forces on a blackboard as he explained to novice artillery students where the artillery pieces should be placed on the battlefield and how they should be employed.

John Gibbon's *Artillerist's Manual* evokes an entirely different set of feelings and associations. Equally well schooled in military science, Gibbon meticulously described the minutest of recent advances in artillery practice, as well as related physics and mathematical principles. Unlike Roberts's treatment, Gibbon's discussion of artillery tactics also evokes the smell of gunpowder and the rush of adrenaline during the crisis of real combat. It is apparent that the author's experiences with the army of occupation during the Mexican-American War and while fighting Indians in Florida had not been ignored and had contributed their share to discussion about artillery practice.

Forever pragmatic, Gibbon went into great detail about how the artillery should deploy rapidly into a battery along the battle line. A battery traveling in single file typically would be ordered into a column of sections doubled on the center. This referred to a column that consisted of two to four tiers, depending upon the number of guns in the battery. There were two guns from the same section along each tier; the center section was at the head of the column. Of course, the artillery column might contain more than one battery. In these cases, the batteries could be formed in several parallel columns by section or, even better, into two columns of sections side by side, producing a column four artillery pieces wide. Although less common, it wasn't totally unheard of for artillery batteries to approach the intended line in closed column four to six pieces wide and with each tier separated from the next by twice the distance in a normal column of sections.

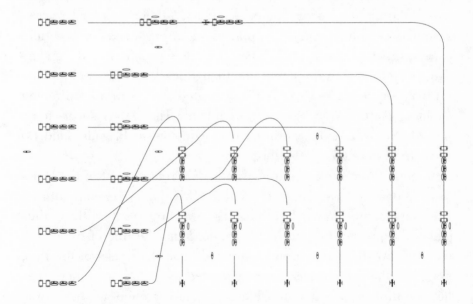

This illustration taken from Gibbon's *Artillerist's Manual* shows how a battery maneuvered into position along a firing line. The second row of wagons are caissons used to store additional ammunition.

The artillerymen were cautioned to dismount from the caissons just before they entered the enemy's range of fire. Otherwise, an explosion caused by a stray bullet or shot hitting a caisson would destroy not just the ammunition but the gun crew as well. It was also wise to leave about half the caissons in the rear. One caisson behind every two guns would suffice until the seriousness of the situation was determined. Meanwhile, as soon as the battery was ordered to ready itself for action, the two guns in the center of the artillery column were to rush forward a slight distance, then halt. The sections in the rear would fan out obliquely on each side and advance to their places along the battery line. The entire deployment process until the first round was fired, Roberts estimated, would take but 25 seconds.

Although officers were to make certain that the ground selected for the artillery was sufficiently wide for all the ordnance, they did not have to guarantee that the proper order between sections within a battery was observed. During a major engagement the batteries would change positions repeatedly, so speed and flexibility were held in greater regard than absolute regularity.

The most significant difference between the Roberts and Gibbon artillery tactics was in where the artillery should be positioned relative to the infantry before the engagement. Gibbon was far less prescriptive. Artillery could be placed in any convenient position, except directly in front of the infantry. To do so would offer the enemy two targets, and hapless infantry thoughtlessly placed behind the artillery would have to endure the heated fire invariably directed against the attractive target in front of them. The batteries were to be placed in the intervals between the regiments or brigades and 60 yards in front of the battle line.

Roberts favored a more linear approach, reminiscent of the Prussians under Frederick the Great and the British more recently during the Napoleonic Wars. In Roberts's own words: "Artillery thus [should] represent the faces of a bastion, and the line of troops the curtain." Artillery was to be positioned upon the flanks of the line, not immediately contiguous but separated by a slight distance so as not to hinder infantry movement. "Convergence of fire" was extremely important. The batteries on either flank would be angled to produce a cross fire toward the center.

Ordinarily, artillery was not to be placed along an infantry line. However, if the infantry line had an extensive front, batteries on the flank would be unable to support the center. The commander then was to place one or two batteries near the center of the line and establish a cross fire between the central batteries and those on the flank. When on the defensive this cross fire had to be directed toward the areas the enemy had to cross. Conversely, when on the offensive the artillery fire must not interdict the movement of friendly forces.

Horse (flying) batteries were always to be placed on the wings, while mounted (foot) artillery was positioned more toward the center of the line. However, before they ordered their pieces "in battery" (unlimbered into a firing line), it was critical that officers and NCOs survey the prospective battlefield to identify the most advantageous positions. Gibbon, for example, believed that terrain properly exploited actually doubled the "force and importance" of artillery. Defensive properties of the position had to be carefully evaluated. It was imperative not to needlessly expose a battery to the enemy artillery fire, and it was wise therefore to position the artillery well before the beginning of engagement to take advantage of available protective cover.

Although stream banks, hollow-ways, buildings, and thin strips of woods were the most obvious forms of protection in the terrain, an experienced artillery officer could find many other forms of protective cover unnoticed by the inexperienced eye. Often a slight rise of ground, as a little as 2 feet, in front of the position could protect the battery from enemy solid shot. Traveling at low trajectories, solid shot would hit the slight elevation and harmlessly ricochet over the batteries. Placing artillery in front of rolling ground often had the same effect. There was an added bonus. Artillerymen generally adjusted the range by looking for the dust that arose where the round shot first struck the ground, then raising or lowering the elevation of their piece accordingly. When firing at an enemy positioned on undulating ground, the contours of the ground often hid these clouds of dust. Gently rolling ground might appear flat in the distance, and failing to see the dust, enemy gunners might think they had fired too high, even though they actually had already acquired the correct range. They would then lower their pieces. All this made it more difficult to be certain of the correct range and ate up valuable time while the opposing artillery remained free to work its destruction unopposed.

Battery commanders were also cautioned against placing their guns on rocky ground. Struck by solid shot or canister, the stones instantly fragmented and caused the same devastation as shrapnel. Furthermore, the officers had to survey the ground *behind the battery*. A battery had to be able to retreat quickly, should it become necessary. Slippery and marshy ground definitely was to be avoided, as was ground intersected with hedges and ditches. Weak positions were to be strengthened by heavy artillery, even siege pieces, if they were available and the position important enough.

Moderate heights along the line were also to be exploited. It had long been a general maxim that artillery should only be placed at the top of a slope which it could defend by itself. The artillery had to be able to direct an unobstructed fire against the base of the hill; otherwise, the enemy force could form in the dead zone and begin its assault up the hill unopposed by the artillery. Officers were cautioned, however, against ever placing artillery on either steep hills or high elevations. Ideally, artillery was placed on elevations whose height was 1% of the distance to the target and were never to be placed upon hills where the elevation was greater than 7% of this distance. When artillery was required to defend a lofty hill or elevation, whose height made it impossible for the artillery to command the

Illustrated from a battlefield sketch submitted by R. E. Small, this is the Lincoln Gun at Fortress Monroe in Virginia. *Frank Leslie's Illustrated Weekly,* July 5, 1862.

base, artillery officers were advised, if at all possible, to place the battery lower along the slope, such as at the halfway point. If this was impossible, infantry should be used to defend that stretch of the line instead, since it was not possible to depress the barrels of artillery pieces as much as the soldier could lower his shoulder arm. Any excess artillery was placed in a reserve in the rear, out of range of enemy artillery fire, ideally in a covered position with a convenient access to the front.

DEFENSIVE CONSIDERATIONS

Regardless of where the artillery was placed, doctrine called for officers to take a number of precautions for its defense. Attacked frontally, a battery could repulse most assaults. Artillery, however, was especially vulnerable to attack from the flank and the rear, and whenever possible batteries had to be protected by either infantry or cavalry "supports." While at West Point, Gibbon, in his course on artillery tactics, taught that in open terrain artillery support was best provided by cavalry. Placed on either side of the battery, at the propitious moment the cavalry could charge the advancing enemy. However, if the battery was very large or likely to receive a "hot and lively" fire, it was better to place the cavalry about 100 yards behind the battery and, if possible, in a protected position. When fighting over broken terrain, cavalry would no longer prove useful. Then it was the infantry's turn to support the artillery, instead. Gibbon suggested that such infantry be kept in squares on both flanks of the artillery and to the rear of its center.

Officers also had to make certain the guns were never placed directly in front of or behind friendly infantry, since this doubled the target and needlessly increased casualties. The exception was when the intention was to initially mask the batteries from the opponent's view so that they could be sprung upon the unsuspecting foe at the crisis of the engagement and inflict maximum carnage and mayhem. In this case Roberts recommended that cavalry, rather than infantry, be used to mask the artillery, since mounted forces could be moved out of the way much more expeditiously. Although during the 1840s and '50s a number of improvements had been made to gun carriages that permitted slightly higher elevations than employed during the

Napoleonic Wars, many artillery experts still warned against trying to fire over friendly troops. Not only was there a chance of injury by a wayward shot or a premature explosion of shell, a commonplace occurrence with Civil War artillery, there was an even better chance of unsettling the troops caught between the enemy to their front and the friendly artillery in the rear.

Regardless of what measures were taken to support the artillery, occasionally, the enemy would threaten to overrun the artillery position and capture the pieces. Because of the expense and diffi-culty in replacing lost artillery, the "defend the guns at all costs" credo was at the heart of defensive doctrine. In the British army, for example, the loss of one's guns was equated with the loss of one's honor, and British artillerymen were encouraged to defend their guns to the death. Although in theory the French espoused the same doctrine, French artillerymen practiced a more mercurial defensive philosophy. Though the guns should be vigorously defended, the gunners were advised to retire at the last possible moment. Not only did this pragmatic approach acknowledge the value of the gunner's lives, but it recognized the fact that gunners who "live to fight another day" would be around to work the guns should they be recaptured, an event which, given the unpredictable ebb and flow of any large battle, might happen during that same engagement.

American opinion by the late 1850s appears to have been much closer to the British position. Gibbon encouraged artillerymen to con-tinue to fire "up to the last moment" in order to protect nearby troops. Concurring, Roberts emphatically declared:

> An artilleryman must never forget that his gun is his proper arm; here lies his strength; that his post of honor and his duty; also the last discharge are always the most destructive and may pos-sible insure the safety of the whole army, or turn the tide of vic-tory in their favor.

FIRING GUNS INDIVIDUALLY
When infantry attacked in line, artillery was to direct its fire against the entire width of the defender's position. On the other hand, if the

infantry was to assault in column, the artillery had to concentrate upon the "real points of attack."

Unless it was necessary to inflict the greatest amount of casualties at a single moment, such as when attackers were crossing a bridge or passing through a narrow defile, salvo fire was to be strictly avoided. Up to the mid-eighteenth century, artillery theory required artillerymen to fire all the guns in a position at the same time, believing that this inflicted the maximum punishment. The drawbacks with general salvos soon became apparent, however. All guns having fired, there would be a 10- to 20-second period in which the enemy could advance unopposed while the artillerymen reloaded. As military tacticians began to examine what we today call the "psychological impact" of artillery fire, it became apparent that salvo fire, though noisy, failed to produce the maximum negative psychological effect upon the enemy. The 10- to 20-second intervals allowed the foe sufficient time to recover and emotionally brace himself for the next salvo. The Confederate troops along Missionary Ridge found out, much to their chagrin, that this could lead to embarrassing results just when artillery fire was the most crucial, that is, in the last moments as the attackers attempted to close to hand-to-hand combat with the gunners (Chattanooga, November 25, 1863).

To avoid the problems caused by artillery silence, in his instructions to his artillery officers (May 10, 1782), Frederick the Great had recommended that officers order salvos whereby every second artillery piece fired. This effectively halved the time during which the battery was denuded of fire. Frederick frowned upon individual fire, whereby every gun was free to fire at its own pace, since this lacked the necessary psychological impact upon the enemy.

Writing about the same issue years later, Gassendi did not feel this was really a problem, and he recommended individual fire. Since the effectiveness of artillery was generally proportional to the number of guns, whenever possible, artillery had to be concentrated into sizable packets to severely punish enemy formations and deliver a decisive blow. There was less of a consensus regarding how the guns were to operate within the battery. Gibbon agreed with Gassendi and thought that the guns should fire individually. Roberts, on the other hand, believed that individual fire was to be avoided, and to ensure continuous fire and mutual support, a minimum of two guns were to participate in each salvo.

HOW THEY FIRED THE PIECE

The officers were to ensure that the artillerymen aimed and fired their pieces carefully, rather than try to maintain an impressive rate of fire. Accuracy was more important than weight of shot. It was recommended to fire slowly and methodically as long as the target formation remained at long range. As the enemy approached, the pace had to be quickened. It was the officer's duty to ensure that the shots were not thrown away, to avoid any waste of ammunition.

Even during relatively ideal peacetime conditions, the operation of artillery demanded the highest degree of teamwork. Not only did each artilleryman have to perform a specific function in a predefined sequence, but all his actions had to harmonize with the others working the same gun. As soon as the piece was fired, the No. 3 artilleryman jumped to his position immediately behind the back end of the barrel. He was responsible for closing off the flow of air by placing his left hand over the vent. Thus starved of oxygen, any lit embers would be extinguished. Although this had to be done as quickly as possible, it was critical that No. 3 always remain alert. If he wasn't careful and some air entered through the vent, an ember might precipitate a premature explosion as the next charge was rammed home, maiming, possibly even killing, his comrades in front of the piece.

The No. 1 artillerymen meanwhile cleaned out the burnt residue inside the barrel with his long sponge-staff. As he finished, he would reverse the staff and after No. 2 inserted the round into the muzzle would ram home the next round with a swinging motion of his body, which by the time of the Civil War was usually a bag charge followed separately by the projectile. Incidentally, during the Civil War, except for large howitzers, ammunition for smoothbores was "fixed," the charge and the projectile bound together for ease of loading. To provide flexibility of range, the charge and projectile had to be loaded separately for rifled artillery. After aiming the piece, as the gunner (the person who aimed the gun) yelled, "Ready!" Nos. 1, 2, and 3 assumed the ready position. The No. 4 artilleryman inserted

the primer, and the piece was ready to be fired. The gunner meanwhile took advantage of the momentary pause between firings to correct any inaccuracies. Paying close attention to where the last round
struck, he would use the elevating screws to raise or lower the barrel
accordingly. The entire process took less than 30 seconds and when
necessary could be performed up to three times a minute for a short
period.

Veteran artillerymen gradually acquired a number of tricks that
would speed up loading and firing, as well as avoid some common
problems. As soon as the gunner saw the flash at the vent, he would
spring forward and hold the wheels of the undercarriage. By doing
this, he was usually able to reduce the recoil about 50%. Not only
did this reduce the amount of time relaying and sighting the gun
before the next shot could be fired; it also reduced the amount of
wear and tear on the ground below and the strain on the carriage's
wheels and axles. Minimizing the impact of the artillery piece on the
ground was not very important during brief engagements or when the
artillery was positioned upon firm ground. However, it often proved
to be an important precaution when on soft or loose earth, as was
frequently found after rainstorms. Then the repeated recoiling of
the piece would cut large furrows in the earth, and eventually the
piece would have to be moved to firmer ground, as happened to
some of Jackson's artillery during the Battle of Port Republic (on the
upper reaches of the Shenandoah, June 9, 1862).

The need to fire quickly was probably greatest when the battery
found itself the target of a frontal attack. The battery's position
imperiled, the men would be urged to load and fire as quickly as
possible and to aim where the enemy's troops were thickest. If the
situation was desperate enough, the men might be instructed to
forego sponging the barrel to achieve a higher rate of fire. Maj.
Henry J. Hunt, who then commanded Light Battery M of the Second
U.S. Artillery Regiment, issued such orders during the First Battle
of Bull Run.

Although many artillery engagements continued for hours, much
of the action tended to be concentrated in short-lived crescendos,
when the team's exertions were strained to a feverish pitch. But
sometimes the artillery crew had to maintain a grueling pace for

longer periods, such as during counterbattery fire or an extended bombardment before an infantry offensive. Despite their exhaustion and even physical pain, the men had to keep up the rapid fire, like so many automatons. The thumb cot (or thumbstall) protecting No. 3's left hand would gradually be burned through from covering the vent between firings to allow No. 2 to load the piece. Then the captain would remind him it was his duty to cover the vent with bare hands, and if the action continued long enough, the fingers on his left hand might be burnt to the bone. On the other end of the artillery piece, the strenuous effort required to clean out the inner barrel would eventually become too much for No. 3, and he would have to trade places with No. 2 for a while as he recouped his energy.

ACCURACY OF ARTILLERY

The potential accuracy of Civil War era rifles is well known, and many anecdotes of expert marksmen hitting enemies at extreme range have come down to posterity. No such recognition was been attributed to period artillery, at least in the mind of the modern public. One tends to think about artillery as only capable of broadstroke action, firing at lengthy lines or massed formations on the battlefield. In reality, rifled and even smoothbore cannon, when handled by skilled artillerists, was capable of surprising accuracy, even at long ranges. During the First Bull Run campaign, the Union forces enjoyed a virtual monopoly on the new rifled guns, and it was the rebels that had to endure the effects of the heightened accuracy of that weapon.

By the next year, however, increasing numbers of rifled artillery had fallen into the hands of the Confederates or were otherwise obtained. As Union troops made their slow, inept move up the York County Peninsula, they too suffered from the effectiveness of this new form of artillery. In a letter written home on May 2, 1862, while in front of Yorktown, Frederick Peet of the First United States Sharpshooters complained that properly handled rifled artillery could "be shot almost as straight as a target rifle, when aimed with a glass." To justify his newly earned respect, he recounted just how accurate these pieces could be when handled by competent artillerists. A group of rebel observers atop their fortifications had been carefully watching the effects of their artillery on the Union batteries all afternoon. Peet and a few subordinate sharpshooters were out on patrol about a mile away from the Confederate fortifications. Just as evening was setting in, Peet allowed one of his patrol to try to pick off a few "traitors" on the rebel fortifications. Despite the distance the shot obviously came close to the mark, for immediately a rebel battery replied with a 6-pound shell whizzing a few feet over the patrol's heads.

At this early stage of the war, some of the men in the regiment were still armed with the highly accurate target rifles with telescopic lenses they had brought with them from home. Borrowing just such a weapon, Peet carefully placed a second shot among the rebels on the opposite fortifications. Once again the rebel rifled artillery replied, and once again it was too close for comfort. Fortunately, the rebel shell failed to burst. The Union sharpshooters saw the writing on the wall and understood what was in store if they continued the duel. Prudently, they decided to seek the safety of their own line of works and started back to the "parallels," which ran slightly to their rear. The Union sharpshooters quickly made their way over their own entrenchments. A few seconds later another rebel shell zipped a foot above where they had crossed over a merlon moments before.

Two years later, as the Union army gradually tightened its stranglehold around Virginia's capital and environs, Union artillerists displayed equal proficiency. A veteran named Lightsey recalled one memorable example. Rebel sharpshooters continually plagued the Union infantrymen, as the latter gradually sought to extend the entrenchments and fieldworks to the south and southwest of Petersburg. Lightsey recalls that like so many times before and after, a work party in front of that city was forced to scatter as a slow but dangerously accurate series bullets of whistled around the men, wounding two and killing one. With the aid of field glasses, they spotted an enemy marksman in a tall pine tree about a mile distant. The men were ordered to lie down as a rifled gun was prepared to strike back. After a few rounds, looking through his field glasses, the captain saw a rebel marksman fall from the trees, and the infantrymen were able to resume their work unmolested.

William Izlar of the Twenty-fifth South Carolina Infantry provides a stunning example of the intrinsic accuracy of the rifled cannon.

During a lull in its 1864 bombardment, a young signal officer by the name of Hugen went to the top of Fort Sumter to observe the Union preparations to retake that fort. Resting his telescope on the parapet, Hugen started to look around the harbor. Although only his head was above the stone parapet, a Union gun at Cumming's Point was able to decapitate the officer with its first shot. However, probably the most famous example of accurate rifled artillery fire occurred during an action at Pine Mountain (June 14, 1864), near Marietta, Georgia, when a round killed Confederate Gen. Bishop Leonidas Polk.

USES OF DIFFERENT PROJECTILES

The Civil War artillerist had a greater choice of projectiles than did his grandfather during the War of 1812. Previously, guns had been generally restricted to firing shot and canister, while howitzers, although they could be made to fire solid shot in extreme cases, were used to throw shells and, at close range, canister. At this earlier point, the effectiveness of spherical case (shrapnel) had yet to become generally recognized, and its use had been limited to British armies. As the results of French experiments with reduction in charges, to allow guns to fire both shot and shell, became known and sturdier shells were manufactured, artillerymen during the decade preceding the Civil War were gradually issued a more varied repertoire of ammunition.

The variety of projectile to be used against each type of target had long ago been worked out by artillery experts, and American artillery doctrine followed suit. Gibbon's instructions about the choice of projectile and the rate of fire to use at various ranges appears to have been largely based on Gassendi's *Aide-mémoire*. The fact that many observations were drawn from leading European sources in no way should lessen Gibbon's reputation as a thought leader in American artillery doctrine. Unlike poetical and fictional works, the goal of the military scientific treatise is not originality for its own sake; rather, it is the uncovering and presentation of the most useful information, regardless of origin.

Most American artillery experts felt that fire should be limited to targets within 1000 to 1200 yards. Although this certainly wasn't the maximum range of smoothbore weapons, it was unwise to fire at more distant targets since the resulting casualties and damage declined greatly. This not only wasted ammunition; it also inadvertently handed the enemy a psychological advantage. Noticing the ineffectiveness of the long-range cannonade, the enemy's morale would be buoyed and he would then advance with even greater confidence and determination.

It was also extremely important that the artillerymen aim and fire slowly and carefully, especially when firing at targets farther than 600 or 700 yards. A consistent message was repeatedly hammered away by European and American authors alike: The effect of artillery depended upon well-directed shots, rather than sheer volume of fire. Gibbon cautioned American artillerymen to fire at targets beyond 600 yards only once per minute. Six-pounder guns were supplied with only 400 rounds, which were intended to last an entire campaign, and the entire amount of ammunition could be spent in 7 hours of continuous fighting even at the suggested slow rate of expenditure. An inexperienced artillery officer could inadvertently fall into a trap if he gave in to the exhortations of nearby infantry and began to fire quickly during feints and exploratory efforts, which were almost always preliminary to the main engagement. Incidentally, artillerymen were advised to first use the ammunition in the caisson rather than in the limber assigned to the artillery piece. This ensured that there was available ammunition near each gun, even should the weapon and its crew be separated from its caisson, an event that happened all too frequently during the pandemonium of the battlefield. If possible, officers were initially to deploy only half the caissons, or one caisson for every two artillery pieces. The remainder were to be kept in the rear and out of harm's way until they were needed.

The type of projectile that should be fired also depended upon the target. Everyone agreed that shot or shell should be used when firing at deep columns, artillery, or a formation taken in flank. Shot was probably preferable against infantry, while shell or shrapnel tended to be more useful when firing at cavalry, especially when in deep columns. Not only was the explosion more likely to inflict wounds on the horses' passengers, but the loud noise and sudden flash startled the horses and caused much more consternation than physical damage. For the same reasons, shell and shrapnel were also useful when the enemy infantry was protected by the contour of the ground and seemed proof against round shot. The officially sanctioned *Instructions for Light Artillery* pointed out that once the enemy cavalry gained speed, however, the artillerymen should discontinue firing either shell or shrapnel and switch to round shot. Shell and shrapnel required precise estimates of range. This was not only time consuming, but impractical given the horses' rate of advance. Solid shot could be fired more quickly, and it was deadly across a much longer dangerous space.

A number of experiments conducted by European tacticians during the 1840s and '50s were similar in spirit and rigorousness to those conducted by the American tactician William Duane 3 or 4 decades before. They sought to determine how quickly infantry and cavalry could advance through the artillery's fire zone and how many rounds the artillery could get off in response. The general consensus was that infantry could traverse 200 yards in 2 minutes, while the cavalry could do the same in about 30 seconds. According to the official instructions for field artillery, the gunner should expect enemy cavalry to traverse the last 1000 yards in about 7 minutes. It would require about 4 minutes to cover the first 400 yards, starting off at a walk and then at a "gentle trot." Then at a full trot it would cross the next 400 yards in 2 minutes before breaking out into a gallop and covering the last 200 yards in 30 seconds. Roberts was more optimistic about cavalry's movement capabilities. Crossing the first half mile at a trot and the remainder at a gallop, it could cover 1500 yards in about 6 minutes. This compared to 16 minutes for their infantry counterpart. Of course, cavalry required much more time to approach over broken ground, and artillery could impede the advance by disordering the formation, especially during the early stages of the advance.

Both Roberts's *Handbook of Artillery* and the official *Instructions for Field Artillery* advocated switching ammunition types as soon as the target had advanced to within a specified range, although there was some disagreement about when to switch and what type of projectile to use in each case. The following chart shows how many rounds of each type could be unleashed before the enemy troops reached the battery, as well as the range where each should be used.

Official Instructions for Field Artillery

Against cavalry

Range (yds.)	No. of shots and ammo type
1000–600	9 solid shot
600–400	2 solid shot
400–200	3 canister
200–close quarters	2 canister

Roberts's Handbook of Artillery

Against cavalry

Range (yds.)	No. of shots and ammo type
1500–650	7 spherical case
650–350	2 solid shot
350–close quarters	2 canister

Against infantry

1500–650	19 spherical case
650–350	7 solid shot
350–close quarters	8 canister
Double quick and the charge	2 canister

At longer ranges, in theory, the artillerymen could fire solid shot, shell, or shrapnel. Roberts advocated firing shrapnel at long range before converting to solid shot at medium range, while the official *Instructions* prescribed the use of solid shot at both these ranges. Presumably, Roberts felt that when the cavalry was 1500 yards away or so, it would be moving slowly enough for shrapnel to be practicable.

The issue most heavily debated was how long to continue to fire solid shot before switching to canister. Finding themselves suddenly attacked by cavalry, novice artillerymen tended to start firing canister at medium ranges. Veteran officers felt that this was premature and that the artillerymen should continue to fire solid shot as long as possible. Although conceding that canister certainly proved effective at ranges up to 600 yards on completely hard, open ground, where it would ricochet, its range was much more restricted when the ground was soft or when fighting in the broken terrain encountered over so much of the North American continent.

Both solid shot and shrapnel could be said to have a "minimum range" within which their effectiveness would drop off. To be effective, solid shot had to follow a relatively precise trajectory. As the enemy neared, the barrel had to be correspondingly depressed, and the charges decreased, to produce this trajectory. When firing solid shot at extremely short range, very small charges had to be used, so the projectile did not have enough velocity to ricochet effectively. Roberts enjoined artillerymen to employ only solid shot at targets that were more than 350 yards distant, while Gibbon argued that solid shot could be used against infantry or cavalry that had advanced to within 200 yards. Relying on the force of an explosion rather than impact, shells could be fired at even the closest range, since the velocity of the projectile was immaterial. Of course, before the advent of the French 12-pounder gun howitzer—known in America as the "light 12-pounder" or "12-pounder Napoleon"—and of rifled artillery, the use of shells had been mostly limited to howitzers. Experts thought, however, that shrapnel, like solid shot, was less effective at very close range and suggested that it only be used against targets 500 yards or more distant.

Artillery experts debated just how far canister could be fired effectively, although by the mid-nineteenth century 400 yards was generally considered to be the limit. Gibbon felt that canister could be used effectively against targets 300 to 400 yards distant; Roberts felt the range when firing at troops in formation was 350 yards, while it was practical to fire away at enemy skirmishers at up to 400 yards. This, incidentally, represented a marked decrease in what was considered to be the maximum range of canister. During the Napoleonic Wars, for example, French artillerists had been instructed to fire canister containing large balls up to 800 meters and those with the smaller balls up to 700 meters. The reason for the change in doctrine did not lie in a diminution of either the force of the projecting charge, the sturdiness of the canister, or the average capability of later artillerymen. The French did not possess the advantage of shrapnel and had to rely more heavily on canister. Spherical case, which could be used at much longer ranges, became much more

Robert's *The Handbook of Artillery*

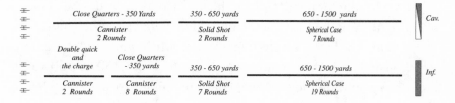

	Close Quarters - 350 Yards		350 - 650 yards	650 - 1500 yards	Cav.
	Cannister 2 Rounds		Solid Shot 2 Rounds	Spherical Case 7 Rounds	
	Double quick and the charge	Close Quarters - 350 yards	350 - 650 yards	650 - 1500 yards	Inf.
	Cannister 2 Rounds	Cannister 8 Rounds	Solid Shot 7 Rounds	Spherical Case 19 Rounds	

Official Instructions for Field Artillery

	200 yards - close quarters	200 - 400 yards	400 - 600 yards	600 - 1000 yards	Cav.
	Cannister 2 Rounds	Cannister 3 Rounds	Solid Shot 2 Rounds	Solid Shot 19 Rounds	

The type of ammunition that was to be used was strictly prescribed by American artillery doctrine and varied according to the range of the target.

prevalent during the mid-nineteenth century. Moreover, those armed with the 12-pounder Napoleon possessed the added advantage of being able to hurl shells up to the maximum range of the weapon.

The rate of fire also varied with both the type of projectile used and the target range. Shells and solid shot required more accuracy than canister and took longer to load and fire. Gibbon felt that the cautious rate of one round per minute should be continued until the enemy had advanced to within 600 yards. The pace of the gunners would increase as the enemy continued to near, and once the enemy forces had closed to within 600 yards, the rate of fire was allowed to be "rapid." It was estimated that gunners could fire solid shot approximately twice and canister three times per minute. As the range continued to decrease, the gunners were instructed to forego sponging the pieces before loading, thereby achieving an even greater rate of fire. In his seminal work *An Account of Some of the Most Remarkable Events of the War & a Treatise on Several Branches of the Military Art,* published just prior to the French Revolution, the great Austrian artillerist J. G. Tielke observed that six rounds per minute was the maximum an artillery piece could be loaded and fired and still achieve accuracy.

If the enemy, undeterred, still advanced, the gunners were to switch to canister, which could be fired around three times per minute. Opinion appears to have been divided as to the best means of action during the final moments of the enemy assault. The official *Instructions for Light Artillery* instructed artillerymen to continue to fire canister until the enemy had closed to about 150 to 160 yards; then they could employ two canisters propelled by a single charge. Gibbon suggested a slightly different expedient. Between 150 and 350 yards, gunners could elect to use a combination of the two types of ammunition. The solid shot was placed in front of the canister inside the barrel. However, Gibbon suggested that once the enemy closed to 150 yards, the gunners were to rely solely on canister, which they would employ up to the last moment. Canister, like solid shot, was to be fired a little low in order that the bullets would ricochet off of the ground and scatter more widely.

Both authors advised that field batteries avoid counterbattery fire, fire targeted at enemy batteries, unless specifically ordered to go after them or prompted by peculiar circumstances, such as when the enemy artillery was exposed and there were no other available targets. When it was necessary to conduct counterbattery fire, the officers were to take a number of precautions. When firing at infantry or cavalry targets, artillery officers usually attempted to bring an oblique fire to bear, since this maximized the number of casualties that would be inflicted. During counterbattery fire, however, the artillery officers were to avoid oblique fire and instead position their artillery directly in front of the enemy artillery. This reduced the oblique angle of the incoming shots and correspondingly decreased the chances that the wheels and carriages would be hit. Distances between individual pieces in the battery were also to be increased beyond normal, the distance just slightly greater than the known maximum deviation of fire for the enemy artillery. This minimized the possibility that enemy artillery that was actually aiming at one friendly artillery piece would accidentally hit its neighbor (a piece destroyed is a piece lost, regardless of whether it was the result of accurate fire or not).

The friendly artillery meanwhile was to concentrate its fire against two enemy guns, destroy these, and then proceed to the next pair.

Experience had shown that the best opportunity to destroy an enemy battery occurred when enfilade fire could be brought to bear at the moment the horses and carriages were turning around in order to place the weapons in battery. Gunners were initially to select an enemy slightly to one side or the other in order to obtain an oblique fire. This increased the likelihood of hitting the wheels and carriage, thereby dismounting the piece.

This, then, was the theory of artillery tactics at the start of the Civil War. In practice it appears that artillery officers were generally left to their own devices or the will of their superior officers. One finds some instructions on artillery usage in the various general orders and circulars that were issued. These were usually fragmentary affairs in which a short discussion about some aspect of artillery usage is briefly sandwiched amid a litany of other pressing matters, such as where and when to attack, and what forces were to be used, or attached as a seeming afterthought.

General Beauregard began the second of his tactical instructions (December 4, 1862,) with a brief discussion of several issues that involved artillery. Beauregard reminded his men that rifled guns were designed for long-range firing and therefore should be placed in positions that commanded expansive stretches of the battlefield but were themselves outside of enemy canister or small arms rifle fire. At the beginning of the battle, the rifled pieces were to be directed primarily at the enemy reserve forces. As the enemy advanced against them, however, they must be turned against the enemy columns. Only after the opposing infantry or cavalry had been routed were the friendly rifled artillery to be directed against Union artillery. Beauregard implored his officers to continuously impress upon their men the necessity of keeping calm in order to fire slowly and accurately. Special care was also always to be taken to keep the battery's horses in a protected position behind cover. For without the horses the mobility of the batteries was greatly reduced. In a circular written to compliment his artillery on their performance (February 25, 1863) D. H. Hill—now commander of Confederate troops in North Carolina—took the opportunity to importune his gunners to reserve their fire primarily for masses of infantry, just as they did at Fredericksburg, and not to withdraw their batteries prematurely.

Chapter 23

ARTILLERY IN PRACTICE

ATTACKED BY INFANTRY

Although by the Civil War, rifled artillery had a theoretical range of more than a mile, the lack of reliable communications between forward artillery spotters and the battery severely limited the effectiveness of indirect fire under battle conditions. During an engagement most of the artillery had to be placed along or near the line of battle in order to see its targets. Despite precautionary measures taken to protect the artillery pieces, it was not uncommon for a battery to be assaulted by either enemy infantry or cavalry during the course of a hotly contested action. The artillery, of course, would vigorously contest any enemy attempt to overrun its position and capture the guns.

Although doctrine prescribed the ranges at which each type of ammunition was to be used, in practice the choice often was based on the officer's personal preference, and there was considerable variation. During the Battle of Williamsburg (Virginia, May 5, 1862), for example, seeing the rebels approaching in the distance, Capt. Charles C. Wheeler ordered Battery E of the New York Light Artillery to fire case shot when the attackers had closed to 300 yards. Nonplussed, the Confederates continued to advance, and Wheeler had his artillerymen switch to canister. In contrast, Capt. Andrew Cowan, who commanded a battery from the same organization at Gettysburg, chose to start firing canister only when rebel skirmishers had approached to within 200 yards.

In an emergency the defending artillerymen set aside formal procedure and utilized any available means to beat back a hotly pressed attack. The Union artillerist Daniel Webster of the First

Wisconsin Battery tells us how during an engagement at Tazewell, Tennessee (August 3, 1862), his battery suddenly came under frontal assault. Despite the fact that the oncoming rebel infantry was clothed in blue Union uniforms, the manner in which the officers among the advancing troops issued their orders quickly dispelled any doubts about their political allegiance. Webster ordered that the shell already loaded in his gun be removed and replaced with canister. The crew, uncertain whether this would be enough to produce the desired effect, augmented the deadly load with parts of broken carriages that were lying about, thus creating an impromptu variety of "double charge."

Whether because of the unavailability of canister or because of choice, the defending battery occasionally would continue to fire shell even as the attackers approached closer ranges. In theory shell was equally effective at any range. The problem at closer ranges of course was to set the fuse so that it would explode just before the projectile reached the desired range. This was a real problem, especially during the early stages of the war, when many of the shells came with preset, unadjustable fuses. Nevertheless, a Union battery at Shiloh, dangerously threatened by Breckenridge's men, extemporized 1-second fuses. Their fire kept low to the ground, and their fire proved deadly. The attacking rebel infantry was ordered to fall down and load and fire in this prostrate position. Nevertheless, the fire from the Union battery proved so accurate that many of the attackers were rendered *hors de combat*.

Although official doctrine required artillery to be protected by infantry or cavalry supports, these protective measures were largely ignored on the battlefield. The most common precaution taken to support an artillery battery was simply to place a battalion of infantry on either flank. Occasionally, infantry was placed between the individual guns. John Urban, a Union infantryman, tells of just such an occurrence during the Battle of New Market Cross-Roads (Seven Days' Battles, June 30, 1862). The First Regiment Pennsylvania Reserves, with which Urban served, initially withheld its fire as the artillery pummeled the Confederate infantry in its front. Finally, the regiment was ordered to fire. Crowding between the guns, the men immediately directed a lively fire at the common enemy. The Confederate forces vainly struggled to take the position with desperate frontal assaults for almost 2 hours, but the "slaughter was horrible in the extreme." Each time, the Confederates managed to advance to within forty to fifty "steps," pushing forward over their fallen comrades and making a heroic effort to remain oblivious to the carnage surrounding them. The Union infantrymen were firing so quickly that their rifle barrels started to heat up and their hands began to blister. Despite these efforts the enemy kept advancing, and for a moment it appeared that the defenders would be overrun. But just at this crisis point, the Confederates succumbed to the beating inflicted by both infantry and artillery and broke, leaving behind the dead, the dying, and those desperately struggling to survive.

It was at this point that fortune seemed to be smile on the Confederate cause. In spite of Captain Kern's frantic efforts to resupply his battery, the Union artillery finally ran out of ammunition, and this officer had to order his guns to withdraw out of the line. It was quite natural that the Confederates confused this tactical withdrawal with a general retreat, so they redoubled their efforts to overrun the position. The defending infantry itself had sustained substantial losses, and the situation now appeared desperate. Col. R. Biddle Roberts, the regimental commander, redressed his thinning and broken ranks. Sure of impending victory, the attackers came on one last time with a loud cheer. Roberts forbade his men to fire, and yelling, "First Regiment, forward, charge bayonets!" ordered his men forward. After one loud preparatory yell, they advanced without firing a shot. Astounded by this unexpected move, the enemy completely broke. In a textbook move of which even Frederick the Great would have approved, the Union infantrymen stopped their pursuit and delivered a murderous fire into their enemies' backs. This, incidentally, was the most murderous of all small arms fire. The victorious infantrymen, no longer threatened, were totally free to aim properly and could "take much cooler aim at a man's back than at his breast."

Even the presence of flanking support, however, did not guarantee a battery's safety, as demonstrated by the fate of the Eleventh Ohio Battery during the Battle of Iuka (Mississippi, September 19, 1862.) Suddenly faced with a much larger Confederate force, which threatened to fall upon the remainder of Rosecrans's force still in column of route, the battery and three infantry regiments attempted to hold off a combined infantry and artillery force four to five times its size. First firing shell, the battery soon switched to double canister, which inflicted horrendous casualties on the advancing Confederate masses, actually three battalions, each in line, two ranks deep. Repulsed, the Confederates rallied and returned to the attack. The inexperienced men of the Forty-eighth Indiana Infantry regiment recoiled, exposing the battery's left flank. The Fifth Iowa Infantry on its right repeatedly drove off the attackers with several bayonet charges, while the battery continued its carnage. Eventually, even the brave men of the Fifth Iowa were driven back, leaving both flanks of the battery now exposed. Still, the cannoneers continued to fire quickly and inflicted staggering casualties on those brave enough to continue the frontal assault. Hand-to-hand combat intermittently broke out as the gunners beat back the first four assaults.

Overpowered, completely outnumbered, the guns were finally captured during the next Confederate charge. The result was the highest percentage of casualties taken by a light battery at any time during the war. Out of the battery's original ninety-seven men and five officers, eighteen were killed, thirty-nine were wounded, many of whom died as a result of their wounds, and two men were taken prisoner. These statistics include the drivers and those stationed with the ammunition in the caissons. The gunners along the front line suffered an even higher rate of casualties, 46 out of 54 killed or wounded; some of these men had been bayoneted at their guns.

Although an artillery commander might have to deploy his battery without being able to count on adequate infantry or cavalry support, a competent officer would try to take advantage of the available terrain. Sometimes, though, an artillery battery might receive unexpected aid from neighboring batteries, which, seeing the former's plight, might redirect their fire upon the common foe and thus create a withering concentric fire.

This happened to Battery B, Fourth U.S. Artillery, near the close of the second day of fighting at Gettysburg. Just as the sun began to set and the artillerymen—then positioned near Cemetery Hill—thought they had escaped combat that day, they espied a long rebel line bearing down upon the XI Corps's position. Wiedrich's and Rickett's batteries occupied lower ground in front of Battery B. The two lower batteries opened with canister just about the same time the infantry unleashed a deadly volley, sounding like "one solid crash, like a million trees falling at once." But it was to little avail. Despite this tremendous firepower, the rebel forces continued to advance and eventually succeeded in pushing back both the infantry and the advanced batteries.

Battery B was attached was slightly to the left and rear of all this action. Apparently, it had been positioned to guard against the possibility of rebel forces issuing out of Gettysburg, the direction the battery was originally facing. With no threat posed in his front, the battery commander ordered the guns to turn 45 degrees toward the right to bring additional pressure against the advancing rebels and restore the crumbling position on this side. The gunners had to wait a few moments before the Union troops (Von Gilsa's Brigade) could disengage from the Confederate attackers.

Two other Union batteries, those of Reynolds and Stevens, positioned 200 yards and 400 yards, respectively, to the right of Battery B, now opened on the enemy roughly at the same time. What followed, though a trivial affair compared to the bloody fighting elsewhere on the battlefield, produced 10 minutes of artillery fireworks. The enemy, two brigades strong, continued its advance in two columns each of regimental frontage. The battery commander ordered the gunners to "Fire by piece; fire by will"—in other words, for the guns to fire individually as soon as each was loaded and aimed at its target.

For a few minutes the issue swayed in the balance. Von Gilsa's brigade broke, exposing Ames's brigade to a flank attack. The column on the right headed straight towards Battery B. However, the terrain the column had to traverse proved to be less than accommodating. The men on the left of the column were in an open pasture, but those on the right were partially sheltered by a small ravine running diagonally toward the Union battery and a stone wall that extended beyond the road at the west base of the hill. Completely exposed, the Confederates in open pasture on their left were quickly disordered by the merciless canister and started to waver. Those on the right, the Louisiana Tigers, rushed up the ravine, jumped over the stone wall, and charged the battery with the ferocious rebel yell. These troops managed to approach to within between 50 to 100 yards of the battery. August Buell, in the history of this battery penned some years after the war, opined that the gunners owed their survival to the Confederate forces' refusal to stop to deliver a devastating volley:

> If they had fired a volley at us then there is little doubt that the remnant of our poor ole Battery would have been wiped out; but for some reason they came on with cold steel alone. It may be imagined that we gave them the best we had, but artillery fire does not have its best effect upon troops coming straight on, and it is plain that we could not have stopped them with our four guns unaided.

Fortunately, it was exactly at this point that Battery B received much-needed succor in the form of Stevens's guns, positioned on its right. Changing its facing to the right, the resulting echelon formation managed to enfilade the advancing Confederates, while Battery B continued to spew out deadly canister directly to its front. The combined fire very quickly proved too much for the attackers, who now broke and fled back to the stone wall and ravine over which they had come. The Confederate officer managed to rally many of the men here, as a sporadic fire erupted. This proved short-lived, however. Within minutes a Union infantry brigade swept past to the right of Battery B and charged the rebel's position behind the wall and ravine. Pushing back the enemy, this brigade succeeded in retaking Wiedrich's and Rickett's guns, thus ending the fighting on the second day.

FILLING IN FOR CASUALTIES

Although some officers frowned upon counterbattery fire and a number of general orders proscribed the practice, during a lengthy, hard-fought engagement, artillery batteries themselves frequently came under enemy artillery fire. The sound of shot and shell would be heard whizzing around their position, and sometimes even the thud of shell fragments hitting the muzzle or gun carriage were heard. Artillerymen were to ignore such threats and go on with their business. Throughout history a number of observers have commented upon the artillerymen's sangfroid in the face of hostile artillery. Whether this resulted from the gunners' feeling that they were partially sheltered by their guns, or simply because they were more completely preoccupied with the mechanical routine required to reload their weapons, is uncertain.

They did not, however, exhibit the same insouciance when subjected to small arms fire. In his memoirs Colonel Scribner, who commanded the Thirty-eighth Indiana Volunteers, could not help commenting upon the artillerymen's sensitivity to musket fire:

> Cannon against cannon they appear to delight in; they seemed to feel complimented when the enemy turns his guns upon them; but a musket-ball they despise, and when they begin to hiss about them or strike their guns with a sound like a spat or a splash, they begin to grumble, and think they are not properly supported.

If the fire became too hot and the position untenable, before the battery retired outright, its commanding officer might first try to move it a small distance laterally. The idea was to move into the new position, resight the guns, and get off a few rounds before the opposing battery could discover the new position and acquire the new range. The Washington Artillery during the "battle" of Blackburn's Ford (July 18, 1861, preliminary to First Bull Run), facing some Union "long ranged guns," in this manner managed to extricate itself several times from a withering fire and was ultimately able to silence its adversary. Of course, this evasive tactic was only possible when a battery was firing at long-range targets that did not pose an immediate threat. A battery that found itself attacked frontally by enemy infantry while simultaneously under artillery fire had to either endure the hail of enemy projectiles or retire from the position entirely. The proximity of enemy infantry made any finessing of its position impossible.

If it was a chance encounter and the artillery had been forced to unlimber in open terrain, the gun crew would have to endure the punishment as long as their officers were determined to continue the fight or hold the position. Frequently, when the army was on the defensive and occupied a position for some time, the artillery was placed in prepared positions, where a number of precautionary steps were taken to shelter the artillerymen. This could be as elaborate as carefully constructed earthworks and embrasures or as simple as jury-rigged sandbags. A survivor of the Nineteenth Massachusetts Volunteers would recall an incident during the 1862 Peninsular Campaign in which rebel gunners threatened by Union artillery, who were then making their first appearance, protected themselves with particular ingenuity:

> The manner in which the rebels erected a sand bag battery was watched with interest. They would run out of their entrenchements with an empty bag. One would hold the bag and two others would drop sand into it with a shovel, working as fast as they could until they saw the flash of Hazard's guns. Then they would scoot back under cover again. Shot after shot would strike the ground where they had been at work. As soon as the shells struck they would dash out again, grab a bag, if filled, and drag it under cover, keeping up the labors in this way between flashes of the Union guns.

In a hard-fought engagement, a battery probably would start to suffer casualties despite precautions. When this happened, some of artillerymen manning the piece had to perform more than one function. Edward Moore, who served as an artillerymen in Stonewall Jackson's command, recalled that at Malvern Hill his battery had suffered so many casualties that he had to assume three different functions while loading and firing his assigned artillery piece (these of Nos. 7, 5, and 2). This continued until he was able to impress a staff lieutenant into service. Many artillery batteries were even harder pressed at Antietam. A number of infantrymen from the Iron Brigade had to assist Campbell's Battery (Battery B of the Fourth U.S.) during its repulse of Hood's counterattack. Ordered to fire double shot, the inexperienced infantrymen simply rammed home two complete canister charges down the barrel and nonchalantly fired away repeatedly. Unaware that they were first supposed to detach the propelling charge of the second canister, they thought that the violent bucking of the piece was a normal part of artillery experience. Fortunately, despite the rough use the piece remained operable throughout the engagement.

A captured enemy gun was always considered a prize worth the casualties suffered taking it. The temporarily victorious side would make every effort to retain possession of captured artillery, and the seesaw struggle over such a piece often resulted in the bitterest fighting. The regimental history of the Nineteenth Massachusetts tells of such a fight on May 12, 1864, at Spotsylvania. Spotting several abandoned Confederate guns just in front of their lines, Captain Hale of Gen. Max Weber's staff called to the mob of Union infantrymen to organize for their possession and defense. The men rushed out and dragged the pieces back. Turning them around, they began to fire the artillery at their former owners. Lacking normal projectiles, the infantrymen loaded the weapons with whatever was readily at hand: ammunition from other caliber pieces, old musket barrels—in fact, whatever debris was available. The memoirist recalling the event had to concede that in retrospect the men firing the captured pieces were probably in as much potential danger as their intended targets.

In the thick of battle, with frequent change of fortunes, it was not always possible to retain possession of even the hardest earned of captured enemy artillery pieces. If there was any possibility of recapture, the captors would make every effort to render the captured artillery pieces inoperable for the remainder of the fight. Probably the two most common methods were either to *spike* the guns, to block the touchhole leading to the detonating charge, and to *dismount* the gun, to take off and destroy the wheels of the gun carriage. "Necessity is the mother of invention," as the age-old expression goes, and it is certainly not surprising to find infantry and cavalrymen resorting to a wide array of unlikely objects to spike the enemy's guns. The Eighth Kentucky Volunteers (Union), capturing several rebels after a futile dawn surprise attack (November 18th, 1862), found a rebel lieutenant with his pockets full of thin, cylindrical rat-tail files. Questioned, he explained that these were to be used to spike any Federal artillery that happened to be overrun.

Of course, if the captors were lucky and persistent enough, it was possible to unspike a gun and make it once again serviceable, so if there were an opportunity, those forced to abandon artillery would frequently take even greater measures to permanently disable these weapons. Driven into near-precipitous retreat when forced to retire from the Cumberland Gap (at the junction of Virginia, Kentucky, and Tennessee, September 17, 1862), the First Wisconsin Battery was forced to leave behind several 30-pounder Parrotts. To prevent the Confederates from being able to use these pieces, they were dismounted. Solid shot was then rammed down the barrels, and the trunnions were knocked off. As an even further precaution, the naked barrels were placed on blocks, and then men hammered away at the middle of the barrels with sledgehammers. Despite all these efforts to destroy the artillery pieces, the Union would later discover that the Confederates were able to repair them.

WHEN ATTACKED BY CAVALRY

As far back as the Napoleonic Wars, a number of formal techniques had been developed to allow cavalry to assault enemy batteries with the greatest chance of success while minimizing the number of casualties that were likely to be suffered. One of these methods was known as an attack *en herse*. In this technique the cavalry split up into two or three parts. Those advancing in the center, directly in front of the guns, were detached as mounted skirmishers. Their desultory fire gave the impression of a feint or haphazard attack and was designed to preoccupy the artillerymen without making them aware of their imminent danger. Meanwhile, the remainder of the attacking forces, as stealthily as possible, continued to advance in column, working their way to one or both flanks of the enemy battery. If the battery continued to fire at the skirmishers pestering them in front, the cavalry columns would rush in and overpower it. Even if the battery discovered the trap and began firing at the cavalry on its flanks, it would be difficult to fend off all three assaults simultaneously.

The *en herse* technique was fairly well known in the French and Prussian armies during the 1840s and '50s, although it is difficult to gage American artillerymen's familiarity with it prior to the Civil War. It is certain that some Union officers were familiar with the *en herse* technique by early 1862, since this was essentially the method that General Buell recommended in his April 15 instructions after the Battle of Shiloh. An infantry regiment required to attack an enemy battery was to detach its flank companies, which would then advance straight ahead as skirmishers. The remaining companies would advance in two groups, on either flank of the skirmishers, in a column by division at half distance. The skirmishers meanwhile would attempt to cut down the gunners with a carefully aimed, deliberate fire. Buell believed that usually the skirmisher fire would be sufficient to drive the gunners from their pieces. However, this failing, the two columns were to rush around the flanks of the skirmishers, deploy, and deliver a deadly cross fire at the enemy artillerymen. If the enemy proved obstinate, the columns were then to rush in with lowered bayonets. Whenever this technique was used, it was important to have another regiment present that could be quickly brought in as support as soon as the enemy battery had been captured.

Regardless of what Federal and Confederate cavalrymen did or did not know about accepted European anti-artillery doctrine, there is ample evidence that by the summer of 1863, if not sooner, Federal cavalry had developed a very similar tactic when attacking an unsupported Confederate battery. George Neese, who served with Chew's Battery (Ashby Horse Artillery), at that point in Stuart's Cavalry Division, was subjected to several Federal cavalry attacks during 1863. One such case occurred while Chew's Battery was posted on the Harpers Ferry Pike a mile below Charlestown, Virginia (July 15, 1863). The Confederate battery had hardly unlimbered, before the Federals began to advance. The frontal assault was delivered by a line of dismounted sharpshooters who began a lively fire with long-range rifles for about 10 minutes. Neese, who commanded one of the rifled guns in the battery, explains that fire was withheld despite the annoyance toward their front because about a mile off, the remainder of the cavalry was forming up in preparation to charge the battery. Neese took matters in his own hand and, as it turned out, broke up the show. When attacked by charging cavalry, artillerists usually aimed at the horses' lower legs, and from an account of another engagement, we know Chew's men were familiar with the technique. Although Neese does not say where the artillerymen aimed in this case, we are told that the first round struck the front of the column squarely. This single round stymied the entire attack; the troopers in the Federal column dispersed, while the line of skirmishers ceased firing and began to retire.

A second effort on the part of Federal cavalry met with greater success. Positioned below Culpepper Court House on September 13, 1863, Chew's Battery found itself once again facing a force of Federal mounted and dismounted cavalry. Observing a body of cavalry moving toward their right, the Confederate battery opened up on this threat to their flank. Soon, however, a line of dismounted skirmishers, followed by a mounted formation, was seen advancing toward its front. The battery changed targets and began to fire canister rapidly at the dismounted skirmishers. Faced with this double threat, the Confederates quickly realized that their position was untenable and after six rounds decided to limber up and unceremoniously retire at the double.

DIFFERENT USES OF RIFLED AND SMOOTHBORE ARTILLERY

Most batteries in the field would inevitably find themselves called upon to employ a wide range of artillery tactics during the course of a campaign. In one engagement accurate, long-range fire might be required, such as when shelling a fixed, immovable target, like field or permanent fortifications. The very next action might see the same battery frantically unloading canister in a desperate bid to drive off a determined infantry assault. When pressed by urgent situations on the battlefield, artillery officers would be forced to utilize whatever artillery was available or in the most suitable location, regardless of the task to be performed.

Artillerymen soon discovered, however, that there were other differences with the motley collection of ordnance hurriedly collected together than simply maximum effective range and weight of shell that was hurled at the enemy. When a battery contained different types of ordnance or when there was more than one battery available, artillery officers at least occasionally applied the most appropriate weapon for a task. Possessing both a longer and a more accurate trajectory, rifled artillery was used for long-range shelling whenever possible, while the smoothbore was more suitable for close-quarters work. Rifled artillery took longer to reload and therefore had a lower rate of fire than smoothbore artillery. Smoothbore guns could be loaded more quickly, which was an important attribute when threatened by charging infantry or cavalry, and a higher rate of fire increased one's chance of survival. This meant that although rifled batteries or sections were supplied with canister and certainly utilized this type of projectile when necessary, whenever a choice was possible, smoothbore weapons were preferred for in-close fighting.

END OF THE WAR

Two unusually detailed sets of official instructions were circulated among Union artillery officers in the Eastern theater during the opening months of 1864. Unlike earlier in the war, these were not naïve regurgitations of oft-repeated precepts taken from military scientific works but reflected the experience of 3 years of hard-fought campaigning. Not only do these instructions provide details of how artillery practices evolved during the Civil War; they also suggest the types of problems artillerymen encountered during actual combat and common mistakes.

The first of these instructions was issued by Brig. Gen. Henry J. Hunt, chief of artillery for the Army of the Potomac. As far as general principles were concerned, Hunt's instructions reaffirmed traditional tactical principles, as found on the pages of Roberts's and Gibbon's works. Like both former West Point instructors, Hunt valued a "concentration of fire," urging artillerymen to converge their fire upon "important points." Whenever possible they were to enfilade targets with an "oblique fire." Although moderately elevated ground was to be exploited, Hunt repeated the old dictum that artillery should never be placed on steep inclinations, since a flat trajectory passing a few feet over the ground was far more preferable to a plunging fire. Like his predecessors, Hunt recommended the use of infantry and cavalry supports placed on either flank to help defend an artillery position, rather than directly behind or among the guns. And, following in the British tradition, Hunt urged his artillerymen to fight "to the last."

However, a majority of Hunt's instructions focused on a level of detail that went beyond that generally covered by peacetime authors, attempting to address problems encountered during actual field operations. In fact, the appearance of both sets of detailed artillery instructions suggests that Union military authorities were aware of a number of endemic malpractices, which they finally decided to address systematically. The single greatest problem was wastage and misuse of ammunition. All too often Union gunners began firing simply because the enemy had approached to within maximum range, rather than waiting until the latter was within an effective range, where "at least one-quarter of the shots are hits." An equally significant problem was that many gunners frequently utilized inappropriate projectiles for the targets at which they fired. Shrapnel and percussion cap shells had captured everyone's imagination, and solid shot, at least unconsciously, was regarded by a majority of artillerymen as passé. Seeing an enemy cavalry column advancing at a quick trot 800 yards away, many artillerymen would cut off the appropriate amount of fuse, and a few seconds later a shell would be rushing toward its mark. Suspecting that a wooded area sheltered lurking rebels, artillery officers would bombard the area with shrapnel or shell.

There was also an excessive reliance upon canister. Too frequently, artillery officers would automatically switch to canister as soon as the enemy had approached to within its theoretical maximum range, rather than waiting until it could be used with greater effect. It was not uncommon for a battery to run out of canister and shell before it had even touched its supply of solid shot. The Union gunners manning 12-pounder Napoleons offer a case in point. Most Union batteries were allocated eight shrapnel shells per gun. Anticipating that shrapnel might be useful when the pieces were used as howitzers, 12-pounder Napoleons had their allotment increased to twelve shrapnel shells per piece. However, this was done with the understanding that generally four of these shrapnel shells would be fired as solid shot, without preset fuses, unless circumstances absolutely dictated otherwise. In practice, this forbearance never occurred, and invariably all twelve were used as shrapnel.

Hunt railed against the excessive use of shell and shrapnel and reminded artillerists handling rifled guns that shrapnel shell minus the fuse was as effective as solid shot. Firing deep into the woods was to be strictly avoided, although it was fine to fire canister into the outskirts of woods inhabited by skirmishers or sharpshooters. Pointing out that shrapnel was the "most effective and powerful of projectiles if well used, it is also the most harmless and contemptible if used badly," Hunt reminded artillery officers that it was to be used against fixed positions and slow-moving or stationary objects, such as bridges, crossroads, and wagon trains. It was almost always ineffective against quickly moving targets. Of course, in neither of these cases was shell or shrapnel appropriate. Correct procedure required instead that solid shot be fired at a distant cavalry column, while no type of fire should be directed at an unseen enemy in a woods.

There was also an almost irresistible temptation to fire at tactically irrelevant targets of opportunity, such as a group of aides-de-camp or a few skirmishers. It was not unheard of for a battery to expend 300 to 400 rounds during a skirmish, the amount of ammunition allocated for an entire campaign. Probably the greatest amount of unproductive expenditure of ammunition stemmed simply from the gunners' firing too quickly. During a general engagement many batteries were known to run out of ammunition after only a half hour, the batteries having fired on average one round per minute for each gun.

Hunt and Gen. William Farquhar Barry, in his own set of instructions 2 weeks later, emphasized the importance of accuracy of fire, rather than sheer volume of fire. Of the two, probably General Barry put it the most succinctly when he stressed:

> The firing in action should be deliberate—never more than will admit of accurate pointing. A few shots effectively thrown is better than a large number badly directed. The object in killing is to inspire terror so as to deter or drive off the enemy, and precision of fire and consequent certainty of execution is infinitely more important in effecting this than a great noise, rapid firing, and less proportional execution.

Hunt's tactical instructions meshed nicely with these observations. Gunners within the same battery were strongly advised not to fire at several different targets but were to focus on a single target. The true value of artillery lay not simply with the physical destruction it was able to achieve, but rather the psychological role it played in destroying the enemy's will to fight:

> It is not the number of killed and wounded that decides a battle, but the panic and demoralization of those who remain; and this panic and demoralization are much sooner created and spread by concentrating the artillery fire on successive points than by distributing it over a wide space. The general rule is that artillery should concentrate its fire upon that part of the enemy's force which, from its position, or from its character, it is the most desirable to overthrow.

Hunt's extensive orders also suggest that all too frequently, artillerymen would deploy their pieces behind friendly infantry some distance to the front. Hunt reminded his artillerymen that this was to be avoided for a number of reasons. Pieces of shell, the bags holding the propellant powder, and so on could maim, even kill, friendly troops. Even if this didn't happen, many of the troops would be demoralized. This artillery fire impeded the infantry advance, forcing them to stop temporarily and cutting up the ground that they had to traverse. When circumstances forced artillery to fire over their infantry, solid shot was the best choice, although in certain rare cases the artillerymen were authorized to use shells. Under no such circumstances were they to use canister or shrapnel.

Although Hunt urged artillerymen ordinarily to avoid counterbattery fire, they were to use it when forced by circumstances. When counterbattery fire became unavoidable, the battery should concentrate its fire against a single enemy piece. Once it was destroyed, the gunners should select and then fire at a second gun and so on until all ordnance within the opposing battery was out of action. The same concept was to be used when firing at enemy infantry or cavalry formations. Initially, fire was to be concentrated on a single unit, which was to be destroyed before moving on to the next target.

During the previous year the fighting increasingly had occurred in and near rough terrain, such as at Chancellorsville in the East and around Vicksburg and Chickamauga out West. Further, extemporaneous field fortifications were more frequently employed on both sides. Both circumstances compelled Hunt to discuss the impact of field fortifications and broken terrain on field tactics. Experience had shown that it was unwise to position artillery within rifle range of a wooded area not controlled by friendly troops. Increasingly, commanders strengthened the battle line by digging rifle pits, erecting abatis or wooden barricades, or by positioning troops behind stone walls. Whenever this occurred, the friendly artillery was not to be placed behind the line, as too often had proved to be the case. Instead, it was to be placed along the line, preferably in some advanced position, so as to take the enemy in flank as it approached during the final moments of the assault.

The artillery was not to be placed directly behind its own side's fieldworks. Instead, it was to exploit existing terrain. The best tactic, terrain permitting, was to place the pieces on the reverse side of a gentle slope, with the muzzle looking over the crest. When natural protection was unavailable, artillerymen were to hastily throw up earthen parapets and simultaneously sink the guns partially into the ground. To do this, the artillerymen would dig a trench about 1½ feet deep, the earth being thrown up in front of the artillery as protection from small arms fire. To protect the caissons in the rear, the artillerymen were to dig two small holes the width of the spade. These were arranged so that the caisson wheels were placed into these holes and the caisson sank into the ground up to the axles, thus lowering the profile offered to the enemy.

The second set of instructions, authored by Brigadier General Barry, inspector of artillery for the entire Union army, appeared on February 2 and was a nuts and bolts description of the various procedures required to maintain armament and ammunition, as well as the precautions that had to be taken to avoid dangerous accidents. Extremely detailed, Barry's instructions encompassed a wide range of what today might be termed "best practices," such as how to properly keep elevating screws clean, where to store various implements and tools, and the most effective method of airing out ammunition and projectiles in the magazines, to name but a few of the topics that were covered. Particularly interesting is Barry's injunction that everyone who entered the magazine was to wear special shoes or moccasins, if possible; otherwise, they were to walk in their stocking feet. Ordinary military shoes and boots had iron plates on the soles and generated sparks as one walked. Under no circumstances was anyone carrying a sword, pistol, or cane or wearing spurs to be admitted regardless of his rank! A sound precaution indeed, considering the potential effects of a single stray spark in a powder magazine.

Although for the most part eschewing tactical issues, General Barry felt compelled to remind artillery officers once again about the most appropriate use of each type of projectile and cautioned against the use of case shot and shell when firing at fast-moving targets. The inspector of artillery felt that a few words of advice about rifled artillery were in order. The sponges used to clean out the residue left after each firing had to be well saturated with oil. Also, coating the projectiles with a thin covering of grease had been found to increase accuracy. For similar reasons the artilleryman was enjoined to ram home carefully in order to make certain no space remained between the cartridge and the projectile after they had been loaded into the artillery piece.

The Parrott rifles, though effective, from the first had suffered from temperamental ammunition, which often forced Union artillerymen to devise a number of workarounds. Those operating Parrotts were to make certain that the brass ring or cup at the rear of the projectile was properly wedged and not clogged with sand or dirt. It was equally important to avoid large-grain powder but to use finer "mortar powder" instead.

Chapter 24

ARTILLERY DEVELOPMENTS
DURING THE WAR

L ong before the outbreak of the Civil War, the number of guns and personnel in each battery had been strictly prescribed by a set of instructions. A company was commanded by four to six officers, depending upon the number of pieces, and each gun was manned by between twenty and thirty artillerymen, NCOs, and artificers. Batteries had to be able to fire both shell and solid shot, so before the introduction of the light 12-pounders, each battery had to include one or two howitzers. The war-time footing of a battery in the U.S. Army was as follows:

Light or 6-pounder battery	Heavy or 12-pounder battery
4 6-pounder guns	4 12-pounder guns
2 12-pounder howitzers	2 24- or 32-pounder howitzers
6 caissons	6 caissons
1 forge	1 forge
1 battery wagon	1 battery wagon
4 horses per carriage	6 horses per carriage

Artillery in the United States Army was divided between heavy artillery—used for coastal defense and siege operations—and light or field artillery that was employed during a campaign. A distinction was also made between horse artillery and mounted artillery. The latter had been introduced by the Russians into central Europe during the Seven Years' War and was copied by Frederick the Great and then eventually by the rest of Europe. Traditionally, the artillerymen had walked beside the artillery teams as they moved onto the battlefields. This limited the artillery pace to that of the foot soldier, hence the name *foot* or *infantry artillery.* In the case of *horse artillery,* most of the artillerymen sat on the caissons or occasionally were mounted on their own horses. For greater speed horse artillery tended to have smaller artillery pieces than their foot or infantry counterparts and they could generally keep up with the cavalry. The U.S. mounted artillery was somewhat of a misnomer, since despite the implication of its name the artillerymen ordinarily walked beside their advancing pieces. In time of urgency, however, they rode on top of the caissons and accompanying wagons, hence the name.

The four artillery regiments in the United States Army were each supposed to include two mounted artillery companies, but only seven of these companies were organized. The remaining forty-one companies were equipped and served as infantry artillery. Faced with the threat of warfare, early in 1861 the Confederate authorities quickly established their own military organization. Authorization was given to raise a Corps of Artillery of forty artillery companies. Each company consisted of eighty men and NCOs commanded by four officers and was initially a little more than half the size of its Union counterpart. As soon as the actual fighting began in the East, it became obvious that the artillery arm was understrength. In August the corps's staff was increased to include one colonel, two lieutenant colonels, and twelve majors. A battery could contain as many as 150 men with the following organization:

Officers	**Men**
1 captain	1 sergeant-major or first sergeant
2 first lieutenants	1 quarter-master sergeant
2 second lieutenants	6 sergeants
	12 corporals
	2 artificers
	2 buglers
	1 guidon
	64–125 privates

At this point, a light battery in Confederate service generally consisted of six artillery pieces, although some had as many as eight, and others as few as four pieces. Each gun and its caisson were considered to be a *detachment,* and two detachments formed a *section.* Initially, most of the artillery pieces were obsolescent 6-pounder smoothbores,

which were quickly replaced by larger calibers and the 3–inch ordnance rifle as these became available later in the war. Batteries that
were fortunate also included two 12-pounder Napoleons, which took
over the traditional role of howitzers. In practice there was tremendous variation in the field.

PROBLEMS WITH DIVERSE MATERIAL

Although most regular Union artillery batteries enjoyed standard-
ized armament, the same certainly could not be said of the Confederate artillery or the Northern volunteer organizations quickly
thrown together during the first year of the war. The First Wisconsin
Battery of Light Artillery, for example, was initially equipped with
two 12-pounder Napoleons, two 6-pounder smoothbores, and two 12-
pounder howitzers. The Eleventh Ohio Battery, destined to play such
a gallant role at Iuka, Mississippi, had a similar organization, except
it had two James pattern rifled 6-pounders instead of the two 12-
pounder Napoleons. The ordnance carried by many Confederate batteries was even more eclectic. In 1861 Carter's battery consisted of
two bronze 8-pounders, one 12-pounder bronze howitzer, and a
3-inch iron rifle. At the First Battle of Bull Run, batteries of the
Washington Artillery were made up of six 6-pounders, four 12-
pounder howitzers, and three 6-pounder rifles, all bronze.

It is difficult to tell whether such eclecticism was the result of a conscious doctrine that each battery had be armed to meet a diversity of
challenges and needs or whether the founding officers simply scrambled to acquire whatever was locally available. One finds many Union
volunteer batteries organized into three sections, each with a different
class of armament: one section of relatively heavy pieces with striking
power, the second more mobile, the third consisting of howitzers.

Regardless of increased specificity of function, such diversity of
materiel made it more difficult to supply, service, and maintain the
pieces. Military authorities on both sides were aware of the problems
and attempted to introduce greater uniformity of armament, even if
only in the same battery. Their complacency driven away by the Bull
Run embarrassment, high-ranking Union artillery officers were the
first to comment about this problem. Brigadier General Barry, the
Army of the Potomac's chief of artillery during the summer of '62,

noted in an official report that only about a sixth of the volunteer artillery organizations brought their own horses and harnesses, and many of those that did were incompletely equipped. Barry estimated that only about 10% of the artillery was equipped for active service when they reported to the Army of the Potomac. These problems were compounded by the fact that that the volunteers' batteries' guns "were nearly all such peculiar calibers, to lack uniformity with the more modern and serviceable ordinance." Though of interest to a military antiquarian, it was obvious that most of this would be useless in action, and Barry was forced to withdraw many of these early volunteer units while they were gradually refitted with more suitable material. It is possible, however, that Barry's critical assessment was influenced by the regular versus volunteer rivalry.

Nevertheless, the problem was slow to disappear. As late as Vicksburg in '63, for example, the Union IX Corps artillery still sported a diverse assortment of ordnance. Its four constituent batteries were equipped with 20-pounder Parrotts, 12-pounder Napoleons, 10-pounder Parrotts, and 3-inch rifles, respectively. The situation was even worse for behind-the-line units, whose main purpose was to garrison important positions. When standardizing light artillery batteries in his military department, General Beauregard had to continue to countenance a wide assortment of materiel, but provided that a battery had no more than two different types of ordnance, in one of five acceptable configurations, it would do.

A number of batteries resisted the movement toward standardization, and some returned to a mix even after uniformity had been achieved. Though by late 1861 the First Wisconsin Battery, whose complement has been mentioned, had managed to replace its motley ordnance with six 20-pounder Parrotts, experience soon showed that a mix of ordnance was preferable to one single artillery type. On March 26, 1862, the battery finally settled on four 3-inch Rodman and two 10-pounder Parrotts for the center section. This, according to Lt. Daniel Webster, made for the "ideal field battery, light to handle, easy on stock and precise and effective."

Although standardization of ordnance and equipment was much less of a problem for batteries supplied by the regular United States army, simply maintaining the required personnel initially proved difficult for those regular army batteries that had been stationed in states that turned rebellious, the soldiers loyal to the Union having to flee. Other batteries lost men through the normal wear and tear of the as yet mild campaigning. Although at first local commanders resorted to stopgap solutions, it quickly became obvious that more systematic measures were needed. Reporting upon the state of the artillery around Washington after the Battle of Bull Run, Maj. Henry J. Hunt noted that the regiments made up of German emigrants, in particular, contained a high percentage of experienced artillerymen. Capt. A. von Morozowicz's company in the De Kalb Regiment (Forty-first New York Volunteers) was composed almost exclusively of old German artillery soldiers. Hunt recommended that these men, if necessary, could be transferred into artillery service.

The situation continued to worsen, and by the time McClellan reorganized the Army of the Potomac during the fall, many regular U.S. batteries were but mere skeletons. Writing to the secretary of war on October 1, McClellan suggested a wholesale transfer of volunteers into these organizations to make up this manpower deficiency. This advice was accepted, and many volunteer infantrymen soon found themselves serving with the regular artillery. The new men were referred to as "detached volunteers," while the original population in these batteries henceforth were known as "old regulars."

LACK OF CONCENTRATION OF ARTILLERY

The problem of inadequate materiel during the first year and a half of fighting was further compounded by organizational inefficiencies. Both sides employed an inadequate form of combined arms support. During the early stages of the war, artillery was invariably parceled out along the line. In order to provide immediate artillery support for close-in fighting, one artillery battery was attached to each infantry brigade, with which it would camp and march. In addition to whatever casualties were actually inflicted upon the enemy, friendly artillery always positively influenced the morale of nearby infantry. Seasoned artillerymen had long known that the roar of the artillery and the accompanying visual pyrotechnics was especially uplifting to raw, inexperienced troops in the volunteer regiments, who during the early stages of the war, made up the great majority of fighting force.

These considerations notwithstanding, this practice was in reality a waste of valuable artillery resources. There was a general shortage of artillery during the opening months of the war, so assigning artillery to individual infantry brigades meant there was little or none to place in reserve. During the summer of 1861, the artillery reserve of the Army of Northern Virginia, for example, consisted of only a few batteries under Col. (later Gen.) William N. Pendleton. This policy also limited the size of the artillery force that could be brought to bear against a target to the six or eight pieces that made up the individual battery. Even more than infantry, however, artillery derived its greatest effectiveness from the volume of fire that could be applied at a target at the same time, or as Gen. E. P. Alexander expressed the converse truth, "artillery fire loses effect if scattered." Battlefield experience would later show the utility of amassing several batteries to fire at a common enemy formation in a critical situation, either to help crush the defenders' will to stand or to repel a determined enemy assault. However, as long as the artillery was scattered along the entire front, this was not even an option for either the senior artillery officers or the commanding field officers.

ARTILLERY REORGANIZATION

When Maj. Gen. George McClellan took command of the Division of the Potomac on July 25, 1861, his artillery force was comprised of portions of nine batteries, or thirty artillery pieces. Recognizing the inadequacy of existing artillery resources Major Barry, chief of artillery of the Army of the Potomac, made a sweeping set of recommendations to McClellan. The amount of artillery available to each fighting force had to be drastically increased. Sufficient artillery had to be acquired so that there would be an average of two and a half artillery pieces for every thousand infantry- and cavalrymen. This was an ambitious target. European armies during the 1756 to 1815 period rarely were able to achieve a ratio of three guns per thousand troops in the field, and at Waterloo opposing armies only had one gun to every 408 soldiers.

Barry recommended that one third of the artillery be Parrott rifled pieces, while most of the remainder should be the 1857 model smoothbore gun howitzer, also known as the 12-pounder Napoleon. The only exceptions were to be a few howitzers reserved for special service. Whenever possible batteries would have six guns and never fewer than four. Barry recommended that henceforth all the ordnance within the same battery be of the same type and caliber and each gun be supplied with 400 rounds.

Probably the most significant of Barry's recommendations, however, was to attach several field batteries to a division rather than to individual brigades. One battery of regular artillery commanded by a captain from the U.S. Army was to form the nucleus for the remaining volunteer batteries. Feeling that an army artillery reserve was essential, Barry also recommended that a hundred guns plus "sufficient number of light 'mounted batteries' " be set aside as the reserve, as well as the formation of a fifty-piece siege train.

Whether or not it was the result of Barry's influence with McClellan, many of these recommendations were in fact adopted soon after the reorganization of the infantry into divisions during the winter of 1861–62. The divisional system of artillery replaced the previous brigade system, and three or four batteries were assigned to a division. As recommended, the senior officer of the regular battery assumed the role of acting chief of artillery for the division.

The creation of McClellan's 100,000-man Army of the Potomac in the spring of 1862 placed an extraordinary burden on the ordnance department and forced Union military planners to adopt a more systematic approach to artillery organization. In May 1862 all artillery within a corps was grouped into an artillery brigade headed by the corps chief of artillery. In theory the artillery was to be attached to the corps headquarters and was to function as a reserve to army headquarters. Although this organization had its own commander, the constituent batteries continued to operate somewhat independently and, when necessary, were temporarily assigned to divisions and even individual brigades in that corps.

A search through the *Official Records* shows that both sides used the notion of an artillery brigade before it was officially adopted by the Union Army of the Potomac. Although Confederate Gen. J. C. Pemberton had command of an artillery brigade in July 1861, this was a paper organization with a purely logistical reason for being. Its constituent batteries never fought together as a tactical unit and were distributed to a number of forces dispersed around Virginia. The next mention in the *Official Records* is a March 1862 return for Maj. Gen. Sterling Price's First Division of Army of the West, which lists the eleven batteries and the cavalry unit in his "artillery brigade." Maj. Gen. Earl Van Dorn's March 17 instructions called for Price's First Division to be completely ready to march on March 25. Its artillery brigade was to move out the 26th, while the rest Price's force was to start on the 27th and 28th. This grouping was still only an administrative function and had no tactical relevance on the battlefield.

The Union forces facing the Army of the Tennessee appear to have quickly adopted this organizational innovation, and by April 30 Maj. Gen. John Pope's Army of the Mississippi contained an artillery brigade, which was made up three light artillery batteries. Given the remoteness of the Confederate Army of the West, it is improbable that its practices influenced the adoption of an artillery brigade by the Army of the Potomac a few weeks later. However, future research in this area may show that these developments might have been the result of commonly shared ideas that emerged among top-level Union and Confederate military authorities in both theaters of operations.

In any case, the artillery brigade was still a logistical unit intended to facilitate supplies and movement and as yet had no tactical significance on the battlefield. In practice this reorganization still did not result in the intended artillery concentrations, since most batteries continued to be assigned to divisions and sometimes even individual brigades. Little effort was made to keep batteries from the same artillery regiment together; in fact, this practice was actively discouraged.

The Confederates were slower to appreciate the need for artillery reform, and their artillery remained dispersed among the infantry brigades when large-scale fighting finally erupted in the East in June 1862. Although at this point the Confederate military machine suffered from several organizational deficiencies, such as the lack of a corps-level organization and the lack of properly trained staff officers, after the war E. P. Alexander felt that the inability to concentrate artillery was the single most important organizational inadequacy. Just how much a disadvantage this could be became evident during the Seven Days' Battle, especially on June 31, when Kirby's and Brady's batteries were able to wreak havoc on the Confederate assaults with close-range canister without once being fired upon by their enemy counterparts.

The problem could no longer be ignored by the rebels, and four to six batteries were now grouped together to form artillery battalions. Five artillery battalions were assigned to the newly formed Confederate corps, one to each of the three divisions, while two artillery battalions were kept as a reserve under the direct control of the corps's chief of artillery. The reorganization took a few months to complete in practice. While preparing for what would become known as the Second Manassas Campaign, nine of the eleven batteries in Longstreet's corps were still assigned directly to infantry brigades, and the artillery reorganization in this corps was still in progress at the time of Antietam, 2 months later.

The hard-fought Peninsula Campaign and the disappointments of the Seven Days' Battles to both sides did much to highlight the tactical poverty of the original artillery organization in both armies. Fall 1862 saw both sides beginning to experiment with more sophisticated artillery organizations.

POPULARITY OF THE 12-POUNDER NAPOLEON

Although the appearance of rifled artillery weapons, such as the Parrott and the 3-inch ordnance rifled guns, spelled doom for most of the old smoothbore pieces, there was one smoothbore that would actually increase its presence on the battlefield as the Civil War progressed. This of course was the 12-pounder Napoleon. Prior to the battle of Bull Run, the Napoleons had accounted for less than 10% of the army's artillery stock. In fact, as Maj. Henry J. Hunt rushed the men and equipment of Battery M, Second Artillery, out of Texas, he would note in an official memo that his battery was the only unit equipped with the new "light 12-pounders." The battery commander, incidentally, thought very highly of the new type of ordnance. In his April 10 memo to Capt. David E. Twiggs, his appraisal of the new weapon probably summed up opinion at the time:

> "Their firing is very accurate, and with equal mobility they
> have much greater power than the 6-pounder. Each is perfectly
> adapted to the use of all the projectiles known in the service—
> shot, shell, spherical case, and canister. The fire of one portion

of the battery is therefore never sacrificed to that of another, as so often happens in ordinary batteries, where the fire of the gun must often be sacrificed to that of the howitzer, and *vice versa.*

When McClellan took command of the Division of the Potomac on July 25, 1861, a few days after the disaster at Bull Run, he inherited a meager artillery accompaniment of thirty pieces, many of which were of either unusual or unserviceable calibers. One of his top priorities, therefore, was to strengthen the artillery establishment. Acquiescing to the opinion of the more experienced officers, he ordered that one third of the batteries should be equipped with 12-pounder Napoleons. This turned out to be a wise decision. This smoothbore proved to be surprisingly popular. Responding to Gen. W. Ripley's demand for an inventory of all weapons then in the possession of the Army of the Potomac, in October 1862 Lt. D. W. Flagler, the army's assistant ordnance officer, admitted that of the 321 artillery pieces, 126 of these were Napoleons. This was more than any other single type of ordnance and represented 39% of the available artillery pieces in the army.

Artillery—Division of the Potomac (July 1861)

4	12-pounder Napoleons
16	10-pounder Parrott rifle guns
10	James 13-pounder rifle guns
14	6-pounder guns
6	12-pounder howitzers
2	20-pounder Parrott rifle guns
1	30-pounder Parrott rifle guns
2	Dahlgren boat howitzers

Artillery—Army of the Potomac (October 11, 1862)

126	12-pounder Napoleons
64	10-pounder Parrotts
20	20-pounder Parrotts
98	3–inch ordnance guns
6	32-pounders
2	12-pounder howitzers
5	30-pounder Parrotts

Artillery—Army of Northern Virginia (Summer 1863)

107	12-pounder Napoleons
103	3-inch ordnance guns
30	12-pounder howitzers
4	6-inch Whitworths

This certainly did not represent the high point of the 12-pounder Napoleon's popularity. In fact, there are incidents of Union artillery batteries exchanging their rifled field pieces for smoothbore artillery at least as late as spring 1863. While preparing for the eventuality of a summer campaign, the gunners of Battery B of the First Regiment of Rhode Island Light Artillery, for example, eagerly exchanged their 10-pounder Parrotts for six brass Napoleons at Harrison Landing early that year. Battery B of the New Jersey Light Artillery fired out all six of its 10-pound Parrotts during the Battle of Gettysburg, which were then also replaced by six Napoleons. Not counting the VI Corps's artillery, which is impossible to identify with certainty, the Union amassed no fewer than 280 artillery pieces at Gettysburg (July 1–3, 1863). Of these at least 122 were Napoleons, that is, 43.6% of its total artillery resources. This trend certainly was not confined to the North, and the Napoleon gun accounted for 43.9% of the artillery in the Army of Northern Virginia. Some writers believe this trend only continued as the war went on and that Napoleons accounted for nearly 50% of all artillery by 1865.

Recognition of these figures has lead some Civil War historians, such as Curt Johnson, to dub the Napoleon as the most popular variety of all Civil War artillery. Others have argued that this weapon was more popular among the Confederates than among Union artillerymen. And in the latter case, Maj. Gen. Henry J. Hunt, chief of artillery for the Army of the Potomac, would write that the Napoleon was more popular among the older, veteran officers than among the younger generation, who tended to prefer rifled artillery.

This trend probably strikes most modern readers as curious, since it is only natural to expect the more accurate, longer-range weapons to quickly and irrevocably supplant older, supposedly less effective technology. It is all too easy, therefore, to ascribe the popularity of Napoleons to an all-too-common aversion to change, which causes many to cling to existing tools and practices even after superior alternatives have become available.

The continued reliance upon the smoothbore Napoleon, however, was thoroughly grounded in pragmatic considerations, rather than symptomatic of widespread resistance to change. This has in fact been long recognized by many Civil War historians, who have pointed to the weapon's greater canister capabilities. Some have also cited Lee's observation about its utility in the broken, wooded terrain that was so frequently encountered:

> Nothing surpasses . . . the impression of 12 pound smoothbores which approaches to within 400–600 paces of the enemy and exercises its influence not only with shell and grape shot, but also with the moral effect of its thundering proximity. In such moments rifled artillery, the advantages of which in open country is fully appreciated, cannot replace the smoothbore."

These were only a few of the reasons for the longevity of the 12-pounder Napoleon, however. Although the new rifled artillery in theory offered its gunners both greater range and greater accuracy, the rush to produce these new weapons only multiplied the number of teething problems that always accompany the introduction of any new technology. One of the most pervasive problems with most rifled artillery during the Civil War stemmed from the gun carriages. Bowing to pressures of time and available resources, many of the new weapons were expeditiously mounted on existing carriages that had been designed many years earlier for conventional smoothbore artillery. Both the 10-pounder Parrott and the 3-inch ordnance rifle, for example, were set atop the standard 6-pounder field carriage, while the 20-pounder and 30-pounder Parrotts were mounted on 12-pounder and 18-pounder field carriages, respectively. This was even true in the case of some of the heavier ordnance that was arriving on the scene. The 100-pounder Parrot army gun utilized either the 8-inch Columbiad or 10-inch ordnance carriage.

The rule of thumb now became to take the bore caliber of the rifled weapon and use the carriage for the smoothbore of similar caliber. The problem of course is that the rifled artillery required long cylindrical projectiles that typically weighed about three times as much as the ammunition used by the same caliber smoothbore. Unfortunately, this significantly reduced the ratio of the weight of the combined gun and carriage compared to the projectile. It had long been the custom to design an artillery piece and its equipage so that there was a 100-to-1 ratio between the weight of the piece and the projectile it fired. Similarly, the ideal ratio of the weight of the piece and carriage to the projectile was 300 to 1.

The result was that the lighter pieces recoiled very much more than their predecessors. During trials conducted at the Washington Arsenal, Norman Wiard, himself a notable artillery inventor whose own weapons saw limited action during the war, noticed that it was not uncommon for some of the 12- and 24-pounder James guns then being tested to recoil between 20 and 27 feet. Not only did this mean that the gunners had to work much harder to reposition the artillery piece, but it simultaneously decreased the weapon's accuracy. It also dramatically increased the strain on the wheels, axles, and under-carriage. An artillery piece recoils so quickly that the wheels do not turn; the piece skids backwards, which means that the wheels and axles have to absorb much of the force of the recoil. Not surprisingly, these light carriages suffered more than their share of casualties. Mr. Watson, the assistant secretary of war, admitted in a conversation with Wiard that the battle reports he received were filled with mentions of broken carriages, and after the Second Battle of Bull Run, Wiard noticed about thirty abandoned 3-inch ordnance or 10-pounder Parrotts, all with broken wheels or bent axles.

AGGRESSIVE USE OF ARTILLERY

The aggressive use of artillery, where a battery or several pieces operated independently, and slightly in advance, of the infantry, had become part of accepted doctrine since the Mexican-American War. At Palo Alto (May 8, 1846), Col. James Duncun, with the adroit maneuvering of his two artillery pieces, was able to completely thwart a Mexican attempt to turn the American left flank. Maneuvered close to the enemy infantry and unlimbered, this artillery confused and then repulsed the Mexican infantry through a well-directed fire. The next day at Resaca de la Palma, S. G. Ridgeley's battery advanced in front of the supporting infantry during each lull in enemy small arms fire and delivered canister. Gen. Persifor F. Smith employed similar aggressive artillery tactics at Contreras (August 20, 1847). John B. Magruder's Battery was ordered to a rock ledge in front of the line, and only later was it supported by infantry which advanced to its proximity.

Noting these accomplishments in his *Artillerist's Manual*, John Gibbon felt that occasionally, the artillery officer was justified in advancing his battery to within 300 paces of the enemy line, where he would attempt to overwhelm the opposition with well-placed canister fire. The master artilleryman had to concede, however, that these tactics demanded "calmness & intelligence," as well as the "tact and resolution in how to profit by them."

There is a certain amount of evidence that this aggressive style of artillery tactics found favor among some professionally trained officers at the start of the Civil War. It might explain McDowell's controversial employment of Ricketts's and Griffin's batteries during the First Bull Run. Although the initial confrontation between Burnside and Bee's forces on the extreme left flank of the original Confederate position could be characterized as a joint artillery-infantry engagement, Union artillery played a much more aggressive role in the moments following Bee's repulse. Griffin's battery, for example, advanced twice incrementally, before being ordered by no less than Gen. Irvin McDowell himself to advance with Ricketts's battery another 800 yards to near the position previously occupied by the Confederate guns in Imboden's battery. The move was bold and at first was completely unsupported by friendly infantry. It also proved to be overly reckless, and the Union gunners were soon cut down by musket fire, and the batteries were eventually overrun and captured.

The ignominious fate of Ricketts's and Griffin's batteries at Bull Run did not put an immediate end to advocacy of such artillery tactics, however. At Shiloh it was the Confederates' turn to use such artillery tactics. Following Gen. Daniel Ruggles's orders to move to the sound of the guns, soon after the start of fighting during the first day, Capt. W. Irving Hodgson, who commanded Fifth Company of the Louisiana Washington Artillery, moved his battery up to within 50 yards of the Union tents. His gunners soon found themselves roughly handled, however. Union infantrymen cut holes in the tents and only a stone's throw from those they aimed at, delivered a deadly fire. Besides disabling a number of horses, this killed three artillerymen and wounded seven or eight.

Two hours later in Rhea's Field, a gun from Polk's Tennessee Battery also attempted to unlimber extremely close to the Union infantry. Accurate Union small arms fire inflicted sufficient casualties that the gun had to be abandoned. Captain Girardey's Washington (Georgia) Light Artillery Battery was the third battery to attempt to deliver close-in fire, and it too suffered heavy casualties. Only a timely nearby Confederate infantry charge saved the battery from further destruction.

Though none of these attempts had proven overly successful, this aggressive tactic was never completely abandoned. In his contribution to *Battles and Leaders,* Gen. James Longstreet admitted that he had contemplated similar artillery tactics during the struggle for Malvern Hill.

It should not surprise anyone that the *most* notable use of aggressive artillery tactics during the Civil War was implemented by Nathan Bedford Forrest. Generally, Forrest's tactical methods epitomized a combination of cleverness, extreme aggression, and an intuitive grasp of sound tactical doctrine. During the engagement at Parker's Crossroads (halfway between Nashville and Memphis, December 31, 1862), young Capt. John Watson Morton's artillery advanced to within 200 yards of the Union line as it followed Forrest's infantry on its advance. Unlike at Bull Run and Shiloh, in this case the artillery-infantry combination successfully broke the enemy's line and then withstood a series of counterattacks.

A much more compelling example occurred during the engagement at Brice's Crossroads, in Mississippi, on June 10, 1864, however. During this meeting, Forrest's forces managed to push back a sizeable contingent of Union cavalry before temporarily stalling in front of Union infantry to the rear. Though now facing superior numbers, Forrest as ever remained undaunted and decided to resort to bold tactics. Riding up to Captain Morton, Forrest ordered him to double-shot his guns. During the upcoming advance, without any accompanying infantry support, these were to precipitously gallop as close as possible to the enemy line, unlimber, and fire a deadly salvo at very close range. Morton obediently complied. As soon as the general signal for the assault was sounded, four of his "bull pups," as mountain howitzers were affectionately known, galloped to within 60 yards of the Union line and quickly unlimbered before the enemy was able to respond effectively. The devastating artillery fire, coupled with the threat of being outflanked by Buford's men on the right and Buell's on the left, completely overawed the defenders, who now turned and fled.

This aggressive use of artillery has occasionally been said to be a holdover from Napoleonic artillery tactics, a characterization that certainly comes as a surprise to those who specialize in the study of Napoleonic warfare. True, during the Battle of Friedland (June 14, 1807), after his artillery had unlimbered 600 paces from the Russian line, General Sénarmont had his artillery rapidly bound to 300 paces, then 150 paces, and finally to within 60 paces of the foe. Firing canister at each stop, the French soon sent the Russians reeling back, and Russian cavalry, attempting to take the French guns, was dealt the same fate. But this employment appears to be an anomaly. During the Battle of Dresden (August 26–27, 1813), the French were able to advance their artillery up to within 100 paces of the enemy infantry in squares, but this was only because they were able to do so with impunity: A torrential rain made it impossible for the defenders to use their muskets. One simply does not find other examples of French artillery, unsupported by friendly infantry, aggressively advancing very close to an enemy, unlimbering, and firing with great alacrity.

By today's standards American and even British military authorities during the 1840s and '50s had a relatively superficial knowledge of the tactical minutiae that was actually used on the Napoleonic battlefield. Consequently, one will never know for sure why American artillerists employed such aggressive artillery tactics during the Mexican-American War. However, it is possible that learning of Sénarmont's feat at Friedland, American artillerists assumed that this was a formal tactic that had been employed by the famed French artillery and hence was worthy of imitation.

Chapter 25

CAVALRY DEVELOPMENTS DURING THE WAR

FIGHTING DISMOUNTED

C alled upon to characterize the nature of Civil War cavalry combat, William F. Fox, in his seminal *Regimental Losses*, was forced to conclude that in most cases rough terrain prevented the use of effective cavalry charges and forced troopers to dismount and rely on their carbines. Horses often were used simply as a means of quick conveyance, rather than a means of attack. To be effective, a charge had to be delivered by a tight, ordered cavalry line traveling at speed, and, of course, movement over broken ground made this impossible. In such cases it was much more practical to dismount and have some of the men guard the horses, while the main body of the cavalry force fought on foot.

The second expedition against the Confederate salt works in Saltville, Virginia, demonstrates not only why cavalry had to dismount so often but also the nature of this rough-and-tumble fighting over difficult ground. In late September 1864 Gen. Nathaniel C. McLean had been sent with 4200 men to destroy the salt works in the southwestern portion of the state. These works were on a high mountain that could only be accessed through a relatively narrow valley, and the Confederate defenders had positioned themselves along the slopes on either side of the valley. McLean decided to attack one of the lesser mountains about a mile from their ultimate goal and upon which rested a rebel battery. Here the defenders were positioned along the lower slope, ensconced behind 3-foot-high rifle pits made of logs and stones. The real challenge, however, was posed by an "almost impenetrable jungle" of thick brush and briars in front of the Confederate position. There was a small stream at the bottom of the valley, which was quite narrow at this point.

The main brunt of the attack fell to the left of the Union line of dismounted cavalry: the Fifth U.S. Colored Cavalry, the Twelfth Ohio Volunteer Cavalry, and the Eleventh Michigan Cavalry. At the start of the affair, the Union force was partway up an opposing slope. The order was given for the assault to begin, and the Union dismounted cavalry moved forward down the slope, a thin skirmish line leading the way. There are conflicting accounts of who fired first. However, it appears that both sides delivered a tremendous initial volley, after which the dismounted Union cavalry crossed the stream and determinedly pushed up the opposite slope until they were about 50 yards from the enemy.

At this point some of the Union colonels ordered their men to charge, and the attackers rushed forward. They succeeded in gaining a toehold along some points of the defending position, and vicious and bloody hand-to-hand fights erupted here and there along the line. In his memoirs F. H. Mason, captain of Squadron I of the Twelfth Ohio Cavalry, recalled the intensity of the fighting as the Union cavalry slowly pushed back its adversaries:

> The rebels returned slowly and stubbornly through the thicket up the hill, the Federals pressing them forward step by step— each soldier fighting according to his own ideas, and often unable to see a comrade or enemy. More than once duels took place between individuals of more than a half-a-dozen paces— each firing through a dense undergrowth at a noise heard beyond until a groan or a cessation of firing announced that the heard but unseen enemy was dead. At other times a rebel would pop out from behind a tree or a rock only a few feet from an advancing Yankee, and then it was he who was the quickest and surest shot of the two who lived to tell the story.

Everyone nearby momentarily shifted their attention to Sergeant Davis, the guidon bearer of Squadron H, as a daring rebel rushed forward and tried to carry off the colors. The two unarmed men grappled for a few moments, before Davis was able to harpoon his opponent with the bottom end of the flagstaff. The injury was fatal, the sharp end protruding from the man's lower back.

The brutal fighting continued until about 5 P.M., and although the attackers managed to seize some of the defenders' position along that hill, they were essentially checked and unable to fulfill their main objective, the destruction of the salt works. McLean would report that his men had run out of ammunition. More probably, they were stopped by a foe that was equally tough and equally determined. The Union force was forced to retire, leaving its wounded with several surgeons on the contested mountainside. Most of the wounded in the "colored" regiment, through prodigious effort and willpower, managed to withdraw, realizing that to stay was almost certain death after capture.

The Fifth U.S. Colored Cavalry fought bravely and effectively in this, its baptism of fire. En route to Saltville, its men, all recent recruits, were reviled and cursed at by their white brothers in arms, much like the black Fifty-fourth Massachusetts had to endure elsewhere. In his report after the battle, the Fifth Regiment's colonel would recount his men's forbearance with pride:

> These insults, as well as the jeers and taunts that they would not fight, were borne by the colored soldier patiently, or punished with dignity by their officers, but in no instance did I hear colored soldiers make any reply to insulting language used toward [them] by the white troops.

And bravely Col. James S. Brisbin's colored troops did fight, storming their portion of the line and quickly seizing the rebel's defenses in their front. As ferocious as they were in the fight, they were caring with their prisoners, carrying water to the wounded Confederates after the fighting was over.

USE OF REVOLVERS

Even when the cavalry was not forced to dismount, the saber could not be used effectively while moving through forests or over broken ground. In such cases, the cavalrymen resorted to the revolver, if so armed. The day after the Battle of Corinth, the Fifth Iowa Cavalry confronted an enemy force along a road that led through "swamp and jungle." The eight troopers in the regiment with revolvers were placed at the front of the cavalry column, where they skirmished with their side arms in the thick timber and undergrowth.

Apart from its rapid fire, one of the virtues of the revolver was the facility with which it could be handled. It was easy to use while mounted or dismounted and could be brought into play quickly, an important quality when the cavalry found itself in an unexpected situation. In pursuit of the enemy in October 1861, the Third New York Cavalry was wending its way in the middle of a forest on the Leesburg, Virginia, road, when its commander spotted the gleam of Confederate bayonets above the heavy brush slightly to the left and in front of their position. Sensing the peril, Maj. John Mix ordered his men to turn toward the threat and fire their revolvers. The Union cavalry thus was able to escape the ambuscade with the loss of several men, despite a heavy enemy volley delivered at only 30 yards.

Quick access to the revolver also meant that cavalrymen could change weapons even during a fight, if required. Sneaking up unnoticed on a rebel encampment near Forsyth, Missouri (August 2, 1862), Capt. Milton Burch of the Fourteenth Missouri Cavalry (State Militia) divided his command into two groups. Those armed with sabers remained mounted and attacked first. The remainder of the regiment, equipped with carbines, followed on foot. The mounted charge was completely successful, however, not only driving in the enemy vedettes but also forcing the main body of rebels back behind a fence in a cornfield. Seemingly stopped by this barrier, Burch expected that the cavalrymen would have to retire and the dismounted force would take over. The Union cavalrymen, however, simply sheathed their sabers, drew their revolvers, and delivered a deadly point-blank fire to the rebels on the other side of the fence. The rebels were completely routed, and the affair was over before the dismounted men came up.

Revolvers, however, are much more closely associated with Confederate cavalry, who frequently used this side arm as the weapon of choice. Even prior to the war, the Texas Rangers had gained a widespread reputation for proficiency with this weapon, and those who expected to fight Texas cavalry had to take into account a new style of mounted tactics, whereby the troopers would advance very close to the enemy cavalry or infantry and then blast away with one or two revolvers. The Texans certainly didn't disappoint their adversaries, and these were the tactics used during the lively engagement at Rowlett's Station, Kentucky.

Of course, that action was a rather small affair and involved only one or two companies of Texas cavalry. An example of a much grander application of these tactics occurred during the Battle of Murfreesboro (also known as Stone's River) when the Cavalry Brigade of the Army of Tennessee under Brig. Gen. John A. Wharton was ordered to work its way around the Union left flank. Seeing a heavy body of cavalry defending the Union wagon train, Wharton decided to seize the opportunity and charge the Union cavalry. After a successful preliminary round of charges, Wharton threw in his entire brigade, which he estimated to be about two thousand cavalrymen. After a short hand-to-hand conflict "in which the revolver was used with deadly effect," the enemy cavalry was chased from the field and was able to regroup only after it crossed Overall's Creek, about 2 miles away.

BREECHLOADERS AND REPEATERS

A number of Union cavalry regiments had been issued various types of breech-loading single-shot carbines and repeaters early in the war. Initially, there were considerable teething problems, and most of these weapons were prone to mechanical malfunctions. The Gallager carbine often jammed after it was fired, and some of its parts were so brittle that they snapped. Responding to Ripley's requests for an evaluation of the weapon, Brig. Gen. Jeremiah T. Boyle concluded that it was "unquestionably worthless." This was the same conclusion that some had formed of the Smith carbine, carried by the First Connecticut Cavalry, and the Joslyn carbine, by the First New York Dragoons and Ninth Pennsylvania Cavalry.

Despite such early teething problems, the breechloader and eventually the repeater proved to be invaluable weapons for cavalry and mounted infantry once they dismounted. The effectiveness of these faster-firing new weapons became evident on March 25, 1863, when the approximately 625 men of the Fourth Cavalry Brigade pursued and then engaged a larger rebel force that had just captured another Union force at Brentwood, Tennessee. Even after the rebels were reinforced by Gens. Wharton and Nathan Bedford Forest, the Union brigade was able to beat back several attempts to overrun and out-flank its position before itself retiring to safety. Brig. Gen. G. Clay Smith, who commanded the Union cavalry, attributed this successful resistance to a much superior force, lasting several hours, to the revolvers of the Second Michigan and the speed with which they could reload their Burnside carbines. These shoulder arms "poured such a constant and deadly volley into their ranks, and felled so many, that but for such overwhelming forces, numbering not less than 5,000, our success would have been unquestioned."

A few months later the Spencer rifle proved as deadly a weapon in the hands of the Eighth Michigan Cavalry as they pursued Morgan and his partisans on a 578-mile chase through Kentucky, Indiana, and Ohio. The regiment's commander would report that the seven-shooter had terrorized the enemy, who "thought us in much stronger force than we were, when each man could pour seven shots into them so rapidly." In most engagements there were generally four times as many men wounded as killed outright. However, the Spencer seemed to invert the ratio, and the lieutenant colonel noticed that there was more of the enemy killed than wounded.

These two incidents, however, were relatively minor and occurred in out-of-the-way places and probably became known only to the forces' immediate superiors and very select circles within the War Department. The reputation of breechloaders and repeaters would grow widespread after the Battles of Gettysburg and Chickamauga, in which relatively small numbers of dismounted cavalry and mounted infantry were able to hold their own against enormously superior odds. On July 1, 1863, between 8 and 9 P.M., the lead elements of the opposing armies began to stumble into one another along the Cham-bersburg Pike northwest of Gettysburg. Union Col. William Gamble's First Brigade of the First Cavalry Division quickly had three squadrons dismount and join the existing skirmish line. For 2 hours this small force, fighting from behind trees and fences, stiffly opposed a division from A. P. Hill's Third Corps. Eventually, forced to retire to a second position 200 yards farther back, they neverthe-less slowed down the Confederate advance enough to allow the infantry from Reynolds's I Corps to get up and into place to take over the defense. That they were able to do so was largely the result of the increased firepower of the Sharps, Smith, Merrill, Gallagher, and Smith carbines with which they were armed.

Samuel Harris, who fought with the Fifth Michigan Cavalry at Gettysburg, provides a vivid description of how his regiment's Spencer rifles altered the normal dynamics of the attack and defense. On the third day of the battle, his regiment, posted behind a rail fence, was assailed by about 1500 dismounted Confederate cavalrymen, who had just come out of a wood on a slight hill to their front. The rebels marched "in perfect time" until they were ordered to charge. When they started to run in, it struck the defenders that the Confederates thought themselves certain of victory. The defending Union cavalry waited until the attackers had closed to within about 100 yards, then unleashed a volley. A Confederate officer was immediately heard to urge the attackers to rush in before the Union cavalrymen had a chance to reload. Of course, the men in the Fifth Michigan didn't have to reload, and they quickly delivered second, third, and fourth volleys, which stopped the onrushing Confederates, who now started to run back faster than they had approached. As he was led away, one prisoner remarked, "You'n load in the morning and fire all day."

Other Union regiments armed with the Spencer reported similar results. The next year Lt. Col. Daniel C. Rodman of the Seventh Connecticut Infantry, who fought on the south bank of the James River during the Overland Campaign, claimed that defenders armed with Spencers would settle an affair in about a minute and a half. In his own report the major of this regiment claimed that so armed and with enough ammunition, his men could hold off any size force and that "nothing can stand before them." So great did the confidence in the repeaters become that when about sixty Confederates with Enfields bested thirty cavalrymen with Spencers, the commander of the Third U.S. Colored Cavalry immediately recommended an investigation to determine the cause of such an anomaly.

CONCENTRATION OF CAVALRY

By June 1864 the idea of the heroic, decisive battle had been replaced by continuous day-to-day fighting through which the Union army attempted to slowly acquire a strategic geographical advantage.

The Union mounted arm, now organized into a large cavalry corps, was repeatedly called upon to probe the countryside to locate the enemy or to quickly protect some vulnerable position suddenly attacked by the Confederates. Opposing cavalry forces frequently clashed; however, the intensity of the fighting and the scale on which it was conducted was unlike anything previously known. Generally, the fighting was undistinguishable from that carried out by infantry. Dismounted, the cavalrymen relied upon their carbines and were frequently called upon to attack even enemy field fortifications.

While moving on the Mechanicsville Road during the engagement at Haw's Shop, Virginia, for example, Gregg's Second Cavalry Division ran into a large body of Southern cavalry ensconced behind temporary breastworks. Initially, both sides proved equally determined, and the engagement dragged on without resolution until late in the evening, when George C. Custer's Brigade attacked in closed column of attack. Finally overwhelmed, the Confederate cavalry finished pushed out of their position. As the war drew to a close during the final year, many such dismounted large-scale cavalry fights can be found.

THE SLOW CLIMB UPWARD

The advent of the breechloaders and the formation of large-scale cavalry formations is only part of the story of the evolution of Union cavalry from its inglorious beginnings and rude defeats at the start of the war to its staunch showing later in the war. The transformation was as much due to the gradual inculcation of the needed discipline and a mastery of the traditional tools of the cavalry arm as it was the result of technological innovation and more effective organization.

General Scott's policy of distributing Union cavalry into "penny packets" had early made it impossible for cavalry to act as a significant military force. During the first 2 years of the war, most of the cavalry regiments had been geographically dispersed or, worse yet, subdivided into smaller corps forced to serve on outpost and picket duty and as escorts and bodyguards. At the start of the Peninsular Campaign, for example, only four companies from the Sixth New York and two companies from the Eighth Pennsylvania Cavalry Regiments were assigned to the II and V Corps, respectively. And, even in those rare cases during the early fighting when cavalry was present in meaningful numbers on the battlefield, it was invariably relegated to a secondary, indecisive role, reflecting the commanders' view of its usefulness. For example, when, ordered by Gen. Fitz-John Porter to prevent stragglers from leaving the battle line during the Second Battle of Bull Run, Hugh Kilpatrick deployed his troopers at close skirmish order to form an equine screen.

When the series of disappointments during the summer of 1862 destroyed the illusions of having a short, decisive war to restore the Union, the necessity of reorganizing the cavalry into an effective fighting force became inescapably apparent. Although in the Eastern theater General George D. Bayard took the first tentative steps to reorganize the cavalry during Ambrose Burnside's tenure as commander of the Army of the Potomac, significant progress in this area had to wait until Gen. Joe Hooker took command. Early in 1863 a number of previously detached regiments were massed near the Potomac Creek Bridge, a few miles north of Fredericksburg, to form the Cavalry Corps of the Army of the Potomac, with Gen. George D. Stoneman as its commander.

This simple organizational change by itself went a long way to reestablishing the men's morale. Now buoyed up by the confidence and self-esteem that usually result from the coming together of a large number of people with a common purpose, the cavalryman no longer saw himself as a relatively useless appendage to the foot soldier, who had up to now done almost all of the fighting. Much more rigorous discipline was imposed than had been hitherto demanded. Camps of instruction were established, along with boards of examination, and officers found incompetent were replaced by more intelligent and energetic ones. Cavalrymen performed squadron and regimental drill daily, while occasional brigade drills and division reviews afforded the experience in the movement of large bodies of troops. Officers and NCOs were not exempt from demanding routine. During the evenings in candlelit tents, the NCOs recited cavalry tactics to the senior captain of the squadron, while the commissioned officers recited their lessons to the major.

Another development was simultaneously taking place that, when combined with better training, would eventually have a profound effect upon the Union cavalry's capabilities during the last 2 years of the war. This was a renewed confidence in the saber. The antisaber articles in *Scientific American* and the *Army and Navy Journal* notwithstanding, there were many veteran regular officers who realized that when facing enemy cavalry on open ground, there was no better tactic than to administer a determined charge with the threat of cold steel.

One of the clearest justifications for the use of the saber was supplied by Col. James H. Carleton of the First California Volunteers in a set of detailed instructions issued to the lieutenant colonel of his regiment on May 2, 1862. The Texans they were to face were known for repeatedly firing their revolvers during aggressive charges. Realizing that the horses, unused to firearms, were noticeably skittish, he counseled that the troopers dismount when they were to use their firearms. Arguing that "cold steel will win against the pistol," the Californian troopers were not to attempt to return the fire but instead, without delay, were to rush in "as quick as thought" with outstretched sabers. As they neared the Texan horsemen, they were to disable their enemies by cutting the reins or killing the horses. As soon as the enemy broke, which the colonel predicted they would if the saber were used judiciously, the troopers were to fire revolvers, making sure that they remained close together. Carleton, incidentally, recommended similar tactics if the Texans attacked on foot. In this case the defenders, themselves dismounted, could use their revolvers or carbines until the enemy was near, then once again they were to draw their sabers and rush in at breakneck speed.

Lest one is inclined to dismiss Carleton's orders simply as naïve, other instructions for Union cavalry in the West must be considered. A few weeks later Maj. Gen. S. R. Curtis issued orders to the Army of the Southwest which, though far more cursory, were similar in their extolment of the saber:

> Emulate the example of the renowned in your arm! Keep your sabers polished; drill daily in the use of them, and watch the opportunity to show the heroic deeds you may accomplish.

Events would soon prove that confidence in this weapon, at least when in the hands of Western cavalrymen, was not misplaced. Granted, on several occasions in 1862, when Union cavalry serving with the Army of the Potomac attempted to charge enemy cavalry, all attempts met with failure. The same could not be said of their comrades in the West, though. The Frémont Battalion of Cavalry had successfully charged at Henrytown, Missouri (October 13, 1861), and elsewhere Western Union cavalry was effective when coming into contact with its enemy counterpart. True, these were rough-and-ready affairs, in which a disorganized body of Union cavalry or mounted infantry haphazardly threw themselves upon equally disorganized defenders with little regard to formal tactics or finesse.

These sporadic successes were not lost on higher-level Union commanders. There is fragmentary evidence that offensive cavalry doctrine based upon a determined saber charge had regained a certain amount of credibility in the Western theater of operations by early 1863. During the very first day of a Union expedition toward Columbia, Tennessee (March 4), the Seventh Pennsylvania Cavalry administered a perfectly delivered saber charge and succeeded in completely routing the opposing rebel force. Impressed with this accomplishment, General Rosecrans brought the affair to the attention of General Halleck 2 weeks later. In a short communiqué he not only praised the heroism of the brigade commander, Col. Robert H. G. Minty, but also applauded the men's choice of tactics, adding that they had wisely "used the saber where the carbine would delay." This was at the height of Rosecrans's effort to secure as many Colt's Revolving Rifles as possible for his cavalry and mounted infantry, and innumerable wires were exchanged between the two Union officials. On April 1, while informing Rosecrans that he was to receive the next shipment of carbines and revolving pistols, almost as an afterthought Assistant Secretary of War P. H. Watson, inquired whether any sabers were needed. Without any hesitancy Rosecrans requested 3000 sabers the same day, de facto testimony to the weapon's usefulness—made all the more compelling since it came from the most ardent champion of arming cavalry with repeating rifles.

Rosecrans was by no means the only Union officer in the West singing the praises of the saber during this period. In his April 4 report on the expedition from Readyville to Woodbury, Tennessee Col. William B. Hazen, a brigade commander in the XXI Army Corps, spoke in the highest terms of the Third Ohio Cavalry and emphasized that a brigade of such troops armed with revolvers and sabers would be "invaluable."

That such sentiments had filtered down among a number of cavalry commanders is demonstrated during a minor engagement less than a month later. While the Union was attempting to counter Gen. John Marmaduke's expedition into Missouri, a small action took place at Chalk River. Faced with rebel infantry-supported artillery, Col. John M. Glover, who commanded a cavalry brigade, repeatedly mentioned to subordinate officers that the Third Missouri, which he personally commanded, was equipped with excellent sabers and that this was a perfect opportunity to test both the effectiveness of this weapon and the mettle of his men. Though the ensuing charge was completely successful, it nevertheless angered Maj. Joseph W. Caldwell of the First Iowa Cavalry. In his own report of the affair, Major Caldwell claimed that Glover had purposely placed the First Iowa so that it was unavailable for the charge and thus could not share in the glory garnered by the Third Missouri and its commander. Caldwell's accusation implies that there had been preexisting consensus that a well-led cavalry regiment had a good chance of overthrowing enemy infantry with a vigorous cavalry charge over open ground.

The first signs of a more effective Union cavalry in the East occurred early in 1863, when a Union cavalry force under Brig. Gen. William W. Averell managed to overthrow Brig. Gen. Fitz Lee's contingent during a small action at Kelly's Ford (Virginia, March 17). Although participants' accounts provide conflicting versions of some of the details, it is nevertheless possible to reconstruct the main events during the day's combat. As the head of the Union cavalry column came out of a small wood, a rebel cavalry force, preceded by skirmishers, was observed to be advancing rapidly toward them. General Averell immediately ordered the Fourth New York and Fourth Pennsylvania to deploy into line to the right and left, respectively. It appears that Averell intended to employ what by this point was a common practice among Union cavalry in the East. He instructed these regiments to position themselves along the fringes of the woods, where they were to deliver carbine fire upon the advancing enemy.

Averell's battle plan was never carried out, at least not in the way it was initially envisioned. Before the troopers along the edge could get into position, the First Rhode Island Cavalry found itself suddenly threatened by the feared Virginia horse. William Meyers in Troop A would forever remember his impressions of this moment:

> How fearfully beautiful appears the grand Virginia cavalry, dashing down the muddy road from the distance; out of the woody road into the field they line up in battle array with red battle flags in which we see the cross of stars, fluttering out right in the wind, they just out of our pistol range.

Meanwhile, as Fitz Lee's cavalry was positioning itself, Col. Alfred N. Duffié, who commanded the Rhode Island regiment, decided upon his own reaction to these fast-breaking events. Riding along his regiment's front, he cautioned his men to remember what he had taught them. During the charge they were not to gallop but instead maintain a carefully controlled gait; after the initial advance, they were then to speed up to a trot, all the while making sure that they remained close enough to touch the "next man's stirrups." They were only to fire when they could literally see the whites of the enemies' eyes. The advice delivered, Duffié gave the order "Draw sabers," the bugles sounded, and the countercharge was delivered.

Duffié's tactics paid off. The relatively novice Rhode Island cavalry managed to maintain enough cohesion that Fitz Lee's troops were forced to spread out or turn around to avoid the shock. A few mounts and their riders unable to evade the blue surge were overturned, and instantly, there was ubiquitous confusion and clouds of dust, punctuated with the rattling of revolvers. The Union riders had held their ground, and their Southern foe had to regroup slightly to the rear. Both sides started to regroup, and the same sequence was repeated twice again, each time with the same result: Fitz Lee's vaunted cavalrymen had been discomfited.

There is some evidence that the specific tactics that the First

Rhode Island Cavalry had used owed more to the teaching and instructions of its colonel than the accepted practice of the Union cavalry in general. Virtually every veteran of the regiment who published his memoirs applauded Duffié's strict discipline. Cavalryman William E. Meyers mentions that the drills did not always conform to officially accepted practice but instead were conducted "in his own French way." The instructions Duffié issued to his troopers before the charge were much more representative of the type of charge doctrine employed by French Napoleonic cavalry than of the more predominant charge tactics employed by most nations, which were based on a system originally devised by Frederick the Great.

Traditional Prussian Charge Doctrine

The basis of eighteenth- and nineteenth-century cavalry practice was laid by Swedish King Gustavus Adolphus (killed 1632) when he ordered his horsemen to strip off much of their armor and attack their heavily armored, cumbersome foes at speeds greater than the customary slow trot. By the 1690s French cavalry had developed its own variant, known as the charge *en fourrageurs,* wherein the emphasis was on speed rather than cohesion of the formation. As the troopers approached at a hell-for-leather speed, spaces would open up between horses. The Imperialists (of the Hapsburg Empire) faced a much more deadly foe, the feared Turkish horsemen, and they developed a very controlled system. They would approach only at a slow trot in order to allow their troopers to remain boot to boot, thus preventing the Turks from penetrating their formation. Emulating this tactic, the English were able to defeat their more ardent but less disciplined French rivals during the War of the Spanish Succession.

This was the situation when Frederick the Great went to war against Maria Theresa of Austria in 1740 (the War of the Austrian Succession). He inherited a particularly clumsy and inept cavalry, which ignominiously scampered off the battlefield at the mere sight of the Austrian cavalry during the Battle of Mollwitz (April 10, 1741). In the middle of a war and hardly able to replace either his mounts or the riders they carried, he realized that the only viable option was to come up with a new set of cavalry tactics, one that would give an advantage to an otherwise lackluster cavalry. At the heart of Frederick's new charge doctrine was the profound realization that the real conscious objective of a cavalry-versus-cavalry action was not to destroy the opponent but rather to force the opponent to flee precipitously.

If the Austrians and British were able to defeat a fast-moving enemy line with a slower-moving counterpart that was better formed, then surely Frederick's own cavalry could in turn defeat the latter if it learned how to attack enemy cavalry at speed but still in well-ordered formations. *The destruction of the enemy cavalry formation was a psychological rather than a physical event.* A closed, well-ordered formation would impart a positive morale benefit to the cavalrymen in it, while the enemy moving at a slower gait, even if in an equally cohesive formation, would inevitably become intimidated, lose its resolution, and become routed. These were the tactics that the Prussian cavalry general Seydlitz and his compeers used to discomfit the Austrian, French, and Russian cavalry—tactics that became the generally accepted model for the next hundred years.

During the French Revolutionary Wars (1792–1800), the French cavalry was in a situation similar to that faced by the Prussians at the start of the War of the Austrian Succession. During the ancien regime, most of the cavalry officers came from the nobility, which quickly disappeared after the execution of Louis XVI. French mounts were also inferior, and the masses of townspeople and city dwellers who were brought in to fill the thinning ranks were completely inexperienced. Like the Prussians before them, the French were able to gradually turn things around, and the French cavalry accomplished prodigious feats under the leadership of such luminaries as Murat, LaSalle, and Kellerman the younger. Nevertheless, the French cavalry utilized a more modest cavalry charge doctrine. Although taught to ride boot to boot, it often charged at a fast trot rather than a true charge *à la sauvage,* as did the Prussians. This was the doctrine specifically mandated by General LaSalle, among others.

And of course, this tactic is very similar to the one William Meyers tells us that Duffié instructed the First Rhode Island Cavalry to employ. Regardless of the inspiration or origin of the tactics, the results, both short term and lasting, cannot be questioned. Writing many years later, George Bliss, who had participated in the charge, would boast that even before the engagement his comrades were confident that they could always beat the Confederate cavalry in a charge. Meyers was probably more honest about how the Rhode Islanders felt going into the action:

> Could we face and beat the "Famous Black Horse"? Could we dare to meet men who were almost born on a horse? We, from the cabin and forecastle, from city office and workshop, could we do it?

Certainly, there had to be more than a trace of fear as they faced off against their feared opponents. However, if Bliss had later exploited the prerogatives of the victor and exaggerated the confidence of the Union cavalry *before* the engagement, he more accurately described the effect of the victory on Averell's cavalry *after* the affair. Their confidence in their tactics and themselves grew enormously, and Bliss could rightly boast:

> Our men were fully convinced that they were superior to the rebel cavalry, and were confident that they could always beat them by a charge with a sabre, and from that day until the war closed our cavalry [the First Rhode Island] never failed to defeat the enemy on every occasion where they had an opportunity to charge with the sabre.

By 1864 Union cavalry in the West had gradually undergone a similar transformation. Pointing out to General Halleck the "conspicuous gallantry and laborious services" that the cavalry had displayed during the Chattanooga Campaign, Rosecrans was elated about the progress that had been made during the previous 12 months. No longer forced to operate in purely a secondary capacity within the lines, the mounted arm had become sufficiently active and aggressive to consistently attack the enemy whenever the occasion presented itself. Rosecrans felt that this change had been brought about by the men's and officers' unrelenting efforts to improve, coupled with better weaponry and the "determined use of the saber." Unlike the previous year, in which whatever instructions to use the saber were couched in the vaguest of terms, a number of instructions now appeared that described when and how a saber charge was to be conducted.

While issuing instructions on May 16, 1864, for an upcoming expedition along the Cache and White Rivers, Col. R. R. Livingston, the Union commander of the District of Northeastern Arkansas prescribed the tactics that had to be used should a rebel force be encountered. All long-range firing was to be strictly avoided, and even if outnumbered, the troopers were to draw their sabers, raise a vigorous yell, and immediately charge home. Several months earlier the chief of cavalry of the Military Division of the Mississippi, Brig. Gen. William S. Smith, in special field orders, had advocated similar cavalry tactics. These orders emphasized that every effort had to be made so that cavalry officers of all ranks understood that a saber charge conducted over "favorable ground" must result in a "most signal and decisive success" against an enemy who had laid aside its sabers, provided, of course, it was performed "resolutely." Cavalry in this department was forbidden to receive an enemy cavalry at the halt; a charge had to be met with a charge.

The constant campaigning provided a vast pool of essential experience, and the Union trooper and the doctrine he employed gradually became more sophisticated. The tactical deficiencies of simply yelling at the top of one's lungs and then riding in hell-for-leather finally began to be recognized, and some fundamental principles first uncovered by Frederick the Great were rediscovered. Solidity of the attacking formation, rather than simply speed, became important:

> The strength of cavalry consisting to a great extent in its momentum, the attack must be made en masse, and with just such rate of speed as is consistent with a maintenance of the organization of each command.

SHENANDOAH VALLEY CAMPAIGN

Probably the most successful use of saber charges occurred during Sheridan's Shenandoah Valley campaign in 1864. Sheridan would proudly report to Ulysses S. Grant that during an engagement over expansive, relatively flat terrain in front of Front Royal (the Battle of Cedarville, August 16), the saber "was freely used" by Devin's and Custer's cavalry brigades. In his more detailed report of operations during that campaign, Sheridan went on to explain that the enemy cavalry had been badly beaten and that most of the 24 officers and 276 men taken prisoner were captured during "handsome saber charges."

Saber charges produced even more spectacular results during the Battle of Winchester on September 19. Ordered to cross the Opequon Creek at Locke's Ford, Custer's brigade was finally able to brush past enemy-occupied rifle pits when two squadrons from the First Michigan Cavalry aggressively charged through the creek, supported by a heavy, well-directed fire by Kidd's Sixth Michigan, whose men had dismounted and were positioned on the reverse slope of a hill near the creek. However, the real test occurred later in the battle when Custer's brigade found itself suddenly threatened by a very large enemy cavalry force. The first of these challenges was posed by the appearance of Lomax's troopers. A series of small charges easily pushed back Lomax's men, who "at no time waited for us to approach within pistol range, but broke and fled."

After linking up with Averell's cavalry division, which had been advancing along the Martinsburg Pike, the augmented Union cavalry now advanced in five brigade columns, each formed in a column of squadrons. These were preceded by mounted skirmishers, who at first were easily able to push back any mounted opposition, producing a sight that General Custer characterized as one of "the most inspiring as well as imposing scenes of martial grandeur ever witnessed upon a battle-field."

The splendor of the sight notwithstanding, the peril had not passed. The advanced skirmishers soon encountered Lomax's and Fitz Lee's cavalry brigades, who had been waiting under cover of a large open forest near the Martinsburg and Winchester Pike. The latter soon charged out of the woods and repulsed the mounted skirmishers and a formed regiment acting as their support. The main body of Union cavalry, not slow to respond, countercharged. According to Custer, "The enemy relied wholly upon the carbine and pistol; my men preferred the saber." Regardless of the techniques employed, the result was the same as the earlier confrontation. The Confederate cavalry was roughly handled, and many prisoners were taken.

Later during the battle Devin's Second Brigade enjoyed equal success with a saber charge, this time against Confederate infantry. During the last stages of the contest, the Confederates attempted to make one last stand with their infantry. Maj. Gen. Wesley Merritt ordered his Union cavalry brigades to charge some enemy cavalry that were blocking the way, but these withdrew before they could be attacked. Devin's command then struck the nearby enemy infantry. Merritt provided the highest accolades for Devin's actions in his report:

> The charge was directed on the enemy's infantry, which was attempting to change front and meet us; they were in confusion; no time was lost; the intrepid Devin, with his gallant brigade, burst like a storm of case-shot in their midst, showering saber blows on their heads and shoulders, trampling them under his horses' feet, and routing them in droves in every direction.

Three stands of colors and 300 prisoners were garnered.

In his own report Devin provided additional details of the slaughter. When ordered to charge, he had to change the cavalry line's direction obliquely to the left, which the men "splendidly executed" at the gallop. They then dashed "like a whirl wind" on the unfortunate rebel infantry and tried unsuccessfully to re-form. The troopers slashed wildly, and scores of prisoners were taken. Some of these had second thoughts, though, and tried to grab the weapons they had just cast down. Those foolish individuals were savagely pistol-whipped into submission.

Sheridan's cavalry would continue to score repeated successes with the saber charge throughout the remainder of the campaign. Merritt's cavalry would again best the opposition with the same tactics at the engagement at Tom's Brook (October 9). The growing number of cases where Union cavalry successfully charged Confederate horse validated this doctrine, and by the end of 1864, in a pontifical tone, Brig. Gen. J. W. Davidson of the Military Division of West

Mississippi declared "the saber is the weapon to be used when mounted and the carbine dismounted." Henceforth, troopers under his command armed with a saber were expressly forbidden to fire their carbines when mounted.

CONFEDERATE REACTION TO UNION CAVALRY SUCCESSES

By August 1864 the consistency with which Union cavalry overpowered Confederate horse on open ground forced a number of Confederate officers to examine Union cavalry practices as they had now evolved and to reevaluate cavalry-versus-cavalry tactics. A number of orders penned by high-ranking Confederate officers bemoaned the limitations of their cavalry's armament and how the lack of sabers greatly restricted the type of tactics that could be used against Union cavalry. The most plaintive of these was Lt. Gen. Jubal A. Early's report of the crushing defeat of Lomax's and Fitz Lee's forces at Tom's Brook.

> This is very distressing to me, and God knows I have done all in my power to avert the disasters which have befallen this command; but the fact is that the enemy's cavalry is so much superior to ours, both in numbers and equipment, and the country is so favorable to the operations of cavalry, that it is impossible for ours to compete with his.

In Lomax's defense Early pointed out that his troopers were armed only with rifles and consequently were not able to fight against enemy cavalry, once the latter decided to charge. Even when his men dismounted, they were unable to hold off this type of attack, so Early had even considered the transfer of all cavalry armed only with rifles into the infantry. Only the recognition that most of these men would have deserted in disgust stopped the general from carrying out this plan.

As the Union offensive gained momentum in both the Eastern and the Western theaters during the summer, this scenario was repeated, and several other Confederate officers filed similar reports, unhappily notifying authorities of cavalry defeats and proffering explanations for the defeats. General Ross had to report that on July 28,

1864, during the Atlanta Campaign, the Ninth Texas Cavalry, despite heroic efforts, was initially repulsed by waves of "better armed opponents," saber-brandishing Union cavalry, and only saved by reinforcements. Ross explained that once the Texans fired their rifles and carbines, they were helpless against a saber charge. Brig. Gen. Bradley T. Johnson had to report like results, with the essentially the same explanation, for the defeat of Confederate cavalry at Moorefield, West Virginia, on August 7.

There was an effort to arm part of the Confederate cavalry with sabers to meet this growing threat. When Maj. Gen. John A. Wharton was ordered to raise two cavalry brigades in early 1865, Gen. E. Kirby Smith instructed Wharton to arm their troopers with sabers and revolvers. Only the flank companies were to carry rifled carbines. Smith promised to send Wharton a thousand sabers, while the needed revolvers were to be supplied by mounted infantry, who would no longer carry this weapon.

By the end of the war, those who advocated the use of the saber and the concomitant charge doctrine could point to a number of cases in which the determined saber charge bested opponents not similarly armed. In the April 22 edition of *Army and Navy Journal*, an anonymous contributor declared that despite recent advances in small arms weaponry, the saber remained the true arm of cavalry. According to this writer the carbine should be used only when the cavalryman was dismounted, and the revolver was a "contingent arm" to be used only when the cavalry was prevented from closing upon its enemy. In open ground a determined charge would always best enemy cavalry that unwisely relied upon firearms:

> A brave enemy, deriding the erring and unsteady aim of thousands of carbines drawn under the motion and restlessness of horses, would melt away before the weight and speed of a few squadrons, with firmly-set and keen-edged sabers.

There were many who did not accept this view and believed that modern cavalry had to rely upon fire arms rather than cold steel. In fact, even as the credibility of the saber and the charge was revitalized among a number of Western Union officers in 1863, there was no lack of brother officers who continued to berate edged weapons. Writing to the commander of the District of Upper Arkansas as late as August 1864, Maj. Gen. James G. Blunt emphatically asked his superior not to send any sabers, arguing that "carbines and revolvers are essential." It seems the criticism originally raised in 1862 never totally disappeared. Broken terrain prevented troops from charging effectively and favored defenders with firearms. Operating in roughly the same general area, the colonel of the First Regiment Nebraska Cavalry, for example, had complained several months before that his troops, armed only with revolvers and sabers, were frequently at the mercy of Confederates, who took advantage of this type of terrain.

COMBINED MOUNTED-DISMOUNTED TACTICS

Although the discussion so far has portrayed the use of firearms and saber charges as mutually exclusive tactics, throughout the war there were a number of officers willing to employ both practices as required. During a skirmish near Greenwich, Virginia, on May 30, 1863, for example, after advancing up to its rebel counterpart and emptying its revolvers at close range, the Seventh Michigan Cavalry then rushed in with drawn sabers. During the ensuing chase the Confederate cavalry was completely scattered, and many rebel cavalrymen were "severely cut with saber, but clung to their horses and fell back into the thicket."

Although this is certainly not the only instance of fire and then charge tactics that can be found, a much more common practice was for a cavalry commander to have a portion of his men dismount while others remained mounted, ready to charge. To be able to do, as we have seen, some Union cavalry regiments, such as the Second Iowa Cavalry, were divided, part being designated saber companies, while the remaining companies were armed with carbines or even rifle muskets. More commonly, a brigade commander would order some regiments to dismount and use their carbines, while one or more other regiments would charge at the appropriate moment.

Forced to respond to Southern Gen. Joseph Wheeler's intrusion into the Sequatchie Valley, Tennessee, in late 1863, Gen. George Crook's cavalry used such tactics very effectively. On October 7 Crook's main force decisively defeated the rebel raiders a few miles from Shelbyville. This time the Union assault was led by mounted infantry, which delivered a "sharp fire" that pushed the rebels back into the woods behind them. Dismounting, the Union mounted infantry delivered several more volleys into the Confederates, who were now pushed back into greater confusion. Seeing the opportunity to crush the confused foe, Crook ordered the Second Brigade to the front, and Col. Eli Long led his men in a saber charge. Completely successful, the charge effectively drove the enemy back several miles, whereupon the rebels rallied in a cedar thicket.

Here the same general process was repeated. The mounted infantry dismounted and threw Wheeler's men into confusion with a few quick volleys. Once the defenders were sufficiently confused, the Second Brigade delivered another saber charge, and once again the rebels were routed. The advantages of alternating mounted infantry fighting on foot and a vigorous cavalry charge as a follow-up became apparent, so Crook continued to use this tactical sequence for the remainder of the day. Not only were the Union cavalry using these tactics able to push Wheeler's force successively back 15 miles; they were finally able to scatter Wheeler's force when he concentrated his men to make a desperate final stand near Farmington.

Similar attempts by some Union commanders to utilize a combination of dismounted fire tactics with mounted cavalry charge continued throughout the war. Confronted by a large Confederate force under S.J. Gholson and Brig. Gen. Daniel Ruggles at Tupelo, Mississippi, on May 5, 1863, Col. Florence M. Cornyn, a brigade commander, after deploying his skirmishers, ordered two squadrons of the Seventh Kansas Cavalry, armed with Colt's Revolving Rifles, to dismount and attack frontally on foot. The Tenth Missouri was held in reserve and ordered to charge as soon as the enemy line showed signs of wavering.

Col. Smith D. Atkins's brigade employed similar tactics when Kilpatrick's temporary headquarters was attacked on November 18, 1864, during Sherman's March to the Sea. Confederate troops charged "in splendid style," closely supported by artillery firing double shot, and another rebel force attempted to work its way around the Union right flank. Undeterred, the defenders, dismounted cavalry, poured in a withering close-range fire that repelled the frontal assault. The threat on the flank was quashed by the simultaneous counterattack of the Ninth Michigan Volunteer Cavalry, dismounted, and Tenth Ohio Volunteer Cavalry, mounted.

One of the best examples of a sophisticated orchestration of dismounted and mounted cavalry tactics was employed by Gen. George A. Custer's command in the Shenandoah Valley. On March 2, 1865 after driving in the enemy pickets, Union commanders determined that the main Confederate position was along a series of hills west of Waynesborough, Virginia. Though only after needlessly bloody fighting did Custer decide that the rebel position could only be taken by frontal attack, he did notice a weakness that could be exploited. The Confederate left flank was not anchored on the South River but thrown slightly forward. Custer decided to try to advance through this gap. The men in three cavalry regiments, armed with Spencer repeaters, were dismounted and led through the woods until they were opposite the point to be attacked, but still unobserved by the enemy. Colonel William Wells's Second Brigade meanwhile preoccupied the enemy with a strong showing of mounted skirmishers. Colonel Henry Capehart's Third Brigade plus two other regiments from the First Brigade were ordered to charge the enemy in front as soon as the attack began. In an effort to further deceive the enemy, the Union horse artillery, initially in plain view, ostentatiously retired, but it was then surreptitiously brought back under the cover of the woods.

The signal given, the Woodruff's horse artillery opened fire, forcing the defenders to lie down behind their cover. The three regiments of dismounted cavalry rushed forward, while the mounted cavalry, including Wells's skirmishers, charged forward. The artillery continued to fire furiously until their line of fire was obscured by the onrushing Union troops. The ploy proved wonderfully successful. Not only were the Confederates pushed out of their seemingly formidable entrenchments with few Union casualties, but they were completely routed and pushed back 12 miles through Rockfish Gap.

Maj. Arthur Wagner was one of the first to recognize that probably the Civil War's most lasting contribution to military science was the development of the new type of field fortification used from the Overland Campaign (May 1864) onward. In a paper read before the Military Historical Society of Massachusetts on December 7, 1897, Wagner contradistinguished the shallow trenches dug by soldiers under fire, what he called "hasty intrenchments," from intricate fortifications built by engineers. Wagner was referring to a practice that was observed from 1864 onward, wherein as soon as a soldier came under fire, he used his tin cup and plate to carve out a shallow trench protected by a small mound of earth.

Although both sides had utilized field fortifications before this 1864 campaign, these had been mostly reserved for strategically important positions, such as the approach to Richmond from the lower peninsula (at Yorktown). Trying to hold onto the Tennessee and Cumberland River waterways during early 1862, for example, the Confederates attempted to strengthen Fort Donelson with an assortment of defensive works, which included earthworks and outlying abatis. Of course, the rows of breastworks and entrenchments that protected Vicksburg are the best-known example of such prepared defenses. Wagner argued that given the effectiveness of the new longer-range weaponry, this new defensive style of warfare should have been employed much earlier during the conflict.

In actuality, even during the early stages of the war, field fortifications were used more extensively in both the Eastern and the Western theaters of operations than recognized by Wagner and his contemporaries. The problem was that, writing a few years after the publication of *The Century War Series* (now known as *Battle and Leaders*) and the *Official Records*, Civil War historians were initially limited to the information that they and a select circle of colleagues could obtain. The days in which one could turn to a number of secondary sources for each campaign or battle were still in the future.

In contrast, a modern-day historian can compile a list of all recorded instances in which entrenchments, abatis, and breastworks were utilized by simply keying in these terms and conducting an electronic search of the *Official Records* on CD-ROM. This yields a much more extensive list of where field fortifications were used during the first stages of the war. As Wagner has pointed out, numerous fortifications of all assortments were constructed near Yorktown almost from the commencement of hostilities in April 1861. However, there is ample evidence that field fortifications were used on a more tactical level to protect some local key point, such as a bridge, crossroads, or mountain pass, or some prominent part of the countryside that would have a commanding influence on any nearby events. This last application certainly was well rooted in existing military scientific tradition; field fortifications had been used with great effect during several famous European battles. The crafty Villars, reinforcing his right wing with a triple row of entrenchments during the Battle of Malplaquet (September 11, 1709), consternated Marlborough and Prince Eugene. At Fontenoy (May 11, 1745) French troops led by the great Marshal de Saxe sufficiently benefited from several adroitly placed redoubts to repulse their perennial foes the British. During the Napoleonic era the Russian redoubts contributed to the staggering bloodletting at Borodino (September 7, 1812.)

Beauregard apparently entertained similar intentions for his Federal guests during their first sortie into northern Virginia. On July 19, 1861, 2 days before the First Battle of Bull Run, Brig. Gen. Irvin McDowell reported stumbling into an "unusually heavy abatis" that the rebels had thrown across the Warrenton Road just beyond the Stone Bridge over the Bull Run. Such precautions certainly were not limited to the rebels, and the day of the battle saw the Union constructing similar defensive works in an effort to protect their left flank, which they had intended to refuse. The pioneers of the Garibaldi Guards, for example, had been ordered to build a redoubt with two embrasures so that the section of guns thus protected could sweep the Old Braddock Road.

If Americans were merely following an established tradition when they fortified part of a battlefield, they definitely had entered "uncharted territory" as soon as they used similar methods to guard a mountain pass or a bridge across an important river. Confronted with Napoleon quickly crossing and recrossing what is today the northern Italian countryside, the Austrians in 1796 and 1800, for example, had never attempted to interdict his movements with strategically placed entrenchments and breastworks along an important mountain pass or crossroad. However, dozens of examples of just such a tactic are found during the first 2 years of the Civil War. Both sides resorted to the same defensive precautions to guard the mountain passes in western Virginia. Not only did Union forces in June 1861 construct entrenchments in a hill overlooking Philippi, but they also used abatis to obstruct the approach to the Cheat Bridge. The Confederates used similar tactics a few months later to guard Carnifix Ferry in the same general area of the state. The next spring, reconnoitering along the Hock Road which led from Purdy, Tennessee, to Corinth, Mississippi, Union forces encountered at a vital crossroads a strong defensive position held by infantry and artillery protected by rifle pits and earthworks.

Of course, such efforts were relatively few and far between and were anything but routine. However, another development was underway, both more spontaneous and widespread, which would eventually evolve into an even more effective set of defensive tactics, which can be thought of as the precursors to the hasty entrenchments that Wagner felt were so important. This was the tendency for many soldiers to exploit whatever defensive cover was available. One of the simplest but most effective methods was simply to lie down as soon as one came under fire.

In many respects this was anathema to the fundamental principles underlying traditional close-order tactics. Though some European officers had occasionally experimented with this tactic, its use was generally frowned upon. The rebellious Scots often would fall to the ground just before the British would level a volley. Quickly jumping up, they would continue to rush in upon their hated enemy. The royalists in La

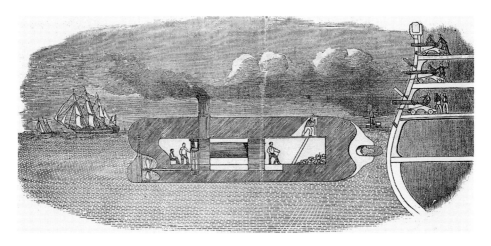

Plate 16. In 1853, James Nasmyth proposed the idea of attaching a large underwater mortar to an almost entirely submerged vessel. This illustration of a submarine mortar frigate from 1853 could have been an inspiration for the *H.L. Hunley. Scientific American, Vol. VIII, no. 23, Feb. 19, 1853*

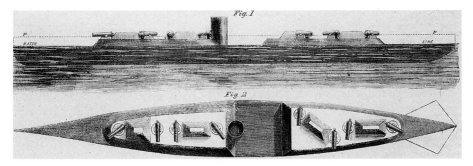

Plate 17. With the start of the war interest in the Stevens Floating Battery was revived. The editors of *Scientific American* touted it as the most progressive vessel ever designed. *Scientific American, Aug. 31, 1861*

Plate 18. This depiction of the Frémont Body Guards's second charge in a forest near Springfield, Missouri shows Union cavalry delivering close range pistol and carbine fire while still mounted, a popular tactic in the rough terrain that covered much of the Western theatre. *Frank Leslie's Pictorial History of the War, 1862*

Plate 19. During the Battle of Dranesville, Virginia, Union commanders utilized open infantry columns to attack. This ensured each tier in the column was outside the "dangerous space" of the preceding one. It is improbable that friendly infantry would have so calmly crossed in front of artillery, even though the latter was positioned on an elevation. *Frank Leslie's Pictorial History of the War, 1862*

Plate 20. The Tennessee River, February 6, 1862; the bombardment of Fort Henry by the Union Mississippi flotilla under Flag Officer Foote. From left to right: *St. Louis, Carondelet, Cincinnati* (flag ship), *Essex, Conestoga, Taylor* and *Lexington. Frank Leslie's Pictorial History of the War, 1862*

Plate 21. Small arms and incoming artillery fire were not the only dangers artillerymen had to face. There was a very real chance that the piece would explode if improperly handled, as in the catastrophic bursting of this rifled artillery gun. *Frank Leslie's Pictorial History of the War, 1862*

Plate 22. New York and Massachusetts infantry conduct a bayonet charge against a 3-gun battery. The Fifty-first New York in a column advances *à la Zouave*, i.e., they are running forward at 180 paces per minute. The Twenty-first Massachusetts is shown on the right. *Frank Leslie's Pictorial History of the War, 1862*

Plate 23. Much Civil War combat occurred over the rough type of terrain shown in this illustration of forested ground with tall grass. *Frank Leslie's Pictorial History of the War, 1862*

Plate 24. The clash between the *USS Monitor* and the *Virginia* (aka *Merrimac*) during the Battle of Hampton Roads, second day (March 9, 1862). *Frank Leslie's Pictorial History of the War, 1862*

Plate 25. This depiction of General Taylor's decisive charge during the Battle of Winchester (March 23, 1862) appears to be a romanticized ideal propogating the myth of bayonet fighting in an open field. Hand-to-hand combat infrequently occurred. However, because of the stonewall, it could have occurred here. (Once again, note the open column of attack in the central background.) *Frank Leslie's Pictorial History of the War, 1862*

Plate 26. This early illustration captures a scene that would be repeated countless times during the Civil War. In the days of black powder, billowing clouds of smoke would quickly obscure the firing line. When fighting in dense woods, the infantrymen could see little other than their comrades immediately beside them, leading to great confusion. Based on a battlefield sketch by M.H. Lowe. *Frank Leslie's Pictorial History of the War, 1862*

Plate 27. The dynamics of a charge—this action at Blue Ridge Pass on September 14 1862 illustrates the dynamics of a typical infantry charge. Since the men in the rear of the defending line have started to retire, this bold offensive might have been successful if the attackers continued to advance. *Frank Leslie's Illustrated Weekly, October 4, 1862*

Plate 28. This cavalry versus cavalry melee occurred between the Sixth US cavalry and opposing force under Stuart. Illustrated from a battlefield sketch submitted by R.E. Small. *Frank Leslie's Illustrated Weekly, June 7, 1862.*

Plate 29. Part of the Union line during an action at Charles City Road, Virginia, on June 30, 1862. In contrast to Napoleonic and Frederickian-era infantry, the men are ordered to kneel while they wait. From left to right are Rush's Lancers, Colonel Porter's First Massachusetts battery, Colonel Platt's Regular battalion, Hexamer Battery and on the right, the Sixteenth New York lying down. Adapted from a sketch by William Wavd. *Frank Leslie's Illustrated Weekly, August 2, 1862*

Plate 30. Fighting over fortifications could result in bloody close-in combat as shown by this illustration of a heroic charge of the Seventy-ninth New York infantry led by Lt.Col. Morrison against the Tower battery on James Island, South Carolina. Illustrated from a battlefield sketch by R.E. Small. *Frank Leslie's Illustrated Weekly, July 12, 1862*

Vendée employed similar tactics. During the Peninsular War (1809–14), Wellington had occasionally ordered his men to crouch or lie down, sheltered by a hillcrest or an undulation in the ground, while awaiting their approaching foe. However, this was considered a novelty at the time and not common practice. The problem was that once they were on the relative safety of the ground, it proved extremely difficult to get most European troops to return the more exposed upright position along the firing line. Near the end of the Battle of Parma (June 29, 1734), for example, a sizeable portion of the infantry was seen to be crawling around and refused to stand up.

In contrast, this technique was used repeatedly during the Civil War, and usually without such embarrassing results. The first examples are found among Western troops a full year before the practice is noticed among their Eastern counterparts. After the battle of Wilson's Creek (Missouri, August 10, 1861), Maj. John M. Schofield, First Missouri Infantry, would report that the rebel forces had advanced to within 30 to 40 yards of the Union artillery in an informal line, three to four ranks deep, and the men in an assortment of postures, some standing and many kneeling and lying down. A few months later during an action near Ironton and Fredericktown, Missouri, (October 21), seeking cover from a brisk artillery, a Confederate regiment lay down behind the crest of a hill. Another observer on the same side of the battlefield noted that most of Lowe's command, ordered to lie down, would roll over on their backs to reload and then fire in either a kneeling or a prone position.

Within weeks Union officers would report that their men had taken similar precautions. Several times during the engagement at Belmont, Missouri (November 7), the Seventh Iowa Infantry had to lie down to escape a hot artillery fire, while at Fort Donelson the Twelfth Illinois Infantry found itself so hotly engaged in small arms fire that its men had to prostrate themselves on the ground to lessen the chances of being hit. After the Battle of Pea Ridge (Arkansas, March 7–8, 1862), Col. Thomas Pattison of the Eighteenth Indiana Infantry attributed the relatively low number of casualties taken by his regiment to this defensive precaution.

It would be several months before troops in the East began to follow suit. The Fifth Wisconsin Infantry did during the Battle of Williamsburg (May 5, 1862), and a number of regiments on both sides did at Fair Oaks (May 31–June 1).

Describing how he ordered his men to take similar evasive action when suddenly faced with a withering small arms fire during the Battle of Richmond, Kentucky (August 20, 1862), Maj. Frederick G. Bracht sheds some light upon, if not the origin of this practice, a factor that may have contributed to its popularity:

> Seeing it was suicide to stand the men were ordered to fall upon the ground, which they promptly did, and continued *(à la Zouave)* from that position to pour into the fields from which the balls were raining so thick upon us a prompt and steady fire.

When he ordered his men to fall on the ground to avoid the enemy fire, Bracht was clearly aware that Zouave doctrine, which had been discussed so frequently in military circles before the war, called for this reaction when under fire. This might explain an otherwise cryptic remark made by Lew Wallace when he was asked to describe the fighting for Fort Donelson for a chapter in *The Century War Series*. Wallace recalled his thoughts as he looked upon the Eleventh Indiana and Eighth Missouri, two regiments that had been part of a brigade he personally commanded: "I knew they had been admirably drilled in zouave tactics. . . . I was sure they would take their men to the top of the bluff."

Although Zouave doctrine might have provided a stimulus to looser, less formalized methods of combat, others may argue that in America the real inducement lay in the nature of the terrain over which the Civil War was fought. Much of the day-to-day campaigning took place over vast distances and on extremely difficult terrain, especially in the West. The densely forested, broken ground seemed to work against neatly orchestrated close-order formations while simultaneously offering the hope of defensive cover. Defensive shelter took many forms. One of the simplest was the stone fence, and the combatants were not slow to appreciate its defensive properties. This was especially true in Jackson's campaigning in the Shenandoah

Valley during the spring and summer of 1862. In this part of Virginia, the stone was used to demarcate individual lots of farmland, so as a result the battlefields in this area were fecund with this type of defensive cover. During the Battle of Kernstown (March 23), Confederate forces operated from behind a stone fence with noticeable advantage. Both sides repeatedly exploited the same type of protected cover during the first Battle of Winchester (May 25). Col. W.S.H. Baylor of the Fifth Virginia Infantry ordered some of his skirmishers to take cover behind this type of barrier.

Chance encounters frequently took place between hostile groups who lacked artillery support, and if the defenders were competently led and had sufficient time, they would hastily erect whatever field fortifications they could. Many instances can be found of defenders transforming houses to something vaguely reminiscent of the frontier blockhouses. On December 21, 1862, for example, Colonel Morgan with 250 Union cavalrymen successfully held off a Confederate force of several thousand men led by General Van Dorn. Learning of the rebels' approach the day before, Morgan and his men started to fortify their position at Davis's Mills, Mississippi, on the Mississippi Central Railroad between Bolivar, Tennessee, and Coffeeville, Mississippi. The old sawmill was converted into a "blockhouse." Its walls were reinforced with old railroad ties, and cotton bales and an earthwork were thrown around its base. These defensive arrangements were completed by 11 o'clock the night before the engagement. This proved to be a valuable investment of time and effort. The next morning the greatly superior Confederate force attacked. The rebels were repulsed, and the Confederates suffered several hundred dead and wounded, compared to only three Union cavalrymen wounded.

A similar scenario had occurred earlier that year at Fort Donelson (February 1862), where another Union force would ward off several brigades of rebel infantry. Once again there were disproportionate losses between the attacker and the defender ensconced behind entrenchments. This time the attackers lost 900 men killed and wounded. The Union defenders had only 13 killed and 51 wounded.

• • •

TYPICAL FIELD ABATIS

Before the advent of rifled artillery, intricate Vauban-style fortresses continued to dominate military engineering. In seafaring nations, such as Britain and France, there was a continued need for strong coastal defenses. Every effort was devoted to make the defenses proof against artillery, and suitable materials, if not available locally, were brought in from afar. Sturdy stone or brick walls were sunk and protected by many feet of tightly compacted earthen inclines, so as to provide no visible target. Military authorities cautioned against the use of wood in a fortification. Though proof against small arms fire, when hit by shell or solid shot, logs or planks were usually torn into hundreds of splinters, which caused serious, even fatal, injuries to the defenders.

In the West the American army for decades had relied upon wooden stockades and blockhouses for protection against Indians on the warpath. Stockade walls consisted of medium-sized logs punctuated every few feet with a loophole. To discourage the enemy from taking shelter close to the walls underneath the loopholes, the fort was designed to allow a deadly close range cross fire. Typically, two log houses were placed on opposite corners of the stockade, while each wall was strengthened by a series of overhanging projections called *tambours*. Often the defensive works consisted of a solitary structure known as a blockhouse. Generally two stories high, it was formed from large logs laid one on top of the other. The second story overlapped the first floor by several feet, creating a *machicoulis*. Loopholes in the floor allowed the defenders to pour in a deadly fire on anyone who ventured up to its walls. The roof, also of thick logs, was covered with 2 feet of earth to prevent it from catching on fire from burning arrows. American Indians never had artillery, so these defenses were more than sufficient against their small arms.

With their high profiles, stockades and blockhouses would be useless against an enemy equipped with even light artillery. Even though both Union and Confederate armies soon possessed a sizeable amount of artillery, the theoretical undesirability of wooden defenses did not deter either side from throwing up wooden and earthen fieldworks to an unprecedented degree. The reasons are not hard to find. Much of the contested land was at least partially forested, so there was always an abundance of timber. The rough terrain over which the day-to-day campaigning took place also meant that it was usually necessary to take additional defensive precautions to prevent from being surprised, while the increased killing power of newly emerging weaponry added other incentives to seek safety behind fieldworks. Sharpshooters armed with the new rifle muskets could pick off an unwary victim from way beyond the picket and vedette lines, so from the summer of 1862 onwards, it became increasingly necessary to find shelter from these depredations.

A big reason for the popularity of wooden defenses came from the combatants themselves, who, especially those from the South or West, were inured to manual labor and generally familiar with carpentry and woodworking. At first the typical breastwork was constructed by piling up several logs, heavy pine whenever possible, one on top of the other. These were often 10 feet high and occasionally as high as 15. Although this afforded some protection against small arms, it was insufficient protection from even small-caliber artillery, so other precautions were necessary. The side of the breastwork facing the enemy was usually banked. Soft dirt was shoveled in front

This blockhouse near Fort Corcoran, Arlington Heights, Virginia, was typical of those used during the earlier Indian Wars. The overhanging second floor, called a *machicoulis*, had openings in the floors so that the defenders could fire upon attackers near the walls. *Frank Leslie's Illustrated Weekly*, Aug. 17, 1861.

and packed down, forming an incline, similar to the glacis of a fortress. Shot or shell hitting the incline would either deflect up into the air or bury itself harmlessly in the thick layer of protective soil.

At Spotsylvania, 2nd Lt. Henry Meyer, a Union cavalryman, discovered that other materials were occasionally banked up in lieu of soil. In need of firewood, he ordered some of his men to steal a few rails from an abandoned breastwork. Hearing a report that someone saw a dead Confederate inside the breastworks, he ordered portions of it dismantled. Great was their dismay when inside they discovered that those who originally had constructed the fieldworks used the bodies of Confederate soldiers instead of the usual earth!

As they acquired practical experience, both sides improved upon the traditional field entrenchments. The defenders, if possible, would place another large log, about 15 inches in diameter, along the top of the breastworks. Enough space was left between the top and bottom sections so that a rifle barrel could stick through. The defenders could crawl behind the entrenchments with relative impunity and coolly aim and fire without exposing their heads. The heavy log at eye level had originally been separated from the lower works protecting the infantryman's body by small blocks every few feet. There was one potential problem, however. Occasionally, a cannonball would strike the log squarely, causing it to roll backwards and onto the infantrymen directly to its rear, resulting in severe injury and even death.

However, at some point before 1864, some unknown Confederate discovered an ingenious solution: placing saplings as "roll bars" under and perpendicular to the topmost log. The saplings extended back 8 to 10 feet behind the fieldworks and sloped downwards from the log to the ground. Now if the top log was struck by solid shot, it would roll along the two nearest saplings, and the crouching infantrymen would be spared a headache! As Colonel Scribner, who commanded the Thirty-eighth Indiana Volunteer Infantry, later observed in his memoirs, "As no patent or caveat had been issued by proper authority [regarding this invention], we did not hesitate to adopt it."

Frequently, a skirmish line was thrown out in front of the entrenchments, usually between 100 and 300 yards. These men took refuge in a series of rifle pits. Back closer to the entrenchments, if possible, a large ditch was dug immediately in front of the abatis. The impedimenta at the

Western Field Defenses

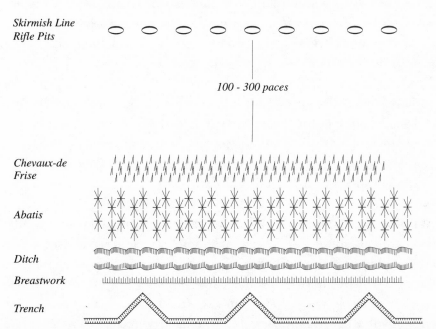

Skirmish Line
Rifle Pits

100 - 300 paces

Chevaux-de
Frise

Abatis

Ditch

Breastwork

Trench

There was tremendous variation among fortifications based on circumstances and personal preferences. However, if there was enough time, an experienced defender would attempt to construct a multi-layered defense.

front of an abatis took the form of rows of long, slender boards and branches, the blunt ends buried into the ground and the sharpened ends facing outward away from the breastwork. In technical manuals these were termed chevaux-de-frise, but they were popularly known as "horse rakes" among Civil War infantrymen. Such formal methods had been used occasionally on the European battlefield.

The heavily forested areas of the American countryside allowed further defensive precautions to be extemporized. Obstacles between the abatis and the rifle pits out front could be quickly formed simply by cutting down rows of small and medium-size trees up to 15 rods in front of the hastily constructed breastworks. The trees were felled so that the branches reached toward the enemy's line. The ends of branches were sharpened to jagged points, becoming abates themselves, and the leaves, foliage, and under-brush were cleared away. Coniferous trees, such as the common pine found throughout much of north-central Virginia, were ideal for this purpose. The ever-present underbrush was also cut and looped over and the tops twisted.

Regardless of which way the branches were pointing, they posed a significant obstacle. To an infantrymen forced to work his way over or through these trees under fire this would appear to be an impossible task:

> Just imagine for a moment a soldier with a knapsack, haversack, tenting outfit, rifle, sixty rounds of ammunition, and his canteen, trying to go from the top of a tree through its branches towards the butt. That would be almost an impossibility, and doubly so under the cruel fire of the enemy.

Trying to avoid just such a fate, most of the enemy's advance would be channeled toward whatever gaps there appeared in the trees, and all semblance of the advancing formations would be lost as men in the ranks made individual choices as to which way to proceed. Of course, counting on just such an eventuality, the defenders trained their small arms and artillery on these narrow passageways.

Even when the attackers managed to reach the abatis by the entrenchments, the grimmest part of the fight was yet to be fought! Crouched on the other side of the breastworks awaited a long row of men with sharp bayonets! Gen. Emory Upton, who though young, was highly respected for his tactical acumen and innovation, would provide a vivid description of how his attack upon Dole's Georgia brigade of Rhode's division was met during the fighting for the salient at Spotsylvania:

> Here occurred a deadly hand-to-hand conflict. The enemy was sitting in their pits with their pieces upright, loaded, and with bayonets fixed ready to impale the first who should leap over, absolutely refused to yield the ground. The first of our men who tired to surmount the works fell pierced through the head by musket balls. Others, seeing the fate of their comrades, held their pieces at arm's-length and fired downward, while others poising their pieces vertically hurled them down upon their enemy, pinning them to the ground.

Seemingly oblivious to the danger around them, some attackers would stand brazenly near the top of the defensive works and fire down at the enemy below them as fast as their comrades could hand them loaded (rifle) muskets. Such frenetic firing was at extremely close range, and foe met foe face to face. Capt. G.B. Adams, who served with the seemingly ubiquitous Nineteenth Massachusetts Regiment, would recall how one of the men in Company C fired at a Confederate soldier just as the latter was himself taking aim. The two were so close that the Union infantrymen's musket was instantly spattered with blood. Many also "clubbed their muskets," trying to hit the enemy with the butt of the musket, or with a rail or a large branch taken from the defensive works.

Though those rash enough to stand out in the open were soon shot down, there was no shortage of replacements. Others searching out

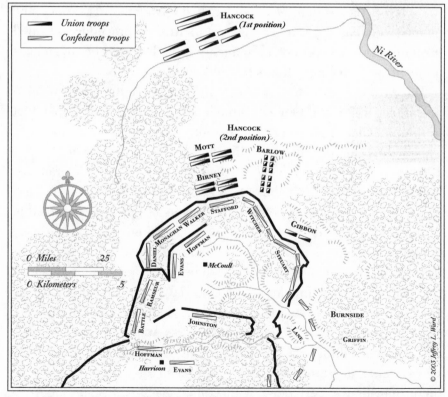

Hancock's Assault on the "Mule Shoe," May 12, 1864. Mott, Birney, and Gibbon's divisions adopted a two-line formation. Barlow's forces had deployed into two rows of columns doubled on the center, similar to columns of division in size and depth, with a different sequence of companies in the column.

crevices and holes in the breastwork would shoot some unsuspecting soldier on the other side, who on his knees thought himself safe from the hand-to-hand above him. Adams remembered one individual who utilized a noticeably different technique. One of the Sixth Wisconsin Infantry was a full-blooded Indian who was used to the more clandestine fighting methods of the West. Cautiously crawling up to the rebel works, he would take careful aim and bring down a man before slowly crawling back to reload his weapon. Closely hugging the ground, he was scarcely visible and repeated the process many times without ever being observed by the enemy.

Sometimes, as at the salient at Spotsylvania, the defender would shore up the defenses with some light artillery. Whenever this happened, the most desperate fighting was over the guns. During Upton's attack Capt. Harry Hale, a member of General Weber's staff, ordered the men around him to sally over the defensive works and retrieve two artillery pieces that the defenders had abandoned. This done, the infantrymen, eager but inexperienced in artillery procedures, loaded them up with whatever potential ammunition they could find, such as projectiles of varying calibers and old musket barrels.

The close-in nature of this type of fighting made the men's position precarious. The viability of one stretch of the line depended upon that of its immediate neighbors. Many would be unable to run to safety when their comrades along the line had broke and fled. On May 12, 1864 the Confederates launched at least five successive counterattacks to retake the outer entrenchments at Spotsylvania. A number of times during the consequent ebb and flow, pockets of rebels were forced to raise a white flag and surrender. Unfortunately, one such group used the white flag as a ruse, firing upon and killing several of the Union soldiers who jumped over the entrenchments to take them prisoner. Enraged, the Union infantrymen along that part of the line gave no more quarter that day, and all potential prisoners were cut down.

This close-in type of fighting of course was extremely deadly. Officials inspecting the Union lines the day after the fighting at Spotsylvania declared that there was even more human carnage there than that experienced at the infamous Bloody Lane at Antietam. The dead on both sides of the entrenchments lay piled high, the bodies "horribly torn and mangled." In fact, there was such a concentration of casualties that several times during the battle, General McGowan had to order that the bodies be removed from the trenches on the right side of the breastworks to clear room for those still able to fight.

The extreme volume of fire in such a limited area also left a visible mark on the natural landscape. When the fighting finally subsided, much to everyone's astonishment entire trees had been felled by the cumulative effect of "minié balls." Several trees 18 inches in diameter had thus met their end, and an oak tree cut down by fire at midnight injured several defenders from a South Carolina regiment.

Yet, for all the suffering and killing, the intensity of the fighting had little impact on how the men on opposing sides felt about each other:

> One of the pleasant features of our fighting is that none of us consider it a personal affair and individually are as friendly to any of our captured antagonists as though no state of war existed. There is no personal animosity whatever, so far as I have seen.

HEMP BALES AND BAGS

Given the vicissitudes of war, a defending force was not always able to construct elaborate field fortifications. Lacking sufficient time to prepare, materials, or human resources, the defender frequently had to extemporize. Caught by surprise, defenders knocked loopholes in a stone or brick house or piled wooden furniture behind a window for added protection. Early in the war troops on both sides discovered that bales of cotton or hemp, even bags of wool, provided protection from small arms fire in an emergency.

One such case occurred on August 29, 1862, when a Confederate force stumbled upon a substantially inferior Union force at Metamora, Tennessee, near the Hatchie River. Positioned in and around the town's railroad depot, Union defenders strengthened their position with a makeshift wall of cotton bales and other material. Though lacking in artillery, the defenders were able to repulse every Confederate attack hurled against them and the latter eventually withdrew. Almost the same scenario was reenacted in October 1863 when 600

Union cavalry under Colonel Clayton's command successfully held off 2500 Confederates and twelve pieces of artillery at Pine Bluffs, Arkansas. Having only 30 minutes to prepare for the upcoming assault, the cavalrymen quickly rolled out bales of cotton from a nearby warehouse. Despite a series of determined attacks, the Confederates were driven off after 5 hours, suffering heavy losses.

Ad hoc field fortifications were certainly never limited to defenders. The value of cotton bales and other similar material during an attack on a strong, prepared position also quickly became apparent to those planning the assault. Light, but nevertheless resistant to even light solid shot, cotton bales could be pushed progressively closer and closer to the defenders. The only drawback was that hemp and cotton were highly combustible and easily set afire by artillery shells. This appears to have been less of a problem with bags of wool. Even with cotton, flammability was not an insurmountable problem, however. Those behind these makeshift defenses simply doused the bales or bags periodically with water.

Probably the best-known use of cotton bales on the offensive occurred during the siege of Lexington, Missouri (September 18–20, 1861). In his official report Confederate Gen. Thomas A. Harris explained that he had ordered the use of the bales. Realizing that the bales were likely to catch fire and had to be thoroughly wetted down, Harris ordered that they be carried first to the nearby banks of the Missouri. Unfortunately, the wet bales were now much heavier, and the Confederate infantrymen, fatigued by the active service of the last few days, were unable to push them up to the crest of the hill. Harris quickly came up with the solution. Dry bales were carried up to the crest, and buckets of water were thrown on them at or near their final position.

Sheltered behind the wet bales, the attackers slowly but irresistibly advanced against the determined, but outnumbered group of Union defenders. All available fire was directed against the moveable "breastworks." Hit by round shot, the bales simply rocked back and forth for a few moments but with no injury to those taking shelter behind. Desperate, the Union cannoneers tried firing red-hot shot, but these also had no effect. The soaked hemp wouldn't catch fire. Realizing that the expected reinforcements would not arrive and the

Confederate assault would inevitably succeed, the Union commander ordered the exhausted group of Union defenders to lay down their arms and surrender.

The lesson doesn't appear to have been thrown away, and one sees similar, albeit more formalized, procedures utilized by Union besiegers in front of Vicksburg in mid-June of 1863. Concentrating their siege effort against the Baldwin's Ferry Road entrance, the Union forces, after completing their parallels, pushed three saps towards the part of the effort occupied by the Second Texas Infantry. To protect the sappers as they labored, large sap rollers were pushed just ahead of each sap. Each sap roller was a 7- to 8-foot long cylinder, about 4 feet in diameter, consisting of a coil of wire.

The Confederates first fired 6- and 12-pounder shot at these sap rollers, but to no effect. Next they threw burning cotton balls impregnated with turpentine but encountered the same results. The three sap rollers continued to advance. Desperate, the defenders wrapped an 18-pounder explosive shell with the same turpentine-cotton solution. The shell exploded in the hands of a Union soldier as he was trying to throw it back, and the resulting fire consumed one of the sap rollers. A second sap roller had a slightly different construction. Its core was formed from two bales of cotton placed end to end. This was set on fire by an artillery fuse fired from a smoothbore musket. An "incessant shower of Miniés" prevented the attackers from putting out these fires, so the attack proved futile.

ATTACKING FIELD FORTIFICATIONS

With the return of peace in 1865, Francis Lippitt, who had served as the colonel of the Second Infantry California and the department commander of California, immediately decided to author a work on military science, as it then existed. The result was *A Treatise on the Tactical Use of the Three Arms* and a *A Treatise on Intrenchments,* both widely acclaimed as cogent and practical syntheses of formal European military scientific theory and the practical experience gained during 4 years of very hard fighting.

Commanders frequently had found it necessary to assault field fortifications, and a portion of Lipitt's *Intrenchments* was devoted to what he considered to be the best methods to be used in such cases.

The tactics described were a sophisticated orchestration of combined arms. The defender's artillery would be overpowered by a bombardment of the attacker's artillery resources. Before the attack it was first necessary to unmask the enemy's artillery. This occasionally could be achieved simply by throwing forward a few companies of skirmishers, as happened at Williamsburg. However, skirmishers frequently were driven off by musket fire before they forced the defending artillery to fire. Often it was more practical to throw forward a few light guns firing canister. The defending artillerymen would usually be soon sufficiently annoyed and return fire, disclosing not only their positions but the number and types of ordnance, as well.

Just before the main assault, a large body of skirmishers would be thrown forward along other points in the line and, unlike with normal assaults, would be encouraged to fire quickly and yell as much as possible. These were sham attacks designed to deceive the enemy as to the true point of the main assault. The artillery would redirect its fire to the portion of the line to be attacked. Ricochet fire would be used to remove the various obstacles usually placed in front of the parapet or abatis. If the area was known to be mined or booby-trapped with mines or grenades to be set off by trip wires, a heavier artillery fire would be ordered. Shells were more useful than round shot in this case. When firing at wooden defenses, it was necessary to use small or at most moderate charges, especially if the artillery was rifled. High-velocity shells would simply pass through the defenses and do little damage. Slower projectiles not only caused more destruction but also generated more splinters, which in turn produced greater collateral injuries among the defenders.

The various obstacles cleared, the artillery would now focus along the length of the breastwork or parapet to be assaulted. This was kept up until the fortifications along that stretch crumbled. Not only would this remove any aboveground obstacles that might delay the advance, but also any ditch in front would necessarily fill up with debris. In the final moments the artillery would lob shells into the open space behind the fortifications to inhibit the movement of the defenders, who, it was hoped, would be driven into underground "bomb-proofs."

Storming the defensive works would be achieved by a determined bayonet charge. Of course, this same tactic was also the best method of defense. Arguing that the bayonet was the most effective method of restoring the defenders' morale and their will to fight, Lippitt claimed:

Experience has proved the bayonet to be the surest reliance for the defense at this moment. In using it, the assailed have the benefit of the moral force acquired by becoming the assailants, are fresher than the climbing enemy, and have the advantage of position.

One way for the attackers to prevent this countermeasure was by the judicious use of hand grenades. Just before leaping over the enemy breastworks, the advancing infantry was to throw the grenades over the defensive works to clear away any of the enemy who still remained. This last step had to be performed with a certain amount of discretion, however, as the enemy, if given a chance, was likely to pick up still unexploded grenades and throw them back at the attackers, as happened during the Union assault on Port Hudson, Louisiana, on June 14, 1863. Around that time at Vicksburg, the Union infantrymen had their own opportunity to discomfit Confederate defenders when the latter attempted to obstruct the besiegers' efforts by throwing lit grenades into the Union ditches. Once more the tables were quickly turned, as the unexploded grenades were sent back to their original owners, where they finally exploded and wreaked havoc.

Such a very careful and highly orchestrated set of combined arms tactics was rarely employed in practice, at least in this full a version. In most cases actual attacks were impromptu affairs with little preliminary planning and virtually no effort to use combined arms techniques. The experience of the Twenty-seventh Georgia Infantry during the battle of Fair Oaks is illustrative of how most attackers responded to a chance discovery of enemy field fortifications during the heat of a hard-fought engagement. They simply overwhelmed the defenders with the weight of musketry, then frightened them away with a determined bayonet charge. The description of the affair is probably best left in Lt. Col. Charles T. Zachry's own words:

> The enemy had concealed himself on the other edge of the abatis, and when we had arrived within this easy range opened a tremendous fire of musketry, with some grape and shell. We replied with greater effect upon the enemy, as shown by their dead and wounded, for a brief period, then charged over the abatis, the enemy's sense of danger on seeing our bayonets intrepidly advancing allowing him to take but little advantage of the exposure of our men in crossing such a place.

Of course, the attacking force was not always as successful as the Twenty-seventh Georgia Infantry had been. More often than not the assault stalled in front of the defensive works, and the operation devolved into a general, but strategically ineffective, firefight, where noise and pandemonium reigned but all forward movement ceased. Col. William R. Morrison of the Forty-ninth Illinois Infantry remembers how the attack of the Union Third Brigade of the First Division was stymied in exactly this way as it advanced against the outlying Confederate defenses around Fort Donelson on February 13, 1862. After throwing out some skirmishers, the brigade quickly marched 200 yards down a hill. Though they had to pass through thick brush, the brigade continued on in "perfect order" and then proceeded up the incline towards the opposite ridge, defended by a rebel redoubt. The Forty-ninth, on the right, had the advantage of passing through a wide slashing and soon was ahead of the rest of the brigade.

When about 50 yards from the enemy breastworks, the regiment encountered an "almost impassible abatis." Up to this point, the Union attackers had been allowed to advance unmolested, but the skirmishers in front of the main line started to draw the defender's fire as they slowly struggled through the impenetrable abatis. In his report Morrison recalled how he appraised the unfolding situation and how he quickly formulated a plan of action:

> We had advanced to within less than fifty paces of the enemy's works without his offering any opposition, and were making our

way slowly but surely, when our skirmishers commenced drawing the fire of the enemy, who was undoubtedly waiting for us. I had now obtained a position from which I could see the nature of the difficulties to our progress, which consisted mostly in the almost impassable nature of the breastworks and the length of time required to climb over them. I at once determined to reserve my fire until the top of the works was reached, when I could create such confusion with one volley as would enable us to get over before the enemy recovered from the shock. Many of my men had already fallen and the others wanted shot for shot. They were undisciplined and had never been under fire, and as I beckoned and called them forward I saw them coming involuntarily to a "ready." Passing quickly to the rear, unfortunately they fired without orders, though with fair precision and some effect.

The Seventeenth and the Forty-eighth encountered similar difficulties as they in turn arrived at the abatis. The advance of the third brigade came to a halt.

It would be equally inaccurate, however, to suggest that all efforts against entrenchments, breastworks, and abatis were such ad hoc affairs in which the result depended upon luck or the pure pluck of the attackers. One also can find examples of more thought-out efforts, such as the first assault on Vicksburg, Mississippi, on May 22, 1863. Here the enemy position in front of Osterhaus's Ninth Division appeared to be impregnable. Large portions of the hill occupied by the Confederates were "perpendicular." All the trees on the slope had been cut down and used to build a "most intricate abatis" which extended almost completely in front of the Ninth Division. To make matters worse, the defenders' rifle pits were so positioned as to deliver a murderous, close-range cross fire wherever the Union could be expected to attack.

The Union forces had several days to prepare for the impending offense, and every yard along the enemy line was thoroughly examined. After carefully deliberating how he would employ his division, Osterhaus decided that his division would launch its attack up the steep acclivity in front of the position then occupied by Captain Lanphere's guns (Battery G, First Michigan Light Artillery). The report issued after the battle provided his reasons. The steepness of the hill at that point produced a "dead spot" in which the Union troops could form without fear of Confederate fire. There were also fewer obstructions than along other portions of the defending line. Most importantly, the ridge at this point was intersected by a number of ravines, or "water drains," varying between 8 to 10 feet deep and 10 to 15 feet wide. Marching at the bottom of these ravines, the men would not be exposed to the deadly enfilading fire so destructive at ranges within 150 yards.

The bulk of Osterhaus's infantry was organized into three columns as follows: right, Twenty-second Kentucky and Forty-second Ohio Inf.; center, 114th Ohio and Forty-ninth and Sixty-ninth Indiana Infantry; left, Seventh Kentucky and the 118th Illinois Infantry. Osterhaus specifically ordered each column to be formed into "columns of divisions at half distance," that is, the distance between each tier in the columns was equivalent to half of its frontage. The broken terrain precluded the use of lines or wider columns. The Sixteenth Ohio Infantry was deployed as skirmishers in front of and between columns, while the 120th Ohio Infantry was to throw out a strong line of skirmishers on the extreme left and open a heavy fire to serve as a diversion. The artillery was to fire at the Confederate fortifications starting at daybreak in order to soften up the position.

The assault began as scheduled at 10 A.M. on the May 21. At first all went well, and the men in the three columns easily cleared the obstructions at the base of the hill. Despite a heavy defensive fire, the attackers made it up the incline to the crest of the hill. They were within 20 to 30 yards of the Confederate works and could distinctly hear the orders issued to the defending infantry.

Unfortunately, at this point they unexpectedly encountered a new set of defensive obstructions and were forced to lie down and seek protection amidst the contours of the ground. Here they remained for the rest of the day, though the sharpshooters and those at the front of the columns maintained a well-directed fire, which forced the gunners to leave their guns. The attack had devolved into a standoff, and finally, at the end of the day, the assault deemed a failure, and the men were called back, though a strong line of pickets and sharpshooters were left at the most advanced position.

WIRES

The first known use of wire obstructions in European warfare was recorded during the Schleswig-Holstein War in 1864. During the siege of Dybböl (March 15–April 17), the beleaguered Danish defenders blocked the approach to their outworks with a network of iron wire. This was positioned to allow the attackers to advance within short range of small arms fire; then the attackers, suddenly checked by a hitherto unnoticed obstacle, would be mowed down by a murderous fire. This defensive measure proved to be very effective, and the Prussian attackers were required to retire several times after taking stiff casualties.

The use of wire during this siege, strictly speaking, was not a first in the art of warfare. The first recorded use of wire as a defensive measure occurred in northern Virginia in 1861. One evening (December 4) while riding along the Old Braddock Road near Fairfax Court House, some troopers of the Sixth Virginia Cavalry espied a wire stretched across the road to snag unsuspecting horsemen. Drawing up, they were immediately fired upon by a small Union force waiting in ambush. Whether inspired by this affair or not, it is impossible to determine, but in any case on April 6, 1862, General Longstreet instructed his cavalry officers to use similar techniques to protect themselves against enemy cavalry. When encamped they were instructed to run wires across any incoming roads to hinder an unexpected enemy charge. Though it is unclear whether his officers followed the advice, soon after the start of the Gettysburg campaign while assaulting a rebel battery (June 14, 1863), the Eighty-seventh Pennsylvania Infantry and the Eighteenth Connecticut encountered "a perfect barricade of telegraph wire wound together and stretched from tree to tree across roads and through woods and fields, so as to completely obstruct the farther progress of cavalry in this direction."

Wire entanglements played a more prominent role during the siege of the Vicksburg, when Union forces placed a stranglehold on this important fortified position overlooking the Mississippi River. Discovering that a "rear line" possessed some vulnerable weak spots, Maj. Samuel H. Lockett, chief engineer of Confederate forces at Vicksburg, ordered his engineers on May 25, 1863, to strengthen the line with a series of abatis, palisades, ditches, and "entanglements of pickets and telegraph wire." This was no isolated incident; the defenders at Vicksburg used such wire entanglements in front of other vulnerable positions. To strengthen the right portion of his position, Gen. F. A. Shoup, who commanded a brigade in M. L. Smith's Division, had a ditch dug in front of his line of troops. The area immediately in front of a redan was further protected by stockades formed of a "brush and wire entanglement" combination. Taking a close look at the defenses after Vicksburg had capitulated, Union engineers noticed that in many places the defenders had carefully woven wire around and between 2- to 8-foot inclining stakes.

The lesson was not lost on the Union military, and engineers soon adopted similar techniques when it became necessary to shore up their own defensive positions. Burnside, in a later report, remembered that although the main defenses at Knoxville had been completed by November 20, over the next several days the men continued to refine the works with "abatis, *chevaux-de-frise*, and wire entanglements . . . wherever they were necessary." After the bloody repulse of a Confederate attempt to capture an outlying portion of the Knoxville defenses known as Fort Saunders, in his own report Lieutenant Colonel Hutchins of the Third Georgia Battalion Sharpshooters recounted how the wire entanglements tied from stump to stump, coupled with a 4- to 6-foot ditch, whose 60- to 70-degree slopes of hard, slippery clay made it difficult to climb, conspired to impede the assault.

The efficacy of the new wire defenses soon became widely known, and their use spread to the Eastern theater of operations the next year, (1864) as both sides settled down for the protracted and bloody struggle around Richmond, Virginia.

PART VI

THE
DISTINCTIVENESS
OF LATER
CAMPAIGNS

Chapter 27

FIGHTING IN THE WILDERNESS

N orth Americans frequently have used the term *wilderness* to refer to the large stretches of dense, untamed forest that once covered so much of the Eastern and central portions of the continent. During colonial times, it was common practice to call the unsettled, forested areas to the West of the colonies the "wilderness."

In the study of the Civil War, the term tends to have a much more narrow meaning. Here "the Wilderness" refers to a "dark, dense and silent forest" that was to occupy a stage well out of proportion to the size of land it covered. Extending roughly from Chancellorsville, Virginia, to a little beyond Mine Run, this relatively small stretch of highly entangled, thickly wooded area would be the scene of some of the most fiercely contested fighting during 1863 and 1864. It was here in 1863 that Joe Hooker's army, severely bloodied and almost completely outflanked, would be forced back across the Rapidan River, nipping the Union's offensive designs in the East before they had a chance to unfold. The very next year in an effort to doggedly fight his way closer to Richmond, Grant choose to start his campaign in almost the exactly same place.

Although the Battles of Chancellorsville and of the Wilderness were two distinct engagements—fought a year apart almost to the day—in this work they will be considered in tandem. They were fought in the same general area, and part of the two battlefields in fact overlapped.

However, there is a more compelling reason to look at both battles side by side than simply proximity of location. In both cases the participants fought and died struggling for possession of the same type of unyielding terrain. In both the nearly impassible forest left an indelible mark on every aspect of combat, restricting not only the tactics that could be used but even which arms would participate. In most other battles, the artillery played an important role, softening up key defensive positions or, conversely, helping to inflict sufficient casualties to dull the enemy's assaults. During the Battle of the Wilderness and much of Chancellorsville, whatever artillery came into play was limited to the few roads and paths. The cavalry was similarly denied any consequential role. Lacking open fields, the mounted arm was doomed to play an even more passive role than usual and forced to remain in reserve in the rear.

Almost the entire struggle devolved upon the infantry, though even the latter's normal modus operandi was also restricted by the terrain. Ranged firefights were limited to the few clearings that were encountered here and there. The generals on either side were denied all but the most basic maneuvering, while the great preponderance of the fighting occurred at extremely close ranges. The men simply couldn't see any farther through the trees and underbrush.

THE NATURE OF THE LAND

Located on the south bank of the Rapidan, the Wilderness was approximately 10 miles West of Fredericksburg. There are conflicting estimates of its size. Recently, Noah Andre Trudeau, in *The Civil War Battlefield Guide*, estimated it to be some 12 miles wide by about 6 miles in depth. Depending on how they defined the region, some others have arrived at smaller estimations. George Ward, who served and fought with the Second Pennsylvania Veteran Heavy Artillery, estimated the Chancellorsville Wilderness to be only 3 to 7 miles long.

There has been no debate, however, about the nature of the ground and the difficulties it posed to soldiers fighting over it. John Robson, a one-legged Confederate veteran, would forever remember this "mournful" country. Its dense forests were thickly congested with a motley assortment of small pines and scrub oak, cedar, and dogwood. This coupled with its extremely thick underbrush and frequent wet, low-lying ground made it almost impossible to traverse. W. A. Smith, a North Carolina officer, would describe the region as a "great, dismal forest containing . . . the worst kind of thicket of second-growth trees . . . so thick . . . [that] one could barely see ten paces." When piecing together a regimental history of the Second Pennsylvania Veteran Heavy Artillery in the years following the Great Rebellion, George Ward provided one of the most atmospheric descriptions of the great forest:

> It is a strip of country . . . which is penetrated here and there by roads, but whose depths furnish safe retreats for the wild cat, the owl, the serpent and the fox. It is a lonely ride along the best traveled highway in time of peace. The hoot of the owl is heard from the dark thickets at noonday, and the deadly moccasin snake leaves his trail in the dust as he crosses the highway to plunge into a denser swamp.

The region had not always been so inhospitable, and the primeval forest encountered by the first settlers would have been much easier to traverse and originally lacking the eerie qualities so frequently attributed to the region during the Civil War era. During the early eighteenth century, Virginia Governor Alexander Spotswood had attempted to tame the wilderness, and hence the name that was bestowed on the forest. German colonists were brought in to work the region's iron mines. During this era mining operations required vast amounts of lumber in order to shore up the mine shafts, fuel the smelters, and plank the roads. To meet these demands, large tracts of the forest were cleared. Unfortunately, the forest proved intractable, and mining efforts were quickly abandoned. Secondary growth soon covered the areas that had been cleared; thus was born an even denser, more inhospitable forest.

With bloodhounds close at their heels, many runaway slaves and fugitives sought refuge inside the impenetrable forest and its swamps. Though safe from slave master and the law once inside, few runaways were ever heard of again. Many fell victim to the deadly snakes. The only traces of civilization were a few small clearings here and there.

Although the name *Chancellorsville* suggests a town or at the least a large village or hamlet, the name is misleading. Chancellorsville was a single large brick mansion with spacious wings that had served as a hotel. Situated in the middle of a large clearing it was surrounded by a number of outbuildings.

MARCHING THROUGH THE WILDERNESS

Although the heavy forest was intersected by a myriad of "obscure and primitive" footpaths which seemed to run in all directions, only three plank roads and the Orange-Fredericksburg turnpike afforded anything resembling continuous, easily negotiable roads through this area. But even these so-called highways were but shadows of their counterparts in more settled parts of the country. George Ward recalled:

> There is not one spot on the main highway where one could see the length of the regiment, on the march, and he would to hide from the whole world has but to take twenty steps to the right or the left.

This dense forest just south of the Rapidan River posed a heavy obstacle to every aspect of military operations. It was extremely difficult simply to march or advance through this area, let alone attempt to overpower a determined, experienced enemy. Clay Mac-Cauley, who served as a lieutenant in the 126th Pennsylvania Volunteer Infantry, vividly recalled the first few moments as his regiment moved past the Chancellorsville Hotel and into the foreboding forest:

> What an advance! Leaving the open field we entered the wilderness. Our progress was for the most part a mere scramble; over logs, through dense underbrush, briers, and in swamp-mud. We were scratched and bruised, and our clothing torn.

When compared to the fate of many others who struggled through this rough country, however, MacCauley was fortunate to have come out with these relatively minor inconveniences. Others, such as the Russian immigrant Peter Petroff, who fought in the same area during Grant's '64 campaign, were literally almost killed by this most inhospitable forest,

which in its seemingly purposive enmity to humankind appears equal to
Tolkien's Old Forest in the mythical Middle Earth. Called up to advance
into combat against the rebel forces, Petroff's regiment formed in battle
line. Regulation order lasted but for a few seconds, as the formation
advanced at the double quick and almost immediately became entangled in the ubiquitous thick brush and vines. Samuel Wing, who fought
in this same string of actions with the Third Maine Infantry, would later
recall how this density of the underbrush made it impossible even to
keep one's eyes open while advancing, so real was the threat of having
one's eyes poked out. Shutting his eyes and determinedly advancing in
the same general direction as his unit, a few moments later Wing was
surprised to find that he had his "gun" (rifle musket) lying across his
colonel's back.

Petroff experienced even greater difficulty during the advance.
Becoming enmeshed in the tortuous web of vines, he was able to
extricate himself only with the greatest difficulty:

> And at the start I found myself entangled and almost stran-
> gled by one of these vine cords or strings. As I was running,
> as all others did, some of these vine cords chanced to come
> around my neck, and through my rapid moving forward they
> formed themselves into a perfect noose, so that I was not only
> stopped in my run, but was violently jerked back. Being in an
> condition that utterly prevented my moving forward, I began
> to extricate and disentangle myself out of the meshes . . .
> having in mine hands my gun, with the bayonet fixed on it,
> and not one soul to help me.

Eventually, Petroff managed to disentangle himself. Out of breath
and deeply chagrined, it was only with the greatest difficulty that he
was able to catch up to his regiment. By this time it had encountered
the enemy and was itself in the greatest throes of disorder.

FEROCITY OF FIGHTING

Both the Battle of Chancellorsville and The Battle of the Wilderness
were strongly contested affairs that pitted the main elements of the
Army of the Potomac against Lee's forces. The main burden of the

fighting during both battles naturally enough devolved upon the infantry. The terrain was so broken, so impassible, however, that even the infantry's actions and capabilities were greatly restricted. Although the two engagements involved a massive number of participants on both sides—along the 4-mile battlefront, there were about 90,000 Union troops versus 65,000 Confederates at the Wilderness— the divisions in each army were never able to deploy fully and exert their true force. And any semblance of cohesion at the regimental, even company, level was soon lost. The troops went into the action seemingly piecemeal, as they encountered the enemy, without any sophisticated grand tactical orchestration. One Union artillery officer would later refer to the infantry's style of fighting in the Wilderness as "a sort of rough-and-tumble fashion, catch as catch can . . . bushwhacking on a grand scale." Here the term "bushwhacking" shouldn't be interpreted in the usual sense, though, whereby one side deliberately waits and delivers an aimed fire at an unsuspecting foe. Not only had the thick forest greatly curtailed the troops' ability to move and maneuver; anything even remotely resembling aimed fire was impossible.

Recounting his regiment's experience during the Battle of the Wilderness, Lt. Josiah Favill recalls that even after they stopped and began to fire, the men along the regimental line were still unable to actually see the enemy. They were only able to aim in a very general way, directing their weapons towards the sound of their opposition's own small arms fire, and they could only speculate at its effect by "the slackening or increasing of the enemy's fire." Friendly troops advancing behind only became aware of the "opening of the ball" with the tremendous crash of musketry and the rolling clouds of smoke that started to billow above the woods in front of them.

Unlike in an open field, where sound waves more readily dissipate, the noise of thousands of rifles firing reverberated through the woods. The result was a continuous, distracting cacophony, the noise of repeated volleys and furious file fire echoing from line to line. The effect was particularly noticeable to those slightly away from the firing lines, such as the cavalrymen and artillerymen relegated to anxious inactivity in the rear. George Neese, a Confederate cannoneer, recalls that on May 6 during the Battle of the Wilderness, the "sharp roar" of musketry was heard literally from dawn to well past dusk. Usually, those in the rear could follow the progress of the battle from the sound, but here those in the rear could neither "make head or tail of it from the sound."

Probably of greater tactical import was the other secondary effect of the small arms, the huge billows of smoke that inevitably accompanied the discharge of weapons in the era before smokeless powder. Once again the dense forest potentiated its effect. Soon after the fighting began, a thick cloud of white smoke could be seen hovering "pall-like" the entire day over each line. Kept from rising by the branches and leaves these clouds often hung so low that it was impossible to see 50 paces even in a clearing. Again we are indebted to Neese for a vivid description:

> At midday the smoke was so thick overheads that I could just make out to see the sun, and it looked like a vast ball of red fire hanging in a smoke-filled sky. A thousand new volumes of smoke rolled up toward the sky that was already draped with clouds of battle smoke. The hissing flames, the sharp, rattling, crashing roar of musketry, the deep bellowing of the artillery, mingled with the yelling of charging, struggling, fighting war machines, the wailing moans of the wounded and the fainter groans of the dying, all loudly acclaimed the savagery of our boasted civilization.

This level of chaos and confusion were certainly not isolated events. Most units at Chancellorsville or the Wilderness found themselves in similar situations. At Chancellorsville the 126th Pennsylvania Volunteer Regiment, for example, was unable to see anything even after it emerged from the thicket and began firing while in "thinner woods." The regimental line halted and the men lay down and began to fire at will:

> It was an ugly give and take. We could not see the enemy, but the whizz and the ting of their bullets showed they were not far away. How long this aimless firing continued I do not know. But, as the excitement grew, many of the men rose to their feet,

fired and remained standing to load and fire . . . The air
seemed full of hissing, shrieking demons, and I expected that
the next moment would bring death.

The firing continued unabated until the Union regiment began to run
out of ammunition. Then the men one after the other stopped firing.

So intense had been the small arms fire that the underbrush was
literally cut down to waist level. The artillery had also left its mark.
Here and there a passage could be seen through the trees and foliage
where a shell had punched its way through, "as neatly as though cut
by an axe," before it exploded. The undergrowth had been quite dry
and caught fire early in the day as a result of the numerous shell
explosions. Neese remembers, "A thousand fires blazed and crackled
on the bloody arena, which added new horrors and terrors to the
ghastly scene spread out over the battle plain." The smoke from the
burning trees and undergrowth quickly became so thick that in many
parts of the front line, even where the thick undergrowth gave way to
the occasional clearing, the men were unable to see anything 20
yards in front.

In this chaotic, in-close action, the setting of the sun did not bring
an automatic cessation of the fighting. As the forest quickly darkened
with the onset of dusk, those slightly behind the front lines could
follow the unfolding of events during its nocturnal phase. The yelling
of those along the firing line, a blurry, indistinctive sound during daylight, now became more audible in the darkness. Judging whether the
sounds were coming nearer or receding, those farther back could
piece together the progress of the battle. Looking up, those in a
clearing or on the border of a wood would see the flash of the occasional volley light up the skyline over the treetops.

CAVALRY IN THE WILDERNESS

Campaigns conducted through forested and mountainous terrain
require different tactics and fighting techniques than those developed in the largely cultivated and relatively level western Europe. By
1863 most frontline cavalry on either side had some practical combat
experience fighting over difficult terrain. When forced to assault a
strong defensive position, such as an enemy ensconced in a woods or

outworks of a farm or village, cavalrymen frequently would dismount and fight like infantrymen. Alternatively, if the woods were sufficiently clear of underbrush, the cavalry could attempt to thwart its opponent with a devil-may-care, albeit necessarily disorganized, all-out charge.

Neither option was available to cavalry during either the Chancellorsville or the Wilderness campaign; in fact, the dense forests almost completely precluded the use of cavalry. Obviously, mounted combat was completely impossible. Cavalrymen were even denied the option of fighting on foot. The vast, continuous stretches of woods meant that the horses could not approach even remotely close to the battle line, which stretched irregularly through the uncharted, dark, smoke-filled woods.

One extremely important exception occurred at Chancellorsville when Maj. Pennock Huey's Eighth Pennsylvania Cavalry found itself almost inadvertently breaking the final forward motion of Jackson's advance along the Orange Turnpike on the right flank of the Union battle line. Gen. Alfred Pleasonton, forever the political creature, would attempt to take all the credit for the affair, claiming in his reports that he consciously sent in the cavalry regiment to interdict Jackson's advance. Huey gives a different and more believable account. Around 6:30 P.M. on May 2, 1863, a staff officer galloped up to Gen. Daniel Sickles's post, then at Scott's Run at Hazel Grove. Excitedly, he informed Sickles that Gen. Oliver Howard's corps had been outflanked and he had been sent for one of Pleasonton's cavalry regiments. Thus ordered, Pleasonton in turn ordered Pennock Huey's Eighth Pennsylvania Regiment to report to General Howard, then thought to be at the Old Wilderness Tavern.

The Eighth Pennsylvania started off through the woods towards its objective. Believing that the rebels were retreating and the battle was almost over, the men were quiet and unconcerned, and some of the formalities of the march were relaxed. Lieutenant Carpenter, who commanded the first squadron, for example, was required by the regulations to march behind his squadron. Instead, he casually rode with Major Huey; Maj. Peter Keenan, commander of the first battalion; Lt. J. Edward Carpenter, commander of the second company; and Ad. J. Haseltine Haddock at the head of the column.

At first the march was uneventful, but as the regiment approached their intended destination, the cavalrymen suddenly received the greatest shock! They had ridden into the center of a large body of rebel infantrymen, apparently the flankers of Jackson's column, who had been completely screened by the thick underbrush. In force on the road in front as well as in the woods on either side, they completely surrounded the Union cavalry column.

Huey immediately ordered the troopers to draw their swords and charge the enemy. Led by the five officers, the Union column plunged down the plank road. Huey claims that the Confederate infantry marching along the road was so closely packed and so surprised that "scores were trampled to death beneath our horses' feet as we went plunging and clashing over them." The major describes the first instants of the charge:

> The order to charge, followed by its instant execution, had such an overwhelming effect upon the enemy that for a space of a few seconds those nearest us seemed utterly to lose the power of motion. Many throwing down their arms, raising their hands, and pleading for mercy and surrender, they doubtless thinking that they had unawares run into the main portion of the Union army . . . We, deaf to their cries, dashed madly through and over them, trampling them under our horses' feet, and using our sabers right and left on all within our reach. Surrounded or cut off, every man of us, thinking it was his last minute on earth, resolved to sell his life as dearly as possible.

The cavalry column was forced to veer to the left, facing the main body of the Confederates. The Eighth Pennsylvania managed to cut its way through the first hundred yards, sabering and running down anyone unfortunate enough to remain in its way. In one sense this actually afforded a momentary advantage to some of the Confederate infantry on the flanks, who were able to thrust and stab the horsemen with their bayonets as they galloped past. A number of Union saddles were thus emptied.

For the first 20 or 30 seconds or so, the defenders failed to offer any coordinated response. Finally recovering, however, the rebel infantry unleashed a single powerful volley, which inflicted many casualties among those near the front of the column. Three officers—Major Keenan, Captain Arrowsmith, and Adjutant Haddock—were killed instantly. So violent was the force striking Keenan that his body was thrown against the next rider at his side, who happened to be Major Huey, before being ridden over by the latter's horse.

Despite the losses inflicted by minié ball and bayonet, most of the forward part of the column managed to barrel its way through the startled defenders. Coming out of the thick woods on the north, or opposite, side of the plank road, the regiment was quickly re-formed behind some artillery, which was just then in the process of forming a line on the left of the plank road. A large, dense wood lay between the artillery and the position where the Eighth Pennsylvania regiment had been momentarily surrounded. Some of the artillery officers were tempted to fire in this direction but were discouraged by the cavalry officers, who realized that to do so was to fire on the cavalry stragglers, who continued to stream out of the woods.

As these events were unfolding in the front of the column a different story was happening in the rear. Drawn out in a thin column during its original advance, the Eighth had stretched out quite a distance. The rearmost portion of the column had not entered the woods for any considerable distance when the regiment found itself trapped. Those in the rear had begun the charge at the same moment as those at the head, but after the Confederate volley they soon found their progress blocked by dead and wounded men and mounts. The rear squadron commanded by Capt. Joseph Wistar thus found itself completely cut off before it was able to reach the plank road. Changing direction, it managed to extricate itself from the woods, clambering over temporary earthworks and entering the open space that surrounded the Chancellorsville House.

In his account of this action, Major Huey opined that the whole affair ended decidedly in his regiment's favor. Dusk now coming on, the Confederate advance as a whole stopped at the plank road, and few rebels crossed over this narrow road running parallel to both lines of battle.

ARTILLERY IN THE WILDERNESS

Of all arms, artillery was the most negatively affected by the density of

the forestation. Given the relatively small explosive shells that were
fired by field artillery of the time, blindly shelling a forest would be
futile and a complete waste of ammunition. During both Chancellorsville and the Wilderness, most artillery assets on both sides sat idly
in the rear, although the hard-fought artillery duel at Hazel's Grove at
Chancellorsville provides a notable exception. A few batteries were
brought up and positioned to command the few pikes and highways
that ran across the battlefield. These soon proved ineffective, however.
Wherever faced with Union artillery along a road, the Confederates
relied upon the simple but highly effective solution of dividing their
forces, which, working their way through the woods, would fall on the
artillery's flanks.

Although many participants thought that the countless fires that soon
sprung up were the inevitable companion to exploding shells, at least
some on the Confederate side would later accuse the Union artillery of
purposely setting these fires, an inconvenience to those who were fortunate to remain uninjured but deadly to many of those less fortunate who
had been struck down. The Confederate artilleryman Neese provided
the following recollection of a duel between opposing artilleries on May
5, 1864, during the Battle of the Wilderness:

> The field that we were in was covered with dry broomsedge
> about two feet high, and the cowardly Yanks, although they had
> the best position and eight pieces to our two, attempted to drive
> us from the field by setting the dry broomsedge on fire by
> shooting some kind of a something of the firework family at us,
> which, from its appearance as it came flying slowly and emit-
> ting a thick volume of inky black smoke, and blazing with
> glaring red fire, looked like a little bit of hell. It ignited the
> grass, which burnt rapidly all over the field and right around,
> and even under our guns, but we stuck to our position and kept
> up our fire at the Yankee battery.

The Wilderness seemed to wreak havoc on the soldiers in all three
arms!

Chapter 28

THE APPEARANCE OF HASTY ENTRENCHMENTS

W ith the exception of a few days in front of Yorktown and again several weeks later as McClellan threw away his best opportunity in front of Richmond, field fortifications did not play a dominant role in the Eastern theater of operations during the first 3 years of war. Setting aside the Confederate lines in front of Richmond, reliance upon fieldworks in the East remained sporadic. In general, fortifications were not a purposive, conscious part of the commander's overall strategy or operational plan; instead, they tended to be a reaction to unexpected developments. As we have seen, fortifications, of both the temporary and the permanent varieties, had played a significantly larger part in the West.

Any paucity of field fortifications in the East, however, would soon vanish with the defenses around Mine Run (Northwest of the Wilderness) in November 1863 and the opening of Grant's 1864 spring campaign. Apart from the stubborn, desperate fighting in the dark, densely forested area known as the Wilderness, this campaign also has become indelibly associated with the sanguinary attacks against hastily thrown up but nonetheless effective field fortifications at Spotsylvania and Cold Harbor and the bloody but absolutely hopeless assaults against semipermanent works in front of Petersburg.

This change in style of fighting from the more traditional open-field battle to an early form of trench warfare has usually been attributed to a sudden tactical awakening among the officers and the rank and file on both sides. Now aware of the lethality of the rifle musket and the futility of relying upon tactically bankrupt, old-fashioned European close-order techniques, soldiers on all levels supposedly gave in to their instincts for self-preservation and started to take advantage of whatever protection they could find or make. The battle-worn veteran is seen as finally setting aside any vestiges of a heroic, idealized mode of warfare and accepting the less chivalrous but more pragmatic approach needed to increase one's chances of staying alive, if only until the next battle. The examples most commonly cited to illustrate the ends of the spectrum are Kershaw's troops (Confederate) at Cold Harbor, reflexively starting to throw up earthen entrenchments, digging with their tin cups or plates, in extreme contrast to the naiveté of the inexperienced Union heavy artillery regiments, so gallantly marching to their destruction in the face of overwhelming fire.

There is mounting evidence that the overall trend towards increased reliance upon field fortifications and defensive works was just as much a reflection of a change in military scientific thinking among high-level officers as it was simply the result of a collective change of values and priorities among the rank and file. One finds several instances in which a corps commander ordered the construction of defensive works before the enemy had even been engaged. On May 5, at the very outset of what would later become known as the Overland Campaign, Gen. Winfield Scott Hancock ordered his divisional commanders to construct breastworks as soon as they completed their advance that day. Elements of the Second Division of Maj. Gen. George Washington Getty's VI Corps had already taken similar precautions even before the arrival of Hancock's men. This was a conscious precautionary step to establish a defensible position if the imminent advance ended in disaster.

This was not an isolated incident, the idiosyncratic product of one corps commander's tactics or style. The very next day Gen. Benjamin Franklin Butler took exactly the same steps after his forces crossed the James River and landed at Bermuda Hundred. In both cases the Union commander halted a general advance to first build precautionary defensive works even though the immediate situation at hand suggested a more pressing need for an immediate advance against a relatively unprepared defending force. Butler's advance was delayed a full 4 days while a line of entrenchments was constructed from the James River at Trent's Reach to the Appomattox River at Port Walthall, even though at this time there were only 6000 Confederate soldiers at or near Petersburg. Had Butler pressed on instead of building works, his forces, in all probability, could have muscled their way into the town.

One finds a third example during the Overland campaign fighting along the North Anna on May 24. In this case the Union forces constructed a strong defensive position 800 yards from the rebel line. A probably even more telling example had been provided 2 weeks earlier, on May 8, By Gen. Gouverneur Warren's Federal V Corps. When forced back by Gen. Robert Rodes's division that evening, his men took refuge in some entrenchments that they had constructed earlier that day. That they did this when on the offensive suggests that this had now become a standard operating procedure ordered by a divisional or corps commander, rather than spontaneous, voluntary work on the part of the men themselves. So commonplace had fortifying become that the ever-perspicacious Lieutenant Favill would record in his diary on May 7:

> We immediately went into position, relieving Gregg's division of cavalry, and commenced at once, *as is usual now-a-days* [italics mine], to throw up a breastwork of logs and rails, and dug a ditch behind them . . . The enemy was discovered to be entrenched on the opposite shore and opened fire as soon as our party showed themselves.

Of course, one could argue that these examples of using field fortifications prior to a major offensive as a precaution against a catastrophic defeat are coincidental. Even accepting this explanation, at a minimum these instances suggest that this defensive measure had been discussed among officers before the start of the campaign and a consensus had been reached regarding its utility. Hancock's example is the most compelling in this regard. Though Butler's fortifications were more extensive, his actions could more readily be justified by established military scientific principles. Having established what we today might call a "beachhead," it was sound practice to first fortify this initial position before moving away from the river. Hancock faced an entirely different situation as his troops completed the defensive works on May 5. One of the army's strategic objectives was to burst through the Wilderness before Lee's forces could react and block the way. Forward motion was critical. To stop a corps's movement just when it was to be set into motion was certainly an action that Hancock could be held accountable for, and it suggests that his decision to do so, if not a direct response to a specific set of instructions, was at least in accordance with a general, prearranged agreement how to proceed.

By late 1863 and early 1864, some top Union military officials were beginning to believe that field fortifications would play an increasing role during day-to-day campaign operations. Rather than a reaction to unexpected developments during the campaign, they were to now to become a standard procedure, one of the integral steps that were to be taken to achieve overall strategic goals. Today we might say they were to become proactive rather than simply reactive.

Recognizing that many detached posts failed to take adequate defensive measures, General William Rosecrans, commander of the Army of the Cumberland, issued a short directive on September 5, 1863, that prescribed the fundamental precautions henceforth to be taken. Although most of these orders dealt with the steps needed to improve the defensive capabilities of blockhouses and stockades, Rosecrans also mentioned the need to surround any defensive work with an abatis, which was to be placed 100 yards in front. Officers were to make certain that the abatis was carefully staked to the ground and that the abatis's limbs and branches were sharpened and "interlaced," manually intertwined for greater strength. These precautions became all the more urgent after the defeat at Chickamauga and the army's retreat into Chattanooga. The day after the battle, Rosecrans instructed that at 6 A.M. the next morning (the 22nd), the army was to dig rifle pits and erect breastworks as quickly as possible. Once again, these were to be preceded by abatis.

Some historians have attributed the increased reliance upon fortifications during 1864 in the East to such efforts found a few months earlier in the West. Arthur Wagner, for example, thought that the increasing tendency to reply upon fortifications, including the impromptu variety dug by individual soldiers under fire, had ultimately been spawned by this type of intellectual cross-pollination:

The intelligence of the men in the ranks and the wide dissemination of military news had rendered the armies in the East and West familiar with the experiences of the other.

When contributing an article to *Confederate Military History*, Jedediah Hotchkiss felt that the new trend was instead the result of the efforts of a few key individuals, such as Robert E. Lee's chief engineer, Martin Smith. Playing an active role in the defense of Vicksburg, Smith had an ample opportunity to see all of the defensive techniques and stratagems used to hold this important position on the middle Mississippi. He was taken prisoner when Vicksburg capitulated in July 1863; after being exchanged, Smith joined the Army of Northern Virginia in early 1864. Impressed with Smith's knowledge and skill, Lee ordered this trusted engineer to fortify defensive positions during the fighting at both the Wilderness and Spotsylvania Court House.

Probably both factors—innovations by individuals and general spreading of techniques between and throughout theaters—played a role in the popularization of fortifying battlefields and encampments. A large number of Eastern troops on both sides had previously been rushed to the West to take part in the critical fighting in southern Tennessee, including Gen. James Longstreet on the Southern side and Gen. Joseph Hooker on the Northern. Although Hooker's corps would never return to the Army of the Potomac, Longstreet's men returned to Lee's army in the spring of 1864. It is possible that this transfer of troops from East to West resulted in a variety of cross-pollination of military practices and might explain the sudden propensity towards field fortifications in the Eastern theater in early 1864.

Even though most of the Eastern troops on the Union side who had been transferred to the West never returned to the Eastern theater, the North still possibly benefited from a trend similar to the South's experience. Some Union officers were transferred to the East. The most notable of these of course was U.S. Grant, who on March 12, 1864, assumed command of the Union armies. Given his authority, Grant was in an ideal position to implement any practices or techniques that had been successfully used by his previous commands.

NEW ENTRENCHING TECHNIQUES

The presence of the Corps of Engineers with the Army of the Potomac is highly suggestive that the trend toward consistent, widespread entrenchment was directed from above. Starting off the 1864 campaign with 2226 men and NCOs led by 50 expert engineer officers, the Corps quickly proved itself adept at the creation of all types of field fortifications, including digging ditches, cutting down trees, and every aspect of the construction process. When it came to the quantity and the quality of fieldworks and entrenchments it was able to construct, Gen. Edward Porter Alexander estimated that this organization had proved itself to be the equivalent of a full fighting corps, about 20,000 regular infantrymen.

A similar phenomenon appeared in the West. While pushing back Joseph E. Johnston's army slowly but ineluctably towards Atlanta, Sherman's army also became heavily dependent upon field fortifications. Increasingly, protective entrenchments were erected each time the Union force advanced. As we have seen, these field fortifications proliferated on both sides during 1864. However, in *The Virginia Campaign of 1864 and 1865*, Gen. Andrew Humphreys would note that many of the rebel defensive works were "entangled in their front in a manner unknown to European warfare, &, indeed, in a manner new to warfare to this country." The entanglements that Humphrey referred to were probably a combination of twisted branches and telegraph wire, a technique that had proven so effective at Vicksburg and appears to have shown up in the East the next spring.

Interestingly enough, it appears that the Federals were the first to utilize wire entanglements in this part of the country, during General Butler's futile attempt to break out beyond the south bank of the James during mid-May 1864. Penetrating the second Union line, Brig. Gen. Johnson Hagood's men had to struggle over a "line of abatis interlaced with wire" near Fort Stevens during the battle of Drewry's Bluff (May 16). Seeing its effectiveness as a defensive measure proven, Maj. Gen. Q. A. Gillmore soon thereafter sent a dispatch to General Butler which requested "a couple of miles or more of telegraph wire" so that he could thus protect his entire front.

As the weeks passed and the Confederates themselves were increasingly forced to fortify their positions around Petersburg and

Richmond, they employed similar precautions. By the first week of July, Henry A. Wise's brigade in W. H. C. Whiting's division had settled down along a line protected by a string of abatis and "wire fencing." A few days later Bushrod Johnson reported that the Forty-first Alabama Regiment had adopted similar measures. A spy, sent out ostensibly to exchange newspapers with the Union troops, came back and reported that the opposing enemy forces, though strongly entrenched, did not yet resort to wire fences. The Confederates, now forced to remain largely on the defensive, began to erect miles of wire fences. By July 30 Maj. Gen. Hancock would write to Chief of Staff Maj. Gen. A. A. Humphreys—commander of the II Army Corps—that Gen. Edward Ord and his division commanders had decided not to attack the Confederates in their front since "there was no place to assault . . . as the line was not only protected by abatis but by wire."

Both sides henceforth would resort to liberal use of wire fences, and as the two armies continued to stare across at one another for the rest of the year, the records show the Union Corps of Engineers busy at work erecting such obstacles in a number of places. As fall set in, Union skirmishers and pickets were occasionally known to pick at the logs in the abatis and other fortifications to get firewood. In November a company of engineers was directed to use wire to close up the unsanctioned "slashings" that now punctuated the line between Fort Fisher to Fort Welch. Although apparently stretching for several hundred yards, this paled in comparison to the wire defenses that had been erected under Lieut. W. R. King, chief engineer of the XVIII Army Corps in October. In this portion of the front, a least 1600 yards stretching south of Fort Harrison were protected by wire fences.

There is at least some evidence that the efficacy of the new wire fences and barricades was appreciated by some high-ranking officers. Near the close of the war, no less than Maj. Gen. A. Humphreys would inquire of Col. James Duane, chief engineer of the Army of the Potomac:

Do you intend putting a fraise around new Fort Fisher? In addition to it *I wish you would have a wire entanglement* [italics mine]. The two picket-lines are very close to the work, and driving away the enemy's pickets will bring on constant firing. The work in its present transition state is, of course, less secure than at any other time, and, if it can be done, I would like the fraise and entanglement put up without waiting for the completion of the parapets, &c.

"HASTY ENTRENCHMENTS"

In his private memoirs, intended for his immediate family, recently published in the late 1980s as *Fighting for the Confederacy,* Gen. E. P. Alexander provided detailed descriptions of not only the new type of defensive works and how they were constructed, but also why they were adopted in the first place. Unlike the Union forces, which were generously equipped with a full range of pioneer tools, most of the Confederate infantry lacked even axes, picks, and shovels. Alexander estimated that they had only 25% of the entrenching tools that were required. Be that as it may, the rough terrain and the fact that their Union counterparts were busily constructing their own entrenchments forced the Confederate infantrymen to extemporize by using whatever was at hand. Usually, this meant stabbing the ground to loosen up the dirt and then shoveling it away with their tin drinking cups and sometimes in desperation with their bare hands.

General Alexander described how the men dug ad hoc entrenchments during the battle of Cold Harbor:

> While Kershaw made his attack, the remainder of the long column halted in the road, expecting the march to be presently resumed. But when the delay was prolonged, and a few random bullets from the front began to reach the line, without any general instructions, the men here and there began to dig dirt with their bayonets and pile it with their tin cups to get a little cover. Others followed suit, and gradually the whole column was at work intrenching the line along which they halted. Gradually it became known that the enemy were accumulating in our front, and then, as the country was generally flat, orders were given to close up the column and adopt its line as the line of battle.

Alexander conceded that the resulting entrenchments, in many places nothing more than knee-deep trenches lacking abatis or any other type of defensive works in front, "were scarcely more than a good beginning." Even at Cold Harbor, where the Confederate infantry had ample opportunity to improve upon them, the works were only 2 feet deep and 3 feet wide with a 2-foot earth parapet in front. There the trenches dug by one regiment or brigade did not necessarily connect to those dug by their neighbors. Only when the Army of Northern Virginia remained in position for several days were the trenches deepened and enlarged. Presumably, in these relatively static situations, the Confederates were able to draw upon another source of construction power: slaves. However, even in enlarged trenches and ditches, the soldiers' scope of movement was still extremely limited. Alexander would forever remember as the period of "greatest hardship [Lee's] army ever endured" when the army was confined to these cramped quarters for 8 consecutive days in the flat, open country around Cold Harbor.

Lacking any natural aboveground protection, the men, two ranks deep in most places, had to keep crouched in their shallow trenches day after day. The sharpshooters on either side would find some spot that overlooked the surrounding neighborhood. There they would further fortify that part of the trenches with logs and, if available, sandbags. Patiently, the martial stalker would wait for the prey to show himself along the opposing row of trenches. Then, with his finger on the trigger, he would aim at the same place to see if his hapless victim was foolish enough to show himself again at the same spot. If so, it was usually the end of one man's participation in the great conflict! Water was a much more valuable commodity than food, and thirst would eventually drive many to risk their lives to go to nearby waterholes. Several sharpshooters would be sure to concentrate their attention on each of these paths.

Soldiers along the Union lines did not have to endure the same privation. Accompanied by the Corps of Engineers and plenty of fresh reinforcements, Union forces were usually able to dig a number of zigzagging, covered approaches to the forward trenches, through which men could come in, provisions could flow, and the wounded could be removed. The Confederates lacked the manpower needed to supply this convenience. Anyone wanting to go to the rear had to rely on stealth and wile while risking enemy sharpshooter fire. Most declined the risk in daytime and waited for the cover of night. It was then that the dead and wounded were removed from the trenches and provisions flowed in the opposite direction. When it was necessary to communicate important messages to the officers at the front, a courier would either utilize the few communications trenches—there was usually about one per mile—or try to take advantage of whatever cover he could find. As soon as he reached the front line of trenches, he would hand the orders to one of the men, and this would be passed hand to hand until it reached the intended recipient.

In his personal memoirs Alexander confided that he did not think much of the extemporaneous ditches and abatis that had been quickly dug out or thrown up. At least as far as he could recollect, these were "never enough even to delay the Federal storming columns a minute." According to many of the Union infantrymen, though, the same could not be said of the more elaborate entanglements and obstructions they had to fight their way through. Samuel Wing felt that the men behind the Confederate abatis and breastworks possessed a "very great advantage." John W. Nesbit, referring to the Union assault on the Confederate defensive position at the Bloody Angle salient at Spotsylvania, observed that while the attackers struggled through the timber and brush, the Union infantrymen "were simply at the mercy of the Rebels. It was murder to attempt to charge these works, and no troops in the world could have taken them."

THE PSYCHOLOGICAL IMPACT OF DEFENSIVE WORKS

The popularization of defensive works ultimately had a much more profound impact than simply aiding the defense of a localized position and increasing the number of casualties inflicted upon the attackers. Not only did it alter the frequency with which opposing armies would engage; it also influenced how combatants conducted themselves both on the battlefield and during day-to-day operations for the remainder of the war. During the campaigns of 1861, '62, and '63, it had been impossible for an army to remain close to its enemy counterpart for any extended period. When two opposing armies approached one another, either they usually clashed in a large engagement, or one side peremptorily withdrew. When a battle did occur, the defeated side quickly retired out of harm's way to gather up its scattered men and await reinforcements, such as happened to the Union army after the First Bull Run or the Confederate army after Shiloh.

All this changed as soon as an army routinely placed field fortifications slightly behind the expected point of contact with the enemy or when the army encamped at the end of each day's march. Now it was possible to maintain the army's position close to the enemy's forces *indefinitely*. In *The Virginia Campaign of 1864 and 1865*, General Humphreys characterized the new tenor of the fighting:

> The marching was done mostly by night, and the contact so close as to require constant vigilance day and night, and allow but little time for sleep. The firing was incessant. The fatigue, the loss of sleep, the watchfulness, taxed severely the endurance of both officers and men. Usually, in military operations, the opposing armies come together, fight a battle and separate again, the strain lasting only a few days. In a siege it is only a small part of the opposing armies that are close together. But with these two armies it was different. From the 5th of May, 1864, to the 9th of April, 1865, they were in constant close contact, with rare intervals of brief comparative repose.

This persistent danger was the most obvious impact of field fortifications on the conduct of war.

There was another change, a much more subtle and one which at first escaped detection by all but the most astute observer. This was the attitude of the men. Defensive works not only introduced an element of pragmatism but by their vary nature suggested the acceptability of taking measures to protect oneself. This is completely the opposite of the values on the traditional battle, wherein every effort was made to inculcate into the soldier the necessity of ignoring one's instinct for survival and to do whatever it takes to win, in spite of personal consequences, such as to coolly advance within effective range of the rifle musket amidst the proverbial hail of bullets.

In stark contrast not only were those ensconced in rifle pits or behind breastworks expected to take every precaution to protect their well-being, but in this protected environment a soldier would be censured for taking any needless risks. On picket duty the infantryman would cautiously peer over the entrenchment; an artilleryman suspecting that he still was vulnerable to small arms fire would add a few extra sandbags to the earth works in front of his gun emplacement. This routine, so different from that of the earlier days, repeated for several weeks, necessarily had a permanent impact on the psyche of the American soldier, who by "nature" (because of socially inculcated values) was already a pragmatist.

The new rhythm of warfare also effected a deeper, even more significant psychological transformation, one that changed how the typical soldier felt about going into battle and the risks that he was willing to take. Previously, the episodic nature of battle rendered a recuperative effect. Weeks of physically demanding but relatively uneventful campaigning would suddenly be interrupted with the "opening of the ball," as the men often referred to the commencement of a battle. All routine was immediately set aside, and the adrenaline flowed freely as every man exerted himself to the utmost to best his opponents. Then, almost as suddenly as it began, the battle was over, and whether beaten or victorious, after a few days the routineness would eventually set back in, and the soldier was allowed to psychologically recover from the trauma of battle. In this sense the battle served as epic punctuation in the martial saga. Unconsciously, it could be viewed as a "heroic" experience in which not everyone, certainly, but most were willing to make the supreme effort and possibly the ultimate sacrifice.

However, almost all heroism is based upon the conviction that the greatest personal risk can lead to the greatest collective gain. *Pedestrianism* and *self-sacrifice* in this regard are antonyms. As long as there are periodic battles, as opposed to continuous fighting, men cling to the expectation or hope that the next battle will be the decisive victory that destroys the opponent's army, cripples the latter's ability to continue to fight, and leads to the end of the war.

However, the amalgamation of the new pragmatic emphasis and lessened willingness to take unnecessary risks profoundly affected the troops' behavior. The continuous proximity of the two armies forced the men to continuously seek means of survival and simultaneously undermined the heroic aspect of the battle. It is not surprising, therefore, that when the two opposing armies now confronted each other on more open terrain after weeks of fighting in the Wilderness and Spotsylvania, the men whenever possible started to dig ad hoc entrenchments on their own without waiting for orders from above to do so.

UPTON'S ATTACK AT COLD HARBOR

The more pervasive use of temporary fieldworks coupled with the advent of hasty defenses and wire entanglements caused the fighting to become even bloodier. The attack of Emory Upton's brigade of the VI Corps at Cold Harbor poignantly demonstrates just how murderous combat could be. Originally raised as the Nineteenth Connecticut Volunteer Infantry, the Second Connecticut Heavy Artillery had served with the Washington defenses for much of the war, and its men eagerly awaited an opportunity to show their mettle under fire. That opportunity came on June 1, 1864, when General Upton, a promising young officer who had graduated from West Point in 1861, ordered the regiment forward to take a line of entrenchments and breastworks at Cold Harbor. These field fortifications were typical of those encountered throughout this period: rifle pits in front, followed by several lines of breastworks.

After lying within its own entrenchments all afternoon, the regiment finally was ordered forward at 5 P.M. Forming into three battalion lines, each of four companies, the regiment advanced at the double through an open field and into a shallow, sparsely populated pinewood, where the men took off their knapsacks. The remainder of the brigade formed the fourth line. Unencumbered, the regiment once more set off in what Upton later described as "beautiful order," its colors in the center and Col. Elisha S. Kellogg at its head. As the Second Heavy Artillery moved quickly down a slight slope and then up the adjoining ascent, the Confederates in the rifle pits quickly abandoned their advanced positions.

Although the attackers had encountered a "constantly ever thickening fire" from the moment they left the security of the pine forest, the first line managed to continue unabated until about 70 yards from the defending line, when it started up a gradual incline. Here a tremendous crash of musketry erupted along the entire length of the defending entrenchments. In his official report of the battle, General Upton explains what happened during this critical moment. There had originally been a thick growth of pine sprouts in front of the rebels' position, but all of the trees and shrubbery within 70 yards of the rebel works had been cut down, probably that morning, and purposely interlocked together to form an ad hoc but highly effective abatis. There were only two paths through these obstacles, each only wide enough for a column of fours. The men in the Second Heavy Artillery dashed up both these paths but "were swept away by a converging fire." A vivid description of this moment is provided in the organization's regimental history:

> A sheet of flame, sudden as lightning, red as blood, and so near that it seemed to singe the men's faces, burst along the rebel breastwork, and the ground and trees close behind our lines was ploughed and riddled with a thousand balls that just missed the heads of the men. The battalion dropped flat on the ground, and the second volley, like the first, nearly all went over.

The authors of this regimental history speculated that the rebel fire directly in front was not sufficient to check their advance. It was the rebels on the left flank, "having nothing in front to engage their attention, and having unobstructed range on the battalion, who opened a fire which no human could withstand." Dudley Vaill, who served with the Second Heavy throughout its career, in his own little regimental history, describes his impressions of that enfilading fire:

> It was the work of almost a single moment. The air was filled with sulphurous smoke, and the shrieks and howls of more than two hundred and fifty mangled men rose above the yells of the triumphant rebels and the roar of their musketry.

Much of the front line dropped immediately, forming a long, blue ribbon of corpses across the battlefield. Dazed and now insensible to reality, a Union colonel rode up to the Confederate defenders and ordered them to cease firing; he was immediately captured. Realizing that the attack had failed, Colonel Kellogg had just ordered his men to about-face and retire, when one shot struck his arm, and a moment later a second pierced his skull, killing him instantly.

The accumulated confusion arising from the gruesome sight of the dead, dying, and severely mangled, as well as from the noise, smoke, and what seemed a myriad of conflicting orders, finally caused the first line to disintegrate. Some of the more seriously wounded collapsed on top of the pine bough abatis, where their bodies were very soon "completely riddled with bullets." Others, more fortunate, at least for the moment, limped or crawled to the woods to the front and right of the regiment's position. Almost all of these men were captured or permanently lost.

The regiment's other two battalions had followed behind in the second and third lines, each about 75 yards to the rear of the other. However, as soon as the devastating rebel fire stymied the attack, Upton immediately ordered the men in the rear to lie down to minimize needless casualties. Their field of fire obstructed by the remnants of the first line, they were ordered to withhold their fire, while those in front lay on the ground and took advantage of any available cover. Unable to either advance or return the fire, the regiment was forced to remain until nightfall in this extremely trying position.

The rebels' fire gradually became more sporadic, with occasional lulls punctuating the activity. Several hundred Confederate infantrymen took advantage of one of these lulls and jumped over their breastworks and surrendered to the Union forces.

As night fell, the three lines gradually became mixed, as the wounded more readily made their way to the rear. General Upton, however, had no intention of accepting the stalemate. Although the Second Heavy Artillery's advance had been stopped, another regiment on the right did manage to capture a small portion of the rebel entrenchments. The companies from the rear lines were rallied and quietly brought up to this section of the rebel breastworks, a feat much more easily accomplished in the dark than it would have been several hours earlier. The line thus formed by the newly arriving companies was gradually extended toward the left, so that it arrived directly in front of where the rebels had repelled the earlier assault.

The fight was now between the two forces on either side of the entrenchments, both firing wildly in the dark. The enemy periodically attempted to retake their works, but their efforts were stymied by Union musket fire. Recognizing the futility of their attempts, the Confederates eventually withdrew to their second line of breastworks. The Second Connecticut Heavy Artillery was finally relieved at 3 P.M. the next day, when it was moved back a slight distance. The regiment encamped behind the captured breastworks for the remainder of the time it spent at Cold Harbor.

The failure of the Second Connecticut's attack in many ways presaged the way much of the fighting for Richmond would henceforth be conducted. An expanded repertoire of defensive measures handed the advantage to the defense, when it was able to take the necessary precautions. Although the Union attacks at Cold Harbor were not the last time Union commanders would order an assault against a prepared position, this tactic became much less common and was usually reserved for unusual or desperate situations. Although operations in front of Petersburg the next month opened with several traditional-style frontal assaults, their bloody and futile results finally convinced everyone that a different approach was needed.

Chapter 29

THE ADVENT OF TRENCH WARFARE

G rant's strategies from May 1864 onward can be characterized as first an effort to break through Lee's forces head-on and then, when the confrontation resulted in only a draw, filing his army to the south and east in an effort to gain Lee's right flank and approach ever closer to Richmond. However, after the bloody fighting at Cold Harbor, continued pursuance of this strategy would have placed the Army of the Potomac astraddle the Chickahominy River, the scene of McClellan's defeats in June 1862.

Instead, Grant decided to redirect the main thrust to the south bank of the James River and then toward Petersburg, in order to irretrievably sever Southern railroad communications to Richmond. Embarking at White House (on the Pamunkey), the lead elements of the XVIII Corps, commanded by Gen. William Farrar "Baldy" Smith landed at the Bermuda Hundred on June 14 to join Butler's forces. Crossing the Appomattox River the next day, lead elements that afternoon approached the heavy fortifications known as the Dimmock Line, which Capt. Charles Dimmock had first erected in front of Petersburg back in 1862. The fortifications appeared intimidating. Their 20-foot-thick walls extended 10 miles and in parts were further protected by dry moats and entanglements. Appearances were deceiving, however. At this point there were only about 2000 Confederate soldiers in the vicinity.

The men in the XVIII Corps that evening were tired, though, and given the memories of the intense, bloody fighting of the preceding 6 weeks, not jubilant about the prospects of attacking such an apparently strong position. Although Grant had specifically called for an assault on Petersburg, while visiting General Butler the previous day,

General Smith decided to hold off the assault until the next morning, after the expected arrival of large reinforcements in the form of Hancock's, Burnside's and Warren's corps. Despite the remonstrations by some of the staff officers in the advanced lines that the way into Petersburg was in effect "open," Smith and his staff treated these reports as "pure romance" and ordered the men to "rest upon their arms" within some of the outlying enemy fieldworks captured earlier in the day. As the men rested under a bright moonlit sky, the general expectation was that on the morrow they would accomplish what had been postponed that evening.

During this 12-hour delay, the Confederates were anything but idle. A large portion of Lee's army was in motion, crossing the James and gradually filtering into positions covering Petersburg. One by one, rebel artillery batteries were moved into makeshift positions, and where needed, new entrenchments were hastily thrown up. Waking up at dawn's first rays, the Union troops were surprised to see a new line of entrenchments defended by a "cloud of gray veterans."

INITIAL ATTACKS

In accounts penned after the war, Union participants in the day's events would recall that June 18 began auspiciously for Union forces. Advancing in column through a thin belt of birch trees, the First Massachusetts Heavy Artillery quickly overran two lines of quickly dug rebel rifle pits. The troops suddenly came up to the Prince George Court House Road where this partially planked thoroughfare made a sharp right-hand turn toward the northwest and, running parallel to the enemy's works, led past the New Market Race Course.

Just beyond the road was an open field approximately 500 yards wide. On the far side stood two forts manned by a number of infantry regiments and several batteries. Situated on a bare ridge called Hare's Hill, a short distance in front of the Hare House, approximately where Fort Stedman would later stand, these works had been constructed by Gen. Alfred Colquitt's Georgians and were known to the Confederates as Colquitt's Salient. A soldier named W.H. Morgan would visit the site 37 years after the engagements and later provide an excellent description of this ridge in his unit's regimental history. The two forts, which formed the principal defense, had been made by digging out the rear of Hare's Ridge and throwing up the dirt to form parapets. Embrasures were then cut out for the artillery. The parapets were unusually low, and the guns were sunk so that their barrels were a mere 2 feet above ground level. Not only did this make the defending artillery less vulnerable to counterbattery fire, but the low line of fire, hugging the ground, helped make the fire unusually destructive. The position was further strengthened by redans or lunettes flanking both forts, which housed additional batteries and were positioned to rake the field with a deadly cross fire. These defensive positions were interconnected by a series of rifle pits for the infantry, who served as support.

To make matters worse for the attacking Union forces, the intervening ground was perfect for effective artillery operations. Batteries placed atop a hill or a ridge often fired high, over the approaching enemy's head. Here this wasn't a problem. Although the field was actually a gentle valley, the slope at either end was gradual, and the

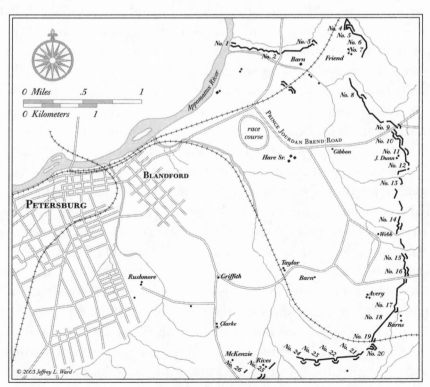

The fortifications around Petersburg. This map shows the Petersburg defenses in 1863. The next year "Colquitt's salient" would be thrown up near the race course near Prince Jourdan Brend Road.

clear field offered the defending artillery an unobstructed field of fire. Although Union witnesses usually only mention the slope at the rebel end of the field, Confederate memoirists describe the slope as being on the Union side. It is possible, therefore that there was a slight incline at either end of the field and that each group of combatants was able to perceive only the slope facing it.

This was the position against which the Union forces found themselves advancing that morning. As soon as they attempted to move past the road, however, their forward motion was checked by a sudden storm of canister and small arms fire that heralded the strength of the Confederate position. To make the situation even less inviting, the approaching forces were also exposed to enfilading fire from a rebel battery on their right.

Fortunately for the Union troops, the road, like many in Virginia, had been built by shoveling the surplus earth to a side, so that there was a long, nearly continuous embankment on the side facing the enemy. The embankment varied between 2 and 5 feet in height and at points was topped by a 5-to 6-foot fork fence. For the most part this afforded protection as the troops awaited further instructions. As the successive tiers of the column came up, the men lay down, huddled close together with their comrades who had preceded them, not paying strict attention to company order. The Confederate fire slackened. Their sharpshooters continued to fire intermittently and eventually managed to pick off a few men and officers.

The attackers did not have long to wait. The Union forces were soon ordered to assault the rebel works. The original instructions called for the Ninety-third and Eighty-fourth New York and the 105th Pennsylvania Regiments to lead the assault. The Fifth Michigan Volunteers as well as the First Maine and First Massachusetts Heavy Artillery Regiments supported from the rear. The first two lines of the Union troops were all veterans all too familiar with the realities of war, especially the nasty, bloodletting form that had been ever-present since the opening of the campaign in the Wilderness. And the men in Hancock's II Corps had borne more than their share of the fighting. During the fighting in the Wilderness, at Spotsylvania, and at Cold Harbor, this 36,000-man force suffered somewhere between 13,000 and 15,000 killed, wounded, and missing, not counting many additional casualties during the first few days on the Petersburg front.

The First Maine was ordered forward. As its inexperienced men näively started to approach the front line, some of the old-timers were heard to whisper impatiently to those behind, "Lie down, you damn fools, you can't take them forts." In his diary S. B. Dearnborn would record how he heard some of his comrades call out to their officers, "Played out. Let the First Maine go! Let the First Maine go!" After a few seconds of indecision, the veterans' advice prevailed, and men lay down once again behind the embankment, refusing to attack the two forts beyond. The officers leading the corps realized that an assault made by such men, even if they finally could be induced to attack, was doomed to failure. About noon the First Maine Heavy Artillery was withdrawn from its forward position to a field slightly to the rear, where it remained until nightfall.

The troops' refusal to advance was duly reported to the acting corps commander. Hancock, the permanent commander of the II Corps, was in a field hospital for a wound suffered the previous year at Gettysburg. Although the rebel position was known to be extremely strong, several attempts to take it had already failed. Gen. David B. Birney, commanding in Hancock's stead, ordered Gershom Mott's Third Division to immediately assault the position. Mott protested, arguing that any attempt on Colquitt's Salient would merely lead to senseless slaughter, as at Cold Harbor, but Birney peremptorily replied, "My orders to you are to assault."

Given no choice but to attack, Mott immediately set about to devise the least of all evils. We are indebted to Capt. G. L. Gilmer, another participant in the suicidal charge, for Mott's explanation of how he decided to proceed:

> I knew that it was useless to expect suicide en masse from my old troops who had seen the wolf, had felt his teeth, and bore the scars. All I could hope was that a heavy artillery regiment, the First Maine, innocent of the danger it would incur, would lead off with a dash and carry the works with a rush.

Brigadier General Mott hoped that the First Maine Heavy Artillery would provide a breakthrough to sufficiently motivate the remainder of the division's troops, so that they would join in the attack. Troops from Mott's Third Division were ordered up to the just-vacated position along the line. When the First Maine H.A. received its new orders, it was still some distance behind the Union line. Every man detailed for extra duty was called in and handed a musket, giving the regiment a total effective force of 832 men.

Later, when asked to provide a firsthand description, for Captain Gilmer's article "Carnage in First Maine Heavy Artillery," of the Maine boy's reaction to the news that that they were to attempt to take the position that others had attempted but failed at, Lt. Low of Company C would write:

> The men's faces had now grown very serious. We knew that many of us were to die. Men turned to their comrades and bid each other good-bye, and with tears trickling down their cheeks dictated messages to wives, fathers, mothers, sisters and sweethearts in case they should be among the slain and their comrades survive. I myself received a number of such messages.

The men were ordered to remove their knapsacks, then fix their bayonets. They were also ordered to remove the caps from their rifle muskets. During the upcoming attack they were to rely entirely on the bayonet. The First Maine Heavy Artillery, which would spearhead the assault, moved up to the Prince George Courthouse Road, whose embankments had sheltered the Union forces in the morning. Some Union artillery was positioned on some slightly elevated ground a little distance to the left rear. It was hoped that the batteries so placed would be able to fire over the onrushing friendly troops and thus support the attack up until the final moments.

Mott's Division was organized into three brigade columns identical in formation. The central column, McAllister's Brigade, was directly in front of Colquitt's Salient and obviously would bear the brunt of the fighting. The three battalions of the First Maine were at the front of this column of battalions. The companies in each battalion were deployed in a line, its men deployed along two ranks. The second battalion, led by Maj. C. V. Crossman, was a short distance behind the first; the third, commanded by Capt. W. S. Clark, was similarly behind the second. The brigade's other regiment was in an identical formation behind the First Maine. At this point Brig. Gen. Robert McAllister was on detached duty; the previous day he had led another force in a futile charge against the same position. As a result, on this occasion the First Maine's colonel was to lead the brigade, while Major R. B. Shepard of the first battalion was in temporary command of the regiment.

The plan was that the first line of the leading battalion would clear away the abatis in front of the two forts and gain the ditch, while the second line was to follow closely and keep the rebels from the tops of their entrenchments as those in the first lines prepared to rush in and capture these works. Once this charge began, it was to be supported by the second line, which would also rush forward. Meanwhile, the third line would come up and serve as a reserve.

After what must have seemed an eternity, the order to advance finally came. The men in the front line of the First Maine H.A. climbed over the embankment, entered the field, and marched forward at the double-quick. They were followed by the other tiers in the column; the brigade columns on the left and right had been ordered to remain in position behind the embankment.

Capt. F. A. Cummings, who was lucky to survive the event, would claim that the attackers began to suffer casualties before they had advanced 5 feet into the open field. These first casualties were probably caused by individual sharpshooters and men in the ranks firing individually, rather than a massed volley. A few moments later, probably not long after the regiment had advanced 50 to 100 yards, the defenders opened a general fire. Capt. G. L. Gilmer, would recall that moment:

> The crash of two thousand muskets rent the air as a long line of flame leaped from the works in our front, and the well known yell of the Army of Virginia mingled with the roar of the Rebel batteries on our right and left as canister followed musket balls of the infantry and tore enormous gaps in our ranks.

Yet, even as the men from Maine began to fall, the officers could still be heard to encourage and order their men forward, a valiant effort made to close up the ranks. This proved to be a futile gesture, only prolonging the ordeal and wasting more lives. William Izlar, who, along with the rest of the Twenty-fifth Virginia, participated in the action on the defenders' side, would recall how the rebel infantry behind the parapets began to fire more quickly as the advance continued. Izlar noticed that a few attackers turned and fled right from the beginning, but most struggled on. However, before the second and third battalions could even form up and proceed across the field, all formal organization of those in front was lost. The first battalion had melted away, and its men and officers lay in heaps.

The situation, hopeless from the onset, became unbearable within minutes. The defenders' artillery fired canister; all cohesion was lost as the attackers broke and fled. Describing his feelings at the moment, Izlar, finding himself on the victorious side, would later write, "The retreat lost much of its inspiring grandeur of the advance, but to those witnessing it, it appeared far more pleasing, if not so spectacular."

How far did the First Maine Heavy Artillery advance before it was forced to admit defeat? There is no clear consensus and the various witnesses who wrote down their observations for posterity contradict one another. Izlar felt that the Union advance made it only halfway down the slope in front of the starting position before the tide of retreat started. This appears to be corroborated by Union observers who later would estimate they had been able to advance only 50 to 100 yards. Some of the Confederates they faced, however, felt that the leading edge of the assault managed to come within 50 to 75 yards of their defensive line.

There can be little dispute about the results of the charge, however. In little more than 10 to 15 minutes after it was launched, the regiment's strength had been shattered. There were 115 men killed, 489 wounded, and 28 missing. Almost 700 of the First Maine Heavy Artillery failed to answer roll call that night. Losses suffered by the regiment (with a single exception) were greater than that taken by any other regiment during the war.

The events of June 16, 17, and 18 were conclusive. Even the most obtuse of generals had to acknowledge that conquest through the direct assault was no longer feasible. If the Second Connecticut Heavy Artillery's action at Cold Harbor and the First Maine's recent assault had been futile, any further attempt to storm the field fortifications, then being upgraded on a daily basis, would be necessarily suicidal. The opportunity to seize Petersburg by surprise had failed. There was nothing left to do but consolidate and fortify the Union position and settle down to a lengthy siege. To this end on June 19 Grant ordered that the Union position around Petersburg be reinforced with trenches and rifle pits, punctuated with the occasional fort. For the next 10 months, approximately 100,000 Union troops attempted to strangle Petersburg and with it the capacity of Richmond to draw food, ammunition, and other supplies from the rest of the Confederacy.

LIFE AT THE FRONT

The staccato fight-march-fight-march routine that occurred continuously throughout May and early June was replaced almost overnight with a much more sedentary counterpart, one which, although it generally required much less physical activity, was no less potentially deadly. In late June the weather turned extremely hot. All physical activity of course became increasingly demanding, and both sides, as best they could, settled down for a long, drawn-out formal siege. The fire from sharpshooters, vedettes, and pickets became almost constant. Over the next several weeks, there were spurts of furious activity, as the Union forces started to construct their own series of earthworks and fortifications, while the Confederates made whatever improvements possible to their own defenses.

Pickets and vedettes were thrown out along their respective fronts to protect the armies against any sudden enemy movements. Seeking cover in hastily constructed rifle pits in front of the lines, they were positioned up to 50 feet from the lines and often were dangerously close to their enemy counterparts. Sharpshooters were sprinkled along the lines in whatever advantageous positions they could exploit, and they began to harass anyone who unwisely exposed any part of his body. These marksmen hid themselves in available trees or bushes or ensconced themselves like the ordinary pickets in rifle pits. Of course, if detected, they would instantly reverse roles and themselves become the targets. Getting sharpshooters in and out of their hiding places became a problem. The solution that was gradually adopted was for the sharpshooters to stealthily crawl out to their positions before daybreak. Here they would remain for 24 hours, when they would be relieved by the next shift.

The difficulties certainly weren't limited to the pickets and sharpshooters, and many units along the front lines became equally restricted in their movement and activity. In his memoirs Dudley Vaill recounts how his regiment, the Second Connecticut Heavy Artillery Volunteers, was forced to occupy "the most intolerable position [it] was ever requested to hold." Half of the regiment was ordered to the lines in front; the remainder lay precariously in a cornfield near Harrison's House. It was a matter of debate as to who were in the greatest danger, those who were "on" or those who were "off" duty. Across a wheatfield lay the enemy's line near a row of trees. The enemy marksmen, familiar with every inch of surrounding terrain, hid in the trees on both flanks and attempted to pick off any man or officer foolish enough to even peek over the hastily constructed parapets. For 2 days the men were forced to lie in their shallow holes from before dawn to long after nightfall. Despite the imminent danger, some men, whether because of thirst, hunger, or sheer boredom, took their chances to change positions or get back to the rear. Most didn't take the risk, however, and were pinned down until zigzag approaches had been dug to connect the rear with the most advanced parts of the front line. Only then was it possible to remove the wounded that had been languishing without succor for almost 48 hours.

The men in the field fortifications quickly adapted to their new environment. Writing to his wife that summer, Capt. Nicholas Baggs of the Second Pennsylvania Veteran Heavy Artillery mused how soon men got used to this constant threat of danger. Most nonchalantly went about their business. During the day food was the most common preoccupation. As soon as they woke up, most of the men built little individual fires and cooked for themselves wherever they were holed up. Coffee in particular was valued, especially by those relegated to rifle pits. It wasn't always possible to savor the java without the unwanted intervention of the enemy. Often bullets spattering upon the nearby ground would scatter earth over the soldier's cup. This was always followed by a deep-felt oath.

In the first part of the summer, camaraderie even developed between some portions of the hostile lines. Where this happened, the sniping at least temporarily abated, and men from the two sides could occasionally be seen trading newspapers, jackknives, and coffee for tobacco. This didn't last, however, when the general fighting eventually became more vicious.

Some of the infantrymen even learned to live underground. Living spaces were created by carving out large dugouts or cellars. These were holes 5 to 6 feet deep. As protection against enemy fire, the earth was thrown up on the front and sides. These mounds were then packed down and covered with logs, bushes, and dirt. During the summer months, the entrance at the rear was left open, but as the weather cooled in the fall the opening in the back was closed by some stockades in the rear, and shelter tents, and fireplaces were added. Sometimes the task of fortification was made easier by the lay of the land. The line occupied by the Twentieth Michigan Infantry near Taylor's Creek ran along a narrow ridge that sloped more gently toward the railroad bed in the rear. Here dugouts were cut out of the rear slope. The ridge itself provided enough protection to allow shelter tents to be placed over the openings in the rear. Gradually, these trenches were connected to the rear via "covered ways," approach trenches that winded their way up to the front lines.

Needless to say, the dugouts were dirty at the best of times and veritable mudholes during rainy weather. Provisioned with a scant supply of food and water, the men were unable to bathe or wash their clothes. The problem was especially severe for those defending the more isolated parts of the line or key advanced positions. Unless they were willing to chance a deadly gauntlet of bullets, they would have to lie in concealment, without food, water, or even a chance to stretch until nightfall, and even then the situation might not improve if there was a full moon.

Eventually, the privations would force many to take their chances. Thirst in the hot sun proved especially hard to bear. A man jumping out of his rifle pit or trench might be protected by the rolling undulation of ground for a while. However, sooner or later as he ran, portions of his silhouette would be exposed, especially his head. Then would follow the inevitable whiz of minié balls. Some men, in fear for their lives, would run as fast as they could, hoping thereby to minimize the chance of being hit; others would continue to walk nonchalantly back to the safety of the rear; still others might vacillate between the two styles, depending upon the intensity and closeness of the enemy fire.

Byron Cutcheon of the Twentieth Michigan Infantry tells about a subterranean ice-well house along the Baxter Road that proved to be an especially strong magnet for thirsty men during that long, hot summer. A considerable quantity of ice had been placed in a hole and then covered with straw. Many men risked, and a few gave up, their lives to quench their relentless thirst with a small piece of ice.

Alexander T. Daugherty, who served as the cook with Battery K of the Second Pennsylvania Heavy Artillery, would recall how difficult it was to distribute food to the men in exposed forward locations:

> I would approach under cover for as far as I could go with safety. Then I would wait until the volley was fired. Then I would run zigzagging with all my might for the breastworks, and frequently passing dead men. I bent my body as low as I could to protect myself. I ran the gauntlet for more than 60 days, morning, noon and evening.

Of course, many others running this gauntlet were not as fortunate and were either killed or severely wounded.

Enemy fire was not the only threat. The hot weather and the emotional strain proved almost as dangerous. Those on the front lines were, in effect, on continual duty. Many eventually succumbed to heat prostration and were evacuated to the rear. Nerves were pushed to the breaking point by lack of sleep, made worse by the incessant annoyance of flies, mosquitoes, "gray-backs," and, of course, enemy sharpshooters. Monotony mixed with sudden danger also took its toll:

> It was hell itself, and it is wondrous to me that so many of us

survived the event. The over-taxing of the men in building rifle pits, batteries, forts and cover ways, in addition to the continuous sharp shooting; the evening and morning duels, which were so deadly in front of the city, was singly awful. One-half of the line would fire while the other worked on the pits or tried to sleep.

To this we must add the strain of constant scares and false alarms. Expecting an imminent attack by the enemy, entire brigades, even divisions, would often be kept on the highest level of alert for lengthy periods. In its regimental history the Second Pennsylvania Heavy Artillery recounted how the July 9–12 period was particularly trying. The besiegers were constantly under fire, and the Union command was convinced a Confederate attack would occur at any moment. Sleeping during the night, consequently, was completely forbidden, and even during the day soldiers were permitted to sleep only in shifts, 2 hours at a time.

Although one is tempted to think that matters could hardly be more difficult, those portions of the line where "colored troops" were positioned were especially subjected to the enemy's ire and thus had to endure even greater hardships. The Confederates maintained a continuous fire against these portions of the line, or at least so it appeared to those on the receiving end. And, of course, bullets and other types of missiles never discriminate according to race, national origin, or sex, so in these areas even the men in the white regiments had to be extremely cautious, since exposing the slightest portion of one's body could have grave consequences.

FIGHTING IN ENTRENCHMENTS

It would be impossible for two such large armies to long remain side by side without the occasional eruption of a martial paroxysm, as one side or the other struggled to obtain some local or strategic advantage. The ten months of the "siege" was punctuated by no fewer than forty-four skirmishes, eleven engagements, nine actions, six assaults, and six set piece battles, not counting the nearly constant sniping that occurred daily along large portions of the lines. These ranged from small, informal clashes between company-sized forces, to large, thoroughly planned, set piece affairs that involved thousands of men on either side.

Often smaller encounters were occasioned simply by the need to push back enemy skirmishers. Such an action occurred on September 10. By this time the Confederate pickets had encroached to a "few roads" from "Fort Hell" (Fort Mahone), and their fire soon became very annoying to both officers and men. At 1 A.M., Gen. Philippe De Trobriand ordered the Twentieth Indiana Infantry to attack the enemy's line near a point known as the Chimneys on the Jerusalem Plank. This they did by threat of the bayonet, with little firing, and their unexpected appearance shook the enemy and guaranteed the success of the operation. The Second U. S. Sharpshooters, meanwhile "perfected the connection" between the captured pits and the old line.

Other times an offensive operation had more ambitious objectives, such as to capture an enemy fort or some other type of defensive strongpoint. Union forces succeeded in taking Battery Harrison, strong defensive works near Richmond on September 30, and then furiously attempted to strengthen the works by extending its line and so on.

Not content to accept this loss of something so valuable, between 2 and 3 P.M. the next day, the Confederates counterattacked, throwing twelve brigades against the position. The three lines of attackers advanced in fine style over slightly descending ground until abut halfway across the field. Part of the defending Union forces, "colored" troops from the Third Division, was armed with Spencer repeating rifles. Gen. Cecil Clay, commander of the Fifty-eighth Pennsylvania Infantry, provides a vivid description of the carnage that ensued:

> The division came on in fine order—officers with their swords drawn, arms glittering and battle flags flying. As soon as it came within range our men began firing, and packed as they were in pits, with the men in the rear loading their pieces and handing them to their comrades in front, kept up a tremendous fire, before which nothing could stand, let alone advance. When the fire opened the men were all shooting low—"an

amiable weakness"—and a long line of puffs of dust plainly to be seen, thrown up some distance on the hither side of the advancing column, marked the impact of the balls. Presently the head of the oncoming mass reached the line of fire, and then! . . . Away went organization, down went men, officers and battle flags; no formation could stand that withering fire. Officers sprang to the front, flags waved and the crowd, for such it now became, struggled to get up to our works; but there was no standing the racket, and the whole mass fell back in confusion.

It was inevitable that this attack would ultimately meet the same fate as the First Maine Heavy Artillery's at Colquitt's Salient in June. Despite their valor the Confederates were driven back. Besides sustaining heavy casualties, Clingman's brigade was almost annihilated; seven battle flags were lost.

MASSIVE ARTILLERY FIRE

It certainly must not be thought that infantry was the exclusive player in this phase of the war. The artillery arm also served a crucial role, and most mornings the stentorian boom of the cannon could be heard, as localized artillery duels erupted here and there along the line. The seasoned veteran could tell the direction of the projectile by both the type of flash and the accompanying sound. Upon detecting inbound shells, everyone would yell, "Cover!" and immediately take their own advice. Occasionally, would then be heard "Stretcher this way!"—a sure indication that at least one shot or shell had found its target. The shells employed by the Confederate artillery were noticeably less reliable than the Union's. Many failed to explode, and soon large piles of them could be seen near the dugouts.

Occasionally, local duels escalated to full-scale artillery battles, with artillery along the entire front vomiting their deadly messengers. Darkness offered little or no respite. These exchanges could occur at any time and resulted in the expenditure of many tons of ammunition. The nocturnal "fireworks displays" were often spectacular. A.S. Twitchell, who served as a quartermaster sergeant with the Seventh Maine Light Battery, provides a vivid recollection of a particularly active series of artillery exchanges when the Confederates launched a nocturnal assault in front of Fort Haskell (March 29, 1865):

> The sky was lit up by the broad flame of mortars and by the twinkling and shooting stars as they passed to and from, high in the air. . . . Sometimes more than twenty shells would be in the air at the same time, looking like twinkling stars shooting and plunging madly out of their spheres; and seldom less than five or six could be seen at the same time. Some, at a low elevation would only rise a few degrees above the horizon; while others would be seen to be mounting away up towards the zenith, then down, down, increasing in rapidity, until near the ground. Then a wide, sudden sheet of flame would terminate its flight, and woe to him or them who came within its deadly circle.

The veteran who authored the regimental history of the First Connecticut Artillery regiment incidentally recorded a noticeable discrepancy in expertise between the Union and the Confederate artillerists at this point. In an action around August 20, he estimated that only about one in a hundred rebel shells reached the intended target, while the prevailing standard was one in five.

SIEGE ARTILLERY

In some ways the situation that Grant and the Army of the Potomac faced by July 1864 was similar to that with which Union authorities had to contend with prior to the start of the 1862 Peninsula Campaign, and once again a large siege train had to be assembled. Of course, the fortifications that now confronted them were more extensive, and their adversaries, profiting from 2 years of constant fighting, were far more experienced. Union commanders were determined, at all costs, to avoid some of the mistakes of the '62 campaign. The high-level Union artillery and engineering authorities were now much more sensitive to the nature of the ground over which the ordnance had to be hauled, and it was decided to utilize much lighter materiel. Brigadier General Hunt suggested that the following ordnance be included in the siege train: Forty 4½-inch siege guns, ten

10-inch siege mortars, twenty 8-inch siege Mortars, twenty Coehorn mortars, plus 1000 rounds per gun, 600 for mortars, and 200 for Coehorns. Col. Henry L. Abbot who was to actually command the siege train, managed to assemble only eighteen 4½-inch siege guns but the full complement of the three types of mortars.

Thus, instead of 200- and 100-pound Parrotts, which were usual for a siege, there were to be numerous 4½-inch rifled guns. The 13-inch seacoast mortars were also left behind. Abbot had also wanted 8-or 10-inch howitzers, but Hunt had purposely rejected these and argued that they were in effect a hybrid between a gun and mortar without the advantages of either. He felt that siege guns and even 12-pounder field guns could provide the same functionality.

The Ordnance Department, however, unable to provide all the necessary 4½-inch guns, substituted twenty 30-pounder Parrotts. As events would turn out, this certainly wasn't a hardship, and the Parrotts proved to be more durable and superior weapons. Capt. J. G. Benton urged Colonel Abbott to take the Parrotts "as a matter of choice." Earlier trials with a 4½-inch gun showed it to burst after 800 rounds, a serious deficiency in a weapon to be fired day in and day out during a protracted siege, as was likely to occur in front of Petersburg and Richmond.

The increasing reliance upon entrenchments, with their sophisticated systems of trenches and subterranean areas, increased the importance of mortars. Entrenched batteries and subterranean storage areas offered little or no vertical profile for howitzers and guns to fire at, making it necessary to lob large explosive shells, instead. Consequently, the siege train in 1864 now carried 50 mortars, compared to the 28 carried by its predecessor in 1862. The highest military authorities thought that even this number might not be sufficient in the upcoming campaign, and General Hunt on May 4 asked Colonel Abbot to experiment with using 12-pounder Napoleons as mortars. The guns would be loaded with much smaller charges than normally required by high-speed, direct fire, and to achieve the necessary high, parabolic trajectory, a hole would be dug under the trail section so that the entire piece could be inclined at a 45-degree angle.

Siege artillery ended up playing a big role in the campaign. On

July 30 during the 4-hour period following the explosion of the mine that started the Battle of the Crater, Colonel Abbot's command fired a total of 3,883 rounds, that is, 7 tons of shot, shell, and canister.

In certain respects the Union siege artillery in front of Petersburg departed from the traditional role. Rather than attempting to annihilate enemy troops and artillery or even destroy inanimate targets, it attempted to reduce the effectiveness of enemy artillery fire and prohibit the Confederates from sending reserves into the areas being attacked. Union siege artillery for the first time began to be used to *suppress* enemy artillery fire and *interdict* enemy troop movement. There had been a shift to depriving enemy functionality, rather than pure physical destruction, in this sense representing a step toward modern artillery tactics.

In a report penned after the battle, Colonel Abbot conjectured that the Battle of the Crater was probably the first instance of heavy mortars being used to fire spherical case. Up to thirty 12-pound canister shot were placed in each 10-inch mortar. These were then fired at selected enemy batteries that had proven to be most troublesome. This technique proved to be "of great utility" and succeeded in suppressing the enemy batteries' fire.

A number of other innovations and improvements appeared around the same time. Artillerymen, like everyone else along the lines, were continuously exposed to enemy sharpshooters, so a number of precautionary measures were quickly taken. One of these was the addition of rope, wood, or iron mantelets to the guns. Some artillerists preferred those made of 6-inch-thick rope (minié balls could only penetrate 2 to 2½ inches), since not only did the iron versions tend to splinter and maim those behind when struck by large shot, but they were soon bent by the repetitive recoils. This, strictly speaking, wasn't an innovation, since they had been first introduced in 1862 by Gen. Richard Delafield, who had in turn drawn from Russian practice at Sebastopol during the Crimean War.

Major General Butler was responsible for another innovation, this time involving the large 13-inch mortar. Its staggering 17,000-pound weight made it unmanageable. Artillerymen on Butler's staff suggested mounting it on an ordinary railroad truck car that was further strengthened by additional iron beams and covered with iron plates.

The experiment was successfully completed after only the second prototype, when the car recoiled only 10 to 12 feet along the track.

The ammunition for these large siege guns also gradually improved. Compliments of Major Birnie of the Royal Artillery, the Tice conflagration shell was used as an incendiary device to set afire rebel buildings. Major Birnie succeeded at destroying houses near a rebel battery at the 1500-yard range. He then proposed to equip two 7-inch Ames guns with these shells and bring these as close to Richmond as possible, then start to burn the Virginia capital.

PART VII

EPILOGUE AND CONCLUSION

Chapter 30

THE EFFECTIVENESS
OF THE RIFLE MUSKET

U ntil recently, Civil War historians have assumed that Civil War firefights tended to be at much longer ranges than when infantrymen had only carried smoothbore muskets. A firestorm of debate and recrimination has broken out, however, since the 1989 publication of Paddy Griffith's *Battle Tactics of the Civil War*. Challenging the traditional view, Mr. Griffith has boldly suggested that the average range of a firefight was considerably less than expected. Griffith claims that the average distance separating both sides during a firefight in 1864-65 was but a modest 141 yards.

At first glance this seems in conflict with a great amount of information that can be culled from primary sources. Many memoirs and battle reports provide instances of accurate, effective long-range rifle fire. Even early in the war, skilled sharpshooters with target rifles equipped with telescopic sights picked off officers at ranges up to a thousand yards. Priv. Frederick Peet of Company H, First United States Sharpshooters, for example, explained to his father in an April 8, 1862, letter how at Yorktown four companies from his regiment were completely able to suppress enemy battery fire, though 1500 yards distant. The Confederate cannoneers were able to resume firing only as evening set in, and then only after taking cover behind sandbags.

Lt. Col. William Ripley, who commanded this regiment, provides an even more compelling example of the long-range accuracy of these small arms. While the regiment was advancing toward Spotsylvania Court House, Virginia, in May 1864, a rebel signal station was espied atop a lofty tree in the distance. Since the rebels there could observe all Union troop movement in the vicinity, they had to be removed from their elevated positions as expeditiously as possible. Unfortunately, the rebel spotters were about 1500 yards away, substantially beyond canister range, and although the Union artillery fired steadily for half an hour, it had no effect.

The men in Company F decided to see what they could do. Few marksmen still carried target rifles with the telescopic sights so common during the regiment's formative months, and they were only able to fire accurately up to the maximum range of their elevated sights, that is, about 1000 yards. This was still 500 yards short of what was needed in the present situation. A description of how the sharpshooters solved this problem is probably best left in Ripley's own words:

> They therefore cut and fitted sticks to increase the elevation of their sights and a few selected men were directed to open fire, while a staff officer with his field glass watched the result. It was apparent from the way the men in the distant trees looked down when the Sharpes bullets began to whistle near them that they were shooting under still, so more and longer sticks were fitted to still further elevate the sights; now the rebels began to look upward, and the inference was at once drawn that the bullets were passing over them. Another adjustment of the sticks, and the rebels began to dodge, first one side then another, and it was announced that the range was found. . . . when all the rifles had been properly sighted and the whole twenty-three opened, the surprised rebels vacated that signal station with great alacrity.

Of course, Confederate sharpshooters enjoyed similar successes. Fighting near Linden Station in Rappahannock County, Virginia, on May 4 1862, a dozen Confederate sharpshooters, called up to stop Union marauders who were killing cattle, poured in a witheringly accurate fire. The Union infantry, though 500 yards away, was able to retreat only after the Confederate sharpshooters had each let off four or five rounds, and about a dozen Union men were left hors de combat.

All of these examples of accurate, long-range fire were achieved by expert sharpshooters who acted independently of a formation. Not forced to participate in volley fire, they were free to select their targets, take as much time as they needed, and choose the exact moment when to fire. However, those who disagree with Griffith in turn point out that the Civil War battlefield abounded with examples of opposing formations blazing away at one another at ranges much greater than the 100 to 150-yard range he has suggested. Indeed, browsing through after-battle reports will uncover many examples of firefights at ranges beyond 150 yards. After the battle of Resaca, Georgia, on May 15, 1864, for example, Surgeon H. Goodman reported that small arms fire had ranged between 20 and 500 yards.

Accounts provided by officers of the Seventh Connecticut Infantry boast one of the longest-range effective fires by infantry in a close-order formation during the entire war. Seeing enemy infantry approaching in the distance during an engagement at Olustee, Florida (February 20, 1864), Colonel Hawley mentally assessed distance and ordered the regiment to raise the "guidesights" (backsights) so that their weapons were ranged for 600 yards. The result proved extremely effective, and the advance was checked. After retiring about 100 yards, the Union regiment was later threatened by a second Confederate attack. This time the men were ordered to set their guidesights to 400 yards. Once again the fire proved effective, and the enemy was forced to abandon the attack.

Although effective very-long-range fire by troops in formation was rare; one doesn't have to look too far to find exchanges of fire within the 150 to 250-yard range. Anyone with sufficient patience to wade through the *Official Records* can extract numerous examples of one or both sides initiating a firefight at such ranges, occasionally even further. An informed reader can reiterate a litany of such encounters from rote. After Fredericksburg, Virginia (December 13, 1862), for instance, Col. William S. Clark, who commanded the Twenty-first Massachusetts Infantry, estimated that his men had begun firing when they had approached to within 40 rods (220 yards) of the defenders. The Ninety-seventh New York Regiment is reported to have begun firing while still 50 rods (275 yards) from the rebels who skirted the woods in front of them. A number of similar examples are found at Gettysburg. On the first day, July 1, 1863, the Sixth Wisconsin Infantry was ordered to deliver a fire against the then-winning rebels, who were about 40 rods distant. This was sufficient to stop the Confederates.

These examples seem to repudiate Griffith's conclusions about the typical range of Civil War small arms fire. Fairness, however, forces us to look at cases in which short-range firefights did occur. When one meticulously compares the ranges during engagements in which the infantry remained in formation, a more varied picture emerges. Rather than the 150- to 400-yard ranges that one might expect, the critical moments of engagements frequently occurred when both sides had closed to 80 to 120 yards. And a number of cases can be isolated in which one or both sides reserved their fire until much closer ranges, as close as 10 to 20 yards! During the first day of the Second Battle of Bull Run (August 29, 1862), the opposing lines had advanced to within this range, with "the men standing in the open and blazing fiercely in each other's faces." At Antietam (September 17, 1862) during one exchange of infantry fire, the men "stood like duelists, firing and receiving fire at fifty or a hundred paces." This would be surpassed later that day during Morell's attack against Jackson's command. The Union assaulting force advanced to within 30 yards of the Confederate position, where, losing all vestiges of cohesiveness, it was completely broken.

Until recently, any comparative analysis of engagements, as described in the 129 volumes of the *Official Records,* would have been an extremely time-consuming process. One would have to wade through an enormous number of reports to find references to telltale tactical parameters, such as the type of fire system that was used, the range the fire was initiated, and so on. With the popularity of home computers and "electronic books" on CD-ROMs, the methodology available to serious researchers has undergone a revolution. By accessing the *Official Records* on CD-ROM and searching for specified combat ranges, it is now possible to list all of the firefights that were *reported* to have taken place at 10, 15, 20, 25, 30, 35, 40 yards ad nauseum.

When such searches are performed, it becomes apparent that of the 7000 or so Civil War skirmishes, actions, and battles, one finds firefights starting at virtually every range between 10 and 250 yards, some at even longer ranges. This is true for actions within larger well-known battles, such as Kernstown, Gaines's Mills, Malvern Hill, Second Bull Run, Antietam, Corinth, Frederickburg, Vicksburg, and Gettysburg as for the little-known skirmishes that took place at Rowlett's Station, Kentucky, Cumberland Iron Works, Tennessee, and Greenland Gap, West Virginia.

In many cases a short-ranged firefight occurred because both sides became visible to one another only at the last moment. There was a great deal of fighting in heavily forested areas during the battles of Fair Oaks, Chancellorsville, and the Wilderness in the East and during countless engagements in West Virginia, Kentucky, Mississippi, and Tennessee in the West. At Fair Oaks, Virginia, a portion of the Fifty-second New York Infantry was only able to square off against the Third Georgia at 15 to 20 paces. The woods were so thick that it was impossible for the troops to see any farther. Despite the proximity of the opposing forces, the firefight lasted half an hour.

In an action at Droop Mountain, West Virginia, on November 6, 1863, the Twenty-eighth Ohio Infantry, obscured by the brush and trees, was able to advance up to 20 yards from the enemy line before it delivered its first fire. Although the rebel forces, yelling wildly "like Indians" immediately launched a wild counterattack, the Union infantry derived an unexpected advantage from the limited visibility afforded by the terrain. The Ohio regiment was ordered to lie down and fire by file. The sudden disappearance of the Federals unsettled the Confederates, who up to this point had been advancing with complete abandon. Unnerved, their attack slowed down and gave time for Union reinforcements to arrive and settle the issue.

Other factors could reduce visibility and force opposing sides closer together. The thick clouds of smoke generated along the firing line sometimes would cover large portions of the battlefield and create visual conditions as limiting as the densest fog. After an engagement at New Berne, North Carolina (March 14, 1862), Confederate Col. H. J. B. Clark reported that once the action began, the smoke made it impossible to see more than a few yards. Although he knew that a Union line was approaching his breastworks, he could only guess its position from the sound of its muskets. He withheld the fire of the Special Battalion North Carolina Militia until he estimated that the approaching enemy was well within range; then he ordered his men to fire by files.

Fog and nightfall could produce exactly the same effect. During an engagement in front of Baton Rouge, Louisiana, on August 5, 1862, Col. T. B. Smith, who commanded the Twentieth Tennessee Infantry, received orders from Gen. Charles Clark to advance upon the enemy and withhold his fire until the Union solders began to fire. Under the cover of fog, his men managed to approach to about 20 yards, when they were finally spotted and fired upon.

With rather surprising frequency, short-range firefights also occurred in clear, unobstructed terrain where the participants easily could have opened fire at longer ranges. Advancing to attack the Union forces at the other side of an orchard at Shiloh (April 6–7, 1862), Brig. Gen. James Chalmers and his men had to march approximately 350 to 400 yards up a gentle incline in full view of an enemy partially sheltered by a fence. To Chalmer's surprise his men were allowed to advance in "most perfect order and splendid style" until they had come within 40 yards of the fence. Only then did the Union infantry unleash a "heavy fire."

Obviously, such short-range firefights in open terrain only occurred when both sides mutually decided to withhold their fire. This decision apparently was prompted by a variety of considerations. So many times the defenders could find at least partial shelter behind a rock fence or other obstructing features. This was a much more frequent occurrence than had been the case in Europe. Since the defenders were hidden along the skirt of a forest or beside a roadway meandering through rough terrain, their exact position was unknown to the opposing side. There was a tremendous potential for surprise and ambuscade. It wasn't uncommon for the defenders to withhold fire until the last possible moment, when it would be the most destructive.

Brig. Gen. James S. Negley recounted how he used just such a tactic against some of Nathan Bedford Forrest's men during a skirmish near La Vergne, Tennessee (October 6, 1862). Spotting a small group of Union cavalry that Gen. Negley offered as bait to his opponents, the Confederates charged along the road. The hidden Union infantry reserved their fire until the rebel horsemen were only 40 yards away, when they stood up and delivered a withering fire. Surprised by the resistance, the rebels retreated in noticeable disorder. A report submitted by Lieut. Col. Adolph Dengler, Forty-third Illinois Infantry, provides greater detail of how the same technique was used a few weeks later along the Lexington Road near Bolivar, Mississippi (December 19, 1862). The advancing Confederate cavalry was clearly visible and thus subject to small arms fire for at 250 yards. Nevertheless, Dengler issued the order to fire only when the Confederates had closed to 30 yards. This produced the same result as in the previous example.

There was another type of situation in which a defending force would withhold its fire to combine the advantage of surprise with the effect of a deadly close-in fire, one that could hardly miss. During a large action one side might temporarily lose track of its opponent, even in a contest taking place over relatively open ground. It was not uncommon for officers to take advantage of undulating terrain and exploit a "reverse slope or rise" much like Wellington 50 years before. During a raid on the Virginia Central Railroad in June 1864, Major Gen. Sheridan's cavalry encountered a sizeable Confederate force on the New Market Road. Initially repulsed, the cavalry retired 15 yards to the other side of a slight crest and lay down to form a battle line. The cavalry opened fire just as the enemy infantry advanced over the crest. This blistering fire from the cavalry's repeaters quickly disrupted the attackers, who were chased back over the plain, losing 250 men and two battle flags.

This is only a small sampling of cases in which infantry advanced up to close range before beginning to fire and is in no way intended to be exhaustive. An attempt to describe every incident reported in the *Official Records* would fill volumes. Nevertheless, as Civil War firefights are tabulated and characterized, the amount of variation in firing ranges becomes clear. One has to concede that when interpreted *from a purely mathematical basis,* Paddy Griffith's statement that during the Civil War the average range of small arms fire in 1864-65 was 141 yards is true at least as a rough approximation.

SMALL ARMS CASUALTIES

Under normal conditions casualty rates were also less than what we might expect. True, one finds numerous cases in which individual regiments, even brigades, were horribly mauled during intense fighting. At Gaines's Mills (June 27, 1862), for example, two regiments in the Union Fourth Brigade lost more than 33% casualties. Nevertheless, even in hotly contested affairs, the rate of casualties suffered by the total number of troops engaged was considerably lower. A contemporary military analyst writing in the *Army and Navy Journal* noted that in most battles, even hard-fought affairs, the overall casualties usually did not exceed 10%.

And it is this casualty rate that one encounters in so many personal memoirs and battle reports. Many soldiers, in fact, commented on how the level of casualties usually did not live up to their expectations. Noticing how many men emerged from a battle unscathed, George Neese, a young Confederate artilleryman, found himself wondering in his diary:

> But it is utterly astonishing and wholly incomprehensible especially to a Tyro, how men standing in line, firing at each other incessantly for hours like they did today, can escape with so few killed and wounded, for when Jackson's infantry emerged from the sulphurous bank of battle smoke that hung along the line the regiment appeared as complete as they were before the fight.

Neese certainly wasn't alone in his astonishment. Amazement at how men could blaze away at each other at close range without total destruction is encountered time and again in veterans' memoirs. Col. B. F. Scribner of the Thirty-Eighth Indiana observed that the number of casualties compared to the rounds fired during a typical engagement resulted in a "great excess of random shots." His Pennsylvania Regiment forced to charge a Confederate line during Second Bull Run (August 29–30, 1862), A. F. Hill could not but wonder how any of the Union infantrymen "could pass unscathed through that storm." Hermann, who fought as a Confederate, echoed exactly the same sentiment:

> I had often thought, how it was possible for so few to be slain when there was such terrific firing. When you consider the

great amount of ammunition expended in battles, the loss is insignificant in comparison.

Gen. James Longstreet, by anyone's standards an experienced professional soldier, not only was aware of this reality but made this fact one of the cornerstones of how the soldier was to conduct himself at the moment of crisis in his tactical doctrine:

Though the fiery noise of battle is indeed most terrifying, and seems to threaten universal ruin it is not so destructive as it seems, and few soldiers after all are slain. This the commanding general desires particularly to impress upon the fresh and inexperienced troops who now constitute a part of this command. Let officers and men, even under the most formidable fire, preserve a quiet demeanor and self-possessed, temper.

Even tacticians required by professional interests to formally examine the dynamics of the battlefield entertained a similar view. Observing that 499 rifle shots out of 500 did not result in a fatality, the author of an 1863 article in the *Army and Navy Journal* concluded that if this analysis was even an "approximate truth,"

it certainly robs war of some of its presumed fatality. As I have before remarked the escape of so large a majority of the men, amid such storms sweeping and yelling around their ears, has always been the greatest mystery.

Lewis A. Stimson, an aide to Gen. David Birney, noted that Maurice de Saxe's saying that a soldier had to fire his weight in bullets to hit an enemy, though "somewhat fanciful," had a loose basis in experience. Stimson was quick to point out, however, that this observation was of little solace to the soldier since "the first bullet may do the trick and the tally of wasted lead be made up afterwards." Stimson remembered occasionally seeing examples of what seemed "personal immunity" and provided a description of one such experience. Noticing a skirmish line advancing across a field, his eyes closely followed the men as they trotted the third of a mile without firing a shot. Safely ensconced in rifle pits, the Confederate infantry tried to stop the attackers with a brisk but deliberate fire. Despite this fire only a single man was struck, and the defenders were driven the short distance back to their next line of defense.

The commanding Union officer in particular appeared to have a charmed existence. Rapidly zigzagging up and down the advancing line to give orders and moral support, he had apparently been selected as a target by many of the defenders. Attracted by a series of uninterrupted puffs from discharged rifles, Stimson was able to detect that throughout the assault a converging fire had been directed towards this officer along the entire length of the defending line, about 200 yards away. Once satisfied that his men's efforts were successful, the officer then galloped back to his own lines unhurt.

If participants sometimes mused about why there were so few casualties when so much ammunition was expended, many also wondered what happened to the shots that were fired. In his highly illuminating memoir, Colonel Scribner quipped that just as the housewife, when wondering about the final resting place for all those little sartorial aids, would sometimes ask, "Where are all the pins?" Civil War veterans were justified in asking, "What becomes of all the bullets?"

Several Confederate soldiers came across the answer. Unlike European wars, which were mostly fought in open fields, many Civil War engagements were fought in wooded areas. When both sides are in completely clear terrain, after the combat it is impossible to easily determine the final resting place for most of the small arms projectiles. If one had enough time and motivation, one could dig all the spent Minié bullets out of the earth. Such an approach, of course, was beyond the means of contemporary observers. However, if the firing line were in front of a row of trees, the trunks and foliage would provide a backdrop. To a keen observer the trees were like the large fabric sheets stretched across a firing range during earlier European experiments to determine where shots actually wound up. One could see where a bullet had struck by looking at the damage to the bark or where the foliage had been torn away.

After Cold Harbor (June 1–2, 1864), looking at the woods through which his unit had passed under fire, Edward Moore, who early in the war fought under "Stonewall" Jackson, noted that not a single medium or large-sized tree was left with fewer than twelve bullet holes in it below the 6-foot mark. Many trees had been perforated all the way to their tops. Several other Confederates made the same observation. Walking over the Spotsylvania Court House battlefield (May 15, 1864), Neese noticed several locations where the small arms fire had been so intense that

> all the bushes and underbrush along in the rear of the lines were cut down clean, and there is not a twig on the trees that does not show the nipping bite of a bullet. The trees that stood in the leaden shower are all splintered and shivered, and look as if all the woodpeckers in creation had been working on them for a month.

Neese went on to observe that many of the pines, some 50 feet high, were hit by "Yankee bullets" from top to bottom.

At Drewey's Bluff, Virginia (May 13, 1864), I. Hermann, a Confederate infantryman, noticed the execution Union bullets were inflicting on a tall pine just within the rebel breastworks. Though the two firing lines had been only a hundred yards apart, Hermann noticed bark, needles, and cones being knocked down the entire height of the tree down to the top of the breastworks. Hermann concluded that even though thousands of shots were fired in a high parabolic trajectory into the upper regions of the tree, thousands more were fired even higher and escaped any sort of visual detection. Hermann confided to his readers that the mystery of how "so few to be slain" was solved when he observed the bullets striking the upper portion of the pine that day.

THEORETICAL VERSUS PRACTICAL EFFECTIVENESS OF THE RIFLE MUSKET

The evidence considered so far has been anecdotal, and although suggestive, it is circumstantial rather than conclusive. To determine if an infantryman carrying a new rifle musket was able to inflict more casualties than his predecessor with a smoothbore, one must also examine the trials of each weapon and the military scientific writings of the period.

Since the late 1700s, military men had tried to determine the "theoretical" accuracy of the musket. Experiments in Britain and France had earlier discovered that between 40% and 60% of the shots fired from a smoothbore musket under ideal conditions hit the target at 100 yards. European military authorities long recognized, though, that these results came from "theoretical performances."

One finds repeated efforts in period literature to estimate the practical effectiveness of the musket in battle. The consensus was that the number of shots that hit an enemy relative to the total fired was discouragingly low. One historian studying the Battle of Czaslau (Moravia, March 17, 1742), for example, concluded that the 6,500 Austrian casualties required the expenditure of about 650,000 Prussian cartridges, a 1.0% casualty rate. Guibert, the influential eighteenth-century French tactician, estimated that of 1,000,000 shots, only 2000 actually hit a man—that is, only 0.2% were effective. Writing after the Napoleonic Wars, Piobert was even more pessimistic, opining that 3000 to 10,000 shots were necessary for a single hit—between 0.01% and 0.03%.

The accuracy of British infantry fire during the Peninsular War (1808–14) appears to have been substantially higher, and British observers estimated it to somewhere between 0.3% and 0.5%. However, a comparison of the rounds fired versus French casualties at Vittoria (June 21, 1813) revealed only a 0.12% accuracy rate.

Estimated Casualties Inflicted by British during Napoleonic Wars

Jackson	Napier	Hughes	Casualties Inflicted at Vittoria
5/1000	1/300	2/100	1/800
0.5%	0.03%	2%	0.125%

Not surprisingly, as the Civil War dragged on, American tacticians became equally concerned with the effectiveness of the small arms, and several American authors tried to uncover the practical effectiveness of the new rifle muskets. An 1863 article in the *Army and Navy Journal* tells us that after the fiercely contested Battle of Murfreesboro, General Rosecrans reported that a total of 14,560 Confederates had been killed and wounded. Rosecrans noted that 20,000 Union artillery shells hit 728 men. This means that the estimated 2 million rounds of small arms fire struck 13,833 Confederates. In other words, 145 "musket" shots were needed to inflict a casualty. "Musket fire" proved to be slightly more effective at the Battle of Gaines's Mills. Here the expenditure of about 100,000 cartridges inflicted a little more than 1000 Confederate casualties, approximately 1 hit per 100 shots.

These two estimates conform rather nicely with that of a British observer who had followed the performance of the American infantry during the Mexican-American War. This officer calculated that during the Battle of Churubusco (August 20, 1847), Mexican infantry had inflicted 1 casualty for approximately every 800 musket rounds expended, while the American infantry were able to kill or wound 1 Mexican for every 125 rounds.

Union and British tacticians were not the only ones interested in determining the effectiveness of small arms fire. I. Hermann, who fought for the Confederate cause, admitted in his memoirs that he had been preoccupied with this same problem. Hermann noted that during a hard-fought affair, most infantrymen went through whatever ammunition they had been handed prior to the battle. Usually this was 40 rounds, although 60 rounds was not unheard of. Thus, during an engagement which lasted several hours, 5000 men would likely fire approximately 200,000 rounds. Based on his experience, Hermann estimated that this resulted in about 500 fatalities, that is, one man killed for every 400 shots fired.

In his analysis Hermann computed only fatalities, which may appear to make it impossible to compare his calculations with the estimates for Gaines's Mills and Murfreesboro. Fortunately, however, the just-cited *Army and Navy Journal* article claimed that typically, there was a five-to-one ratio between wounded and killed. Using this guideline to extrapolate the amount wounded, Hermann's analysis yields a total of 5 wounded and 1 killed for every 400 shots, a 1.50% casualty rate. This estimate is fairly similar to the 1.0% and 0.68% casualty rates computed for Gaines's Mills and Murfreesboro, respectively.

Rate of Casualties During Civil War			**Mex./Am. War**
Murfreesboro	Gaines Mill	Hermann	British Observer
1/145	1/100	6/400	1/125
0.68%	1.0%	1.5%	0.80%

Although this type of statistics is provided by only a handful of contemporary works, it is possible to add to this analysis by carefully collating fragmentary data provided by other sources. The Battle of Chickamauga (September 19–20, 1863) is a case in point. Examining official reports, it is possible to estimate the number of shots fired by the Union infantry and the number of resulting Confederate casualties. Depending upon the amount of ammunition that was actually captured by the Confederates, the estimated percentage of hits per total shots is calculated to be between 0.60% and 0.80%.

An analysis of the casualties suffered during the Battle of the Wilderness (May 5–7, 1864) provides similar figures. Surgeon Thomas A. McParlin, medical director for the U.S. Army, reported that he heard the chief ordnance officer claim that Union infantrymen had on average fired only eleven rounds during the entire battle. This would mean that the Army of the Potomac (less the IX Corps, which at that moment was operating independently) fired about 752,900 rounds. Traditionally, it has been thought that the Confederates sustained 7,450 casualties during these several days of fighting, although recent studies have pushed this figure up to 11,125. This results in an average hit rate between 0.99% and 1.5%. Although the estimated percentage of shots that caused casualties during the Wilderness and Chickamauga are merely that—estimates which have been extrapolated to show an overall tendency—they both fall within the range of the estimates provided by the primary sources described.

To help visualize the implications of these statistics, it is necessary to rephrase them in practical terms. If a British infantryman at Vittoria in 1813 somehow had been able to fire 3 rounds per minute, he would have been likely to achieve a hit only after 4 hours and 27 minutes, whereas an American infantryman during the Civil War probably would have achieved the same result after only 23 to 49 minutes, depending upon which estimate is accepted. On average, therefore, a 500-man regiment would have inflicted somewhere between 3.4 and 7.5 casualties per volley.

Most readers will probably find all of these estimates surprisingly low, even though they are based strictly on contemporary primary sources. Our appreciation of the theoretical accuracy of the rifle musket leads one to expect a much higher casualty rate. Today's black powder gun enthusiasts are able to achieve accurate fire at considerable ranges. It isn't uncommon for a modern marksman with a Springfield to hit a bull's-eye eight times out of ten shots on a range. The overwhelming temptation is to assume that a competent shooter could repeat this performance on the battlefield. Surely, if an infantryman on a target range can hit a human-sized target at 200 yards 40% to 50% of the time, shouldn't he be able to hit the same size target 5% to 10% of the time on the battlefield?

However, the calm emotional atmosphere encountered on a target range does not remotely resemble the pandemonium on the battlefield. It is unreasonable to expect anyone to achieve the same accuracy under fire as he would when leisurely firing on a range where he is in no personal danger.

To understand how the human factor affects the accuracy on the battlefield consider the following example. Let's say a modern military rifle, with laser-guided sights, and so on, has a theoretical accuracy of 99% at 500 yards. However, suppose the person firing the weapon suffers from severe muscular dystrophy. No matter how much this person concentrates, no matter how much training and practice, not only will almost all the shots miss the mark; they will be widely scattered. Although this might appear as an outlandishly extreme case, it paints a picture very close to what happened along the firing line during combat.

Not that it was impossible to hit a man at ranges up to, and even surpassing, a thousand yards. Experienced expert sharpshooters routinely hit the enemy 500 to 800 yards away. It must be remembered that in none of the sharpshooter cases presented at the beginning of this chapter were the men fighting in close-order formations and *exposed to enemy fire in return.* They were aiming and firing as individuals, positioned according to their own inclinations and choosing the exact moment to fire. Separated from their neighbors, they usually took advantage of available cover, and their targets, far distant, were frequently unaware of their danger. The marksmen had the time and presence of mind to estimate the range accurately, set the backsights, and take precise aim. This was critical, for the Minié rifle, in either its Enfield or its Springfield incarnation, had a relatively slow initial muzzle velocity, and the bullets had a parabolic trajectory. To fire accurately, it was critical to estimate the range accurately, to within 10 to 20 yards, and then adjust the backsight accordingly.

Regular infantrymen found themselves in a very different situation from the sharpshooter. Fighting in formations, albeit a slightly looser version than their European counterparts, they were exposed to return fire of companies or regiments firing in volleys. Even when an action had devolved into individual fire, the overall weight of return fire still could be heavy. This destroyed the typical soldier's presence of mind. Memoirs are full of descriptions of the pandemonium of the firefight. Some men became like robots with a fixed gaze, oblivious to everyone around them, including their targets. Others, in a furious frenzy, would load and fire as quickly as possible, disregarding not only the prescribed manual of arms but, more importantly, the steps essential for accurate aimed fire.

Soon everyone along the firing line was enveloped in smoke. The poor visibility and the din caused by the firing and yelling exacerbated the emotional chaos. The negative effect this had on accurate fire did not escape observation. A contributor to the *Army and Navy Journal* observed that the low percentage of actual hits was due to this lack of presence of mind, especially among inexperienced troops. In his memoirs Hermann would concur. In his own memoirs, the oft-quoted Confederate artilleryman Neese would observe:

Some men and not a few—when they get under a heavy infantry fire become wild with excitement, while others are frenzied with fear, and while in that state they shoot anywhere and everywhere; some of them fire at the moon.

All small arms weapons consist of three technologies: the way to load the ammunition to be fired, the method of aiming and firing the weapon, and the mechanism that imparts a ballistic performance upon the projectile. A weapon's accuracy is a function of the second and third of these technologies. The ballistic performance is purely a hardware issue, a characteristic of the weapon. The technology used to aim and fire by necessity involves a human and therefore is influenced by the way the shooter tends to react in stressful situations. In other words, small arms fire during the Civil War was demonstrably less accurate under battlefield conditions than what we would expect by considering its theoretical performance from practice range experiments.

If there is a conclusion that can be made from these anecdotes, estimates, and experiences, it is that in terms of the ratio of hits to shots fired, small arms fire during the Civil War was statistically more effective than that during eighteenth and early-nineteenth-century European warfare. As already shown, various sources estimated casualties ranging between 0.68% and 1.5% during a few selected Civil War battles, compared to an estimated 0.3% to 0.5% hit rate for British infantry during the Napoleonic Wars. If these figures are accurate, then one must conclude that the fire of a Civil War infantryman was two to three times more effective than his British counterpart fifty years previous. At first glance this tends to suggest that the new rifle musket was indeed very much more accurate under battle conditions and was the cause for these increased rates of casualties.

However, there are two reasons not to accept this line of reasoning unequivocally. A British observer during the Mexican-American War had estimated that the American small arms fire, when considering the total shots fired, had inflicted a 0.80% casualty rate. These American infantrymen were armed with Model 1840 flintlock smoothbores; the Model 1842 musket with percussion cap did not enter production until late 1844. Yet Americans during the Mexican American War were observed to achieve a casualty rate 266% to 160% greater than British infantry during the Napoleonic Wars. At the same time this 0.80% casualty rate was 118% of the casualty rate observed at Murfreesboro, 80% of that at Gains's Mills, and 66% of the estimates provided by Hermann. And they achieved this with a weapon that Civil War buffs usually consider an order of magnitude less accurate than either the Enfield or Springfield rifle musket.

A French medical and surgical gazette published at Lyons, after the Battle of Solferino (1859) reported what may be regarded as the converse of the above anomaly. Firing 8,400,000 rounds, Austrian small arms caused 2000 deaths and 10,000 casualties, or a hit for every 700 shots fired. This meant that the Austrian infantrymen inflicted a rate of casualties very much in line with the British during the Napoleonic Wars, despite now being armed with the new rifle muskets. This suggests that the American infantrymen who achieved these higher rates of accuracy did so because of reasons other than the inherent characteristics of the muskets they used (which in 1848 were identical to those used by European armies).

The second problem lies in the intrinsic nature of all Minié type rifles, regardless of their country of origin. As we have seen, the relatively slow initial muzzle velocity meant that at ranges over 150 yards, it was critical to estimate the target's range correctly and then adjust the backsight accordingly. A soldier firing at a man 200 yards away who simply looked down the two sights on his gun and failed to adjust for the range would be guaranteed a miss! Accurate fire demanded careful estimation of range and a corresponding adjustment of the backsight every time the range changed by 10 to 15 yards or so. Except for sharpshooters and Gen. Patrick Cleburne's men, who were disciplined in the formal British methods of aiming, there is little evidence that any other Civil War soldiers ever did this during the heat of battle. Almost all contemporary sources talk about the confusion and the hurriedness, but nowhere is there a mention of adjusting the backsights!

Yet there remains the real possibility that small arms fire during the Civil War was indeed more accurate than it had been in earlier European warfare. Could there have been another reason for this increased casualty rate? A contributor to the August 29, 1863, edition of the *Army and Navy Journal* provides a clue:

> The great disproportion in our battles between the number of ball cartridges discharged and the number of killed and wounded was due mainly to the want of presence of mind in our raw troops, but the very limited investigation . . . has convinced me that our troops take much better aim, and consequently waste far less ammunition than is usual in European warfare.

This author suggests the increased casualties, instead of the increased capability of the rifle muskets, was the result of greater marksmanship among American infantrymen compared to their European counterparts! To some European readers, this might appear to be pure American chauvinism and bombast. However, writing in the *Journal of the Royal United Service Institute* in 1857, Lieutenant Colonel Wilford, chief instructor at the British School of Musketry, was

highly critical of the average British infantryman's ability to deliver anything remotely resembling accurate fire prior to the adoption of the
formal firing techniques at Hythe:

> Being placed in position to commence firing or to charge, the
> soldier was left to his own resources, virtually, in firing, he shut
> his eyes, opened his mouth, threw his head back, and pulled
> the trigger; and, if this was not enough he was sometimes
> exhorted to "aim low" . . . an almost certain mode to issue their
> balls flying over the heads of their opponents, as any ball will
> ricochet at the same angle with which it strikes the ground.

According to Wilford, the best a great many British infantrymen
could do when discharging their weapons was to point their muskets
vaguely in the enemy's direction. There was very little effort to aim
and only a minimal attempt to even "level" their weapons. Results
were completely random.

This may strike the reader not only as completely ineffective, a
complete waste of effort, but also as idiotic. After all, everyone knows
to have any chance of hitting the target, you must align the weapon
using its sights. However, what is overlooked is that today almost
everyone in our society has grown up with a basic familiarity with
firearms, even if they have never held one in their hands. Television
and the movies are replete with action episodes, and everyone grows
up watching fictitious SWAT teams hunting from room to room and
Plains Indians picking off teamsters as they drove the great wagon
trains Westward-ho. From the time we are small children, we are
exposed to the basic operating procedures of these weapons, just as
if we watched army training films!

Wilford's descriptions of the typical British firing methods were
based upon soldiers who, at the beginning of their careers, lacked
any familiarity with the weapons they were expected to use. Until he
became a soldier, a young man might never have even seen a musket
up close or witnessed one fired, much less have any idea of the
proper way it should be held or effectively used.

The same could not be said for a great many of the young American men who enthusiastically entered the ranks to serve their

country in the crises of 1812, 1846, or 1861. Coming from Pennsylvania, Tennessee, Ohio, or any Southern state, a sizable number grew up learning how to hunt to augment their families' food supplies. As they donned their first uniforms, many of these young men already possessed more than some notion of how a musket was used. This type of recruit would be much less inclined to "shut his eyes, open his mouth, throw his head back, and pull the trigger" than his European counterpart. This is not to say that he was necessarily an expert marksman, a candidate for immediate entrance into the special sharpshooter units. Chief Instructor Wilford, in an 1857 article that appeared in the Journal of the Royal United Service Institution, claimed that the only truly "expert shots" were men who received formal training and who consistently followed the proper procedure. According to Wilford, these trained men always bested self-proclaimed marksmen who taught themselves how to fire while hunting birds or game. Nevertheless, the informally trained might be counted on to achieve much more accurate fire, even under battle conditions, than a British lad of the same age who before entering the army had been a clerk or chimney sweep.

If the increased effectiveness of small arms fire during the Civil War was more attributable to the men carrying the rifle musket than to any increase in its capabilities, one important question remains: Was this greater familiarity with small arms, and hence proficiency, a trait exhibited by a majority of those mustered into service, or did a few highly proficient marksmen account disproportionately for the casualties that were inflicted?

Since most of the information needed to resolve this question has been lost to posterity, this must forever remain a theoretical issue. Nevertheless, a few clues can be found to suggest that the latter possibility is the more plausible explanation. Occasionally, in period documents one finds descriptions of these types of men. Capt. John De Forest of the 12th Connecticut tells of a certain Bradey, one of his "old" soldiers, a "heroic" twenty-year-old, who would load and fire with a "murderous pugnacity." Lt. Josiah Favill, who served with a New York infantry volunteer regiment, would never forget noticing just such a man who, although a civilian, fought with his regiment during the First Battle of Bull Run:

There served with us throughout the whole fight a tall, elderly gentleman, wearing plain clothes and a tall silk hat, in the front rank, who loaded and fired away in the most deliberate manner, apparently wholly indifferent to danger; he must have done a good deal of execution, as the excitement did not seem to affect him in the least. They say he is a noted abolitionist, and desired to do his share in the field.

Searching through period memoirs, one can find similar descriptions of other individuals who stood out during the heat of battle, made remarkable by their composure, the steadiness with which they loaded, aimed, and fired, and the carnage they appeared to cause.

The tangible effect of several such individuals, capable of inflicting far more casualties than those in the ranks beside them, may not be obvious. The following hypothetical example, however, demonstrates the statistical impact of the addition of a few good shots in a regiment composed of otherwise mediocre riflemen. Consider the case of a 300-man regiment that on average inflicts casualties equal to 0.3% of the total shots fired, the casualty rate Colonel Napier estimated for British infantrymen during the Peninsular War. Let's say five new replacements are experienced hunters who achieve a 50% hit rate under fire whenever they encounter an enemy formation within 200 yards. The remaining 295 men in the regiment continue at the 0.3% rate. The new average for the regiment would now be [(295 x 0.003) + (5 x 0.5]/300), or 1.1%. In other words, the addition of five extremely good shots would result in an overall increase of 267% in the average rate of casualties per total shots fired by the regiment. Of course, this hypothetical example, with five men achieving a 50% success rate, has been "taken out a hat." Rarely has anyone been able to achieve a 50% casualty rate under fire. However, the same results would have been obtained if 25 new soldiers were capable of achieving an average 10% hit rate under fire. This is probably a much more realistic scenario.

Regardless of the exact figures involved, the point is that putting a few real marksmen into a regiment of otherwise average shooters would result in a significant increase in the unit's performance during fire combat. How many Union regiments, formed primarily from mechanics, bankers, and clerks, were able to boast at least a few men with extensive hunting experience? How many on both sides in the West? The answer is probably the great majority of Civil War regiments!

All these observations will probably strike the reader as a rather serpentine look at the debate as to whether the new rifle musket was indeed significantly more effective than the smoothbore it replaced. Did it inflict more casualties and produce longer-range firefights?

Although the theoretical range of the rifle musket was several times that a smoothbore, much of the fighting nevertheless occurred at ranges equal to or only slightly more than that found during previous wars. In almost all cases in which firefights were conducted by men in close-order formation, the targets were less than 500 yards distant and many examples can be found of opposing forces facing off against one another at almost every range increment between 10 and 250 yards.

This forces the conclusion that although the average range at which the opposing sides exchanged fire was indeed *slightly greater than in previous wars,* at the same time it was *considerably less than what modern readers have come to expect.*

On the surface the ability of the rifle musket to cause a greater number of casualties than the old smoothbore musket appears less open to question. Contemporary and modern sources suggest that the average number of casualties inflicted compared to the total shots fired was between 0.60% and 1.50%. This compares quite favorably to the 0.125% observed for the British infantrymen during the Battle of Vittoria and the 0.01% to 0.1% range estimated by various authorities for continental armies. However, before claiming that this is incontrovertible proof that the rifled musket was indeed more effective, the one statistic available for the Mexican-American War must be considered. It will be remembered that a British observer estimated that American infantrymen armed with percussion cap smoothbores inflicted casualties in 0.80% of the total shots fired, while Austrian infantrymen carrying rifle muskets in 1859 only achieved a 0.14% hit rate. Despite the suggestiveness of these two statistics, they are too narrow a sampling to be conclusive.

To resolve the question, it will be necessary to unearth additional information about the fire effectiveness of American forces during the 1846–48 conflict in Mexico. If a lower ratio of casualties per shots fired is determined for smoothbores of the period, then one must conclude that the rifle musket was indeed more effective on the battlefield. If, on the other hand, the future data is in line with the British observer's Mexican War estimates, then one would be forced to conclude that the increased casualties inflicted during Civil War battles were the result of greater proficiency with the weaponry rather than any improvement in the performance of the weapons themselves.

Chapter 31

THE BAYONET: MYTH AND UTILITY

ORDERS TO USE THE BAYONET

When viewed from tactical directives issued before an engagement, Civil War commanders exhibited noticeable conservatism. Rather than prescribing the tactics based on the "scientific method of rifle firing" and the long-range capabilities of the rifle musket, they consistently espoused doctrine that required their men to remain calm, withhold their fire, and, when finally ready to fire, to aim low. The other key element in this system was the judicious use of the bayonet. Before the Battle of Bull Run, for example, Beauregard predicted, "Great reliance will be placed on the bayonet at the proper juncture," while the next year McClellan emphatically instructed his men to "above all things rely upon the bayonet." Before the Battle of Murfreesboro, Rosecrans gave similar advice to troops in the Army of the Cumberland: "Close steadily in upon the enemy, and, when you get within charging distance, rush on him with the bayonet."

Even as the war continued and a trend toward entrenching eventually emerged, many high-ranking officers continued to advocate the use of cold steel. During the Atlanta Campaign (spring 1864), Union Maj. Gen. James B. McPherson advised the troops in the Army of the Tennessee never to wait until the enemy's final assault but instead "fix bayonets and meet him halfway." At about exactly the same time, one of his adversaries, Maj. Gen. William Bate, reminded Confederate officers that a firefight "should be followed by a determined charge to break the enemy's line, thereby producing further demoralization and confusion." This was almost identical to instructions issued by Maj. Gen. Gouverneur Warren (V Corps, Army of the Potomac) in the East. Warren advised that a firefight should continue until "but few bullets come back." Then the officer was to order a cease-fire and either an advance or a charge, depending upon circumstances. McPherson, Warren, and Bate all stressed the psychological importance of the bayonet. McPherson did not want his troops standing idly by during the crisis of the battle, while Bate wanted his troops to deliver a final coup de grâce after delivering injurious fire.

THE EFFECTIVENESS OF THE BAYONET

Despite its frequent mention in tactical instructions, as a viable tool in the infantryman's arsenal of weapons, the bayonet is probably held in relatively low regard by most modern Civil War historians. When it came turn to discuss the bayonet in a work devoted to the description of Civil War weapons, one modern author has concluded that Civil War infantrymen only carried this weapon because their officers failed to appreciate that the advent of the percussion lock, rifled gun barrels, and the conical Minié bullet rendered "virtually all previous forms of weapons obsolete." The author went on to imply that its only real utility occurred once it was jammed upside-down in the ground, where it could now serve to hold a candle, or when it was held over an open fire to serve as a spit for chicken or ham. Although slightly less sarcastic in tone, McWhiney and Jamieson, in their well known work *Attack and Die,* have exhibited an equally low opinion of the usefulness of the bayonet in real combat situations.

The utility of the bayonet has been held in poor regard by most modern Civil War military historians for several reasons. It did not seem to have any demonstrable use, and, indeed, there is a great temptation to conclude that is was rarely employed. As infantrymen gained experience, they noted that bayonet fighting, much expected at the outset of the war, never materialized. According to Heros von Borcke:

> Accounts of bayonet-fights are current after every engagement, and are frequently embodied in subsequent "histories," so called; but as far as my experience goes, recalling all the battles in which I have borne a part, bayonet-fights rarely if ever occur, and exist only in the imagination.

Capt. John William De Forest of the Twelfth Connecticut Regiment echoed this conclusion in his widely read description of the Battle of Labadieville, Louisiana. Still naïve to the true nature of combat, as his men advanced forward, the captain drew both his saber and his revolver, expecting "a severe hand-to-hand struggle; not having yet learned that bayonet fighting occurs mostly in newspapers and other works of fiction."

Unwilling to so easily give up their belief in bayonet fighting, records tell us, after hard-fought battles survivors would wander around the previously contested area examining the types of wounds inflicted on the lifeless bodies lying about. Once again we are indebted to Von Borcke for just such a description. After Gaines's Mills, many stories immediately began to circulate around the Confederate camp about a ferocious hand-to-hand bayonet struggle that had allegedly occurred between a Texan regiment and New York Zouaves. One apocryphal story even told of two antagonists who, even after repeatedly bayoneting each other, remained upright in death. Giving in to a mixture of skepticism and curiosity, Von Borcke the next day hurried to the spot to see for himself. He would later note his observations in his well-known memoirs:

> An obstinate struggle had indeed taken place there between the troops named, which had ended in utter annihilation of the much vaunted Zouaves, whose bodies, dressed in flashy red uniforms, were scattered about all over the ground like scarlet poppies in a corn-field; but the never-erring bullet of the Texan marksman had brought them down, not the bayonet. I carefully examined many of the corpses, and found only three or four with bayonet-wounds, and these had been received evidently after the bullets.

Von Borcke's observations are substantiated by another group that had a more professional interest in such issues: surgeons and medical directors. Surgeon Daniel G. Brinton, who was the medical director for the Army of the Cumberland, reported similar findings after an engagement in the Lookout Valley, near Chattanooga, on October 28–29, 1863. Noting that almost the entire action had occurred at extremely close range, what he characterized as "a hand-to-hand contest," he expected to find some bayonet wounds. Contrary to his expectations, none were found, nor any heard of, despite the effort to find this type of wound.

As the war dragged on, the administrative side of the operations gradually became more organized, and a more exacting recording system was introduced. Surgeon Thomas A. McParlin, Brinton's counterpart in the Army of the Potomac, for example, assembled a periodic report on the casualties suffered by each corps, the location of the wound, as well as the cause (shell versus small arms and so on). The chart that follows summarizes the five reports he submitted from the opening of the Overland Campaign to the end of July that year.

Casualties: Army of the Potomac May–July, 1864

Cause	Wilderness	Spotsylvania	North Anna	Petersburg	July
Shell	231	712	95	639	435
Cannon-shot	6	37	3	38	4
Bullet	7,046	8,218	959	6,693	2,538
Bayonet	4	14	1	3	14
Sword	2	1	-	1	1

These findings support the anecdotal evidence provided by Von Borcke and Brinton and are further corroborated by the subsequent monthly reports McParlin submitted until the end of the war.

As infantrymen began to observe the paucity of bayonet wounds, some speculated that the edged weapon, eclipsed by the new rifle musket, no longer possessed the tactical usefulness it had during the Napoleonic Wars. This view, however, was itself based on the misconception that in earlier times it had been more common for opposing groups of infantrymen to stand up to one another and fight with the dreaded weapon, just as one would do in the bayonet exercise.

However, those who study warfare during the eighteenth century and the Napoleonic Wars know that this type of personal combat, at least on open ground, was equally rare during the pre–Civil War era. Although during the Napoleonic Wars opposing infantry frequently advanced within close range of each other, after the wars

French veterans often said that the Battle of Amstetten was the only example in which both sides actually stood up and fought with the bayonet in open terrain. Similarly, military historians specializing in eighteenth-century warfare tell us that the Battle of Moys (Liegnitz, Silesia, September 5, 1757) was the only instance in which infantry on both sides engaged in wholesale bayonet fighting on open terrain. Hand-to-hand combat with the bayonet between opposing formations on open ground had been a very rare occurrence throughout the entire history of this weapon.

BAYONET FIGHTING VERSUS BAYONET CHARGES

The rarity with which the bayonet was used to inflict immediate casualties did not diminish the confidence of military tacticians in this weapon. They had long realized that its effectiveness was not to be measured by the casualties it inflicted. Writing before an era when late-nineteenth-century historians would create the myth that the long string of British successes against the French arose from the superiority of British firepower, Gen. John Mitchel of the British Army, a veteran of the Napoleonic Wars, declared that the single most important factor that accounted for these consistent victories was

> a charge of bayonets—a thing that hurt nobody, but was out of the conventional rules of European warfare—invariably put the whole to flight, though generally with what might be deemed a trifling loss. This was the constant tale from Vimiera to Waterloo, whenever the British were the attacking party.

Many modern military historians have failed to appreciate the psychological dimension of edged weapons and have confused the idea of bayonet charges with that of bayonet fighting—which nowadays, unfortunately, are often used interchangeably. Here a *bayonet fight* refers to one in which both sides have managed to advance to extremely close range and stare at one another face to face as the action devolves into a confused melee wherein an individual attempts to stab his opponent by lunging with bayonet or to crack his skull by clubbing the musket and hitting the opponent with its butt.

A *bayonet charge*, on the other hand, is a formal, predefined tactic whereby infantrymen "charge bayonets," that is, extend their muskets in front of them and rush in upon the enemy, threatening to "run in" whoever contemplates standing up to them.

The problem is that the bayonet did not live up to the soldiers' expectations. Inexperienced recruits arrived at training camps during the war's first year with the expectation that much of the upcoming combat would devolve into hand-to-hand fighting, resolved by cold steel, with drawn saber and revolver for the cavalry and by bayonet thrusts in the case of the infantry. These expectations were only heightened as they spent hours in bayonet drills learning how to block the opponent's thrust and execute their own lunge in turn. Unaware that the true power of the bayonet lay in its psychological impact on the opponent, most soldiers, recruits, and officers alike thought that a bayonet charge was only the prelude to bayonet fighting.

If the goal was to overpower the enemy *only after a ferocious and bloody bayonet fight,* then repeat the bayonet indeed proved to be a useless appendage during the Civil War. Of course, it should be obvious to anyone, especially those concerned with military science, that the purpose of any weapon system is to achieve the desired tactical objective, the discomfiture of the enemy, rather than simply to impose *how* the conflict will be resolved. In other words, if we measure the bayonet's role by what it *actually achieved during combat,* then we are forced to conclude that it indeed proved to be an invaluable tool during many Civil War engagements.

The fact is that the bayonet was not, nor ever was, an instrument of physical destruction. This is sure to surprise many readers, since we have just seen that bayonet fighting, if it did ever take place on any scale in open terrain, was extremely rare and that casualties inflicted by this weapon were very uncommon. However, when one combs through the vast material that has come down to us about the Civil War, one quickly finds seemingly innumerable cases of the bayonet *charge.*

How a Bayonet Charge Works

The effectiveness of the bayonet lay in the psychological realm rather than as a means of physical destruction. When properly executed, it buoyed the morale of those who were delivering the charge, while it so intimidated the enemies in front that they instantly turned and fled, usually without a single casualty on either side.

When properly orchestrated, all physical acts can have a momentary positive effect on troops' morale. Cavalry officers long knew, for example, that the simple act of pulling out one's saber and standing up in the stirrups with outstretched sword buoyed a cavalryman's spirits, if but for a moment or two. The act of rushing in with lowered bayonets was one of the most positively psychotropic motions available. In his memoirs a veteran of the Napoleonic wars described the effect of a charge on participants:

> No movement in the field is made with greater confidence of success than that of the charge; it affords little time for thinking, while it creates a fearless excitement, and tends to give a fresh impulse to the blood of the advancing soldier, rouses his courage, strengthens every nerve, and drowns every fear of danger or of death; thus emboldened amidst shouts that anticipate victory, he rushes on and mingles with the fleeing foe.

In later years Civil War veterans would recall experiencing similar feelings during bayonet charges. I. Hermann, a Confederate veteran, remembers that the excitement of the charge evoked a "careless, reckless indifference" despite running through sulphurous smoke and lurid flashes of bursting shells. Alonzo F. Hill, who had fought with the Union Army of the Potomac, recollected that the exultation experienced was so profound that it induced men to face death without a "thought of fear."

Of course, a bayonet charge had the opposite effect on the defenders. In the final moments those who stood awaiting the charge in most cases would literally panic when it became apparent that the onrushing opponents were determined to resolve the affair with cold steel. This panic set in at about the moment at which the defenders had just enough time to retire precipitously and save themselves. Of course, if the attackers became convinced that the defenders were completely determined to stand and fight, the bayonet charge generally stalled, and a lengthy firefight ensued.

On open ground bayonet charges were all-or-nothing affairs. At some point one side invariably would lose its resolve, and either the defenders fled, or the attackers stopped their charge. The reason for this binary nature of combat lay in how soldiers in formation collectively managed their morale. In clear terrain the individual soldier's resolve was inextricably linked to the status of the formation as a whole. As long as the adjoining line remained firm, most soldiers, although struggling with tremendous fear, suppressed their survival instinct and stayed and fought. However, regardless of individual bravery, the soldier's resolve immediately and irrevocably crumbled as soon the formation started to break. Individual soldiers on open ground could never stand up to an oncoming enemy formation that had remained intact. Once his comrades started to flee, inexorably an individual was swept along in the current toward the rear, regardless of his own inclinations.

Although all bayonet charges conformed to these general psychological dynamics, there were some variations in detail. Two styles of bayonet charges had quickly developed after the introduction of this weapon in the late 1600s. Each employed a different set of psychological dynamics. The first could be called the "all-out aggressive school," as used by many French regiments during the eighteenth century and the Napoleonic Wars. This tactic required the attacker to charge as quickly as possible, all the while doing everything to intimidate those receiving the charge. The men were encouraged to shout and yell; officers ran in front of their men, swords drawn, to serve as an example. All the focus was on the initial effort.

During the Peninsular War (1809–1814) the British employed a different type of bayonet charge. All initial effort was made to control the men's emotion. The officers would attempt to slow the advance, while cautioning their men to remain steady. They would advance to 40 to 80 paces and then deliver a crushing volley. Then, while the enemy was still recoiling from the shock, they would rush in with lowered bayonets. The enemy, staggering from casualties and totally overawed by the ferocious charge, delivered to him in a moment of vulnerability, in most cases turned and fled.

• • •

BAYONET FIGHTING IN BROKEN TERRAIN

A number of bayonet fights did occur during the Civil War, but invariably, just as in past wars, they took place on some sort of broken ground, such as in densely wooded terrain, around houses and outlying buildings, and around various types of field fortifications. Certainly, the most famous case occurred during Gettysburg on Little Round Top, when Col. Joshua Chamberlain's Twentieth Maine repulsed Col. William C. Oates's Fifteenth Alabama's intense effort to take the position and turn the extreme left of the Union line. The regiment, deployed along a ridge that ran through rocky and wooded land, had already repulsed two previous attacks and was almost completely out of ammunition. Thinking that Oates and his men would resume the attack and seeing the enemy fast coming up the slope, Chamberlain believed that he quickly had to order a bayonet charge. The effect was immediate. The order ran "like fire" along the regimental line. The men rose shouting and sprang upon the enemy, who at this point were about 30 yards away. Though many along the first line of the attackers surrendered, here and there men fought hand to hand. Some were bayoneted; others were clubbed. Chamberlain himself was almost fatally shot by a rebel officer who was in the process of surrendering his sword.

During the Civil War bayonet fighting most frequently occurred during the frenzied fighting that took place as the attackers attempted to storm an entrenchment, rush through an abatis, and so on. One of the most desperate cases occurred on May 12, 1864, when Gen. Winfield Hancock's II Corps of the Army of the Potomac stormed the salient at Spotsylvania in front of the Landrum House. In his report Brig. Gen. Lewis A. Grant of the Second Brigade, Second Division, VI Corps, observed:

> It was emphatically a hand-to-hand fight. Scores were shot down within a few feet of the death-dealing muskets. A breast-work of logs and earth separated the combatants. Our men would reach over the breast-works and discharge their muskets in the very face of the enemy. Some men clubbed their muskets and in some instances used clubs and rails.

Many other cases of hand-to-hand fighting around entrenchments can be found. Close-in fighting took place at Chancellorsville when the Twenty-seventh Indiana Infantry struggled to retake an abatis that had been temporarily lost to a massive Confederate assault. Similar dynamics occurred when a Union force attacked and captured enemy breastworks at Cloyd's Mountain, West Virginia, on May 9, 1864. This scenario was repeated frequently, and on an even larger scale, during the Atlanta Campaign.

The reason why hand-to-hand fighting could occur on broken ground once again is related to the psychodynamics of morale. As the infantrymen moved over rough ground, they tended to spread out to move around trees, bushes, and other obstacles, and the structure of the formation loosened. The sense of security normally arising from being part of an ordered, tight-knit formation was replaced by that which arose from being physically protected by an obstacle. A man standing behind a tree no longer drew his confidence solely from the proximity of his comrades immediately around him but rather from the fact that there was a physical object directly in front of him which could stop not only a bayonet but even a bullet or canister. To a large degree the sense of security supplied by an ordered formation on open ground was now replaced by the physical nature of the ground or obstacles around them.

The focus shifted from safety in numbers to safety as a result of one's own particular situation and actions. Men behind an abatis would sense the openness surrounding their small "island" of shelter. To retire was to move back into open ground. If, while in the forest or behind an entrenchment, the formation had been transformed into an amorphous mass, the only way to retire through the clear terrain behind them was by complete and uncontrolled flight. Thus, the group as a whole no longer dictated individual actions, and hand-to-hand fighting could occur.

There was another factor that could occur on the battlefield that could lead to hand-to-hand fighting. This was when two groups previously unaware of the other's presence "bumped into" one another. A classical example occurred during the Peninsular War (1809–1814) when men from a French regiment quickly jumped over a stone wall only to find themselves facing a group of British soldiers.

Given the variation of terrain found on the American continent, this kind of sudden up-close encounter was even more common during the Civil War. Advancing into the Cornfield at Antietam, the Fifth Ohio and the Twenty-eighth Pennsylvania (Second Division, XII Corps) pushed back a tenacious Sixth Georgia regiment out of the East Woods and into another cornfield. The fight was bloody and frequently at extremely close quarters. Many of the Ohioans had no bayonets and were forced to attack their foes by clubbing their muskets. In his report Maj. John Collins boasted that his regiment got the best in this affair and the enemy was "severely punished . . . and, being closely pursued, sustained great loss."

FREQUENCY OF BAYONET CHARGES

Unlike bayonet fighting, which almost never occurred between opposing formations on open ground during the Civil War, a great number of bayonet *charges* occurred. In many cases the writer consciously labeled these charges as such; in others he simply recounts how after the regiment fired, it quickly rushed toward the enemy, who, if events unfolded as planned, then turned around and quickly fled.

Of course, many bayonet charges failed. Some abortive attempts were doomed to failure from the onset. During the affair at Big Bethel, Virginia (June 10, 1861), the Third New York Infantry's charge stopped almost as soon as it began, as the men confusedly spread out and fired at long range instead of advancing. Other charges, though executed with alacrity and determination nevertheless ended in total failure, with the virtual destruction of the attacker. Pickett's Charge at Gettysburg and the desperate succession of aggressive but hopelessly futile Union attacks against Longstreet's position on Marye's Heights at Fredericksburg are among the most notable instances of failed bayonet charges.

However, when the full litany of battles and engagements are considered, many, many examples of successful charges can be identified. Probably the most famous bayonet charge during the first two campaigns occurred during the Battle of Mill Springs, Kentucky, on January 19, 1862. After the Confederate surprise attack failed to sweep up the Union forces, the action devolved into desultory long-range firefight. The Ninth Ohio was ordered to advance with the bayonet, which it did with "vociferous cheering." Advancing quickly, the regiment soon turned the Confederates' left flank, and the latter, though partially sheltered by several small buildings and fences, was completely routed. The success of the Ninth Ohio Infantry certainly impressed Union military authorities, and there was frequent mention of the regiment's performance in newspapers and specialty journals, such as the *Army and Navy Journal.*

The defender was also able to repel attacks with the judicious use of bayonet charges during First Bull Run. Harassed by an opposing force on the other side of Bull Run Creek at Blackburn's Ford, small groups of Confederate infantrymen crossed the creek and scattered the Union infantry with a series of bayonet charges. In his report after the battle, Stonewall Jackson attributed the Confederate victory to the adroit use of the weapon at the critical moment:

> At 3.30 A.M. the advance of the enemy having reached a position which called for the use of the bayonet, I gave the command for the charge of the more than brave Fourth and Twenty-seventh [Virginia Regiments], and, under commanders worthy of such regiments, they, in the order in which they were posted, rushed forward obliquely to the left of our batteries, and through the blessing of God, who gave us the victory, pierced the enemy's center, and by co-operating with the victorious Fifth and other forces soon placed the field essentially in our possession.

In these above cases the bayonet charge was used as a means of counterattack; it was employed by troops on the defensive, grand tactically.

Examples can also be found in which bayonet charges were successfully employed by infantry on the grand tactical offense. Though the Union army had been battered and pushed to the brink of destruction during the first day of fighting at Shiloh (April 6–7, 1962), it switched to the offensive the next day. Arriving on the field of battle, the Thirty-second Indiana Infantry originally was positioned 200 yards behind the second line of infantry in Gen. Alexander McCook's division. Seeing that this portion of the battle had temporarily devolved into a stalemate, the regiment's commander, Col. August Willich, requested permission to conduct a bayonet charge. The regiment "ployed" into a "double column on the center" and worked its way through the two lines of Union infantry. As soon as it had advanced to within 200 yards of the Confederates, the latter turned and retired, without awaiting the charge.

This example highlights one of the most noticeable features of this type of tactic, the achievement of its objective without the necessity of spilling any blood. However, it is this very bloodlessness that has so consistently led to a misunderstanding of the bayonet and its effectiveness. It is easy to read Colonel Willich's report without realizing that any tactic was used at all.

Another very notable case was the first instance of the rebel yell in the Shenandoah Valley, during the Battle of Winchester (May 25, 1862). After Gen. Richard Ewell's division managed to outflank Gen. George Gordon's regiment on the Union right, Stonewall Jackson's division sprang forward and overwhelmed the Union forces on the higher ground in front of them. James Wood, who served with Company D of the Thirty-seventh Virginia, recalled that moment:

> Our advance was begun in fine order, without rush or confusion—meanwhile shot and shell played upon us. The greater elevation of the Federals caused them to overshoot, hence we did not suffer greatly. At the order to charge our whole line leaped forward with a terrifying Confederate yell, rushed onto and over the stone wall. The loss of the fleeing enemy was heavy.

It is well known that Jackson was one of the staunchest advocates of the bayonet charge, as well as one of the most successful of its proponents. According to John Cooke, J. E. B. Stuart's chief of staff, the bayonet was Jackson's "favorite weapon, his chosen mode of fighting." So much so, that Jackson's nearly predictable reliance on the bayonet charge might be described as a "conspicuous weakness." With Jackson riding back and forth behind the line before an engagement, one would frequently hear the commander enjoining his troops to "Press him [the enemy] with the bayonet!" And the more determined the enemy, the more obstinate his stance, the more likely Jackson was to attempt to resolve the issue with cold steel. This was especially the case whenever Jackson found himself on the defensive and confronted by a numerically superior enemy that tried to punch its way through Jackson's position by sheer weight of numbers.

Cooke's seeming criticism of Jackson's use of the bayonet charge appears to be more of a fond poke at one of his leader's traits than a cold, analytical criticism of Jackson's chosen mode of fighting. Cooke concluded that unless the enemy was able to withstand the charge of the Old Stonewall Brigade, invariably a study in ferocity, all was soon over, and moments later the enemy line would be reduced to a disorganized band of fugitives.

THE BAYONET LATE IN THE WAR

The premeditated use of bayonet charges certainly was not limited to the earlier stages of the war, before the proliferation of field fortifications and a newfound willingness to seek protection behind any available cover. As late as the summer of 1864, one can still find determined assaults that clearly relied on the threat of shock and cold steel, rather than trying to overpower one's opponent with a withering fire. The most obvious of these are Hancock's multibattalion columns at Spotsylvania in May and the First Maine Heavy Artillery's doomed rush against Colquitt's Salient near Petersburg in late June. In both cases many of the men were ordered to advance against the rebels with unloaded (rifle) muskets. This is an unequivocal indication that the commanders intended to drive the enemy back by a show of unbreakable determination coupled with the threat of the bayonet.

This tactical philosophy was not limited to the Union side. In his memoirs Gen. Johnson Hagood, who commanded a South Carolinian brigade, provides an excellent example of how Confederate commanders would at least on occasion purposely eschew firepower in order to threaten the Union infantry with the *determined advance*. Ordered forward to take a fortified Union position on August 21, 1864, the last day of the Battle of the Weldon Railroad (south of Petersburg), Hagood's brigade found itself a few hundred yards in front of a series of Union rifle pits. Directing his brigade to form in order of battle, Hagood dismounted and positioned himself in front of the center of the Twenty-first South Carolina Infantry regiment. As soon as the line was formed, the brigade was ordered forward at the quick step, with instructions to withhold fire on any account. To help repress the men's excitement or any misplaced eagerness to come to grips with the enemy too quickly, Hagood turned his back to his opponents and, with carefully measured step, marched backward, sword drawn and upright, just as he would during drill or a review. As the brigade reached the crest of the hill in front of the enemy's position, Hagood sidestepped his front ranks, and then along with his staff followed the advancing brigade. The Union infantrymen began a rapid fire on the attackers. The discipline of Hagood's brigade remained unbroken, and they refrained from returning the fire.

Chapter 32

BREECHLOADERS AND REPEATERS: THE DEBATE CONTINUES

RIPLEY'S OPPOSITION TO BREECHLOADERS & REPEATERS

Realizing that Chief of Ordnance James W. Ripley would effectively stonewall all attempts to introduce rapid-fire small arms, early in the hostilities Oliver Winchester wrote directly to Simon Cameron, the secretary of war. Arguing that the Henry rifle was "free of most, if not all objections to the breech-loading arms now in use," Winchester requested that trials be conducted. Several tests were indeed performed, and by mid-November Winchester's weapon had received some encouraging praise. On November 16, 1861, Col. Charles P. Kingsbury, then chief of ordnance for the Army of the Potomac, wrote to Ripley and suggested that enough Henry rifles be purchased to arm a regiment. Kingsbury felt that it was a useful weapon for skirmishers, and the carbine version appeared to be as good as any other weapon currently in service. The fact that it could be fired fifteen times without reloading made it an attractive weapon for cavalry. Three days later Capt. G. D. DeRussy of the Fourth Artillery was ordered by Col. H. J. Hunt to test the Henry rifle. DeRussy concluded that the new repeater would be "a most useful addition to the weapons we now have in service."

General Ripley remained obdurate. In a reply to Winchester, he maintained that the repeater, with its many moving parts, was less sturdy than a muzzleloader. He cited the oft-repeated concern that troops equipped with breechloaders would succumb to temptation and fire too rapidly, quickly depleting all available ammunition. However, continued pressure was applied to the Ordnance Department, and by the year's end Ripley felt compelled to justify his views in a report to the secretary of war.

Though in his December 9, 1861, correspondence, Ripley had to acknowledge that the preliminary reports for both the Henry and the Spencer rifles had been quite favorable, he continued to advance new objections. The first was the matter of weight. A participant in the debate about the virtues of the original Minié rifle, Ripley was aware of the Hardinge Committee's criticism. The .69-caliber, cylindrical-conical ammunition weighed several times a same-caliber ball, so it would be difficult for men to carry forty to fifty rounds during active campaigning, thus resulting in the adoption of the .577 and .580 calibers of the British Enfield and American Springfield musket rifles.

The weight issue was never forgotten. Both the Henry and the Spencer rifles were "magazine guns." Ripley felt that these were too heavy for the soldier to carry easily and were thus impractical in the field. Here the weight of the small arm itself was not the concern but the combined weight of the weapon plus the rounds in the magazine. The seven to fifteen rounds in the rifle added between 1 and 2 extra pounds that had to be carried. This might seem a trivial increment, but anyone who has been forced to run around a field with a heavy Richmond rifle musket knows how difficult it becomes to deal with only a slight increase in weight.

The ammunition for the new small arms was even of greater concern. The repeating action meant that the detonating charge had to be housed within the cartridge, so the traditional ball-and-powder cartridge could not be used. The very sophistication of these new cartridges prompted Ripley to doubt their reliability. Wouldn't they be crushed when carried by horsemen? Would the fulminate inside the cartridge survive the rigors of active campaigning? These were by no means imaginary concerns, having arisen out of recent experiences. Several reports had come in from the field that decried the fragility of some of the new ammunition. Maj. John J. Mudd, Second Illinois Cavalry, recounted how during a recent expedition from Bolivar to Grand Junction and La Grange, Tennessee, the ammunition for the Sharps and Merrill rifles proved to be of very poor quality: "They shake to pieces in riding, and at the end of each day's march many of the men find instead of cartridges only a mixed mass of powder, ball, and paper."

This problem would continue to plague soldiers throughout the war. As late as July 1864, Brig. Gen. August V. Kautz complained that all paper cartridges were susceptible to such problems. Normally, only small amounts could be distributed among the troops, since the cartridges tended to deteriorate after a few days of hard marching. This was a real inconvenience for cavalry forced to move quickly through the enemy countryside, since the ammunition train that carried the reserve ammunition could not keep up with them.

Ripley also objected to the cost of breechloaders and repeaters. A December 31, 1862, report showed that it was possible to acquire old smoothbores and even many of the early European rifle muskets, such as the Austrian and Belgian rifles, for $10 to $12 apiece, while Springfield rifle muskets were available in quantities for $18.50. The Sharps, Merrill, and Colt rifles were considerably more expensive, ranging between $42.50 and $45. The newer carbines, though less expensive, were still more than 60% more costly than the rifle muskets. Given the relatively high price of such weapons, Ripley felt the money was much better spent on rifle muskets or single-shot breechloaders, all of which, he argued, were more reliable. Claiming that neither the Henry nor the Spencer possessed any important advantages over other breechloaders that were being examined, he reasoned that the adoption of any additional rifles or carbines would create a logistically impossible assortment of ammunition types. Though admitting that these questions could be resolved through extensive testing, Ripley protested that his department lacked both the time and personnel for such trials.

SMALL SUCCESSES FOR THE ADVOCATES OF BREECHLOADERS

Fortunately, General Ripley was unable to completely quash the breechloader issue. The various manufacturers encountered no such formidable roadblock when dealing with the Navy. J. A. Dahlgren, commander of ordnance at the Washington Navy Yard, was much more open-minded than his army counterpart and ordered trials for the new weapons to determine both reliability and effectiveness. Tests conducted by the navy in 1861 demonstrated both the Henry and Spencer rifles to be durable, reliable weapons. The amount of firepower that could be delivered in an extremely short time also was evident. A navy man armed with a Henry rifle could fire 125 rounds in 5 minutes 40 seconds, while the 7 rounds in a Spencer rifle could be unleashed in 10 seconds. The Spencer was also found to be extremely robust, only a single misfire occurring in 500 rounds. Impressed, the navy placed an order for 700 Spencer carbines in July of that year.

The navy was not the only entity with an open mind. Several Union regiments acting independently of the Ordnance Department had shown marked interest in the new weaponry. Reluctant to accept the standard Springfields and Enfields, they either lobbied for breechloaders or purchased these weapons at their own expense. As the war became more general and the number of volunteer regiments began to multiply, the War Department was less able to interfere with every aspect of operational minutia. As a result several infantry regiments temporarily escaped the fate of the Ellsworth's Zouaves and managed to outfit themselves partially with breechloaders.

The Twenty-first Indiana was one such regiment. Sufficiently intrigued with the possibilities afforded by the new breechloaders, the state government purchased enough Merrill rifles to arm Company K of the regiment. As soon as his men received the Merrill rifles in December 1861, Captain Hesse, who commanded this company, began the trials. Approval was immediate and complete. Writing to the manufacturer, Hesse would boast:

> Gentlemen: My Company having armed themselves with your 'Breech-Loading Infantry Rifle', I challenge the world to compete with them. A target placed at the distance of a thousand yards or under is riddled to atoms by a squad of six or eight men at every fire. I have tested the qualities of your Rifle until I am satisfied it merits all the praise bestowed upon it. The facility, the rapidity and ease with which it can be used has no equal. The ingenuity and simplicity which celebrated your Gun far supersedes any that has come under my observation. Let the noble men of the gallant Twenty-First sum up their interests as to what they need to sustain their honor in his deplorable war, and equip themselves with the 'Merrill Breech-Loading Rifle', and then they can laugh at opposition.

Also impressed with the Merrill rifle, Col. James W. McMillan, the commander of the regiment, wrote to his congressman, W. McKee Dun, and asked that the entire unit be equipped with the new breechloaders. The state did not volunteer the necessary funds, however. Undeterred, the regiment's men and officers seized the initiative and decided to purchase the weapons themselves. Each soldier had $15 deducted from three successive payrolls in order to pay for the Merrills.

This trend certainly did not reflect the official policy of either the War or the Ordnance Department. As the president of the New Haven Arms Company, Winchester was eager to equip Union troops with the Henry rifles. If the authorities in Washington were unwilling to officially approve the weapon, then the next option was to sell breechloaders to individual regiments or even companies. Arguing that this precluded standardization and further exacerbated an already difficult logistical situation, the War Department once again ordered regiments to return all unsanctioned small arms.

This latest round of official instructions does not appear to have completely stopped the practice, however. It will be recalled that in the summer of 1861, Gen. Winfield Scott had encouraged Major General Butler to arm some flank companies with breechloaders. Not only did Butler comply with this request, but there is evidence that the next summer a number of other Union regiments followed suit. At Shiloh (April 6–7, 1862), Company L of the 154th Tennessee fought with Maynard rifles and acted independently from the main body of the regiment to unmask the enemy's movement on its right. During the Seven Days' Battles, Company B of the Second New Hampshire Infantry, equipped with breech loaders, was often called on to serve as skirmishers in front of the regiment. At Corinth (October 3–4, 1862), for example, the Sharps Reserve Company of the Twenty-sixth Missouri unleashed such a rapid fire as to rout the enemy opposing the regiment.

There is evidence that the War Department did not necessarily disapprove of these practices. Inquiring whether companies so armed would be allowed to remain in the field, Winchester was informed by Assistant Secretary of War P. H. Watson in an August 19, 1862, letter that the official stance remained unchanged. Watson replied that regiments which chose to equip themselves entirely with the same type of repeater or breechloader could do so—provided, of course, that it was completely at their own expense. As the number of volunteer organizations continued to multiply, it proved impossible to maintain complete control over every unit, and a number of regiments continued to arm their elite companies with better-quality rifles. The flank companies of the Seventh Connecticut, which operated in South Carolina, were similarly armed.

The First United States Sharpshooters would become the first Union infantry regiment to be completely armed with breechloaders. Recruited from many of the best marksmen available, it was only natural that sharpshooter regiments sought the most effective weapons. Although the consensus among the men was that the Sharps rifle was the most desirable, General Ripley stymied the men's and officers' efforts to be equipped with that rifle. Instead, he ordered that the regiment be armed with the standard Springfield, a ridiculous choice for men whose very reason for being was their ability to deliver highly accurate fire even up to extreme ranges. A regimental howl immediately went up, and Ripley finally had to relent in March 1862, when he authorized the use of the Colt's Revolving Rifle. Although this certainly did not placate the men, their exploits around Yorktown in May of that year and throughout the remainder of the Peninsular Campaign provided much-needed positive advertising for what the new breechloaders and repeaters could do in the hands of an adept.

The Debate Becomes Public

Historians have always criticized General Ripley for his intransigence. Armed with hindsight, it is easy to see that a Union army equipped with sizable quantities of breechloaders and repeaters would have emerged victorious much earlier than it finally did that day at Appomattox after almost 4 years of bitter fighting. Ripley doggedly opposed the introduction of breechloaders ever since some of the problems arose with the Hall rifle years before. Ripley's stance was probably motivated by two factors: an underlying, unconscious set of emotions and conscious pragmatic considerations. The 67-year old Ripley had been one of the leading advocates of replacing the obsolescent percussion smoothbores with the Springfield rifle musket before the war and was hostile to the new types of shoulder arms.

Indeed, it is all too likely that James W. Ripley was one of those individuals who, once committed to a particular decision, takes a proprietary interest in this stance and treats any opposing view as a direct assault on his own being or ego. In fairness to Ripley, however, it must be pointed out that at the beginning of the war the production facilities needed to produce large numbers of repeaters and breechloaders had yet to be developed. Arming large numbers of Union infantry with these weapons was still not a viable option.

Regardless of Ripley's personal motives, a rather public debate soon showed that the chief of ordnance was not alone in his views and that as late as spring 1863 his views represented the majority opinion on both sides! On August 10, Col. J. R. Chambliss, Jr., commander of Lee's Cavalry Brigade, complained to Col. A. R. Boteler that Union cavalry enjoyed superiority in equipment, weapons, and occasionally even in tactical practices. He urged the adoption of a series of improvements; chief among these was that the Confederate cavalry adopt breechloaders. Boteler forwarded this letter to James A. Seddon, the Confederate secretary of war. Seddon and Col. Josiah Gorgas both enclosed "endorsements" to support Chambliss's recommendations. Gorgas, who incidentally was the chief of the Confederate Ordnance Bureau, did include one caveat: He was forced to point out that, Chambliss's enthusiasm notwithstanding, there was no consensus among the officers regarding the value of breechloaders and that, in fact, "officers of great experience pronounce in favor of the muzzle-loading carbine." This was a stance remarkably consonant with his Union counterpart, General Ripley! Of course, breechloading shoulder arms were not really an option for the rebels, since the South lacked the manufacturing facilities for these weapons.

The American scientific community appears to have supported Ripley's position as late as the spring of 1863. Frustrated with the seemingly insurmountable opposition of the Ordnance Department, Oliver Winchester had a letter published in the March 7, 1863, edition of *Scientific American.* Venting long pent-up frustration, Winchester opened with a strongly worded declaration that the day for reasonably questioning the utility and feasibility of breechloaders had passed. Knowing that Ripley's facetiousness, though effective in back room politics, wouldn't pass pubic scrutiny, the writer told readers how the chief of ordnance had scornfully speculated that nine out of ten officers would prefer their men to be armed with old-fashioned flintlock muskets rather than accept breechloaders or repeaters.

Acknowledging that in terms of accuracy, no military weapon could compare to specialty target rifles, which unfortunately were impractical because of their weight, the gun manufacturer insisted there was little difference between the traditional muzzleloaders and breechloaders or repeaters. According to Winchester, accuracy was a function of weight of barrel and the finish of the bore, and for all practical matters this was about the same for both types of small arms. The critical differentiator was the speed with which each could be loaded and fired. Winchester estimated that a muzzleloader on average required about 60 seconds to load, compared to 4 seconds for the Burnside rifle and 2 seconds for the Henry. The time needed to aim and fire was the same in all cases, about 4 seconds.

The objection most consistently encountered was the concern about wastage of ammunition. Countering that it was an incontrovertible fact that at least 95% of all shots fired with muzzleloaders missed their mark, Winchester then asked rhetorically whether it was reasonable to expect any other type of small arm to be less accurate. The crux of Winchester's argument was that the extreme rapidity of fire allowed by breechloaders and repeaters, rather than increasing the wastage of ammunition, instead promoted more accurate fire and therefore *saved* ammunition. The reason cited was how the infantrymen tended to react under fire:

> If, as we think, it is a consciousness of power that makes men brave, and a sense of imminent peril that makes "cowards of us all," and often times strikes with panic the best armies, it is not unreasonable to suppose that such a weapon would give a soldier the courage and coolness needed to send each of his fifteen shots with more unerring certainty than his trembling opponent could send with his single shot? If *to save ammunition,* it is essential that every soldier should remain for sixty seconds while reloading, a helpless target, to receive his opponent's fire from one to fifteen shots, why not reverse the order of progress

and turn the ingenuity of inventors to the production of a gun that will require twice the length of time or more to reload, and thus *double the saving of ammunition?* Saving of life does not appear an element worthy of consideration in this connection. Yet this is West Point opinion—the deductions of West Point science! Are these results worth their cost to the country?

Even as late as early 1863, Winchester's views were still considered sufficiently radical that the editors of the *Scientific American* were anxious that his opinions were not interpreted as those of the magazine, running a house article entitled "Breech-loading versus Muzzle-loading Guns" several pages later in the same issue. The tone of this article showed that the views of military editors had nevertheless shifted slightly from 2 years before, when the magazine had argued mildly for the retention of traditional smoothbores and rifled muzzleloaders that fired "tight fitting conical bullets." Though in 1863 it still believed that at short ranges the older smoothbores firing "one ball and two buckshot" were more effective than rifle muskets, it finally conceded that for military service the latter were more effective overall since they were much more effective at long ranges. *Scientific American* stopped short of endorsing the adoption of breechloaders, however, and disagreed with Winchester's claim that they were as accurate as muzzle-loading rifle muskets.

Citing recent trials with the new weapons, the editors argued that breechloaders as they then existed were intrinsically less accurate than Enfield or Springfield rifle muskets. They felt that muzzleloaders were easier to keep clean and that the very act of ramming the ball projectile down the barrel removed much of the fouling. It was thought that the projectiles fired by breechloaders had to push the grime up and out the barrel and were thus given an irregular and unpredictable trajectory. The editors also argued that this same act of ramming allowed the musket's projectile to be more evenly centered than when inserted at the breech. Finally, they resurrected the often-cited issue of reliability.

ROSECRANS'S EFFORTS TO INTRODUCE THE BREECHLOADER

As this debate unfolded in back room offices in Washington City and on the pages of Eastern-based magazines, another development occurred which, though it appeared trivial at the time, would eventually have far-reaching consequences. There was one Union general, more than all others, who was absolutely convinced that that the breechloader was the shoulder arm of choice and it was absolutely imperative that he make every effort to equip as much of his command with this weapon as possible. This was William S. Rosecrans. In an effort to obtain breechloaders, at first for his cavalry and then later for part of his infantry, during a 9-month span Rosecrans directed no fewer than 19 missives to the secretary of war, his assistant, the commander-in-chief, and the chief of staff. Ranging from rational arguments on why the weapons were necessary to purely emotional appeals, these letters covered the full gamut of possible arguments.

By mid-1862 Rosecrans claimed that his cavalry had dwindled in strength and was now forced to confront superior rebel numbers on a front 60 miles in extent. Reasoning that the solution was to improve their combat effectiveness by giving them "superior weapons," on July 19 he wrote to Col. F. D. Callender at the St. Louis arsenal and asked for 1250 revolvers and 1100 carbines or "repeating rifles." To justify his request, Rosecrans carefully avoided the pros and cons of the weapon itself and argued instead what has become a thoroughly modern consideration: the overall cost-effectiveness of the troops to be armed. Opponents to breechloaders frequently had cited the relatively high cost of these arms, usually between three and four times as much as for a conventional small arm. Rosecrans expanded the equation also to include the cost of maintaining a force equipped with less effective weaponry. Rosecrans pleaded that his demands be met and, abandoning any attempt at tact, forcefully concluded that "impossibility or imbecility alone could refuse or delay the supply."

Apparently subscribing to the theory that out of sight is out of mind, Rosecrans bombarded authorities with a series of urgent requests. Without waiting for a reply from Callender, the very next day Rosecrans appealed to General Halleck, general-in-chief of the Union Army. Expanding upon his argument, Rosecrans claimed that the cost of maintaining a regiment without arms of for 1 month was approximately the same as that needed to purchase repeating or breech-loading rifles. As the months passed and letters, orders, and reports were repeatedly exchanged, Rosecrans would frequently resort to this cost argument. On August 6, for example, he again wrote to Halleck and claimed that the total cost of the government for not equipping its troops with the best possible weaponry amounted to about $500,000 per day, and on November 9 he would tell the secretary of war that the wastage for his command alone was $10,000 a day. This analysis was predicated on the belief that troops armed with breechloaders were two to three times as effective as those with muzzle-loading weapons. Thus, Rosecrans reasoned, for every 1,000 men armed with breechloaders that the government paid to maintain, it saved on the cost of maintaining the twice or even three times as many rifle muskets needed to achieve the same result. The total maintenance costs thereby would be cut at least in half.

Rosecrans's campaign of incessant badgering eventually did produce results. In October 1500 revolvers were forwarded to his command, along with about two thousand breech-loading carbines and rifles. It is difficult to identify the types of small arms that were shipped to the West at this point, but in a November 17 correspondence, Halleck does mention that all "all revolving rifles that can be spared will also be sent." Pestered by Rosecrans's continuous pleas and demands, Halleck attempted to explain the reasons for the government's seeming unresponsiveness: "Each army receives its proportion of each kind of arms as fast as they can be procured. This rule must be followed, for we cannot 'rob Peter to pay Paul.' "

The next day Edward M. Stanton, secretary of war, sent even more promising news. The entire inventory of revolving rifles, literally all that had been recently manufactured in the United States, was on a train traveling to Louisville. Rosecrans's army was to receive another 4000 as soon as they were manufactured! One detects the first note of admonition in this communiqué, however. Stanton closed the short letter with a promise and a caution: "No effort shall be spared to supply what you ask for, but something is expected from you." P. H. Watson, assistant secretary of war, echoed similar sentiments several weeks later (December 8) when explaining to Rosecrans that receiving 3600 carbines and revolving rifles meant he had been allocated "a far larger proportion of cavalry arms [repeaters and breechloaders] than any other commander."

Initially, the general limited his effort to arm his cavalry with the new small arms. Gradually, however, references to infantry armed with breechloaders or "revolving rifles" also begin to appear in his correspondence. At first he mentioned them only to substantiate his central argument about increased effectiveness and lower costs and to support his plea to rearm his cavalry. In a November 16 letter to the secretary of war, he first mentions equipping some of his infantry with the same weapon to create a more effective body of skirmishers. His plan was to put saddles on packhorses so that they could be used for a "double purpose." When required by circumstances, a portion of his infantry would be employed as a "very swift-moving body of light artillery." Their primary goal would be find large enemy columns, then "surprise and cut them to pieces." To implement this plan, he informed Stanton that he required 4000 revolving rifles, that is, Colt's Revolving Rifles. The same day he sent Major General Halleck another telegram to inform the "general-in-chief" of his plans.

A February 1, 1863, communiqué to Halleck elaborated upon this proposal. Each brigade was to supply an "elite" battalion formed from select men taken from each company and one officer and five NCOs from each regiment. Rosecrans likened these corps to "flying artillery," and they were to have the most effective shoulder arms available.

On February 14 Rosecrans followed through with his plans: General Orders No. 19 called for the formation of "light battalions." Each was to be formed by extracting one officer, two sergeants, and three corporals from each regiment in his army, along with a field officer from each brigade. Its men were to be armed with the best arms, Colt's Revolving Rifles whenever possible. Although the men were to be taken from the infantry, they were to serve as mounted infantry as soon as the horses could be provided. They were to be considered "the élite of the army" and "from them will be expected such deeds of daring and enterprise as will prove them worthy of the distinction conferred upon them, and justify the choice of their companions." As such they were exempted from routine chores, such as picket duty, and when not on detached service, they were to camp at brigade headquarters.

There was at least one subordinate officer who enthusiastically threw himself behind Rosecrans's efforts to create a mobile infantry force armed with repeating breechloaders. Col. John T. Wilder approached Rosecrans with the request to raid the countryside for mounts, and this permission was given eagerly. The problem of mounting his brigade solved, Wilder next turned his attention to its armament. Like Rosecrans, Wilder had a healthy respect for the new repeating breechloaders. After meeting Christopher Spencer in March 1863, Wilder became convinced that the Spencer was the best weapon for his mounted infantry. Realizing that they would never get the Spencers through official channels, Wilder and his men decided to pay for the new weapons themselves. Each trooper signed a promissory note for $35.

OPINION STARTS TO TURN

Rosecrans's efforts to arm his forces with as many breechloaders as he could beg, cajole, and coerce out of authorities would eventually have an effect beyond simply what his men would accomplish in the field. Hundreds of infantrymen and cavalry troopers armed with these weapons went on picket duty, fought the endless variety of small actions that made up the daily routine of an active campaign, and occasionally participated in large, hotly contested battles. Gradually, this provided regimental and brigade commanders, then, more slowly, higher-level commanders, with a body of firsthand, practical experience with which to judge the capabilities of these weapons more realistically. The result was that after a few months the whole tenor of the debate had been transformed. From a theoretical discussion that had focused exclusively on issues in the domain of gunsmiths, military engineers, and expert target shooters, the argumentation shifted to a practical discussion of how these weapons had performed under battlefield conditions.

One of the first examples of this change was provided on the pages of *Scientific American*. A Union officer known only as "the Rifleman" took umbrage at the editors' unwillingness to endorse the general idea of the introduction of breechloaders and repeaters. His opening arguments in a May 9, 1863, article were a technical discussion which, in terms of the issues and approach, were in much the same character as other letters and articles that had appeared during the previous several years in magazines such as *Harper's, Scientific American,* and the *Military Gazette.* Supporters of muzzle-loading weapons had long argued that the process of ramming the ball home also helped clean the weapons, so they were less prone to become fouled. The Rifleman thought this was pure nonsense and asked why, if this were indeed so, did the barrel of a muzzleloader after a few rounds become "so foul that the ball cannot be forced down without difficulty—often bruising and jamming it out of shape," an occurrence that certainly did not lend accuracy to the weapon. He thought that the editors' claim that the marksman could more easily center the traditional ball or Minié bullet in the barrel even more absurd. Mass-produced cartridges had a uniform shape, so the shooter was guaranteed that the bullet was placed in the proper position with every shot. In contrast, the soldier ramming home a minié ball could inadvertently push the ball off center by unconsciously angling the ramrod.

However, a more compelling portion of his argument was based on his own personal experiences and those of men he had interviewed in the field. Detractors had long claimed that the sophisticated new small arms had an odious reputation in the field. The Rifleman assured readers that nothing he had encountered during actual campaigning substantiated this accusation. As to the charge that the latest Sharps rifles still leaked at the breech, he wrote that though he had repeatedly fired repeaters and breechloaders since the start of the war, not only had he never encountered the problem, but he never heard this complaint from anyone else.

Ripley had superciliously declared that 90% of officers would rather arm their men with old smoothbores than either breechloaders or repeaters. The Rifleman's experiences suggested quite the opposite. Visiting a number of field hospitals, he was able to interview many of the wounded, some of whom, as either skirmishers or mounted soldiers, had been armed with Sharps, Henry, Spencer, and other rifles. He was struck by their enthusiastic support for these weapons. Many of the less seriously wounded hung onto and jealously guarded their breechloaders even while they recuperated in the hospital. Often he heard how the soldier intended to purchase the weapon and bring his "pet" home after being discharged, if the government allowed.

His experiences had shown that the claim that breechloaders fouled more easily and were impractical during the rigors of combat was equally groundless and he observed:

> It is usually the first dozen or so of shots that decide a battle—rendering the attack or defense successful or unsuccessful, according as the one or the other side pours in the most rapid and effective fire; and as there is no pretense that the breech-loader will not remain sufficiently clean for up to several dozen rounds at least, its decided superiority over the muzzle-loader, in such a case, is beyond the possibility of dispute.

Unlike earlier advocates this anonymous writer was now able to cite instances in which the new weaponry had been very effectively employed during actual combat. At Fredericksburg a single company armed with Sharps rifles was able to suppress a rebel battery for several hours, while at Springfield the Frémont Body Guard, each of whom was armed with two Colt revolvers and a Colt's revolving rifle, conducted a successful charge, firing all the way without having to stop and reload. The anonymous Rifleman was particularly impressed with the Sharps rifle and claimed that if there had been "anywhere in this war, better shooting or more effective service than has been furnished by Sharpe's rifle" he hadn't heard of it. Ripley's claim to the opposite notwithstanding, the Rifleman was convinced that if the Union soldiers actually doing the fighting were polled, 80% would vote to immediately adopt breechloaders.

Almost 6 months would go by before the breechloading controversy would reappear in a professional publication. Then it would briefly resurface in a periodical published by the Union armed services. Finally forced to acknowledge that the war would be a long, drawn-out affair and that there was a need for a permanent, regularly issued publication to communicate with all Union officers and to provide a forum for informed military debate, in August 1863 Federal authorities set up the *Army and Navy Journal*, a weekly periodical for Union army and naval officers. Announcing promotions and various official orders and regulations, the journal was vaguely similar to New York state's prewar *Military Gazette*. However, given the seriousness of the existing military situation, there was much less attention to purely theoretical matters, and the articles and letters to the editors had a practical focus. It is also probable that the wartime need for a united front and doctrinal consistency led the magazine's editors to avoid, even suppress, any public debate about tactics, since this inevitably could undermine the officers' authority in the field.

Nevertheless, in the October 17 edition, a correspondent wrote decrying the practice of arming cavalry with sabers. He argued that the cause was much better served if 80% of a cavalry force were armed with "repeating or breech-loading rifles" and only one-fifth with the traditional weapon, sabers. This was especially important for mounted infantry during raids, who were always to fight dismounted.

THE TURNING POINT IN THE DEBATE

Though by late 1863 the breechloader debate had slackened off in the press, the matter was anything but dormant. For the most part the arena of debate had shifted onto the field itself, where soldiers lucky enough to carry the new weapons were eager to show their value. The true power of the breechloader would only be first truly revealed on a large scale during the Battle of Gettysburg and then again at Chickamauga (September 19–20, 1863). At Gettysburg, Col. William Gamble's brigade, armed with an assortment of breechloaders, stopped the advancing Confederates long enough for the Union I Army Corps to come up. At Chickamauga, John T. Wilder's brigade of five regiments encountered a much larger rebel force that had already pushed through the entire XX Army Corps. Alone and unsupported, Wilder's small force managed to hold the up-to-then victorious attackers at bay for 4 hours.

Wilder's success was obvious, indisputable, and much commented upon, and it further marks the symbolic turning point of the struggle to introduce breechloaders and repeaters among the infantry. During the next several months, a number of supporters would come out publicly and declare themselves in favor of breechloaders. The first of these, not surprisingly, was Wilder himself. In a January 7, 1864, letter, he urged that all infantry in the Army of the Cumberland be armed with the Spencer rifle, which he argued was

> a most perfect weapon, when used by cool men, and I have no hesitancy in saying (after commanding a brigade armed with them . . . for nearly a year) that men so armed can always defeat at least double their number, and my command have repeatedly driven three times their number of rebels.

He cited his own voluminous experience, pointing out that his command, once armed with the Spencer, had never been repulsed but had been victorious in over thirty fights, most of these against larger odds. During the affair at Framlington, for example, four of his regiments broke through Gen. Joseph Wheeler's forces and, fighting dismounted, captured a battery and scattered two rebel divisions of mounted skirmishers. He believed that a 10,000 man strong Union force armed with Spencers would be able to completely disrupt the enemy's railroad operations and do more damage than 100,000 soldiers carrying conventional weapons. The only change he recommended was to add a ring on the side of the breech-piece so it could be carried by mounted troops like a cavalry carbine.

The next call in favor of the breechloaders came from a somewhat unexpected quarter. As acting examiner of the U.S. Patent Office, a certain W. C. Dodge, Esq., had become fascinated with the weapon and the possibilities it afforded, probably because of the number of submissions for patents that he received. Convinced that as a class these rapid-fire weapons were immeasurably superior to any of the Minié-style rifle muskets, he published a pamphlet advocating the adoption of the new weapons. In addition to providing J. T. Wilder's January 7 letter in its entirety, Dodge cited more than forty Union officers who approved the wide-scale introduction of the breechloaders, including such prominent officers as McClellan, Hooker, Frémont, Rosecrans, Burnside, and Franz Sigel.

The performance of Wilder's Lightning Brigade at Chickamauga and the growing support among seasoned army officers was finally enough, at least to convince the editorial staff at *Scientific American.* In its March 12, 1864 issue, the magazine announced that in its opinion a single infantry regiment armed with breechloaders could outfight at least three, and possibly ten, times as many opponents. Ironically, to support its sudden change of stance, it advanced arguments that had been made by Winchester and the Rifleman on its pages, which up to then it had rejected:

> With a breech-loader the soldier consumes but one or two seconds of time in the labor of loading, and he can pour an almost constant stream of balls into the ranks of the enemy. It has been objected that when a soldier could load with so much facility, he would throw away his ammunition in careless firing; but we never doubted that this difficulty might be overcome by a proper drill. In the case where the soldier can load so quickly, he may be taught to make all his movements slowly and to take a much cooler and better aim than he will when he hurries through the operation of loading.

The tide of public opinion had turned; clearly, most people now wanted the adoption of breechloaders as quickly as possible. Still, there were signs of procrastination at the War Department. A few infantry regiments, such as the 102nd Illinois, were armed with breechloaders, but this was still very much the exception. In September 1864 tidings came in regarding the power of the Prussian needle gun during the Schleswig-Holstein War, then underway. And closer to home the effectiveness of the more efficiently armed units during Sherman's advance on Atlanta could be neither denied nor overlooked. The War Department now finally took its first steps to ensure that all Union forces were apportioned breechloaders for a portion of their infantry. Henceforth, one regiment within each division was to be equipped with these fast-firing weapons. General Hancock chose, based on its meritorious conduct, the 148th Pennsylvania Regiment.

At this point the Ordnance Department appears to have endorsed the more general use of breechloaders by the infantry, but there was still some equivocation at the top levels of the War Department.

Although admitting to E. M. Stanton, the secretary of war, that experience with breechloaders, even by this late date (October 22, 1864), had largely been limited to cavalry, Officer A. B. Dyer, who had replaced Ripley as chief of ordnance, thought it advisable to further expand the experiment to the infantry, especially in light of similar efforts among European powers. Dyer explained that a series of trials and tests had to be conducted to determine the most efficient breechloader. Then the manufacturer would have to modify the machinery to mass-produce this weapon. Factoring in cost and logistical issues, Dyer opined that conversion of the current model of the Springfield to a breechloader was a "very desirable measure."

It was probably no coincidence that the first letter calling for the adoption of breechloaders appeared in the *Army and Navy Journal* 2 days later. The writer challenged anyone who still supported the use of the rifle musket to

> come to the front armed with a Springfield musket, and oppose themselves to an equal number of Rebs. armed with repeaters or breech-loaders. If they can stand that, let them go to the picket line, and while fumbling for a cap and trying to get it on the cone on one these cold days offer themselves as a target to some fellow on the other side who has nothing to do but cock his piece and blaze away.

In another letter to Stanton 2 weeks later (December 5), Dyer was more emphatic. As far as he was concerned, experience had unequivocally demonstrated that breech-loading arms were "greatly superior" to muzzleloaders for both infantry and cavalry and the time had come to immediately start mass-producing breechloaders at the National Armory in Springfield, Massachusetts. To this end he had already requested the convening of a board of cavalry, infantry, and artillery officers to select the new weapon.

One of those chosen to test candidates for the new weapon was Maj. Gen. J. L. Wilson, whom Dyer instructed to evaluate the Gallager carbine. Suspecting that the selection of a successor to the Springfield rifle musket was imminent, Wilson immediately sent a preemptive reply that "all carbines are bad by comparison with the

Spencer, and that the troops of this army will receive no other without protest." Not only arguing that this weapon was the most economical with ammunition, producing the greatest physical and moral effect, he claimed his officers considered it the equivalent of any three other shoulder arms. Wilson cited recent experiences during the Nashville Campaign in which it had a profound effect on his men's confidence:

> A common belief amongst them is if their flanks are covered they can go anywhere. I have seen a large number of dismounted charges made with them against cavalry, infantry, and breast-works, and never knew one to fail. . . . The confidence in the arm is so widely spread that I have now applications from every regiment in the corps, not already supplied with them.

For whatever reasons, the selection of the new weapon did not occur as quickly as Dyer had originally hoped. On March 1, 1865, five weeks before the conclusion of the war, Stanton finally issued a formal recommendation that breechloaders be universally introduced. However, many months would go by before this was acted upon. In a report released on October 20 of that year, the chief of ordnance explained that extensive testing had indeed been performed, but as of yet no weapon had been selected as the definite successor to the rifle musket. He did admit that he found a plan submitted by the master armorer at the Springfield National Armory to convert the existing rifle muskets into breechloaders to be the most promising.

A new executive order (January 3, 1866) called for the establishment of a second review board to evaluate the various breechloaders and also consider the feasibility of converting rifle muskets. The board convened on March 10 and finally submitted its recommendations on June 4. In light of the existing weapons, its recommendation was to convert the Springfield rifle muskets into breechloaders.

Chapter 33

TACTICAL DEVELOPMENTS IN EUROPEAN
WARFARE, 1859–71

T hose who have studied the Civil War have generally been per-
plexed by the European military's lack of interest in this conflict during the years immediately following Appomattox. Taught to
view this conflict as a watershed of innovation, a trove of technological and tactical firsts, Civil War students cannot understand why
European military thinkers so adamantly turned their backs on the
American experience and made little effort to uncover any lessons it
could yield. This unwillingness has often been attributed to a type of
cultural arrogance, an unstated conviction that those who regarded
themselves as denizens of the "civilized world" could learn little from
what they considered to be little more than colonial bushwhacking.

This perception of the intransigent reluctance of Europeans to
explore valuable military lessons, however, in large part has arisen
from an unawareness of how military technology evolved during the
1850s. Many historians have mistakenly attributed to the Civil War a
number of "first in kind" developments that already had been introduced in earlier European conflicts. Progressive European military
thinkers did not have to look beyond their own continent for most of the
emerging military technology, examples of their use in battle, or how
they were likely to transform warfare. Even a well-informed civilian in
a European metropolis in 1860 would read all the hoopla about the new
French or British ironclads, the successful use of French rifled artillery
against the Austrians the year before, as well as the seemingly promising introduction of breechloading artillery by the British during its
war against China. Someone with access to the leading European military scientific journals would read about the host of other recent innovations, such as the mine, mortar boats, the use of trains to transport

troops, the mechanical grenade, and submarines, all of which had been either used in anger or at least experimented with by European armies before Confederate artillery attacked Fort Sumter.

Certainly, the face-off of the *Monitor* against the *Virginia* (formerly the *Merrimac*) attracted notable attention in the European press. However, its significance to European military authorities was not that it afforded much that was truly new, but rather that it convincingly vindicated those who had for years argued for the adoption of ironclads, as well the British and French governments' decision to build this new type of vessel. A British naval architect designing a large ironclad man-of-war in 1862, for example, would have been inspired by existing European examples of this genre rather than those proffered by his American cousins. The same was true about reports coming in on American rifled artillery. European artillery officers naturally would have been more excited by its use at Solferino and the latest trials at Royal Arsenal at Woolwich than they would have been by comparable developments on the other side of the Atlantic.

The same may be said of the fighting methods employed during the Civil War. If one temporarily sets aside the use of hasty entrenchments and Grant's strategy of attrition, a great majority of the tactics and grand tactics employed during the Civil War fell squarely within existing military scientific practice. When rebel and Federal forces faced off in opposing lines, as they often did, they employed techniques utilized not only in the Crimea but also during the numerous wars of the eighteenth century. Columns of companies and divisions, of course, had been used frequently during the Napoleonic Wars and consequently were well studied. Frequently, when a Union army was preparing for a set-piece action, instructions prescribed the employment of a multitiered grand tactical formation, with a standard line in front, followed by one or two tiers of battalions in columns. Though probably one of the most progressive grand tactical systems found during the Civil War, it was nevertheless structurally similar to French grand tactical practices of the time—hardly surprising, since both systems were inspired by Jomini's writings.

Unlike the Union tacticians the French seem to have favored a simpler form of Jomini's grand tactical system, in which the battalions were positioned along two lines of division or company columns. However, variants actually used during the Franco-Prussian War (1870–1871) suggest that the French gave more thought to minimizing the destructiveness of enemy small arms fire. During an engagement at Ladonchamps, during the seige of Metz, General Deligny threw out a skirmish line across the entire 600 meters in front of a line of companies, each at a full interval from its neighbor. The remainder of the force was positioned in line of columns 600 meters still farther to the rear.

Elsewhere the Army of the Loire took even greater precautions. The main body was screened by two lines of skirmishers, separated by 600 meters from one another. Another 600 meters to the rear were two lines of columns, again separated by 600 meters. Except for the volume of skirmishers and, in Deligny's case, the line of companies at open interval, this was the same grand tactical system expostulated by Jomini during the 1830s and '40s. However, now faced with opponents armed with Prussian breechloading needle guns, it became imperative to screen the main body with at least two tiers of troops that operated in much looser order.

The American version of these formations, at least those described in the orders of Generals Buell, French, and Rosecrans, did not offer the same protective cover, suggesting that the officers issuing these orders either did not take into account, or did not attach the same importance to, the heightened range and precision of the new small arms. It is not unnatural, therefore, that a French tactician familiar with these Union grand tactical systems might conclude that they were but minor variations of the same grand tactical system. Offering less protection from the new small arms fire by the post-1865 period, they were now outmoded.

Although French tacticians attempted to modify their existing grand tactical system by increasing the numbers of skirmishers that preceded the main force and/or masking the entire front with a very thin linear force (companies deployed at full interval), during the next war (1870–71) these tactical countermeasures proved inadequate. Despite these iterations to Jomini's grand tactical system, ultimately, the French grand tactical system remained based on dense columnar formations that had originated in an era in which combatants had been armed with muzzle-loading flintlocks. Once an attack began, the battalion-size columns in the rear were to advance quickly and attack, generally without firing.

Ironically, the basis of this conservatism lay in the relatively easy French victory over the Austrians in the short but much publicized war in 1859. Here French columns, marching quickly, were able to overwhelm the Austrians with their élan and grim determination, even though the defenders were armed with the new rifle muskets. Unfortunately, that success engendered a false sense of confidence, a belief that the new weaponry was less effective under battlefield conditions than originally supposed, and the notion that the traditional formations and grand tactics remained viable. It is equally unfortunate that the Austrians, the vanquished, naturally impressed with the French who beat them, unquestioningly adopted their adversary's methods and attitudes.

Given the advantage of 130 years of hindsight, one can conclude that a study of the American Civil War might have been useful to French authorities during the period leading up to the Franco-Prussian War, not for the formations and tactics that the Americans employed, but the difficulties posed by the new weaponry and the frequent failure of traditional methods. In the months that followed the Civil War, there were some indications that the great American struggle would indeed capture the imagination of some of the more open-minded of Europe's military thinkers. Now free from his duties with the Second California Volunteer Infantry, Colonel Lippett attempted to synthesize the lessons just learned with the established body of military science. The resulting *Treatise on the Tactical Use of the Three Arms* was well received, earning laudatory mention not only in a number of American journals but the *Edinburgh Review*, as well.

Events, however, soon conspired to redirect the attention of the European military much closer to home. Though not rocked by the scale of conflict that had shaken Europe at the turn of the century, the 1850s had seen a number of minor military conflagrations in Europe. Prior to the eruption of the Civil War, western European armies had fought in the Crimean War (1853–56), the Indian Mutiny (1857–58), the Second Opium War (1856–1860), and the Italian War of 1859. However, it was two wars that soon followed the Civil War that would absorb military scientists until the twentieth century. This was, of course, the Austro-Prussian War, which broke out less than 14 months after the cessation of hostilities at Appomattox, followed by the bloodier and by far more influential Franco-Prussian War of 1870–71.

This latter war captured everyone's attention, not simply because the Prussians managed to trounce the French, a nation that dominated all things military for more than 80 years, but much more importantly, because this war had seen the introduction of entirely new tactical and grand tactical systems which completely superceded the traditional methods that the great Napoleon had used to gain hegemony over much of western Europe.

The traditional system, employed to such disastrous effect by the French, had its roots in (1) the system of maneuvers devised by Frederick the Great and his generals during the short respite between the War of the Austrian Succession and the Seven Years' War and (2) the very sophisticated lexicon of grand tactical methods introduced by Napoleon and his marshallate during the Wars of the Empire. In recognition of these origins, people more versed in military history sometimes referred to this combined system as the Prussian school of tactics and the French school of grand tactics.

Although throughout the period the battalion remained the tactical quantum, its commander was rarely free to act independently, having to ensure that his command conformed to the movements and overall formation of the brigade or division. During the Seven Years' War, although a battalion advancing in the front line might maneuver individually to avoid obstructing terrain, it otherwise had to strictly conform to the movements of the overall grand tactical formation (the line), such as advancing when the line did and halting when it halted. During the Napoleonic era, a tactical unit occasionally might be ordered to operate semi-independently of its brigade organization for short periods, such as when the brigade or divisional commander ordered a battalion to attack a suddenly appearing enemy flank. Nevertheless, in the great majority of cases, it still had to operate within a brigade-level formation, such as a mixed-order or two-tiered line of columns.

The new Prussian system broke precedent on both accounts. The battalion ceased to be the basic tactical unit, while the new tactical quantum, the company, was no longer strictly required to conform to the structure and motions of its parent brigade or division. Prussian authorities proved to be truly prescient, and as far back as 1843, the Prussian infantry regulations called for the establishment of the company column. The decision to adopt this formation demonstrates a remarkable farsightedness, since with the exception of Swedish experimentation with the Norwegian breechloaders and a few regiments of chasseurs in Algeria, at this point there was no significant threat posed by potential enemy forces armed with the modern small arms.

Probably the most informative description of the Prussian company column and how it was used appeared in an 1875 article in Frederick Engle's *International Review*. It was penned by Emory Upton, who was preeminently qualified to discuss the nuances of tactical issues. The Prussians utilized a large, 900-man battalion, which was organized into four companies, each of which consisted of two "subdivisions." When column was to be formed from line, the third rank of each company about-faced and marched 12 paces to the rear. The first and second ranks of the right half of a company then turned left and marched into the space between the second and third ranks of the left half, while its third rank took its place in front of the third rank of the left. The two center companies, now with a "subdivision" front, marched toward the center and formed a half-battalion column, which was two company columns side by side. The other two company columns, each a subdivision in width, were positioned about 24 yards on either side of the central column. These columns were six ranks deep. The men in each pair of ranks (1st and 2nd, and so on) were also rather confusingly referred to as a "platoon" or a "subdivision." The men in the 5th and 6th ranks in each column were the "shooting subdivision," which frequently had to act independently of the close-order formation, just like the "small parties" and "commanded men" had in eighteenth-century warfare.

The Prussians greatly limited the use of the larger, battalion-size columns. This was not only because the company-size columns offered less of a target to artillery but also because they had greater mobility and could more readily take advantage of available cover.

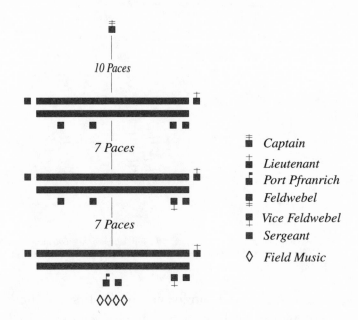

10 Paces

7 Paces

7 Paces

◊◊◊◊

■ Captain
■ Lieutenant
■ Port Pfranrich
■ Feldwebel
■ Vice Feldwebel
■ Sergeant
◊ Field Music

The light Prussian company column was developed in 1843 after the introduction of the *zundnadel-gewehr* or "needle igniting musket." Its effectiveness was only fully demonstrated almost 30 years later during the Franco-Prussian War (1870-71).

This capability became increasingly important as artillery shells and the new small arms became more popular.

On a superficial level the Prussian grand tactical system appears to have some similarities to the older Napoleonic system it replaced. The infantry brigade continued to be deployed in depth. The battalions in each of its two regiments were positioned along three tiers, one battalion behind the other. The battalion in front was formed in the four columns just described. However, this was where any resemblance between the Prussian and the older French system ended. Not only did the new Prussian system allow for greater numbers of infantrymen to be sent to the front as skirmishers—as much as 50% of the entire battalion—but the skirmish chain tended to be at a greater distance from the close-order formation than previously. There was also a more sophisticated system of supports at varying distances between the chain and the columns in the rear.

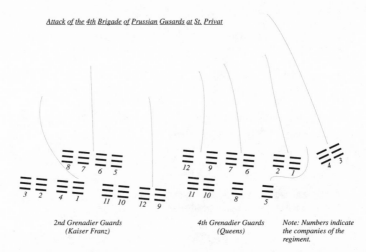

Attack of the 4th Brigade of Prussian Gusards at St. Privat

2nd Grenadier Guards
(Kaiser Franz)

4th Grenadier Guards
(Queens)

Note: Numbers indicate
the companies of the
regiment.

The small Prussian company columns (shown here in the Russian form) afforded much more flexibility than Jomini's linear formations, giving the Prussians a grand tactical sophistication reminiscent of that enjoyed by the French at the height of the Napoleonic Wars in 1805-06.

However, the shooting subdivision of the first and fourth companies were deployed as skirmishers and covered the entire frontage of the battalion. The remainder of these two companies, known as the column's "front body," followed behind as supports and were either grouped together to form a half-battalion column or, alternatively, were kept 80 to 100 yards apart. Generally, the skirmishers were kept about 400 yards in front of the main body, the central companies. There was a small group kept 150 yards behind the skirmish chain, while the front body of the two flank companies was 100 yards before the first supports. The two companies in the main body were 150 yards behind these second supports.

The second battalion, 250 yards behind the first, was not as dispersed and was generally maintained in two half-battalion columns about 250 yards from one another. The third battalion was positioned 250 yards directly behind the second but formed in a traditional battalion-size column of attack. The depth of the brigade was about 900 yards.

It wasn't always possible to position the brigade in such a highly articulate formation, so it would be forced into a two-tiered formation. When this happened, the first battalion positioned itself as normal; however, the second and third battalions were deployed in line or a line of columns about 250 yards to the rear.

In any case the result was a very deep brigade formation, with several layers of highly dispersed troops near the front and the heaviest forma-tions, battalion-size columns, 900 to 1000 yards behind the skirmishers. The spacing between the tiers in the brigade formation was greater than the "dangerous space" of any small arms then existent; in other words, bullets that could strike infantry in one tier could not possibly hit those behind. The troops along the first five tiers were also in skirmish order or in small columns, company-size or even smaller, and thus offered less of a target to artillery that fired shells.

There was another difference from the Napoleonic system that was probably more significant. The traditional system had been designed for fighting on open, relatively flat terrain. Of course, there was obstructing terrain and obstacles on almost every European battlefield. However, where possible, the troops generally maneuvered to avoid this terrain, or small amount of forces would engage in what might be termed exceptional activity. In other words, the great majority of the combatant troops were stationed in the open ground, over which most of the battle was fought. There was little systematic attempt to exploit broken ground; some maneuvers were considered, but there was nothing in the grand tactical system then in use that facilitated such efforts. The other difference from earlier in the century was the greatly expanded role of skirmishers. Until then skirmishers were primarily intended either to pester or annoy the enemy or to offer some brief resistance to attack. The main assault or the brunt of the defense had traditionally fallen to the closed-order formations.

The new Prussian system utilized what was referred to as an attack *en tenaille.* Rather than by a broad-stroke force, an assault was deliv-ered by a series of echelons, each usually directed at the flanks between the enemy formations. In this way groups of skirmishers and/or their supports in separate locations were able to combine their efforts and direct their fire concentrically toward a common target. This mutual support proved highly effective and not only maximized the casualties that would be inflicted but also proved to be psychologically overpowering. It also seemed to take a page from the Zouave methods. The numerous skirmishers were to take advantage of the terrain, hiding behind shrubs, declines in the ground, or whatever was available. When appropriate, they were to rush forward. Other times they were to lie on the ground and fire and reload from this position.

The local commander was to commit a small skirmisher force, initially. The shooting division of each column might send out a section while it followed as the first support about 100 to 150 yards behind. If the enemy did not give ground, the remainder of the shooting subdivision might be sent out to skirmish section by section. The rest of that company, up to then slightly behind the first support, would move up into the latter's position. Generally, it was expected that the entirety of the first and fourth companies would have been deployed as skirmishers when they had approached to within 300 to 400 yards of the defender's position.

The second and third companies meanwhile would continue to advance by a series of short advances. Periodically halting, they were to send out skirmishers in front of them who would then prostrate themselves on the ground. However, once they had closed to within 150 to 200 yards of the enemy, the entire force, skirmishers and all, broke into loud cheers and immediately rushed forward.

If the attack was unsuccessful, the second battalion moved up while the first would re-form and then the two battalions would rush the enemy. If the first battalion was repulsed during the attack, the officers would attempt to rally it on the flanks of the second battalion; that failing, the officers would then rally from behind the third battalion at the rear of the brigade.

Superficially, the new Prussian tactical and grand tactical system appears to be simply a slightly more evolved variation of the Napoleonic-Jominian model it replaced. However, although it is tempting to interpret the increased number of the skirmishers and the smaller of columnar formations as purely a *quantitative* change, the adoption of the new methods reflected a fundamental paradigmatic shift.

This becomes clearer when one compares the Napoleonic system to the linear system of warfare prevalent during the eighteenth century. During the classical linear period, the army tended to act as a whole during battle. The commanding general would often order the entire front line forward, with the second line and reserve following behind. Occasionally, he might order an attack by *wing*, the left or right half of the line. Once the army had positioned itself, it simply wasn't possible to order the battalion along part of the line to operate in one direction while its neighbors were angled somewhere else. All of the component parts of a wing or line had to act as a single block, being *unarticulated* in the sense that movement of the parts had to conform to the whole. There was a strong tendency for an army or a wing during this period to act as an *indivisible body* and along a *single axis of operations*.

The French innovation of dividing an army into discrete corps and these, in turn, into divisions dramatically reduced such limitations. The new command structure facilitated the delegation of command to mid-level organizations, such as the division. This, coupled with the Prussian school of tactics (developed by Frederick the Great) allowed each division, even individual brigades, to operate independently of the corps or army. Brigades and divisions could act *differentially* so that a French army, if necessary, could act along *multiple axes of operations*. Whereas the movement of an army during the eighteenth century had been essentially a binary proposition—the army either remained stationary or moved in toto—by the zenith of the Napoleonic era (about 1805), a commander could throw sizable forces against his opponent in a phased attack.

The system used by the Prussians during the Austro- and Franco-Prussian Wars was quite different on the structural and functional levels. The new tactics systematically utilized broken terrain, which, instead of being an annoyance to be avoided as much as possible, was now sought after. The lengthy chain of skirmishers and its supports assumed a serpentine form, as pockets of the men exploited protective cover. Firefights along the winding "front line" devolved into numerous foci, each with a concentration of fire coming in from divergent points.

This skirmishing phase of the battle, instead of a mere preamble to the main event that would inevitably be superceded by an assault with close-order formations, now assumed equal importance to a formal assault and often was sufficient to win local enemy positions. Meeting with stiff pockets of resistance, the chain and its supports would work their ways to the enemy's flank. Its position no longer tenable, the enemy frequently was forced to withdraw tactically. The tactical components in this first phase of the general attack, involving the skirmish chain and its supports, thus functioned as a type of fluidal membrane operating to the front and the sides of close-order formations, which themselves had shrunk to company- or half-battalion-size columns.

The new Prussian methods in this regard were a hybrid or transitional method of warfare. It marked the beginning of the end of the traditional close-order formations and in many ways was a precursor of the small-unit tactics that would emerge during World War II. Of course, in terms of its sophistication, the new Prussian tactical system represented a quantum leap from anything that had come before. Its apparent success immediately captivated the military intelligentsia in Europe and North America. Most other European armies quickly emulated these Prussian developments and implemented their own varieties of company columns. Grand tactical systems reliant upon battalion-size formations all of a sudden appeared hopelessly archaic and the Civil War suddenly seemed as though it had little to offer to future military scientific analyses.

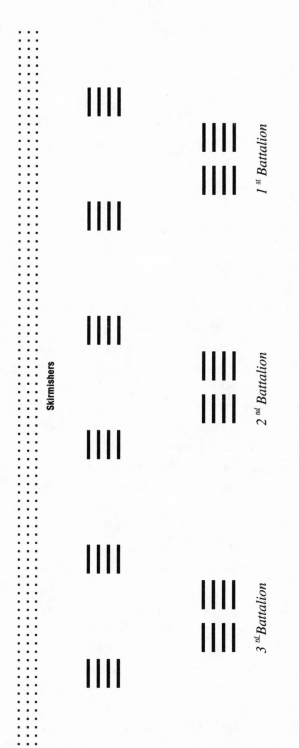

Attack Formation of a Russian Regiment in 1877

Skirmishers

3ʳᵈ *Battalion*

2ⁿᵈ *Battalion*

1ˢᵗ *Battalion*

Within several years of the Franco-Prussian War, most European armies had adopted some form of the Prussian company column. The reader should compare this Russian variant with the *ordre mixte* of Napoleonic times and Jomini's more linear approach.

Chapter 34

CONCLUSION

T he Civil War, if not at center stage, has been at least the back-drop in a truly vast number of printed works. Many a unit produced its regimental history, even if often only a pamphlet printed in limited quantities in its hometown or county. This interest in America's greatest moment of internal peril has continued over the years virtually unabated. Great wars have erupted, been fought, and eventually resolved. Troops have gone reluctantly to Asian soil. From the time when Northern armies marched to quell the great Southern rebellion, our way of life has been fundamentally transformed by a series of incredible inventions: the electric light, the telephone, the automobile, the airplane, the computer, the Internet. From 1861 when Americans leisurely traveled to church in a carriage or buggy, where an army of men took almost 2 entire days to traverse the 23 miles separating Washington and Centreville, Virginia, now a businessman takes 6½ hours to go from a meeting in Manhattan back to his home in the San Fernando Valley in California.

Despite the constant ebb and flow of international incidents and the complete transmogrification of our lifestyle, interest in the American Civil War persists undiminished. It is not unnatural, therefore, that many have sought to determine the Civil War's place in the overall scheme of military history? To what extent were its fighting methods an evolutionary dead end, characteristic of an earlier era? Conversely, how much did its methods, practices, and technologies contribute to the future conflicts that would eventually define the twentieth century?

When the great body of Civil War histories, memoirs, and studies are considered, one can say questions remain regarding its final place in military history. Was the American Civil War the first "modern war," or is it more accurate to characterize it as "the last war of the musket era"? In American literature, at least, the general consensus is that its affinity toward modern warfare greatly outweighs any resemblance to early-nineteenth-century antecedents. A few historians, mostly European, however, maintain the opposite view, arguing that it was in fact the last war of the musket era.

Those who emphasize the Civil War's ties with twentieth-century warfare cite a string of inventions and innovations. These include the military use of the submarine, mines (then called torpedoes), trains to move troops and supplies, the telegraph to transmit orders, the advent of ironclads, and, of course, the proliferation of rifled cannons, the revolver, and repeating breech-loading small arms.

Much of the conviction about the modern-ness of the Civil War is also tied to the belief that the new rifle musket represented a significant improvement over the smoothbore musket it replaced. According to common wisdom the "rifle" was a more deadly weapon, able to inflict a greater number of casualties and at a much longer range than the smoothbore musket. This point of view argues that a large part of the bloodiness of the American Civil War is attributable to the rifle musket's significantly greater range and accuracy, combined with a tactical bankruptcy stemming from most generals' misplaced determination to use outdated tactical methods, which were in effect procedural hand-me-downs from the Napoleonic age. Many of the traditional weapons and methods, such as bayonet charges during direct frontal assaults and stoically marching into a withering enemy defensive fire on an open field, strike the modern reader as absolute folly, an absurd holdover from an earlier age in which less effective weapons had made reliance upon such seemingly crude methods unavoidable.

However, this interpretation of the Civil War's place in military history fails to survive a closer scrutiny based on a rigorous and systematic comparison of the weapon systems and tactical practices actually employed during this conflict, as well as the state of military arts and science as it existed at the commencement of hostilities. This latter type of analysis produces a much more complex and textured picture that, if not inimical to the preceding point of view, differs from it in a number of fundamental ways.

Contrary to modern claims to the opposite, the Civil War was a war of fewer technological firsts than has been thought. Depending upon how one classifies the Lancaster gun, for example, the Civil War was not the first, but rather the fifth or sixth, war in which rifled artillery was used. The Lancaster was unsuccessfully used during the Crimean War. Beaulieu rifled artillery was first tentatively used in Algeria but received great acclaim only during the Italian War of 1859. The Armstrong gun gave a disappointing performance during the Second Opium War, but the Spanish army successfully used rifled artillery during the Moroccan War of 1860.

Similar observations can be made about the origins and first use of rifle muskets, revolvers, and breechloaders. Rifle muskets firing self-expanding bullets arose out of the desultory fighting between French colonial forces and native peoples in North Africa during the 1830s and '40s. A number of British and French infantry regiments during the Crimean War were equipped with rifle muskets that fired self-expanding bullets, while even greater numbers of the British infantry were armed with the rifle musket, which was used to great effect during the Indian Mutiny in 1857–58. The Colt revolver was very successfully used during the Eighth Kaffir War (1850–53), the Crimean War, and the Indian Mutiny. Ironically, breechloaders had even a lengthier service record, and the Civil War was the fifth war in which this type of small arm was employed. One of the earliest breechloaders, the Prussian needle gun, first saw service during the Schleswig-Holstoin Revolt of 1848, British engineers turned to the Colt's revolving rifle for personal protection during the Crimean War, some British cavalrymen employed the Sharps carbine during the Indian Mutiny, and key units within Garibaldi's forces fought with the Colt's Revolving Rifle in 1859.

The same can be said of mortar boats, the use of the telegraph to transmit orders, ironclads, and torpedoes. We learn from Delafield's report to Congress that all of these technological accomplishments first saw service during the Crimean War. Mechanical hand grenades had been developed before this war, and this weapon was used in an unsuccessful assassination attempt on Napoleon III in 1858. Submarines had a much longer history; the first was the *Turtle* of the American Revolution. The Russians attempted to build their first submarine in 1833, while the French and Americans intensified their experiments with this new type of naval vessel during the 1850s. Incidentally, the use of trains to transmit troops, although commonly thought to have originated during the Civil War, was actually first used by the French National Guard to help stop the 1848 Rebellion. The Russians meanwhile advanced their troops along the Warsaw-Vienna line to help quell the Hungarian Revolt that was taking place. The next year Badenese revolutionary forces exploited the rail system to retreat out of the Prussian army's way, while a decade later Napoleon III was able to mobilize a superior force against his Austrian foes by adroit use of the new system of transportation.

When judged strictly by first-time use under battlefield conditions, the Crimean War saw a greater number of technical innovations: mines, ironclads, mortar boats, rifled artillery, nurses, wartime photography, the new system of earthen fortifications, mantelets to protect artillerymen from small arms fire, and the telegraph to transmit military orders. Against this impressive list the Civil War can only boast the introduction of wire entanglements, metallic cartridges, percussion-capped mortar shells, and the first sinking of a ship by a submarine, as well as the first unsuccessful attempts to use a primitive machine gun under fire.

The belief that the new rifle muskets were much more accurate than the smoothbore under battlefield conditions, inflicted greater casualties, and forced firefights to be fought at significantly longer ranges also appears to be overly simplistic. Sharpshooting feats performed at Yorktown and throughout the conflict convincingly demonstrated what could be achieved when the new rifle muskets were placed in the hands of expert marksmen not constrained by a close-order formation and *who had the freedom to choose their targets and when to fire.* Firefights between troops in formation invariably took place at closer ranges, however. Though there are numerous examples of long-range firefights, in the 300- to 400-yard vicinity, one can find many more examples of the attacker approaching much closer, and on the average, fighting took place at ranges much smaller than has been generally thought. Before the nearly ubiquitous use of ad hoc fortifications from 1864 onward, it was still possible for an attacking force to overpower a defender with a quick rush and the threat of the bayonet. Even at close range, when fired by men under fire who were in massed formations, the rifle musket inflicted statistically few casualties compared to the number of shots fired. The chaos of the situation made it impossible for the average man to aim or even level his piece properly in the confusion of battle.

The notion that the bloodiness and indecisiveness of the early battles came about because Union and Confederate commanders had no choice but to rely on outdated doctrine and tactics also must be reevaluated. As early as the late 1840s, a number of tactical systems had been devised in response to the new weapons, such as those proposed by Captains Wittich and Gilluim. In 1843 the Prussian army had issued new regulations that moved away from traditional, battalion-size columns and placed greater emphasis on aimed individual fire. These developments were noted by knowledgeable militarymen, such as Cadmus Wilcox, Jefferson Davis, John Gibbon, Richard Delafield, and Alfred Mordecai, all of whom made every effort to keep abreast of the latest European military developments. Unfortunately, in the late 1850s Napoleon III, with his return to traditional doctrine that emphasized the importance of bayonet charges at the expense of long-range aimed fire, confused matters and deflected many away from more progressive trends. This doctrine, incidentally, was referred to as "Napoleonic tactics," an unfortunate choice of terms which, though perfectly clear to those writing in 1859–60, succeeded in confusing generations of Civil War historians, who mistakenly cast aspersions on the doctrine and practices of Louis Bonaparte's famous uncle, instead.

That the American army ultimately settled upon Jomini's much more conservative grand tactical system was the result of the efforts of Halleck and other American proponents of Jomini. One must wonder what would have happened had Jefferson Davis remained secretary of war for a second term. Already responsible for the introduction of an American Enfield-like rifle musket, taking a close look at the 12-pounder Napoleon (it would be adopted during Floyd's tenure), and the translation of the chasseur regulations, "Hardee's Tactics," Davis might have shifted his focus to the grand tactical doctrine and effected similar reforms. As it was, the indolent atmosphere during Floyd's tenure as secretary of war largely quashed all investigative efforts, and Jomini's retrogressive effort to intertwine Napoleonic concepts within a linear framework appealed to the more conservative sensibilities of the new Buchanan administration.

Although the Civil War can boast fewer firsts than has been previously thought, when considered in its totality, it still represented a departure from the way in which warfare had been fought. Despite the numerous innovations that appeared during the Crimean War, the method of fighting in practice had remained remarkably unchanged. The British infantry at Balaklava still fought in their now-traditional two-rank line; the cavalry continued to employ the walk-trot-gallop method of charge introduced a hundred years before by the Prussians. The infantry, many still equipped with smoothbores, still engaged at very close ranges.

The same certainly cannot be said of the American Civil War. Although during the first 3 years of the war, many field battles were still vaguely similar to the traditional European set piece battle, the rough, forested terrain colluded with the new weaponry to force the creation of new methods. By the summer of 1864, it is undeniable that the troops in both the Eastern and the Western theaters were daily following a modus operandi substantially different from their European counterparts or their own fathers and grandfathers. Great armies, periodically seeking shelter behind field fortifications, now remained in proximity to each other throughout the entire campaign. Shielded from the rain of long-range small arms and artillery fire, defenders were able to beat back determined assaults more readily than they had previously. By late June of that year, even the most obdurate of commanders realized that assault of a prepared position was doomed to failure and an extremely high causality toll, so they sought alternative measures to strike at the enemy or take an important position.

All of these considerations force the adoption of a much more intricate model of Civil War warfare. Metaphorically, warfare during Civil War was an anisotrope, its characteristics varying according to the point of view of the observer or what is focused upon. It was the first modern war in the sense that by the closing campaigns the *decisive battle* strategy had been set aside for lengthy lines that remained indefinitely in contact with the enemy.

However, at the same time it was the last war of the musket era, to the extent that its infantrymen were armed with Enfields and Springfields. Though these new rifle muskets theoretically enjoyed much greater range and accuracy on the target range than did their predecessors, their mechanism of loading tremendously reduced their practical effectiveness under battlefield conditions. Most firefights occurred at much closer ranges than have normally been attributed to the Civil War battlefield. Given these limitations, until combatants would routinely and quickly erect field fortifications at every available opportunity, the traditional offensive and defensive doctrine that required the men to withhold fire until at close range and then charge in with lowered bayonet appeared to remain practical. Though causing few casualties, the bayonet, a weapon of psychological terror, remained a very effective weapon, and hundreds of cases can be found in which, facing the threat of imminent impalement, the opposing line fled at the last moment.

History has similarly maligned the saber and the cavalry charge doctrine. Although originally subjected to ridicule, the importance of this weapon was revitalized during 1863 by Union cavalry, and the saber's superiority to muzzle-loading firearms when fighting enemy cavalry over open ground was demonstrated conclusively during the Shenandoah Campaign in 1864. Although there was an ever-increasing clamor to arm both infantry and cavalry with the new repeaters and breechloaders, relatively limited numbers were to be had by troops until very late in the war.

Von Moltke's infamous remark that Civil War battles were no more than engagements between armed mobs notwithstanding, the failure of Europeans to seriously study the Civil War and properly learn from its lessons was less the result of complacency and snobbery than it was the inevitable result of an ever-increasing rate of change not only in weapons technology but in the doctrines that could best exploit these innovations. By the late 1860s European armies had universally adopted breechloaders and repeaters. The newly introduced steel-barrel artillery was as radical a departure from the heavy Parrotts and Rodman pieces as these weapons had been from the smoothbores they had replaced. Just as importantly, by 1868 the Prussians had developed a completely new fighting system, one that rejected the battalion-size formations like those used during the Civil War. Seemingly vindicating their views with the swift and decisive victory over the French in 1870–71, in the eyes of the world, the Prussians appeared to be justified when, as far as relevance to modern fighting was concerned, they relegated all earlier conflicts to the realm of "ancient history."

Some modern historians have criticized European military authorities for not learning the lessons provided by the 1864 and '65 campaigns about the value of constant entrenchment and the futility of open-field assaults against prepared positions, arguing that this failure somehow led to the suicidal and completely useless wave attacks during the First World War. An example of historical analysis at its worst, this argument utilizes a 20-20 hindsight established during the 1950s and '60s. It then uses these conclusions as a yardstick against which to evaluate the merit of doctrine and military art developed during the 1870s. It is absolutely preposterous to expect military men to deduce after several years of fighting what moderns have been able to learn only after decades of research and analysis performed in the relative comfort and stability of peacetime conditions.

THE IMPACT OF SYSTEMATIC BIASES UPON MILITARY HISTORY

Molded by the received wisdom that permeates Civil War literature, we unquestionably accept the traditional view of the Civil War and its place in history. However, an in-depth look at mid-nineteenth-century military science and Civil War combat practices has shown that many commonly accepted beliefs about the Civil War are largely unfounded. Unfortunately, the very universality and longevity with which these views have been held appear to make them unassailable. Intuitively, it is difficult to accept analyses and conclusions contradicted by hundreds of other works, no matter how thorough the research or meticulous the treatment.

To a large degree, however, the present work reflects the sensibilities of a new generation of enthusiasts and military historians. Over the last 4 decades, several developments, which at first glance might appear to be trivial, nevertheless have materially affected the study of military history. Not only has the introduction of complex military simulations and living history groups—reenactors—swelled the number of enthusiasts intensely interested in military history; this trend is also responsible for the explosion in the number of recently published historical works. These are not neutral developments; they also have modified *what* is examined, as well as *how* the subjected matter is analyzed.

To fully appreciate the import of this change and why it has occurred, one must momentarily consider the "history of military history." Although today the military historian is generally a scholar who teaches and writes within a university setting, this was not always the case. The study of military history can be divided into four distinct periods according to the historians' backgrounds and methodologies. Originally, military historians were mostly military officers. Works used to instruct prospective officers covered the complete military spectrum, ranging from higher-level grand tactical and strategic issues to procedural minutiae, such as how to maneuver onto the battlefield and defend oneself against enemy cavalry. The writings of Baron de Jomini, Cadmus Wilcox, and Capt. Lewis Nolan are representative of this period.

As time passed, there was a gradual shift in what was considered worthy of study. New weapons technology significantly changed the tactical landscape. Strategic and grand tactics, on the other hand— long considered the progeny of immutable principles and theorems— and campaign studies were still thought to offer valuable lessons. The more tactical components of the military arts did not fare as well. Past exploits and practices inextricably connected to obsolete weapons technology were now viewed as irrelevant.

After the First World War, military history underwent yet another change as the custodial role as keeper of the history shifted to academic-based historians. *Scholarly interest* now replaced *military utility* as the underlying consideration that drove the selection of material and focus. The new military historians possessed more formalistic, academic backgrounds than their martial predecessors, and as the social sciences came into vogue, there was a proliferation of works with an obvious sociological or psychological orientation. This wave of historians tended to study the events and personalities purely for their own sake or as part of some larger sociological or historiographical quest. Increasingly, works limited their studies to *what* had occurred. The imperative to systematically examine the *how* and *why* had long since disappeared. Academic historians were content to limit discussion of tactics to a few pages per work, and these brief descriptions tended to be an encapsulation of existing received wisdom. Relegating detailed descriptions of the tactical practices to dusty shelves, military writers by this point had completely forgotten that they had ever been useful at all.

The recent entry of large numbers of military historical enthusiasts and hobbyists into the arena has affected how military history is studied. Seeking to satisfy the specialized needs of this emerging market, many historians have begun to return to a level of detail long ago abandoned. Books like *Gettysburg July 1*, *Stand Firm Ye Boys From Maine!*, and *The Battles for Spotsylvania Court House and the Road to Yellow Tavern* provide a thoroughness of treatment that would have been foreign to previous generations. There has also been a gradual shift in what is considered worthy of study. It is difficult to provide the reenactor with too much information about how soldiers dressed, the experiences of the campaign, and even the types of food that were consumed and how these were prepared. Those involved with sophisticated military simulations crave detailed information about how the troops fought, the tactics that were used, and how men reacted under fire. Narrative and chronology become less important. Dissection of purely political issues is reduced to secondary importance.

This in turn has helped foster a new perspective, even when treating oft-visited topics. Like the surveyor who changes his vantage point, this not only affords a new, slightly different view of the subject matter under scrutiny but also allows the observer to assay the qualities of the original perspective, in this case the methodology employed by previous generations of historians. As one attempts to trace the development of military practices in detail, a number of intellectual trends become discernable. Despite the truly vast number of books that appear to deal with some aspect of this epic American struggle, or possibly because of this very profusion of information, by the end of the nineteenth century, a number of "myths" had arisen. These were not caused by the intellectual or professional deficiencies of individual authors, many of whom were gifted historians, but are indicative of a pervasive collective mind-set that unconsciously influenced many who operated within this intellectual environment.

The problems that arose for the most part were the unwitting result of subliminal attitudes and beliefs, which, though seeming trivial and harmless, nevertheless profoundly influenced the investigative and analytical processes. Once interwoven throughout the intellectual tapestry, feelings and convictions inevitably become transformed into self-evident and indisputable "truths." A sociologist who believes that progress almost inevitably leads to positive change and a general higher level of well-being, for example, might never question this belief in the context of his professional work. If polled, most graduate students would agree that a consensus of opinion among current thought leaders, though still capable of further refinement, provides a lasting framework upon which all future opinion on the subject will be based. Unconscious attitudes can affect an analyst's ability to place historical phenomena into a broader context; they also can insidiously influence what is considered important and hence worthy of study. Unconsciously held, these attitudes rarely, if ever, come under self-examination; thus, they are tenaciously resistant to change.

These biases generally fall into two broad categories: the urge to simplify and the desire to validate one's "place in the universe." The laws of inertia and entropy appear to be equally applicable on the purely intellectual plane. Seeking an understanding with the least amount of effort, the human mind tries to reduce complex, multilayered phenomena to easily digestible, "bite-size" intellectual units or "high concepts." This last term refers to the tendency of Hollywood pitchmen to describe the gist of a book or a script in a single, easily grasped sentence. Historians have been known to employ similar artifices, and in recent years a number of works have appeared which attempt to explain important but complex events as due to one all-powerful causative factor or dynamic. The study of the Civil War is not unique in this regard, for this problem has plagued the study of every period within military history.

Of course, apart from a brief period of notoriety and brisk sales, this type of work rarely achieves lasting credibility; historians and readers eventually recognize it is overly simplistic and offers, at best, only partial truths. There are, however, two other attitudes that arise from the urge to simplify which have had a much greater impact. The first is the tendency of many military historians to specialize in a particular era or topic. This is based upon the conviction that a historian can learn more by devoting all of his attention to his chosen specialty. Authors who write about eighteenth-century warfare, for example, specialize in this, their chosen period. The same is true for those studying the Napoleonic period or the Civil War.

Specialization offers obvious benefits. Not forced to divide his attention, the historian can more closely examine his own area. This not only heightens the expertise that can be developed but also increases the amount of detailed information that can be collected. Unfortunately, there is a downside that imposes its own set of limitations. Whatever knowledge is acquired about other subjects or periods beyond the specialization is generally derived from secondary sources. This limits the historian's ability to perform any meaningful comparative analysis. It hinders his ability to accurately recognize what is truly new in a particular period and what owes it's origins to previous developments. One of the clearest examples is found in the study of Napoleonic warfare. Unwilling to systematically investigate eighteenth-century warfare, most Napoleonic historians until recently have assumed that the battalion-size closed columns so noticeable during the French Revolutionary Wars originated during the tempestuous period following the storming of the Bastille. However, a detailed look at the development of military arts and science during the earlier period shows that columns of attack not only were sometimes used during the Seven Years' War but in fact can even be traced back to as early as the War of the Spanish Succession.

Civil War historians again are not exempt from this problem, sometimes being as isolationist as some late-nineteenth-century British historians who wrote about the Napoleonic Wars and succumbed to the same intellectual trap. Lacking sufficient knowledge about contemporary European warfare, as well as several important European tactical developments during the 1840s and '50s, it would be impossible to reconstruct the full story of the development of Civil War weaponry.

This, however, did not occur for want of clues and potential leads in the contemporary American official reports, journal articles, and even newspaper reports that have periodically found their way into Civil War bibliographies. From our perspective it seems only logical that the seemingly innumerable references to European antecedents in Mordecai's and Delafield's reports to Congress, Cadmus Wilcox's *Rifles and Rifle Practice,* and John Gibbon's *The Artillerist's Manual,* for example, would have aroused Civil War historians' curiosity and encouraged them to the follow the succession of clues back to the beginning of the story, wherever this might lead. Unfortunately, all too often Civil War historians have proven to be like the hunter who relentlessly tracks his prey over vast expanses of open land, only to give up at the last moment because the tracks unexpectedly take him into a dense, threatening forest. The Civil War historian has proven himself a competent analyst who can indefatigably and competently plough through a truly daunting amount of primary sources as long as these deal *directly* with the great conflict. Unfortunately, he has also demonstrated a proclivity to immediately abandon or deflect the research the moment the clues lead into literally or metaphorically foreign territory. Of course, specialization is neither avoidable nor undesirable. Nevertheless, those who specialize must be aware of these potential problems and consciously strive to avoid tunnel vision.

If specialization has narrowed the historian's focus, another attitude has systematically limited what will be examined even within the chosen area. Unwilling to adequately tackle the intricacies of military science, many military historians exude a distain for tactical-level analysis, which they unconsciously regard as essentially a banausic activity. Believing that such details have little or no relevance to "more important issues," their works studiously eschew such minutiae and unwittingly become self-fulfilling prophecies. This tendency has plagued all of military history, and once again the study of the Civil War is no exception. Only a handful of works have taken a detailed look at the nature of combat on the Civil War battlefield, and fewer still have sought to reconstruct the theoretical art of war as it existed during the 1850s and '60s, a vital precondition if there is ever to be a meaningful comparison between theory and practice or an accurate assessment of the Civil War's place in military history.

Ironically, the study of this aspect of the Civil War got off to an auspicious start with the writings of Lt. Col. Arthur Wagner. An instructor in The Department of Military Art at the U.S. Infantry and Cavalry School in the 1880s, Wagner was what Paddy Griffith has referred to as the "rarest of species, the true tactical military historian." An authority on contemporary warfare, he was also preeminently knowledgeable about warfare during the Napoleonic and Civil War periods. Unfortunately, the foundation laid by Wagner was never exploited and with the exception of several master's and doctoral theses, this important aspect of the Civil War was essentially disregarded until the late 1970s. By this point a number of works on period weaponry had appeared, but these offered little more than an unreflective regurgitation of received wisdom that had developed over the years.

If the urge to simplify reduces the types of information the historian is willing to explore, the desire to validate one's place in the universe insidiously influences the evaluative processes. One of the most common ways of amplifying the meaning of one's life is to feel superior either to one's peers or predecessors. The first often takes the form of cultural chauvinism; the second is an arrogance of the present over the past. Not the obvious, strident form of chauvinism that overtly denigrates and mocks the actions and contributions of other nationalities, chauvinism in the English-speaking world is generally subtler. Instead of a direct attack, it simply minimizes or ignores foreign accomplishments. It is rarely a self-conscious sentiment and, subliminally interwoven into the foundation of one's intellectual psyche, is part of the process that decides what is important and what can be dismissed out of hand.

This problem, prevalent among almost all European societies at the turn of the twentieth century, was compounded in America by cultural insecurity. Denizens of a youthful country and sensitive to the criticism and mockery that inevitably is hurled by those who style themselves as sophisticated and mature (in this case Europeans) at those deemed cultural adolescents (Americans), many early Civil War historians unconsciously attempted to compensate for this emotional vulnerability. All too often the historian succumbed to the urge to discount any shortcoming of the Civil War soldiers and commanders and exclusively focused upon, or even magnified, their positive qualities. Statements that tout some aspect of the Civil War as the "the most," "the first," or "the best" when unaccompanied by a detailed analysis to substantiate the claim are usually symptomatic of this tendency.

Such unsupported claims remind one of driving into a town and seeing a store sign that advertises "the world's best coffee." Does the proprietor belong to some international coffee tasting society where this offering won first prize? Did he or she travel extensively and taste every conceivable blend and roast from Sumatra to Hawaii? Certainly not! The reality is that the storeowner, recognizing that his coffee is better than any other offered locally, resorts to hyperbole and boasts that it is the best coffee existent! This tendency to appreciate accomplishment in a specific context and then elevate this performance to "best in kind" without adequate comparative analysis to substantiate the claim is frequently encountered in twentieth-century Civil War literature.

The other potential bias is probably the least noticed yet the most pervasive. This of course is the rather smug belief that we are somehow better off than our predecessors, and armed with our sophisticated technological and scientific capabilities and vast reservoir of knowledge, we can do things better. If people back then knew what we know, they would have done things differently. How many times, for example, does one find in a modern work in which the author seems to be saying, "How could military authorities have armed their infantry with bayonets and cavalry with swords? Wasn't it obvious that the increased range of the new rifle made all edged weapons obsolete?" This tendency to deprecate edged weapons and bayonet charges is a biased arrogance of the present over the past whenever an author adopts such pejorative views without at least first trying to determine how these weapons functioned.

WHAT MUST BE DONE?

The goal of history is to study and understand the past. The successful study of history is like returning to a previous era via a fantastical time machine; there, totally invisible, the modern is able to observe events unnoticed. Having consciously placed modern sensibilities and values completely on hold, the time traveler is able to appreciate what is observed without bias, in other words, to understand the past *on its terms, not our own.* It is this last criterion that so frequently defies accomplishment. It is relatively easy to piece together "cold, hard facts"; it is much more difficult to sympathetically reconstruct the emotional and intellectual worldviews of those in long-ago times. Many of our views about the Napoleonic era and the Civil War, for example, have been influenced by much more recent values: the strident nationalism common at the turn of the twentieth century and the smug yet unreflective arrogance of the denizen of the television era.

At this stage of military history, the challenge is less in finding completely new repositories of historical information than in learning to interpret the vast storehouse of available data more accurately. In this sense historians at the start of the twenty-first century are in a situation rather akin to that faced by physical scientists 120 years ago. Faced with a submolecular reality that defied comprehension using existing terminology and concepts, scientists had to consciously create a new intellectual universe. The philosophically more astute among these thinkers realized that this necessarily was an artificial process. No matter how pragmatically correct the new theorems proved to be, new concepts, such as the dual wave-matter properties of light, were artificial intellectual metaphors that allowed the human mind to understand atomic- and subatomic-level phenomena and were not necessarily reality itself. Appreciative of the unavoidable gap between reality and the understanding of reality, scientists like Werner Heisenberg realized that the very process of observing electrons altered the position of these tiny particles, and hence he formulated his famous Law of Uncertainty.

The study of history appears to be influenced by its own Law of Uncertainty. The values, attitudes, and sensibilities of the historian will always to some degree influence his appreciation of what is under study. In this sense the historiographical process can never be a completely neutral event but will always have some impact upon what is studied, even if it is only slight and trivial. To minimize this impact, the historian must first examine his own set of values and beliefs and determine how these are likely to influence the subject under study. Only then can he, as with eyes that become acclimatized to the darkness, begin to discern the deepest, most basic, and most pervasive values of those under study.

If the pitfalls of past military historical efforts are to be avoided, it is important that the military historian's conceptual, informational, and methodological armamentarium be expanded. One of the key challenges, therefore, is to reinstitute a working knowledge of a period's military science as a core competency for all military historical efforts, regardless of the period or specific area of focus. Surely the time is past when some academes, who after merely reading Jomini, von Clausewitz, and a handful of other top-level writers, are encouraged to masquerade as experts in mid-nineteenth-century military science simply because of the degrees they hold or the prestige of the institutions where they teach. This is not to belittle the scholastic approach or the vital role it will always play in furthering our understanding of all aspects of history. Rather, it is simply to lobby for improvement in several areas, previously thought to be of little import, in which the present level of knowledge is noticeably deficient.

It is equally important to compensate for an exclusive preoccupation with the microspecific. Civil War literature is filled with excellent "microhistories," in which the historian, utilizing a *vertical* approach to the subject matter, is able to go into incredible detail about a single, easily defined topic. Such studies usually have a predominant *point of focus* and often serve purely a descriptive function, such as when an author provides a chronology or narrative of events. Works that focus upon a single battle, an army during one campaign, a particular regiment, or the exploits of an individual usually employ a vertical approach. The advantages are obvious. The boundaries of the topic distinctive and intuitively identifiable, the historian is able to exclude extraneous issues quickly and drill down upon the core subject matter. The problem is that when unsupported by more general works, these studies tend to compartmentalize information. Someone interested in ironclads, for example, might know about the recent research tracing the origins of this type of vessel to the Crimean War and before, while someone who is only interested in the Western theater of operations might only be aware of the "received wisdom" originally propagated by late-nineteenth-century historians.

The sheer volume of even recently published secondary sources forces ultraspecialization, and critically important information unearthed by these microhistories tends to be appreciated only by their specific readership.

As a result there is a pressing need for new studies to somehow bring together the interesting and significant findings of the micro-histories to make this information available to a broader cross section of the public. Such works by their nature would have to utilize a *relational* or *horizontal* approach that attempts to follow a theme, topic, or issue through many areas, much like following a single strand of cord through a large entanglement. This type of analytical work, generally, is characterized by multiple points of focus and is *comparative;* a sizable portion of the intellectual effort is spent showing how the issues and practices evolved and what distinguishes them from others during that same period.

Although this might appear to be a formidable challenge, the modern Civil War community has the assets immediately available to undertake such a challenge. In many respects this amalgamation of traditional historical approaches with military historical simulations and living historical reenactments marks a new phase of Civil War historiography. The scholastic-based military historian, the military professional, the dedicated enthusiast, the living historian or reenactor, and the simulation designer or miniature rules writer each brings a slightly different set of interests and competencies to the table, thus greatly expanding the types of analysis, data, and conclusions that can be generated.

The reason and emotion that compels this renewed, reinvigorated approach to the study of the Civil War, incidentally, is not simply an abstract quest for verisimilitude, the pursuit of truth for its own sake. It should be motivated by a sincere respect for our forefathers who fought in this great conflict, white and black, Northerner and Southerner, *and to accept them for what they really were, not what we wish them to be.* Throughout history and in all cultures, there is a tendency to magnify the accomplishments of those we love and respect. However, this very act of embellishment suggests a deep, unconscious sense of insecurity, as though somehow the original story, if left unaltered, would reveal something less than perfection. Why else is the story embellished? This is actually disrespectful to those under scrutiny, since it suggests a lack of acceptance or appreciation of who they really were or what they actually achieved. In this regard, the appreciation of one's heritage is like a long-term marriage or close personal relationship. In the beginning one can only see the virtues and positive qualities; one is blind to flaws or shortcomings. As time goes, however, the emotive bond is only strengthened by the recognition, acceptance, and ultimately, the appreciation of *all* of the other's qualities.

So too is it in the study of one's favorite subject. America has come a long way since the 1890s, not only in the technology and popular culture that it has introduced to the world but in its mature appreciation of its own self-worth. Emotionally, there should no longer be a need for the adolescent cultural chauvinism encountered all too often in the Civil War's late-nineteenth- and early-twentieth-century historiography. Besides, studies that transcend the unconscious urge to portray their subjects as "the best," "the bloodiest," and "the bravest" generally provide not only a more accurate but a far more human and interesting story as well.

KEY TO ABBREVIATIONS IN ENDNOTES

JCCW-HA = Joint Committee on the Conduct of the War, Report on Heavy Ordnance, 38th Congress 2nd Session.
JRUSI = *Journal Royal United Service Institute*
MG = *Military Gazette*
OR = *Official Records*
SA = *Scientific American,* Original Series
SA-NS = *Scientific American,* New Series
SLM = *Southern Literary Messenger*

All citations to the *Official Records* (OR) should be read without "Vol." and "No."

CHAPTER 1

5. "An advance was ordered . . . routed them completely.": OR Vol. I, No. 3, p. 113.
8. "The Union regulars . . . battle on Oak Hill.": Watson, p. 217.
9. "Now, however, the advancing infantry . . . lowered the men's morale.": De Forest, pp. 60–61. *Harper's Magazine,* vol. XXIX, no. 72, (Sept. 1864) pp.475–482.
10. "The mistake, however . . . back on their feet.": De Forest, p. 62.
12. "Of course there was some . . . my own soldiers.": De Forest, p. 69.
13. "In one part of the field . . . around 10 A.M.": In his official report, Colonel Fuller states that the attack commenced at 11 A.M.
13. "Taking advantage of the sudden . . . 'to close upon them.' ": OR Vol. I, No. 17 (1), p. 185. One of the Arkansas regiments was probably the Third Arkansas Cavalry, which also was serving as infantry.
15. "Again the Union defenders . . . not to return that day.": Jackson O, p. 73.
18. "While reading Watson's description . . . the Battle of Caldiero.": This was either November 12, 1796, or October 29–31, 1805, depending upon whether Duhèsme was referring to the First or Second battle of Caldiero.
19. "Well then! Hardly had . . . separated us, retreated.": Duhèsme, pp. 442–44.
19. "Similarly, while reading of the Twelfth . . . *Military Discipline* (1727.)": Bland, 1st ed.; pp. 145–147.

CHAPTER 2

22. "Their first response . . . in 1776–77.": Blackmore, p. 83.

23. "French riflemen during . . . pick up smoothbores.": "R.E.C.", pp. 7–8.

24. "What a melancholy object . . . tree is a fortress.": Wilford, JRUSI, Vol. I, no. 3, pp. 239–240.

24. "The French troops, encumbered . . . proper blow in return.": "R.E.C.", p. 14.

25. "This failing, in desperation . . . two hundred years previously.": Fox, JRUSI, Vol. II, no. 8, p. 463; Wilford, p. 241.

25. "In trials conducted during . . . number in *15 minutes.*": Chesney, p. 265.

26. "In hot weather, however . . . part of the powder.": Chesney, p. 275.

26. "Once again, officers began . . . find on the battlefield.": "R.E.C.", pp. 7–8.

26. "However, it would require . . . powder should be used.": Dixon, JRUSI, pp. 98–100.

26. "These slender projectiles were . . . impact as larger calibers.": Chesney, p. 266, citing H.J. Paixhans *Constitution militaire de France,* Paris 1849, pp. 225–226.

27–28. "Hollowing out the . . . a thin iron cup.": Some contemporaries observed that Minié, had frequently been invited to Delvigne's earlier experiments with conical bullets and was inspired by Delvigne's work and ideas.

28. "Pressed against the barrel . . . there was no windage.": Dixon, pp. 98–100.

28. "It was rumored that at . . . anyone standing behind!": "R.E.C.", p. 9.

28. "The French Imperial . . . these converted rifles.": Wilford, pp. 241; Dixon, pp. 98–100.

29. "All infantrymen were . . . cylindrical-conical bullet.": Dixon, pp. 100–101.

29. "It possessed greater accuracy . . . the limits of its sights.": Wilford, p. 241.

29. "Not only was the . . . of the weapon's development." *Report of Experiments with Small Arms,* p. 33.

29–30. "The same year, both . . . old smoothbore muskets.": Dixon, pp. 98–100.

30. "Beyond 80 yards it . . . a target at 300 yards.": Wilford, pp. 239–240.

30. ". . . when the target was . . . no balls ever retrieved.": Blanche, pp. 8–11. Other tests conducted about the same period suggested that the effective range of the traditional musket was 80 to 100 yards greater than what was just stated. In another experiment, a soldier was able to place twelve consecutive rounds within a 12-inch target at 150 yards, an 18-inch target at 200 yards and a 6-foot target at 300 yards; Dixon, p. 98.

30. "Incidentally, the new rifle . . . target at that range.": Chesney, pp. 268–269.

31. "French tests revealed . . . velocity of 1115 feet per second.": Wilcox, pp. 171, 177.

31. "In 1844 Major Mordecai . . . 947 feet per second, respectively.": *U.S., Report Small Arms* (1856), p. 108; Wilcox, pp. 171, 181.

31. "Thus, the velocity of . . . for traditional small arms.": These values are corroborated by findings published by an Englishman, Andrew Steinmetz of the Queen's Militia; Steinmetz, JRUSI, Vol. V, No.18, p. 391.

31. "In other words, if . . . 100 and 225 yards from the shooter.": *Report of Experiments,*

Appendix II, p. 25; citing the results of experiments from *Report of Experiments with small arms carried out at Enfield (Eng.) 1852* by Honorable A. Gordon, Lt.-Col. London, 1853.

31. "The limits of this narrow band was called the *dangerous space*.": Wilcox, p. 66.

32. "If a shooter adjusted . . . 986.5 and 997.25 yards.": Wilcox, p. 67.

32. "The Enfield rifle was . . . 800 yards, respectively.": Wilcox, p. 179–180.

33. "Although a rifleman . . . charge began in earnest.": Steinmetz, Vol. V, No. 18, pp. 387, 391.

33. "Alexander would later recall . . . fellow drop at my shot.' ": Alexander, *Fighting*, p. 143.

34. "Soon after the adoption . . . (Instructions on Firing).": Wilcox, p. 68.

34. "Similar schools were established . . . long-rang small arms.": Wilcox, pp. 239–241.

35. "He then pulled the trigger . . . the detonating cap.": Mordecai, pp. 192, 196.

35. "The resulting trials pitted . . . a Prussian jäger rifle.": Chesney, p. 261; citing *Royal Engineer Corps Papers*, 1849–50 prepared by Lieutenant Colonel Portlock of the Royal Engineers.

36. "Nevertheless, the Swedish king . . . 500 of the new rifles.": Chesney, p. 265; citing *Royal Engineer Corps Papers*.

36. "Unfortunately, excessive ramming . . . at the breech instead.": Mordecai, p. 193.

36. "Dreyse was more fortunate . . . Prussian infantry in 1842.": Blanche, p. 66.

36. "Its inventor claimed . . . six rounds per minute.": Chesney, p. 270.

37. "During the Eighth Kaffir War . . . Cape Town colony.": SA, Vol. 7, No. 23, (Feb. 21, 1852), p. 184.

37. "Reliable and highly accurate . . . met with general approval.": SA, Vol. 8, 19, (Jan. 22, 1853), p. 149.

37. "Within moments the rebel . . . upon the battlefield." Busk, pp. 44, 47.

37. "The editors of *Scientific American* . . . prove to be 'humbug.' ": SA, Vol. 1, No. 49, (Aug. 27, 1846), p. 2.

37. "The magazine's overtly acerbic . . . only several months earlier.": SA, Vol. 1, No. 36, (May 21, 1846), p. 3.

38. "The duke was inclined . . . victor of Waterloo.": Pliny, p. 12.

38–39. "Although it received . . . by British military authorities." Blanche, p. 61.

CHAPTER 3

42. "The Prussian officer argued . . . converted into 'mounted infantry.' ": Chesney, pp. 286–293 citing Captain Wittich, *Das Fahnlein oder die Compagnie als die wahre tactische Einheit, etc.*, Wesel, 1849, pp. 16–63, 74–80.

43. "The target was hit 28 times . . . a 70% hit rate.": *Report of Experiments with Small Arms*, Appendix, p. 34.

43. "Two targets were erected . . . one-quarter of its frontage.": Wilford, p. 241.

43. "Fortunately, the second target . . . its dangerous space.": Wilcox, pp. 179–180.

44. "The front row of skirmishers . . . the rear rank, twice.": Wilcox, p. 180; *Report of Experiments*, pp. 34–3.

45. "It may be added . . . sangfroid are proverbial.": Dixon, p. 115, citing Captain Gilluim, *Belgian Artillery* 1856, p. 331.

46. "Chesney concluded that . . . remain largely unchanged.": Chesney, pp. 300–303.

46. "An army would cease . . . attacks on isolated points.": Dixon, pp. 109–111.

47. "This would not only . . . 'a distinction as promotion.' ": Dixon, p. 104.

47. "Unlike a skirmisher carefully . . . possible weight of fire.": Dixon, pp. 103–104.

47. "The old time-consuming . . . had to be abandoned.": Between 1748 and 1756 Frederick the Great introduced a new lexicon of infantry maneuvers that would serve as the basis for virtually all European drill booklets until the 1840s. In recognition of this, some military experts referred to this tactical tradition as the "Prussian School."

47. "The cavalry could still . . . enemy fleeing the field.": Dixon, pp. 112, 114.

48. "The main walls of the . . . moved farther to the front.": Dixon, p. 114.

49. "Like Dixon, Wilford emphasized . . . defender's small arms.": Wilford, p. 247.

49. "(Some modern firearms . . . soldiers were undistinguishable.)": Opinion of Joseph Bilby, expressed directly to the author.

49. "A light company firing . . . less than a minute.": Rumsby, p. 18–22.

50. "Ditches would have to . . . attackers at longer range.": Tyler, JRUSI, Vol. III, no. 10, (1859), p. 180.

50. "Though agreeing with the artillery . . . embarrass field artillery.": Tyler, pp. 170–171.

50. "The difficulty in getting . . . its value in practice.": Tyler, p. 174.

51. "They will wisely avail . . . assistance of the spade...": Tyler, p. 177.

51. "Both taught at the United States . . . the American Civil War.": Faust, p. 309; Boatner III, p. 918.

51. "During his lecture Tyler . . . 'interfere with extreme ranges.' ": Tyler, p. 172.

52. "Hurrying from one position . . . 'judgement or his aim.' ": Dixon, pp. 103–104.

52. "Add to this the groans and shrieks of the dying and wounded.": Steinmetz, p. 390.

52. "The earth would literally shake . . . wobble from leg to leg.": Steinmetz, p. 468.

52. "The best that could . . . the Napoleonic Wars.": Steinmetz, p. 390.

53. "If we could make . . . but that is impossible.": Steinmetz, p. 387.

53. "The discrepancy in . . . in initial muzzle velocities.": Steinmetz, pp. 391.

55. "These would prove . . . other French skirmishers.": "R.E.C", p. 15.

55. "If they had adopted . . . by those in the third.": Rose, p. 254.

55. "This latter step, . . . 180 paces per minute.": "R.E.C.", pp. 15–16.

56. "The heavy version of the . . . to be an instant success.": Rose, p. 255.

56. "The two organizations learned . . . new Tirailleurs maneuvers.": "R.E.C.", pp. 16–17.

57. "After hard-fought operations . . . Europe and North America.": Rose, p. 255.

57. "If infantry continued . . . forward to the attack.": *Southern Literary Messenger*, pp. 15–16.

58. "Around 1858 the maximum . . . down to 400 yards.": Scoffern, pp. 328–329.

58. "Starting at 400 meters, . . . at the enemy's waist": Wilcox, pp. 176–177.

59. "When the intended victim . . . range was 250 meters.": Steinmetz, pp. 456–457.

59. "Experience had demonstrated . . . amount of ammunition.": Wilcox, pp. 176–177.

59. "It is not absolutely necessary . . . good practice in firing.": Steinmetz, pp. 463–464.

CHAPTER 4

61. "The assortment of artillery . . . *Instructions for Heavy Artillery*.": Gibbon, *Artillerist's Manual*, also U.S. Army, *Instructions for Heavy Artillery*.

62. "Guns were generally limited . . . harmlessly in the ground.": Hughes, *British Smoothbore Artillery*, p. 27–34. When massed, guns sometimes were elevated more than 15 degrees to hit long range targets.

62. "This created the need . . . Austrian Succession (1740–48).": de Tousard, Vol. I, p. 270; They were adopted by the French army in 1747–48. Victors at the Battle of Fontenoy in 1745, the French captured several howitzers and were satisfied with their performance at the sieges of Bergen-op-Zoom (July to September 1747) and Mastreicht (May 1748).

63. "The length of a howitzer's . . . diameter of the bore.": Hughes, *Firepower* p. 13.

63. "Nevertheless, shells were . . . slowly moving cavalry.": Tielke, Vol. I, p. 200.

63. "The noise and confusion . . . the cavalry to regroup.": Okounef, p. 342.

64. "A 32–pounder howitzer . . . feet of earth per shot.": Gibbon, *Artillerist's Manual*, p. 246, also U. S. Army, *Instructions for Field Artillery*, p. 12.

64. "It was recognized that . . . was highly useful.": Haythornthwaite, p. 60.

64. "In the center of . . . explosive charge inserted.": United States Army, *Instructions for Field Artillery*, p. 12.

64. "Since they were intended . . . weight of the projectile.": Gibbon, *Artillerist's Manual*, p. 147.

65. "Not only could shrapnel . . . fire and cavalry charges.": Great Britain, (*Madras Gunner*), pp. 119–120.

65. "In 1835 the Ordnance . . . resumed the next year.": Ripley, Warren, pp. 19–20.

65. "Known as a *canon* . . . ship-to-ship fighting.": Gibbon, *Artillerist's Manual*, p. 242.

66. "According to this version, . . . innovation into French service.": *Harper's Magazine, The Artillerist, Harper's Magazine* Vol. XXIV, No. CXLII, pp. 545–549, March, 1862, p. 547.

67. "The American expert . . . who put it all together.": Dahlgren, pp. 14–15.

67. "At this distance . . . would soon be silenced.": Chesney, pp. 279–280; 300–301; citing *Constitution militaire de la France.* 1849, Paris H. J. Paixhaus pp. 41, 42, 72.

67. "Since our last war, . . . power at long range.": Favé, p. 14.

69. "Prior to taking over . . . gun *and* a howitzer.": Mordecai, p. 141.

69. "The theoretical evidence . . . less damage to the gun.": Favé, p. 7–8, 10–11.

69. "The French artillery engineers . . . shell was now feasible.": Favé, p. 14.

70. "Although all three . . . different types of ordnance.": Favé, pp. 50–112.

70. "To remedy this problem . . . of the entire piece.": It was reduced from 10 to 2 millimeters.

71. "The positioning of the trunnions . . . other types of ordnance.": Favé, pp. 12–13.

71. "By 1854 enough . . . with the gun howitzer.": Mordecai, p. 143.

71. "One of the oldest known . . . St. Petersburg arsenal.": Mordecai, p. 109.

71. "Looking closely they noticed . . . a hundred years old.": SA, Vol. 5, No. 5, New Series, Aug. 3, 1861, p. 80.

72. "A bronze piece . . . pointed leaden projectiles.": Scott, R.A.E., pp. 6–7.

72. "Reichenbach combined two . . . used by Colonel Beaulieu.": Taylor, Note A, p. 29.

74. "Rather than spinning, . . . all accuracy was lost.": Delafield, pp. 8–9.

74–75. "The Belgian, Dutch, Russians . . . muzzle-loading rifled artillery.": Taylor, p. 7 citing *Canon Rayé Prussien Paris*, p. 79.

75. "On two separate occasions . . . prevented them from charging.": Steinmetz, p. 467.

75. "Their stock of Wahrendorf . . . assigned to fortifications.": Taylor, pp. 10–11, citing *Le Canon Prussien Jugé*, Paris, 1861, p. 23.

75. "However, after rave reports . . . Wahrendorf artillery.": Taylor, pp. 14–15, citing *Canon Rayé*, pp. 55, 58–59, 77; and *Canon Prussien*, pp. 15, 63.

75. "The Italians were predisposed . . . school of rifled artillery.": Taylor, pp. 16, citing *Canon Rayé Prussien*, pp. 48, 78.

75. "Clearly, by the opening . . . by the new weapon.": Taylor, p. 7, citing *Le Canon Prussien Jugé*, p. 15 and the appendix of *Canon Rayé*, p. 6.

CHAPTER 5

77. "We possess a nucleus . . . in time of peace": Delafield, pp. 2–3.

78. "These tests took place . . . Springfield in 1855.": Moseley, p. 94, 97.

78. "The military had to be . . . employed as 'light troops.' ": Armstrong, p. 100, fn 16.

79. "That fall the new manual . . . using the Cadet Corps.": Armstrong, pp. 89–91.

79. "Recruits who were forced . . . as the 'Shanghai Drill.' ": "R.E.C.", p. 17.

79. "A January 1858 article . . . original French document.": "R.E.C.", p. 17.

79. "Benjamin F. Evans . . . 'nothing but a translation.' ": Moore, Frank; *The Rebellion Record*, Vol. I, Section 3, p. 111; also cited in Moseley, pp. 263–265, fn 55, 56.

81. "That Hardee had plagiarized . . . 'Hardee's name attached.' ": Grant, U.S., p. 108.

81. "Davis directed these commissioners . . . the need for howitzers.": Delafield, p. v.

81. "Presumably, the title . . . the opening chapter.": McClellan, *The Armies of Europe*, Washington, 1861.

81–82. "His chapter on "rifled cannon" . . . April 12 of the same year.": Mordecai, pp. 109–115.

82. "There was also mention . . . Arsenal in May 1856.": Mordecai, pp. 117–119.

82. "A fuse was mechanically . . . that still used today.": Mordecai, p. 154.

82. "Delafield was also . . . powered transport ships.": Delafield, pp. 109–110.

83. "The ordnance department . . . the United States Army.": Gibbon, *Artillerist's Manual*, p. 324; Mordecai, p. 145; *Military Gazette*, p. 339.

83. "The latest technological . . . *Études sur l'artillerie*, and more.": Mordecai, pp. 5–10.

84. "A thorough treatment . . . for more than 5 years.": Mosely, p. 297.

84. "Although the breechloader . . . French-inspired rifle musket.": Outside this area, only the *Cent Gardes* in France were equipped with these weapons; Wilcox, p. 214.

84. "The paper of the cartridge . . . cartridge is inserted.": "R.E.C.", p. 11.

84. "In August, Congress . . . experiments were halted.": Report of the secretary of war, executive documents of the 1st session, 35th congress, Vol. 920, pp. 19–20; "R.E.C." p. 7; *Experiments with Small Arms* p. 25; and Armstrong, p. 83, citing Carl L. Davis, *Small Arms in the Union Army 1861–65*; Ph.D. Thesis, Oklahoma State University, pp. 138, 140–141.

85. "When another board . . . recommend the weapon.": Wilcox, pp. 217–218.

85. " 'Some of these arms . . . force, at long range.' ": Report of the secretary of war, executive documents of the 1st session, 35th congress, Vol. 920, pp. 18–19.

85. "It must sustain unharmed . . . firearm in a few weeks.": "Improvement in Arms," *Military Gazette*, Vol. 2, No. 18, Sept. 15, 1859, p. 282.

86. "In either case . . . stage of the battle.": "R.E.C.", p. 11.

86. "Gibbon, for example . . . accurate barrage of fire.": Gibbon, *Artillerist's Manual*, p. 231.

86. "Troops in fieldworks . . . construction of trenches.": Wilcox, pp. 215–216.

86. "Capable of expending . . . armed with rifle muskets.": "R.E.C", p. 11; Gibbon, *Artillerist's Manual*, p. 230; Wilcox, pp. 215–216.

87. "Although this work largely . . . *Treatise on Normal Gunnery*.": Specifically, these were: Colonel Huger's report on experiments at Harpers Ferry Armory during the Fall of 183 and Winter 1854; Lt. Benton's report of his experiments at Harpers Ferry Armory during 1854 and the next year at Springfield Armory.

88. "This author placed . . . the Minié's advantages.": "R.E.C.", p. 19.

88. "The author of this article . . . Sixteenth Virginia Infantry Regiment.": Warner, Generals in Gray, pp. 58–59.

90. "The infantryman would now . . . under fire as artillerymen.": Wilcox, pp. 238, 243.

90. "Cavalry would now . . . than artillery bombardment.": Wilcox, pp. 242–243, 246–248.

91. "In general, the infantry . . . the mass of troops.": Gibbon, *Artillerist's Manual*, pp. 230–231.

92. "Captain Gibbon confidentially . . . than plot its demise.": Gibbon, *Artillerist's Manual*, pp. 144–145.

92. "Believing that the frailties . . . with the new weapons.": Gibbon, *Artillerist's Manual*, p. 145.

92. "It would seem difficult . . . before venturing to disapprove.": Wilcox, p. 177.

93. "These weapons, warned . . . formidable only at a distance.": Gibbon, *Artillerist's Manual*, p. 145.

93. "It was essential that . . . a peculiarly French arm.": *Military Gazette*, Vol. 2, No. 14, July 15, 1859, p. 214.

93. "The French soldiers were . . . practiced hands, lungs and legs.": Steinmetz, pp. 382–383.

93. "Though a long-range exchange . . . point of the bayonet.": Citing Captain Brabazon; *Military Gazette*, Vol. 3, No. 10, May, 15, 1860, pp. 152, 155.

93. "Interviewed after the short war . . . 'made lots of prisoners.' ": Steinmetz, p. 383.

94. "Gunpowder, crossbows, long bows . . . Hurrah for the bayonet!": *Military Gazette*, Vol. II, No. 14, July 15, 1859, p. 214, writing from Paris June 28, 1859.

95. "Remarking that the only . . . to render their verdict.": *Military Gazette*, Vol. II, No. 16, Aug. 15, 1859, p. 243.

95. "All 48 shots hit the mark . . . within a 2 foot square.": Wilcox, p. 218.

95. "Within minutes the raiders . . . plus others wounded.": Blanche, pp. 73–74.

96. "More pointedly, some of . . . waste precious ammunition.": *Military Gazette*, Vol. 3, No. 18, Sept. 15, 1860, p. 276.

96. "As a result only . . . for continued testing.": Wilcox, pp. 216, 218.

97. "The writer concluded . . . 'double line of Kentucky rifles.' ": *The Atlantic Monthly*, October, 1859, Vol. 4, XXIV, pp. 444–455, *Military Gazette*, Vol. 2, No. 22, Nov. 15, 1859, p. 345.

97. "As events would turn out . . . lone military 'iconodule.' ": Antonym of "iconoclast," literally one who venerates icons — *Webster's Third New International Dictionary*.

98. "Colston went on to . . . as it turned out.": "R.E.C.", p. 18.

98. "Attempting to explain . . . movement of 'The Zouaves.' ": *Frank Leslie's Illustrated Newspaper*, Vol. XI, No. 285, New York, May 4, 1861, p. 385.

98. "The 'individuality, self-reliance . . . his most valuable qualities.' ": *Military Gazette*; Vol. 3, No. 14; July 15, 1860, pp. 210–211.

99. "If the French have . . . trained in the same way?": "R.E.C.", p. 18.

99. "The second and more believable . . . their own deprecations.": *Military Gazette*, Vol. 3, No. 14, July 15 1860, pp. 212–213.

99. "The most publicized . . . 'exhibition of athletic soldiership.": *Frank Leslie's Illustrated Newspaper*, Vol. X, No. 244, New York, July 28, 1860, pp. 145–146, 152.

100. "Once they fired . . . stomachs to fire again.": SA-NS, Vol. III, No. 5, July 28, 1860, p. 71.

101. "Paying closer attention . . . iron artillery pieces.": Testimony of Major T. J. Rodman, JCCW-HA; Rep Com. No. 121; pp. 97, Washington, Feb. 6, 1864.

102. "Now, since the shrinkage . . . the layers apart.": Brig Gen. George D. Ramsey, Chief of Ordnance; JCCW-HA, Rep Com. No. 121; p. 7, Washington, Jan. 27, 1864.

102. "Assured there was not . . . a 50% share.": Major T. J. Rodman JCCW-HA, Rep Com. No. 121; p. 97, Washington, Feb. 6, 1864.

102–103. "Though this weapon . . . gun was flawed.": Capt. James Benton, JCCW-HA, Rep Com. No. 121; p. 65, Washington, Feb 2, 1864.

103. "In every case Rodman's . . . traditional counterpart.": Mr. Charles Knap, JCCW-HA, Rep Com. No. 121; p. 84, Washington, Feb. 4, 1864.

103. "Unfortunately, a design . . . beneath the breech.": Capt. James Benton, JCCW-HA, Rep Com. No. 121; p. 65, Washington, Feb. 2, 1864.

103. "Finally, on November 16 . . . at Pitt Foundry.": Brig Gen. George D. Ramsey, Chief of Ordnance; JCCW-HA, Rep Com. No. 121; p. 7, Washington, Jan. 27, 1864.

103. "According to cannon, . . . European military circles.": Parrott, p. 4.

103. "The Rodman mortars . . . rounds had been fired.": Capt. James Benton to the JCCW, JCCW-HA, Rep Com. No. 121; p. 65, Washington, Feb 2, 1864.

103. "A standard 24–pounder . . . at Fort Monroe.": Gen. William F. Barry to the JCCW-HA, Rep Com. No. 121; p. 49, Washington, January 19, 1864.

104. "This piece, which . . . only the fifth round!": Dickey, p. 18.

104. "Offering this statement . . . with this assessment.": *Military Gazette*, Vol. 2, No. 20, Oct. 15, 1859, p. 310.

105. "The ordnance used . . . way to 32-pounders.": *Military Gazette*, Vol. 3, No. 1, Jan. 1, 1860, p. 9.

105. "The tests at Fort Monroe . . . perform ongoing trials.": *Military Gazette*, Vol. 3, No. 1, Jan. 1, 1860, p. 2.

105. "Disappointed, Treadwell recognized . . . would be futile.": Treadwell, pp. 10–12.

106. "Experience soon demonstrated . . . was $10 apiece.": Captain James Benton JCCW-HA, Rep Com. No. 121; p. 67, Washington, Feb 2, 1864.

106. "Thus armed, some . . . adoption that year.": Taylor, F. pp. 22–23, citing *Les canons rayé Études Militaire*, J. Schmoelzl (Lt. Col. Artillery). Translated from German by E. Heydt (Sous-Lt. artillery), Paris, 1860, p. 41.

106. "Parrott began to . . . in 1857 or '58.": Captain Alfred Mordecai, JCCW-HA, Rep Com. No. 121; p. 54, Washington, Feb 1, 1864.

106. "So that the piece . . . band near the breech.": Hazlett, p. 88.

107. "This, however, was . . . the Read projectile.": Dickey, p. 18.

107. "The Virginia authorities . . . twelve Parrott rifles.": Wise, pp. 63–64.

107. "Though praising this . . . 'will be rifled also.' ": *Military Gazette*, Vol. 3, No. 22, Nov. 15, 1860, p. 339.

158. "The only other tangible . . . to rifled artillery.": Wise, Vol. I, p. 80.

107–108. "If we wait for . . . better than none.": *Military Gazette*, Vol. 3, No. 23, Dec. 1, 1860, p. 354.

CHAPTER 6

109. "An oared vessel . . . batter enemy ships.": Dupuy and Dupuy, p. 464; Greene, p. 16.

109. "The homely 800 to 1000 . . . outlying Japanese islands.": *Army and Navy Journal,* Vol. I, No. 20, Jan. 9, 1864, p. 306.

110. "If the illustration . . . on-board artillery.": Citing "A Man of War," C. N. Robinson, *The Graphic,* Feb. 10, 1894, in SA-NS , Vol. LXX, No. 7, April 28, 1894, p. 260.

110. "Disillusioned with his . . . vetoed the plan.": *Atlantic Monthly,* Vol., VIII, No. 46, p. 227.

111. "There was a sharp . . . serve as a ram.": SA-NS, Vol. VII, No. 21, May 24, 1862, p. 328.

111. "Seeing little need . . . John Stevens's proposals.": Tucker, p. 13.

111. "Both conditions were . . . was promptly rejected.": *United Service Magazine,* p. 211, excerpting Sir Howard Douglas' *Treatise on Naval Gunnery.*

112. "A decade later in . . . 'direction to ricochet.' ": Gardiner, p. 51; citing Samuel Eliot Morison *Old Bruin: Commodore Matthew C. Perry,* Boston, 1967, p. 129.

112. "This time, however . . . their latest proposal.": This board consisted of Stewart and Perry and Colonels Thain and Totten; SA-NS , Vol. VIII, No. 6, Feb. 7, 1863, p. 81.

112. "The last hurdle was . . . to complete the project.": Tucker, pp. 13–14.

112. "Secondly, although thick . . . ignite the wood.": House Report, No. 448, 2nd session, 27th congress, p. 10.

113. "Not discouraged, in . . . obstruct enemy passage.": Fishbourne, E.G., Capt. (R.N.); p. 359.

113. "Fresh air would . . . a ventilation system.": Tucker, pp. 14–16.

113–114. "The Stevenses intended . . . 'any now in use.' ": SA-NS, Vol. V, No. 9, (Aug. 31, 1861) p. 129.

115. "John Laird, who . . . Navy of their value.": Gardiner, p. 48.

115. "In both cases . . . were easily repaired.": Halsted, *Iron-Cased Ships Pt. 1* Vol. 5, No. 17: P. pp. 128, 132.

116. "French tests in 1834–35 . . . to protect naval vessels.": Fishbourne, E.G., Capt. (R.N.); *Iron Ships and Iron Plates,* p. 359.

116. "Although none of the . . were greatly shattered.": Halsted, JRUSI, Vol. 5, No. 7; *Iron-Cased Ships Pt. 1;* p. 129.

117. "The writer of 'Iron-Clad . . . the closest examination.": *Blackwood's Edinburgh Magazine;* Vol. 88, No. 541, p. 626.

117. "Though it was too . . . troop transport ships.": Gardiner, p. 49.

118. "Numerous difficulties were . . . *Lave,* and *Tonnante.*": Osbon, p. 189.

118. "Their masts cut down . . . or were burned alive": *Manufacturer and Farmer's Journal:* Feb. 18, 1861 Vol. LX, No. 14, p. 1 citing *The NY Post.*

119. "In return, the British . . . existing British designs.": Greenhill, pp. 301–303.

120. "One of these vessels . . . loosening of three rivets.": Tyrrell, p. 311; Greenhill, p. 305.

120. "The admiralty took . . . more floating batteries.": Greenhill, p. 305.

120. "Had the dispute . . . Venice and Trieste.": Greene, p. 31; *Blackwood's Edinburgh Magazine*, Vol. 88, No. 541, p. 622.

120. "At 250 feet long . . . 4.3 to 4.7-inch iron plates.": Chesneau, p. 286.

123. "Both shared three . . . profile on the water.": Coles, pp. 280–281.

123. "Delivering a talk . . . outgrowth of Coles's ideas.": *Journal of the Franklin Institute*, 3rd series, Vol. XIII, No. 6 (Dec, 1861) pp. 369-370.

124. "Unlike Coles's second design . . . single two-gun cupola.": *Journal of the Franklin Institution*, 3rd Series, Vol. XLII, Dec. 1861, No. 6, pp. 369–382, describing "A Proposal for a Class of Gunboats capable of engaging Armour-plated ships at sea, accompanied with Suggestions on Armour-Plates" in Proceedings from the British Association in the *London Athen'um*, Sept. 1861.

124. "The crew will be . . . cannot ignore it.": SA-NS, Vol. IV, No. 3, Jan. 19, 1861, p. 37; These are *canonnières* nos. 1–5 & 11 cited in *Conway's* p. 285.

124–125. "Confidence in the . . . type of armored ship.": SA, Vol. 4, No. 15, April 13, 1861, p. 235.

125. "In 1854 Ericsson . . . deflect enemy shot easily.": Dorr, p. 13.

125. "Napoleon commissioned . . . complete the vessel successfully.": SA, Vol. VIII, No. 23, Feb. 19, 1853, p. 178.

125. "The most interesting . . . three Congreve rockets.": Mazing, pp. 72–73, 94–95.

126. "He created what . . . for this purpose.": SA, Oct. 13, 1849, Vol. V, No. 4, p. 24.

126. "In 1852 Day came . . . American naval authorities.": SA, Vol. VII, No. 26, March 13, 1852, p. 204; Vol. 7, No. 34, May 8, 1852, p. 268.

126. "On July 20, 1855 . . . 'Deep Diving Boat.' ": *The Engineer*, March 7, 1856, p. 121.

126. "Neither variant succeeded . . . the Crimean War.": Greene, pp. 21–22.

126. "As soon as the . . . below the waterline.": SA, Vol. VIII, No. 23, Feb. 19, 1853, p. 178.

CHAPTER 7

129. "Such preparations only . . . with twenty-four artillery pieces.": Wise, Vol. I, pp. 62–63.

129. "The article concluded . . . 'of this Union.' ": D. Eldredge, p. 1, citing *Military Gazette*, Nov. 15, 1861.

130. "In the December 10 . . . 'revolution in the country.' ": D. Eldredge, p. 1, *Military Gazette*, Dec. 15, 1861, pp. 1–2.

130. "The day this warning . . . on a 'war footing.' ": *Manufacturer and Farmer's Journal*, Jan. 3/61, Vol. XL, No. 1; p. 1.

130. "Less than 2 weeks . . . recruiting 2000 men.": *Manufacturer and Farmer's Journal*, Jan. 14/61, Vol. XL, No. 4, p. 1.

130. "By January 21 . . . and Worcester, Massachusetts": *Manufacturer and Farmer's Journal*, Jan. 21/61, Vol. XL, No. 6, p. 1.

130–131. "However, it was widely . . . ineffective garrisons.": Grant, p.138.

131. "In April 1861 . . . miles from Richmond.": Henderson, *The Science of War*, p. 134; Others have supplied varying numbers. The British military historian Henderson estimated there were 16,000 men while the Confederate Eggleson placed the entire Federal force at only 10,000 men; Henderson, p. 106, Eggleson, p. 22.

131. "The District of Columbia, . . . contribute 1680 men.": Bishop, p. 17.

132. "The state's governor . . . for volunteers, instead.": Croffut, p. 43.

132. "Stationed at the . . . remainder stood guard.": *New York Times*, April 19, 1861; Vol. X, No. 2988, p. 1.

133. "The situation dramatically . . . way into the capital.": Foote, *Battles and Leaders*, Vol. I, pp. 53–54.

133. "The regiment began . . . its destination, the capital.": Clarke, pp. 4–17.

134. "Once there, they . . . to Washington City.": The travels of the Second Rhode Island Regiment were typical of New England regiments that were sent to the "front." On June 19 the regiment embarked on the steamer Kill Van Kull at India Point (Fox Point, just outside of Providence) during the late afternoon. It put in for a few hours at New York City then shoved off to Elizabeth where the men disembarked at 10 *a.m.* on the next day. Travelling via rail, the regiment passed through Harrisburg in the early morning of the 21st and arrived at Baltimore at 8 *a.m.* The march through hostile Baltimore was without incident and the men were once again entrained by 10 *a.m.* The only sign of the hostile populace was a few bricks thrown at the train as it pulled away from Washington Station. Woodbury, p. 24 and Reichardt, pp. 6–7.

135. "We wished for morning . . . long looked for halt.": Marvin, p. 32.

136. "In Pennsylvania the . . . the Twelfth Pennsylvania.": When the company along with its parent regiment was disbanded three months later nearly all of its men reentered service as commissioned officers. By the end of the war, sixty-nine officers had started one—major general, nine colonels, four lieutenant colonels, six majors, twenty captains, twenty-nine lieutenants, plus one O. S. and a sergeant not counting one major serving with rebels; Donaghy, pp. 14–15.

136. "There were cases . . . served as officers.": Cox, *Battles and Leaders*, Vol. I, p. 97.

136. "Originally, a regiment . . . man regimental staff.": Curry, p. 125.

137. 1 Principal Musician [list]: Beecher, p. 16.

137. "Its ten infantry companies . . . and officers, respectively.": Bennet G.

138. "The Second New Hampshire . . . use in late July.": Reichardt, pp. 13.

138. "The following sequence . . . 7th, and 2nd companies.": Curry, p. 71.

138. "The existing height . . . from 5'4" to 5'3".": Eldredge, pp. 16–18.

CHAPTER 8

141. "More theoretical subjects . . . left to the evening.": Cox, in *Battles and Leaders*, Vol. I, p. 96.

141. "Major General Jacob Cox . . . fours from double ranks.": Cox, *Battles and Leaders*, Vol. I, pp. 94–95.

141. "Col. Benjamin F. Scribner . . . the soldier's duties.": Scribner, p. 15.

141. "In Butterfield's opinion . . . 'company in the regiment.' ": Butterfield, p. 1.

142. "Remembering back to this . . . 'knowledge of war.' ": Henderson; *The Science of War*, p. 135; citing *Memoirs of General Sherman*, Vol. I, pp. 181–82.

142. "The men in this regiment . . . the word 'F-O-R-W-A-R-D!' ": Curtis, Newton Martin; p. 26.

142. "Col. Scribner records . . . at Muldrough's Hill.": Scribner, p. 24.

142. "Donaghy was forced . . . 'as some of them.' ": Donaghy, pp. 5–6.

143. "Once again, whatever . . . started all over again.": Scribner, p. 15.

143. "Despite all official . . . had previously served.": Bishop, p. 31.

144. "Needless to say . . . for his negligence.": Donaghy, p. 28.

144. "Someone walking around . . . his new profession.": Curtis, Newton Martin; p. 26.

145. "It was a cruel . . . from the east.": Marvin, pp. 15–16.

146. "The men rushing to . . . old-fashioned smoothbore muskets.": Alexander, *Military Memoirs*, p. 8.

146. "The most impractical . . . he knew the best.": Eggleson, p. 20.

146. "As a result of . . . on the battlefield.": Orweig, p. 15.

146. "Despite the conscientious . . . a 'modern soldier.' ": Eggleson, p. 29.

146. "And yet they acquitted . . . insubordination in camp.": Eggleson, p. 38.

147. "True, on the exercise . . . drills under study.": Eggleson, p. 31.

147. "To ensure proper order . . . 'breeding of the men.": Morgan, W. H., p. 26.

148. "It rests then upon . . . known as family.": Eggleson, p. 31.

148. "Pendleton eventually left, . . . rest of the journey.": Baylor, pp. 19–20.

148. "It was inevitable . . . commissions during elections.": Robson, p. 25.

149. "Von Borcke had to . . . this was accomplished.": Borcke, Vol. I, pp. 19–20.

149. "Throughout the war . . . and hungry looking.": Alexander, *Military Memoirs;* p. 8.

149. "Death has few terrors . . . the field of battle.": Eggleson, p. 38.

150. "Their Northern foe . . . or the local store.": Ripley, William, p. 3.

150. "But most of all . . . as you would poison.": *New York Times*, April 24, 1861; Vol. X, No. 2993, p. 2.

151. "This could be tied up . . . sun was too strong.": *Manufacturer and Farmer's Journal*, April 25/61, Vol. XL, No. 33 p. 4.

152. "The January 19, 1861 . . . of men now living.": SA-NS, Vol. 4, No. 3, January 19, 1861, p. 48.

152. "Napoleon III, is . . . any other person living.": SA-NS, Vol. 4, No. 5, Feb 2, 1861, p. 73.

153. "Cavalry must now . . . riflemen and artillery.": SA-NS, Vol. 4, No. 19, May 11, 1861, p. 292.

153. "If our raw recruits . . . account of themselves.": *New York Times*, May 1, 1861; Vol. X, No. 3000, p. 4.

154. "The campaigns in Sicily . . . soldiers in this crisis.": *New York Times*, May 1, 1861, Vol. X, No. 3000, p. 4.

155. "The saber bayonet is . . . intend to rely upon.": SA-NS, Vol. IV, No. 24, June 15, 1861, p. 379.

156. "The difference in these . . . spirit of the volunteers.": *Manufacturer and Farmer's Journal*: May 20/61, Vol. XL, No. 40 p. 1.

156–157. "Passes from camp were . . . have a good time.": Favill, p. 50.

157. "This was apparently a . . . was doing the same.": Barrett, p. 9.

157. "Many young officers . . . within the regular army.": Cox, in *Battles and Leaders*, Vol. I, p. 94.

158. "Faced with the necessity . . . the Seventh Indiana.": Scribner, pp. 13–14.

158. "The Confederate army . . . around the Southern states.": Henderson, *The Science of War*, p. 134.

158. "In practice the officers . . . in the regular army.": Cox, *Battles and Leaders*, Vol. I, p. 94; also Grant, p. 124.

CHAPTER 9

160. "A sharp-eyed person . . . Napoleon III in 1858.": *London Illustrated News*, Vol. XXXII, No. 896, Feb. 27, 1858, p. 222.

160. "The reader would also . . . during the same period.": *The Engineer*, March 7, 1856, p. 121.

161. "If this was not . . . the piece inoperable.": SA-NS, Vol. IV, No. 3, Jan. 19, 1861, p. 48.

161. "Citing the Armstrong's . . . muzzle-loading rifled artillery.": SA-NS, Vol. IV, No. 5, Feb. 2, 1861, p. 73; Vol. IV, No. 3, Jan. 19, 1861, p. 48.

161. "In contrast, writers for . . . Europeans' the previous year.": *New York Times*, May 8, 1861, Vol. X, No. 3004, p. 4.

162. "Moreover, the extreme . . . to buckle or strip.": SA-NS, Vol. IV, No. 5, Feb. 2, 1861, p. 73.

163. "Since the Whitworths . . . 3 miles distant.": Testimony of Gen. William F. Barry, JCCW-HA; Rep Com. No. 121; pp. 48–49, Washington, Jan. 19, 1864.

163. "In Virginia . . . employed at Antietam.": Johnson, Curt; p. 26.

163. "Artillery destined for . . . Corps of Artillery.": *Manufacturer and Farmer's Journal*: April 25/61 Vol. XI, No. 33 p. 1, p. 4. Incidentally, this battery was present with the First Rhode Island at Bull Run.

163–164. "The manufacturer wired . . . allowed to do so.": Springfield Republican cited in the *Manufacturer and Farmer's Journal*: April 25, 1861 Vol. XI, No. 33 p. 1, p. 4.

164. "This projectile, incidentally, . . . in the United States.": Taylor, p. 23.

164. "This conveniently converted . . . or James rifles.": Curry, pp. 42–44.

164–165. "He explained that . . . 'best he had seen.' ": Ripley, W, p. 169.

165. "When Union Gen. . . . number of James Rifles.": OR Vol. I No. 2, pp. 345–346.

165. "After the battle . . . nine such weapons.": Wise, Vol. I, p. 72.

165. "After capturing the fort . . . 'that can be desired.' ": OR Vol. I No. 6, p. 164.

165. "The trick was to . . . negate the windage.": Curry, pp. 42–44.

166. "To the gunners . . . mouth of the barrel.": Johnson, Curt, p. 25.

166. "The projectile, instead of . . . inserted into the tube.": Beecher.

166. "Having fallen into disfavor . . . year of the war.": Ripley, Warren; p. 169.

166. "Ripley immediately overturned . . . Parrotts on May 23.": Captain James Benton, JCCW-HA, Rep Com. No. 121; p. 67, Feb. 2, 1864; Hazlett, p. 88.

166. "When Barry returned . . . Parrott artillery pieces.": JCCW-HA, Rep Com. No. 121; p. 50, Gen. William F. Barry, Jan. 19, 1864.

166. "Encouraged even more . . . 300-pounder weapons.": JCCW-HA, Rep Com. No. 121; pp. 39, Capt. S. V. Benèt (Ordnance Dept.), Jan. 28, 1864. Also Capt. Alfred Mordecai, Feb 1, 1864, p. 54 of the same source.

168. "Other than this . . . 'very desirable' weapon.": OR Vol. I No. 2, p. 100.

169. "Hundreds of Jackson's pupils . . . carried much weight.": Wise, Vol. I, p. 66.

169. "He countered with the Anaconda Plan.": Reed, pp. 5–6, 389.

170. "With ninety ships, 1200 . . . resources for the task.": Coombe, p. 9.

170. "Out of the forty . . . available for action.": Soley, *Battles and Leaders,* Vol. I, p. 614.

170. "Although these more . . . in November 1860.": Proceedings from the British Association: from the *London Athen'um,* Sept. 1861; *Journal of the Franklin Institution,* 3rd Series, Vol. XLII, No. 6, (Dec 1861); pp. 369–382; *Military Gazette,* Vol. 3, No. 1, Jan. 15, 1860, p. 12.

170. "The *Blackburne* articles . . . known in history.": *Blackwood's Edinburgh Magazine,* Nov. & Dec. 1860, pp. 616–632, 633–49; March 1861, pp. 304–317.

171. "The editors of *Scientific* . . . 'of pasteboard soldiers.' ": SA-NS, Vol. IV, No. 3, Jan. 19, 1861, p. 41.

171. "The *New York Times* . . . Armstrong rifled cannon.": *New York Times,* May 8, 1861, Vol. X, No. 3004, p. 4.

172. "He recommended that . . . should be constructed.": Soley, *Battles and Leaders,* Vol. I, pp. 616.

172. "Only 2 years before . . . a monument to folly.": *Military Gazette,* Vol. II, No. 5, March 1, 1859, p. 69.

172. "On July 16 . . . Congress to take action.": *The World: Morning Courier and New York Enquirer,* Friday, July 16, p. 4.

173. "We would urge . . . before it is too late.": SA-NS, Vol. V, No. 9, Aug. 31, 1861, p. 132.

174. "E. H. Derby, a friend . . . American iron-cased ships.": *The Congressional Globe,* Washington City, 1861, 37th congress, 1st session, p. 210.

174. "Citing articles recently . . . be an abysmal failure.": *The Congressional Globe,* Washington City, 1861, 37th congress, 1st session, p. 256.

174–175. "It appears the project . . . would capsize and sink.": *Manufacturer and Farmer's Journal:* Feb. 18, 1861 Vol. XI, No. 14, p. 1.

175. "On May 28 . . . its own motive force.": *Manufacturer and Farmer's Journal:* June 6, 1861 Vol. XL, No. 45, p. 1.

175. "Both the converted . . . blockading New Orleans.": *Manufacturer and Farmer's Journal:* July 15, 1861 Vol. XI, No. 56, p. 1, p. 2; Sept 26, 1861, Vol. XL, 77; p. 1; Aug 12/61 Vol. XL, No. 63; p. 1.

176. "The gun weighed 6700 pounds . . . static defensive situations.": Frank *Leslie's Illustrated Newspaper,* Vol. XI, No. 286, New York, May 11, 1861, p. 414.

176. "Dickenson and the gun . . . Annapolis under guard.": *Frank Leslie's Illustrated Newspaper,* Vol. XII, No. 287, New York, May 18, 1861, pp. 1–2.

176. "Apprehended, De Villeroi . . . its crew were confiscated.": *New York Times,* May 18, 1861; Vol. X, No. 3013, p. 1.

Chapter 10

177. "A report submitted to . . . best breech-loading firearms.": SA-NS, Vol. IV, No. 4, Jan. 26, 1861, p. 57.

177–178. "Jefferson Davis specifically . . . 'breech-loading carbines.' ": OR Vol. IV, No. 1, p. 420.

178. "Writing to Floyd on . . . patent breech-loading rifles.": OR Vol. III, No. 1, p. 122.

178. "Though it is highly . . . equipped with this weapon.": *Rebellion Records,* Vol. I, section 3, p. 95, citing the *Intelligencer* of Oxford, Mississippi.

178. "In the weeks following . . . Zouaves with beechloaders.": SA-NS, Vol. IV, No. 24, June 15, 1861, p. 379.

178. "After the humiliating events . . . by their namesake.": OR Vol. III, No.1, p. 460.

178. "Several weeks earlier . . . with the same weapon.": OR Vol.III, No. 1, p. 262.

178. "He went on to . . . Colonel Duryea's command.": OR Vol. I, No. 2, p. 668.

179. "In retrospect, we . . . on the battlefield.": Marvin, pp. 18–19; see also OR Vol. III, No.1, p. 93.

179. "The point being made . . . obviously bogus, as well.": *Rebellion Records,* Vol. I, section 3, p. 95.

180. "Though acknowledging . . . or extremely accurate.": SA-NS, Vol. IV, No. 4, Jan. 26, 1861, p. 57.

181. "These opinions, mostly . . . and the *Military Gazette*.": *Military Gazette*; Vol. II, No. 22; Nov. 15, 1859; p. 345.

181. "They reasoned that . . . as accurately as any other.": Cited in SA-NS, Vol. IV, No. 9, March 2, 1861, p. 134.

181. "He argued that the . . . surface of the barrel.": Cited in SA-NS, Vol. IV, No. 9, March 2, 1861, p. 134.

181. "Unfortunately for many rifle . . . in May 1861.": Drury & Gibbons, p. 58.

182. "It was feared that . . . all of their ammunition.": SA-NS, Vol. VIII, No. 10, March, 7, 1863, p. 150.

182. "It was reported, for . . . on the Ibernian Peninsula.": *Army & Navy Journal,* Vol. I, No. 1863, p. 11.

182. "This prompted one . . . cause a single death.": *New York Commercial,* May 21; cited in *Rebellion Records,* Vol. I, section 3, 95.

183. "Not only would breechloaders . . . 'breech-loading toys.' ": SA-NS, Vol. IV, No. 24, June 15, 1861, p. 379.

183. "Lt. Col. Ferdinand Lecomte . . . among Union infantry.": Lecomte, p. 65.

183. "There was no standardization even of caliber size.": Bishop, p. 25.

183. "Originally, the Eighth . . . hunting rifles and shotguns.": Wright, T. J., p. 19.

183–184. "One of its companies . . . to take any weapons.": Bennet, L, pp. 59–60.

184. "The Second Minnesota . . . until March 29, 1863.": Bishop, p. 85.

184. "The First Rhode Island . . . for percussion caps.": Rhodes, p. 10.

184. "These were put aside . . . muskets shortly thereafter.": Ward, p. 14.

184. "Although some Union troops . . . of the Austrian weapon.": Bilby, *Civil War Firearms,* pp. 62–67.

184. "However, of the five . . . Lorenz rifle musket.": Bilby, Remember, pp. 608–622.

185. "Edwin Porter Alexander . . . with rifle muskets.": Alexander, *Fighting for the Confederacy,* p. 61.

185. "These latter, however, . . . about 20 rounds.": Ross, F., p. 156.

185. "On April 21 . . . South Carolina Volunteers, respectively.": OR Vol. I, No. 14, p. 481.

186. "The center companies . . . be supplied locally.": OR Vol. 1, No. 9, pp. 464–465.

186. "It is unclear whether . . . across the regiment.": Dixon, pp. 114–115.

186. "Captain Fitzgerald Ross, . . . and Springfield rifles.": Ross, F., p. 155.

186. "In his personal memoirs . . . rid of smoothbore muskets.": Alexander, *Fighting for the Confederacy;* p. 122.

186. "Arming the flank companies . . . time-consuming, disruptive task.": OR Vol. I, No. 34 (2), p. 1002.

187. "The men in Brig. Gen . . . very primitive arms.": Snead, pp. 269–271.

187. "Forrest of course . . . on December 17 1862.": Jordan, p. 195.

187. "The other companies . . . smoothbore percussion cap muskets.": Watson, p. 162.

188. "Although this is a . . . was sufficiently armed.": Ross, F., p. 155.

188. "The fate of many . . . upon an advancing column.": Gibbon, *Artillerist's Manual,* p. 355.

189. "When the men in the . . . themselves with revolvers.": Rhodes, p. 10. Prior to Bull Run, this artillery battery had been attached to the First Rhode Island Infantry.

189. "In her history . . . probably an exaggeration.": Whitcomb, p. 19; Opinion of Joseph G. Bilby expressed directly to the author.

189. "For the purpose of . . . to the 'unloaded gun' ": Webster, pp. 34–35.

189–190. "Again, some modern . . . conclusion of the Civil War.": Opinion of Joseph G. Bilby expressed directly to the author.

190. "In 1863 the Ordnance . . . self-defense at close range.": Buell, p. 58.

190. "Few details are provided . . . marksmen in the regiment.": OR Vol. I No. 3, p. 437.

191. "During the charge . . . in rapid succession.": SA-NS, Vol. VIII, No. 19, May, 9, 1863, pp. 293–294.

191. "Placing ads for expert . . . to Washington City.": *Manufacturer and Farmer's Journal:* May 13/61 Vol. XL, No. 47 p. 2.

191. "The shooter was allowed . . . upon his shoulder.": Ripley, William, p. 5.

195. "Most of the two . . . rifles for a while longer.": Peet; letter to father from Camp Porter 1st regiment USSS, Near Hampton, Va., Porter's Division, March 30th, 1962.

192. "Many complained that although . . . dangerous to its owner.": Ripley, William; pp. 11–12, 16.

193. "Union veterans would . . . during this last battle.": Nesbit, p. 19.

193. "However, the manufacturer . . . muzzle in a crisis.": Drury & Gibbons, p. 58.

194. "Even the single-shot . . . they were to replace.": Curry, p. 71.

CHAPTER 11

195. "A few days before . . . 'know how to retreat.' ": Woodbury, p. 41.

196. "Captain William H. P. Steere, who served . . . search of the enemy.": Rhodes, *The First Campaign*, pp. 15–19.

196. "Strawberry and blackberry . . . an irresistible temptation.": Sherman, *Memoirs*, Vol. I, pp. 181; cited in Henerson, *The Science of War*, p. 135.

196. "In a rare moment . . . for any great distance.": Henderson, *Science*, p. 135; citing H. C. Fletcher, *History of the American War*, Vol. I, pp. 129–130.

196. "Though more refreshing . . . as the hours passed.": Woodbury, pp. 41–42.

196. "On July 20 General . . . 'the time they should.' ": OR, Vol. I, No. 2, p. 308.

197. "Despite the urgency . . . the preceding days.": Woodbury, pp. 41–42.

197. "Fortunately for the Union . . . attempts at its destruction.": Monroe, A, *Rhode Island Artillery*, pp. 14–16.

198–199. "The stampede was only . . . of the Rhode Islanders.": Favill, p. 32.

199. "I was in this . . . doing much of anything.": Favill, p. 33–34.

199. "Ordered to select available . . . 'I think I can hit him,' ": Estvan, Vol. I, p. 85.

199. "George Baylor, at this point . . . 'located by our people.' ": Baylor, p. 21.

200. "He would later confide . . . nothing to run from.": *Manufacturer and Farmer's Journal*, Aug. 1, 1861, Vol. XL, No. 61, p. 1.

200. "So upon this field . . . in order was repose.": Monroe, A; *Rhode Island Artillery*, p. 24.

200. "Capt. James R. Fry . . . efforts to stop men.": Capt. James R. Fry, *Battles and Leaders*, Vol. I, p. 191.

201. "According to this . . . a military organization.": Henderson, *Science*, pp. 135–136 quoting John G, Nicolay, The Outbreak of the Rebellion, pp. 195–195.

202. "But old soldiers will . . . embarked on ships.": Scribner, p. 259.

202. "According to Curtis . . . up Franklin's division.": Curtis, Newton, p. 44.

203. "Three years later . . . of active service.": Bishop, p. 195.

203. "The lure of leadership . . . with the regular forces.": Cox, in *Battles and Leaders*, Vol., I, p. 94.

204. "Partly to put a stop . . . of existing regiments.": Vaill, pp. 4–5; also McClellan, G. *Battles and Leaders*, Vol. II, p. 170.

205. "The other side of . . . the same errors.": McClellan, G; *Battles and Leaders*, Vol. II pp. 170–171.

205. "Those failing these . . . from active service.": Ward, p. 18.

206. "The rallied force . . . instructed to fall back.": Donaghy, p. 53.

206. "Not surprisingly, his men were initially indignant.": Reichardt, p. 15.

206. "A cordon of defensive works was hastily thrown up.": Woodbury, pp. 47–48.

206–207. "The men now . . . fall of Fort Sumter.": Vaill, p. 4.

207. "To set an example . . . were actually preferred.": Curtis, Newton; p. 54.

207. "Recruits with previous . . . attention to their advice.": Favill, pp. 45–50.

208. "Gradually, experience taught . . . a comfortable bed.": Scribner, p. 24; Webster, p. 41.

208. "As they gained experience . . . that pointed away.": Webster, p. 84.

208. "By his second campaign . . . plus a few essentials.": Robson, pp. 8–9.

208. "The unit became . . . reduced in size.": Bishop, pp. 198–199.

Chapter 12

211. "Bending over, he . . . with human fat.": Webster, p. 64.

212. "Reduced by the distance . . . 'swarms of bees.' ": Estvan, Vol. I, pp. 133–134.

213. "On a sunny day, . . . approaching the observer.": The bright finished Springfield was more telling in this regard than a blued Enfield; De Brack, p. 74.

213. "It was only at about . . . of individual soldiers.": De la Pierre, p. 30.

213. "Although most field . . . flat, open terrain.": Steinmetz, JRUSI, Vol. V, No. 19, p. 458.

214. "These of course . . . action was imminent.": Nesbit, p. 10.

214. "At first each company . . . per regiment was retained.": Izlar, p. 23.

215. "The adjutants then repeated these orders along the line.": Dinkins, p. 35.

215. "Every one of them . . . in the atmosphere.": Johnson, Charles F., p. 190.

215. "Bodies would lie . . . muskets as crutches.": Blackford, p. 131.

216. "Unlike the smoke . . . if any was present.": Noyes, p. 196.

216. "As the process . . . once more re-formed.": Blackford, p. 132.

217. "Coming all too close . . . close to one's ears.": Congdon, p. 99.

217. "One Northern newspaper . . . 'tumble at a great fire.' ": SA-NS, Vol. VII, No. 18, Nov. 1, 1862, p. 279.

217. "To John Robson . . . 'again along the line.' ": Robson, p. 98.

217. "George Noyes later . . . single battery or brigade.": Noyes, p. 196.

217. "He never forgot the . . . of those around him.": Hill, p. 384.

217–218. "Very occasionally, a caisson . . . throughout the immediate area.": Robson, p. 98.

218. "Then, without delay, . . . tragedy is re-enacted.": *History of the Nineteenth Regiment*, p. 182.

218. "This gap was produced . . . to get out its way.": Blackford, pp. 28, 32–33.

219. "It was impossible to . . . all dodging together.": *History of the Nineteenth Regiment*, p. 63.

219. "This reaction was so . . . 'grain in the wind.' ": *History of the Nineteenth Regiment*, p. 179.

219. "No matter how much . . . fire nearly unabated.": Joseph E. Johnston was in the process of chiding his officers at Seven Pines saying, "There is no use dodging like that, Colonel. When you hear the things they have passed," when a shell exploded seriously wounding him; Picket (Mrs.), p. 103.

219. "Other times the soldier . . . just tried to stop.": Phisterer, p. 17.

220. "Fired upon by . . . enemy pieces were rifled.": Neese, p. 30.

220. "The cannon turned out . . . and Confederate artillerymen." Monroe, p. 106.

221. "I watched it until . . . descending to earth.": Neese, p. 30.

221. "A second or so . . . feet to their rear.": Harris, p. 30.

221–222. "His comrades in the rear . . . broke out in laughter.": Phisterer, pp. 16–17.

222. "It was the burning . . . shot by or burst.": Moore, Edward, pp. 146–147.

222. "If both sides were . . . could be hit randomly.": Robson, p. 98.

222–223. "Glancing off the rifle . . . with the other.": De Forest, pp. 64–65.

223. "Another would convulsively . . . gushing from his wound.": Hill, p. 306.

223. "Though the bullet . . . colors as he fell.": De Forest, pp. 64–65.

224. "But more to the point . . . in time of battle.": Wing, pp. 69–70.

224–225. "Occasionally, one might . . . holding each corner.": Blackford, pp. 121–122.

225. "In many regiments musicians . . . to the surgeons' area.": *History of the Nineteenth Regiment,* p. 75; Ward, p. 2.

225. "The ambulances which . . . their ghastly cargo.": Robson, p. 98.

226. "The 'prayers, the curses' . . . of the roaring battle.": Blackford, p. 28.

226. "A soldier was slumped . . . moment or two more.": Abner, p. 68.

227. "The groans and moans . . . made the stoutest quail.": Hutchins, pp. 14–15.

327. "I was as sore . . . all over with a club.": SA-NS, Vol. VII, No. 22, Nov. 29, 1862, p. 283.

228. "What struck Davidison . . . 'as natural as life.' ": Davidson, p. 28.

228 "He always attributed . . . smell of the torn soil.": Congdon, p. 99.

228. "Horses, cannoneers, dismounted guns . . . like gibbets on high.": Hutchins, pp. 14–15.

229. "Roemer attributed this . . . the Confederates' diet.": Roemer, Jacob p. 89.

229. "Once again, he reasoned . . . in the opposing armies.": Moore, Edward, pp. 121–122.

229. "It was not uncommon . . . through the ground.": Roemer, Jacob, p. 55.

229. "The heavy rains soon . . . gruesome of scenes.": Favill, p. 121.

230. "Busy examining the skulls . . . full of teeth.": Peck, pp. 50–51.

230. "The bodies were then . . . a mortal wound." Blackford, p. 123.

231. "I do not mean . . . effect was that described.": Blackford, pp. 132–133.

231. "In one particular case . . . the dead and dying.": McLaughlin, pp. 56–57.

231. "Artillery tears its sheaves . . . well heaped windrows.": Blackford, p. 44.

231. "These of course were . . . on a major battlefield.": Jackson, pp. 64–65.

232. "Men can, in the . . . waste of human life.": Bishop, p. 54.

232. "Paradoxically, almost perversely . . . 'strawberries in a meadow.' ": Jackson, p. 64.

CHAPTER 13

233. "Often weighing up to . . . a torturous experience.": Robson, pp. 8–9.

235. "In his *Detailed Minutae* . . . after foraging expeditions.": McCarthy, pp. 20–26.

235. "McCarthy estimated that . . . forty of his comrades.": McCarthy, pp. 68–69.

236. "The salty liquid . . . sleeves of the blouse.": *History of the Nineteenth Regiment*, p. 213.

236. "Riding along these roads . . . to the side or front.": Bliss, *Reminiscences in the Service of the First Rhode Island Cavalry*, p. 26.

236. "This time the dust . . . 'of the rising moon.' ": *A History of the 102d Illinois*, p. 5.

236. "They appeared more . . . young and sturdy men.": Scribner, p. 56.

237. "In the fall . . . benefit of a fire.": Stevenson, William, p. 123.

237. "During one particularly . . . with exhausted stragglers.": Stevenson, William, p. 124.

237. "As this happened . . . not have recognized him.": Bliss, *Reminiscences in the Service of the First Rhode Island Cavalry*, p. 26.

237. "This extra effort . . . fell by the wayside.": Favill, pp. 88, 96.

237. "Cavalrymen would encounter . . . like the infantry.": Roemer, Jacob, p. 107.

238. "During this Herculean . . . water-soaked ground.": Holden, pp. 49–50.

238. "At some points . . . other clothing was found.": Bishop, p. 90.

239. "The situation did not . . . something 'nice" to eat.' ": Montgomery, pp. 61, 64, 68.

240. Two or three days' . . . one or two sittings.": Montgomery, p. 80.

241. "This austere regimen . . . adequate provisions.": Worsham, William, pp. 29–30.

241. "Unfortunately, the result . . . blow them apart!": Worsham, William, p. 97.

241. "Lying down, they . . . rain, snow, or sleet.": McCarthy, p. 25.

242. "William Worsham of the . . . completely empty stomachs!": Worsham, William, p. 29.

242. "Valuable time had . . . spokes and felloes (rims).": Davidson, p. 22.

244. "The countryside now . . . more relaxing sleep.": *102nd Illinois*, pp. 121–122.

244. "Some would be waiting . . . onto a steer or two.": Bishop, p. 161.

CHAPTER 14

247. "Faces turned pale . . . their {rifle} "muskets:". Adams, p. 34; June 30 at Glendale during the 1862 Peninsular campaign.

247. "And they had all . . . had been wounded.": Stimson, pp. 21–22.

248. "One might check if . . . with his clothing.": Jackson, O.; p. 71.

248. "A third would count . . . rained around them.": Scribner, pp. 75–76.

248. "For some the physical . . . twitch their fingers.": Curtis, Newton, p. 26.

248. "Once the paroxysm . . . 'have never came near.' ": De Forest, p. 59.

248. "Though not exempt . . . or withstand an assault.": Curtis, Newton, p. 269.

248. "De Forest observed . . . 'brilliantly as veterans.' ": De Forest, p. 59.

249. "Only with difficulty . . . behind which to hide.": Ward, p. 110.

249. "The next time the . . . closer to friendly troops.": Stimson, p. 18.

250. "Thus the shirks . . . fear and anxiety.": Scribner, p. 273.

250. "The man who appreciates . . . trusted to keep going.": Stimson, pp. 24–25.

250. "Abner, a Union private . . . 'in spite of themselves.' ": Abner, p. 185.

251. "I do not go into . . . ashamed to run.": Wing, p. 55.

251. "The shock from . . . the leaves overhead.": Abner, p. 185.

251. "In his experience . . . its mind and retire.": Bishop p. 127.

251–252. "Scribner had also . . . flying for safety.": Scribner, pp. 273–274.

252. "In Scribner's words . . . 'performance of duty.' ": Scribner pp. 75–76.

254. "They thought if . . . afford to be brave.": Ward, p. 66.

254. "On their part . . . 'help towards victory.' ": De Forest, pp. 65–66.

255. "The flag was recaptured . . . out of the position.": Scribner, pp. 282–283.

255. "Whether the men . . . orders had failed.": Bliss, *How I Lost my Sabre*, pp. 8–14.

256. "The colonel had realized . . . by constant practice.": Lippett, *Tactical Use of the Three Arms*, p. 32.

256. "During the Battle of Antietem . . . Charge at Gettysburg.": Adams, p. 44; Webster, p. 102; Wert, p. 196.

257. "The Union men . . . 'coarse and harsh.' ": Morgan, W. H., p. 70.

Chapter 15

259. "Tactical talent consists . . . he is entirely unprepared.": "Marmont p. 49. The marshal defined tactics as "the art of handling troops upon the field of battle, and of manoeuvring them without confusion . . . it is the science of the application of manoeuvres."

259. "The marshal was merely . . . final and crushing blow.": Bülow, p. 97.

260. "Although the psychological . . . Fortuné de Brack.": Bugeaud de la Piconnèrie in *The Practice of War*, Richmond, Va., 1863; De Brack, Fortuné, *Cavalry Outpost Duties*, New York, 1893; and Nolan, L.; *Cavalry: Its History and Tactics*, Columbia, S.C., 1864.

260. "Cautioning against thrusting . . . impaling an enemy.": De Brack, pp. 42–43.

260. "When slashing at an enemy . . . the victim's forehead.": De Brack pp. 42–43.

262. "According to the *à prest* . . . from the enemy.": Quincy, op. cit., Vol. VII, p. 60.

262. "Following the established . . . moments of the assault.": Colin, p. 25.

264. "The attackers, on the other . . . a now-defenseless enemy.": Cited in Colin, p. 25.

265. "The defenders, who . . . with lowered bayonets.": Cited in Le Blond, pp. 416–417.

266. "Bland informs us that . . . on the advancing forces.": Bland, First Ed.; pp. 145–147.

266. "The cadenced manual . . . as late as 1811.": Müller, William, Vol. II, p. 186.

267. "Only when ordered . . . with lowered bayonet.": Wolfe, pp. 47, 49, 52.

267. "More recent studies . . . for British victory.": Nosworthy, Sir Charles Oman, London, 1999, pp. 231–263.

268. "The French, for example . . . fury was unleashed.": This is discussed in much

greater detail in a previous work, specifically, Nosworthy, *With Musket Cannon and Sword*, pp. 219–244.

269. "Captain Henry Heth's . . . the Confederate cause.": Mosely; p. 297.

269. "On the Southern side . . . upon its adoption.": Morrow, pp. 26–28.

270. "The overwhelming consensus . . . 'queen of the battlefield.' ": *Military Gazette*, Vol. II, No. 22, Nov. 15, 1859, p. 345.

270. "In firing, each man . . . object in full view.": OR Vol. I, No. 51 (2), p. 175.

271. "As they neared . . . forerunners of success.": Mahan, p. 41.

271. "They must keep . . . rely upon the bayonet.": OR Vol. I, No. 14, p. 192.

271. "Then all would be . . . to 'aim low.' ": OR Vol. I, No. 14, p. 606.

272. "Men were never . . . see the enemy.": OR Vol. I, No. 22 (1), p. 83.

272. "Despite the enormous . . . with which it is given.": OR Vol. I, No. 38 (4), p. 42.

272. "In Circular No. 109 . . . 'the enemy's line powerless.' ": OR Vol. I, No. 42 (2), p. 344.

272. "In a letter to Gen. . . . at their knees.": OR Vol. I, No. XLI (3), p. 412; OR Vol. I, No. 22 (1), p. 83.

273. "Do not kill . . . to take prisoners.": OR Vol. I, No. 34 (2), p. 190.

273. "In a letter to Brig. Gen. . . . to a 'deadly range.' ": OR Vol. I, No. 41 (3), p. 663.

273. "Three weeks before . . . 'the enemy's eyes.' ": OR Vol. I, No. 41 (3), p. 412.

273. "Hindman's orders give . . . 'take deliberate aim.' ": OR Vol. I, No. 22 (1), p. 83.

273. "As to its effectiveness . . . stand such a fire.": OR Vol. I, No. 41 (3), p. 412.

273. "His August 20, 1864 . . . first and rear ranks.": OR Vol. I, No. 42 (2), pp. 343–344.

273–274. "Earlier in the war . . . 'volley and by ranks.' ": OR Vol. I, No. 30 (1), p. 168.

274. "Instead, he recommended . . . *fire by company*.": OR Vol. I, No. 10 (2), p. 326.

274. "In either case . . . front and rear ranks.": OR Vol. I, No. 38 (4), p. 671.

275. "The marshal did concede . . . the need arise.": Ney, *Memoirs*, Vol. II, pp. 368–369.

275. "Howard of course . . . blow to fall elsewhere.": OR Vol. I, No. 38 (5), p. 605.

275. "Regardless of the officers' . . . fire by file instead.": OR Vol. I, No. 19 (1), p. 608.

276. "Offensive tactics, which had . . . strength of the defenders.": McWhiney & Jamieson, p. xv.

278. "Patti Griffith's assertion . . . closest to the mark.": Griffith, *Battle Tactics;* p. 147.

CHAPTER 16

280. "The only way cavalry . . . type of 'mounted infantry.' ": Chesney, pp. 286–293, citing Capt. Wittich, *Das Fahnlein oder die Compagnie als die wahre tactische Einheit, etc.*, Wesel, 1849, pp. 16–63, 74–80.

280. "Like Wittich, Captain . . . combat as formerly.": Tyler, pp. 170–171.

280. "This was in line . . . a broken army.": Dixon, p. 114.

281. "He also argued that . . . accuracy at long range.": Steinmetz, JRUSI, Vol. V, No. 19, pp. 391–392, citing Renard *De la Cavalerie*, p. 147.

281. "This would waste . . . of the infantry line.": Steinmetz, pp. 391.

281. "Although he felt that . . . against equestrian foes.": Steinmetz, p. 455.

282. "Rather than the direct . . . opposing infantry position.": Steinmetz, pp. 474–475.

282. "In 1859 Capt. Cadmus . . . about 1200 yards.": Wilcox, p. 246.

282. "The same article . . . with riflemen and artillery.": SA-NS, Vol. 4, No. 19, May 11, 1861, p. 292.

283. "The journalist's argument . . . than 1500 infantrymen.": *New York Times*, April 23, 1861; Vol. X, No. 2992, p. 1. Another small article appeared in the *New York Times* on the April 26. This time the journalist advocated the use of the Second U.S. Cavalry regiment.

283. "This argument was . . . from the Indian territories.": *Manufacturer and Farmer's Journal:* April 25, 1861 Vol. XI, No. 33 p. 1, p. 4; *New York Times*, April 26, 1861; Vol. X, No. 2995, p. 8.

283. "During the initial rush . . . the secretary of war.": Starr, Vol. I, p. 65, citing James H. Stevenson, *Boots and Saddles: A History of the First Volunteer Cavalry of the War*, Harrisburg, Pa., 1979, pp. 37–38.

283. "Displaying initiative, McClellan . . . his military department.": Starr, Vol. I, p. 64, citing Charles D. Rhodes, *History of the Cavalry of the Army of the Potomac*, Kansas City, MO, 1900, No. 6; Thiele, "The Evolution of Cavalry," p. 33.

283. "Though cavalry played . . . mail delivery roles.": Glasier, pp. 21–22.

284. "However, spotting the Stars . . . obliqued left) and charge.": OR Vol. I, No. 2, p. 483.

284. "With no time to . . . over his shoulder.": Blackford, pp. 28–29.

285. " 'The Black Horse Cavalry . . . fearful to think of.' ": Starr, Vol. I, No. 65 citing James H. Stevenson, *Boots and Saddles: A History of the First Volunteer Cavalry of the War*, Known as the First New York (Lincoln) Cavalry (Harrisburg, Pa. 1979), pp. 37–38.

285. "Senator Ira Harris . . . Light Cavalry Regiment.": Glasier, p. 22–23.

285. "The rebellious mounts . . . been totally misplaced.": Glasier, pp. 35–36.

286. "Ross theorized that . . . fought on foot.": Ross, F., p. 30.

286–287. "By 1854 the Colt . . . sort of sword.": Steffen, Randy, Vol. II, pp. 20–21.

287. "This long continued . . . companies' received carbines.": OR Vol. I, p. 13.

287. "At the start of . . . May 23, 1861.": OR Vol. I, No. 2, p. 869.

287. "However, 6 weeks later . . . carbines and sabers.": OR Vol. I, No. 2, p. 722.

287. "In Missouri most . . . old-fashioned squirrel rifles.": Hubbard, p. 16.

287. "This problem certainly . . . interminably long time.": Tarrant, p. 26.

288. "Traveling much faster . . . into hopeless confusion.": Curry, p. 69.

288. "If not in the exact . . . Seven Years' War.": Bland, Eighth Edition, pp. 407–412; also Hinde, pp. 56, 90–92; and Dalrymple, pp. 320–321.

288. "De Brack had . . . the art of war.": De Brack, p. 209.

289. "In order to guarantee . . . within 50 yards.": OR Vol. I, No. 10 (1), p. 64.

289. "Panicked, the Confederates . . . a running fight.": OR Vol. I, No. 3, p. 239.

289. "McDonald complained . . . as most unequal.": OR Vol. I, No. 5, pp. 205–206.

290. "His cavalry had to . . . revolvers and sabers.": OR Vol. I, No. 8, p. 335.

290. "Only twenty or . . . his men to retire.": OR Vol. I, No. 12 (1), pp. 815–816.

290. "Unable to even approach . . .' more than spectators.' ": OR Vol. I, No. 23 (1) p. 196.

291. "He aborted the charge . . . the enemy position.": OR Vol. I, No. 8, p. 61.

291. "The Fourth Illinois Cavalry . . . charge could commence.": Avery, pp. 61–62.

291. "Writing to the secretary . . . 1000 Burnside carbines.": OR Vol. I, No. 9.

291. "The Second Iowa choose . . . 'battalion of riflemen.' ": OR Vol. I, No. 27 (1), p. 501; OR Vol. I—24 (2), p. 674, 677; OR Vol. I, No. 32 (1), p. 300, 301; OR Vol. I, No. 39 (1), 317.

291. "Two saber companies . . . from the front.": OR Vol. I, No. 17 (1), p. 20.

292. "Texan Cavalry in particular . . . relished these tactics.": OR Vol. I, No. 49 (3), p. 1046.

292. "Caught off guard . . . emptied their revolvers.": Wulsin; p. 22.

292. "The act was twice . . . with the same result.": OR Vol. I, No. 7, pp. 15, 17.

292. "It is believed that . . . the year 1600.": Daniel Père (1721), *Histoire de la Malice Françoise*, Vol. II, p. 498, citing Cavalier Melzo's *Regole Militari Sopra Il Governo Della Cavalleria*.

292. "The number of men . . . could join the fight.": Mason, p. 88.

293. "Not only were they . . . break from routine.": Whittaker, p. 16–19.

293. "The Seventh Missouri . . . (March 10, 1862).": OR Vol. I, pp. 334–335.

293. "Charged by enemy cavalry . . . forced to retire.": OR Vol. I, No. 22 (1).

294. "Still not satiated . . . with a single punch.": OR Vol. I, No. 3, p. 240.

294. "One man, Louis Farley, . . . the rebels' horses.": OR Vol. I, No. 2, p. 135.

295. "The major later . . . a left-handed man.": Baylor, p. 157.

295. "Writing at the end . . . wounds often survived!": Grandmaison, pp. 16–17.

295. "Thrust! Thrust! as often . . . and never uncovered.": De Brack, p. 42.

297. "Bliss was nearly knocked . . . painfully bruised ribs!": Bliss, *How I Lost My Sabre*, p. 8–14.

297. "This was especially . . . while in motion.": OR Vol. I, No. 6, p. 281.

298. "In the same letter . . . for cavalry service.": OR Vol. I, No. V 1, p. 965.

298. "By late 1861 . . . throughout the Confederacy.": OR Vol. I, No. 3, p. 573.

298. "Benjamin added that . . . provide the lances.": OR Vol. IV, No. 1, p. 948.

298. "Writing to the governor . . . *'of that arm'* [italics mine].": OR Vol. I, No. 10 (2), p. 334.

298. "While writing to . . . effective in battle.": OR Vol. I, No. 11 (3), p. 390.

298. "Instead of a long . . . close-in fighting.": OR Vol. I, No. 2, p. 953.

299. "To send cavalry . . . the fleetest hussar.": SA-NS, Vol. VI, No. 4, Jan. 25, 1862, p. 50.

299–300. "On April 7, 1862 . . . 'for a columbiad.' ": OR Vol. I, No. 8, p. 673.

300. "The remaining fifth . . . and charge tactics.": *A & N Journal*, Vol. 1, 8, p. 118 (Oct 17, 1863.)

300. "Although the first reference . . . in May that year.": OR Vol. I, No. 6, p. 331; Dyer's Compendium, Pt. 1 (Campaigns etc.), Union Regimental Index, Missouri, p. 172.

301. "After a skirmish . . . 'Stock's mounted infantry.' ": OR Vol. I, No. 10 (1), p. 18.

301. "When faced with . . . .2 days later.": OR III 2, p. 666; OR Vol. I, No. 13, p. 596.

301–302. "Proclaiming that this force . . . the Union position.": OR Vol. I, No. 17 (1), p. 49.

302. "Portions of the Minnesota . . . by mid-October.": OR Vol. III, No. 2, p. 666.

302. "On October 15, 1862 . . . the other at Paducah.": OR Vol. III, No. 2, p. 665.

302. "As a countermeasure . . . near year's end.": OR Vol. I, No. 17 (2), p. 462.

302. "To add to their efficiency . . . of the same character.": OR Vol. I, No. 27 (2), pp. 375–376.

303. "Although it had long . . . expose a weakness.": Bland, First Ed., p. 91.

303. "At Shiloh the Fourth . . . the charge was aborted.": Avery, pp. 61–62.

303. "Despite heavy defensive . . . bemired in a morass.": Jordan, p. 127; Hurst, p. 89.

305. "The latter unceremoniously . . . knapsacks, and blankets.": Baylor, pp. 163–164; OR Vol. I, No. 29 (1), p. 441.

305. "The first 400 yards . . . gallop in 30 seconds.": U.S. Army, *Instructions for Field Artillery*, p. 42.

306. "Some believed it was . . . fast-approaching cavalry.": Steinmetz, pp. 484–485.

306. "According to Bugeaud . . . of the assault.": Bugeaud "Instructions to the Fifty-sixth Regiment" in the *Practise of War*, p. 177.

307. "The instinct for survival . . . training and doctrine.": *Essai sur . . .* , Book I, pp. 275–276.

307. "The cavalry seeing them . . . when it is all over.": Thomkinson, p. 280.

307. "Many of the men . . . then on the other.": Jackson, p. 71.

308. "Only several men . . . were able to escape.": Leslie, pp. 324–326.

Chapter 17

314. "However, no sooner . . . again with the next.": Wulsin; p 23; citing Colonel Kennett's "A March from Cincinnati to Nashville."

314. "Dead animals placed . . . suitable drinking water.": Wulsin, p 20.

315. "It was only by 10 . . . the march resumed.": *A History of the 102d Illinois Infantry*, p. 4.

316. "The inside set of . . . over the precipice.": Webster, p. 83.

316. "In more difficult spots . . . inches at a time.": Webster, p. 52.

316. "This was a dangerous . . . out of control.": Roemer, Jacob, pp. 150–151.

317. "A series of sharp . . . action was imminent.": Blackford, p. 121.

319. "The battle had begun in earnest.": Robson, pp. 94–97.

320. "However, the precipitous . . . large college building.": OR Vol. I, No. 10 (1), p. 886.

321. "Most conspicuous among . . . Colonel Wolford himself.": Tarrant, pp. 81–90.

322. "The chaplain of the . . . relinquish their prized captive.": OR Vol. I, No. 10 (1), p. 886.

Chapter 18

324. "Operating generally within . . . their clandestine activities.": OR Vol. III, No. 2, pp. 301–303.

324. "In *International Law,* . . . guerrillas as synonymous.": Halleck, *International Law, or Rules Regulating the Intercourse of States in Peace and War,* San Francisco, 1861, 386, cited in OR Vol. III, No. 2, p. 307.

326. "Henry A. Wise . . . motion and quick raids.": OR Vol. I, No. 5, p. 151.

326. "Maj. Gen. M. Lowell . . . in May 12, 1862.": OR Vol. I, No. 6, p. 889.

326. "The formation of such . . . Ranger Act in 1862.": OR Vol. IV, No. 2, p. 31.

326. "General Van Dorn . . . of 'partisan officers.' ": OR Vol. I, No. 13, 828.

326. "Col. J. D. Bingham . . . Poindexter, and Cobb.": OR Vol. I, No. 13, pp. 12–13.

326. "Trains and wagon convoys . . . groups of foragers.": OR Vol. I, No. 16 (1), pp. 630.

327. "It was also a convenient . . . occasional artillery piece.": OR Vol. I, No. 13, pp. 33.

327. "The effort paid off . . . Trans-Mississippi Department.": OR Vol. I, No. 13, pp. 45.

328. "When partisans came . . . the same results.": OR Vol. I, No. 34/2, pp. 244.

328. "Early in his career . . . Eighth Pennsylvania Infantry.": OR Vol. I, No. 10/1, pp. 632–633.

328–329. "Stopped by patrols, . . . with their comrades.": OR Vol. I, No. 13, p. 215.

329. "Probably the simplest . . . columns or camp.": Tarrant, pp. 90, 92, 95.

330. "A great many stragglers . . . and permanent end.": *A History of the 102d Illinois Infantry,* pp. 42–43.

330. "First there were . . . Morgan, Forrest, and others.": Tarrant, p. 95.

331. "Not content to raise . . . they stumbled upon.": OR Vol. I, No. 13, pp. 12–13.

331. "Usually armed with only . . . and relatively powerless.": OR Vol. I, No. 41 (1), p. 72.

331. "But certainly the sabre . . . use against gunpowder.": Mosby, p. 30.

332. "Sabers tended to clank . . . in a close-in fight.": Williamson, James, p. 21.

332. "It was hoped that . . . posed such a problem.": OR Vol. I, No. 13, pp. 506.

332. "Watson advised those . . . to do the same.": OR Vol. I, No. 10 (2), pp. 181–182.

332. "As soon as irregular . . . and sentry posts.": OR Vol. I, No. 12 (3), pp. 175–176.

332. "This would free . . . the rebel guerrillas.": OR Vol. I, No. 12 (3), p. 534.

333. "All small posts were . . . 'and with vigor.' ": OR Vol. I, No. 13, pp. 564.

333. "About the same time . . . into larger bodies.": OR Vol. I, No. 16/1, pp. 36.

333. "It is much easier . . . spies, pickets, or couriers.": OR Vol. I, No. 13, p. 806.

333. "Following the trail . . . 'views' of them.": OR Vol. I, No. 15, pp. 126.

333. "In his report David . . . beaten 'by strategy.' ": OR Vol. I, No. 13, pp. 313–314.

333–334. "Colonel William R. Penick . . . the secessionist cause.": OR Vol. I, No. 13, p. 234.

334. "Union authorities did not . . . 'plunder and murder.' ": OR Vol. I, No. 13, pp. 14; 688–89.

334. "Even suspects against . . . bond was posted.": OR Vol. I, No. 13, pp. 420.

334. "If guerrillas fired . . . burned down immediately.": OR Vol. I, No. 12 (2), pp. 51.

334. "They were also . . . all property destroyed.": OR Vol. I, No. 13, pp. 446–447.

335. "Sherman wrote to . . . on its own people.": OR Vol. I, No. 13, pp. 741–743.

335. "Noting a lull in such . . . horses and provisions.": OR Vol. I, No. 17 (2), pp. 218, 234, 272–273.

335. "Faced with guerrilla . . . support the guerrillas.": OR Vol. I, No. 17 (1), pp. 480.

336. " 'He is nothing more than a good raider.' ": Hurst, p. 139.

336. "Cool in the presence . . . paralyze most men.": Jordan, p.105.

336–337. "Finding himself nearly . . . that soon passed nearby.": Jordan, p. 180.

337. "Attacked on both flanks . . . in complete disorder.": Hurst, pp. 78–79.

337. "At Brice's Crossroads . . . the enemy's flanks.": Morton, pp. 178–179.

338. "The Union discomfiture was immediate and complete.": Jordan, pp. 212–13.

CHAPTER 19

339. "Bushnell & Company of New . . . call the *Monitor*.": Ericsson himself used the term "floating battery" to refer to this vessel as late as 1862 when writing to the secretary of the navy, Ericsson, *Battles and Leaders*, Vol. I, p. 731.

339. "Of the three . . . Roads (March 9, 1862).": Alternatively spelled "Merrimack." The author has chosen to use the spelling more popular during the 1861–1890 period.

340. "Of course, Soley . . . of these events.": Soley, *Battles and Leaders*, Vol. I, pp. 616–618.

340. "A few days later Ericsson received the contract.": Wheeler, Francis, pp. 4–6.

341. "The "port-stoppers" . . . Delamater Iron Works.": A handwritten note in the margin seemingly written by an expert reader personally associated with the project says, 'Novelty Iron Works.'

341. "The remainder of February . . . solve such shortcomings.": Dorr, pp. 7–10.

342. "Summoned to Richmond . . . the public's imagination.": Porter, John L., *Battles and Leaders*, Vol. I, p. 717.

342. "The vessel had taken . . . on February 9, 1860.": *Frank Leslie's* , Feb. 9, 1861, p. 189.

343. "It thus became feasible . . . above the surface.": Brooke, John; Vol. I, pp. 715–716.

343. "The protective 4–inch . . . 24–inch pitch-pine.": Porter *Battles and Leaders*, Vol. I, p. 717.

344. "In early March . . . long-expected adversary.": Charles Martin, pp. 4–5.

344. "The *Virginia* ignored . . . toward its intended victims.": Reaney, Henry; *Battles and Leaders*, Vol. I, pp. 714–15.

345. "The next round demolished the *Cumberland's* after pivot gun.": Charles Martin, p. 6.

346. "The destruction of the *Minnesota* . . . wait to the morrow.": Wood, John, *Battles and Leaders*, Vol. I, pp. 698–700.

346. "Steaming beside the ironclad . . . all wooden vessels.": Cannon, p. 8; These included the *Jamestown*, the *Patrick Henry*, and the *Teazor, Monitor Versus the Merrimac S&S*, p. 25.

347. "Few on shore had . . . and the frigate.": Colston, R.E., *Battles and Leaders*, Vol. I, p. 714.

347. "Both vessels remained . . . adversary once again.": *Monitor versus the Merrimac S&S*, p. 26.

348. "In his chapter . . . of the two combatants.": Wood, *Battles and Leaders*, Vol. I, pp. 700–702.

349. "It was impossible . . . at the *Virginia*.": Greene, Dana, *Battles and Leaders*, Vol. I, pp. 723–725.

350. "Blinded by burnt powder . . . commander to safety.": Cannon, pp. 8–9.

350. "This shield was pushed . . . of the concussion.": Wood, *Battles and Leaders*, Vol. I, pp. 702.

350. "The *Virginia*, thought . . . scuttled on May 11.": Wood, *Battles and Leaders*, Vol. I, pp. 703 & 710.

351. "Although this vessel . . . even shallower waters.": OR Vol. I, No. 53, pp. 491–492.

351. "No more than 170 . . . not exceed 395 tons.": OR Vol. III, No. 2, pp. 814–815.

351. "The agreed-upon specifications . . . protected by iron plates.": OR Vol. III, No. 2, pp. 817–832.

352. "These gunboats, the *Lexington* . . . 7 to 10 knot speed.": Coombe, pp. 24.

352. "Offensive armament appears . . . and four 8 inch Dahlgrens.": Walke, Henry, *Battles and Leaders*, Vol. I, p. 359.

352. "While retiring after . . . during the war.": Gosnell, p. 49, citing James Laning excerpted in Walke's *Naval Scenes and Reminiscences*.

354. "The fuses were correspondingly . . . 10 and then 5 seconds.": Gosnell, p. 51, citing Walke's *Naval Scenes and Reminiscences*.

355. "Their eight 32–pounders . . . to fire prematurely.": Taylor, Jesse; *Battles and Leaders*, Vol. I, p. 369.

356. "In his report . . . more than 2 hours.": OR Vol. I, No. 7, p. 125; OR Vol. I. No. 7, p. 136.

356. "The defending gunners . . . declined to return fire.": Gosnell, p. 59, quoting Lt. H.L. Bedford, Vol. XIII, Southern Historical Society Papers.

357. "Once again the armored . . . a "moderate speed.": Walke, *Battles and Leaders*, Vol. I, p. 433.

358. "Unfortunately for the defenders . . . Confederate 32–pounders.": Gosnell, p. 65 citing Lt. H. L. Bedford, Vol. XIII, *Southern Historical Society Papers*.

358. "The *St. Louis*, . . . lobbed conical shells.": Coombe, p. 67.

358. "As at Fort Henry . . . ten in Fort Donelson.": Gosnell, p. 66 citing Lt. H. L. Bedford, Vol. XIII, *Southern Historical Society Papers*.

358. "To make matters worse . . . in front of them.": OR Vol. I, No. 7, p. 166; Coombe, p. 67.

inia, thought . . . scuttled on May 11.": Wood; *Battles and Leaders*, I, pp. 703 & 710.

360 "A pamphlet in which Ellet . . . be used offensively.": SA-NS, Vol. VI, No. 8, Feb. 22, 1862, p. 121.

360. "Crewed by local landsmen . . . with one or two guns.": Coombe, p. 122.

363. "This boat, however . . . mortar boat's blinds.": OR Vol. I, No. 10 (1), p. 889.

363. "Overpowered and suffering . . . finally beaten back.": Gosnell, p. 86–91.

363. "Moreover, the Union . . . that campaign, Memphis.": Coombe, p. 124.

364. "Davis apparently expected . . . gunboats and Ellet's rams.": Crandall, p. 52.

365. "The captain of the *Switzerland* . . . behind as a reserve.": OR Vol. I, No. 10 (1), p. 909.

365. "Once through . . . *Price,* on the right.": Ellet, Alfred, *Battles and Leaders*, Vol. I, p. 456.

365. "She began to take on water.": Crandall, p. 54; Ellet, *Battles and Leaders*, Vol. I, p. 457.

366. "The *Monarch* attempted . . . in shallow shoal water.": OR Vol. I, No. (10) 1, p. 907–908.

366. "Only the *General Van Dorn* . . . the river and escape.": Coombe, pp. 129–131.

367. "In 1863 *Scientific American* . . . inventors of the ironclad.": SA-NS, Vol. VIII, No. 6, Feb. 7, 1863, p. 81.

367. "As if to dispel . . . 'ship ever commenced.' ": "The Great Naval Revolution," *The Cornhill Magazine*, May 1862, p. 557.

367. "In the weeks . . . known as ironclad.": SA-NS, Vol. VI, No. 21, May 24, 1862, p. 328; also, Vol. VIII, No. 6, Feb. 7, 1863, p. 81.

367. "Acknowledging the role . . . 'execution of an idea.' ": *Army and Navy Journal*, Vol. I, No. 4 (Sept. 19, 1863), p. 59.

368. "In his own chapter . . . Washington and Richmond.": Ericsson, John; *Battles and Leaders*, I. P. 730.

368. "In an 1893 article . . . by *Scientific American*.": Citing "A Man of War," C. N. Robinson, *The Graphic*, Feb. 10, 1894, in SA-NS, Vol. LXX, No. 17, April 28, 1894, p. 260.

CHAPTER 20

369. "Charged with the evaluation . . . more accurate weapons.": OR Vol. I, No. 1, p. 74.

371. "The shot fired . . . now lay dead.": Ripley, William, pp. 22–24.

372. "In his memoirs . . . issued similar instructions.": Dinkins, p. 34.

372. "After the battle . . . rode along his lines.": Wheeler, Richard, p. 123.

372. "He urged his shooters . . . enemy artillery horses.": OR Vol. I, No. 22 (1), p. 83.

372. "The regimental history . . . by the regulations.": *History of the Nineteenth Regiment Massachusetts*, pp. 151–152.

373. "The French quickly . . . in French service.": *Military Gazette*, Vol. 2, No. 12, June 15, 1859, p. 187.

373. "Called to take . . . enlisted men's clothing.": Favill, p. 125.

373. "Thus looking like . . . own personal reconnaissance.": Ward, p. 88.

374. "This included a request . . . 'and ball' cartridges.": OR Vol. I, No. 1 pp. 450–451.

374. "In January that year . . . cap smoothbore muskets.": OR Vol. I, No. 1, p. 495.

374. "Finding that his troops . . . be immediately sent.": OR Vol. I, No. 2, pp. 53–54.

374. "General George H. Thomas . . . in September 1861.": OR Vol. I, No. 4, p. 260.

374. "The chief ordnance officer . . . fighting at Antietam.": OR Vol. I, No. 12 (3), p. 767; OR Vol. I, No. 19 (2), p. 321.

374. "On the Confederate . . . '(especially buck and ball).' ": OR Vol. I, No. 24 (1), p. 317.

375. "Colonel A. J. Brown's Fifty-fifth . . . of this formation.": OR Vol. I, No. 8, p. 151.

375. "Reflecting upon events . . . accuracy of their fire.": OR Vol. I, No. 11 (2), p. 721.

375. "No idle boast, . . . Battle of Malvern Hill.": OR Vol. I, No. 11 (2), p. 214.

376. "The back elevating . . . skirmishers or sharpshooters.": Willard, p. 12.

376. "Willard admitted that . . . role as a result.": Willard, p. 7.

376. "He argued that . . . 'when at close quarters.' ": Willard, p. 3.

376. "There was no need . . . as the enemy neared.": Willard, pp. 5–6.

377. Instead of the ten . . . each of 150 men.": Ward, p. 27.

377. "Unlike with regular infantry . . . by senior lieutenants.": Shaw, p. 99.

378. "This was a far cry . . . charged to train.": Shaw, p. 101.

379. "The horrors of the . . . 'out dig the diggers.' ": Shaw, p. 111.

379. "In fact, by the height . . . almost every major engagement.": From a conversation with Richard Patterson, executive director of Old Barracks Museum, Trenton, New Jersey.

379. "Despite these precedents . . . of fighting material.": Sherman, George, pp. 5–6.

379. "Though this regiment . . . and the experiment abandoned.": *Manufacturer and Farmer's Journal,* May 9, 1861, Vol. XL, No. 37, p. 1.

380. "So intense was this . . . laws or ordinances.": Califf, p. 3.

380. "Even most ardent . . . any meaningful use.": Sherman, George, p. 6.

380. "The Union Articles . . . return fugitive slaves.": Sherman, George, pp. 10–11.

380. "Given the enormity . . . annulled these acts.": Rickard, p. 6.

380. "In June slaves . . . of African descent.": Sherman, George, pp. 10–11.

380. "Three weeks later . . . for black troops.": Califf, pp. 2–3.

380. "On May 22 . . . began in earnest.": Sherman, George, pp. 10–11.

381. "Writing to Grant . . . garrison important positions.": OR Vol. I, No. 24 (3), p. 497; OR Vol. 26 (1), p. 653.

381. "Although confiding to . . . the Mississippi River.": OR Vol. I, No. 24 (3), p. 584.

381. "Some white troops . . . by their peers.": Morgan, Thomas J., p. 20.

381. "On the march . . . by the white soldiers.": OR Vol. I, No. 39 (1), p. 557.

381. "Of course, there . . . and their officers.": Califf, p. 4.

382. "General Butler, who . . . for servile labor.": Califf, pp. 2–3.

382. "Writing to Secretary of War . . . be accurately assayed.": OR Vol. I, No. 29 (2), p. 596.

382. "Other commanders, such . . . resolve these problems.": OR Vol. I, No. 26 (1), pp. 663–664; OR I 28 (2), p. 95.

382. "About 50,000 freedmen . . . colors during 1863.": Sherman, George, p. 12.

382. "At this point . . . permanently to a halt.": Higginson, p. 5.

382. "Even such a seasoned . . . 'well as this one.' ": Morgan, Thomas J., p. 22.

383. "Henry S. Clapp . . . white volunteer regiments.": Clapp, p. 26.

383. "They gave themselves . . . regiment second to none.": Sherman, George, pp. 16–17.

383. "Being more attentive . . . learned more quickly.": Higginson, p. 11.

384. "The man was . . . forehead, of course.": Rickard, p. 10.

387. "No less a personage . . . men would fight.": Sherman, George, pp. 21–31.

387. "By the war's end . . . never return home.": Sherman, George, pp. 12, 31.

CHAPTER 21

394. "Recent research suggests . . . during the early 1790s.": Lynn, pp. 241–260; Ross, pp. 68–69.

394. "In desperation French . . . the defender's position.": For a more detailed analysis of the evolution of French grand tactics during the Napoleonic Era the reader is directed to Nosworthy, *With Musket, Cannon and Sword*, pp. 103–186.

398. "Finally, Jomini also . . . V or an 'inverted V' formation.": Jomini, pp. 189–195.

398. "However, during a series . . . in their entirety.": Warner; *Generals in Blue*, p. 195. The reader is also asked to compared the ideas and information presented in Jomini's *Art of War*, pp. 178–203 and 277–320, with those in Halleck's *Elements of Military Art and Science*, pp. 114–135 and pp. 257–274.

398. "His lectures a resounding . . . *and Science* in 1846.": Halleck, H. W.; *Elements of Military Art and Science*; New York, 1846.

398. "In his preface . . . 'part of the work.' ": Halleck, p. 5.

400. "During the battle . . . original corps assignment.": Swinton, pp. 103, 115.

401. "Union reports contain references . . . during the Atlanta Campaign.": OR Vol. I, No. 11 (2), p. 290; OR Vol. I, No. 30 (1), p. 319; OR Vol. I, No. 45 (1), pp. 244–245; OR Vol. I, No. 38 (3), pp. 343–344.

401. "Such tactics were . . . (southwest Virginia, May 9, 1864).": OR Vol. I, No. 31 (1), p. 526; OR Vol. I, No. 37 (1), p. 57.

402. "A little later, when . . . was long [that is, wide]." Jackson, p. 71.

402. "There was a 5-pace . . . paces between brigades." Rhea, *The Battles for Spotsylvania Court House* . . . p. 225.

403. "The resulting column . . . from front to back.": Alexander, *Fighting for the Confederacy*, pp. 375–376.

404. "Each of Ruggles's battalions . . . frontage of a company.": OR Vol. I, No. 10 (1), p. 470.

404. "The orders to employ . . . General Braxton Bragg himself.": OR Vol. I, No. 10 (1), pp. 494–495.

404. "The Seventeenth Kentucky . . . two companies wide.": OR Vol. I, No. 10 (1), p. 241.

404. "The five regimental . . . with the artillery.": OR Vol. I, No. 12 (2), p. 394.

404. "When ordered by Major General . . . tier of the column.": OR Vol. I, No. 38 (1), p. 877.

405. "This practice, incidentally . . . the Seven Years' War.": Warnery, pp. 51–55.

405. "Brigade commanders . . . along the first line.": OR Vol. I, No. 52 (1), pp. 238–239.

406. "The regiments in the first . . . companies or divisions.": OR Vol. I, No. 29 (1), p. 746.

406–407. "During the Battle . . . half distance on center.": OR Vol. I, No. 20 (2), p. 290.

407. "During the Union advance . . . 100 yards farther back.": OR Vol. I, No. 10 (1), p. 848.

407. "During an action . . . deployed in line.": OR Vol. I, No. 12 (2), p. 542.

407. "Similar brigade-level line . . . the Chickamauga Campaign.": OR Vol. I, No. 20 (1), p. 309; OR Vol. I, No. 30 (1), pp. 796–797.

407–408. "It is not clear how . . . at the defending troops.": OR Vol. I, No. 12 (1), p. 368.

408. "Each brigade was 200 yards behind the one in front.": OR Vol. I, No. 19 (1), p. 380.

409. "Each division advanced . . . at least five times.": OR Vol. I, No. 21, p. 226.

409. "Although Major General . . . the brigades in line.": OR Vol. I, No. 21, p. 222.

409. "True, division-size columns . . . front of Petersburg.": OR Vol. I, No. 46 (1), p. 976.

409. "Examples of brigade-size columns . . . on June 3, 1864.": OR Vol. I, No. 31 (2), p. 189; OR Vol. I, No. 38 (2), p. 360; OR Vol. I, No. 26 (1), p. 548; OR Vol. I, No. 36 (2), p. 456.

411. "In a note that accompanied . . . deployed on the center.": Jomini, Fig. 28, pp. 282–284.

411. "Although Jomini's writings . . . entered the Civil War.": Jamieson; p. 35.

416. "Jomini's works were . . . all aspects of daily life": The French Restoration can be thought to start with the return of monarchy in 1814 or the ascension of Louis Philippe in 1830 after the July Revolution that year. However, when referring to cultural and artistic trends, normally,the term is used to refer to the 1830–1848 period of French history.

CHAPTER 22

420. "The artillerymen were . . . gun crew as well.": Gibbon, *Artillerist's Manual*, pp. 354–355.

420. "One caisson behind . . . situation was determined.": Gibbon, *Artillerist's Manual*, p. 345.

420. "The entire deployment . . . but 25 seconds.": Roberts, p. 50.

420. "During a major engagement . . . than absolute regularity.": Gibbon, *Artillerist's Manual*, , p. 355.

420. "The batteries were . . . of the battle line.": Gibbon, *Artillerist's Manual*, p. 356.

421. "Conversely, when on the . . . of friendly forces.": Roberts, p. 52; Gibbon, *Artillerist's Manual*, pp. 354–358.

421. "Gibbon, for example . . . 'importance' of artillery.": Gibbon, *Artillerist's Manual*, p. 355.

421. "Although stream banks . . . by the inexperienced eye.": Roberts, p. 52.

422. "Struck by solid shot . . . devastation as shrapnel.": Gibbon, *Artillerist's Manual*, p. 357.

422–423. "When artillery was required . . . the halfway point.": Gibbon, *Artillerist's Manual*, p. 358.

423. "If this was impossible . . . his shoulder arm.": Tielke, Vol. I, p. 175.

423. "Any excess artillery . . . access to the front.": Roberts, p. 52.

423. "Gibbon suggested that . . . rear of its center.": Gibbon, *Artillerist's Manual*, p. 356; Roberts p. 52.

424. "Not only was there . . . artillery in the rear.": Roberts, pp. 47–48.

424. "In the British army, . . . guns to the death.": In his "Orders to detachment of cavalry going to Cape of Good Hope prior to landing Dec 12, 1805," Wilson provides an excellent example of this attitude: "The commanding officer is confident that the cavalry will never abandon the gun without orders from him. Till that moment they should regard it as committed to their charge of their courage; and therefore consider its loss incompatible with their honour." Wilson, Vol. I, pp. 335, 338.

424. "Not only did this . . . during that same engagement.": *Strictures*, p. 25.

424. "Gibbon encouraged artillerymen . . . protect nearby troops.": Gibbon, *Artillerist's Manual*, p. 359.

424. "An artilleryman must never . . . victory in their favor.": Roberts, p. 52.

425. "Frederick frowned upon . . . impact upon the enemy.": Frederick II, Vol. IV, pp. 57–58.

425. "Writing about the same . . . recommended individual fire.": Gassendi, p. 386.

425. "Gibbon agreed with Gassendi . . . should fire individually.": Gibbon, *Artillerist's Manual*, p. 343; Roberts, pp. 47, 49–51.

425–426. "Roberts, on the other hand . . . in each salvo.": Roberts p. 49–50.

426. "It was the officer's . . . waste of ammunition.": Roberts, pp. 47, 49–51.

427. "Not only did this . . . wheels and axles.": Sumner, J. Albert Monroe, p. 16.

427. "Then, the repeated . . . Shenandoah June 9, 1862).": Moore, Edward, pp. 73–74.

427. "Maj. Henry J. Hunt . . . Battle of Bull Run.": OR Vol. I, No. 2, p. 379.

428. "On the other end . . . recouped his energy.": Sumner, J. Albert Monroe, pp. 16–18.

429. "A few seconds . . . merlon moments before.": Peet, p. 122; Camp Winfield Scott near Yorktown 1st U.S. May 2, 1962.

429. "After a few rounds . . . their work unmolested.": Lightsey, p. 41.

430. "Although only his head . . . with its first shot.": Izlar, pp. 43.

430. "However, probably the most . . . Bishop Leonidas Polk.": Sherman, *Memoirs of William T. Sherman*, Vol. II, pp. 52–54.

430. "Gibbon's instructions about . . . Gassendi's *Aide-mémoire*.": Compare the distances/times and uses of projectile types provided by Gassendi, p. 386 with those supplied by Gibbon, *Artillerist's Manual*, p. 343, 359.

431. "An inexperienced artillery . . . to the main engagement.": Gibbon, *Artillerist's Manual*, p. 343.

431. "The remainder were . . . they were needed.": Gibbon, *Artillerist's Manual*, p. 359.

431–432. "For the same reasons . . . against round shot.": Gibbon, *Artillerist's Manual*, p. 232.

432. "Solid shot could . . . longer dangerous space.": U.S. Army, *Instructions for Field Artillery*, p. 43.

432. "The general consensus . . . about 30 seconds.": These figures published in Gassendi's work were quoted by Gibbon, *Artillerist's Manual*, p. 356; U.S. Army,

Instructions for Field Artillery, p. 42; Gassendi, p. 386. Colonel Maude in his *Letters on Tactics* would be even more optimistic and stated that cavalry only required 20 seconds to travel 200 yards, p. 268.

432. "The following chart . . . each should be used.": Roberts, p. 50; U.S. Army, *Instructions for Field Artillery,* p. 42.

433. "Although conceding that . . . North American continent.": U.S. Army, I*nstructions for Field Artillery,* p. 42.

434. "Of course, before . . . limited to howitzers.": Gibbon, *Artillerist's Manual,* p. 235.

434. "Experts thought, however . . . or more distant.": *Instructions for Field Artillery,* p. 43.

434. "Gibbon felt that canister . . . up to 400 yards.": Roberts, pp. 49–50.

435. "The pace of the gunners . . . allowed to be 'rapid.' ": Gibbon, *Artillerist's Manual,* p. 343.

435. "It was estimated . . . times per minute.": Roberts p. 49–50; U.S. Army, *Instructions for Field Artillery,* p. 42.

435. "In his seminal work . . . still achieve accuracy.": Tielke, Vol. I, p. 186.

436. "If the enemy, . . . around three times per minute.": Roberts, pp. 49–50.

436. "The official *Instructions* . . . by a single charge.": US Army, *Instructions for Field Artillery,* pp. 42–43.

436. "Canister, like solid shot . . . scatter more widely.": Gibbon, *Artillerist's Manual,* p. 359.

436. "Both authors advised . . . no other available targets.": Gibbon, *Artillerist's Manual,* p. 358.

437. "This increased the likelihood . . . dismounting the piece.": Gibbon, *Artillerist's Manual,* p. 358.

437. "Special care was . . . was greatly reduced.": OR Vol. I, No. 14, pp. 698–699.

437. "In a circular written . . . their batteries prematurely.": OR Vol. 18, pp. 894–895.

CHAPTER 23

438. "Nonplussed, the Confederates . . . switch to "canister.": OR Vol. I, No. 11 (1), pp. 531–532.

438. "In contrast, Capt. Andrew . . . to within 200 yards.": OR Vol. I, No. 27 (1), p. 690.

439. "The crew uncertain . . . of 'double charge.' ": Webster, p. 68.

439. "Nevertheless, the fire . . . hors de combat.": Stevenson, William, p. 154.

440. "In a textbook . . . their enemy's backs.": Urban, pp. 156–157.

440. "The victorious infantrymen . . . than at his breast.": Hill, A. F. p. 307; see also Shaw, p. 130.

441. "The gunners along . . . bayoneted at their guns.": These statistics were taken from Neil, pp. 5–10. This account of this action is a distillation that is provided in OR Vol. I, No. 17 (1), pp. 90–92, 94–95, 99.

443. "Pushing back the enemy . . . on the second day.": Buell, pp. 82–83; Report No. 22, pp. 97–98. *Note:* Although Buell attempted to pass this very informative work off as an autobiography, modern research has shown that it was a compilation of

oral history from Pvt. Frank McCormick, Pvt. Peter Andrews, and a veteran of the 7th Wisconsin. Nevertheless, its content appears highly detailed and accurate and remains a valuable source for anyone studying the Civil War, Felton, p. 39.

444. "Cannon against cannon . . . not properly supported.": Scribner, pp. 294–295.

444. "The Washington Artillery . . . silence its adversary.": Morgan W. H., pp. 57–58.

445. "As soon as the shells . . . of the Union guns.": *History of the Nineteenth Regiment Massachusetts*, p. 63.

445. "This continued until he . . . lieutenant into service.": Moore, Edward, p. 88.

446. "Fortunately, despite the rough . . . throughout the engagement.": Johnson, Curt, p. 21.

446. "The memoirist recalling . . . their intended targets.": Adams, p. 91.

446. "Questioned, he explained . . . happened to be overrun.": Wright, T. J., p. 114.

447. "Despite all these efforts . . . to repair them.": Webster, p. 78.

447. "If the battery continued . . . three assaults simultaneously.": Nolan, p. 143, Decker, p. 168.

448. "Whenever this technique . . . had been captured.": OR Vol. I, No. 52 (1), p. 239.

448–449. "When attacked by charging . . . with the technique.": Captain Chew ordered his men to take "careful aim at the horses' knees and fire as rapidly as possible," during the affair at Brandy Station, Neese, p. 177 (June 9th, 1863.) Similar orders were issued to "L" Battery of 2nd NY artillery regiment at Cedar Mountain; Roemer, Jacob, pp. 43–44.

449. "This single round . . . and began to retire.": Neese, pp. 199–200.

449. "Faced with this double threat . . . retire at the double.": Neese, pp. 209–210.

450. "This meant that although . . . for in-close fighting.": Buell, p. 57.

452. "During a general engagement . . . minute for each gun.": OR Vol. I, No. 42 (2), pp. 574–582.

453. "The object in killing . . . less proportional execution.": OR Vol. III, No. 4, pp. 65–66.

453. "The general rule . . . desirable to overthrow.": OR Vol. I, No. 42 (2), pp. 578.

454. "These were arranged . . . offered to the enemy.": OR Vol. I, No. 42 (2), pp. 574–582.

455. "It was equally important . . . 'mortar powder' instead.": OR Vol. III, No. 4, pp. 61–65.

CHAPTER 24

456. "Batteries had to be . . . one or two howitzers.": U.S. Army; *Instructions for Field Artillery*, p. 3; Gibbon, *Artillerist's Manual*, p. 344.

456. "6 horses per carriage." [in list]: Gibbon, *Artillerist's Manual*, p. 344.

458. "In practice there was tremendous variation in the field.": Wise, Vol. I, pp. 108–110.

458. "The First Wisconsin . . . two 12-pounder howitzers.": Webster, pp. 34–35.

458. "The Eleventh Ohio . . . 12-pounder Napoleons.": Neil, p. 15.

458. "At the First Battle . . . rifles, all bronze.": OR Vol. I, No. 2, p. 515.

459. "Though of interest . . . more suitable material.": Barnard, p. 109.

459. "Its four constituent . . . 3-inch rifles, respectively.": Roemer, Jacob, p. 119.

459. "When standardizing light . . . it would do.": OR Vol. I, No. 14, pp. 698–699. A battery could have either four 6-pounder smoothbores, two 6-pounder smoothbores and two 12-pounder or two 24-pounder howitzers, four 12-pounder Napoleon guns, four rifled guns of same caliber, or two 12 (or two 24-pounder) howitzers and two rifled guns.

459. "This, according to Lt . . . 'precise and effective.' ": Webster, pp. 40–41.

460. "Hunt recommended that . . . into artillery service.": OR Vol. I, No. 2, pp. 768–769.

460. "Writing to the secretary . . . this manpower deficiency.": OR Vol. I, No. 5, p. 10.

460. "The new men were . . . known as 'old regulars.' ": Buell, pp. 17–19.

460. "In order to provide . . . camp and march.": Buell, p. 56.

461. "Even more than infantry . . . 'effect if scattered.' ": Alexander, *Fighting for the Confederacy*, p. 104.

461. "European armies during . . . every 408 soldiers.": Chesney, pp. 102–103.

462. "Feeling that an army . . . a fifty-piece siege train.": OR Vol. I, No. 5, p. 66–69.

462. "Although this organization . . . brigades in that corps.": Buell; p. 56.

462–463. "Although Confederate Gen. J. C . . . . dispersed around Virginia.": OR Vol. I, No. 2, p. 983.

463. "The next mention . . . his 'artillery brigade.': OR Vol. I, No. 8, pp. 788.

463. "Its artillery brigade . . . the 27th and 28th.": OR Vol. I, No. 8, pp. 793.

463. "The Union forces . . . light artillery batteries.": OR Vol. I, No. 10 (2), pp. 147.

463. "Little effort was made . . . was actively discouraged.": Buell, p. 56.

463–464. "Just how much . . . their enemy counterparts.": Alexander, *Military Memoirs . . .*, p. 90.

464. "Five artillery battalions . . . chief of artillery.": Ross, F., pp. 153–154; Alexander, *Fighting for the Confederacy*, p. 105.

464. "While preparing for what . . . Antietam, two months later.": Johnson, Curt; p. 5.

464. "Prior to the battle . . . army's artillery stock.": OR Vol. I, No. 2, pp. 345–346.

464–465. "The fire of one . . . and *vice versa.*": OR Vol. I, No. 1, pp. 370–371.

465. "This was more . . . pieces in the army.": OR Vol. I, No. 19(2), p. 412.

466. "Artillery—Army of Northern Virginia (Summer 1863)" [List Heading] : Luvaas, p. 67, fn 40, citing Wise, *The Long Arm of Lee*, Vol. II, p. 571.

466. "While preparing for . . . Landing early that year.": Rhodes, *The Gettysburg Gun*, pp. 8–9.

466. "Of these at least . . . total artillery resources.": Naisawald, pp. 553–556.

466. "This trend certainly . . . Army of Northern Virginia.": Luvaas, p. 67, fn 40, citing Wise, Vol. II, p. 571.

466. "Some writers believe . . . all artillery by 1865.": Luvaas, p. 66, fn 40, citing "Artillery" in M.H.S.P. XIII, p. 115.

467. "In such moments . . . replace the smoothbore.": Luvaas, p. 66, fn 40; citing Scheibert in *Der Bügerkrieg*, p.78.

467. "The 100-pounder Parrot . . . 10-inch ordnance carriage.": *Ranges of Parrott Guns*, p. 15; Wiard, pp. 4–5.

468. "Mr. Watson, the assistant . . . wheels or bent axles.": Wiard, pp. 4–5.

468. "John B. Magruder's . . . to its proximity.": McWhiney, Grady and Perry D. Jamieson, p. 38.

469. "The master artilleryman . . . 'profit by them.' " : Gibbon, *Artillerist's Manual*, p. 342.

469. "Union infantrymen cut . . . wounded seven or eight.": OR Vol. I, No. 10 (1), p. 513.

469–470. "Accurate Union small arms . . . had to be abandoned.": Daniel, pp. 34–35.

470. "Only a timely nearby . . . from further destruction.": OR Vol. I, No. 10 (1), p. 565.

470. "In his contribution . . . struggle for Malvern Hill.": McWhitney, p. 117.

470. "Unlike at Bull Run . . . series of counterattacks.": Jordan, pp. 212–214.

471. "The devastating artillery fire . . . now turned and fled.": Hurst, pp. 190–191.

Chapter 25

472. "Horses often were . . . means of attack.": Fox, p. 426.

472. "In late September . . . portion of the state.": OR Vol. I, No. 39 (1), pp. 555–556.

473. "The injury was fatal . . . the man's lower back.": Mason, pp. 64–65.

474. "McLean would report . . . out of ammunition.": OR Vol. I, No. 39 (1), p. 553.

474. "As ferocious as they . . . fighting was over.": OR Vol. I, No. 39 (1), p. 557.

474–475. "The eight troopers . . . timber and undergrowth.": OR Vol. I, No. 17 (1), p. 307.

475. "The Union cavalry thus, . . . at only 30 yards.": OR Vol. I, No. 5, p. 335.

475. "The rebels were completely . . . men came up.": OR Vol. I, No. 13, p. 199.

476. "The Texans certainly . . . at Rowlett's Station.": OR Vol. I, No. 7, p. 17.

476. "After a short . . . about 2 miles away.": OR Vol. I, No. 20 (1), pp. 967–969.

476. "The Gallager carbine . . . 'unquestionably worthless.' ": OR Vol. I, No. 16 (1), p. 750.

476. "This was the same . . . Ninth Pennsylvania Cavalry.": OR Vol. I, No. 33, p. 892; OR Vol. I, No. 44 (1), p. 361.

477. "These shoulder arms . . . 'have been unquestioned.' ": OR Vol. I, No. 23 (1), p. 181.

477. "However, the Spencer . . . killed than wounded.": OR Vol. I, No. 23 (1), p. 667

478. "As he was led away . . . 'and fire all day.' ": Harris, pp. 30–31.

478. "In his own report . . . 'stand before them.' ": OR Vol. I, No. 36 (2), pp. 60, 63.

478. "So great did the . . . such an anomaly.": OR Vol. I, No. 49 (2) p. 236.

479. "Dismounted, the cavalrymen . . . enemy field fortifications.": Fox, p. 111.

479. "Finally overwhelmed . . . out of their position.": Bliss, *Reminiscences* . . . , OR Vol. I, No. 36 (1), p. 793.

479. "At the start . . . and V Corps, respectively.": Starr, Vol. I, pp. 262–263.

480. "For example, when . . . an equine screen.": Meyer, Henry p. 16.

480. "Early in 1863, . . . as its commander.": Bliss, *Reminiscences* . . ., p. 13.

480. "During the evenings . . . lessons to the major.": Bliss, *Reminiscences* . . ., p. 13.

481. "In this case . . . at breakneck speed.": OR Vol. I, No. 49 (3), p. 1046.

481. "Keep your sabers . . . you may accomplish.": OR Vol. I, No. XIII, p. 406.

482. "In a short communiqué . . . 'carbine would delay.' ": OR Vol. I, No. 23 (1), p. 127.

482. "Without any hesitancy . . . with repeating rifles.": OR Vol. I, No. 23 (2), p. 199.

482–483. "In his April 4 . . . would be 'invaluable.' ": OR Vol. I, No. 23 (1), p. 204.

483. "Caldwell's accusation implies . . . over open ground.": OR Vol. I, No. 22 (1), p. 262.

483–484. "He instructed these . . . the advancing enemy.": OR Vol. I, No. 25 (1), p. 49.

484. "Both sides started . . . had been discomfited.": Meyers, pp. 32–33.

486. "Although taught to ride . . . LaSalle, among others.": Ardant du Picq, p. 187.

486–487. "Writing many years . . . cavalry in a charge.": Bliss, *Reminiscences . . .*, pp. 18–19.

487. "Our men were fully . . . charge with the sabre.": Bliss, *Reminiscences . . .*, pp. 18–19.

487. "Rosecrans felt that this . . . 'use of the saber.' ": OR Vol. I, No. 30 (1), p. 80.

488. "All long-range firing . . . immediately charge home.": OR Vol. I, No. 34 (3), p. 620.

488. "The strength of cavalry . . . of each command.": OR Vol. I, No. 32 (2), p. 358.

488–489. "Sheridan would proudly . . . Custer's cavalry brigades.": OR Vol. 43 (1), p. 822.

489. "In his more detailed . . . 'handsome saber charges.' ": OR Vol. 43 (1), p. 19.

490. "The Confederate cavalry . . . prisoners were taken.": OR Vol. 43 (1), pp. 456–457.

490. "Three stands of colors . . . prisoners were garnered.": OR Vol. 43 (1), p. 445.

490. "Those foolish individuals . . . whipped into submission.": OR Vol. I, No. 43 (1), p. 482.

490. "Merritt's cavalry would . . . Tom's Brook (October 9).": OR Vol. I, 43 (1), p. 447.

491. "Henceforth, troopers under . . . carbines when mounted.": OR Vol. I, No. 41 (4), p. 688.

491. "Only the recognition . . . out this plan.": OR Vol. I, No. 43 (1), p. 559.

492. "Ross explained that once . . . against a saber charge.": OR Vol. IV, No. 38 (3), p. 964.

492. "Brig. Gen. Bradley T. Johnson . . . West Virginia, on August 7.": OR Vol. I, No. 43 (1), p. 6.

492. "Smith promised to send . . . carry this weapon.": OR Vol. I, No. 48 (1), p. 1352.

492. "A brave enemy . . . and keen-edged sabers.": *A & N Journal*, Vol. II, No. 35, April 22, 1865, pp. 549.

493. "Writing to the commander . . . revolvers are essential.": OR Vol. I, No. 41 (2), p. 612.

493. "Operating in roughly . . . this type of terrain.": OR, SI, 34 (3)

493. "During the ensuing chase . . . 'back into the thicket.' ": OR Vol. I, No. 25 (1), p. 1119.

494. "Not only were . . . stand near Farmington.": Wulsin; pp. 44–46.

494. "The Tenth Missouri . . . signs of wavering.": OR Vol. I, No. 23 (1), p. 257.

495. "The threat on the . . . Volunteer Cavalry, mounted.": OR Vol. I, No. 44 (1) p. 392.

495. "Not only were . . . through Rockfish Gap.": OR Vol. I, No. 46 (1), pp. 502–503.

CHAPTER 26

496. "Wagner argued that . . . during the conflict.": Wagner, "Hasty Intrenchments.", p. 131.

497. "On July 19, 1861 . . . over the Bull Run.": OR Vol. I, No. 2, p. 308.

497. "The pioneers of the . . . Old Braddock Road.": OR Vol. I, No. 2, pp. 334–335.

498. "Not only did Union . . . to the Cheat Bridge.": OR Vol. I, No. 2, pp. 237–238.

498. "The Confederates used . . . area of the state.": OR Vol. I, No. 5, p. 133.

499. "Near the end . . . refused to stand up.": Skrine, p. 168.

499. "After the battle . . . and lying down.": OR Vol. I, No. 3, p. 61.

499. "A few months later . . . the crest of a hill.": OR Vol. I, No. 3, p. 227.

499. "Another observer on . . . or a prone position.": OR Vol. I, No. 3, p. 233.

499. "Several times during the . . . chances of being hit.": OR Vol. I, No. 3, p. 296; OR Vol. I, No. 7, p. 217.

499. "After the Battle of Pea . . . this defensive precaution.": OR Vol. I, No. 8, p. 252.

499–500. "It would be several . . . (May 31–June 1).": OR Vol. I, No. 11 (1), p. 555; OR Vol. I, No. 11 (1), p. 773.

500. "Seeing it was suicide . . . prompt and steady fire.": OR Vol. I, No. 16 (1), p. 927.

500. "Wallace recalled his thoughts . . . 'top of the bluff.' ": *Battles and Leaders*, Vol. I, p. 422.

501. "Both sides repeatedly . . . this type of barrier.": OR Vol. I, No. 12 (1), p. 748.

501. "The Union defenders . . . 51 wounded.": Lippitt, pp. 2–3.

502. "The roof, also . . . from burning arrows.": Lippitt, pp. 61–62.

504. "Great was their dismay . . . of the usual earth!": Meyer; p. 78.

504. "As Colonel Scribner, . . . hesitate to adopt it.": Scribner, pp. 260–261.

505. "In technical manuals . . . among Civil War infantrymen.": *A History of the 102d Illinois Infantry*, p. 85.

505. "The ends of branches . . . underbrush were cleared away.": Nesbit, p. 29.

506. "Of course, counting . . . these narrow passageways.": Wing, pp. 67–68.

506. "Others, seeing the fate . . . them to the ground.": Alexander, *Military* . . ., p. 516.

507. "The two were so . . . spattered with blood.": Adams, p. 91.

507. "Many also 'clubbed their muskets' . . . the defensive works.": OR Vol. I, No. 36 (1), p. 704.

507–508. "Others searching out crevices . . . hand-to-hand above him.": Wing, p. 68.

508. "This done, the infantrymen . . . and old musket barrels.": Adams, pp. 91, 93.

508. "Enraged, the Union . . . prisoners were cut down.": Wing, p. 68; Adams, p. 91.

509. "Several trees 18 inches . . . a South Carolina regiment.": Wing, p. 69.

509. "There is no personal . . . as I have seen.": Favill, pp. 296–297.

509. "Though lacking in artillery . . . latter eventually withdrew.": Hubbard, p. 33.

510. "Despite a series . . . hours, suffering heavy losses.": Lippitt, Intrenchments, p. 6.

510. "Those behind these . . . periodically with water.": Lippitt, Intrenchments, p. 6.

510–511. "Realizing that the expected . . . arms and surrender.": Mulligan in *Battles and Leaders* Vol. I, pp. 311–312; in footnote that quotes General Harris' official report.

511. "An 'incessant shower' . . . the attack proved futile.": OR Vol. I, No. 24 (2), pp. 391–392.

512. "These were sham attacks . . . of the main assault.": Lippitt, *A Treatise on Intrenchments*, p. 125.

512. "In the final moments . . . underground 'bomb-proofs'.": Lippitt, *A Treatise on Intrenchments*, pp. 114–117.

513. "In using it . . . advantage of position.": Lippitt, *A Treatise on Intrenchments*, p. 144.

513. "Once more the tables . . . and wreaked havoc.": Lippitt, *A Treatise on Intrenchments*, pp. 129–130.

514. "We replied with greater . . . crossing such a place.": OR Vol. I, No. 11 (1), p. 953.

515. "Passing quickly to . . . and some effect.": OR Vol. I, No. 7, pp. 212–213.

516. "The attack had devolved . . . most advanced position.": OR Vol. I, No. 24 (2), pp. 20–21.

517 "This defensive measure . . . after taking stiff casualties.": Lippitt, p. 55.

517. "Drawing up, they were . . . waiting in ambush.": OR Vol. I, No. 51 (1), p. 49.

517. "When encamped they were . . . unexpected enemy charge.": OR Vol. I, No. 18, p. 963.

517–518. "Though it is unclear . . . 'in this direction.' ": OR Vol. I, No. 27 (2), p. 85.

518. "Discovering that a 'rear . . . and telegraph wire.' ": OR Vol. I, No. 24 (2) XXIV/2, p. 331.

518. "The area immediately in . . . 'wire entanglement' combination.' ": OR Vol. I, No. 24 (2) p. 408.

518. "Taking a close look . . . 2-to 8-foot inclining stakes.": OR Vol. I, No. 24 (2) p. 179.

518. "Burnside, in a later . . . 'they were necessary.' ": OR Vol. I, No. 31 (1) p. 276.

518. "After the bloody repulse . . . to impede the assault.": OR Vol. I, No. 31 (1), p. 519.

CHAPTER 27

522. "Recently, Noah Andre Trudeau . . . 6 miles in depth.": Trudeau, pp. 203–206 in Kennedy.

522. "George Ward, who served . . . 7 miles long.": Ward, p. 163.

522. "John Robson, a one-legged . . . this 'mournful' country.": Robson, p. 134.

522–523. "W.A. Smith, a North . . . 'barely see ten paces.' ": Trudeau, pp. 203–206 in Kennedy.

523. "The hoot of the owl . . . into a denser swamp.": Ward, p. 163.

523. "Unfortunately, the forest . . . were quickly abandoned.": Trudeau, pp. 203–206, in Kennedy.

523. "The only traces . . . clearings here and there.": Ward, p. 163.

524. "Although the heavy forest . . . through this area.": Urban, p. 242; MacCauley, p. 10.

524. "There is not one spot . . . the right or the left.": Ward, p. 163.

524. "We were scratched and bruised, and our clothing torn.": MacCauley, p. 14.

525. "Shutting his eyes . . . his colonel's back.": Wing, p. 64.

525. "By this time . . . throes of disorder.": Petroff, p. 26.

526. "One Union artillery officer . . . 'on a grand scale.' ": Buell, pp. 161 & 167.

526. "They were only able . . . 'of the enemy's fire.": Favill, p. 290.

526. "The result was a . . . from line to line.": Favill,. p. 288.

527. "George Neese, a Confederate . . . to well past dusk.": Neese, pp. 261.

527. "The hissing flames . . . our boasted civilization.": Neese, p. 261.

528. "So intense had been . . . to waist level.": MacCauley, p. 14.

528. "The undergrowth had been . . . numerous shell explosions.": Favill, p. 288.

528. "Neese remembers 'A thousand . . . over the battle plain.' ": Neese, pp. 261.

528. "The smoke from the . . . 20 yards in front.": Favill, 288.

528. "Looking up, those in . . . skyline over the treetops.": Buell, p. 166.

530. "Surrounded or cut off . . . dearly as possible.": Huey, fn p. 14.

531. "Dusk now coming on . . . both lines of battle.": Huey, pp. 10–16.

532. "Wherever faced with . . . on the artillery's flanks.": Buell, p. 162.

532. "It ignited the grass . . . at the Yankee battery.": Neese, p. 260.

Chapter 28

534. "On May 5 . . . their advance that day.": OR Vol. I, No. 36 (1), p. 319.

534. "Elements of the Second . . . of Hancock's men.": OR Vol. I, No. 36 (1), p. 696.

534. "In this case the Union . . . from the rebel line.": Alexander, *Fighting . . .*, pp. 354, 390, 392.

535. "We immediately went . . . our party showed themselves.": Favill, p. 292.

536. "Officers were to make . . . for greater strength.": OR Vol. I, No. 30 (3), pp. 362–363.

536. "Once again, these were to be preceded by abatis.": OR Vol. I, No. 30 (1), pp. 158.

537. "The intelligence of . . . experiences of the other.": Wagner, *Hasty Intrenchments,* p. 141.

537. "Impressed with Smith's . . . Spotsylvania Court House.": Rhea, *To the North Anna River,* p. 321, citing Jedediah Hotchkiss, *Confederate Military History,* Vol. III, pp. 210–11.

537. "Some Union officers . . . of the Union armies.": Grant, *Battles and Leaders,* Vol. IV, p. 98.

538. "Starting off the 1864 . . . of the construction process.": Humphreys, p. 14. Technically, the Corps of Engineers was an umbrella organization of the Regular Army, with officers and men stationed in many areas and military organizations. However, apparently there was a disproportionate number with the Army of the Potomac. A good portion of the engineering troops that accompanied the Army of the Potomac was supplied by volunteer units, such as the Fifteenth and Fiftieth New York Engineers. There was only one battalion of Regulars.

538. "When it came to . . . 20,000 regular infantrymen.": Alexander, *Fighting . . .*, p. 370. A corps had no real fixed strength. Grant's army at the beginning of the Overland Campaign had four corps with an aggregate strength of over 90,000 infantrymen. Therefore, it is probably fair to say that Alexander estimated the Engineer force was worth perhaps 20,000 infantry or more.

538. "However, in *The Virginia* . . . 'to this country.' ": Humphreys, p. 117.

538. "Penetrating the second . . . Drewry's Bluff (May 16).": OR Vol. I, No. 36 (2), pp. 203, 253–254.

538. "Seeing its effectiveness . . . protect his entire front.": OR Vol. I, No. 36 (3) p. 238.

539. "A spy, sent out . . . resort to wire fences.": OR Vol. I, No. 40 (1) pp. 776–777, 779.

539. "By July 30 Maj. Gen . . . 'abatis but by wire.' ": OR Vol. I, No. 40 (3), p. 153.

539. "In November a company . . . Fisher to Fort Welch.": OR Vol. I, No. 42 (1) p. 179.

539. "In this portion . . . by wire fences.": OR Vol. I, No. 42 (1) p. 664.

540. "The work in its present . . . of the parapets, &c.": OR Vol. I, No. 46 (2), p. 354.

540. "Usually, this meant . . . with their bare hands.": Alexander, *Fighting* . . ., p. 381.

540–541. "Alexander conceded that . . . 'than a good beginning.' ": Alexander, *Military Memoirs* . . ., p. 536.

541. "Only when the Army . . . deepened and enlarged.": Alexander, *Fighting* . . ., p. 381.

542. "As soon as he . . . the intended recipient.": Alexander, *Fighting* . . ., pp. 408–409.

542. "At least as far as he . . . storming columns a minute.": Alexander, *Fighting* . . ., p. 381.

542. "Samuel Wing . . . 'very great advantage.' ": Wing, p. 68.

542. " 'It was murder . . . could have taken them.' ": Nesbit, p. 29.

542. "From the 5th of May . . . brief comparative repose.": Humphreys, pp. 117–118.

545–546. "Although the attackers . . . up a gradual incline.": Vaill, pp. 30–31; Izlar, p. 61.

546. "The men in the Second . . . 'by a converging fire.' ": Vaill, pp. 34–35.

546. "The air was filled . . . roar of their musketry.": Vaill, pp. 31–32.

546–547. "Dazed and now . . . was immediately captured.": Izlar, p. 61.

548. "The regiment encamped . . . spent at Cold Harbor.": Vaill, pp. 34–35.

CHAPTER 29

549–550. "Although Grant had . . . Burnside's and Warren's corps.": Symonds, p. 91.

550. "Waking up at dawn's . . . 'cloud of gray veterans.' ": Shaw, pp. 118–119.

550. "The troops suddenly came . . . New Market Race Course.": Roe, p. 174.

550. "Situated on a bare . . . as Colquitt's Salient.": Izlar, p. 75.

551. "These defensive positions . . . who served as support.": Roe, pp. 175–176.

551–552. "Although the field . . . unobstructed field of fire.": Roe, pp. 175–176.

552. "Although Union witnesses . . . on the Union side.": Izlar, p. 73.

552. "As the successive tiers . . . attention to company order.": Roe, pp. 174–175.

552. "Their sharpshooters continued . . . few men and officers.": Roe, pp. 179–180, quoting S.B. Dearborn's diary published by the *Wakefield Banner*, August 14, 1886.

552. "The Fifth Michigan Volunteers . . . supported from the rear.": Roe, p. 181; citing Dearborne's diary.

552–553. "During the fighting . . . on the Petersburg front.": Izlar, pp. 74–7 provides the lower estimate, citing "Carnage in First Maine Heavy Artillery" by Capt G.L. Gilmer, Military Editor, American Press Association.

553. "In his diary…Let the First Maine go!": Roe, p. 181, citing Dearborne's diary.

553. "All I could hope . . . the works with a rush.": Izlar, p. 75.

554. "Troops from Mott's Third . . . position along the line.": Roe, pp. 174–175.

554. "Every man detailed . . . force of 832 men.": Izlar pp. 75–76. citing Capt. Gilmer, who relied on a verbal quotation from Lt. Fred C. Low of Company C.

554. "During the upcoming . . . entirely on the bayonet.": Izlar, pp. 76–77.

554. "It was hoped that . . . until the final moments.": Shaw, pp. 121–122.

555. "The brigade's other regiment . . . behind the First Maine.": Izlar, p. 76, citing "Carnage in First Maine Heavy Artillery" by Capt. G.L. Gilmer, Military Editor American Press Association.

555. "Meanwhile, the third line . . . serve as a reserve.": Shaw, p. 122.

555. "Capt. F.A. Cummings . . . feet into the open field.": Izlar, pp. 74–75, quoting "Carnage in First Maine Heavy Artillery" by Capt. G.L. Gilmer.

555. "The crash of two . . . gaps in our ranks.": Izlar, p. 77.

556. "Yet, even as . . . close up the ranks.": Roe, p. 180.

556. "The first battalion had . . . officers lay in heaps.": Izlar, p. 77, citing Capt. G.L. Gilmer.

556. "The defenders' artillery . . . attackers broke and fled.": Roe, p. 180.

556. "The retreat lost much . . . if not so spectacular.": Izlar, p. 73.

556. "This appears to be . . . only 50 to 100 yards.": Roe, pp. 175, 180.

556. "Some of the Confederates . . . their defensive line.": Izlar, pp. 73, 77.

556. "Almost 700 of the . . . roll call that night.": Shaw, p. 122.

557. "Over the next several . . . their own defenses.": Roe, p. 184.

558. "Here they would . . . by the next shift.": Ward, p. 73.

558. "Only then was it . . . almost 48 hours.": Vaill, pp. 44–45, in front of Petersburg June 20–21, 1864.

559. "This was always . . . a deep-felt oath.": Ward, p. 77.

559. "This didn't last . . . became more vicious.": Shaw, p. 146.

559. "During the summer months . . . fireplaces were added.": Shaw, p. 144, Citing "Carnage in the First Main Heavy Artillery."

559. "Provisioned with a scant . . . wash their clothes.": Cutcheon, p. 137.

560. "Some men, in fear . . . of the enemy fire.": Ward, p. 77.

560. "Many men risked, . . . small piece of ice.": Cutcheon, p. 137.

560. "I ran the gauntlet . . . noon and evening.": Ward, p. 70.

561. "One-half of the line . . . or tried to sleep.": Ward, quoting letter written by Corporal Chambers of Battery L, p. 76.

561. "Sleeping during the night . . . 2 hours at a time.": Ward, p. 74.

561. "And, of course, bullets . . . have grave consequences.": Ward, p. 70.

562. "The 10 months of . . . portions of the lines.": Christopher M. Calkins in Kennedy, pp. 251–252.

562. "The Second U. S. Sharpshooters . . . pits and the old line.": OR Vol. I, No. 42 (1), p. 342.

563. "Officers sprang to the front . . . fell back in confusion.": Ward, p. 112–113.

563. "Despite their valor . . . battle-flags were lost.": OR Vol. I, No. 42 (3), p. 163.

563. "These exchanges could . . . tons of ammunition.": *History of the First Connecticut Artillery*, p. 102.

564. "Then a wide, sudden . . . within its deadly circle.": Twitchell, p. 47.

565. "In an action around . . . was one in five.": *History of the First Connecticut Artillery*, p. 102.

565. "Col. Henry L. Abbot who . . . three types of mortars.": *History of the First Connecticut Artillery*, p. 49.

565. "He felt that siege . . . the same functionality.": *History of the First Connecticut Artillery*, p. 49.

565. "Earlier trials with . . . of Petersburg and Richmond.": Abbot to Hunt Fort Richardson, April 26, *History of the First Connecticut Artillery,* p. 49.

565. "The guns would be . . . at a 45-degree angle.": *History of the First Connecticut Artillery,* pp. 49–50; Letter to Abbot from Hunt, May 4, Army Headquarters, Army of the Potomac.

566. "This technique proved to be . . . the enemy batteries' fire.": *History of the First Connecticut Artillery,* pp. 84–85.

566. "This, strictly speaking . . . during the Crimean War.": *History of the First Connecticut Artillery,* p. 56; OR Vol. I, p. 348.

566. "The experiment was . . . feet along the track.": *History of the First Connecticut Artillery,* p. 103.

566. "He then proposed . . . burn the Virginia capital.": *History of the First Connecticut Artillery,* pp. 118, 123.

Chapter 30

571. "Griffith claims that the average . . . a modest 141 yards.": Griffith, *Battle Tactics of the Civil War,* p. 147.

571. "The Confederate cannoneers . . . cover behind sandbags.": Peet, pp. 108–109, in camp near Yorktown.

572. "Another adjustment of the sticks . . . with great alacrity.": Ripley, William, p. 158.

573. "The Union infantry . . . left hors de combat.": Peck, p. 14.

573. "After the battle of Resaca . . . between 20 and 500 yards.": OR Vol. I, No. 38 (2), p. 149.

573. "Accounts provided by officers . . . during the entire war.": OR Vol. I, No. 35 (1), pp. 304–305. Although the returns indicate that the regiment was armed with Spencer carbines and Springfield rifle muskets, they must have possessed quantities of Enfields. The back sight on a Springfield had a maximum range of 500 compared to the Enfield's 800–900 yards.

573. "Seeing enemy infantry . . . ranged for 600 yards.": Although the returns indicate that the regiment was armed with Spencer carbines and Springfield rifle muskets, they must have possessed quantities of Enfields. The back sight on a Springfield had a maximum range of 500 compared to the Enfield's 800–900 yards.

573. "Once again the fire . . . abandon the attack.": OR Vol. I, No. 35 (1), p. 308.

573. "After Fredericksburg, Virginia . . . of the defenders.": OR Vol. I, No. 21, p. 327.

573. "The Ninety-seventh New York . . . in front of them.": OR Vol. I, No. 21, p. 506.

573–574. "On the first day . . . about 40 rods distant.": OR Vol. I, No. 27 (1), p. 276.

574. "During the first day . . . 'in each other's faces.' ": Henderson, *Stonewall Jackson and the American Civil War,* Vol. II, p. 147.

574. "At Antietam (September 17, 1862) . . . or a hundred paces.": Henderson, *Stonewall Jackson and the American Civil War,* Vol. II, p. 248.

574. "The Union assaulting . . . was completely broken.": Henderson, *Stonewall Jackson and the American Civil War*, Vol. II, p. 174.

575. "Despite the proximity . . . lasted half an hour.": OR Vol. I, No. 9 (1), p. 785.

575. "Unnerved, their attack . . . and settle the issue.": OR Vol. I, No. 24 (1), p. 511.

575–576. "He withheld the fire . . . to fire by files.": OR Vol. I, No. 9, p. 267.

576. "Under the cover . . . spotted and fired upon.": OR Vol. I, No. 15, p. 89.

576. "Only then did . . . unleash a "heavy fire.": OR Vol. I, No. 10 (1), p. 549.

577. "Surprised by the resistance . . . in noticeable disorder.": OR Vol. I, No. 16 (1), p. 259.

577. "This produced the same result as in the previous example.": OR Vol. I, No. 17 (1), p. 558.

577. "This blistering fire . . . and two battle flags.": OR Vol. I, No. 36 (1), p. 800.

578. "A contemporary military . . . did not exceed 10%.": *Army & Navy Journal*, Vol. I, p. 12.

578. "But it is utterly . . . before the fight.": Neese, p. 35.

578. "Colonel B.F. Scribner observed . . . 'excess of random shots.' ": Scribner, pp. 271–273.

578–579. "When you consider . . . insignificant in comparison.": Hermann, pp. 55–56.

579. "Let officers and men, . . . and self-possessed, temper.": OR Vol. I, No. 11 (3), pp. 606.

579. "As I have before . . . been the greatest mystery.": *Army & Navy Journal*, Vol. I, p. 12.

580. "Once satisfied that his . . . his own lines unhurt.": Stimson, p. 26.

580. In his highly illuminating…'What becomes of all the bullets?'" : Scribner, pp. 271–273.

580. "Such an approach . . . of contemporary observers.": Thomas, Dean S.; *Ready . . . Aim . . . Fire! Small Arms Ammunition in the Battle of Gettysburg*, Biglerville, Pa., 1981.

581. "Many trees had been . . . way to their tops.": Moore, Edward, pp. 83-84.

581. "Neese went on to . . . from top to bottom.": Neese, pp. 270–271.

581. "Hermann concluded that . . . sort of visual detection.": Hermann, pp. 55–56.

581. "Hermann confided to his . . . the pine that day.": Hermann, pp. 55–56.

582. "Experiments in Britain . . . target at 100 yards.": Hughes, *Firepower*, p. 27 citing Picard, *La campagne de 1800 en Allemange*.

582. "One historian studying . . . a 1.0% casualty rate.": Anonymous historian cited in Duane, Vol. I, p. 207.

582. "Writing after the Napoleonic . . . between 0.01% and 0.03%.": Du Picq, p. 245.

582. "Estimated Casualties Inflicted by British during Napoleonic Wars." [Chart title]: Greener, p. 218; Estimates figures for Guibert, Gassendi, Piobert cited in Ardant Du Picq, p. 245; anonymous historian cited in Duane, Vol. I, p. 207, Jackson in Jackson, p. 262; Decker in *Army & Naval Journal*, 1863, Vol. I, No. 1, p. 11, fn.

583. "This officer calculated . . . for every 125 rounds.": *Army & Naval Journal*, Vol. I, p. 11.

583. "Based on his experience . . . every 400 shots fired.": Hermann, pp. 55–56.

583. "Fortunately, however, the . . . wounded and killed.": Out of these wounded another 10% would eventually succumb to their wounds in the field hospitals. *Army & Naval Journal*, Vol. 1, p. 12.

584. "Depending upon the amount . . . between 0.60% and 0.80%.": Capt. Horace Porter, Chief of Ordnance for the Army of Cumberland reported that Union infantry fired 2,529,952 bullets; OR I 30 (1), p. 233. The Confederates lost a total of 16,986 killed and wounded during the engagement. Presuming 8% of the casualties were caused by the artillery and 2.4% by cavalry, about 15,219 casualties were inflicted by Union infantry. Thus, Union infantrymen succeeded in hitting an enemy 0.60% of the time. However, this is probably too low an estimate. Captain Porter reported 150,280 rounds had been captured or lost. Longstreet, on the other hand, claimed he captured 393,000 rounds of Union small arms ammunition. And this was just on the Confederate left, alone, OR I, 30 (2), p. 290. Subtracting the number of rounds mentioned by Longstreet, the adjusted percentage of hits becomes 0.67% And, if the Union left lost as much ammunition as did the right, the new hit rate becomes .080%.

584. "Surgeon Thomas A. McParlin . . . during the entire battle.": OR Vol. I, No. 36 (1), p. 219.

584. "This results in an . . . between 0.99% and 1.5%.": Army strengths from Rhea, *The Battle of the Wilderness*, p. 34.; Numbers of Union officers and men at Gettysburg from Busey and, pp. 21–89; Confederate casualties from Trudeau, p. 341; Young, p. 26.

586. "A contributor to the Army . . . among inexperienced troops.": *Army & Naval Journal*, Vol. I, p. 11, Aug 29, 1863.

586. "In his memoirs Hermann would concur.": Hermann, p. 56.

586. "Some men and not . . . fire at the moon.": Neese, pp. 270-271.

587. "This meant that . . . the new rifle muskets.": Moore, Frank, Vol. I, Section 3, p. 95.

589. "The great disproportion . . . in European warfare.": *Army & Naval Journal*, Vol. I, p. 11, Aug 29, 1863.

589. "Being placed in position . . . it strikes the ground.": Wilford, p. 245.

590. "Capt. John De Forest . . . with a 'murderous pugnacity.' ": De Forest, pp. 184–185.

591. "They say he is a noted . . . share in the field.": Favill, pp. 32–34.

CHAPTER 31

594. "Before the Battle of Bull . . . upon the bayonet.": OR Vol. I, No. 51 (2), p. 175; OR Vol. I, No. 14, p. 192.

594. "Before the Battle of . . . him with the bayonet.": OR Vol. I, No. 20 (1), p. 183.

594. "During the Atlanta campaign . . . and meet him halfway.": OR Vol. I, No. 38 (4), p. 42.

594 "At about exactly . . . demoralization and confusion.": OR Vol. I, No. 38 (4), p.671.

595. "Then the officer was . . . depending upon circumstances.": OR Vol. I, No. 42 (2), p. 344.

595. "The author went . . . for chicken or ham.": Davis, William, pp. 6, 12.

595. "According to Heros . . . only in the imagination.": Borcke, Vol. I, p. 64–65.

596. "Still naïve to the true . . . other works of fiction.": De Forest, pp. 65–66.

596. "I carefully examined . . . evidently after the bullets.": Borcke, Vol. I, p. 63.

597. "Contrary to his . . . this type of wound.": OR Vol. I, No. 31 (1), pp. 99–101.

597. "Casualties: Army of the Potomac May-July, 1864" [Chart Title]: OR Vol. I, No. 36 (1), pp. 225–226, 237–238, 251–252, 261–262.

597. "These findings support . . . end of the war.": OR Vol. I, No. 42 (1), pp. 200–202.

597–598. "Although during the . . . bayonet in open terrain.": Ardant du Picq, p. 127.

598. "Similarly, military historians . . . on open terrain.": Duffy, p. 79.

598. "This was the constant . . . the attacking party": Mitchell, pp. 64–65.

600. "No movement in the field . . . with the fleeing foe.": Anton, pp. 107–108.

600. "In later years . . . flashes of bursting shells.": Hermann, p. 70.

600. "Alonzo F. Hill, who had . . . a 'thought of fear.' ": Hill, A.F.; p. 384.

601. "The enemy, staggering . . . turned and fled.": For a more thorough treatment of the difference between French and British bayonet charges, see Nosworthy, *With Musket Cannon and Sword,* pp. 235-241.

602. "Chamberlain himself was . . . surrendering his sword.": OR Vol. I, No. 27 (1), p. 624

602. "Some men clubbed . . . used clubs and rails.": OR Vol. I, No. 36 (1), p. 704.

603. "Close-in fighting . . . massive Confederate assault.": OR Vol. I, No 25 (1) pp. 711–712.

603. "Similar dynamics occurred . . . on May 9, 1864.": OR Vol. I, No. 37 (1), p. 21.

604. "In his report Major . . . 'sustained great loss.' ": OR Vol. I, No. 19 (1), p. 507.

604. "During the affair . . . instead of advancing.": OR Vol. I, No. 2, p. 84.

605. "Advancing quickly, the regiment . . . was completely routed.": OR Vol. I, No. 7, pp. 79-80, 94; Lippett, *Tactical Use of the Three Arms,* p. 25; Bishop, p. 41.

605. "Harassed by an opposing . . . series of bayonet charges.": OR Vol. I, No. 2, p. 443.

605. "At 3.30 A.M. . . . in our possession.": OR Vol. I, No. 2, pp. 481–482.

606. "As soon as it . . . without awaiting the charge.": OR Vol. I, No. 10 (1), p. 318.

606. "Another very notable . . . Winchester (May 25, 1862).": Henderson, Stonewall Jackson, p. 340.

606. "The loss of the fleeing enemy was heavy.": Wood, James, p. 53.

607. "Cooke concluded that . . . band of fugitives.": Cooke, John, p. 43.

608. "The discipline of Hagood's . . . from returning the fire.": Hagood, p. 291; OR Vol. I, No. 42 (1), p. 936.

CHAPTER 32

609. DeRussy concluded that . . . 'now have in service.' ": McCauly, pp. 40-41.

609. "He cited the oft-repeated . . . all available ammunition.": Drury & Gibbons, p. 58.

610. "The .69-caliber cylindrical . . . Springfield musket rifles.": Dixon, pp. 100-101.

610. "Maj. John J. Mudd . . . ball, and paper.": OR Vol. I, No. 17 (1), p. 143.

611. "This was a real inconvenience . . . not keep up with them.": OR Vol. I, No. 40 (3), p. 250.

611. "The newer carbines, though . . . than the rifle muskets.": OR Vol. III, No. 2, p. 621.

612. "Impressed, the Navy placed . . . July of that year.": Drury & Gibbons, pp. 58, 61.

613. "Undeterred, the regiment's . . . pay for the Merrills.": McCauley, pp. 61–62.

613. "At Shiloh (April 6–7 . . . movement on its right.": OR Vol. I, No. 10 (1), p. 451.

613. "During the Seven Days' . . . of the regiment.": OR Vol. I, No. 11 (2), p. 130.

613. "At Corinth (October 3–4, 1862) . . . opposing the regiment.": OR Vol. I, No. 17 (1).

613–614. "Watson replied that . . . their own expense.": OR Vol. III, No. 2 Vol. II, pp. 412-413.

614. "The flank companies . . . were similarly armed.": OR Vol. I, No. 14, p. 167.

615. "Arming large numbers . . . not a viable option.": Bilby, *A Tale . . .*, citing the yet-to-be published, unpaginated manuscript.

615. "This was a stance.... counterpart, Union Gen. Ripley!": OR Vol. IV, No. 2, pp. 720–721.

617. "Yet this is West Point . . . cost to the country?": SA-NS, Vol. VIII, No. 10, March, 7, 1863, p. 151.

617. "Finally, they resurrected . . . issue of reliability.": SA-NS, Vol. VIII, No. 10, March, 7, 1863, p. 154.

618. "Rosecrans pleaded that . . . or delay the supply.": OR Vol. I, No. 17 (2), p. 105.

618–619. "Expanding upon his . . . or breech-loading rifles.": OR Vol. I, No. 17 (2), p. 108.

619. "On August 6, for . . . was $10,000 a day.": OR I 17 (2), p. 154; OR Vol. I, No. 20 (2), p. 31.

619. "This analysis was predicated . . . muzzle-loading weapons.": OR Vol. I, No. 20 (2), p. 58.

619. "Rosecrans's campaign of . . . carbines and rifles.": OR Vol. I, No.17 (2), p. 282.

619. "This rule must be . . . 'Peter to pay Paul.' ": OR Vol. I, No. 20 (2), p. 60.

619. "Stanton closed the short . . . 'expected from you.' ": OR Vol. I, No. 20 (2), p. 64.

619–620. "P.H. Watson, assistant . . . than any other commander.": OR Vol. I, No. 20 (2), p. 135.

620. "The same day he sent . . . of his plans.": OR Vol. I, No. 20 (2), p. 58.

620. "Each brigade was to . . . shoulder arms available.": OR Vol. I, No. 23 (2), p. 31.

620. "As such they were...at brigade headquarters.": OR Vol. I, No. 23 (2), pp. 67-68.

620. "Each trooper signed . . . promissory note for $35.": Couzzins, pp. 14-15.

623. "Ripley's claim to the . . . immediately adopt breechloaders.": SA-NS, Vol. VIII, No. 19, May 9, 1863, pp. 293–294.

624. "This was especially . . . always to fight dismounted.": *Army & Navy Journal*, Vol. I, No. #8, p. 118–Oct 17, 1863.

626. "In the case where . . . the operation of loading.": SA-NS, Vol. X, No. 11, March 12, 1864, p. 170.

626. "In September 1864 . . . War, then underway.": *Army and Navy Journal*, Vol. I, No. 50, Aug. 6, 1864, p. 822.

626. "Henceforth, one regiment . . . 148th Pennsylvania regiment.": Fox, p. 302.

Chapter X, 148th Pennsylvania Infantry; Brooke's Brigade--Barlow's Division--2nd Corps.

627. "Factoring in cost . . . 'very desirable measure.' " : OR Vol. III, No. 4, p. 802.

627. "If they can stand that . . . piece and blaze away...": *Army & Navy Journal*, Vol. 2, p. 278, 18, Dec. 24, 1864.

627. "To this end he . . . select the new weapon.": OR III 4, Vol. IV, pp. 971–972.

628. "The confidence in the arm . . . supplied with them.": OR Vol. I, No. 45 (2), Vol. XLV (2), p. 488.

628. "On March 1, 1865 . . . be universally introduced.": OR Vol. III, No. 4, p. 1208.

628. "He did admit that . . . to be the most promising.": OR Vol. III, No. 5, pp. 142–143.

628. "In light of the existing . . . muskets into breechloaders.": OR Vol. III, No. 5, pp. 1034–1035.

CHAPTER 33

631. "Another 600 meters...separated by 600 meters.": Lyman, pp. 49–50.

632. "The resulting *Treatise...Edinburgh Review*, as well.": Lippitt, *A Treatise on Intrenchments*, pp. i–iv.

637. "It also seemed to . . . the Zouave methods.": Lyman, pp. 45–46.

638. "If the first battalion . . . rear of the brigade.": Upton, pp. 304–306.

CHAPTER 34

643. "A few historians . . . of the musket era.": Griffith, *Battle Tactics of the Civil War*, 1989.

644. "Mechanical hand grenades . . . Napoleon III in 1858.": *London Illustrated News*, Vol. XXXII, No. 896, Feb 27, 1858, p. 222.

644–645. "The Russians attempted . . . during the 1850s.": *The Engineer*, March 7, 1856, p. 121.

645. "The next year . . . system of transportation.": Wawro, p. 10.

650. "The study of military . . . backgrounds and methodologies.": The analysis of the contributions by various types of enthusiasts first appeared in Nosworthy, *The Current State of Military History.*

655. "An instructor in the Department . . . tactical military historian.": Griffith, *Forward into Battle*, p. 14.

Bibliography

To assist those wishing to consult the following sources, the location of ultrarare works not listed in the National Union Catalog or the electronic Worldcat OCLC database has also been provided. [in brackets]

-A-

Adams, John G. *Reminiscences of the Nineteenth Massachusetts Regiment.* Boston, 1899.

Addeman, J.M. *Reminiscences of Two Years with Colored Troops* Personal Narratives of the Events in the War, series 2, no. 7, Providence, Rhode Island, 1880.

Adts, V. (Lt., Fourth Belgian Artillery Regiment). *Des canon rayés: Research nouvelles.* Paris, 1862.

Alexander, Edward Porter (Gen.). *Military Memoirs of a Confederate.* Bloomington: Indiana University Press, 1962.

Alexander, Edward Porter (Gen.). *Fighting for the Confederacy.* Chapel Hill, N.C., 1987.

"American Military Literature," *United Service Magazine,* London, pt. 2 no. 391, June 1861, pp. 207–210.

Anderson, John Q., ed. *Campaigning with Parsons' Texas Cavalry Brigade CSA: The War Journal and Letters of the Four Orr Brothers, 12 Texas Cavalry Regiment.* Hillsboro, Texas, 1967.

Anton, James. *Retrospect of a Military Life.* Edinburgh, Scotland, 1841. Facsimile reprint, Cambridge, 1991.

Ardant du Picq (Col.). Charles J.J.J., *Battle Studies: Ancient and Modern Battle,* trans. Col. John N. Greely and Robert C. Cotton. Harrisburg, Pa., 1947.

Armstrong, Marion Vincent. "United States Tactical Doctrine, 1855–1861." Master's thesis, Old Dominion University, Dec. 1991.

Army and Navy Journal, New York, vol. 1–3, 1863–65.

Arnold, James. *Marengo and Hohenlinden: Napoleon's Rise to Power.* Lexington, Va., 1999.

"The Artillerist," *Harper's Magazine,* New York, vol. 24, no. 142, March 1862, pp. 545–549.

Avery, P.O. *History of the Fourth Illinois Cavalry Regiment.* Humboldt, Nebraska, 1903.

-B-

Barnard, J.G. (Gen.), and W.F. Barry (Gen.). *Report of the Engineers and Artillery Operations of the Army of the Potomac.* New York, 1863.

Barrett, Edwin S. *What I Saw at Bull Run,* Boston, 1886.

Baylor, George (Capt.). *Bull Run to Bull Run, or, Four Years in the Army of Northern Virginia.* Richmond, 1900.

Beecher, Herbert W. *History of the First Light Battery Connecticut Volunteers, 1861–65. New York, 1901.*

Benham, Calhoun (Maj.). A System for Conducting Musketry Instruction, Prepared and Printed by Order of General Bragg for the Army of Tennessee. Richmond, 1863. Facsimile reprint, Ashburn, Va., 1998, with an introduction by Joseph Bilby.

Bennett, Charles. *A Historical Account of the Development of Small Arms.* Fort Monroe, Va., 1886.

Bennet, L.G., and William M. Haight. *History of the Thirty-Six Regiment Illinois Volunteers.* Aurora, Ill., 1876.

Bercher, Dr. Harvey H. *Record of the 114th New York State Volunteers.* Norwich, N.Y., 1866.

Bilby, Joseph G. *Civil War Firearms.* Conshohocken, Penn., 1996.

Bilby, Joseph G. "A Tale of Technology: Union Cavalry Arms in the Civil War." *History Channel Magazine,* summer 2003.

Bishop, Judson W. (Col.). *The Story of a Regiment, Being a Narrative of the Service of the Second Regiment, Minnesota Veteran Volunteer Infantry,* St. Paul Minn., 1890.

Blackford, W.W. (Lt. Col.). *War Years with Jeb Stuart.* New York, 1945.

Blackmore, Howard L., *British Military Firearms, 1650–1850.* London, 1961.

Blanche, H.J. *A Century of Guns.* London, 1909.

Bland, Humphrey (Col.). *A Treatise of Military Discipline.* 1st ed., London, 1727. 8th ed., London, 1759.

Blessington, Joseph P. *The Campaigns of Walker's Division.* New York, 1875.

Bliss, George, N. *Reminiscences of the Service in the First Rhode Island Cavalry.* Personal Narratives of the Events in the War, ser. 1, no. 3. Providence, Rhode Island, 1878.

Bliss, George, N. *How I Lost My Sabre in War and Found It in Peace.* Personal Narratives of the Events in the War, ser. 2, no. 6. Providence, Rhode Island, 1903.

Boatner, Mark M., III. *The Civil War Dictionary.* New York, 1959.

Bonie, Jean Jacques *et al, Cavalry Studies from the Two Great Wars.* Kansas City, Mo., 1896.

Borcke, Heros von. *Memoirs of the Confederate War for Independence.* 2 vols. New York, 1938.

Brackett, Albert G. *History of the United States Cavalry.* New York, 1965.

Brady, Cyrus Townsend. *The Sioux Indian Wars.* New York, 1992.

Buell, Augustus. *The Cannoneer.* Washington, 1890.

Bugeaud, Thomas Robert. *The Practice of War.* Richmond, Va., 1863.

Bülow, A. H. *The Spirit of the Modern System of War by a General Prussian Officer.* London, 1806.

Busey, John W., and David G. Martin. *Regimental Strengths and Losses at Gettysburg.* Hightstown, N.J., 1986.

Busk, Hans. *The Rifle: And How to Use It.* 5th ed., London, 1859.

Butterfield, Dexter (Sergeant). *A Brief History of the "Abbott Grays" (Second Massachusetts Volunteer Infantry).* Lowell, Mass., 1911.

Butts, Francis B. *The Monitor and the Merrimac.* Personal Narratives of the Events in the War, ser. 4, no. 6. Providence, Rhode Island, 1890.

Butts, Francis B. (Corporal). *The Origin and First Campaign of Battery "E", First Rhode Island Light Artillery.* Personal Narratives of the Events in the War, ser. 5, no. 2, pp. 1–85. Providence, Rhode Island, 1896.

-C-

Califf, Joseph, attr. *Record of the Services of the Seventh Regiment of U.S. Colored Troops.* Providence, R.I., 1878.

Cannon, Le G. B. *Recollections of the Iron Clads, Monitor and Merrimack.* Burlington, Va., 1875.

Chesney, Charles (Capt.). *Observations on the Past and the Present State of Firearms and on the Probable Effects of the New Musket.* London, 1852.

Chesney, Charles. *The Military Resources of Prussia and France.* London, 1870.

Chesneau, Roger, and Eugene M. Kolesnik, eds. *Conway's All the World's Fighting Ships, 1860–1905. London, Conway, 1979.*

Clarke, Charles H. *History of Company "F" First Regiment of Rhode Island Volunteers during the Spring and Summer of 1861.* Newport, Rhode Island, 1891.

Clapp, Henry S. *Sketches of Army Life in the Sixties.* N.p., n.d.

Coates, Earl J., and John D. McAulay. *Civil War Sharps Carbines and Rifles.* Gettysburg, Penn., 1996.

Coffin, Charles Carleston. *Following the Flag from August 1861 to November 1862.* Boston, 1865.

Coggins, Jack. *Arms and Equipment of the Civil War.* New York, 1983.

Coles, Cowper P. (Capt. R.N.). "Shot-Proof Gun Shields as Adapted to Iron-Cased Ships." *Journal of the United Service Institute,* pp. 280–290.

Colin, Jean Lambert Alphonse. *L'infanterie au XVIIIe siècle: La Tactique.* Paris, 1907.

Congdon, Don, ed. *Combat: The Civil War.* New York, 1992.

Conrad, Mark, trans. "The Moscow Infantry Regiment at Alma (Part 2)." *The War Correspondent* (journal of the Crimea Research Society), Barnham, West Sussex, England vol. XV, no. 4, January 1998, Barnham, West Sussex, pp. 12–19.

Considerations on Tactics; More Particularly on the Combination of the Three Arms of War. London, 1853.

Cooke, Jacob B. *The Battle of Kelley's Ford.* Personal Narratives of the Events in the War, ser. 3, no. 19. Providence, R.I. 1887.

Cooke, John Esten. *Stonewall Jackson and the Old Stonewall Brigade.* Charlottesville, Va., 1954.

Coombe, Jack D. *Thunder along the Mississippi.* New York, 1996.

Cozzens, Peter. *This Terrible Sound: The Battle of Chickamauga.* Urbana, University of Illinois Press, 1992.

Cox, Jacob, D. (Maj. Gen.). "War Preparations in the North." in *Battles and Leaders*, vol. I., pp. 84–98.

Crandall,W.D., and J.D. Hewhill. *History of the Ram Fleet and the Mississippi Marine Brigade.* St. Louis, 1907.

Croffut, W.A., and John M. Morris. *The Military and Civil History of Connecticut during the War of 1861–65.* New York, 1869.

Currie, George E. *Warfare Along the Mississippi: The Letters of Lieutenant Colonel George E. Currie*, ed. Norm E. Clarke, Sr. Mount Pleasant, Michigan, 1961.

Curry, John P. *Volunteer's Camp and Field Book.* New York, 1861.

Curtis, Bill. "Infantry Shoulder Arms (Part 10)." *The War Correspondent* (Journal of the Crimea Research Society), Barnham, West Sussex, England, vol. XV, no. 4, January 1998, pp. 30–32.

Curtis, Newton Martin. *From Bull Run to Chancellorsville: The Story of the Sixteenth New York.* New York, 1906.

Cutcheon, Byron M. *The Story of the Twentieth Michigan Infantry.* Lansing, Mich., 1904.

-D-

Dahlgren, J.A. *Shells and Shell-guns.* Philadelphia, 1856.

Dalrymple, Campbell (Lt. Col., King's Own Regiment). *A Military Essay Containing Reflections on the Raising, Arming, Cloathing, and Discipline of the British Infantry and Cavalry.* London, 1761.

Daniel, Larry J. *Cannoneers in Gray.* Alabama, 1984.

Daniel, R.P. (Père). *Histoire de la Malice Françoise*, 2 vols., Paris, 1721.

Davidson, Henry M. *History of Battery A, First Regiment of Ohio Volunteer Light Artillery.* Milwaukee, 1865.

Davis, Lucius (Col.). *The Trooper's Manual or Tactics for Light Dragoons and Mounted Riflemen*, 3d ed. Richmond, 1862.

Davis, William C. *Weapons of the Civil War.* New York, 1991.

De Brack, Antoine Fortuné (Col.). *Cavalry Outpost Duties.* New York, 1893.

Decker, Karl. D. *De la tactique des trois armes: Infanterie, cavalerie, artillerie*, trans. F. De Brack. Paris, n.d.

De Forest, John William (Col.). *A Volunteer's Adventures: A Union Captain's Record of the Civil War.* New Haven, Conn., 1946.

deKay, James Tertius. *Monitor: The Story of the Legendary Civil War Ironclad and the Man Whose Invention Changed the Course of History.* New York, 1997.

Delafield, Richard, (Col.) *Report on the Art of War in Europe in 1854, 1855, and 1856.* Washington, 1861.

De la Pierre, E.H. *Simples elements d'art militaire.* Paris, 1847.

de Sionville [generally ascribed to François Alexandre Aubert de la Chesnaye Desbois]. *Œuvres Militatires*, 3 vols., n.p., 1756. [Rare Book Room, McLellan Library, McGill University, Montreal]

Denison, Frederic. *Sabres and Spurs, First Rhode Island Cavalry*. Centry, R.I., 1876.

Dickey, Thomas S., and Peter C. George. *Field Artillery Projectiles of the American Civil War*. Rev. and suppl. ed. Mechanicsville, Va., 1993.

Dinkins, James. *1861 to 1865, by a Johnnie; Personal Recollections and Experiences in the Confederate Army*. Cincinnati, 1897.

Dixon, Lt. Col. (R.A.) "The Rifle—Its Probable Influence on Modern Warfare," *Journal of the Royal United Service Institution*, vol. 1, no. 2, 1857, 95–120.

Donaghy, John. *Army Experience of Capt. John Donaghy, 103rd Pennsylvania Volunteers*. De Land, Florida, 1926 (written 1886).

Dorr, Eben P. *A Brief Sketch of the First Monitor and Its Inventor*. 2d ed. Buffalo, N.Y., 1874.

Douglas, Sir General Howard. "The Attack of Bomarsund." *United Service Magazine*, London, pt. 1, February 1855, pp. 209–213.

Douglas, Howard, Sir General. "General Sir H. Douglas on Iron Defences and Armour-Plated Ships." *United Service Magazine*, London, Jan. 1861, pp. 46–84.

Dowd, Ira. *One Young Soldier* New York, 1918. Originally published as *The Song of the Rappahanock* (1898).

Drury, Ian, & Tony Gibbons. *The Civil War Military Machine*. New York, 1993.

Duane, William. *The American Military Library; or, Compendium of the Modern Tactics*. Philadelphia, 1809.

Duhèsme, Guillaume P. (Comte de, Lt. Gen.) *Essai sur l'infanterie légère: Traite des petites opérations de guerre*. Paris, 1814.

Duffy, Christopher. *The Army of Maria Theresa*. New York, 1977.

Dupuy, R. Ernest, and Trevor N. Dupuy. *The Encyclopedia of Military History*. 2d revised ed., New York, 1986.

Dyer, Frederick Henry. *A Compendium of the War of the Rebellion*. Des Moines, Iowa, 1908.

-E-

Early, Jubal Anderson (Gen.). *War Memoirs, Autobiographical Sketch, and Narrative of the War between the States*. New York, 1989.

Eby, Henry *Observations of an Illinois Boy in Battle, Camp, and Prisons: 1861–1865*. Mendota, Ill., 1910.

Eggleson, George Cary. *A Rebel's Recollections*. 2d ed. New York, 1887.

Eldredge, D. (Capt.). *The Third New Hampshire and All about It*. Boston, 1893.

Elliot, General Issac H. *History of the Thirty-Third Regiment Illinois Veteran Volunteer Infantry in the Civil War*. Gibson City, Ill., 1902.

Essai sur la tactique de l'infanterie. Geneva, 1761. [Boston Pulic Library]

Estvan, B. *War Pictures from the South*, 2 vols. London, 1863.

-F-

Faust, Patricia L., ed. *Historical Times Illustrated Encyclopedia of the Civil War.* New York, 1986.

Favé (Capt.). *The Emperor's New System: Field Artillery,* trans. William Hamilton Cox. London, 1854.

Favill, Josiah Marshall (Lieut.). *The Diary of a Young Officer: Serving with the Armies of the United States during the War of the Rebellion.* Chicago, 1909.

Fay, Charles (Chef de escadron). *Conférence de qulques récents travaux sur la tactique.* Conférences du Ministère de la Guerre, 1869–1870, 1st ser., no. 5. Paris, 1869.

Felton, Silas. "Pursuing the Elusive 'Cannoneer'." *The Gettysburg Magazine,* no. 9, July 1993, pp. 33–39.

Fenner, Earl. *The History of Battery H: First Regiment of Rhode Island Light Artillery.* Providence, R.I., 1894.

Fishbourne, E.G., (Capt. R.N.). "Iron Ships and Iron Plates." *Journal of the Royal United Service Institution,* 1861, pp. 354–369.

Foote, Shelby. *The Civil War: A Narrative,* 3 vols. New York, 1958–1974.

Fox, Lane (Lieut. Col.). "On the Improvement of the Rifle—As a Weapon for General Use." *Journal of the Royal United Service Institution,* vol. 2, no. 8, 1858, pp. 453–493.

Fox, William F. *Regimental Losses of the Civil War.* Albany, N.Y., 1889.

France, Ministre de la Guerre. *Ordonnance du Roi du Juillet 1845 sur l'exercise et les manoeuvres des bataillons de chassuers d'Orléans.* Paris, 1845.

Frank Leslie's Illustrated Newspaper, New York, vol. 10, no. 244, July 28, 1860, pp. 145–146, 152.

Frederick II. "Instruction du Fredéric, pour l'artillerie." *Spectateur Militaire,* Paris, vol. 4, 1828, pp. 55–60.

Fuller, Claud. *The Rifled Musket.* Harrisburg, Pa., 1958.

"The Future of Cavalry: Part II." *United Service Magazine,* London, pt. 3, no. 394, Sept. 1861, pp. 46–53.

-G-

Gardiner, Robert, ed. *Steam, Steel, and Shellfire: The Steam Warship, 1815–1905.* Annapolis, Md., 1992.

Gassendi Jean-Jacques Basilien. *Aide-mémoire a l'usage des officers d'artillerie.* 2d ed., Paris, 1844.

Gibbon, John (Capt.). *The Artillerist's Manual, Compiled from Various Sources and Adapted to the Services of the United States.* 2d ed. New York, 1863.

Gibbon, John (Brig. Gen.). *Personal Recollections of the War.* Dayton, Oh., 1978. Facsimile reprint of 1928 edition, New York.

Gill, John. *Reminiscences of Four Years as a Private.* Baltimore, 1902.

Glasier, Willard. *Three Years in the Federal Cavalry.* New York, 1870.

Gosnell, H. Allen. *Guns on the Western Waters*. Baton Rouge, La., 1949.

Gould, Richard A. *Recovering the Past*. Albuquerque, N.M., 1990.

de Grandmaison (Gen.). *On the Military Service of Light Troops in the Field and in Fortified Places*, trans by Major Lewis Nicola. Philadelphia, 1777. Originally published as *Petit guerre; au traite du service des troupes legers en campagne*, Paris, 1756.

Grant, Ulysses, S. (Gen.) *Personal Memoirs of Ulysses S. Grant*. New York, 1994.

Great Britain, War Office. *Rules and Regulations for the Guidance of Officers and Non-commissioned Officers of Artillery*. London, 1808. Also known as *The Madras Gunner*.

"The Great Naval Revolution." *The Cornhill Magazine*, London, no. 5, May 1862, pp. 550–559.

Greene, Jack. *Ironclads at War: The Origin and Development of the Armored Warship, 1854–1891, Conshohocken, Penn., 1998.*

Greenhill, Basil, and Ann Gifford. The British Assault on Finland, 1854–1855. London, 1988.

Griffith, Paddy. *Forward into Battle: Fighting Tactics from Waterloo to Vietnam*. Chichester West Sussex, England, 1981.

Griffith, Paddy. *Battle Tactics of the Civil War*. New Haven, Conn., 1989.

-H-

Hagood, Johnson (Gen.). *Memoirs of the War of Succession from the Original Manuscripts of Johnson Hagood*. Columbia, S.C., 1910.

Hale, Edward Everett. *Stories of War Told by Soldiers*. Boston, 1879.

Halleck, Henry Wagner (Gen.). *Elements of Military Art and Science*. New York, 1863.

Halsted, Pellew E. (Captain, R.N.). "Iron-Cased Ships." *Journal of the Royal United Service Institution*, London, vol. 5, no. 17, 1861, 121–171.

Hardee, William J. (Gen.), *Rifle and Light Infantry Tactics*, New York, 1861.

Harris, Samuel. *Personal Sketches of Samuel Harris*. Chicago, 1897.

Haythornthwaite, Philip. *Weapons and Equipment of the Napoleonic Wars*. Poole Dorset, 1979.

Hazlett, James C., Edwin Olmstead, and M. Hume Parks. *Field Artillery Weapons of the Civil War*. Newark, N.J., 1983.

Heintz, M. (Chef de bataillon). *Conférence sur la tactique de l'infanterie prussienne*. Conférences du Ministère de la Guerre, 1869–1870, 1st ser., no. 6. 1869.

Held, Robert. *The Age of Firearms: A Pictorial History*. Northfield, Ill., 1970.

Henderson, G.F.R. *The Science of War*. London, 1905.

Henderson, G.F.R. *Stonewall Jackson and the American Civil War*. New York, 1898.

Hermann, I. *Memoirs of a Veteran*. Atlanta, 1911.

Higgenson, Thomas Wentworth (Col.). *Army Life in a Black Regiment*. Boston, 1962, originally published in Boston, 1870.

Hill, Alonzo F. *Our Boys: The Personal Experience of a Soldier in the Army of the Potomac.* Philadelphia, 1864.

Hinde Robert (Capt.). *The Discipline of the Light-Horse.* London, 1778.

Hohenlohe-Ingelfingen (Crown Prince). *Conversations on Cavalry,* trans. Lt. C. Reichmann. London, 1897.

Holbrooke, William C. (Col.) *History of the Seventh Regiment Vermont Volunteers.* Burlington, Vermont, 1891.

Holden, Leverett D. *My First and Last Fights: Memoirs of the Civil War.* Maldon. Mass., 1914.

Hubbard, John Milton. *Notes of a Private.* St. Louis, 1911.

Huey, Pennock (Col.). *A True History of the Charge of the Eighth Pennsylvania Cavalry at Chancellorsville.* Philadelphia, 1883.

Hughes, B.P. (Maj. Gen.). *Firepower: Weapons Effectiveness on the Battlefield, 1630–1850.* London, 1974.

Hughes, B.P. (Major-Gen.), *British Smooth-bore Artillery: The Muzzle Loading Artillery of the 18th and 19th Centuries,* London, 1969.

Hulot, Jean Baptiste (Chef de bataillon au corps Imperial d'Artillerie). *Instruction sur le service de l'artillerie.* 3d ed. Paris, 1813.

Humphreys, Andrew A. (Gen.) *The Virginia Campaign of 1864 and 1865.* New York, 1995. Originally published in 1865.

Hurst, Jack. *Nathan Bedford Forrest: A Biography.* New York, 1994.

Hutchins, E.R. *The War of the Sixties.* New York, 1912.

-I-

"Iron Clad Ships of War." Parts 1–3. *Blackwood's Edinburgh Magazine,* vol. 88, no. 541, Nov. 1860, pp. 616–632; no. 542, Dec. 1860, pp. 633–649; vol. 89, no. 545, March 1861, pp. 304–317.

Izlar, William Valmore. *A Sketch of the War Record of the Edisto Rifles, 1861–1865.* Columbia, S.C., 1914.

-J-

Jackson, Oscar J. (Col.). *The Colonel's Diary.* Sharon, Penn., 1922.

Jamieson, Perry D. "The Development of Civil War Tactics." Ph.D. diss., Wayne State University, Detroit, 1979.

Jeffers, William N. "Remarks on the Rifle." *Journal of the Franklin Institute,* 3d ser., vol. 24, no. 3, Sept. 1852.

Johnson, Ben C. *A Soldier's Life: The Civil War Experiences of Ben C. Johnson.* Kalamazoo, Mich., 1962.

Johnson, Charles F. *The Long Roll, Being a Journal of the Civil War.* East Aurora, N.Y., 1911.

Johnson, Curt, and Richard C. Anderson. *Artillery Hell: The Employment of Artillery at Antietam.* College Station, Tex., 1995.

Jomini, Antoine Henri, Baron de. *The Art of War*, trans. W.P. Craighill, 1862.

Jordan, Thomas (Gen.), and J.P. Pryor. *The Campaigns of General Nathan Bedford Forrest and of Forrest's Cavalry.* New York, 1996. originally published New York, 1868.

Journal of the Franklin Institute, 3rd ser., vol XLII, no. 6, (Dec. 1861).

-K-

Kennedy, Frances H., ed. *The Civil War Battlefield Guide.* Boston, 1990.

-L-

Lallemand, H. *A Complete Treatise on Artillery,* trans. James Renwick, 2 vols. New York, 1820.

Le Blond, M. *Elemens de tactique.* Paris, 1758.

Lecomte, Ferdinand. *The War in the United States: Report to the Swiss Military Department,* New York, 1863. Originally published in French.

Lendy, Auguste F., Capt., trans. *Maxims, Advice and Instructions on the Art of War.* New York, 1862. Orig. in French.

Leslie, Edward. *The Devil Knows How to Ride: The True Story of William Clarke Quantrill.* New York, 1996.

Lightsey, Ada Christine. *The Veteran's Story.* Meridian, Miss., 1899.

Lippitt, Francis James (Col.). *A Treatise on Intrenchements.* New York, 1866.

Lippitt, Francis James (Col.). *A Treatise on the Tactical Use of the Three Arms: Infantry, Artillery, and Cavalry.* New York, 1865.

Loehr, Charles. *War History of the Old First Virginia Infantry Regiment.* Richmond, 1884.

Longacre, Edward G. *The Cavalry at Gettysburg.* Lincoln, Neb., 1986.

Luvass, Jay. *The Military Legacy of the Civil War: The European Inheritance.* Chicago, 1959.

Lyman, Wyllys (Maj.). *A Collection of Tactical Studies.* New York, 1874.

Lynn, John A. *The Bayonets of the Republic: Motivation and Tactics in the Army of Revolutionary France, 1791–1794.* Chicago, 1984.

-M-

MacCauley, Clay. *Through Chancellorsville, Into and Out of Libbey Prison.* Personal Narratives of the Events in the War, ser. 6, no. 7. Providence, Rhode Island, 1904.

MacDougall, Patrick (Col.). *Modern Warfare as Influenced by Modern Artillery.* London, 1864.

Mahan, Dennis, H. *Elementary Treatise on Advanced-Guard, Out-Posts, Etc.* New York, 1862.

"Mail-Clad Steamers." *Atlantic Monthly,* New York, vol. 8, no. 46, Aug. 1861, pp. 227–235.

Marmont, Auguste Frederic Louis Viesse de (Marshal). *The Spirit of Military Institutions, or Essential Principles of the Art of War,* trans. Henry Coppée. Philadelphia, 1862.

Martin, Charles. *Personal Reminiscences of the Monitor and Merrimac Engagement.* New York, 1886.

Marvin, Edwin E. *The Fifth Regiment Connecticut Volunteers.* Hartford, Conn., 1889.

Mason, F.H., (Capt.). *The Twelfth Ohio Cavalry.* Cleveland, 1871.

Matter, William D. *If It Takes All Summer: The Battle of Spotsylvania.* Chapel Hill, North Carolina, 1988.

Maude, Frederick, N. (Lt.-Col.). *Letters on Tactics and Organization, or English Military Institutions and the Continental Systems.* Leavenworth, Kansas, 1891.

Maude, Frederick N., (Capt.) *Cavalry versus Infantry.* London, 1896.

Maude, Frederick N. (Lt.-Col.) *Cavalry: Its Past and Future.* London, 1903.

May, E.S. (Maj.). *Guns and Cavalry: Their Performances in the Past, and their Prospects in the Future.* London, 1896.

Mazing, Georgii Yur'evich. *Karl Andreevich Shil'der, 1785–1854.* Moscow, 1989.

McAulay, John D. *Civil War Breech Loading Rifles.* Lincoln, R.I., 1987.

McCarthy, Carlton. *Detailed Minutiae of Soldier Life, The Army of Northern Virginia, 1861–1865.* Cambridge, Mass., 1882.

McClellan, George B. (Maj. Gen.). *The Armies of Europe.* Philadelphia, 1862.

McClellan, George B. (Maj. Gen.) "The Peninsular Campaign," *Battles and Leaders,* vol. 2., pp. 160–188. Secaucus, N.J., c. 1992.

McElwee, William. *The Art of War: Waterloo to Mons.* London, 1974.

McLaughlin, John. *A Memoir of Hector Tyndale.* Philadelphia, 1882.

McWhiney, Grady, and Perry D. Jamieson. *Attack and Die: Civil War Military Tactics and the Southern Heritage.* Alabama, 1982.

Meyer, Henry C. (Capt.). *Civil War Experiences under Bayard, Gregg, Kilpatrick, Custer, Raulston, and Newberry.* New York, 1911.

Meyers, William E. *The Sailor on Horseback.* Personal Narratives of the Events in the War, ser. 5, no. 7. Providence, Rhode Island, 1912.

Military Gazette, Albany, N.Y., vol. 2, 1859; vol. 3, 1860.

Mitchell, John (Lt. Col. R.A.). *Thoughts on Tactics and Military Organization.* London, 1838.

Montgomery, George, ed. *Georgia Sharpshooter: The Civil War Diary and Letters of William Rhadamanthus Montgomery.* Macon, Georgia, 1997.

Monroe, John Albert. *The Rhode Island Artillery at the First Battle of Bull Run.* Personal Narratives of the Events in the War, ser. 1, no. 2. Providence, Rhode Island, 1878.

Moore, Edward A. *The Story of a Cannoneer under Stonewall Jackson.* New York, 1909.

Moore, Frank, ed. *The Rebellion Record: A Diary of American Events,* 11 vols. New York, 1861–68.

Mordecai, Alfred (Maj.), Military Commission to Europe in 1855 and 1856. *Report of Major Alfred Mordecai of the Ordnance Department to the House of Representatives.* 36th Cong., 2d Sess., vol. 1037. Washington, 1861.

Morgan, Thomas J. *Reminiscences of Service with Colored Troops in the Army of the Cumberland.* Personal Narratives of the Events in the War, ser. 3, no. 13. Providence, Rhode Island, 1885.

Morgan, W.H. *Reminiscences of the War of 1861–65.* Lynchburg, Va., 1911.

Morrow, John Anderson. *The Confederate Whitworth Sharpshooters.* N.p., 1989.

Morton, John Watson (Capt.) *The Artillery of Nathan Bedford Forrest's Cavalry.* Marietta, Ga., 1995.

Mosby, John S., Col. *Mosby's Memoirs.* Nashville, Tenn., 1995.

Moseley, Thomas Vernon. "Evolution of the American Civil War Infantry Tactics." Ph.D. diss. University of North Carolina at Chapel Hill, 1967.

Müller, William. *The Elements of the Science of War, 3 vols.* London, 1811.

Mulligan, James A. (Col.) "The Siege of Lexington, Mo.," *Battles and Leaders of the Civil War,* vol. I, pp. 307–313.

-N-

Naisawald, L. Van Loan. *Grape and Canister: The Story of the Field Artillery of the Army of the Potomac.* New York, 1960.

Neese, George, M. *Three Years in the Confederate Army.* New York, 1911.

Neil, Henry M. (Captain, Twenty-second Battery). "A Battery at Close Quarters." Paper presented before the Ohio Commandery of the Loyal Legion, Columbus, Oh., Oct. 6, 1909.

Nesbitt, John W., comp. *General History of Company "D," 149th Pennsylvania Volunteers.* Oakdale, Pennsylvania, 1908.

Ney, Michel. (Marshal) *Memoirs of Marshal Ney, 2 vols.* London, 1833.

Nichols, George Ward (Capt.). *The Story of the Great March.* New York, 1865.

Nixon, Liberty Independence. "An Alabamian at Shiloh: The Diary of Liberty Independence Nixon." *The Alabama Review,* no. 2, April 1958, pp. 144–158.

Noé Viscomte de, Lt. Col. "Les chasseurs d'Afrique." *Revue de Deux Monde,* vol. 29, Sept. 1, 1860, pp. 204–225.

Nolan, Lewis E. *Cavalry: Its History and Tactics.* Columbia, S.C., 1864.

Nosworthy, Brent. *The Anatomy of Victory: Battle Tactics, 1689–1763.* New York, 1990.

Nosworthy, Brent. *With Musket, Cannon and Sword.* New York, 1996. Published as *Battle Tactics of Napoleon and His Enemies* in the U.K.

Nosworthy, Brent. *The Current State of Military History.* The Age of Napoleon, no. 35, London, 1999.

Nosworthy, Brent. "Sir Charles Oman on Line versus Column," in *A History of the Peninsular War,* vol. 9, edited by Paddy Griffith. London, 1999.

Noyes, George, F. *The Bivouac and the Battle-field.* New York, 1864.

-O-

Okounef, Nikolai Alexsandrovich. *Examen raisonne des propriétés des trois armes de leur emploi dans les batilles et de leur rapport entre elles.* Paris, 1832.

Orwig, Joseph R. (Capt.) *History of the 131st Penna. Volunteers.* Williamsport, Penn., 1902.

Osbon, G.A. "The First of the Ironclads." *The Mariner's Mirror,* London, vol. 50, no. 3, August 1964, pp. 189–198.

Osbon, George A. "The Crimean Gunboats (Part I)." *The Mariner's Mirror,* London, vol. 51, no. 3, May 1965, pp. 103–115.

Our Regiment: A History of the 102d Illinois Infantry Volunteers. Chicago, 1865.

-P -

Page, Charles D. *History of the Fourteenth Regiment Connecticut Vol. Infantry.* Meriden, Conn., 1906.

Palmer, Edwin F. *The Second Brigade, or Camp Life.* Montpelier, Vt., 1864.

De Parades de la Plaigne, H. (Captain Adjutant-major). *De armement de l'Europe.* Conférences du Ministère de la Guerre, 1869–1870, 2d ser., no. 9. 1870.

Parrott, R.P. *Facts as to the Hooped Gun.* New York, 1862. [Special Collections, Providence Public Library]

Patterson, A. Temple. "Captain Cowper Coles and 'Palmerston's Folly'." *The Mariner's Mirror,* London, vol. 51, no. 1, February 1965, pp. 19–26.

Peck, R.H. *Reminiscences of a Confederate Soldier.* Fincastle, Va., 1913.

Peet, Frederick Tomlinson. (Civil War Letters and documents, Newport, 1917.

Pepper, George W. (Capt.). *Personal Recollections of Sherman's Campaigns in Georgia and the Carolinas.* Zanesville, Oh., 1866.

Petroff, Peter. *Ante-Mortem Depositions of Peter Petroff.* San Francisco, 1895.

Picket, Lasalle Corbell. *What Happened to Me.* New York, 1917.

Phisterer, Frederick. *The Regular Brigade of the Fourteenth Army Corps . . . in the Battle of Stone River, or Murfreesboro.* Albany, N.Y., 1883.

Pike, James. *Scout and Ranger, Being the Personal Adventures of James Pike of the Texas Rangers, in 1859–60.* Princeton, N.J., 1962.

Piobert, G. *Traité d'artillerie theorique et pratique,* 3d ed. Paris, 1852.

Pliny, Miles. *Perkins' Steam Gun.* N.p., n.d. [Providence Public Library, Special Collections.]

Polk, J.M. *The Confederate Soldier and Ten Years in South America.* Austin, Tex., 1910.

"Proceedings from the British Association: From the London Athenæum, Sept. 1861." *Journal of the Franklin Institution,* 3d ser., vol. 4, no. 6, Dec. 1861, pp. 369–382.

-Q -

Quincy, C. S. (Marquis de, Lt. Gen. d'artillerie). *Maxims et instructions sur l'art militaire.* in vol. 7, *Histoire de regne de Louis le grand.* Paris, 1726.

-R -

Ranges of Parrott Guns with Notes for Practice. New York, 1863.

R.E.C. (probably Raleigh Edward Colston). "Modern Tactics," *Southern Literary Messenger,* Richmond, Va., vol. 26, no. 1, January 1858, pp. 1–20.

Reed, Rowena. *Combined Operations in the Civil War.* Annapolis, Md., 1978.

Reichardt, Theodore. *Diary of Battery A, First Rhode Island Light Artillery.* Providence, R.I., 1865.

Renard, Jean Baptiste (Gen.). *Considerations sur la tactique de l'infanterie en Europe.* Paris, 1857.

Recherches sur le feu de l'infanterie. Paris, 1826.

Rhea, Gordon C. *The Battle of the Wilderness: May 5–6, 1864.* Baton Rouge, La., 1994.

Rhea, Gordon C. *The Battles for Spotsylvania Court House and the Road to Yellow Tavern, May 7–12, 1864.* Baton Rouge, La., 1997.

Rhea, Gordon C. *To the North Anna River.* Baton Rouge, La., 2000.

Rhodes, Elisha H. *The First Campaign of the Second Rhode Island Infantry.* Personal Narratives of the Events in the War, ser. 1, no. 1. Providence, Rhode Island, 1878.

Rhodes, John H. *The Gettysburg Gun.* Personal Narratives of the Events in the War, ser. 4, no. 19, Providence, Rhode Island, 1892.

Rickard, James H. *Service in the Colored Troops in Burnside's Corps.* Personal Narratives of the Events in the War, ser. 5, no. 1. Providence, Rhode Island, 1894.

Ripley, Warren. *Artillery and Ammunition of the Civil War.* New York, 1970.

Ripley, William Y. W. (Lt. Col.). *Vermont Riflemen in the War of the Union: A History of Company F, First United States Sharp Shooters.* Rutland, Vt., 1983.

Roberts, Joseph. *The Handbook of Artillery.* 2d ed. New York, 1875.

Robertson, Robert S. *Personal Recollections of the War: A Record of Service with the Ninety-Third New York.* Milwaukee, 1885.

Robson, John S. *How a One-Legged Rebel Lives, or the Reminisces of the Civil War.* Durham, North Carolina, 1898.

Roe, Alfred Seelye. *History of the First Regiment of Heavy Artillery Massachusetts Volunteers, Formerly the 14th Regiment of Infantry.* Boston, 1917.

Roemer, Jacob. *Reminiscences of the War of the Rebellion.* Flushing, New York, 1897.

Roemer, Jean. *Cavalry: Its History, Management, and Uses.* New York, 1863.

Rose, W.J. "The Chasseurs à Pied." *Atlantic Monthly,* vol. 11, no. 64, February 1863, pp. 250–259.

Rosecrans, William S. "The Battle of Corinth," in *Battles and Leaders of the Civil War,* vol. 2, pp. 737–757. Secaucus, N.J., c. 1992.

Ross, Fitzgerald. *A Visit to the Cities and Camps of the Confederate States.* London, 1865.

Ross, Steven. *From Flintlock to Rifle: Infantry Tactics, 1740–1866.* London, 1979.

Rumsky, John. "Enfield versus Tulwar: The Effectiveness of British Weapons in the Indian Mutiny." *Indian Military Historical Society,* vol. 15, no.1, spring 1998, pp. 17–37.

-S-

Sargent, Epes. "Ericsson and His Inventions." *Atlantic Monthly*, New York, vol. 10, no. 47, July 1862, pp. 68–81.

Schalk, Emil (A.O.). *Summary of the Art of War*. 2d ed. Philadelphia, 1863.

Schön, J. (Capt. Saxon Infantry). *Modern System of Small Arms*. 2d ed., trans. J. Gorgas. Dresden, 1855. English Translation provided entire in Mordecai, Report.

Scientific American, original and new ser., New York, 1846–1864, 1894.

Scoffern, J. (Prof.). *Projectile Weapons of War and Explosive Compounds with Specific Reference to Rifled Ordnance*. 4th ed., London, 1859.

Scott, John (Maj.). *Partisan Life of Colonel John S. Mosby*. New York, 1867.

Scott, R.A.E. (Commander, Royal Navy). "The Progress of Ordnance Abroad Compared with that of Ordnance at Home." *Journal of the Royal United Service Institution*, vol. (1862), no. 21, pp. 5–27. [Special Collections, Providence Public Library]

Scribner, B.F. *How Soldiers Were Made, or, the War as I Saw It*. New Albany, Ind., 1887.

Sharpe, Michael, *Historical Maps of Civil War Battlefields*. San Diego, CA, 2000.

Shaw, Cladius (Maj.). "Remarks upon the Effect of the New Armament of Cannon and Rifles Lately Adopted in the British Army." *United Service Magazine*, pt. I, London, no. 387, Feb. 1861, pp. 193–201.

Shaw, Horace. *The First Maine Heavy Artillery, 1861–1865*. Portland, Me., 1903.

Sherman, George C. *The Negro as Soldier*. Personal Narratives of the Events in the War, ser. 7, no. 7. Providence, Rhode Island, 1913.

Sherman, William T. (Gen.) *Memoirs of William T. Sherman*, 2 vols. New York, 1891.

Skrine, Francis Henry. *Fontenoy and the War of the Austrian Succession*. London, 1906.

Small, Abner R. and Harold Adams Small, ed. *The Road to Richmond*. Berkeley, Cal., 1939.

Smith, Graham, ed. *Military Small Arms*. London, 1994.

Smith, M.W. *Modern Tactics of the Three Arms*. London, 1869.

Snead, Thomas L., (Col.) "The First Year of the War in Missouri," in *Battles and Leaders of the Civil War*, vol. 1. pp. 262–277, Secaucus, N.J., c. 1992.

Soley, James R. "The Union and Confederate Navies," in *Battles and Leaders of the Civil War*, vol. I., pp. 611–631, Secaucus, N.J., c. 1992.

Starr, Stephen Z. *The Union Cavalry in the Civil War*, 2 vols. Baton Rouge, La., 1979.

Steffen, Randy. *The Horse Soldier: The United States Cavalryman*, 2 vols. Norman, Okla., 1978.

Steinmetz, Andrew, Esq. (Queen's Own Light Infantry Militia). "Military Gymnastics of the French." *Journal of the Royal United Service Institute*, vol. 5 (1861), no.18, pp. 370–395.

Steinmetz, Andrew. "Musketry Instruction for the Cavalry Carbine and Pistol." *Journal of the Royal United Service Institute*, vol. 5 (1861), no. 19, pp. 454–496.

Stevens, George T. *Three Years in the Sixth Corps*. Albany, N.Y., 1866.

Stevenson, B.F. *Letters from the Army*. Cincinnati, 1884.

Stevenson, William G. *Thirteen Months in the Rebel Army*. New York, 1864.

Stillé, Charles, J. *How a Free People Conduct a Long War*. Philadelphia, 1862.

Stimson, Lewis A. *Civil War Memories of Lewis A. Stimson*. New York, 1918.

The Story of One Regiment: The Eleventh Maine Infantry Volunteers. New York, 1896.

Strictures on the Army. Dublin, Ireland, 1809.

Sumner, George. *Recollections of Service in Battery "D"*. Personal Narratives of the Events in the War, ser. 4, no. 11. Providence, Rhode Island, 1891.

Sumner, George. *J. Albert Monroe: Recollections of Him as Commander, Battery "D," First Rhode Island Light Artillery*. Personal Narratives of the Events in the War, ser. 4, no. 18, pp. 5–25. Providence, Rhode Island, 1892.

Swinton, William. *Decisive Battles of the Civil War*. New York, 1992.

Symonds, Craig L. *A Battlefield Atlas of the Civil War*. Baltimore, 1996.

-T-

Tarrant, E. (Sergeant). *The Wild Riders of the First Kentucky*. Louisville, Ky., 1894.

Taylor, Frank. *Rifled Field Pieces: A Short History of What Is Known*, pamphlet. Washington, 1862. [Special Collections, Providence Public Library]

Taylor, John C. and Samuel P. Hatfield *History of the First Connecticut Artillery and of the Siege Trains of the Armies Operating against Richmond, 1862–65*. Hartford, Conn., 1893.

Tenney, Harris. *War Diary of Harris Tenney*. Cleveland, 1914.

Thatcher, Marshall P. (Capt. Co. "B"). *A Hundred Battles in the West: St. Louis to Atlanta, 1861–65, the Second Michigan Cavalry*. Detroit, 1884.

Thompkinson, William (Lt. Col.). *Diary of a Cavalry Officer in the Peninsular and Waterloo Campaigns, 1809–1815*. London, 1894.

Three Rebels Write Home: Including the Letters of Edgar Allan Jackson, James Fenton Bryant, and Irwin Cross Wills. Franklin, Va., 1955.

Tielke, J.G. *An Account of Some of the Most Remarkable Events of the War & A Treatise on Several Branches of the Military Art*, trans. Capt. C. Craufurd and Capt. R. Craufurd, 2 vols. London, 1787–88.

de Tousard, Louis. *American Artillerist's Companion, or Elements of Artillery*, 2 vols. Philadelphia, 1809–1813.

Transactions of the Institution of Naval Architects, London, vols 1 & 2, 1860–1861.

Treadwell, Daniel. *On the Construction of Improved Ordnance*. Cambridge, Mass., 1862. [Special Collections, Providence Public Library]

Trinque, Bruce A. "Arnold's Battery and the 26th North Carolina." *Gettysburg Magazine*, no. 12, January 1995.

Trinque, Bruce A. "Confederate Battle Flags in the July 3rd Charge." *Gettysburg Magazine*, issue no. 21, January 2000.

Trudeau, Noah Andre. *Bloody Roads South.* Baton Rouge, La., 1989.

Tucker, Spencer C. "The Stevens Ironclad Battery." *American Neptune*, Salem, Mass., vol. 51, no. 1, winter 1991, pp. 12–22.

Twitchell, A.S. (Quartermaster-Sergeant). *History of the Seventh Maine Light Battery in the Great Rebellion, Boston.* 1890.

Tyler (Captain). "The Rifle and the Spade, or the Future of Field Operations." *Journal of the Royal United Service Institute*, vol. 3 (1859), no. 10, pp.170–194.

Tyrrell, Henry. *History of the War with Russia.* London, c. 1858.

-U-

United States Army. *Instruction for Heavy Artillery.* Washington, 1851.

United States Army. *Instructions for Field Artillery.* Philadelphia, 1860.

United States Government. *The Congressional Globe.* 37th Cong., 1st sess., Washington, 1861.

United States Government. Serial Set: *Senate Reports*, vol. 1211, Rep. Comm. no. 121, Joint Committee on the Conduct of the War, "Report on Heavy Ordnance." 38th Congress, 2d sess. Washington, 1865.

United States Army Ordnance Department. *Reports of Experiments with Small Arms.* Washington, 1856.

United States Government. Serial Set: *Report of Committees*, vol. 916, Executive Doc. no. 1, "Report of the Secretary of War," "The Report of Captain George B. McClellan." 35th Cong., Special Session. Washington, 1857.

United States Government. Serial Set: vol. 408, House Report No. 448, "Harbor Defense." 27th Cong., 2d sess. Washington, 1841–42.

United States Government. *The War of the Rebellion: A Compilation of the Official Records of the Union and the Confederate Armies.* 128 vols. Washington, 1880–1891.

The United States Journal and Gazette of the Regular and Volunteer Forces. New York, 1863. Later *The Infantry and Navy Journal.*

United States Navy Department. *Reports of the Naval Engagements on the Mississippi River.* Washington, 1862.

United States. War Dept. *A System of Target Practice for the Use of Troops when Armed with the Musket, Rifle-Musket, Rifle, or Carbine.* Washington, 1862. Facsimile reprint, Ashburn, Va., 1998, with an introduction by Joseph Bilby.

Upton, Emory (Brevet Maj. Gen.). "The Prussian Company Column." *The International Review*, New York, vol. II, January 1875, pp. 302–316.

d'Urtubie, Théodore. *Manuel de l'artillerie.* Paris, 1795.

Urban, John W. *Battle Field and Prison Pen.* Philadelphia, 1882.

"The Use of the Rifle." *Atlantic Monthly*, vol. 9, no. 43, March 1862, pp. 300–306.

-V-

Vaill, Dudley Landon. *The County Regiment: A Sketch of the Second Regiment of*

Connecticut Volunteer Heavy Artillery (Originally 19 Vol. Infantry), Winsted, Connecticut. 1908.

Von Schmidt, Karl, Maj. Gen. *Instructions for Training, Employment, and Leading of Cavalry,* transl. Capt. C.W. Bowdler Bell. London, 1881. Reprinted New York, 1968.

-W-

Wagner, Arthur L. (Maj.). "Hasty Intrenchments in the War of Secession." *Papers of the Military Historical Society of Massachusetts,* vol. XIII, Boston, 1913.

Wagner, Arthur L. (Maj.). *Organization and Tactics.* 3d ed. Kansas City, Mo., 1899.

Walsun, Lucien (Private Co. "A"). *The Story of the Fourth Regiment Ohio Veteran Volunteer Cavalry.* Cincinnati, 1912.

Ward, George. *History of the Second Pennsylvania Veteran Heavy Artillery.* 2d ed. Philadelphia, 1904.

Warner, Ezra J. *Generals in Gray: Lives of the Confederate Commanders.* Baton Rouge, La., 1959.

Warner, Ezra J. *Generals in Blue: Lives of the Union's Commanders.* Baton Rouge, La., 1964.

Warnery, Emanuel von. *Remarks on Cavalry.* London, 1802.

Watson, William. *Life in the Confederate Army.* New York, 1888.

Watt, Ernest L. (compiled by) *History of the Nineteenth Regiment Massachusetts Volunteer Infantry, 1861–1865,* Salem, Mass., 1906.

Wawro, Geoffrey. *The Austro-Prussian War: Austria's War with Prussia and Italy in 1866.* New York, 1996.

Webster, Dan, and Don C. Cameron. *History of the First Wisconsin Battery of Light Artillery.* Washington, 1907.

Wert, Jeffry D. *Gettysburg Day Three.* New York, 2001.

Wheeler, B. Francis. *The First Monitor and Its Builders.* Poughkeepsie, N.Y., 1884.

Wheeler, Richard. *Voices of the Civil War.* New York, 1976.

Whitcomb, Caroline. *History of the Second Massachusetts Battery (Nim's Battery) of Light Artillery, 1861–1865.* Concord, N.H., 1912.

Whittaker, Frederick. *Volunteer Cavalry: The Lessons of the Decade.* New York, 1871.

Wiard, Norman. *Wiard's System of Field Artillery.* New York, 1863. [Special Collections, Providence, Rhode Island, Public Library]

Wilcox, C.M. (Capt.) *Rifles and Rifle Practice as an Elementary Treatise upon the Theory of Rifle Firing.* New York, 1859.

Wilcox, C.M. (Capt.) *Evolutions of the Line as Practiced by the Austrian Infantry.* New York, 1860.

Wilford, (Lt. Col.) "On the Rifle: Showing the Necessity for Its Introduction as a Universal Infantry Weapon." *Journal of the Royal United Service Institution,* vol. 1 (1857), no. 3, pp. 238–253.

Willard, George L. (Col. 125 NY). *Comparative Value of Rifled and Smooth-Bored Arms.* N.p., 1863. [Special Collections, Providence, Rhode Island, Public Library]

Williams, John A. B. *Leaves from a Trooper's Diary.* Philadelphia, 1869.

Williamson, James J. (Co. "A"). *Mosby's Rangers: A Record of the Operations of the Forty-third Battalion of Virginia Cavalry.* NewYork, 1896.

Wilson, Sir Robert. *The Life of General Robert Wilson,* 2 vols. London, 1862.

Wing, Samuel. *The Soldier's Story: A Personal Narrative of the Life, Army Experiences, and the Marvelous Sufferings since the War.* Phillips, Me., 1898.

Wise, Jennings Cropper. *The Long Arm of Lee,* 2 vols., Lynchburg, Va., 1915. Reprinted Lincoln, Neb., 1991.

Wolfe, James. (Gen.) *General Wolfe's Instructions to Young Officers.* 2d ed. London, 1780.

Wood, Sir Evelyn (Gen.). *Achievements of Cavalry.* London, 1897.

Wood, James Harvey. *The War: Stonewall Jackson, His Campaigns and Battles.* Cumberland, Md., 1910.

Woodbury, Augustus. *The Second Rhode Island Regiment: A Narrative of Military Operations.* Providence, R.I., 1875.

Worsham, John H. *One of Jackson's Foot Cavalry: His Experience and What He Saw during the War, 1861–1865.* New York, 1912.

Worsham, William Johnson. *Old Nineteenth Tennessee Regiment, C.S.A., June, 1861–April, l865.* Knoxville, Tenn., 1902.

Wright, Charles. *Experiences in the Ranks of Company C, 81st Vol. Infantry.* Philadelphia, 1887.

Wright, Thomas J. (Capt.). *History of the Eighth Regiment Kentucky Volunteers Infantry.* St. Joseph, Mo., 1880.

Wulsin, L. *The Story of the Fourteenth Regiment Ohio Veteran Volunteer Cavalry.* Cincinnati, 1912.

-Y-

Young, Alfred. "Numbers and Losses in the Army of Northern Virginia." *North & South,* vol. III, no. 3, March 2000

ACKNOWLEDGMENTS

Any work that attempts to examine not only the full range of Civil War tactical-level minutiae and combat experience, but how these are interwoven into the overall development of military practice, is a huge undertaking, one, by necessity, beyond the exertions of a single author. Fortunately, this project benefited from the expert assistance of a large number of Civil War enthusiasts and professional historians. Foremost among these are Bruce Trinque and Dean West, who unselfishly and untiringly answered a seemingly unending stream of requests and queries, undeterred by time of day or the dauntingness of the task. The same must be said for Stewart Gibson who executed all custom drawings and, of course, my agent, Bob Roistacher and the Carroll and Graf editorial staff. I would also like to thank Professor Richard Gould, a marine archeologist at Brown University, Richard Patterson, executive director of the Old Barracks (Trenton, NJ), Dr. David Martin, Stefan Patejak, Ted Sharp, Mark Conrad, Roger Kennedy, Lenny Millman, Lou Giorgino, Brian McLaughlin, and Larry O'Donnel for their assistance during the extensive research phase of this project. All supplied interesting research materials that otherwise, in all probability, would not have been considered.

Dana Lombardy, Matt de la Matter, Dave Clark, Bill Proal, Dick Bryant of *The Courier*, Howie Muir, Mark Donkelman, Lee Jones and Joe Pereira also worked hard reviewing the manuscript in its various stages and offered very helpful critical insight and feedback. Rich Berg and John Hill, old game design colleagues, contributed invaluable advice, while William Keyser did an excellent job photographing the illustrations. Of course, I am also deeply indebted to Gordon Rhea, Paddy Griffith, Joseph Bilby, and Jack Greene for their evaluation of this work as well as Norris Darrel, Rick Devine, Doug Dwyer, Arthur Ianelli, and Scot Mingus, Sr.

Special thanks also goes out to all of the curators and librarians encountered during my long informational peregrinations, specifically, the staff of the New York Public Library, especially the staff of the Tenth Avenue Annex; as well as those at Boston Library, Harvard College Libraries, Rhode Island Historical Society, McLellen Library at McGill University; and the Providence Public Library, especially Greg Frazier, Betty Lilly, Shirley Long, and Phil Weimerskirch, curator of its Special Collections. A special word of appreciation goes out to Peter Harrington, curator of the Ann S. K. Brown Collection, as well as James Andrew Moul, Patricia Sirois, and Jean Rainwater of the Hay Library at Brown University for enduring so courteously 5 years of academic pestering and making available what might be best described as a delightful "scholarly theme park."

Finally, I want to acknowledge genuine appreciation for all of the reenactment and living history communities, especially the Twelfth Georgia Volunteer Infantry Regiment, of which I am a member, for providing such a fun, interesting, and naturalistic learning environment.

INDEX

ABOUT THE AUTHOR

Brent Nosworthy is an independent scholar whose two previous books on military history, *The Anatomy of Victory: Battle Tactics 1689-1763* and *With Musket, Sword and Cannon: Battle Tactics of Napoleon and His Enemies*, are widely considered classics in their field. *The Anatomy of Victory*, which examined (linear) warfare after the advent of the flintlock musket and the socket bayonet was praised by Booklist as "an exhaustive study of how warfare was conducted on the 18th century European battlefield . . . a scholarly yet readable book, very probably the best ever on this particular subject." The Military Book Club wrote that *With Musket, Sword and Cannon* "will undoubtedly gain status as a classic," and Army magazine praised that "this is the clearest and most complete interpretation of Napoleonic warfare yet written; it is sure to become a classic." A graduate of McGill University, Nosworthy lives in Providence, Rhode Island.